Early Childhood Curriculum

Developmental Bases for Learning and Teaching

Early Childhood Curriculum

Developmental Bases for Learning and Teaching

Sue C. Wortham
University of Texas at San Antonio

Merrill, an imprint of
Macmillan College Publishing Company
New York

Maxwell Macmillan Canada
Toronto

Maxwell Macmillan International
New York Oxford Singapore Sydney

Cover photo: Mary Kate Denny/PhotoEdit
Editor: Linda Sullivan
Production Editor: Mary Irvin
Photo Editor: Anne Vega
Cover Designer: Robert Vega
Production Manager: Pamela A. Bennett
Electronic Text Management: Marilyn Wilson Phelps, Matthew Williams, Jane Lopez, Vincent
      A. Smith

This book was set in Souvenir by Macmillan College Publishing Company and was printed
and bound by R. R. Donnelley & Sons Co. The cover was printed by Phoenix Color Corp.

Macmillan College Publishing Company
866 Third Avenue
New York, NY 10022

Macmillan College Publishing Company is part of the
Maxwell Communication Group of Companies.

Maxwell Macmillan Canada, Inc.
1200 Eglinton Avenue East, Suite 200
Don Mills, Ontario M3C 3N1

Library of Congress Cataloging-in-Publication Data
Wortham, Sue Clark
      Early childhood curriculum : developmental bases for
learning and teaching / Sue C. Wortham.
            p.   cm.
      Includes bibliographical references and indexes.
      ISBN 0-02-429471-3
      1. Early childhood education—Curricula. 2. Curriculum
planning. 3. Child development. I. Title.
   LB1139.4.W67   1994
   372.19—dc20   93-14620
                                                       CIP

Printing: 1 2 3 4 5 6 7 8 9   Year: 4 5 6 7

Photo credits: Barbara Schwartz/Macmillan, pp. 359, 374, 384, 419, 429, 447; Dan
Floss/Macmillan, p. 402; Anne Vega/Macmillan, pp. 407, 421; All other photos supplied by
author.

Preface

Early Childhood Curriculum: Developmental Bases for Learning and Teaching was written for teachers of children from infancy to eight years of age. It was prepared in response to the need of present and future teachers to understand the role of the child's development in the curriculum; the curriculum that we discuss is prepared for the very youngest children, whether they be in a child-care, private preschool, or public school setting. Teachers in the primary grades in elementary schools are particularly aware of the difficulty in providing successful learning experiences for children who come to them from diverse backgrounds, especially at a time when they may be expected to cover learning objectives more rapidly than in the past.

Regardless of the age of the child in the early childhood program, the teacher needs to understand that the nature of the child's development has implications for the kinds of experiences that are appropriate. Likewise, teachers can benefit from understanding the role of developmental theories in the practice of teaching in an early childhood program. This text concerns the issues of bridging and making transitions—it offers information and suggestions for bridging theory and practice, and it includes suggestions for guiding children through transitions in developmental stages, especially as they move from preschool into the primary grades.

Chapters 1 and 2 establish the background setting and context for the early childhood curriculum that will be described. Chapter 1, "The Changing Role of the Teacher in Developing Curriculum for Diverse Populations," discusses the diversity of children entering programs for those who are under the age of eight; it also describes the teacher's changing role in developing curriculum for very young children. Chapter 2, "The Need for Developmentally Appropriate Practice in Early Childhood Settings," examines issues and practices in early childhood programs; the historical heritage of early childhood education is reviewed, leading to a discussion of current practices that are inappropriate for young children and suggestions for how developmentally appropriate practices can lead to appropriate learning experiences in early childhood classrooms.

Chapter 3, "Developmental Characteristics of Young Children from Birth to Eight Years: Implications for Learning," describes the theoretical bases of development and the way in which they facilitate understanding of the young child's development. Characteristics of development are explained in regards to the sensorimotor, preoperational, and concrete operational periods; characteristics and competencies in physical, cognitive, language, and social-emotional development are discussed for children from birth to two years of age, two to five years of age, and five to eight years of age.

Chapters 4 and 5 address programs for infants and toddlers. Chapter 4, "Organizing Infant–Toddler Programs," traces the history of programs for children under age two and describes the characteristics of a model program for infants and toddlers. Chapter 5, "Infant–Toddler Curriculum: Birth to Age Two," discusses how development is nurtured in physical, cognitive, language, and social development and suggests activities that can be used with very young children.

Chapters 6, 7, and 8 address the developmental needs and programming for preschool children ages three, four, and five. Chapter 6, "A Developmental Model for Preschool Programs," addresses the qualities needed in a developmentally appropriate program for preschool children. It describes the characteristics of such a model and the way in which it is implemented. Chapter 7, "Preschool Curriculum: Ages Three to Five: Language and Cognitive Development," describes curriculum for language development and cognitive development. Chapter 8, "Preschool Curriculum: Ages Three to Five: Social and Physical Development," addresses how to plan and implement appropriate activities for social and physical development. Within each category of development in chapters 7 and 8, the nature of development in the preschool years is applied to planning the curriculum, play activities, and the environment to support learning experiences.

Chapters 9, 10, and 11 move to programs for children from age five to eight. Chapter 9, "A Model for Programs for Children Age Five to Eight," describes how developmental changes during those three years have implications for the way quality curriculum and instruction are designed and implemented as children make the transition into the concrete operational period and toward literacy. We describe characteristics of an ungraded primary model and discuss how such a model is put into practice. Chapter 10, "The Transitional Curriculum: Ages Five to Eight: Language Arts, Mathematics, and Science," and chapter 11, "The Transitional Curriculum: Ages Five to Eight: Social Studies and Physical Education," discuss the goals and topics that are the foundations for each of the curriculum content areas.

A basic principle held throughout the curriculum descriptions for each developmental level is that curriculum and instruction are based on developmental needs and possibilities of young children. Even more important is the premise that integrated curriculum, which guides children to understand the interrelatedness of learning, is the effective mode for designing and implementing child-centered, developmentally appropriate curriculum and instruction. Beginning with very simple unit themes for infants and toddlers, integrated thematic units are discussed within the developmental curriculum of the preschool years and content areas in the primary grades.

Chapter 12, "Teaching in the Real World," takes a final look at the world of early childhood teachers as they encounter and address problems and possibilities present in early childhood programs today. Readers are introduced to the realities of practice that are experienced by contemporary teachers; these teachers often struggle with making decisions within the context of many kinds of programs from different philosophical perspectives and within their own developmental stages. New teachers entering the field will find both opportunities and frustrations as they join teachers who are working to provide quality programs for the very youngest children in our society.

Students are excellent sources of information in developing a new textbook. I wish to thank students in ECE 4303, Approaches to Learning, PreK to Third Grade, who used information from the first drafts of the manuscript and provided questions and suggestions for providing further information and improving the writing. Special thanks are due to Lisa Cinadr, Laurel McCurdy, Christina Denton, Barbara Walthers, and Marina Montez, who allowed me to adapt their unit plans for the appendixes. My colleagues, Cindy Soto and Laurie Pariseau, were especially helpful as they used the manuscript and made suggestions for revisions. I also wish to thank the reviewers of the book, who asked questions and made extensive suggestions for improvements at all stages of writing and revision: Sandra DeCosta, West Virginia University; Mildred Fischle, State University College at Buffalo; Kathy Fite, Southwest Texas State University; Barbara Graham, Norfolk State University; James Hoot, State University of New York at Buffalo; Sherill Richarz, Washington State University; Marcia Rysztak, Lansing Community College; and Elaine Surbeck, Arizona.

At this point in the preface of a textbook, writers frequently thank their editor. Linda Sullivan, my editor at Merrill, an imprint of Macmillan, provided both support and patience in great measure. I thank her for guiding me through my delays and frustrations "con calma."

I also thank my daughter-in-law, Mary Blanche, who suggested that I consider taking up knitting, which probably accurately reflects the feelings of many in my immediate and extended family. I thank my family for continuing to understand me. I will consider the possibility of learning to knit at some future time, which is as yet beyond my perception.

Contents

CHAPTER THREE
Developmental Characteristics of Young Children from Birth to Eight Years: Implications for Learning   **55**

CHAPTER FOUR
Organizing Infant–Toddler Programs   **101**

CHAPTER FIVE
Infant–Toddler Curriculum: Birth to Age Two   **137**

CHAPTER SIX
A Developmental Model for Preschool Programs   **175**

CHAPTER SEVEN
Preschool Curriculum: Ages Three to Five: Language and Cognitive Development

221

CHAPTER EIGHT
Preschool Curriculum: Ages Three to Five: Social and Physical Development 277

CHAPTER NINE
A Model for Programs for Children Age Five to Eight 317

CHAPTER TEN

The Transitional Curriculum: Ages Five to Eight: Language Arts, Mathematics, and Science   **359**

CHAPTER ELEVEN

The Transitional Curriculum: Ages Five to Eight Social Studies and Physical Education   **419**

CHAPTER TWELVE
Teaching in the Real World
447

APPENDIX A
Preschool Unit: "Seeds"
455

APPENDIX B
Preschool Unit: "Farm Animals"
467

APPENDIX C
Kindergarten–Primary Unit:
If You Give a Mouse a Cookie
480

APPENDIX D
Primary Unit: *Alexander and the Terrible, Horrible, No Good, Very Bad Day*
491

Index
501

Early Childhood Curriculum

Developmental Bases for
Learning and Teaching

CHAPTER ONE

The Changing Role of the Teacher in Developing Curriculum for Diverse Populations

Teachers make decisions about curriculum; what to teach, how to organize the content, what instructional approaches to use, what to give major emphasis and what to exclude; how and what to evaluate. Teachers decide how to present material, how explicit to make explanations, how much to leave to inference. They decide how to supplement the prescribed curriculum, what materials to use, what risks they may expose themselves to and whether the educational benefit warrants the risk. They decide how to evaluate student progress and what to report to parents. They decide, perhaps implicitly through their personal style, about classroom climate, about group work and interpersonal relationships, about housekeeping and discipline. They decide what professional inservice work to undertake, and they make judgments about their needs to become more effective instructors (Manley-Casimir & Wassermann, 1989, pp. 288–293).

The decade of the 1990s is a time of change. People are experiencing changes in how they live, how their families are structured, how and where they work, and what they want and can expect for their children. As has been true in all periods of U.S. history, we are a nation of diverse people.

Early childhood programs in the United States are also in a period of change, as educators respond to various expectations for care and learning and to the diversity of families, of children's backgrounds, and of the needs and possibilities that children bring to the programs. This book was written for teachers and future teachers of children from birth to age eight; it discusses how to develop curriculum and instruction appropriate for the development of these children in a time of change.

The field of early childhood education is in an exciting period of growth and expansion. Early childhood programs now serve young children in public schools, child-care and nurture centers, private schools, religious institutions, and other settings. Teachers of these young children have significant opportunities, in cooperation with parents, to guide the children's development and learning. The conditions that affect young lives can significantly influence the learning process—thus the first chapter addresses the complex combination of factors that form the characteristics that very young children present when they enter a group setting. The young children we teach come from diverse backgrounds that affect our role as teachers as we design programs to facilitate their journey of development and learning.

Teachers entering the field in the 1990s and into the new century have a perception of what education for young children should be that is based on their own childhood school experiences. If the new teacher entered school in the 1970s or earlier, the memory might be of an open classroom that was part of a popular school design during the 1960s and 1970s. Kindergarten classrooms were likely to have had learning centers and a variety of toys and materials available for exploration and play. Elementary school teachers during those years were developing an awareness of diverse needs of different student populations as a result of federally funded programs like Head Start. Such programs were established to improve education for children who were considered to be at risk for failure in school achievement.

However, students preparing to become teachers during the 1950s were still likely to expect young students entering elementary school to come from middle-class families. Teachers in schools that had been based on a middle-class model were just beginning to understand that U.S. children came from backgrounds that represented differences in culture, ethnicity, income, and family structure. They were beginning to consider how curriculum and instruction in the classroom needed to be adapted for different kinds of student needs. At this time, having children younger than five years enter public schools was not yet a consideration; and the growth of early childhood programs associated with child care was yet to make a major impact. Likewise, the concept of mainstreaming children with disabilities into regular classrooms was just being implemented.

Today, the diversity of student populations has widened. Not only have families and life-styles in this country changed, but some issues in education now reflect a global view rather than a more isolated national perspective. Rapidly changing conditions have expanded the differences among children who reside in this country and attend early childhood programs of various types. College and university students preparing to teach tomorrow's children must understand the complexity of diversity represented by the populations of children they will teach and the implications that those differences have for how they will plan and implement instructional programs. As Manley-Casimir and Wassermann (1989) describe the teaching role, "Teachers make hundreds of decisions every day—from the very trivial to the very complex" (p. 288). Instructional decisions include considerations for the varied needs of the young children they teach.

Change in education is now the rule in contemporary schools, just as it is in other facets of society. In previous periods of the history of early childhood education, cycles of change in instructional methods alternated with times of stability, when the same approaches were used for several decades. The organization of early childhood curriculum and instruction in today's programs is a response to the issues that confront the community, educators, and families in a period of continuing transition. Tomorrow's schools will be engaged in constant evolution and evaluation if the challenges to educate changing student populations and their varied learning needs are to be met. The issues discussed in this chapter focus on the diversity of children enrolled in early childhood programs, the complexity of early childhood settings that serve children in these programs, and the effect of change and diversity in early childhood programs that in turn require a changing role for teachers of young children.

CONDITIONS THAT HAVE CURRICULUM IMPLICATIONS FOR EARLY CHILDHOOD PROGRAMS

The Diversity of Children Enrolled in Early Childhood Programs

The typical (over 50 percent) American child in the year 1990 will experience a major family disruption due to divorce. Consequently, the child will live in a one-parent home with a parent who holds regular employment outside the home. He/she will enter several substitute child care arrangements and spend a great deal of time alone. By school age, the child's time will be occupied in terms of duration by television, school and family in that order, with family a poor third. TV programs watched will grow rapidly from PG to R to X *rated,* with all forms available in most homes. During the teen years, the child will use one or more illicit drugs plus alcohol and tobacco, and will father or mother a child or have an abortion. The child will be subjected to abuse by a parent or friend of the family and some of his/her friends and acquaintances will attempt suicide (Frost, 1986, p. 243).

In 1986 Frost accurately predicted the status of children in 1990. If anything, he was conservative in his estimation of the changing conditions of childhood during the last decade of the twentieth century. In addition to the possibilities he listed, children are also encountering homelessness and increasing domestic and environmental violence. Regardless of family income, some children are experiencing stress from factors in their own families and in the larger society that affect their ability to learn in school. Teachers of tomorrow's young children need to be aware of these differences in family environments, as well as cultural and ethnic differences that will have an effect on the interests and experiences that they will bring to the beginning years in educational settings.

Cultural and Ethnic Differences.   The United States has always been a nation of many cultures, with populations representing a variety of races and ethnic groups. Nevertheless, there was a time when the education of children was based on a belief that curriculum and instruction could be the same for all. With the advent of the civil rights movement after World War II, there was an increasing awareness that elementary school education had been designed with the middle-class child and teacher in mind. In reality, curriculum and instruction needed to be organized for diverse cultures and economic populations (Weber, 1984).

During the War on Poverty and Great Society years of the 1960s, various federally funded programs were initiated to meet the needs of different populations of students. For instance, programs such as Head Start and Follow Through focused on the needs of children from economically disadvantaged populations; Head Start served preschool children from three to five years of age, and Follow Through programs sought to extend the benefits of Head Start into elementary school. In addition, bilingual education, Title I programs, and programs for migrants were introduced to public schools through federal funding for children who were at risk for school failure. Migrant students were at risk because, as they and their families moved about the country following the harvest of crops, their sporadic school attendance caused them to fall further behind in academic achievement each year. Some students from low-income homes also needed supplementary instruction through Title I teachers because they were at risk for falling behind their peers in reading and mathematics. These and other federally funded initiatives were used to identify and address the learning differences in children from diverse populations. Although not all children needing programs were served through these initiatives (e.g., Head Start served only 20 percent of the economically disadvantaged preschool population), the programs reflected efforts to plan for children from different cultural and economic populations.

Awareness of cultural, racial, and ethnic differences has broadened since the 1960s. In addition, an influx of new immigrants and refugees to the United States has widened the diversity of groups entering the schools. Families have come from Cuba, Central America, Indochina, Eastern Europe, the former Soviet Union, and many other regions as political crises, wars, and changes in government leadership have forced families to seek safety and economic opportunity in other countries. Children from these families entering schools and other early childhood programs bring unique cultural experiences to their new nation. Their parents range from professionals with affluent circumstances to uneducated people from underdeveloped nations. Some of these children are either under foster parent care, have been adopted by U.S. parents, or are otherwise of a race that is different from that of the parents. In addition, mixed-race adoptions are becoming more common in this country. Teachers of the future will need a broad understanding of the differences in nationality, culture, and life events that affect every child entering their classrooms (DiMartino, 1989; Wardle, 1990).

Lucy Wu

Lucy is six years old. Her parents came to the United States from Vietnam when they were teenagers. Lucy's mother went with her family to Houston, where they were sponsored by a Lutheran church; her father's family went to Houston to stay with relatives until they could get settled. Lucy's mother and father met in a local community college. They worked in a small grocery store that her father's family opened in a leased building in an older neighborhood in eastern Houston. Recently, the store burned as a result of faulty wiring. The contents of the store were not insured; thus, Lucy's mother is working as a maid in a Holiday Inn and her father is working at a drive-in grocery until the debts are paid and they can try to get another start in a family business. Lucy and her parents are living temporarily with her maternal grandparents in a small apartment until they can afford their own place.

Differences in Family Environments.   As mentioned earlier, early childhood education prior to the 1960s, particularly in public schools, was oriented to the middle-class child (Weber, 1984). The child was assumed to come from an intact family with both parents present in the home. The typical mother did not work outside the home and devoted her time and energy to the family, especially the children. Although this was never an accurate picture of all populations of children, in recent decades it has become the exception rather than the rule. Many factors have affected the makeup of the family structure. In addition to families in which a father and mother are present, there are single-parent families, stepfamilies and blended families (which result from multiple marriages or cohabitation, where children from two or more family combinations live as a single family), teenage parents, and working mothers.

Billy and Bobby

Billy and Bobby are two-year-old twins. Their mother, Susan, is seventeen and not married. They live in the family room in the basement of Susan's parents' home in Evansville, Indiana. Susan works at a Kmart department store during the day and attends night school three evenings a week. She receives a check each month through Aid to Families with Dependent Children. Billy and Bobby stay in a family day home during the day; their grandmother takes care of them on the evenings when Susan attends school.

Susan and her mother have recently been fighting over the amount of time Susan has been out on dates each week with her new boyfriend. Susan believes she is going to have to move out. Her boyfriend is not working and does not want to get married and have the responsibility of the twins. At the moment, Billy and Bobby face an uncertain future.

Children live with a single parent for various reasons, divorce being the most common. Although dual custody is a frequent possibility when parents divorce, most children spend the majority of their lives with one parent. Fathers who are single parents are increasing in number, as are split-custody decisions where siblings are divided between the parents. Single adults are now able to adopt children as well as act as foster parents to children needing temporary homes. In addition, children may live with a grandparent when the parents are unable or unwilling to care for their children. The number of children living in single-parent homes has increased dramatically in recent decades. Edelman (1989) reported that 8.9 million children under the age of ten lived in single-parent households, a 48 percent increase from the 6 million reported in the early 1980s.

Children who have experienced a divorce in their family may be at risk for learning difficulties. Children from divorced families are more likely to become juvenile delinquents, have trouble in school, need psychiatric help, and experience depression, loneliness, low self-esteem, and low achievement. During the first two years after a divorce, they are often neglected because the parent who is to care for them is overworked, absorbed with problems of surviving, and trying to cope with meeting the increased responsibilities of single parenting (Clarke-Stewart, 1989). Some of the children will also experience having to adjust to a new stepparent and siblings in a stepfamily. An additional factor can be reduced family income because of the changed economic circumstances caused by the divorce.

Although the results of experiencing a divorce may or may not be long-lasting, the classroom teacher must be sensitive to trauma these children are going through. Teacher support is needed to reassure the affected students that they are valued at school and that school life will provide some consistency in their young lives. The school community can also provide support to the large numbers of young children and their parents who are affected by separation and divorce each year.

Children of teenage parents are also at risk. Many of these parents are barely more than children themselves, with little in the way of parenting skills or financial resources. Although the teen birth rate actually dropped in the 1970s and remained stable in the 1980s, in 1986 there were almost half a million births to women younger than twenty. It is also predicted that by the year 2000 only six in ten young single mothers will have a high school diploma, and almost one in five will have two or more children (Children's Defense Fund, 1989).

Children born to teenage mothers are more likely to live in a one-parent home at or below the poverty level than those born to older females. Their mothers are likely to be unemployed or working at low-paying jobs. Because of the stressful circumstances for the mothers, children are likely to be at risk from poor nutrition, inadequate housing, and inappropriate parenting. Although there are programs across the United States to assist and counsel teenage mothers, only a low percentage of young mothers can be reached (Children's Defense Fund, 1989). Children entering school from a home headed by a teenage parent frequently need security, nutritious meals, and positive experiences, which the parent is often unable to provide. The parent in turn may need support and assistance from the school in finding social services and in learning how to help the child.

Not all families needing consideration are poor or close to poverty. Upwardly mobile families with two parents working at professional positions are the norm in many communities. Educated parents have high expectations for their children's achievement in the early years of schooling; they expect their children to be prepared for entry into higher education and a profession. Middle-class and upper-class parents are more likely to put pressure on teachers to provide accelerated educational experiences that will ensure that their children will excel in school. Schools receiving these children are responsible for providing appropriate curriculum and instruction in early childhood classrooms; they must also help parents understand what expectations they should have for their children's learning at this stage of their development (Elkind, 1987). Teachers are challenged to successfully communicate with parents and guide their understanding of what constitutes a good educational program for young children.

Families in Stress.   Contemporary life-styles are stressful. Circumstances of daily living can cause stress in families whether the family unit is at the poverty level, in the working class, or a part of affluent society. Moreover, children from all types of families can be neglected or maltreated. Although much more concern is expressed for the stressful life of the child living at the poverty level, children of affluent parents can also be troubled or deprived if, for example, the parents travel frequently or are busy with social or professional obligations, usually leaving the children in the care of a housekeeper or nanny.

Stress goes beyond the economic circumstances of the family. In addition to divorce and poverty, which are major causes of stress for families, other factors can be equally important. Pressures are found in families with working mothers, families who are homeless, families in which parents are addicted to alcohol or drugs or both, families who experience domestic violence or live in violent neighborhoods, and families in which children are abused or neglected.

Working Parents.   Although the perception before 1970 that the father was the breadwinner and the mother maintained the home and cared for the children was never true for many families, the percentage of mothers employed outside the home has risen dramatically since the 1970s. Edelman (1989) reported that by the 1990s, 55 percent of mothers of young children would work outside the home, an increase of 80 percent since 1970. Whether the working mother is a single parent or married, the changes in family life-style can cause problems for family members. Working parents are faced with time management problems, concerns for quality child care, and the matter of balancing priorities between work and home (O'Neil, 1991). Children from families in which both parents or the single parent are employed face adjustments that may range from attending a combination of child-care and educational settings each day, to self-caring before and after school, to accepting family responsibilities that are difficult to manage at their level of maturity.

Working parents often find it difficult to meet with teachers for conferences or attend school meetings. They must frequently hurry their children and themselves as they seek to reconcile family and work schedules. Working parents of all types need support systems to make their tasks and responsibilities easier to manage and to ease their concern for their children's welfare (Brazelton, 1989). Although the federal government has failed to acknowledge the reality of the needs of working parents in the United States and the implications for a federal role in assisting families, some schools are providing needed services for parents and children. Many schools now offer before- and after-school care and training and support groups for parenting skills and other issues that are unique to working parents.

Homelessness.   When attention first focused on the growing numbers of homeless people in the United States, those affected were described as mentally ill individuals who had been released from mental institutions with no local services to provide the assistance they needed. Others without homes were drug- and alcohol-addicted individuals or vagrants who did occasional work. Within the last few years, the homeless have included families who have lost their homes for a variety of reasons (Eddowes & Hranitz, 1989). One factor involved in homelessness is the nature of employment for the working poor. A large percentage of U.S. workers are employed in temporary or part-time jobs that do not offer health insurance and other benefits associated with permanent employment. In addition, the types of jobs that many individuals are engaged in are within the service industry. Workers are hired and fired as business trends improve or deteriorate. As a result, there is little financial stability and security (Children's Defense Fund, 1989).

The reality of life for many of the working poor is that financial security is impossible, even if both parents work. These families live marginal lives that are governed by the availability of work. If one parent loses employment, the rent cannot be paid and the family must move. Any combination of financial problems, such as the serious illness of a family member and an unexpected expense, can wipe out the family's resources. Another difficulty for the working poor is the unavailability of affordable housing. The decrease and deterioration of low-cost housing has made it impossible for many families to afford rent for even the most modest apartment or home (Eddowes & Hranitz, 1989). It is estimated that one hundred thousand children go to sleep homeless in the United States each night (James, Smith, & Mann, 1991).

As families join the ranks of the homeless, children become victims of their living conditions. Many homeless families are forced to seek housing in shelters that are not designed for children. Shelters are frequently located in old buildings or houses; consequently, they may not be equipped to provide minimum safety standards for infants and young children. Lead poisoning from painted surfaces can affect the health of homeless children, who also are susceptible to illnesses that spread through the shelters; recovering from illness is difficult if shelter residents are required to leave during the day (Children's Defense Fund, 1990). In addition, families must often separate because certain shelters receive only one gender.

Homeless children usually have to give up their toys and other items that provide security. It is difficult for them to attend school because of the transient nature of their existence. As a result, regular school attendance is impossible for many. They are frequently teased by schoolmates who do not understand their plight. If they are able to attend school, their teachers need to be aware of and sensitive to their stress. Like many other populations of at-risk children, they need nutritional meals at school, particularly because shelter meals are not usually prepared for the needs of growing children. For some, mere availability of food may be uncertain outside of the school (Eddowes & Hranitz, 1989). Special planning is required in every community if homeless children are not to become invisible and forgotten.

 Cassandra

Cassandra is four years old. She and her parents had been living in an old farm house ten miles from Natchez, Mississippi. Her father worked on a nearby farm, but it was recently sold by the owner. Cassandra, her two older brothers, and her parents then moved into Natchez, where they are now staying with Cassandra's aunt. The home is large, but Cassandra's four cousins make a total of ten people living in the home. Many of Cassandra's toys and clothes are in a storage building behind the house.

Cassandra's mother found work at a dry cleaner, but her father is still looking for work. Her aunt heard of a vacancy in the Head Start program located near her home and is going to take Cassandra to the center to enroll her in the program. Cassandra's brothers have been enrolled in an elementary school, but they feel like strangers and make excuses not to attend classes.

Substance Abuse.   Children who live in a home where the adults are addicted to alcohol or chemicals are also living with stress. When substance abuse is a problem, the whole family is affected. Parents who are under the influence of drugs or alcohol are more likely to neglect or abuse their children than those who are not addicted. Nearly six thousand cases of child neglect or abuse were reported in the District of Columbia between January and June 1989, an increase of 64 percent since 1988; drugs, including alcohol, were a factor in more than half the cases. More serious is that there were 1,225 child abuse fatalities reported in 1988. An investigation of child fatalities in Georgia revealed that one-third of the deaths were linked to parents who were using drugs or alcohol (Children's Defense Fund, 1990). More recently, crack, the cooked form of cocaine, has affected young children. Since the drug became widely available in 1985, it is estimated that as many as one million children have been affected by in utero exposure. The first of these children are now in school (Hutchinson, 1991; Newman & Buka, 1991).

Violence, Neglect, and Abuse.   Domestic violence is found in every socioeconomic group. It is also found in all racial and ethnic groups. Shelters for battered women and children are necessary in most midsize and larger communities to provide a haven for victims of domestic violence (Hranitz & Eddowes, 1990).

Violence is increasing not only in the home but also in many neighborhoods and schools. Neighborhood violence is rampant in urban areas, particularly in inner cities where crack cocaine is sold and used. Children growing up in these neighborhoods experience violence and are sometimes random victims of violent incidents (O'Neil, 1991). A survey of 536 south-side Chicago elementary school children revealed that 26 percent of the children had seen someone shot and 29 percent had seen someone stabbed. Violent crime among youths is also increasing, with evidence that there is a history of abuse or family violence among delinquent youths (Children's Defense Fund, 1990).

Schools and teachers have a particularly important responsibility when teaching children who are at risk for neglect or abuse. Children who are dressed inappropriately or who frequently attend school in dirty clothing may exhibit other symptoms of neglect. Likewise, children who have been physically, sexually, or mentally abused may show signs of their condition that may alert the teacher that the child's situation may need to be reported to the proper authorities. Children who are frequently bruised, exhibit burn marks, or have other unusual physical characteristics may have been physically abused. Schools need to help children who are experiencing abuse or neglect; such children are unable to attend to learning. Schools must take responsibility for these children, because teachers may be the adults outside the family who have the most frequent and consistent contact with the children and are most likely to have an opportunity to initiate intervention. There are indications that numbers of neglected and abused children will continue to rise in the immediate future. For these children, schools are a haven, and possibly their only source of security (Santrock, 1990).

Teaching Stressed Children

The difficult part of teaching is not the academics. The difficult part is dealing with the great numbers of kids who come from emotionally, physically, socially, and financially stressed homes. Nearly all of my kindergarten kids come from single-parent families. Most of the moms really care for their kids but are very young, undereducated, and financially strained. Children who have had no breakfast or who are fearful of what their moms' boyfriends will do to them—or to their moms—are not very

good listeners or cooperative partners with teachers or with their peers. We are rais-
ing a generation of emotionally stunted and troubled youth who will in turn raise a
generation of the same. What is the future of this country when we have so many
needy youngsters? (a kindergarten teacher in Minnesota, cited by Ernest L. Boyer in
"What Teachers Say About Children in America," Educational Leadership, 46, no. 8,
May 1989, p. 73).

▲

Differences in Learning Needs.   Children enter school as unique individuals. They bring with them their experiences from their homes and communities. They also bring their own combination of interests, styles of learning, and personalities. As a group they represent a range of aptitudes for learning, as well as strengths and weaknesses that may be so minor that they are hidden or so extreme that they are serious impediments. Despite their differences, they are all similar in that they have hopes of being successful students. The first years in early childhood classrooms are important because it is during this time that the children form perceptions of themselves and their competence as individual students and as members of groups of students.

Many children have exceptionally high aptitudes and abilities. They have a high potential for learning that allows them to learn quickly and often independently. They are self-starters and voracious in their desire to acquire information. They can accomplish by themselves much of what is to be learned. The teacher's responsibility with children having high learning potential is to keep them challenged and help them discipline themselves to work to achieve their best, without being pushed unreasonably to excel.

Other children are also competent, but they are steady rather than fast-paced learners like the high achievers. They do consistently well in school and are a stable influence on the other children in the class. These students may have occasional difficulties but are easily redirected toward a positive outcome in their class experiences.

A large percentage of young students are at risk for school failure. For a child to be at risk academically means that he or she has some condition that might be a deterrent to successful learning. The number of children in this category is expected to increase in the decades to come. Children can be at risk because of health factors, social factors, or both (O'Neil, 1991). They may be at risk academically because of low birth weight or prematurity that has had residual effects on development. Children who enter school with a home language other than English or have limited language skills are also at risk (Au & Kawakami, 1991; Haycock, 1991).

Children who live in homes that are experiencing one or more types of stress can be at risk for success in school (Reed & Sauter, 1990). Children from poverty-level families commonly are at risk. Because they are likely to be unable to have their basic needs met for nutrition or security, they may encounter problems in performing well in the school environment. Poverty is frequently combined with other negative forces in a child's life experiences; the child living at or below the poverty level is also more likely to be a minority child, experience the effects of drug and alcohol abuse, or be exposed to domestic and neighborhood violence. However, whether these

conditions happen to a child from a low-income home or one from more affluent financial circumstances, they cause the child to be at risk for lower achievement.

Children who are at risk academically need early intervention to remediate the negative factors that can affect their ability to learn. Because early intervention is the most effective in eliminating or minimizing risk factors, early childhood programs, many beginning in infancy, enhance the possibilities that children can overcome the conditions in their lives that can negatively affect their learning (Children's Defense Fund, 1990; Taylor, Willits, & Lieberman, 1990).

Cautions About Using the Term *At Risk*

Anthony Pellegrini discussed concerns about using the term at risk *in emergent literacy programs. He proposed that being at risk implies that something is wrong with children and their families or the school. Instead of viewing the term as describing probabilities of certain groups for encountering difficulties, it implies blame of implied locus of responsibility.*

One assumption is that children are at risk for failure because the locus of responsibility lies with the family; something is lacking or deficient in the home environment. The other assumption is that the locus of responsibility lies with the school. Children are at risk for failure because of the curriculum, school organization, and teaching styles.

Pellegrini recommends not using the term at risk *because it assigns blame. Instead, he proposes that materials familiar to families be used when encouraging them to engage in emergent literacy activities with their children (A. D. Pellegrini, "A Critique of the Concept of at Risk as Applied to Emergent Literacy," Language Arts, 68, 1991, pp. 380–385).*

Children who have physical factors that can affect their learning are frequently described as having special needs. Physical impairments include hearing and visual disabilities as well as other physical disabilities. Hearing impairments range from slight to severe and affect speech and language development (Mayer, 1990; Moran, 1990; Patterson & Wright, 1990). Visual impairments such as nearsightedness (myopia) and farsightedness (hyperopia) can be corrected with eyeglasses. More severe visual impairments include conditions such as congenital cataracts or glaucoma and atrophy of the optic nerve, all of which can have more serious implications for handicaps to learning (Silberman, 1990).

Some students can be seriously disabled by mental retardation or emotional disturbance. Emotionally disturbed children are characterized by an inability (not related to a physical disability) to benefit from instruction. They have difficulty relating to their peers and exhibit wide variations in mood (Edwards & Simpson, 1990). Children with mental retardation have a condition that affects academic learning differently, depending upon the amount of retardation. Children with mild retardation are described as educable mentally retarded, and those with moderate retardation are characterized as trainable mentally retarded. Children with severe or profound mental retardation also have serious physical conditions that require extensive medical attention and services from time of birth (Yoshida, 1990).

Children at the other extreme of mental ability are also exceptional. The child who has an extremely high potential for learning or shows signs of exceptional skills or talents also has unique learning needs and requires individual intervention so that the instructional program nurtures that child's interests and potential. School districts commonly have teachers who have been specially trained to work with students who are gifted and talented. Such students usually are assigned to a regular classroom and work with the special teacher in a resource room designed and equipped for that purpose (Jenkins-Friedman & Nielson, 1990).

Some children exhibit learning difficulties that are not associated with mental retardation. They have difficulty academically and sometimes socially and do not respond to the usual instructional methods. Children with this condition are described as learning disabled but may also be characterized as hyperactive, perceptually handicapped, brain injured, dyslexic, or neurologically impaired (Graham, Harris, & Reid, 1990). A more recent and currently popular label for hyperactivity is attention deficit disorder (ADD) (Buchoff, 1990).

Children with special needs exhibit many different types of possible interference with learning, as well as variations in the seriousness of the interference. Many of the children can be served by or at least included in the regular classroom within the

instructional program used with other students. Other conditions are severe enough to require the services of a special teacher or a combination of specialists to provide therapy or instruction (or both) that is planned for the student's individual needs. Children with special needs also have to interact and learn in the regular classroom as much as possible with their peers who are not disabled. This process, called mainstreaming, inclusion, or integration, is planned for each student with special needs to determine the balance needed between special services and experiences in regular classrooms (Meyen, 1990).

Early childhood education is very important for children who are at risk academically or have special needs. Early intervention with any kind of risk factor or impairment is important to maximize the child's opportunity to overcome, minimize, or adapt to the disability. Whether the young child is at risk because of economic, physical, or social factors, early attention to the problem is essential. If the child is experiencing more than one risk factor, the possibility of long-term damaging consequences multiplies (Schorr, 1989). Early modification or elimination of risk factors is essential to prevent permanent damage to the child's outcomes. At-risk factors that are economically or socially based are addressed in programs such as Head Start and prekindergarten programs in the public schools, whereas conditions that are based on physical or mental disabilities need the type of services that are provided through PL 94-142, the Education for All Handicapped Children Act, and PL 99-457, which extends services to infants and their families (Morrison, 1988). Programs under PL 94-142 provided for children with handicaps have been based primarily in public schools; however, under PL 99-457 infants and families can be served from a variety of agencies and settings. The programs provided by public schools for children ages three to five with disabilities and by Head Start projects for at-risk preschool children are but two types of educational settings that serve children in the early childhood years.

THE COMPLEX NATURE OF SETTINGS FOR EARLY CHILDHOOD PROGRAMS

Early childhood education encompasses the years from birth through age eight. The teacher who is preparing to teach children of these ages can be overwhelmed by the various types of settings that serve such children. The large majority of primary-age children attend school in some type of institutional setting, be it public, private, or parochial. (Home schooling, where a parent conducts instruction with his or her own children, is a growing method of education but still does not account for more than a small percentage of children.) Preschool children, on the other hand, can attend a variety of programs, including those offered by schools, parochial institutions, agencies, corporations, and hospitals.

The role of the teacher varies in the programs, as does the salary. Financing for the programs ranges from publicly funded schools and projects to settings that are entirely supported by fees paid by parents. For purposes of this discussion, the programs have been categorized as public school programs, nonpublic school programs, Head Start, and child-care programs.

Public School Programs

Kindergarten.   Public schools have served children under the age of six for more than a century through kindergarten classrooms. The purpose for kindergarten has evolved during the decades it has been associated with the public schools. Designed as a program for five-year-olds, it was originally developed following the philosophy and methods of Friedrich Froebel in the nineteenth century. Not all states have kindergartens in the public schools, but as the trend toward expanding early childhood programs in public schools continues, more states are implementing kindergarten classrooms.

In the 1940s and 1950s, kindergartens were perceived as programs for middle-class children. Since the 1960s, they have served all populations of children. They have been joined by preschool programs that serve children who are at risk for academic failure (Coleman, 1990). These newer programs can include prekindergarten or other programs for four-year-olds, bilingual programs, classes for children with special needs, and extended-care programs.

Prekindergarten Programs.   Prekindergarten programs have been established in some states for four-year-old children who have language or cognitive limitations. Usually from low-income homes and sometimes from homes where the primary language is not English, prekindergarten children attend programs that emphasize learning experiences to develop the language and concepts needed for later success in school.

Bilingual Programs.   Bilingual programs serve children who speak a language other than English. Although bilingual programs may begin in the preschool years, they usually extend into the elementary grades. In school districts where non-English-speaking children enter school for the first time beyond the intermediate grades, bilingual education may be offered at the secondary level.

Programs for Children with Special Needs.   Children who are falling behind in achievement in the elementary grades can receive supplementary instruction through a federally funded program titled Chapter I (formerly Title I and other federal programs). Children who are not demonstrating adequate achievement in mathematics and reading receive additional instruction beyond that provided by the regular classroom teacher.

Children with special needs are also served in preschool classes and elementary grades. At the preschool level, children are screened and identified for an early childhood special education program for early intervention that can begin at age three. Following an Individualized Education Program (IEP) developed for each child, the special education teacher and classroom teacher conduct the program with other specialists to optimize the child's potential to learn and develop skills to compensate for the disability.

Extended-Care Programs.   Many schools are now implementing extended care before and after classes for students needing child care during out-of-school hours (Kagan, 1989). These programs can be developed and conducted by school-based personnel or by a community agency that works in a cooperative manner with the school district. Parents can enroll their child in the program; the fees they pay support the payment of program expenses.

Nonpublic School Programs

Parochial and private schools frequently have preschool programs. The starting age may be about three years old, and the program may have a class for three-, four-, and five-year-olds for a few hours each day. Other programs are called nursery schools or mother's-day-out programs and are not offered every day. Preschool programs can also be offered by a local college or university and be labeled as a laboratory school or child development center.

Nonpublic preschool programs serving children with special needs are available in some larger communities that are funded with local, state, and/or federal monies. Preschools for children who are visually or hearing impaired or for infants, toddlers, and preschoolers with multiple disabilities provide programs of early intervention with teachers who are trained to work with individual disabilities.

Head Start

Head Start is a publicly funded program. Developed in the 1960s for intervention with minority and low-income children who were at risk, it is a comprehensive program that addresses the educational, nutritional, and social needs of the at-risk child. It can be associated with public school districts or be conducted as a separate program through a community agency. The large number of children that Head Start serves has increased in recent years. However, only one-fifth of the poor three- and four-year-olds in the United States that would benefit from the program are able to attend (Schweinhart, 1989).

Child-Care Programs

Child care has grown to become a major industry in the United States as a result of the rising numbers of working mothers. In 1987, 52 percent of mothers of children under age five were employed, compared with only 14 percent in 1950. As a result, three of every ten children under the age of five are in day-care homes, day-care centers, or nursery schools (Schweinhart, 1989). Parents who find it necessary to locate daily care for their children have many options from which to choose.

Family day care is characterized by child care provided in an individual home. The provider cares for a small number of children and has adapted the home to accommodate the children who come to the home each day. Center-based child care, in contrast, involves a setting that serves larger numbers of children, usually divided by age groups. The children are assigned to classrooms for their age level and the room is equipped for the programmatic and developmental needs that are characteristic for that age.

Child-care centers are established in various community contexts. Centers that are conducted as businesses may range from a single center to a chain of more than

one hundred centers (such as Kinder Care or La Petite Academy). Child care is also provided at church settings. The church sponsors the child-care program or leases the facilities to an individual or group during the week. Employer-sponsored child care is also a growing service (Magid, 1989). Large companies or corporations may build a center or negotiate with an existing center to serve the children of their employees. Another option is for a cluster of companies, such as a group located in an industrial park, to sponsor collectively a center that provides care to children of workers in the sponsoring companies. Hospitals frequently offer child-care facilities for employees' children but may also provide service for chronically ill children in the community.

Employer-sponsored care may or may not be provided at a special or reduced rate for employees. Convenience of location may be the primary consideration for the parent. Federally supported child care, in contrast, funds child care for low-income parents and assists them in obtaining job training or employment that will allow them to become wage earners rather than continue as welfare recipients. Although care for infants and preschool children while parents work is the primary service provided by child-care centers, educational programs are also conducted.

Continuing Complexity in Preschool Programs

It must be obvious to the reader by now that it is a difficult task to describe early childhood programs in neat categories. In reality, over time, programs have had to modify and provide additional services to adapt to the changing needs of families. Public schools are accepting prekindergarten children and are offering child care, and child-care centers are strengthening their instructional programs. Private preschools are also extending their programs to include child care. The field is becoming comprehensive, and the various components will no longer be able to function as separate entities in the future. There are many issues (Kagan, 1989; Mitchell, 1989; Willer & Bredekamp, 1990) and problems (Boyer, 1989), in addition to opportunities for early childhood educators, as different programs interact and cooperate rather than compete (Caldwell, 1989; Morgan, 1989; Smith, 1989). More about this topic will be discussed in chapter 2.

THE CHANGING ROLE OF THE TEACHER IN DEVELOPING CURRICULUM FOR EARLY CHILDHOOD PROGRAMS

It is clear that many challenges face tomorrow's teachers of young children in the early childhood years. Gone are the days when young children could be perceived as coming from similar homes and family backgrounds. Gone are the days when curriculum and instruction for young children could be designed from a commercial program prepared by a specialist in some distant city. No longer can the teacher be concerned only with the instructional program when working with a classroom of young children. The teacher of tomorrow will be concerned with an educational program for diverse populations of students that will acknowledge and appreciate their differences and include the involvement of their families as well. A major challenge will be to learn how to design curriculum that is appropriate for all young children and compatible with their development and interests, as well as their unique needs. Development of quality programs for young children will include design of curriculum that is dynamic, child centered, and responsive to the diverse populations that are represented in each classroom.

The Role of the Teacher in Developing Curriculum for Diverse Populations

Every classroom of small children is diverse. No matter what the background of the children, even if their circumstances seem to be similar, their individual families are different, with varied family routines, rituals, and observances. If the children come from more varied ethnic groups, socioeconomic groups, and cultures, the diversity will be more pronounced. These and other considerations are kept in mind when preparing learning experiences in the early childhood classroom.

Multicultural Curriculum.   There is now an emphasis on multicultural curriculum in early childhood programs in recognition of the diversity of young children. One focus of the multicultural curriculum has been to study different cultures around the world; the social studies curriculum might include the study of, for instance, an African culture, the Eskimos, or the culture in a South American country. The definition of *multicultural curriculum* intended here is more specific to the developmental needs of young children in the early childhood years.

The multicultural curriculum reflects the cultural representation within the group of children in a particular classroom (Seefeldt, 1990). Topics studied incorporate the unique reflections of those topics in the child's family. If foods are being studied, family recipes can represent the multicultural makeup of the classroom. The multicultural curriculum celebrates the contributions of the cultures of children who are learning together at a particular time of their lives (Au & Kawakami, 1991).

Curriculum for Children from Diverse Family Environments.   Earlier in the chapter we discussed the complex diversity of family environments in which children live. Children come to early childhood programs from all types of housing arrangements and family structures. They have parents who represent many kinds of employment or lack thereof. Some of the children come from very secure family lifestyles, whereas others are experiencing stress that can originate from many causes. Although children from every socioeconomic group can come from stressful home environments, children at the poverty level are more likely to be affected by more than one source of stress. Teachers of young children need to be sensitive to how the program designed for these children demonstrates awareness of their needs and provides continuity and support when needed. The curriculum for social development is particularly relevant when accommodating differences in family environments.

Curriculum for Children with Special Needs.   Although public school programs are most likely to serve children with special needs within a preschool or primary-grade program, other early childhood settings also serve children with disabilities or other types of exceptionalities. The teacher of young children not only needs to be aware of the adaptations that must be made to accommodate a child with special needs into the classroom environment but must also consider how learning experiences can be prepared to include the child's special learning needs. Children with attention deficit disorder may work better in small rather than large group activities. The child with limited vision will need to have visual activities modified to take advantage of his or her best avenue for exploring the environment. Each child with special needs will have individual strengths and requirements that will be factors in how the teacher and other students can assist him or her.

The Role of the Teacher in Involving Parents in Curriculum Development

Earlier in the chapter we discussed factors that are causing changes in family lifestyles and structures. Many of the changes have put families in stress. Teachers in early childhood programs must be more perceptive and sensitive to the needs young children may bring to school that reflect possibly stressful family circumstances. Therefore, teachers will want to know and involve parents and families in their programs (Nuckolls, 1991). Changes in family life-styles require that different types of programs be available to fit individual family requirements (Coleman, 1990). Cooperation between program and family will be necessary if the unique needs of individual family circumstances are to be fulfilled.

There are more important reasons for involving parents in the early childhood program. The extensive research conducted on intervention programs for young children in recent decades has revealed that parent involvement is an essential factor in successful programs. Although the majority of parents of young children are employed, they need information on how they can help their children and the educational or caregiving setting. They also may need help in understanding how important their role is for the child's success in development and learning (Boyer, 1989). Parents may need training in parenting skills or help in seeking assistance for themselves or their children. Partnership relationships among the teacher, other early childhood program staff members, and the family are important ingredients in the development of a successful program.

Parents can also make a very important contribution to the school. In addition to assisting the teacher or staff within possible time limitations, parents can give valuable input to the development of the school curriculum. Parents can serve as resources for learning experiences and share their interests and skills with teachers and children. They can provide needed assistance to the teacher in organizing materials and other resources for the instructional program. Parents can help teachers understand their interests and goals for their child's development and learning while serving as a source of support for the teacher in developing the best possible program for the child (McCormick, 1990).

The Role of the Teacher in Addressing Conflicts between Theory and Practice in Curriculum Development

Early childhood settings have evolved from different traditions. As was discussed earlier, early childhood programs today are moving toward a comprehensive, overlapping system as educators seek to develop quality programs that are responsive to changing family needs. The task of developing quality programs for young children is complex. The teacher not only must plan the program for all types of children but must also understand the contributions of various types of early childhood settings, the contributions of research to the development of quality program models, and the relationships between theory and practice in program planning.

Over the course of the history of early childhood education various theories and influences have affected how programs are designed for young children. These historical and theoretical factors will be discussed in chapters 2 and 3. In the 1990s, teachers are experiencing a complex task in determining how best to use current theories and influences to teach young children. Research on how children develop and learn has come into conflict with educational reform that puts pressure on educational programs to accelerate children's learning in early childhood classrooms. Teachers of young children are groping to understand the implications of these conflicting approaches and will be working to resolve the resulting issues in the years to come. The purpose of this textbook is to help practicing and future teachers understand variables that influence the development of appropriate programs for young children. It also is intended to assist teachers and future teachers of young children in sorting out the issues and developing the knowledge and ability to develop quality instructional programs.

Summary

We are just beginning to understand the challenges and opportunities that young children bring to early childhood programs. Because we are a nation of people whose origins are from many nations, we represent many cultures, ethnic groups, races, and languages. Children enter early childhood settings from families that also represent the full range of economic levels, from poverty to affluence. Their potential for learning is affected by their intellectual aptitude as well as other negative and positive conditions in the family. Their ability to fully participate in the program may be affected by physical handicaps. Children who have an individual or family situation that can be a deterring factor in their participation and learning in a program are said to be at risk. Some children have several risk factors in their lives that compound the possibility that they will later experience difficulty in school.

Because the early childhood years between birth and age eight are very important in the formation of the child's potential for development and learning, early childhood programs can make a major difference in preventing or remediating a risk factor. Various early childhood programs located in public schools, private institutions, and community agencies provide services that aim to reduce risk factors for preschool and primary school children.

Growing numbers of preschool children, including infants, require weekday care while their parents are at work. Because of this growing need, various settings—ranging from family day homes, for-profit child-care centers, churches, and schools—are providing care to accommodate these young children in the preschool years. School-age children may need extended care before and after school until their parents are able to return home with them. The separation between caregiving and educational programs is diminishing as early childhood settings expand and adapt their programs to fit family requirements.

Teachers in these varied settings work with children in the same age ranges. Although the purpose for establishing their program originally may have been distinctly different from that for other programs, services and educational programs offered by early childhood settings now tend to be more similar because of the characteristics they share in meeting contemporary family needs. Teachers and caregivers in all settings will want to be perceptive to the positive and negative factors that affect each young child and to what their role should be in helping the child continue to develop and learn to his or her full potential.

This chapter discussed many variables that contribute to the diversity in young children. Indeed, the reader may come away with the impression that there is "something wrong" with almost every child who is in the early childhood years. That is not the case. A large percentage of children come from stable, happy homes and are in good health. Even if they have experienced divorce, economic downturn, or a health condition, they may exhibit no characteristics that indicate that they are having problems. Likewise, not all children from low-income homes exhibit limited potential as a result of the home environment. It would be equally unbalanced to give the impression that most young children in early childhood programs are similar to the precocious, well-adjusted children in family sitcoms on television. Nevertheless, it is important for those preparing for or engaged in the teaching and care of young children to be knowledgeable about and sensitive to the conditions in the young child's life to which they will respond in planning their instructional program. Teachers in early childhood programs have many challenges and opportunities when they work with the complexity of factors that affect each student.

Teachers in the future will have complex roles; moreover, they will be in partnership with the parents and other persons who may be serving and influencing the child's development and learning. They will be developing a curriculum for young children that will facilitate physical, social-emotional, and cognitive development and learning. They will be teaching the "whole child" in whichever early childhood setting they are located.

Summary Statements

1. Children entering early childhood programs reflect the growing diversity in the general population in the United States.
2. Teachers entering the field of early childhood education in the 1990s will need to understand the diversity among their students and plan curriculum and instruction to match their unique backgrounds and potential.
3. Changing family circumstances and diversity of populations require that early childhood settings accept the reality of constant change in their programs to reflect possibilities for improvement in the field and individual family needs.
4. Since the 1960s, attention to the need for early intervention for children who are at risk for successful learning in the elementary grades has resulted in the implementation of federally funded programs such as Head Start, bilingual education, and Chapter I.
5. New populations of refugees and immigrants who have entered the United States during the last twenty years have widened the diversity of young children in early childhood programs.
6. Changes in family structures, which are frequently the result of divorce, have caused changes in the family environment for many populations of young children, putting them at risk for learning.
7. Children of teenage parents and homeless families can be at risk for learning, as can children of families in which both parents are (or the single parent is) employed.
8. Children from all segments of society may be at risk academically because of parents' drug or alcohol abuse, child neglect or abuse, or violence in the home.
9. Teachers of young children need to be aware of how differences in learning potential and abilities affect planning for appropriate learning experiences.
10. Children who are at risk academically from physical or social causes need early intervention and remediation to minimize long-term effects of their condition.
11. Physical impairments can include visual and hearing problems, as well as other physical handicaps.
12. In addition to programs offered by public schools, there are various other programs that provide a variety of types of early childhood experiences for young children. These programs are offered in such settings as parochial schools, private preschools, and child-care facilities. They also include federally funded programs such as Head Start.
13. Public school early childhood programs include kindergarten; prekindergarten; classes for children who are at risk because of limited English proficiency; bilingual classrooms; special education and classes for children with special needs; and Chapter I programs for at-risk students in the primary grades.
14. With the advent of large percentages of working parents, schools are also providing extended care before and after school in some communities.
15. Child care is also provided in various other settings, including for-profit centers, family day care, employer-sponsored child care, and non-profit programs provided by churches or community agencies.
16. The role of teachers in early childhood programs reflects the complexity of the field and the diversity of young children.
17. Curriculum development also reflects the complexity of early childhood settings and diversity of young children.
18. An important component of all successful early childhood settings is the active participation and involvement of parents.
19. Parents not only need to know how important they are to the child's success in school and the success of the early childhood program, but they can make individual contributions to the instructional program.
20. Teachers entering the field of early childhood education in the 1990s and beyond will need to understand the changing and sometimes conflicting influences on the field; they must also decide how to resolve programmatic decisions that will provide the best learning program for the children they teach in the setting where they are employed.

Study Questions

1. Why do teachers of young children need to get to know their students before they enter the early childhood program?
2. What kind of information can teachers obtain from the parents and their children that will help them in designing their instructional program?
3. What factors will teachers in early childhood programs need to consider when determining in which type of setting they would like to teach?
4. Why do teachers of young children need to understand risk factors that can affect young children's success in elementary school?
5. Why do students from low-income homes sometimes need early intervention programs prior to the elementary years?
6. What are the implications of cultural and ethnic differences in young students for planning the instructional program?
7. Family environments are changing because of social and economic factors. What are some of these changes, and how can young children be affected by them?
8. Why are young children who are born to teenage mothers likely to have more than one condition that puts them at risk in the preschool years?
9. How can it be that contemporary life-styles are stressful in all types of families and at all income levels?
10. Why is the population of homeless children increasing? What are the effects of homelessness on young children?
11. How can inappropriate adult life-styles negatively affect young children?
12. Violence is increasing in U.S. society. How are children most affected by this phenomenon?
13. Why will teachers and settings serving children in the early childhood years have ever expanding responsibilities for children and families beyond the instructional or caregiving program in the 1990s and beyond?
14. How can children vary mentally and physically in how they are able to learn?
15. What is meant by the term *exceptional children?*
16. How are early childhood programs especially helpful for children who are at risk academically or have some type of exceptionality?
17. How are the varied early childhood settings that serve preschool children different yet also increasingly more similar?
18. Why are public schools expanding their programs for the preschool years?
19. Why will teachers of young children under the age of eight have to continually learn about curriculum development for early childhood programs?
20. Why is ongoing communication with parents essential for teachers in early childhood programs?
21. Teachers frequently report that parents are too busy to become involved with school programs. How and why should teachers find ways to convince parents of how vital their interaction and participation is for their child's progress in school?
22. How is the field of early childhood education both challenging and potentially exciting as we approach the end of one century and the beginning of another?

References

Au, K. H., & Kawakami, A. J. (1991). Culture and ownership: Schooling of minority students. *Childhood Education, 67*, 280–284.

Boyer, E. L. (1989). What teachers say about children in America. *Educational Leadership, 46*, 73–75.

Brazelton, T. B. (1989, February 3). Working parents. *Newsweek*, pp. 66–70.

Buchoff, R. (1990). Attention deficit disorder: Help for the classroom teacher. *Childhood Education, 67*, 86–90.

Caldwell, B. M. (1989). A comprehensive model for integrating child care and early childhood education. *Teachers College Record, 90*, 404–414.

Coleman, M. (1990). Planning public preschools. *Dimensions, 19*, 7–9.

Children's Defense Fund. (1989). *A vision for America's future.* Washington, DC: Author.

Children's Defense Fund. (1990). *S. O. S. America! A children's defense budget.* Washington, DC: Author.

Clarke-Stewart, K. A. (1989, January). Single-parent families: How bad for the children? *NEA Today*, pp. 60–64.

DiMartino, E. C. (1989). Understanding children from other cultures. *Childhood Education, 66*, 30–32.

Eddowes, E. A., & Hranitz, J. R. (1989). Educating children of the homeless. *Childhood Education, 66*, 197–200.

Edelman, M. W. (1989). Economic issues related to child care and early childhood education. *Teachers College Record, 90*, 342–351.

Edwards, L. L., & Simpson, J. D. (1990). Emotional disturbance. In E. L. Meyen (Ed.), *Exceptional children in today's schools* (2nd ed.) (pp. 223–254). Denver: Love Publishing.

Elkind, D. (1987). *Miseducation: Preschoolers at risk.* New York: Alfred A. Knopf.

Frost, J. L. (1986). Children in a changing society. *Childhood Education, 62*, 242–249.

Graham, S., Harris, K. R., & Reid, R. (1990). Learning disabilities. In E. L. Meyen (Ed.), *Exceptional children in today's schools* (2nd ed.) (pp. 193–222). Denver: Love Publishing.

Haycock, K. (1991). Reaching for the year 2000. *Childhood Education, 65*, 276–279.

Hranitz, J. R., & Eddowes, E. A. (1990). Violence: A crisis in homes and schools. *Childhood Education, 67*, 4–7.

Hutchinson, J. (1991). What crack does to babies. *American Educator, 15*, 31–32.

James, W. H., Smith, A. J., & Mann, R. (1991). Educating homeless children. *Childhood Education, 67*, 305–308.

Jenkins-Friedman, R., & Nielson, M. E. (1990). Gifted and talented students. In E. L. Meyen (Ed.), *Exceptional children in today's schools* (2nd ed.) (pp. 451–494). Denver: Love Publishing.

Kagan, S. L. (1989, October). Early care and education: Beyond the school house doors. *Phi Delta Kappan*, 107–112.

Magid, R. Y. (1980). The consequences of employer involvement in child care. *Teachers College Record, 90*, 434–443.

Manley-Casimir, M., & Wassermann, S. (1989). The teacher as decision-maker. *Childhood Education, 65*, 288–293.

Mayer, M. H. (1990). Hearing impairment. In E. L. Meyen (Ed.), *Exceptional children in today's schools* (2nd ed.) (pp. 287–316). Denver: Love Publishing.

McCormick, J. (1990, Fall/Winter). Where are the parents? *Newsweek*, pp. 54–55, 58.

Meyen, E. L. (Ed.). (1990). *Exceptional children in today's schools* (2nd ed.). Denver: Love Publishing.

Mitchell, A. (1989, May). Old baggage, new visions: Shaping policy for early childhood programs. *Phi Delta Kappan*, 665–672.

Moran, M. R. (1990). Speech and language disorders. In E. L. Meyen (Ed.), *Exceptional children in today's schools* (2nd ed.) (pp. 255–286). Denver: Love Publishing.

Morgan, G. (1989, Winter). Stalemate or consensus? Barriers to national policy. *Theory into Practice*, 41–46.

Morrison, G. S. (1988). *Education and development of infants, toddlers, and preschoolers.* Glenview, IL: Scott, Foresman.

Newman, L. F., & Buka, S. L. (1991). Clipped wings. *American Educator, 15*, 27–33, 42.

Nuckolls, M. E. (1991). Expanding students' potential through family literacy. *Educational Leadership, 49*, 45–46.

O'Neil, J. (1991). A generation adrift? *Educational Leadership, 49*, 4–10.

Patterson, K., & Wright, A. E. (1990). The speech, language or hearing-impaired child: At-risk academically. *Childhood Education, 67*, 91–95.

Reed, S., & Sauter, R. C. (1990, June). Children of poverty. *Phi Delta Kappan*, K1–K12.

Santrock, J. W. (1990). *Children.* Dubuque, IA: William C. Brown.

Schorr, L. B. (1989). Early interventions to reduce intergenerational disadvantage: The new policy context. *Teachers College Record, 90*, 362–374.

Schweinhart, L. J. (1989, Winter). Early childhood programs in the U. S. today. *High/Scope Resource*, 9–14.

Seefeldt, C. (1990). *Continuing issues in early childhood education.* Columbus, OH: Merrill.

Silberman, R. K. (1990). Visual impairments. In E. L. Meyen (Ed.), *Exceptional children in today's schools* (2nd ed.) (pp. 317–358). Denver: Love Publishing.

Smith, M. M. (1989, Spring). Excellence and equity for America's children. *Tennessee's Children*, 5–12.

Taylor, R. L., Willits, P., & Lieberman, N. (1990). Identification of preschool children with mild handicaps: The importance of cooperative effort. *Childhood Education*, *67*, 26–31.

Wardle, F. (1990). Endorsing children's differences: Meeting the needs of adopted minority children. *Young Children*, *45*, 44–46.

Weber, E. (1984). *Ideas influencing early childhood education.* New York: Teachers College Press.

Willer, B., & Bredekamp, S. (1990). Redefining readiness: An essential requisite for educational reform. *Young Children*, *45*, 22–24.

Yoshida, R. K. (1990). Mental retardation. In E. L. Meyen (Ed.), *Exceptional children in today's schools* (2nd ed.) (pp. 395–422). Denver: Love Publishing.

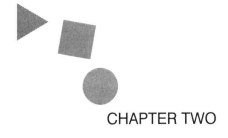

CHAPTER TWO

The Need for Developmentally Appropriate Practice in Early Childhood Settings

In this chapter we will explore current trends and issues in curriculum and instruction used for young children in early childhood programs. We also will discuss how young children learn and the kinds of learning experiences they should have. Because we are in a period of interest in early childhood, and early childhood programs of various types are growing and expanding, we will also include information about how trends in education in elementary schools affect curriculum and instruction for young children.

One current trend is acceleration of curriculum and instruction. Kindergarten and prekindergarten programs are becoming more academically oriented as schools increase curriculum difficulty to meet demands for higher achievement standards. Testing of young children has also increased, both to provide accountability for achievement and as part of the effort to find solutions for those children who cannot perform well in the more difficult curriculum now used in kindergarten and first grade. These trends contribute to the concern expressed by early childhood specialists and early childhood organizations about inappropriate practices in many early childhood classrooms. They call for a return to developmentally appropriate curriculum and practices in early childhood programs.

To say that curriculum is developmentally appropriate means that it is suitable for the physical, emotional, social, and cognitive characteristics and changes that occur in young children; furthermore, such curriculum is also responsive to individual differences in development (Bredekamp, 1987). A developmentally appropriate curriculum is both age appropriate and individually appropriate. This chapter will discuss the issues introduced above, as well as possibilities for working toward solving current problems.

A CONTEMPORARY UNDERSTANDING OF EARLY CHILDHOOD EDUCATION

What does the term *early childhood* mean? When is a child in the period known as early childhood? Answering these questions is not simple because not all child development experts use the same description. The Swiss psychologist Jean Piaget, one of our most influential sources for understanding cognitive development, described stages of development characterized by qualitative differences in thinking. He defined the infant stage as sensorimotor because the child learns primarily through the senses and physical actions until about eighteen months of age. Piaget's next stage, preoperational, extends from the end of the sensorimotor stage to about seven years, when the concrete operational stage begins. Using Piagetian guidelines, some educators prefer to define early childhood as spanning infancy through the end of second grade, or about the time when the child is moving into the concrete operational stage (Mitchell & Modigliani, 1989). As will be further explained in chapter 3, the end of early childhood coincides with the advances in mental reasoning that evolve within the concrete operational stage.

Another perspective is taken from a school organizational point of view. For some, early childhood involves those years prior to kindergarten, whereas for others it includes the years prior to first grade. Yet another approach includes all programs for children beyond the infant-toddler stage through the primary grades, or from age three to eight. In this book, early childhood refers to the period that spans the ages from birth to age eight. Infants and toddlers will be part of our consideration, as will children in the primary grades in elementary school. It is our intent to help the reader understand the continuum of development across these ages; we also aim to show how teachers' understanding of development will help them acquire strategies for instruction that will be developmentally appropriate throughout the early childhood period.

The term *early childhood education* also has many definitions. The care and education of young children originated in many types of different programs early in this century; as a result, the term could be attached to each category with different meanings. In addition to various types of public school programs that have served young children, there are nursery schools that originated in child development programs in universities. Child-care programs, originally designed to care for children of the poor, have become a necessity for all types of families in which both parents work or a single parent is responsible for the family and the home. Federally funded programs such as Head Start also fall within the category of early childhood education. In recent decades, all of these programs have continued to grow and develop, responding to economic and sociological changes in our society that have resulted in an expanding need for programs for children from birth to the age of eight. In effect, early childhood education has become a comprehensive concept that encompasses all types of early childhood programs (Caldwell, 1989; Schweinhart, 1989). How and why this has happened will be discussed later in the chapter.

Historical Roots of Early Childhood Education

For many years after this country was first settled there were no schools for older elementary-age children, much less for those who were of primary age and younger. The first priority for education in the colonies was to establish colleges and then academies that would prepare young men for university work. Later, secondary schools were established. All of these early educational institutions were for white male students (Snyder, 1972).

Younger children were taught in the home. Children of the poor were trained through apprenticeships for a vocation or labored in factories, in mines, or on farms. It was not until after the Civil War that public school systems were developed with access to education for all populations.

The first form of education for children in the early childhood years during the colonial period was the Dame School. A group of parents would pay a nonmarried female or a widow to teach their children in her home. The children received instruction in reading and writing. The Bible was the common source for instruction. Girls also were taught household tasks, whereas boys learned tasks needed for farming (Bonn, 1976).

As the new nation expanded across the West and in the South during the nineteenth century, rural schools were established to provide education. Based on the agricultural calendar, schools frequently were in session only during the winter months when weather prevented outdoor farm work. The facilities, usually one-room schoolhouses, served students as young as three and as old as those in late adolescence. Uneducated adults and older farm workers frequently attended school when their work and the weather permitted. As the country became urbanized and consolidation of school districts caused the closing of one-room schools at the end of the nineteenth century, children younger than six were gradually excluded from attendance in the rural schools (Gulliford, 1984).

The history of early childhood education in this country reflects influences dating back to the eighteenth century in Europe. In the Middle Ages children did not have a childhood as we perceive it today. Children worked alongside their parents at a very early age to provide food and clothing needed for survival. It was not until Jean-Jacques Rousseau (1911) wrote the novel *Emile*, in 1762, that the development of the child was considered a separate stage in life. Rousseau's belief in nature and in the child's right to the period called childhood had a great impact on education. Rousseau believed in a natural approach to educating children that would permit growth without interference and restrictions. Johann Pestalozzi, a Swiss educator, is considered to have been the first early childhood teacher. Influenced by Rousseau's perceptions of children and childhood, Pestalozzi established several schools for poor and orphaned children (Braun & Edwards, 1972).

The German educator Friedrich Froebel was in turn influenced by Pestalozzi. He visited Pestalozzi's school in Yverdun on several occasions. Although he was unable to understand clearly what Pestalozzi was trying to achieve, he was able to develop his own philosophy of how children should learn, and he used his ideas to establish the first school with an organized curriculum for preschool children. Froebel created the *Kindergarten,* or "child garden," because he believed that his classes were gardens for children rather than school rooms. He believed that part of each day should be spent in play; the rest of the day was spent on a teacher-directed curriculum based on what Froebel called gifts and occupations. Gifts were to be handled by the child to achieve a sense of reality, whereas occupations were used to train the eye, hand, and mind (Braun & Edwards, 1972).

In the United States, the kindergarten movement marked the introduction of the first program designed specifically for children younger than age six. It was brought to this country by one of Froebel's students, Mrs. Carl Schurz, who began a kindergarten in her own home in Watertown, Wisconsin, in 1855 (Snyder, 1972). The first kindergartens were private and organized for children whose parents could afford to pay a tuition, but as the kindergarten movement became more popular, kindergartens for poor children were established in settlement houses, churches, and wherever an advocate could find a space where a kindergarten could be opened (Weber, 1969).

Kindergartens soon became affiliated with public schools. In 1873 the first public school kindergarten was established in the St. Louis public schools by Superintendent William T. Harris and Susan Blow, a leader in the kindergarten movement. Gradually, as more kindergartens were absorbed into the public school system, private and philanthropic kindergartens were discontinued. The kindergarten program itself changed as students of the child-study movement clashed with traditionalists who felt that Froebel's methods must be maintained without any change. Leaders of the new field of psychology and of the child-study movement that evolved after 1890 taught new information about child development and the purposes of education; this information influenced teachers to reconsider how young children should be taught (Braun & Edwards, 1972; Weber, 1969).

During the 1920s and 1930s, which were considered part of the progressive era in education, educational leaders and psychologists used their work in child study to propose teaching methods for preschools and elementary schools. Whereas early public schools in the nineteenth century had stressed reading, writing, and mathematics skills with an emphasis on rote learning, new leaders such as John Dewey, Alice Temple, Francis Parker, and William Heard Kilpatrick proposed that schooling for young children should be more child centered and meaningful. John Dewey proposed that the classroom should be a miniature community where children could engage in purposeful learning related to the society in which they lived. The child-centered curriculum proposed by progressive educators included study through projects and preparation for life as adults. Children took responsibility for their learning; and teachers involved them in instructional planning.

One of the influential leaders in the child-study movement was Arnold Gesell, a student of G. Stanley Hall, who had originated child-study research at university-based centers. Gesell did extensive study of children at Yale University and contributed the first descriptions of children at different chronological ages based on normative data. His theory of child development, called the maturational theory, was based on the belief that the child unfolded like a flower and developed readiness for learning as he or she matured (Gesell & Ilg, 1946). Gesell's influence was strong during the 1930s through the 1950s. The maturational theory had a major influence on the evolution of public school organization and curriculum during those decades.

There were also other sources of influence on early childhood education in the early decades of the nineteenth century. The nursery school movement that originated in England with the work of the McMillan sisters was adopted in the United States; nursery schools were implemented in this country as part of the child-study movement. Such schools had been developed to improve health and nutrition for poor preschool children in England; thus they were similar to the day nurseries developed in this country for custodial care that were later to become child-care programs.

Dr. Maria Montessori, a leader in early childhood education in Italy, also influenced educators in the United States. Dr. Montessori was the first woman to earn a degree in medicine in Italy. In 1907 she was invited to start a school in a slum in Rome. Montessori believed in training of the senses. The curriculum she designed for poor preschool children included activities that were developed for the sense of touch, as well as for thermal, visual, and auditory senses. Her materials were designed to be didactic (and interesting as well as educational when used over and over) and self-correcting. Although Montessori's approach to early education was not received well in the 1920s, when it was first introduced in the United States, her method became popular in private and parochial schools after 1950 (Braun & Edwards, 1972).

Urbanization of public schools after 1900 brought other changes as well. As small school districts consolidated and urban schools became larger, the graded school came into being. Although rural schools had teachers who taught whatever levels were needed by the students, consolidated schools and graded schools focused on one age or grade. With the advent of standardized, commercially produced curriculum designed for graded elementary schools, teachers were trained for grade-level teaching, with expectations of what the children should be able to accomplish in a particular grade.

Beginning with the early years when kindergartens became part of primary schools, there were differences between the philosophies and teaching approaches held by kindergarten teachers and elementary school teachers. The source of their training was different, as was their approach to the needs of their students. Although kindergarten teachers had a tradition of Froebelian training that was later influenced and modified by training in child development, primary-grade teachers were the product of teachers' colleges and normal schools where the emphasis in teacher preparation was in teaching methodology. The differences continued until recent decades as universities and colleges maintained separate programs for child development and public elementary school training. Kindergarten teachers have had, and continue to have, a mixed identity, as they are part of both levels of education (Granucci, 1990).

The 1950s and 1960s brought a new group of psychologists and educators whose work focused on the importance of the early years of childhood for later development and learning. Benjamin Bloom, Piaget, and J. McVicker Hunt were some of the leaders of the period who emphasized the significance of the early years in child development. Bloom (1964) found that the first five years were the most rapid period of development and the most significant in determining the course of further development. He believed that deprivation during the preschool years could have serious consequences for both cognitive and affective development. Jean Piaget also believed the nature of the experiences provided a child during the early years could make a difference in the child's intellectual development. Piaget proposed that the child constructed knowledge through active interaction with the environment. The child proceeds through stages of cognitive development as an active initiator of learning, and responses to information are dependent upon the level of understanding at that stage of development (McCarthy & Houston, 1980; Schickedanz, Hansen, & Forsyth, 1990). Hunt (1961) further supported Piaget's proposal of the role of experience during the early years. He questioned the notion of fixed intelligence and suggested that early experiences were important for the development of intelligence. Quality encounters with the environment during the early years made a higher adult level of intellectual capacity possible.

In the 1960s, federal intervention programs, intended to enhance learning for children from deprived environments, brought a new emphasis to the importance of the early childhood years. Projects such as Head Start, Follow Through, and Home Start; programs funded for migrant and bilingual children; and programs for children with special needs all had research components. Projects involved experimentation into theories of learning and development of innovative approaches to curriculum and instruction. Although early evaluation reports of the Head Start program were disappointing when measuring long-term intellectual gain, longitudinal studies found positive outcomes for students who had been in Head Start when compared with their peers who had not been enrolled in the program (Berruta-Clement, Schweinhart, Barrett, Epstein, & Weikart, 1984). The instructional materials and teaching methods developed in these projects in the 1960s were used in early childhood programs, particularly public school programs, in the 1970s. Younger children were also served in public school settings when federal programs funded school districts to implement classrooms for migrant children as young as age four. Preschool children who were at risk for inadequate achievement in the primary grades, including children with disabilities and other special needs, were served in early intervention programs.

Developers of policy and curriculum in elementary education also reacted to the national revolution in education, sparked by the Cold War and the launching of *Sputnik* by the Soviets. In an effort to improve public education there was an emphasis on mathematics and science in the curriculum. At the same time, federal funding for children who were considered to be "disadvantaged" brought new expectations for teachers to teach according to students' individual needs. In the 1970s innovations in instruction, many of which were federally funded, were available to schools to explore new models and teaching strategies. The Open Classroom,

Individually Guided Education, and Competency-Based Instruction were but a few of the instructional innovations used in elementary schools. The Open Classroom was based on the concept of open education borrowed from the British educational system. Instruction was child centered, with the teacher serving in the role of instructional facilitator. Learning centers were used in elementary classrooms. In addition, new schools were designed without interior walls to provide large, open learning areas where teachers and students from multiple classrooms learned together.

Individually Guided Education was a process of individualized instruction that used a team of teachers to plan and implement instruction based on individually paced instruction. Teams of teachers often worked in an open environment, although it was not a requirement of the process. Competency-Based Instruction also was a form of individually paced education. It was based on specific learning objectives, and progress through the curriculum was based on mastery of the sequenced objectives.

In spite of the influx of information and curriculum methods and materials brought into the public schools from federally funded programs, differences in philosophy and methodology continued to exist between programs for children under the age of six and programs for children in the primary grades. Such differences had an impact on how problems in implementing school reform were addressed in the 1980s and 1990s (Morgan, 1989). Teachers now need to bridge the theoretical and methodological differences in how young children should be taught so that the needs of children in the early childhood years are matched appropriately with teaching methods and materials that are complementary to how they learn (Kagan, 1989).

A Changing Concept of Early Childhood Education

Providing developmentally appropriate instruction for children in the early childhood years means that we must have a new understanding of early childhood education. The philosophical separation of preschool and kindergarten from primary education has resulted in a perception that instruction at these two levels is different. First grade is taught like higher grades in elementary school, whereas kindergarten is perceived as the level where children are prepared for the transition from early childhood to elementary education. The error in this understanding has been a factor in the difficulties many young children are experiencing in kindergarten and first grade because teacher expectations for their students do not match what the children are able to do at their level of development.

The changing concept of early childhood education is due partially to growing recognition that early childhood does span the years from birth to age eight (Bredekamp, 1987). Children in the early childhood years are in a continuous state of development that makes their method of learning more similar than different. Children in the primary grades are in the later stages of early childhood, but they still retain some of the learning characteristics that describe all of the early childhood years.

The understanding of development as continuous, rather than age related, comes from the influence of Piaget. During the 1920s and 1930s, our schools were strongly influenced by Gesell's maturational theory of development. Gesell's influence was dominant when public schools were becoming urbanized. The U.S. system of dividing the elementary schools into grade levels was compatible with Gesell's theory of how children develop and learn. Graded curriculum materials produced for the schools reflected Gesell's explanation of what students were capable of learning at each age.

Through Piaget's work, our concept of development has been altered. Piaget helped us to understand that children move through stages of development at different rates. The individual child's developmental progress depends in part upon the opportunities the child has to experience the world and also in part upon genetic potential and maturation. Piaget's stages (Piaget & Inhelder, 1969) demonstrate that there is a continuum in development that is uneven. A child may progress more rapidly in one area of development than in another. Development is not described by ages but by how the individual child is advancing. Teachers do not wait for a period of readiness to commence instruction but plan activities that can facilitate learning at the child's level of development. It is the child's incorporation of new experiences into existing knowledge combined with maturation that allow progress to higher levels of development.

In the Piagetian understanding of development, there is no difference between how children learn when they are five and how they learn when they are six or seven. All through the years of early childhood, the child is developing and acquiring more sophisticated thinking mechanisms. The early childhood teacher needs to understand the nature of the continuity in development when planning for instructional methods and materials. The methods of instruction in the years between three and eight, particularly, should reflect an understanding of the nature of cognitive development and individual variations in development. Each year of early childhood education, including the primary grades, should build on the child's developmental progress, rather than on the methodological expectations dictated by age-graded curriculum materials (Bredekamp, 1987).

Early Childhood Education Curriculum Practices Today: Historical Influences Revisited

The field of early childhood education reflects its history. From the early considerations expressed by Rousseau and Pestalozzi of what childhood is and how young children should learn, through Froebel's design of a school for preschool-age children, to the various influences contributed by students of child development and many types of programs for children, early childhood education as a field has maintained and yet modified all of the advances that have fashioned what it is today (Lanser & McDonnell, 1991). Although the curriculum practices at a private preschool or Montessori school may be very different from those at a public school or child-care center, early childhood education encompasses all of these contributions of programmatic approaches to the field. The history of early childhood education curriculum practices can be thought of as cumulative. Teachers in early childhood programs are more likely to take an eclectic approach to instruction whereby the methods and materials used reflect the many positive influences in the history of such education.

The history of public school curriculum practices can be represented as more of a pendulum. During different periods, teaching practices have reflected trends of the time, and some of those trends have been extremely different. Early public schools stressed reading, writing, and mathematics skills with an emphasis on rote learning. Later, John Dewey's influence resulted in a more child-centered approach (Dewey,1899). Children were to take responsibility for their learning, and teachers were to involve them in instructional planning. This trend came to be called progressive education, and it increased in popularity in the 1930s and 1940s at all levels of public education.

The 1960s and 1970s were a period of innovation and experimentation in schooling as educators attempted to improve educational achievement for diverse populations of children. The federal government funded intervention and compensatory education projects targeted at improved achievement for children who were at risk for learning.

By the 1980s the pendulum was again moving to more traditional teaching methods. With the loss of federal funding and a downturn in national economics and SAT scores, a new reform movement sometimes called Back to Basics was embraced on a national level. Some states and school districts implemented any of a variety of measures—including tighter academic standards, elimination of social promotion, increased retention in grades, and an emphasis on the instruction of basic skills to be measured by standardized tests—to solve some of the problems that were thought to be caused by lax instructional methods and a lack of rigor in the curriculum. Whole-class instruction (rather than instruction geared to the individual student) based on state-mandated curriculum objectives was the trend in some states. As in many previous trends, the negative effects of the extremes of current instructional practices are resulting in reconsideration of the extensive testing of young children, the long-range effects of retention in a grade in the early childhood years, and curriculum that is driven by standardized testing. If public elementary schools follow previous trends, curriculum practices may change in an extreme manner once again. It is hoped that instructional improvement instead will reflect comprehensive contributions from throughout the history of early childhood education and that instructional practices will include the best of the past, as well as new possibilities in the future.

FACTORS LEADING TO INAPPROPRIATE PRACTICES IN EARLY CHILDHOOD EDUCATION

At the same time that public schools are assessing the effects of the latest reform movement in curriculum and instruction on students in elementary schools, particularly those in preschool and primary grades, there is renewed general interest in the early childhood years and early childhood education. Early childhood programs of all types are being expanded or extended, whether they are part of public schools, private institutions, or local, state, or federally funded programs for young children and their families.

The Expanding Role of Early Childhood Education

Early childhood education is in a period when attention is again being focused on the importance of the early years, a focus that is coming from different sources; nevertheless, the renewed emphasis on early childhood programs is enhancing possibilities for better funding and program improvement. This interest comes from parents concerned about the growth and development of their own children, from public schools that are eligible for federal and state funding for new early childhood programs, and from the day-care industry and privately funded preschool programs that are expanding to meet the needs for care and programming for infants, toddlers, and preschool children. Mitchell (1989, p. 37) proposed that the high level of interest in early childhood programs stems from the following:

1. The increased demand for child care from the growing numbers of working mothers in all income groups

2. Concern about present and future productivity, international competitiveness, and the changing nature of the work force, which will include more women and be characterized by greater ethnic and racial diversity as the minority becomes a majority
3. The centrality of child care among efforts to move mothers off AFDC support and into the labor force
4. A desire to provide a better start for poor children in school and in life
5. An accumulating body of evidence that high-quality early childhood programs have long-term positive effects for disadvantaged children and high cost/benefit ratios (on the order of five to one)

Parental Interest in Learning in the Early Childhood Years.   Parents are increasingly becoming interested in their children's opportunity for learning in the preschool years. Parents are aware that the early childhood years are important for their child's academic achievement. More parents are buying books on parenting and child development to acquire information on what kinds of experiences they should provide for their child. There is a high interest in parenting classes among some parent populations. Affluent parents frequently enroll their babies in physical development classes, swimming classes, and other programs advertised to enhance the growth and learning of infants and toddlers. Whether these programs are a wise choice is a separate issue (Elkind, 1987), but their success does indicate that parents are interested in providing good experiences in the early years.

As more parents are placing their children in child care during the day by necessity or by choice, parental concern extends to the educational program offered by caregiving centers (Gullo, 1990; Kagan, 1989). Although day care was once thought of as a service for the poor so that mothers could seek employment, today all types of parents seek quality caregiving programs for their babies and preschool children. According to Mitchell (1989), parents want choices. Parents have different needs for caregiving programs. They want child-care centers to be affordable, convenient, and easy to choose, and they want them to reflect their own values and child-rearing practices.

The Expansion of Child Care.   Providers in the child-care industry are becoming aware of the importance of quality programming as a part of caregiving. The title "day care" is rapidly being abandoned by centers as they seek to be identified as facilities with a good educational program for young children. Terms such as *enrichment, school,* and *discovery* or *creative* are increasingly used as part of the name of child-care centers. People involved in child care are now aware that when parents look for a center, convenience is not their only priority. They look for cleanliness, characteristics of the staff, the quality of materials available to the children, and the type of learning activities that are used with the children.

The child-care industry is expanding because of the increasing numbers of children needing care (Schweinhart, 1989). The federal government is becoming more aware of the need for expanded and improved care. Although initial efforts to pass legislation that would help improve child-care services failed, the 1990s mark a period of increased federal involvement in child-care issues (Mitchell, 1989). In 1991 the Child Care and Development Block Grant was approved and funded by Congress to provide states with new money to subsidize child care for low-income families

(Children's Defense Fund, 1991). Organizations such as the National Association for the Education of Young Children (NAEYC) and the Children's Defense Fund continue in their efforts to educate the public and Congress about the need for federal support for quality child care. At the same time, competition is increasing for clients as churches, employers, public schools, and other agencies offer child care.

Child care is part of the early childhood program system in this country. As caregiving institutions perceive themselves as part of the field of early childhood education, many will continue to improve their programming to maintain a respected position in the field. Evidence of this trend can be found in the growing numbers of child-care centers seeking national accreditation through the NAEYC.

Public schools are a growing resource for children needing care before and after school. Hymes (1990) reported that in 1989, 17 percent of the public school districts in this country offered some form of child care or allowed child-care groups to use school buildings for that purpose. Some states have recognized that many of their students require care before and after school hours. Children are being shuttled back and forth between child-care centers and school, but if the parents cannot afford child-care services, the young often become latchkey children. As a result, public schools are offering services for these children at their facilities. Hymes and others predict that this trend will continue as schools become more like community centers.

This concept has implications for early childhood programs. There is a current trend to extend kindergartens from half-day to full-day programs (Gullo, 1990). Working parents strongly favor full-day programs because they can eliminate situations in which the child must adjust to several settings during the course of a single day. If the school also offers care before and after school hours, the convenience to them and their children is enhanced.

School districts that have empty or partially empty schools because of population shifts also may consider using the space for child care sponsored by the district or leasing it to a child-care organization. Regardless of the organization of the combination of school and care, these arrangements for preschool and primary-age children are becoming a part of the field of early childhood education as school-based programming for these children is perceived as a better alternative than custodial care or self-care during the off-school hours.

Expansion of Preschool Programs in Public Schools.   In recent years, public schools have expanded many of their preschool early childhood intervention programs. One major expansion has been in prekindergarten programs, those for four-year-old children at risk for successful achievement in the elementary grades. Mitchell (1989) reported that in 1979 only seven states had appropriated funds for preschool programs, but by 1989 thirty-one states had appropriated funds for state-initiated prekindergarten programs.

Federal funding has broadened support for early childhood and early intervention programs. The Elementary and Secondary School Improvement Act of 1988 reauthorizing Chapter I funds created Even Start, a joint parent–child education program. The purposes of Even Start were to improve adult literacy and offer early childhood education to children between the ages of one and seven. In addition, Chapter I funding expanded the migrant program to include three- and four-year-olds.

The Family Support Act of 1988 changed the rules by which parents could receive financial support from AFDC. The new act not only required parents of children older than three to work or attend job-training programs but also funded child care required by AFDC recipients in such programs. In addition, this legislation made child care possible for teenage parents while they continued their secondary education. The existing programs that serve young parents and their babies frequently provide these services in the public schools (Mitchell, 1989).

The services to children with handicaps and children with special needs that were initiated with PL 94-142 in the 1970s were joined in the 1980s by extended services mandated by PL 99-457 to infants and toddlers and their families (Kagan, 1989). Although programs for infants and toddlers can be and often are initiated by nonpublic school agencies and institutions, many public school systems are also implementing programs for the youngest children with special needs.

As the field of early childhood education continues to extend and expand, programs for young children are beginning to overlap and merge. It is becoming obvious that the traditional labeling of types of early childhood programs is outdated. A new conceptualization of a comprehensive field of early childhood education that encompasses all types of programs is emerging (Kagan & Rivera, 1991). Mitchell (1989) terms the broader field an "early childhood ecosystem" that requires new ways of relating and interacting among the ecosystem components. Before public school early childhood programs can address membership in an early childhood ecosystem, they must resolve problems within their own early childhood systems, particularly the programs serving children between the ages of four and eight. These age groups in the public schools are the subject of much concern and debate because of current practices in instruction and policies of promotion and retention that are adversely affecting students. In the next section we will discuss these issues and how they affect students, teachers, and parents.

CURRENT ISSUES LEADING TO INAPPROPRIATE PRACTICES

In the late 1970s and during the 1980s, a period of educational reform swept the United States. The major concern was that U.S. students did not achieve as well as their counterparts in Japan and European countries. Looking to the future, national leaders expressed the fear that the United States was falling behind in research and design, as well as in manufacturing. Because German and Japanese products and industries were making inroads on manufacturing that had traditionally been dominated by U.S. corporations, illiteracy and inferior secondary schooling were thought to be major causes of the decline of this country's domination in industrial design and manufacturing.

Efforts to reform the public school systems began within the secondary schools. Increased credits for graduation, tightened standards for grading, and competency testing were some of the policies implemented by individual states to increase achievement and raise the level of learning. As the reform movement continued to expand, similar policies were passed for elementary schools. State departments of education determined curriculum standards to be followed by all schools; such standards included the instructional objectives that were to be used at every grade level. Accountability for student learning was measured by standardized tests, with school districts within a state compared for levels of student achievement. Standards for achievement were raised, and teachers were required to teach more curriculum content that was more difficult than in the past in an effort to increase achievement test results.

When academic reform policies reached the early childhood classrooms, the developmental nature of young children's learning came into conflict with practices that were being initiated as part of educational reform. These practices are inappropriate when applied to children in the early childhood years.

The Impact of Educational Reform on Early Childhood Curriculum

It is difficult to determine which came first: the escalation of the amount and difficulty of the curriculum content, or increased testing. In any case, both have had a major role in the use of inappropriate practices for young children. Shepard and Smith (1988) reported that there has been a consistent escalation of academic demand on both kindergartners and first-graders. Elementary principals, other school district administrators, and middle-class parents have all put a high priority on advancing or accelerating student academic achievement in the elementary grades. As a result, what was formerly expected in the next grade has been pushed down into the lower grade. Day (1988) termed this practice the "push-down curriculum." Part of the rationale in this practice stems from the perception that the large numbers of children who have attended public and private preschool programs and child care are more advanced in their development than are previous populations of students. Therefore, it is assumed that increasing the demands for learning is appropriate because children are ready for more advanced instruction. However erroneous this assumption is, it is a rationale used by teachers, parents, and administrators for using formal academic teaching materials and strategies and increasing expectations for achievement.

The escalation of expectations for learning has been accompanied by an increase in testing (Freeman, 1990; National Council of Teachers of English, 1990). Standardized achievement tests are the common means for determining whether students are learning at an acceptable level. In some states, schools administer an achievement test that has been designed to reflect the curriculum objectives that have been designated for all schools in the state. In other states, individual school districts select standardized tests that have been developed by testing corporations to measure achievement across the nation. Some school districts elect to administer both types of achievement tests. As schools set a high priority on high test scores, curriculum and instruction are modified to ensure that the students will do well on the test (Bredekamp & Shepard, 1989). A common practice is for teachers to focus on teacher-directed instruction centered on reading and mathematics skills that will be on the test, rather than a well-rounded curriculum that is child centered and balanced to include all areas of development and learning. The combination of an increased amount of curriculum content to be learned with increased testing has had a negative effect. More young children are not achieving well in school. They are not mastering the curriculum, nor are they doing well on the standardized achievement tests. The more difficult the curriculum and the greater its content, the lower the percentage of students who are succeeding academically.

The problem of how to assist the students who are not able to perform within the existing curriculum and instructional strategies used in first-grade classrooms has resulted in placing these students in transitional classrooms, withholding them from school entry, and retaining them in kindergarten. Bredekamp and Shepard (1989) point out that instead of using curriculum that is developmentally appropriate for the child, the school holds the child responsible for failing.

Selection for retention and placement requires more testing. The most commonly used tests for this purpose are readiness tests and screening tests. Although they are suitable for screening or curriculum planning purposes only, these tests are also being used for placing children in special programs or to delay their entry into school (Bredekamp & Shepard, 1989; Freeman, 1990; Kamii, 1990; Meisels, 1987; Shepard & Smith, 1989). There are many factors involved with such practices being used inappropriately for children in the early childhood years, including the academic curriculum that requires children to perform at a level beyond their development; the failure children experience when they are retained or placed in a special program, such as a transitional or pre-first-grade classroom; and the tests used that are not appropriate for making placement and retention decisions. All these factors represent issues that need resolution (Nason, 1991; Shepard & Smith, 1990).

Conflicts between Developmental Theories and Practice

The current practices used in early childhood classrooms in many public schools are antithetical to the components of a high-quality early childhood program. Curry (1990) characterizes the back-to-basics approach as retrenching to earlier modes of practice. She compares this practice with the medical field and proposes that we would be appalled if medical doctors returned to earlier strategies with patients. The use of readiness tests to determine if the child is ready for kindergarten or first grade is a policy that fits Curry's perspective on current practices. The concept of readiness based on Gesell's maturational theory that can characterize children as immature or unready for kindergarten or first grade is an old one that has been superseded by Piaget's work on how young children learn. Children's modes and styles of learning are different when they are younger than seven years old, but they are not "unready." The maturational theory of development that embraces "readiness" for learning is in conflict with Piaget's theory of cognitive development that presumes that children are always ready to learn but proposes that the learning experiences must match their mode of learning at their current stage of development.

Practices that perceive the child as deficient because he or she is unable to succeed at tasks that are beyond his or her developmental level reflect a return to a mode of curriculum and instruction used by teachers who do not understand Piaget's work or have opted for a different theoretical explanation of how children learn. Teachers who use instruction that reflects the evolving development of the child in Piaget's preoperational stage perceive the child as an active learner who is normal and successful. The curriculum is designed to effect a developmental match with the child instead of vice versa, where it is the child's responsibility to fit the curriculum.

Seven years has been identified as the average age at which young children become capable of concrete operational thinking. Some researchers question the tasks Piaget used to determine the ability to conserve; they believe that children understand conservation earlier than Piaget indicated. Researchers have altered the conservation tasks (or the verbal instructions about a task) and have found that younger children demonstrated more understanding (Gelman & Gallistel, 1978; Rose & Blank, 1974). Whether or not children achieve concrete operational thinking at an earlier age, there is individual variation in the timing. There is a significant difference in the child's thinking when comparing preoperational thinking with concrete operational thinking. The teacher who is knowledgeable about these differences in quality of thinking can adjust expectations to the individual child's developmental timetable.

The issues concerning appropriate instructional strategies for early childhood programs go beyond the conflict between the maturational theory and the cognitive developmental theory. Another major difference in philosophy of learning and instruction contrasts formal academic instruction and developmental instruction. These two approaches to instruction are in opposition when public schools respond to education

reform with the "push-down" curriculum. The curriculum that is being transferred from second grade to first grade, and from first grade to kindergarten, can be a formal academic one that ignores developmental appropriateness when used with younger children. Teaching approaches used by educators with the two models of instruction have implications for teacher and student behaviors that are quite different.

A fundamental difference between the two approaches regards the philosophy of how children learn. The academic approach is based on the behaviorist theory that assumes that learning is external. The child acquires knowledge through the teaching behaviors used by the teacher (Greenberg, 1990). Elkind (1989) further describes the academic type of instruction as psychometric. Knowledge is something that is measurable. The aim of psychometric instruction is to produce children who score high on achievement tests.

Conversely, the developmental approach is based on the belief that learning is initiated by the child, not the teacher. The child is viewed as having developing mental abilities and learns through creative activity. The developing child creates and re-creates knowledge as a result of experiences with the environment. The teacher facilitates learning by providing materials and activities that match the child's development, but the child as active learner acquires the knowledge through interaction with the experiences, with other children, and with relevant materials.

Classrooms using the contrasting approaches for instruction have different characteristics. The academic classroom is likely to have teacher-directed instruction, workbooks, and drill exercises, and the student makes few choices for activities or experiences. The classroom that uses a developmental approach is full of an array of hands-on materials, both man-made and natural, that are available for exploration and use by the child. The child has many opportunities for choices, planning, and carrying out creative activities. Play and interaction with other students is encouraged as the teacher seeks to facilitate social, cognitive, personality, and motor development (Elkind, 1989; Greenberg, 1990). Because growth is seen as holistic, the teacher does not separate cognitive development from the other aspects of development (Morgan, 1989).

Katz (1988) cautioned educators about the long-term effects of early academic instruction. She pointed out the contrast between what young children can do and what they ought to be doing. She noted that the preschool child is able to complete workbook tasks and other activities in academic classrooms; however, early introduction to academic work can be counterproductive because it affects the child's disposition to be a learner. A young child may be able to learn phonics and other beginning reading skills but may not develop the disposition to be a reader. Likewise, the academic classroom may provide for the acquisition of skills and knowledge but may give little opportunity for social development and verbal communication (Curry, 1990). Katz (1988) emphasized that the disposition for learning can be damaged by inappropriate teaching in the early years.

Greenberg (1990) stressed that few classrooms fit either the academic or the developmental approach in a pure form. Most classrooms have some of both types of instruction; nevertheless, the developmental approach is of particular significance for children in the early childhood years because the long-term development of a feeling of confidence and positive self-esteem cannot be acquired when the type of instruction used is inappropriate. Instruction leading to the acquisition of skills and knowledge is not inappropriate in itself. When skills and knowledge are taught developmentally, both successful learning and positive self-esteem can be experienced by the young child.

What Research Indicates about Inappropriate Practices in Early Childhood Education

As was discussed before, inappropriate practices in early childhood education include the use of testing with young children for placement in school. The placement issue results from another inappropriate practice, that of using tests for retention in both prekindergarten and pre-first-grade classrooms, sometimes referred to as transitional classrooms. A third inappropriate practice, the use of a "push-down" curriculum instead of a developmentally appropriate curriculum in kindergarten classrooms, has resulted in increased failure in young children. This section will discuss the research that is available about these practices.

Testing of Young Children. Testing of young children is increasing across the United States. Testing of children as young as four has become a widespread practice for early identification of children who are at risk for later learning. Some of the children are screened for special education intervention programs, whereas others may be evaluated for at-risk factors such as bilingualism or limited language and cognitive development, which will make them eligible for other preschool intervention or compensatory education programs. In addition to standardized achievement tests, developmental screening and readiness tests are being used. The testing of young children has come under attack because of the dangers of labeling children at an early age and using test scores for determining the placement of children in early childhood programs (Freeman, 1990; Kamii, 1990).

One concern about the tests is that they have limited reliability or validity. Meisels (1987) was also concerned that many of the testers lacked proper training and supervision. Another concern was the accuracy of the tests in identifying children for special programs (Shepard & Smith, 1986). Specific caution was recommended for the use of the Gesell School Readiness Test when it is used to delay entry into school and placement into a prekindergarten classroom or a pre-first-grade classroom. A study by Graue and Shepard (1989) on the test's predictive validity found that its low predictive value does not support its use in placement decisions. Meisels (1987) reported that no systematic study of the test's validity is in the literature. Likewise, Shepard and Smith (1986) reported that the Gesell test does not meet the standards of the American Psychological Association for validity and reliability. Shepard and Smith reported on a study to evaluate the predictive validity of the Gesell test. Only half of the children selected as "potential kindergarten failures" were correctly identified.

Although the Gesell School Readiness Test and other such tests, like the Metropolitan Readiness Test (Nurss & McGauvran, 1976), are useful tools for assessing children's individual abilities and planning for their instruction, they are misused when they are used for placement purposes. They harm individual children when they are labeled as failures before they begin school, misidentify them as being behind the other children in their peer group, and put the responsibility for success or failure on the child rather than on the program. The Metropolitan Readiness Test is not advertised for the purpose of identifying which children are ready for kindergarten or first grade; however, the Gesell test is recommended by its authors for screening children for developmental pre-first-grade programs (Shepard & Smith, 1986).

School Placement of Young Children.   The practice of retaining children in early childhood classrooms is spreading. Although extra-year programs may not be described as retention, in reality an extra year has been added to the child's tenure in elementary and secondary education. The intentions for placing children in extra-year programs are positive. Such programs are perceived as alternative in-between programs to protect children from the increased academic demands of kindergarten or first grade and are the result of a misunderstanding of the term *developmentally appropriate* (Bredekamp & Shepard, 1989). Teachers and administrators are convinced that such early retention does not have negative effects on the child. They strongly believe that the child will later achieve more academically and socially with less stress.

Research about retention and placement in extra-year programs does not support the practice. In many studies on early retention conducted to date, the major finding was that there was no difference between retained and promoted children (Gredler, 1984). Controlled studies of kindergarten retention conducted in Colorado did not show improved achievement in retained children (Shepard & Smith, 1987). In these and other studies conducted between 1984 and 1988 Shepard and Smith (1989, p. 1) summarized the major findings:

1. Kindergarten retention does nothing to boost subsequent academic achievement.
2. Regardless of what the extra year may be called, there is a social stigma for children who attend an extra year.
3. Retention actually fosters inappropriate academic demands in first grade.

Inappropriate Curriculum Used with Young Children.   As was discussed before, failure of children in kindergarten and first grade is primarily caused by the use of inappropriate curriculum and teaching methods. The escalation of academic demand on kindergartners and first-graders has been constant and persistent. The widespread practice of lowering formal academic instruction into early childhood classrooms has already been discussed.

Current statistics indicate that the trend is continuing. One Colorado school district that was studied mandated an academic kindergarten with a prescribed number of minutes spent in the content areas (Shepard & Smith, 1988). Kindergarten programs in Ohio were increasingly academic and skill oriented (Freeman, 1988), and Florida kindergartens were expected to meet two hundred content area objectives during the school year (Webster, 1984).

Many teachers do not agree with the use of academic curriculum in early childhood. Some have described kindergarten and primary grades, especially first grade, as hostile environments from which young children need to be protected. School district coordinators and administrators may require that teachers use a formal method with their students. The fear of low test scores on achievement tests puts pressure on them to stress skills acquisition in mathematics and reading over other components of the curriculum. These teachers have what Bredekamp and Shepard (1989) termed "philosophy-reality" conflicts. They believe that their program should be developmental, but they feel forced to teach the academic curriculum. Moreover, teachers feel they lack the power to influence curriculum and assessment (Bredekamp & Shepard, 1989). Seefeldt and Barbour (1988) suggest that teachers blame external pressures coming from parents, administrators, or legislators for the academic approach to instruction that they use.

Although kindergarten teachers report that they find it increasingly difficult to provide developmentally appropriate programs because of outside pressures, Charlesworth (1989) feels that energy should be focused on improving the schools so that children can receive developmentally appropriate instruction. Freeman (1990) advises that kindergarten teachers will have to take control of their curriculum and resist conforming to practices that they believe are inappropriate. They should insist on using a developmentally appropriate curriculum that best meets the needs of their students.

There is support and information available for teachers and schools seeking to provide appropriate instruction in early childhood classrooms. The National Association for the Education of Young Children began to address the issue of devel-

opmentally appropriate teaching practices in the mid-1980s. A series of position papers describing developmentally appropriate teaching and testing practices was issued by the organization. Relevant articles were published frequently in the organizational journal *Young Children*. In 1987, the publication titled *Developmentally Appropriate Practice in Early Childhood Programs Serving Children from Birth through Age 8* (Bredekamp, 1987) was published. It provided indicators of appropriate practice and inappropriate practice for all ages between birth and age eight and was supported by the National Council of Teachers of Mathematics (1989), the National Association of Elementary School Principals (1990), and the National Association of State Boards of Education (1989). Subsequently, a position statement regarding guidelines for appropriate curriculum content and assessment published in 1990 (National Association for the Education of Young Children & National Association of Early Childhood Specialists in State Departments of Education, 1991) was endorsed or supported by ten national or regional organizations. The Association for Childhood Education International has a publication titled *Developmental Continuity across Preschool and Primary Grades* (Barbour & Seefeldt, 1993) that will provide teachers in both preschool and primary grades with additional information on appropriate instruction for children in early childhood years.

PROVIDING DEVELOPMENTALLY APPROPRIATE PRACTICES FOR ALL TYPES AND LEVELS OF EARLY CHILDHOOD EDUCATION

Now is an opportune time to address the many issues that concern early childhood educators. There are indications that some of the inappropriate practices discussed earlier are being reconsidered and corrected. Hymes (1990) reported that the adverse information researched and published about the Gesell School Readiness Test resulted in a decline in the use of the test. Greenberg (1990) likewise reported that the pendulum is swinging away from the academic preschool. Awareness of the issues related to developmentally appropriate teaching practices has led some teachers and administrators to revise their approach to instruction in preschool and primary grades. As policymakers reassess the issues and make plans to improve their early childhood programs, it would be wise to reflect upon what we have learned about children from the history of early childhood education. As well we should carefully consider how we will design curriculum and instruction for early childhood programs to meet the future needs of children, their families, society, and the early childhood programs themselves. Toward accomplishing this task, we can make some statements about resolution of the issues and how they apply to future directions in providing quality learning experiences for young children.

Sorting Out the Issues

Early Childhood Education as One Comprehensive Program.   To meet the future needs of children in the early childhood years we will need to move rapidly to accept the concept of early childhood education as an ecosystem—that is, a system that incorporates all of the various early childhood programs into a comprehensive support system. The commonalities of all of the various types of programs serving young children are greater than their differences. Public school systems and universities can take a leadership role in developing networks for improved services to families. Models for new cooperative organizations already exist. Hymes (1990) described a cooperative venture in Miami, Florida, where the Dade County Public Schools opened a combined kindergarten–child-care center at the downtown headquarters of the American Bankers Insurance Group that has since added the first grade. This is just one example of the creative possibilities that can be developed to make the best use of the resources of an early childhood ecosystem.

Acceptance of the Continuity of Development at All Levels of Early Childhood. Accepting the span of early childhood as the years from birth through age eight and planning and applying instruction accordingly will accomplish much toward resolving the issue of how young children should be taught in preschool and primary-level classrooms. If all teachers understand the continuity of development in the preoperational period and the implications for instruction as children move from infancy to early and later stages of early childhood, the perception of preschool and primary grades as separate kinds of schooling can be eliminated. Likewise, teachers in prekindergarten and kindergarten programs can visualize how their children are developing toward the later stages of early childhood in the primary grades. Children from ages three to eight in the public schools can be conceptualized as progressing through the developmental stage of preoperational thinking that will gradually evolve to concrete operational thinking. Each grade level can build on the child's developmental accomplishments. Teachers in primary grades can gradually help their students make the transition to activities that are possible in the concrete operational stage, within a child-initiated style of learning combined with teacher-directed instruction.

The Child as Normal and Competent. The majority of children progress through the stages of early childhood in a normal manner. They do not progress at the same rate when compared with other children, nor do all areas of intraindividual development progress at the same rate. These differences are to be accepted and, if understood, will facilitate the teacher's planning for appropriate learning experiences. The curriculum should reflect the child's developmental learning abilities and needs and, if implemented, will eliminate the need for testing children for readiness and placement into extra-year programs. It is more appropriate to nurture every child's competence and success than to sort out the ready from the unready because of a rigid, fixed curriculum that assumes a more advanced, unrealistic stage of development.

Appropriate Instruction in Early Childhood Classrooms

This textbook proposes to help teachers in all kinds of early childhood programs to understand development in the young child and the methods by which learning experiences can be planned so that they are beneficial for early childhood classrooms serving children from infants through primary-age youngsters. Teachers in the past have not had preparation for teaching children across these age levels as a continuous process. Teachers who have prepared for elementary classrooms have not had enough information on how developmental learning in the preschool years gradually makes a transition into learning in the content areas, such as reading and mathematics, in the primary grades. The transition is gradual as the teacher responds to children's development and guides them into writing and more formal methods of performing as they develop the competencies to successfully make the changes. The goal of this text is to help all early childhood teachers to acquire and apply these developmentally based methods in their particular early childhood programs. To be able to teach children appropriately now and in the future, we must have a broadened appreciation of the early childhood years and enhanced competencies to be able to "bridge" the preschool and primary grades with our students. We must be able to do the following:

1. Understand development as well as the relationship between development and instruction
2. Understand how curriculum and instruction respond to and facilitate development
3. Understand how to accommodate instruction to changing levels of development in the early childhood years—to bridge curriculum and instruction across the preschool and primary years

In chapter 3 we will discuss how children grow and develop between birth and age eight. To better understand the nature of development, we will describe social, physical, and cognitive development in infants and toddlers, children of the preschool years, and children between the ages of five and eight. How development affects the child's ability to socialize and learn will also be discussed, along with the implications that developmental characteristics have for parents and teachers when designing instructional programs for young children. If teachers are to understand how to accommodate instruction appropriately to changing levels of development in the early childhood years, they must first have an understanding of how development advances and changes during those years.

Summary

Early childhood education has entered a new period in its history. The field encompasses many types of programs located in a variety of settings. Although the variety of ways to serve and instruct young children may have had different beginnings, social and economic changes in our society are bringing them together into one vast ecosystem with many components.

Early childhood education programs have many commonalities; however, there are numerous concerns. Child-care programs suffer from financial problems as they are restricted by limits on what parents can pay for care. Fortunately, local and state governments, as well as the federal government, are taking a stronger advocacy role in seeking ways to financially support child care. Business and industry support is increasing as this sector of the community recognizes the advantages to assisting parents in this capacity.

Public school early childhood programs also have problems as they seek to resolve issues that are caused in part by a traditional separation in philosophy and training between kindergarten and other preschool programs and the primary grades. Another source of difficulty has been the academic reform movement with raised expectations for achievement standards and testing. This in turn forced formal academic instruction into preschool classrooms with negative impact on young students. One solution to the problems stemming from developmentally inappropriate instruction and testing has

been to place some children identified as at risk into extra-year programs or to withhold them from school entrance.

A new, broader understanding of early childhood education considers the inclusion of all early childhood education programs under one system and emphasizes the continuity of development from birth to age eight. With this understanding, parents, teachers, administrators, policymakers, and others involved with the care and education of young children can comprehend the nature of developmentally appropriate instruction and the methods by which schooling in all early childhood programs can best meet the learning styles and strengths of children at all levels of early childhood.

Summary Statements

1. Issues of testing and appropriate instruction for young children need to be resolved in early childhood classrooms because some current practices are not congruent with children's developmental capabilities.

2. The field of early childhood education is both diverse and interrelated, with many types of programs serving children of the same age.

3. Public school early childhood classrooms reflect the historical heritage of public school education in the United States.

4. A broader understanding of development and learning of students in the early childhood years can modify current instructional practices to a more developmentally appropriate model.

5. The continuum of development and individual developmental differences have implications for curriculum and instruction in the early childhood years that in turn affect all types of early childhood programs.

6. Current teaching and assessment practices responding to pressures for educational reform have had negative effects on the achievement and self-image of many young children.

7. As more children are placed in child care during the preschool years, parents have raised their expectations for the educational programs provided by child-care centers.

8. As a response to changing family needs, public schools are expanding the ages of children served in the preschool years and some are implementing before- and after-school care.

9. Federal programs have expanded services provided to children with handicaps and other high-risk children in the preschool years.

10. Formal academic instruction that is suitable in elementary grades can be inappropriate when used for children in early childhood classrooms.

11. Current research does not support continuation of inappropriate instructional practices for young children.

12. The use of standardized tests for young children is questioned because of problems with validity and reliability, as well as inappropriate use of test results for determining the placement or retention of children in early childhood classrooms.

13. There is now a trend toward addressing the concerns about inappropriate practices used for children in the early childhood years that is resulting in the redesign of curriculum and instruction.

14. If appropriate instruction is to be provided for children in the early childhood years, school organization will need to be modified from a preschool and primary-grade configuration to early childhood as one comprehensive period of schooling.

Study Questions

1. Why are the present practices used for instruction and assessment of the early childhood years considered to be inappropriate?
2. How did the instructional problems currently found in early childhood classrooms develop?
3. Why do the developmental theories of Gesell and Piaget sometimes result in conflicts in early childhood instructional and placement practices?
4. How has educational reform of the 1980s affected early childhood education?
5. What factors are causing growth and expansion in early childhood programs?
6. How does standardized testing of young children affect developmentally inappropriate practices in the early childhood years?
7. What does research have to contribute to the issues regarding testing of young children?
8. What are some positive alternatives that can restore developmentally appropriate practices to early childhood classrooms?

References

Barbour, N. H., & Seefeldt, C. (1993). *Developmental continuity across preschool and primary grades.* Wheaton, MD: Association for Childhood Education International.

Berrueta-Clement, J. R., Schweinhart, L. J., Barrett, W. S., Epstein, A. S., & Weikart, D. P. (1984). Changed lives: The effects of the Perry Preschool programs on youths through age 19. *Monographs of the High/Scope Educational Research Foundation, 8.* Ypsilanti, MI: High/Scope Press.

Bloom, B. (1964). *Stability and change in human characteristics.* New York: John Wiley.

Bonn, M. (1976). An American paradox. In E. H. Grotberg (Ed.), *200 years of children.* Washington, DC: U.S. Department of Health, Education, and Welfare.

Braun, S. J., & Edwards, E. P. (1972). *History and theory of early childhood education.* Belmont, CA: Wadsworth.

Bredekamp, S. (1987). *Developmentally appropriate practice in early childhood programs serving children from birth through age 8.* Washington, DC: National Association for the Education of Young Children.

Bredekamp, S., & Shepard, S. (1989). How to best protect children from inappropriate school expectations, practices, and policies. *Young Children, 44,* 14–24.

Caldwell, B. M. (1989). A comprehensive model for integrating child care and early childhood education. *Teachers College Record, 90,* 404–414.

Charlesworth, R. (1989). "Behind" before they start? *Young Children, 44,* 5–13.

Children's Defense Fund. (1991). *State of America's children: 1991.* Washington, DC: Author.

Curry, N. E. (1990). Presentation to the Pennsylvania State Board of Education. *Young Children, 45,* 17–23.

Day, B. (1988). What's happening in early childhood programs in the United States? In C. Warger (Ed.), *A resource guide to public school early childhood programs* (pp. 3–31). Alexandria, VA: Association for Supervision and Curriculum Development, 3-31.

Dewey, J. (1899). *The school and society.* Chicago: University of Chicago Press.

Elkind, D. (1987). *Miseducation: Preschoolers at risk.* New York: Alfred A. Knopf.

Elkind, D. (1989, October). Developmentally appropriate practice: Philosophical and practical implications. *Phi Delta Kappan,* 113–117.

Freeman, E. B. (1990). Issues in kindergarten policy and practice. *Young Children, 45,* 29–34.

Gelman, R., & Gallistel, C. R. (1978). *The child's understanding of number.* Cambridge, MA: Harvard University Press.

Gesell, A., & Ilg, F. A. (1946). *The child from five to ten.* New York: Harper.

Granucci, P. L. (1990). Kindergarten teachers: Working through our identity crisis. *Young Children, 45,* 6–11.

Graue, M. E., & Shepard, L. A. (1989). Predictive validity of the Gesell School Readiness Tests. *Early Childhood Research Quarterly, 4,* 303–315.

Gredler, G. R. (1984). Transition classes: A viable alternative for the at-risk child? *Psychology in the Schools, 21*, 463–470.

Greenberg, P. (1990). Why not academic preschools? *Young Children, 45*, 70–80.

Gulliford, A. (1984). *America's country schools.* Washington, DC: Preservation Press.

Gullo, F. (1990). The changing family context: Implications for the development of all-day kindergartens. *Young Children, 45*, 35–39.

Hunt, J. M. (1961). *Intelligence and experience.* New York: Ronald Press.

Hymes, J. L. (1990). *Early childhood education. The year in review. A look at 1989.* Washington, DC: National Association for the Education of Young Children.

Kagan, S. (1989, October). Early care and education: Beyond the schoolhouse doors. *Phi Delta Kappan,* 107–112.

Kagan, S., & Rivera, A. M. (1991). Collaboration in early care and education: What can and should we expect? *Young Children, 47*, 51–56.

Kamii, C. (Ed.). (1990). *Achievement testing in the early grades.* Washington, DC: National Association for the Education of Young Children.

Katz, L. G. (1988). What should young children be doing? *American Educator, 12*, 28–33, 44–45.

Lanser, S., & McDonnell, L. (1991). Creating quality curriculum yet not buying out the store. *Young Children, 47*, 4–10.

McCarthy, M. A., & Houston, J. P. (1980). *Fundamentals of early childhood education.* Cambridge, MA: Winthrop.

Meisels, S. J. (1987). Uses and abuses of developmental screening and school readiness testing. *Young Children, 42*, 4–6, 68–73.

Mitchell, A. (1989, May). Old baggage, new visions: Shaping policy for early childhood programs. *Phi Delta Kappan,* 665–672.

Mitchell, A., & Modigliani, K. (1989). Young children in public schools? *Young Children, 44*, 55–61.

Morgan, G. (1989, Winter). Stalemate or consensus? Barriers to national policy. *Theory into Practice,* 41–46.

Nason, R. B. (1991). Retaining children: Is it the right decision? *Childhood Education, 67*, 300–304.

National Association for the Education of Young Children & National Association of Early Childhood Specialists in State Departments of Education. (1991). Guidelines for appropriate curriculum content and assessment in programs serving children ages 3 through 8. *Young Children, 46*, 21–38.

National Council of Teachers of English. (1990). On testing young children. *Language Arts, 67*, 92–93.

Nurss, J., & McGauvran, M. (1976). *Metropolitan readiness tests teachers manuals: Part 2. Interpretation and test results.* New York: Harcourt Brace Jovanovich.

Piaget, J., & Inhelder, B. (1969). *The psychology of the child.* New York: Basic Books.

Rose, S. A., & Blank, M. (1974). The potency of context in children's cognition: An illustration through conservation. *Child Development, 45*, 499–502.

Rousseau, J. J. (1911). *Emile* (B. Foxley, Trans.). London: J. M. Dent & Sons.

Schickendanz, J. A., Hansen, K., & Forsyth, P. D. (1990). *Understanding children.* Mountain View, CA: Mayfield.

Schweinhart, L. J. (1989, Winter). Early childhood programs in the U.S today. *High/Scope Resource, 1*, 9–14.

Seefeldt, C., & Barbour, N. (1988). "They said I had to. . .": Working with mandates. *Young Children, 43*, 4–8.

Shepard, L. A., & Smith, M. L. (1986). Synthesis of research on school readiness and kindergarten retention. *Educational Leadership, 48*, 78–86.

Shepard, L. A., & Smith, M. L. (1987). Effects of kindergarten retention at the end of first grade. *Psychology in the Schools, 24*, 346–357.

Shepard, L. A., & Smith, M. L. (1988). Escalating academic demand in kindergarten. Counterproductive policies. *The Elementary School Journal, 89*, 135–145.

Shepard, L. A., & Smith, M. L. (1989). *Escalating kindergarten curriculum.* Urbana, IL: ERIC Clearinghouse on Elementary and Early Childhood Education.

Shepard, L. A., & Smith, M. L. (1990, May). Synthesis of research on grade retention. *Educational Leadership,* 84–88.

Snyder, A. (1972). *Dauntless women in childhood education 1856–1931.* Washington, DC: Association for Childhood Education International.

Weber, E. (1969). *The kindergarten.* New York: Teacher's College Press.

Webster, N. K. (1984). The 5s and 6s go to school, revisited. *Childhood Education, 60*, 325–330.

CHAPTER THREE

Developmental Characteristics of Young Children from Birth to Eight Years: Implications for Learning

The twentieth century has been a period of research concerned with how infants and young children develop and learn. The child-study movement established at the turn of the century involved researchers interested in developing information about the physical, social, emotional, cognitive, and language development of children. The studies of children conducted at various institutions of higher education in the United States resulted in the accumulation of extensive information that continues to be gathered as the twenty-first century approaches. The interest in child development and in the factors that affect such development and growth has not waned. Instead, research efforts build on earlier data collection, and changing conditions create a demand for investigative studies on how factors affect young children in the early childhood years.

THE THEORETICAL BASES OF DEVELOPMENT

As the field of child study has advanced, psychologists and philosophers have developed different theories on the nature of development and on the influence that such theories have regarding how children develop and learn. Although some of these views have been important since the 1950s, other ideas were the result of the child-study movement or coincided with the establishment of child-study efforts around 1900.

As was discussed in chapter 2, each of the theories involves a different way of approaching child development, and the conflict among theories has led to difficulties in developing the most appropriate model of instruction for children in early childhood programs. The maturational theory focuses on physical and intellectual development, whereas the psychoanalytic and psychosocial theories are concerned with social and emotional, or personality, development. The behaviorist and social learning theories focus on intellectual and personality development. The cognitive-developmental theory is concerned with intellectual development and how it affects cognitive and social growth. Each of the theories has relevance for child development and learning; nevertheless, none offers a complete explanation for all aspects of development. More important, the various theories significantly affect how parents, caregivers, and teachers understand development and learning.

The Maturational Theory

The early observations of children that were made in an effort to understand their development were led by G. Stanley Hall, who wrote *The Content of Children's Minds* (1883). Observation of children and subsequent descriptions of babies and young children were expanded by many researchers; however, Arnold Gesell, a student of G. Stanley Hall, is credited with establishing norms for the ages at which behaviors emerged in young children (Gesell & Ilg, 1946). Gesell, a physician, conducted his work at the Yale Clinic of Child Development. He collected data on the effects of maturation in children and subsequently explained development and learning based on his theory of maturation. Gesell believed that skills such as walking, talking, and learning to read occurred as a result of the individual child's biological timetable. Biological readiness, rather than any influence of experience, was the predominant factor in the child's ability to learn (Weber, 1984).

The Psychoanalytic Theory

The Austrian physician Sigmund Freud was investigating social and personality development in the early part of the twentieth century. Freud believed that sexual energy is the force that influences children's behavior and that children progress through a series of psychosexual stages. In his psychoanalytic theory, Freud (1925) proposed that personality development is composed of the instincts of id, ego, and superego and that these three components control the child's innate drives to release sexual energy through oral gratification, warmth, love, pleasurable body sensations, and elimination of body wastes. If the child's instincts are not under- or overgratified by parents, the child will progress naturally through oral, anal, phallic, latent, and genital stages (Morrison, 1988; Schickedanz, Hansen, & Forsyth, 1990).

The Psychosocial Theory

Erik Erikson, a student of Freud, developed his theory of psychosocial development based on Freud's work. Erikson (1963) proposed that the child's personality development is strongly determined by social contexts such as the family and school, and that the individual's interactions with environmental influences within eight life stages create his or her personality.

Erikson believed that the individual's adaptation at each developmental stage determined personality growth. The resolution of the conflict at each stage determined the course of personality development. In the early childhood years, the child progresses through the stages of trust versus mistrust, autonomy versus shame and doubt, initiative versus guilt, and industry versus inferiority. Figure 3.1 lists Erikson's stages of psychosocial development in the early childhood years and describes important adult behaviors that affect the child's resolution of each stage.

The Behaviorist Theory

The behaviorist theory stemmed from the work of Ivan Pavlov, the Russian physiologist who determined that animals could learn new physiological responses to the environment through stimuli. Pavlov used the process of conditioning to teach a dog to salivate at the sound of a bell by ringing the bell each time food was offered. Because the dog salivated each time the food was offered, it became conditioned to salivate each time the bell rang, even when food was no longer offered (Schickedanz, Hansen, & Forsyth, 1990).

STAGE	AGE	CHARACTERISTICS
1. Trust versus mistrust	Birth to eighteen months	If the infant's needs are met by loving, dependable adults, trust is developed. If adults fail to meet the infant's needs, mistrust develops.
2. Autonomy versus shame and doubt	Eighteen months to three and a half years	If the child is allowed to explore and develop a sense of self as an individual, autonomy develops. If parents are rigid, severe in toilet training, and impatient, the child will develop a sense of shame and doubt.
3. Initiative versus guilt	Three and a half to six years	Physical and mental abilities expand. If the child is encouraged to explore and parents encourage sociodramatic play and imaginative thought, the child will develop initiative. If parents are restrictive and punitive, the child will develop a sense of guilt.
4. Industry versus inferiority	Six to twelve years	Achievement becomes important. If adults help the child find learning and achievement rewarding, the child develops a sense of industry. If the child does not experience success in achievement, a sense of inferiority develops.

Figure 3.1   Erikson's Psychological Stages of Development in the Early Childhood Years

Later behaviorists applied the so-called S-R (stimulus-response) theory to children and their development. For current behaviorists, the critical factors in growth and development are the environment and the opportunity to learn. Development results from the reward system in the environment and is unrelated to ages and stages. The direction of behavior is shaped through control of the learning environment and the individual's experiences (Morrison, 1988).

Through B. F. Skinner's work (1953), the behaviorist theory was applied to parenting and schooling. Skinner proposed that if the environment is arranged to facilitate the desired behavior, and expectations are set for that behavior, the child will be influenced to use the appropriate behavior. Adult rewards for appropriate behavior will strengthen or condition the behavior. According to Skinner, because all behavior is learned it can be shaped or modified. Strategies for behavior modification are based on positive reinforcement (Weber, 1984). Parents and teachers of young children have found the concept of positive reinforcement especially helpful in managing behavior. Praising the young child for an appropriate behavior is more effective than inadvertently reinforcing a behavior that the adult wants the child to stop performing. For example, if a parent buys a toy in the grocery store to stop his two preschoolers from fighting, he may find himself faced with inappropriate behavior the next time the children are shopping with him. The children have learned that the parent will reward them for misbehaving. Likewise, the teacher who picks up and holds the toddler who is disturbing story time has reinforced the unwanted behavior by singling out the child for attention. Parents and teachers find that unwanted behavior is best ignored whenever possible and that appropriate behavior should be strengthened through positive reinforcement.

The Social Learning Theory

More recently, behavioral theorists have expanded the nature of learning to include imitation and observation. Social learning theorists such as Albert Bandura (Bandura & Walters, 1963) believe that many behaviors are not learned through shaping but develop through the individual's reactions to and interpretations of situations. The same stimulus or situation will elicit different responses depending on the individual's interpretation of the event. Verbal instruction, plus the individual's observations within a social context, affect that individual's expectations, abilities, and other inner qualities used to determine their response. Thus, a child who observes another child being punished for an inappropriate behavior can learn the appropriate response. Likewise, the child can learn a new behavior by imitating another child who is using the behavior correctly.

Terry and Julio

Terry and Julio are playing in the manipulative center in the class for three-year-olds. Julio cannot manage to string large colored beads on a shoelace. A teacher notices Julio's difficulty and comes over to show him how to hold the string and push a bead over the end of the shoelace. Terry, who has been working on a puzzle, watches the teacher showing Julio how to string beads. He puts the puzzle away and gets another shoestring. Watching Julio intently, he attempts to put beads on the string. After losing several beads he finally gets one on and pushes it to the end of the shoelace. He now attempts to duplicate the pattern of colored beads that Julio has placed on his shoestring.

The Cognitive-Developmental Theory

The cognitive-developmental view of development has had a major influence on the understanding of how children acquire and use knowledge. Jean Piaget's work has extended our understanding of how cognition develops. Piaget's (1963) studies of cognition led him to propose that children have different levels of understanding at different ages. Further, and more important, according to the cognitive-developmental theory the child has an active role in development. Unlike the maturational theory, which proposes that biological readiness controls the ability to learn, or the behaviorist theory, which suggests that the environment shapes behavior and learning, the cognitive-developmental theory says that the child's interaction with the environment and cognitive organization of experiences results in intelligence. The child's knowledge is constructed gradually as continued experiences permit an expanded understanding of the information encountered.

Piaget believed that knowledge is acquired and changes over time by taking in new information through assimilation and by incorporating or accommodating the new information into the existing knowledge structure, called a scheme. Through the process of assimilation and accommodation, the child not only acquires new knowledge but reorganizes existing knowledge. As the child progresses through stages of development, cognitive styles of organizing and structuring knowledge change. The child's mode or quality of thinking is different in each stage of development. In the early childhood years the child moves through the sensorimotor and preoperational stages of development. According to cognitive-developmental theorists, the early childhood years end when the child moves from the preoperational to the concrete operational stage of development (Weber, 1984). Figure 3.2 describes more about the sensorimotor, preoperational, and concrete operational stages of development.

STAGE	AGE	DESCRIPTION
Sensorimotor	Birth to eighteen months	The infant acquires knowledge through physical actions. Understanding is constructed by coordinating sensory experiences and physical actions.
Preoperational	Two to seven years	The young child acquires and represents knowledge through symbolic actions such as speaking words. The child is able to use symbolic thinking that is also intuitive. Understanding is controlled by perception.
Concrete operational	Seven to eleven years	The child is able to acquire knowledge symbolically and logically. The child reasons logically about concrete events. Logical thinking replaces intuitive thought as long as the concrete objects or events are present.

Figure 3.2 Piaget's Stages of Cognitive Development in the Early Childhood Years

The remainder of this chapter is devoted to a description of the child's development from birth to age eight; it also describes how the developmental stages affect the way in which the child learns. The implications of the characteristics of each age level for early childhood programs are also discussed.

BIRTH TO TWO YEARS: THE SENSORIMOTOR STAGE

Cognitive Development

Piaget described the first stage of cognitive development as the sensorimotor stage because infants come to know and understand their world by using their senses and physical actions. That is, infants construct understanding by using sensorimotor schemes, which are constructed by using innate reflexive actions such as sucking. Sensorimotor schemes in turn help infants acquire new ways of interaction. As the infant continually engages in reflexive action, behavior becomes more complex and predictable.

During the sensorimotor stage the infant moves through six substages of development, beginning with the **reflexive** stage. Reflexive actions in the first stage are gradually replaced by voluntary actions in the second stage, the **primary circular reactions** stage. In the third stage, that of **secondary circular reactions,** the infant is able to increase responses to people and objects, initiate activities, and develop object permanency. In the fourth stage, which involves **coordination of secondary circular reactions,** the infant actively searches for hidden objects and comprehends the meaning of simple words.

At the beginning of the second year, the fifth stage, that of **tertiary circular reactions,** commences. The toddler spends time experimenting with objects and begins to understand space, time, and causality. During the last stage, **symbolic representation** occurs. The toddler is able to mentally represent objects that facilitate symbolic imitative behavior (Morrison, 1988). The sensorimotor substages might be described as follows:

- Reflexive (birth to one month)—The neonate primarily uses reflexes for learning.
- Primary circular reactions (one to four months)—The infant repeats pleasurable behaviors and coordinates reflexes.
- Secondary circular reactions (four to ten months)—The infant discovers new capabilities by chance and repeats them (e.g., accidentally hits crib mobile; repeats the action intentionally). Cause and effect is learned.
- Coordination of secondary circular reactions (ten to twelve months)—The child is able to apply schemes or learned behavior to new situations; attains object permanence (i.e., knows that objects exist even when they cannot be seen).
- Tertiary circular reactions (twelve to eighteen months)—The child experiments with cause and effect; repeats behaviors to achieve variety (e.g., repeatedly drops toy from high chair).
- Symbolic representation (eighteen to twenty-four months)—The child begins to think before acting; can use imagery to represent objects and action (e.g., pretends to drink from cup).

The infant at first uses reflex actions such as sucking and grasping. When the reflexes can be coordinated, the infant can intentionally grasp and pick up objects. After object permanence is achieved, the infant can remember actions and locate objects. The infant learns that he or she can cause events to happen and can retain a mental image of events and objects that have been experienced (Lawton, 1988; Morrison, 1988; Schwartz & Robison, 1982; Seefeldt & Barbour, 1990).

Physical Development

In the first two years, infants and toddlers achieve more physical growth and development than in any other period of their childhood. By their first birthday, they triple their birth weight and acquire mobility skills that include crawling, standing, and walking. During the second year, they practice and refine mobility skills. Motor development proceeds in proximodistal development (from the center of the body out to the fingers) and in cephalocaudal development (from the top of the body down to the legs). By the age of five months they can reach and grasp a toy. Fine and gross motor development is controlled both by biological maturation and stimulation and opportunities for physical activities.

Teething begins at about seven months and is completed at three years, when the full set of "baby" teeth has erupted. Bladder and bowel control are not achieved until age two and a half or three, with boys more likely to achieve control at a later age than girls (Santrock, 1990).

Language Development

In the first two years, infants and toddlers move from prelinguistic utterances to the use of primitive sentences. Crying and cooing during the first few months evolve to babbling at about five or six months. Babbling includes the intonation patterns of the language by about ten months, with the first real word occurring soon thereafter. Use of single words or holophrastic speech for many types of meaningful communication is gradually extended at about eighteen months to combinations of two- and three-word utterances. With what is called telegraphic speech, toddlers express more complex thoughts through intonation and various combinations of the words they are rapidly adding to their vocabulary (Menyuk, 1969).

Social-Emotional Development

In infancy, the emotional tie between infant and parent or caregiver is called attachment. A positive attachment is crucial in the social and emotional development of the infant and toddler. Parental behavior, as well as the child's temperament, can affect development. Inappropriate parental behavior can cause anxious/avoidant or anxious/ambivalent patterns of attachment (Connell & Goldsmith, 1982). Anxious/ambivalent children are wary of strangers and new situations and have difficulty separating from the mother. Anxious/avoidant children, to the contrary, have no difficulty in separating from the mother; in fact, they show little preference for the parent over a stranger and may ignore the mother. For example, a toddler who was abused as an infant or whose needs were neglected shows anxious attachment in a day-care setting by fussing frequently and is fearful if routines or caregivers are changed (George & Main, 1979). Children with anxious attachment histories are at a higher risk of having later emotional difficulties that can include becoming emotionally dependent, aggressive, inattentive, or hyperactive. During the preschool years, children who were anxiously attached as infants are at increased risk for becoming bullies or victims of bullies (Troy & Sroufe, 1987).

Social development during the first two years includes the development of social signals among peers. Social style in toddlers is related to attachment history; toddlers with secure attachment histories relate more positively toward peers. Prosocial behavior, or empathy, the understanding of another person's feelings, begins to emerge at about twelve months, when babies respond to the distress of others. At twelve months they show distress themselves, and by eighteen months they can try to comfort a distressed peer. Children of parents who have been nurturing and responsive are more likely to respond to the distress of another person (Schickedanz, Hansen, & Forsyth, 1990).

The sensorimotor period is one of rapid development in physical, language, and social development. In the pages that follow is a discussion of infant and toddler development, followed by checklists that list some major milestones and behavioral characteristics for each age period. The sections on characteristics and competencies describe the attributes that children in each age group have in common; in addition, the lists also describe individual differences in children. These sections are included to help readers who may not have had extended experience with young children acquire a realistic picture of what children are like at each age and what can reasonably be expected in their behaviors and abilities. It is also important to remember that the description for any age group is general. Each child is unique and develops on an individual timetable.

In the sections that follow, characteristics of age levels from birth through five years are discussed; also included are the Wortham Developmental Checklist for Infants and Toddlers and the Frost-Wortham developmental checklists for the preschool years. The lists are for caregivers, parents, and teachers to use to further understand the normal characteristics in physical, social-emotional, and cognitive development for various age groups. The checklists may be consulted to determine if the child is achieving the listed behaviors during the normal age range. Likewise, parents, teachers, and caregivers can refer to the lists for suggestions about appropriate activities that can be conducted with the child. The checklists can be used in early childhood settings or by parents to record achievement of developmental milestones or mastery of listed competencies in the preschool years. The checklists have boxes in which the child's developmental progress can be tracked. The information to be recorded may vary depending upon the context in which the checklists are used; therefore, the labels for recording progress may be changed to reflect the characteristics the user wishes to document. For example, the infant and toddler checklists might have boxes for dates of mastery rather than dates of observation. Likewise, the preschool checklists might have boxes to indicate when relevant activities or lessons were conducted.

The checklists may also be adapted for use with children with special needs. PL 99-457 extends the guarantee of a free appropriate education for young children, beginning in infancy. Intervention for infants and toddlers with disabilities is funded through the Infants and Toddlers Program. Intervention plans for children with special needs can include checklists of characteristics adapted for the individual educational plan for that child. Mentally retarded children will progress through the categories of cognitive development much later than will children with normal intelligence; nevertheless, teachers of mentally retarded children can also use the checklists to determine the developmental needs of children whose chronological age is different than their mental age. Children with physical handicaps may also be working on motor skills that are typical of younger children with normal development; teachers can adapt the checklist to include the physical characteristics that the child has the potential to develop and can use it for record keeping and reporting progress to parents. Because each child with special needs is different, teachers and specialists will need to determine potential abilities and use developmental checklists to fit the profile of the individual student.

CHARACTERISTICS AND COMPETENCIES: BIRTH TO SIX MONTHS

The newborn baby is often described as being helpless. In many ways he or she is. For the first few weeks of life the baby seemingly sleeps, eats, and cries only. The mother or other adult must take care of the infant's needs. However, in spite of physical helplessness, newborn babies can develop a relationship with the family members and others in their life. They can see faces and hear voices. The baby responds to voices by turning his or her head or quieting to listen.

The new infant communicates his or her needs by crying and using facial expressions and body movements. Later, smiling, cooing, and gurgling are used to attract and hold the attention of significant people. The baby signals the need to withdraw from an interaction by turning his or her head away, yawning, crying, or fussing.

Babies come with all kinds of temperaments. From the beginning weeks of life, babies have unique personalities. Some enjoy being held or cuddled, whereas others do not respond to these activities. Each has his or her own style of being. Infant temperament has been classified into three types: the easy child, the slow-to-warm-up child, and the difficult child (Thomas, Chess, & Birch, 1970). Each type of infant has different personality and temperament characteristics that affect his or her moods, responsiveness, and activity levels. An infant's personality can affect adult interaction. Adults react positively and negatively to infant personalities, which in turn can cause difficulties for the infant. Parents and caregivers can have a positive effect on the infant's and toddler's emerging personalities by recognizing personality differences and modifying their responses positively and appropriately, especially with the child who is classified as difficult (Soderman, 1985).

Figure 3.3 provides a checklist for the developmental characteristics in the newborn child until it is about six months of age. Because no two infants develop at the same rate, the time line will differ for individual babies.

 Hunter

Hunter is nine months old. He can be characterized as having a slow-to-warm-up temperament. As a very young infant Hunter was very serious. He did not smile easily, and he studied other people in his environment. Both of Hunter's parents are professionals. Hunter's father manages real estate, and his mother is an accountant. Hunter stays with a nanny during the day. Now that he is approaching his first birthday, Hunter is physically very active, eager to explore, and obviously larger than average.

CHARACTERISTICS AND COMPETENCIES:
SIX TO TWELVE MONTHS

During the second six months of life, the baby experiences one of the most significant periods of growth and development in the entire life cycle. In physical development, the infant learns to sit, crawl, stand, and perhaps walk. Fine motor development allows

AGE: BIRTH TO SIX MONTHS			
PHYSICAL-COGNITIVE DEVELOPMENT	Date	Date	Date
1. Lifts head when held at shoulder			
2. When on stomach lifts or turns head			
3. Follows a moving person or object with eyes			
4. Looks at suspended object			
5. Grasps and holds a person or object for several seconds			
6. Moves arms and legs actively			
7. Sits in lap with support			
8. Close hand on dangling toy			
9. Learns to roll over			
10. Looks at objects and realistic pictures			
11. Uses eye-hand coordination in reaching			
12. Turns head to sound of bell or rattle			
13. Plays with hands and feet			
14. Brings object to mouth			
SOCIAL-EMOTIONAL DEVELOPMENT			
1. Looks attentively at an adult			
2. Adjusts body to the way the adult holds him/her			
3. Responds to talking, smiling, touching			
4. Quiets when picked up			
5. Stops crying when someone plays with him/her			
6. Vocalizes in association with pleasure, displeasure, eagerness, and satisfaction			
7. Cries to get a bottle, attention, or to be held			
8. Knows familiar people or things by sight or voice			
9. Chuckles and laughs			

Figure 3.3   Wortham Developmental Checklist: Infants and Toddlers, Birth to Six Months

AGE: SIX TO TWELVE MONTHS

PHYSICAL-COGNITIVE DEVELOPMENT	Date	Date	Date
1. Sits alone			
2. Transfers object from one hand to another			
3. Drinks from a cup			
4. Picks up small things with thumb and forefinger			
5. Uncovers hidden toy			
6. Looks at picture book			
7. Holds two toys			
8. Imitates speech sounds			
9. Creeps or gets from one place to another			
10. Attains sitting position independently			
11. Stands holding on			
12. Walks holding on			
13. Drops or places objects into a container			
14. Manipulates objects			
15. Says single words such as "mama" and "dada"			
16. Imitates actions			
17. Attempts self-feeding with a cup and spoon or fingers			
SOCIAL-EMOTIONAL DEVELOPMENT			
1. Shows likes or dislikes of people, objects, places			
2. Plays with image in mirror			
3. Understands "No"			
4. Responds to presence of a new person			
5. Squeals with joy or pleasure			
6. Demonstrates anxiety over departure of parents			
7. Enjoys and plays games with others (e.g., "Pat-a-Cake")			
8. Uses motions or gestures to communicate (holds out arms to be picked up)			

Figure 3.4 Wortham Developmental Checklist: Infants and Toddlers, Six to Twelve Months

the child to explore and manipulate toys and other objects by putting them in the mouth, turning them over and over, and performing other actions that permit learning the physical properties. The baby is very interested in its body as he or she practices motor skills such as rocking on hands and knees or clapping. The child may begin to feed him- or herself and imitates the physical actions of other family members.

The baby enjoys increasing social interactions with others. Babbling, smiling, and making gestures such as waving are used to initiate and respond to social encounters. The baby also uses gestures and tone of voice to communicate wants and needs. Likewise, the baby is gaining an understanding of the language and intonation used by others and can respond to simple commands, particularly "No." As the first birthday approaches, he or she may be able to use a few simple words.

A significant stage in social-emotional development is based on the attainment of memory. The baby begins to recognize and react negatively to the presence of strangers. The baby also develops a new awareness of separation from the mother and other family members and fusses and cries when separation occurs. For a period of time, the infant may be more selective about social interactions and be wary of entering new situations.

Figure 3.4 is a checklist for babies six to twelve months old; it lists the new competencies the baby acquires in physical, cognitive, and social-emotional development during the second half-year of life.

CHARACTERISTICS AND COMPETENCIES: TWELVE TO EIGHTEEN MONTHS

The months after the first birthday are an exciting period of development for the toddler. New abilities enable the child to not only get around without assistance but also

to communicate using language. Freed from the dependence of infancy, the toddler literally blooms as he or she practices and masters emerging competencies.

Learning to walk affords the toddler with true mobility. By eighteen months, he or she will not only leave tentative steps behind and walk well but will also learn to climb stairs and throw a ball. Fine motor development enables the toddler to become more proficient at feeding him- or herself and to learn a few skills in putting on and removing clothing.

Although gestures are still used to communicate wants, emerging language permits the child to use words to interact verbally with others. The baby understands more language than he or she can speak; nevertheless, the baby can name things in the environment and use words to initiate and respond to adult language.

AGE: TWELVE TO EIGHTEEN MONTHS			
PHYSICAL-COGNITIVE DEVELOPMENT	Date	Date	Date
Motor Development			
1. Throws ball			
2. Builds two-block tower			
3. Walks well			
4. Walks backward			
5. Walks up stairs (with difficulty)			
6. Removes clothing (with difficulty)			
7. Takes off shoes and socks			
8. Uses spoon with little help			
9. Turns pages in a book			
10. Drinks from cup or glass unassisted with some spilling			
11. Scribbles			
Language Development			
1. Says single words (may add two and three words)			
2. Points to a body part on request			
3. Imitates words			
4. Responds to a single request			
5. Says the names of at least five things			

Figure 3.5 Wortham Developmental Checklist: Infants and Toddlers, Twelve to Eighteen Months (pp. 69-70)

Motor skills help the child to carry out new abilities in cognitive development. The toddler uses mobility and dexterity to expand exploration and manipulation of things in the environment. Through active play with toys and independent movement, the toddler enlarges his or her understanding of the world and the things that are available for play activities. Language and motor skills enhance the child's social and emotional development. The toddler exchanges words for crying when he or she needs or wants something. The toddler initiates social interactions with others more freely and can control the length of the interactions with others by advancing or withdrawing physically.

	Date	Date	Date
Cognitive Development			
1. Pursues and retrieves a toy that is out of sight			
2. Puts objects in and out of container			
3. Role plays with familiar objects			
4. Recognizes and responds to self in mirror			
5. Solves simple puzzles or constructions			
SOCIAL-EMOTIONAL DEVELOPMENT			
1. Cooperates in games with caregivers			
2. Offers objects to another person			
3. Plays independently or in parallel play			
4. Helps with simple tasks			
5. Maintains interest in activities for longer periods			
6. Looks at speaker who is talking			
7. Carries, hugs toys			

Figure 3.5 Wortham Developmental Checklist: Infants and Toddlers, Twelve to Eighteen Months *(continued)*

The characteristics listed in Figure 3.5 describe the toddler's development during the first six months of the second year. As the characteristics of development become more complex, the descriptions of development can be put into categories. Thus, physical-cognitive development now is divided into motor development, language development, and cognitive development.

 **Katilynn**

Sixteen-month-old Katilynn looks like a little angel but behaves like the opposite. Even before she could move around she wiggled and squirmed. She was not interested in infant toys and only briefly interested in anything else. Now that Katilynn can walk and climb, nothing is safe. She is into everything she can reach. She is a happy toddler but a source of exasperation for her parents. Katilynn is definitely on the go, but her parents are reluctant to take her to restaurants and other public places that will restrict her activities. She defies confinement. She will not sit in a high chair and stubbornly ignores all attempts to curb her behavior. Her attention span is still very brief, and constant activity fills her busy day.

CHARACTERISTICS AND COMPETENCIES: EIGHTEEN TO TWENTY-FOUR MONTHS

During the second half of the second year, the toddler seems to have an inexhaustible source of energy. Development of new abilities seems to be constant and rapid. A few weeks brings many changes in motor development, language, cognitive learning, and social development. The child develops simultaneously in more than one area as he or she tries out new competencies.

The older toddler is physical, or "on the go." He or she can now run, climb, and accomplish some self-help skills in dressing and washing. The child is proficient in feeding him- or herself and engages in all physical activities with enthusiasm.

Language development is accelerating. The child can make him- or herself understood by using words and is expanding the number of words he or she can string together when talking. Role playing or pretending now includes talking as the toddler begins to verbalize what he or she is doing while playing. More words are used correctly, although the toddler uses the same vocabulary to express many different thoughts.

Toys and problem-solving activities are appealing to the competent toddler as he or she is able to apply past experiences to new learning situations. The toddler is learning to work simple puzzles and is developing an awareness of concepts such as color, shape, and number.

Social awareness allows the toddler to enjoy group activities. Although the toddler is just beginning to actually interact in play activities with other children, he or she is aware of others and is expanding interactions with peers and adults.

AGE: EIGHTEEN TO TWENTY-FOUR MONTHS			
PHYSICAL-COGNITIVE DEVELOPMENT	Date	Date	Date
Motor Development			
1. Washes and dries hands			
2. Builds tower of three to four cubes			
3. Kicks ball forward			
4. Throws ball overhand			
5. Walks up steps			
6. Runs			
7. Pounds and rolls clay			
8. Jumps			
9. Removes clothing			
10. Drinks from cup or glass			
11. Uses spoon			
12. Climbs furniture, play equipment			
Language Development			
1. Combines two to three different words			
2. Follows two of three directions			
3. Names pictures			
4. Imitates adult speech without prompting			
5. Engages in make-believe telephone conversation			
6. Uses at least fifteen different words in right way			

Figure 3.6   Wortham Developmental Checklist: Infants and Toddlers, Eighteen to Twenty-four Months

The toddler is eager, interested, challenging, quick, busy, full of energy, and, for adults, exhausting. Toddlers require constant supervision as they explore and experiment with their new abilities. This is the age with the highest potential for toddler accidents, as they move through one of the peak periods of growth and learning. Figure 3.6 lists characteristics of the child during the second half of the second year and describes the toddler's continuing development.

Cognitive Development	Date	Date	Date
1. Demonstrates perception of correct function of toy			
2. Solves a two- or three-piece puzzle			
3. Places correct shape in shape box			
4. Uses housekeeping toys			
5. Recognizes self in photograph			
6. Matches familiar objects by color			
7. Matches familiar objects by shape			
8. Understands "one more"			
9. Returns toy to correct place			
SOCIAL-EMOTIONAL DEVELOPMENT			
1. Uses words to make wants known or express feelings			
2. Puts away toys on request			
3. Engages in affectionate interchanges with adults and children			
4. Sings with adults or other children			
5. Shows interest in exploring new places			

INFANT AND TODDLER DEVELOPMENT: IMPLICATIONS FOR LEARNING

Adults who are responsible for children during the first two years of life have the opportunity to facilitate growth and development within an exciting time of beginnings. Whereas infants used to be considered as helpless human beings, they are now described as capable and competent. Weiser (1982) stated: "This new baby is capable of selecting stimuli to which to respond or ignore, to physically withdraw from an external cause of pain, or to react with total body movement to internal distress" (p.

22). White and Watts (1973) wrote: "The 10- to 18-month period of life is in effect a critical period for the development of the foundations of competence" (p. 245).

Parents, teachers, and caregivers can best serve as facilitators of competence and learning if they understand how the child grows and develops during the first years. Although young infants cry and need to be fed, changed, and burped, they can also coo, attract the adult's attention, use their bodies to express themselves, and enjoy social interactions with others. Toddlers are busy and active. They are noisy and interested in everything.

During physical development, motor and perceptual skills need to be encouraged. Motor skills include running, jumping, using alternate feet on stairs, and manipulating construction toys. Adults need to provide opportunities and activities to encourage the use of both large and fine motor skills. The baby uses the five senses of hearing, tasting, seeing, smelling, and touching to learn about the world. Activities and opportunities to explore using the senses should be included in daily experiences.

The child learns concepts through exploration and exposure to new experiences in cognitive and language growth. Through the development of language, the child becomes able to communicate and express him- or herself. Adults need to plan for opportunities to explore toys, nature, the home and school environment, books, and other items that can enrich children's understanding of their world and expand their receptive and expressive vocabulary.

Social growth includes the development of emotions, the management of fears, and the development of a sense of self. Because babies are in a stage of trust versus mistrust, adults can enhance a positive outlook and confidence by providing a dependable, consistent environment in which they can flourish. Babies need to experience continuity and security in their daily lives that will allow them to become explorers and discoverers. Additional information on how adults can facilitate development and learning with infants and toddlers will be discussed in chapters 4 and 5.

Koby

Koby, Katilynn's brother, is four years old. He fits in the category of the easy child. He has always been agreeable and able to adjust to changes in routines, caregivers, and playmates. He has his own ideas about his choices of activities and clothes. He has preferred to dress like his dad since he was a toddler and usually sports a hat.

Koby recently had his first experience on a soccer team. He finally learned not to lie down on the field during the second half of the game at the end of the season. As the first grandchild on both sides of the family, he usually had extended family representation at the soccer games. Koby now attends a preschool program at a local elementary school.

AGES TWO TO FIVE: THE PREOPERATIONAL STAGE

Between the ages of eighteen months and two years, the toddler enters the preoperational stage. The older toddler between the ages of two and three is making a transition from babyhood into the preschool years. By age two and a half, the toddler is developmentally closer to the preschool three-year-old than to the younger two-year-old toddler. Because two-year-olds are typically preoperational in their thinking, their development is included with that of preschoolers three to five years of age. Similarly, children between the ages of six and seven are making a transition into the concrete operational stage. Although they are progressing through the latter stages of preoperational thinking, their development is discussed with primary-school-age children (Santrock, 1990).

Cognitive Development

Children who have reached the preoperational stage have entered a new period of thought; that is, they can use symbolism, or pretending. They are able to represent objects and events mentally. However, they are controlled by their perceptions. They focus on appearances. They are also limited in that they center on one characteristic at a time and see things from their own egocentric point of view.

Within the preoperational stage is the symbolic function substage. This substage occurs between the ages of two and four. Symbolic thought allows the child to mentally picture things that are not present. Young children who have achieved symbolic function can use art experiences, especially scribbling, to represent things in their environment such as houses, trees, flowers, and people. Symbolism also allows them to engage in pretend play.

Egocentrism in this substage results in the child's inability to distinguish between his or her own perspective and the perspective of another child or adult. In play, the child assumes that other children share his or her feelings and thoughts. The child may have difficulty relating to another child's ideas or emotions that are different from his or her own.

Children in the symbolic function substage also believe that inanimate objects are alive and capable of action. Thus, they are likely to think, for example, that clouds are propelling themselves in the sky. They might also believe, for instance, that a rock or tree can take action or cause something to happen.

Between the ages of four and seven, the preoperational child enters the intuitive thought substage, when primitive reasoning begins. The child's thought process is

changing from one of symbolic thinking to intuitive, or inner, thinking. The child can organize objects into primitive collections but is unable to use categories of classification in a consistent manner. As a result, the child might start organizing an array of objects by a color, then change to another color or move to arranging by shape or size. This primitive system of organization is caused by centration. The child tends to center or focus on one characteristic or attribute. Two attributes cannot be considered at one time. As a result, the child may change from one attribute to another when trying to organize a group of objects. Once the child is able to move beyond centering, levels of thought characteristic of the concrete operational stage—such as classification and seriation—can emerge (Santrock, 1990; Schickedanz, Hansen, & Forsyth, 1990).

Children between the ages of two and five need opportunities to explore. Parents and caregivers can provide experiences for cognitive development through excursions in the nearby environment as well as trips of longer distances. Children also benefit from experiences with books, pictures, and concrete materials related to concepts in their world. Activities with materials combined with conversations facilitate their process of sorting out and internalizing information and ideas.

Physical Development

As children move from toddlerhood to the preschool years they begin to lose their chubby appearance. Their bodies become more proportional as they get taller and thinner. In a slower rate of growing, they gain about three pounds a year and grow approximately two and a half inches.

Children at this stage become agile at climbing, running, and jumping. Later, they can master hopping, skipping, and galloping as they achieve more coordination and control. They acquire some mastery of throwing and catching a ball and move from marked-time climbing of stairs to using alternate feet when both ascending and descending.

Preschoolers gain more fine motor control over hands and fingers and use this control to develop skills in drawing, cutting, coloring, and pasting. They can put on and remove some clothing items, and they enjoy using their developing fine motor skills to become independent.

Indoor and outdoor play environments can provide opportunities for practice of motor skills. Three-year-olds can build block towers and work simple puzzles. They are constantly on the move outdoors as they ride tricycles, move up and down play structures, learn to pump a swing, and run in the playground while pretend playing. Rough-and-tumble play occurs, particularly in boys (DiPietro, 1981), whereas girls are more likely to enjoy using fine motor skills in, for example, scribbling or playing with puzzles. When playing outdoors, boys are more active than girls and use more space in their play. Girls are more likely to prefer indoor play using fine motor skills in manipulative or art activities (Frost, 1992; Johnson, Christie, & Yawkey, 1987).

Adults facilitate physical development by providing daily opportunities for gross motor play both indoors and outdoors. In addition to providing space and equipment for gross motor exercise, adults can engage in games and activities that will extend preschoolers' interests and attempts to try new skills. There are many manipulative toys that attract preschoolers to engage in fine motor activities. Adults need to provide a selection of puzzles, small construction toys, and art media that will entice young children to work with fine motor skills. Because first attempts with scissors and crayons may prove difficult, adults provide support and encouragement through activities that permit the child to enjoy the process.

Language Development

After the age of two, young children move beyond telegraphic speech in that they are able to use longer and more complete sentences. They are learning morphological rules. This is evidenced by their use of plural and possessive forms of nouns and verb endings. They make errors in the use of rules, such as overgeneralizations (e.g., they might apply inappropriate verb endings when using the past tense).

In syntax or sentence construction, children learn the proper word order for asking questions. Their sentences become more complex as they expand their vocabulary and expressive speech. They are gradually able to use negative sentences (Brown, 1973).

At about three years of age, young children begin to understand and use rules of conversation. They are able to talk about things that are not present; consequently, they can use language as they engage in pretend play or talk about imaginary people and things. As prosocial awareness develops, four-year-olds are able to understand others' feelings or needs expressed in conversations. Four-year-olds can also vary their speech style when talking to different audiences such as younger children, peers, or adults (Gleason, 1988).

Word meanings develop continuously. Young preschoolers use environmental contexts to understand the meaning of new words. Locative expressions such as "on" and "under" emerge between ages two and three, but others such as "beside" and "between" take longer to understand and use. Santrock (1990) reported that between the ages of one and five the child learns an average of five words a day. After age five, the rate of acquisition of new word meanings accelerates.

Development in writing and reading, or literacy, is also an important area between the ages of two and five. Actually, literacy is important in the infant and toddler years and is encouraged when parents and other caregivers share with babies books, stories, and pictures. When parents point out labels on a food product, indicate why they are making a grocery list, or explain how they can find a telephone number in the directory, they are helping develop the child's understanding of the functions of reading and writing (Dailey, 1991).

Building on oral language development with books and environmental print, preschool children develop strategies for becoming literate. When parents and teachers talk with children about things the children are interested in and take them on outings that will expose them to new experiences and information, they are helping the child build conceptual foundations and language that is later used in reading and writing (Mavrogenes, 1990). As a result of their experiences, they gradually come to understand that print, not just pictures, gives meaning to books. They come to recognize print, as well as knowledge of the spacing between words, and that individual letters are used to form words (Fields, Spangler, & Lee, 1991).

Young children also develop literacy through writing efforts. They use scribbles, mock letters, letter reversals, and other print efforts as part of their natural growth toward literacy. Preschool children use trial and error and hypothesis testing in their journey to understand reading and writing, just as they do in acquiring oral language. Their literacy emerges gradually as they engage in reading and writing experiences each day (Lindfors, 1987; Morrow, 1989).

Social-Emotional Development

Between the ages of two and five, young children gradually learn how to become part of a social group. A major task during these years is socialization. This process of socialization is affected by parenting styles, the relationship they have with their siblings and peers, and the family and environmental conditions where they live. To become successful members of social groups, young children must learn appropriate behaviors. They must learn what behaviors their parents desire them to use, how to interact with their siblings, and how to successfully play with friends. One major accomplishment is the acquisition of prosocial behaviors when the young child uses cooperating, sharing, and helping behaviors (Doescher & Sugawara, 1989). Another desired behavior is the development of respect for others. Despite the contrary influences of society and television, adults in young children's environment help them acquire appropriate social behaviors that demonstrate respect by modeling and reinforcing concern for others (O'Brien, 1991).

Parenting styles will affect how the child learns self-control and meets parental expectations. Parents may be authoritarian, authoritative, or permissive (Baumrind, 1971). Authoritarian parents place firm limits on children and expect them to follow their directions, whereas authoritative parents, in addition to using limits and controls, encourage their children to be independent. Permissive parents can be indulgent or indifferent (Maccoby & Martin, 1983). Permissive-indulgent parents place few controls on their children but are involved with them, whereas permissive-indifferent parents are not involved in their children's lives. Whichever style they use, consistency or inconsistency in parenting behaviors will affect the child's social and emotional development. The child needs dependable guidelines in the long process of acquiring self-discipline. If the parent and teacher approach the discipline process indifferently or vacillate in how they guide the child's behavior, the child's confusion may result in inappropriate behavior.

The parent or other adult can teach the child social skills in a variety of ways. Styles of guiding or correcting behaviors may include instruction, inductive reasoning, reinforcement, or punishment. These parenting strategies can have either positive or negative consequences in the child's long-term social development. If positive guidelines are to be communicated to the child, parents and teachers will want to focus on teaching the child appropriate behavior rather than on punishment of inappropriate behavior (Clewett, 1988).

At the age of two, the older toddler is learning how to interact with peers through play. He or she is moving from engaging in mostly solitary play or parallel play near another child to gradually increasing the frequency and level of interaction with children in play activities. Peers are an important source of socialization in that they help the child learn how to fit into group situations outside the family. Young children learn how to engage successfully in social play largely through trial and error. They discover it is less successful to hit than to offer a toy when trying to gain acceptance in a play group. Cooperation and sharing become recognized as successful social behaviors. Parents and teachers can help young children acquire successful social behaviors by discussing such behaviors and modeling appropriate peer relationships.

During the preschool years, the young child is exposed to both negative and positive social influences. Children can learn aggression as well as prosocial behavior. Various influences in their lives help mold the socialization characteristics they acquire. Changing social influences affect which socialization patterns the child will ultimately adopt. Because the child is in the stage that Erikson describes as initiative versus guilt, the child is in the process of discovering what kind of person he or she will become. The child is beginning to develop a conscience. The child's initiative and enthusiasm will result in both rewards and punishments from parents. Whether the child will resolve this stage with initiative or guilt is influenced by how the parents respond to the child's attempts at independence and self-control. If parents can set effective limits yet encourage children's curiosity, children will develop a positive outlook about their ability to manage self-control. If parents and teachers are punitive and controlling, children will possibly doubt their ability to achieve independence (Clewett, 1988; Soderman, 1985). Television, changing family patterns, working mothers, quality of child care, and school settings all contribute to the environmental influences that socialize the child positively and negatively.

CHARACTERISTICS AND COMPETENCIES: TWO TO FIVE YEARS

As children move through the preschool years, development is more individually paced. In the preoperational period, development may be more rapid in one area than in another. Developmental change is more dependent on the individual child's maturation and experiences than on chronological age. In discussing developmentally appropriate practice in programs for three-year-olds, Bredekamp (1987) described the developmental continuum in the preschool years: "At $2\frac{1}{2}$, many children begin to display skills and behaviors most typical of 3-year-olds. Thus, children between $2\frac{1}{2}$ and $3\frac{1}{2}$ years of age are often similar developmentally; and some $3\frac{1}{2}$-year-olds share traits of 4s" (p. 47).

To accommodate a developmental continuum, the checklists in Figures 3.7 (pp. 81–83), 3.8 (pp. 84–87), and 3.9 (pp. 88–91) describe children within three levels of development rather than by chronological age. The checklists are an adaptation of the Frost-Wortham developmental checklists (Wortham, 1984) that were originally organized by developmental category. In this context, they have been arranged by level of development, with categories of development grouped together within each level. The language and reading development skills in Level V have been updated to reflect the whole-language, or emergent literacy, approach to reading and writing.

The checklist items include characteristic accomplishments or behaviors for each level. They are not intended to be all-inclusive. For example, in the area of concept development, typical concepts the child can learn at a given level are described, yet there are many more concepts that could be added.

The categories of development are further delineated when compared with those on the infant and toddler checklists. Cognitive development is now more specifically described as concept development and math (quantitative and problem solving). Concept development is further divided into identification, discrimination, and classification skills.

	Introduced	Progress	Mastery
CONCEPT DEVELOPMENT			
Identification, Discrimination, and Classification Skills			
1. Discriminates between two smells			
2. Verbalizes that smells are "different"			
3. Discriminates between sounds and verbalizes that they are "different"			
4. Identifies sounds verbally			
5. Points to different food objects on request			
6. Discriminates differences in the shape of objects (round, square, triangular)			
7. Discriminates differences in the size of objects (big/little, long/short)			
8. Classifies objects by weight (heavy/light)			
9. Classifies objects by height (tall/short)			
Math: Quantitative and Problem Solving			
1. Manipulates and experiments with simple machines			
2. Counts by rote from one to five			
3. Forms creative designs with materials			
4. Uses construction materials for multiple purposes			
5. Perceives objects from different visual perspectives			
LANGUAGE DEVELOPMENT			
Oral Language			
1. Produces language that is mostly intelligible			
2. Recognizes and verbally labels common objects			
3. Responds correctly to simple instructions involving locations in the classroom			
4. Uses sentences of four to five words			
5. Asks questions to gain problem-solving information			

Figure 3.7 Frost-Wortham Developmental Checklist: Level III (pp. 81-83)

Language development has been categorized as oral language at Levels III and IV. At Level V it is further divided into language and vocabulary, oral comprehension, and emergent reading and writing.

Social and emotional development is described under social play and socializing and is also reflected in the continued complexity of social interactions in dramatic play.

Physical development is now categorized as motor development. Gross and fine motor skills are described as gross movement and fine movement.

	Introduced	Progress	Mastery
DRAMATIC PLAY			
1. Imitates grownups (plays house, store, and so forth)			
2. Expresses frustrations in play			
3. Creates imaginary playmates			
4. Engages in housekeeping			
5. Paints and draws symbolic figures on large paper			
6. Builds simple structures with blocks			
7. Uses transportation toys, people toys, and animal toys to enrich block play			
8. Imagines any objects as the object he or she wants (symbolic function)			
SOCIAL PLAY AND SOCIALIZING			
1. Engages in independent play			
2. Engages in parallel play			
3. Plays briefly with peers			
4. Recognizes the needs of others			
5. Shows sympathy for others			
6. Attends to an activity for ten to fifteen minutes			
7. Sings simple songs			
MOTOR DEVELOPMENT			
Gross Movement			
1. Catches a ball with both hands against the chest			
2. Rides a tricycle			
3. Hops on both feet several times without assistance			
4. Throws a ball five feet with accuracy			
5. Climbs up a slide and comes down			
6. Climbs by alternating feet and holding on to a handrail			
7. Stands on one foot and balances briefly			

Figure 3.7 Frost-Wortham Developmental Checklist: Level III *(continued)*

	Introduced	Progress	Mastery
8. Pushes a loaded wheelbarrow			
9. Runs freely with little stumbling or falling			
10. Builds a tower with nine or ten blocks			
Fine Movement			
1. Places small pegs in pegboards			
2. Holds a paintbrush or pencil with the whole hand			
3. Eats with a spoon			
4. Buttons large button on his or her own clothes			
5. Puts on coat unassisted			
6. Strings bead with ease			
7. Hammers a pound toy with accuracy			
8. Works a three- or four-piece puzzle			

DEVELOPMENT IN THE PRESCHOOL YEARS: IMPLICATIONS FOR LEARNING

The older toddler and preschool child in the preoperational period undergo dramatic growth in development between the ages of two and five. They are active learners in every aspect of their development. They need constant experiences to help them refine emerging social, cognitive, physical, and language competencies. Improved large and fine motor control allow them to become more independent. They need indoor and outdoor play activities that will encourage practice and enjoyment of their motor skills.

The curiosity of the preschool child is nurtured through the provision of field trips, exploration of the natural environment, experiences and discovery with real materials, and opportunities for creativity and expression through music, drama, and various art media. The reading of books, storytelling, and other literary experiences will spark their interest in writing and reading their own stories and the stories and books written by others.

Preschool children learn social skills through opportunities to interact with members of the family and to play with peers. As a result of social interaction they learn self-control as well as sharing, helping, playing together, and successfully resolving problems with family and friends. The child learns these social skills both within the home and at caregiving or school environments that foster the development of positive social relationships. The young child needs time to work and play with family members and other children with modeling, discussion, and encouragement, which will help the child learn to use positive rather than negative social behaviors. Adults provide the personal and environmental support that facilitate learning and growth in

	Introduced	Progress	Mastery
CONCEPT DEVELOPMENT *Identification, Discrimination, and Classification Skills*			
1. Points to basic shapes (circle, square, rectangle, triangle) on request			
2. Names basic shapes:			
a) circle			
b) square			
c) triangle			
d) rectangle			
3. Labels tastes verbally			
4. Identifies primary colors (red, yellow, blue)			
5. Identifies likenesses and differences in two or more objects (shape, size, color)			
6. Discriminates differences (opposites) in:			
a) sound (loud/soft)			
b) amount (full/empty)			
7. Identifies spatial relationships:			
a) far/near			
b) in/out			
c) front/back			
d) high/low			
8. Identifies and discriminates time relationships:			
a) before/after			
b) earlier/later			
9. Identifies and discriminates actions:			
a) run			
b) walk			
c) jump			
10. Classifies objects by more than one property			
11. Reverses simple operations:			
a) stacks/unstacks/restacks			
b) arranges/disarranges/rearranges			
12. Classifies by condition:			
a) hot/cold			
b) wet/dry			

Figure 3.8   Frost-Wortham Developmental Checklist: Level IV (pp. 84-87)

	Introduced	Progress	Mastery
13. Identifies and discriminates value relationships:			
a) right/wrong			
b) good/bad			
c) pretty/ugly			
d) sad/happy			
Math: Quantitative and Problem Solving			
1. Counts by rote from one to ten			
2. Demonstrates the concept of numbers through five			
3. Orders the numbers one to five			
4. Understands the concepts of first and last			
5. Identifies:			
a) penny			
b) nickel			
c) dime			
6. Compares differences in dimension (taller/shorter, longer/shorter, thinner/wider)			
7. Demonstrates one-to-one correspondence			
LANGUAGE DEVELOPMENT			
Oral Language			
1. Uses simple position words such as "over" and "under"			
2. Uses simple action words such as "run" and "walk"			
3. Uses complete sentences			
4. Uses language for specific purposes (directions, information)			
5. Verbalizes routine events ("We're going out to play.")			
6. Averages five-word sentences			
7. Follows simple sentences			
8. Repeats nursery rhymes			
DRAMATIC PLAY			
1. Role plays in the housekeeping center			
2. Role plays some adult occupations			
3. Participates in dramatization of familiar stories			
4. Uses puppets in self-initiated dialogues			

	Introduced	Progress	Mastery
5. Differentiates between real and make-believe			
6. Pretends dolls are real people			
7. Constructs (paints, molds, and so forth) recognizable figures			
8. Participates in finger plays			
SOCIAL PLAY AND SOCIALIZING			
1. Leaves the mother readily			
2. Converses with other children			
3. Converses with adults			
4. Plays with peers			
5. Cooperates in classroom routines			
6. Takes turns and shares			
7. Replaces materials after use			
8. Takes care of personal belongings			
9. Respects the property of others			
10. Attends to an activity for fifteen to twenty minutes			
11. Engages in group activities			
12. Sings with a group			
13. Is sensitive to praise and criticism			
MOTOR DEVELOPMENT			
Gross Movement			
1. Balances on one foot			
2. Walks a straight line forward and backward			
3. Walks a balance beam			
4. Climbs steps with alternate feet without support			
5. Climbs on jungle gym			
6. Skips haltingly			
7. Throws, catches and bounces a large ball			
8. Stacks blocks vertically and horizontally			
9. Creates recognizable block structures			
10. Rides a tricycle with speed and skill			

Figure 3.8   Frost-Wortham Developmental Checklist: Level IV *(continued)*

	Introduced	Progress	Mastery
Fine Movement			
1. Pounds and rolls clay			
2. Puts together a five-piece puzzle			
3. Forms a pegboard design			
4. Cuts with scissors haltingly; pastes			
5. Eats with a fork correctly			
6. Holds a cup with one hand			
7. Puts a coat on a hanger or hook			
8. Manipulates large crayons and brushes			
9. Buttons buttons and zips zippers haltingly			

social and all other areas of development. More detailed information on how teachers facilitate development and learning in the preschool years will be discussed in chapters 6, 7, and 8.

Miles and Elizabeth

Miles and Elizabeth are siblings. Miles is almost five, and Elizabeth is eight. Their mother is of Hispanic ancestry and their father is Anglo. Neither the children nor their parents speak any language other than English, although they hear grandparents and other extended family members speaking Spanish. Their father works as a graphic artist and their mother is a dental assistant. Both children have been in child care since they were young infants. Elizabeth is now in the second grade, and Miles will enter kindergarten next fall.

Elizabeth can be described as somewhat shy and eager to please. She participates in dancing lessons and Brownie Scouts. Her teachers find her a cooperative and diligent student. She enjoys Barbie dolls, books, and art activities. She is enjoying trying out her new skills in writing and spelling by describing the pictures she creates.

Miles engages in rough-and-tumble outdoor play with his friends. He lives in a neighborhood full of boys his age who spend many hours playing together in the evenings and on weekends. Wheel toys and other props facilitate "superhero" and other fantasy play themes that move across the yards of homes on their block. Miles enjoys playing with miniature vehicles and is able to keep himself occupied for long periods of time in self-initiated play when he is indoors. He is easy to manage if firm limits are set for his behavior.

	Introduced	Progress	Mastery
CONCEPT DEVELOPMENT			
Identification, Discrimination, and Classification Skills			
1. Identifies spatial relationships:			
a) top/bottom			
b) over/under			
2. Identifies and discriminates value relationships (like/dislike)			
3. Identifies and discriminates time relationships:			
a) morning/noon/night			
b) today/tomorrow			
c) yesterday/today			
4. Labels smells verbally			
5. Identifies colors (green, orange, purple, brown, black, white)			
6. Identifies the simple properties of an object (color, shape, size)			
7. Classifies colors by intensity (dark/light, darker than/lighter than)			
8. Classifies foods (fruits, vegetables, meat)			
9. Classifies tastes (sweet, sour, salty)			
10. Classifies surfaces by textures (smooth, rough, soft, hard)			
11. Identifies and classifies common objects by shape (circle, rectangle, triangle, oval, square)			
12. Seriates (arranges) objects by size			
13. Classifies by function:			
a) food/eat			
b) vehicle/ride			
Math: Quantitative and Problem Solving			
1. Counts to fifty			
2. Demonstrates the concept of numbers through ten			
3. Orders the numbers one to ten			
4. Writes numbers for sets one to ten			
5. Identifies pairs of familiar objects (shoes, socks, gloves, earrings)			
6. Groups objects into sets of equal number			
7. Compares elements of unequal sets (more than/fewer than)			

Figure 3.9 Frost-Wortham Developmental Checklist: Level V (pp. 88-91)

	Introduced	Progress	Mastery
8. Combines (adds) the total number in two small groups			
9. Uses ordinal concepts up through concept of third			
10. Identifies:			
a) penny			
b) nickel			
c) dime			
d) quarter			
11. Compares distance (height, width) to an independent object			
12. Compares volumes in separate containers			
13. Tells time to the hour			
LANGUAGE DEVELOPMENT			
Oral Language			
1. Communicates ideas, feelings, and emotions in well-formed sentences			
2. Uses the correct form of more verbs in informal conversation			
3. Uses the correct prepositions to denote place and position			
4. Uses most personal pronouns correctly			
5. Explains the operation of simple machines			
6. Uses language to get what she or he wants			
7. Can follow instructions containing three parts			
Reading Readiness			
Language and Vocabulary			
1. Listens to and follows verbal directions			
2. Identifies the concept of word			
3. Identifies the concept of letters			
4. Invents a story for a picture book			
Oral Comprehension			
5. Locates elements in a picture (tallest, largest, and so forth)			
6. Retells in the correct sequence a story read to him or her			
7. Reorganizes pictures to show the correct story sequence			
8. Answers recall questions about a story			
9. Draws analogies from a story to his or her own experience			
10. Makes value judgements about story events			

	Introduced	Progress	Mastery
Emergent Reading and Writing			
11. Tells experiences for an experience story			
12. Follows left-to-right progression as an adult reads			
13. Identifies recurring words on an experience chart			
14. Suggests titles for experience stories			
15. Uses invented spelling to write stories			
16. "Reads" familiar storybooks			
DRAMATIC PLAY			
1. Role plays a wide variety of roles in the housekeeping center and in other centers			
2. Role plays on the playground			
3. Role plays a variety of adult occupations			
4. Recognizes that pictures represent real objects			
5. Participates in a wide variety of creative activities: finger plays, rhythm band, working with clay, painting, outdoor play, housekeeping, singing, and so forth			
6. Produces objects at the carpentry table and tells about them			
7. Produces art objects and tells about them			
8. Searches for better ways to construct			
9. Builds complex block structures			
SOCIAL PLAY			
1. Completes most self-initiated projects			
2. Works and plays with limited supervision			
3. Engages in cooperative play			
4. Listens while peers speak			
5. Follows multiple and delayed directions			
6. Carries out special responsibilities (for e.g., feeding animals)			
7. Listens and follows the suggestions of adults			
8. Enjoys talking with adults			
9. Can sustain an attention span for a variety of duties			
10. Evaluates his or her work and suggests improvements			

Figure 3.9 Frost-Wortham Developmental Checklist: Level V *(continued)*

	Introduced	Progress	Mastery
MOTOR DEVELOPMENT			
Gross Movement			
1. Catches and throws a small ball			
2. Bounces and catches a small ball			
3. Skips on either foot			
4. Skips rope			
5. Hops on one foot			
6. Creates Tinkertoy and block structures			
7. Hammers and saws with some skill			
8. Walks a balance beam forward and backward			
9. Descends stairs by alternating feet			
Fine Movement			
1. Cuts and pastes creative designs			
2. Forms a variety of pegboard designs			
3. Buttons buttons, zips zippers, and ties shoes			
4. Creates recognizable objects with clay			
5. Uses the toilet independently			
6. Eats independently with a knife and fork			
7. Dresses and undresses independently			
8. Holds and manipulates pencils, crayons, and brushes of various sizes			
9. Combs and brushes hair			
10. Works a twelve-piece puzzle			

FIVE TO EIGHT YEARS: THE TRANSITION FROM PREOPERATIONS TO CONCRETE OPERATIONS

The ages from five to eight are described here as transitional because the young child is experiencing several kinds of transitions. In terms of schooling, the child is making a transition from home, child care, or preschool into a public or private elementary setting. If the school has preschool classes for four- and five-year-old students, the transition is being made from preschool into primary classrooms.

The child is also making developmental transitions. Although the child is in the last years of early childhood, he or she is gradually moving from preoperations into concrete operations. Development is uneven during this period, both within the individual child and when comparing children of the same chronological age.

It is during this transitional period between preschool and primary grades that the historical heritage of American schooling comes into conflict with developmental theories of how young children learn during the early childhood years. American primary grades have traditionally been organized by chronological age. Following

Gesell's description of norms for different ages, educators and curriculum developers in the years from 1930 to the 1950s organized instruction in the primary grades to complement the child's abilities at ages six, seven, and eight. The organizational pattern by chronological age persists today, with the expectation that children should be prepared to learn using similar curriculum and tasks as their chronological peers. The problems encountered by young children in successfully achieving in spite of individual developmental characteristics are further complicated by the continuing escalation of curriculum difficulty as a response to school reform discussed in chapter 2. The lack of flexibility in adapting curriculum to individual developmental characteristics has resulted in difficulties for both teachers and students in the primary grades, especially in first grade. The need to understand the nature of development and the implications for learning are particularly significant in the years between ages five and eight.

Cognitive Development

Between the ages of five and eight children move from the preoperational stage into the concrete operational stage. Some current researchers disagree with Piaget's position that concrete operations occur at about age seven and have demonstrated that some children can achieve conservation at much earlier ages than was previously thought. Likewise, young children acquire concrete operational concepts gradually, rather than as a synchrony in development, as Piaget believed (Beilin, 1989). There is much individual variation in when and how children move from preoperations to concrete operations. It can begin in some children as young as age four, but it is a gradual process, with characteristics of concrete operations emerging differently in young children (Santrock, 1990).

As young children make the transition to concrete operations, the quality of their thinking changes. They cease evaluating situations based on perception and begin to use logic and mental operations to understand their experiences. This advance in thinking leads to improvement in memory and length of time at each task.

The ability to conserve is the central characteristic that signals the child's achievement of the concrete operational stage. Whether the conservation activity involves number, mass, length, volume, or other type of quantity, the child who can conserve understands that the physical appearance of something doesn't change its quantity. The classic conservation task involving the quantity of liquid usually comes to mind as an example. The child understands that changing the width and height of the container holding the liquid does not change the original amount of the liquid. Likewise, rearranging an array of objects does not change the number of objects.

The ability of the child to think logically using specific thinking skills leads to his or her ability to think about and solve problems mentally; nevertheless, children are limited to things they are familiar with or can see. They are not yet able to think or solve problems as adults do (Bredekamp, 1987).

Children in the concrete operational stage are able to use mental strategies to learn new information. They can use rehearsal of information to store the information in memory. They can also play with their thoughts to think about thinking. Called metacognition, this thinking strategy permits the child to make up jokes or play games that require planning strategies (Santrock, 1990; Schickedanz, Hansen, & Forsyth, 1990). Regardless of the child's new sophistication in thinking skills, the process of learning new information remains the same. The child reconstructs knowledge through active involvement with information. New information is not acquired through rote memory but through engaging in experiences and modifying what is already understood using individual processes and learning paces.

Physical Development

As children move from kindergarten into the primary years, they grow more slowly than during the preschool years. Weight gain occurs in the muscles; the average weight gain is five to seven pounds a year. The trunk and legs grow more rapidly than the head; the legs grow longer and the trunk becomes slimmer. Muscle tone improves, and boys are usually stronger than girls.

Children begin to lose their first teeth at age six and have their permanent teeth by eleven or twelve. Their facial appearance becomes longer and slimmer, as the face and jaw become more balanced with the upper part of the head.

During the primary years, children refine their gross and fine motor skills. They gain better control of their bodies and have longer attention spans. Handwriting skills are acquired through expressive art activities and opportunities for emergent writing experiences. Gross motor skills are developed through sports, games, and other physical activities. Children need to be active because they become fatigued if long periods of sitting are required. The change and progress in motor development is steady and predictable if children have plenty of opportunity for fine and gross motor experiences. They need opportunities for running, jumping, bicycling, and learning sports such as baseball and gymnastic activities such as using a balance beam. For fine motor skills they need abundant experiences with art, including drawing, painting, working with clay, cutting, and playing with manipulative materials (Santrock, 1990; Schickedanz, Hansen, & Forsyth, 1990).

Language Development

The process of language development in the years from five to eight is similar to that of motor development. Children are refining and extending the language learned in the preschool years. They have mastered the basics of syntax and semantics; that is, they have learned how sentences are structured and how words are used to communicate meanings. However, they are still confused by the meanings and usages of some words. Metacognitive thinking allows them to think about language; in other words, children can be described as having metalinguistic awareness. This allows them to enjoy jokes and riddles and the ambiguous use of words (e.g., using words that sound similarly or sentences that can be understood in different ways) (Schickedanz, Hansen, & Forsyth, 1990).

Oral language development can be occurring in more than one language. Continuing immigration to this country and concomitant diversity of cultures results in many children entering school whose first language is not English. Schools serving these children must provide services so that they can acquire English. Since the predominant theory of second-language acquisition is that the young child learns English in the same way as he or she learned the first language, opportunities to hear and use English are important. The child needs to hear English modeled by other children and adults so that he or she can gradually use the vocabulary and sentence structure of English as well as the first language (Abramson, Seda, & Johnson, 1990; Quintero & Huerta-Macias, 1990).

Written language development in the primary grades becomes as important as oral language development. The whole-language approach to reading and writing, beginning in kindergarten, has become a sound and increasingly popular way for children to acquire literacy. Whole-language instruction proposes that elements of the language arts should not be separated but taught as a whole. This approach suggests that children need an extensive oral vocabulary prior to beginning to read. Children are encouraged to "write" stories using scribbling and invented spelling as steps to writing accurately. Written language follows the same hypothesis testing and trial and error as does oral language (Fields, Spangler, & Lee, 1991; Morrow, 1989).

In the whole-language approach, reading follows a similar pattern in that children gradually obtain meaning and recognition of words from books that have become familiar through repeated readings before moving into books that have unfamiliar words. The traditional-skills approach to reading, to the contrary, includes early introduction of phonics and other beginning reading skills as part of the introduction into reading. Alphabet knowledge, letter sounds, sight-word strategies, and other decoding skills are thought to be essential to break the reading code (Freeman & Hatch, 1989).

There is adequate research into how literacy develops in young children to support the whole-language approach. Sulzby (1985), Teale (1986), and Goodman (1986) reported on how children learn about literacy through interaction with literacy in their world and that they develop an awareness of the functions of written language. Further, new theory and research reveals that the components of literacy (reading and writing) develop simultaneously and should not be taught in isolation.

Many schools are not taking an either-or approach to reading and writing; rather, they perceive literacy as being facilitated by both approaches. The child uses natural strategies, such as the whole-language method, in reconstructing his or her own understanding of reading and writing. Information taught about beginning reading and writing skills facilitates an efficient acquisition of literacy (Krogh, 1990).

Social-Emotional Development

The transition into school and the new roles to be encountered are of considerable importance in the years from five to eight. Despite the rising numbers of children in caregiving or preschool settings outside the home during the preschool years, entry into the primary grades is an important transition socially and emotionally.

Children within this age range are entering the stage that Erikson called industry versus inferiority. Achievement and social acceptance become important parts of the child's life. If the child feels successful and achievement is a rewarding effort, the child develops a sense of industry. To the contrary, if the child feels unsuccessful, unpopular, and feels he or she cannot succeed in achieving, a sense of inferiority develops.

Children's social development is affected by their emerging social role-taking abilities. They are aware of other people's thoughts, feelings, and attitudes; in addition, they are becoming more aware and concerned about what others think about them. The child's positive or negative self-image is affected by whether he or she is successful in social interactions (Hartup, 1983).

Perception of social acceptance also affects self-image. Children who have established friendships have been able to develop positive social strategies that are less accessible for children who are disliked. The latter have lower self-esteem, achieve less in school, and are more likely to become antisocial, disruptive, and destructive in later elementary years unless intervention is effective in changing their behaviors and outlook (Asher & Williams, 1987).

Children's early school experiences in successful learning are particularly critical for the development of positive self-esteem and a sense of industry. Success in first grade is significant because this is the first level at which children become aware of whether they perceive themselves as competent and successful learners. It is in first grade that children receive feedback on achievement that makes a major impact on whether they believe themselves to be capable of succeeding in school.

The kind of school setting the child encounters can be an important factor in whether the child will develop a positive or negative picture of his or her ability (Bredekamp, 1987). A school that recognizes the normal variation in children's development in this transitional period, as well as normal differences in language, motor, and social development, will organize kindergarten and primary grades to maximize the child's developmental strengths to ensure success and a positive self-image. Schools where grade-level curriculum is fixed and achievement on standardized tests controls curriculum and instruction in the primary grades are more likely to have many young students who receive negative feedback and subsequently develop a negative self-image and feelings of inferiority (Santrock, 1990).

CHARACTERISTICS AND COMPETENCIES: FIVE TO EIGHT YEARS

Implications for Learning and Instruction

Children are developing more slowly between the ages of five and eight than they did previously, and characteristics of development emerge gradually over a period of years. Developmental characteristics are acquired within the remaining years of early childhood and beyond into the middle childhood years. Developmental checklists are no longer useful for charting development because milestones are achieved gradually and continuously. Characteristics and competencies acquired between the ages of five and eight are best described as evolving within the later ages of early childhood.

Likewise, because children between the ages of five and eight are entering the first grades of formal schooling, it is helpful to now include a discussion of how schooling should complement developmental characteristics. Thus, this section focuses on how parents and educators should respond to rather than overlook development. Characteristics, competencies, and implications for learning and curriculum and instruction are again discussed by category of development.

Cognitive Development

Despite the gradual shift from preoperational to concrete operational thinking during this period, children are still not ready to learn in the abstract. They still need real things to focus their thinking or serve as reference points when using symbols such as words and numbers. Although they can use thinking skills to mentally manipulate concepts and ideas, there is a continuation of the need for concrete materials and experiences in the learning process.

During these years, learning is a continuation of the reconstruction of knowledge. Experience is the method used to facilitate the construction of knowledge. Children need many opportunities to interact with concepts and use their developing thinking skills to identify and solve problems related to new information.

Emerging social and communication skills allow the child to understand and appreciate the thoughts and views of others. Consequently, these children are able to learn in small groups. Through group activities and discussions about group efforts, children can utilize the thoughts and perspectives of their peers to expand their own understanding. At the same time, they are also developing their language and social skills through group involvement in learning experiences.

Physical Development

Children between the ages of five and eight are gaining better control of gross and fine motor skills. They develop longer attention spans and can maintain interest in learning activities. However, these new physical capabilities do not imply that children should be expected to sit for long periods of time engaged in passive, fine motor activities.

Physical activity is essential for children during these years. Their developing gross motor skills require generous time periods for outdoor play, both structured and unstructured. Physical action indoors and outdoors is needed to practice and enjoy new physical competencies. Because children in the primary grades become fatigued from sitting for long periods, they need to be active in the classroom. In addition, their cognitive style as active learners dictates that they interact with concrete examples for meaningful learning to occur. Therefore, physical activity is also needed for cognitive learning. Physical interactions through hands-on, center-based activities should be part of the ongoing experiences with new and familiar concepts. Children need to be actively engaged in self-initiated projects and lessons using manipulative materials as part of the learning process.

Social-Emotional Development

Social competence is a major achievement in the years between five and eight. Children who fail to develop social competence during these years are more likely to develop serious social and emotional problems in later years. The development of competence in achievement is also a major factor in the development of a positive self-image.

Because adults and the school environment are major factors in developing social and learning competence, teachers have an important responsibility in guiding positive acquisition of feelings of success and competence. Teachers can use direct and indirect strategies with young children to assist in the struggle for social acceptance and positive social interaction.

Teachers likewise can be sensitive to structuring classroom experiences to facilitate a sense of industry rather than inferiority. School-age children are able to evaluate their own efforts in learning. If they are enabled to be successful in achieving during the primary grades, they will become self-directed and will develop a sense of industry. If they encounter frequent failure in their efforts to learn, their self-esteem will suffer, and they will develop the perception that they are failures. As a result of their understanding of the implications of development for learning during these years, teachers must organize learning experiences that are not beyond the child's ability to learn successfully. Activities should be carefully designed to facilitate positive motivation to learn and foster the child's belief in his or her ability to succeed.

Children are also developing a conscience and an understanding of moral rules of behavior. They are in the process of learning self-discipline and self-control. Teachers who use positive guidance techniques and model appropriate behaviors are more successful in helping children internalize rules of behavior than if they criticize and punish.

Organization of programs and classrooms for children from age five to eight will be described in chapter 9. Planning for curriculum and instruction for children of these ages will be discussed in chapters 10 and 11.

Summary

The years from birth to age eight are described as the early childhood years. This period of life is most significant in terms of development. Development is more rapid during this period than during any other period in the life span. Understanding how the infant and young child develop physically, cognitively, and socially and how they acquire language and literacy is necessary for adults who are rearing, providing care for, and planning learning experiences for children during this period. An understanding of how the theories of learning and development enable adults to guide the child in the early childhood years also helps adults to plan appropriate kinds of learning experiences.

The younger the child, the more rapid his or her growth and development. Consequently, development of infants and toddlers during the first two years is charted in six-month intervals. Cognitively, babies under the age of two are in what Piaget termed the sensorimotor period. Physically, they develop from neonates to toddlers who have acquired basic locomotor skills. Socially and emotionally they are developing an awareness of self and important others in their lives.

Older toddlers and preschool children from ages two to five are still in active periods of growth. Because these young children are in what Piaget called the preoperational stage, we can describe their development in three levels, rather than by age. Children in the preoperational period are rapidly developing language and concepts as they discover and explore everything they come in contact with at home, outdoors, and at locations away from home. Socially, they are developing abilities to interact and play with other children and develop a positive self-concept as they acquire social and self-help skills. They work toward independence.

Preoperational children are very active physically. They practice and enjoy both gross and fine motor movement. Two- and three-year-olds seem to be in perpetual motion. Throughout these years, much of the children's day is spent in physical activity as they challenge themselves to achieve new physical capabilities.

At this point, children are acquiring the foundations of their language, and by age four or five they have mastered the basic language components. Their language structure has evolved from prelinguistic utterances to a language structure that is similar to that of adults. They have developed an awareness of the nature of written language and reading and may be well on their way to developing literacy.

Children from the age of five to eight are in the latter stages of early childhood. They are also moving from preoperations into concrete operations. We describe these children as in a transitional period because they are changing developmentally; moreover, they are making a transition from one level of schooling to another.

The cognitive transition to concrete operations signals new levels of thinking. The child is no longer perception bound but is now able to think using mental strategies and can think about the thought processes being used. Physical development is slower. Over a period of time the child extends physical capabilities as body length and muscle development predominate. Regular physical activity is important for optimal continued physical development.

Sophistication in language continues. Oral language becomes more complex as the child extends vocabulary and receptive language, as well as more mature expressive language. The move toward literacy, including reading and writing, is an exciting development during the primary grades. Children master the basics of reading and can enjoy written expression and literature.

Social and emotional development are significant during this period because children have a need to become competent in social and learning interactions. It is during this period that they determine if they are popular with their peers and successful as learners.

Development during each period has its own competencies. Learning experiences provided by adults for each period need to complement the individual characteristics of each child. Developmentally appropriate curriculum and instruction are important for preschool children, as well as children making the transition from preschool into primary grades. The transitional years are particularly critical for successful learning. Understanding how to match development with learning experiences is the key to successful schooling in kindergarten and primary grades if students are to develop a positive self-image, believe themselves to be competent, and become success oriented.

Summary Statements

1. Each theory of child development contributes to our understanding of how children develop and learn and how adults can provide experiences that will facilitate learning.

2. Between birth and eighteen to twenty-four months, infants are in what Piaget termed the sensorimotor stage; they learn through using their senses and physical actions.

3. Physical, social-emotional, and cognitive development are major characteristics in the description of infants, toddlers, and young children.

4. The younger the individual, the more rapidly developmental changes occur. Development slows down as the young child matures.

5. Between the years of two and seven, the child is in the preoperational period, when symbolic thinking is possible; however, physical appearances and egocentrism limit their perceptions.

6. The years between five and eight are marked by the child's transition into the concrete operational period, when conservation of quantity is possible, as well as the use of mental strategies.

7. Each stage of development has implications for the role adults can play and the type of experiences that will encourage growth.

8. At each state of development the child acquires competencies that become increasingly more sophisticated and complex as maturation and experiences facilitate progress toward a higher developmental stage.

Study Questions

1. Why is knowledge of various theories of development important when planning instructional programs for young children?
2. How do theories conflict when explaining how young children learn?
3. Why is the psychosocial theory more useful than the psychoanalytic theory of personality development?
4. What contribution did Albert Bandura make to the behaviorist theory of how children learn? Why is his theory important?
5. Why was the maturational theory significant in the evolution of urban public schools?
6. How does Piaget's cognitive-developmental theory explain the cognitive development of children?
7. How do the maturational and cognitive-developmental theories differ on how children develop and learn?
8. How does cognitive development affect social development?
9. What implications do Piaget's stages have for how teachers should plan learning experiences for young children?
10. Why are the ages of six and seven the most difficult when matching instruction to children's development?

References

Abramson, S., Seda, I., & Johnson, C. (1990). Literacy development in a multilingual kindergarten classroom. *Childhood Education, 67,* 68–72.

Asher, S. R., & Williams, G. A. (1987). Helping children without friends in home and school contexts. In *Children's social development: Information for teachers and parents* (pp. 1–26). Urbana, IL: ERIC Clearinghouse on Elementary and Early Childhood Education.

Bandura, A., & Walters, R. (1963). *Social learning and personality development.* New York: Holt, Rinehart & Winston.

Baumrind, D. (1971). Current patterns of parental authority. *Developmental Psychology Monographs, 4*(1, Pt. 2).

Beilin, H. (1989). Piagetian theory. In R. Vasta (Ed.), *Annals of child development* (Vol. 6). Greenwich, CT: JAI Press.

Bjorklund, D. F. (1989). *Children's thinking.* Belmont, CA: Brooks/Cole.

Bredekamp, S. (Ed.). (1987). *Developmentally appropriate practice in early childhood programs serving children from birth through age 8.* Washington, DC: National Association for the Education of Young Children.

Brown, R. (1973). *A first language: The early stages.* Cambridge, MA: Harvard University Press.

Clewett, A. S. (1988). Guidance and discipline: Teaching young children appropriate behavior. *Young Children, 43,* 26–31.

Connell, J. P., & Goldsmith, H. H. (1982). A structural modeling approach to the study of attachment and strange situation behaviors. In R. J. Emde & R. J. Harmon (Eds.), *The development of attachment and affiliative systems* (pp. 213–243). New York: Plenum.

Dailey, K. A. (1991). Writing in kindergarten. *Childhood Education, 67,* 170–175.

DiPietro, J. A. (1981). Rough and tumble play: A function of gender. *Developmental Psychology, 17,* 50–58.

Doescher, S. M., & Sugawara, A. I. (1989). Encouraging prosocial behavior in young children. *Childhood Education, 65,* 213–216.

Erikson, E. H. (1963). *Childhood and society.* New York: Norton.

Fields, M. V., Spangler, K. L., & Lee, D. M. (1991). *Let's begin reading right.* New York: Merrill.

Freeman, E. B., & Hatch, J. A. (1989). Emergent literacy: Reconceptualizing kindergarten practice. *Childhood Education, 66,* 21–24.

Freud, S. (1925). Instincts and their vicissitudes. In S. Freud, *Collected papers* (Vol. 4). London: Institutes for Psycho–analysis & Hogarth Press.

Frost, J. L. (1992). *Play and playscapes*. Albany, NY: Delmar.

George, C., & Main, M. (1979). Social interactions of young abused children: Approach, avoidance, aggression. *Child Development, 50,* 306–318. New York: McGraw–Hill.

Gesell, A., & Ilg, F. (1946). *The child from five to ten*. New York: Harper.

Gleason, J. B. (1988). Language and socialization. In F. Kessel (Ed.), *The development of language and language researchers*. Hillsdale, NJ: Erlbaum.

Goodman, Y. (1986). Children coming to know literacy. In W. H. Teale & E. Sulzby (Eds.), *Emergent literacy: Reading and writing* (pp. 1–14). Norwood, NJ: Ablex.

Hall, G. S. (1883, May). The content of children's minds. *Princeton Review*, pp. 249–253.

Hartup, W. W. (1983). Peer relations. In P. H. Mussen (Ed.), *Handbook of child psychology* (4th ed., Vol. 4). New York: Wiley.

Johnson, J. E., Christie, J. F., & Yawkey, T. D. (1987). *Play and early childhood development*. Glenview, IL: Scott, Foresman.

Krogh, S. (1990). *The integrated early childhood curriculum*. New York: McGraw-Hill.

Lawton, J. T. (1988). *Introduction to child care and early childhood education*. Glenview, IL: Scott, Foresman.

Lindfors, J. W. (1987). *Children's language and language learning* (2nd ed.). Englewood Cliffs, NJ: Prentice–Hall.

Maccoby, E. E., & Martin, J. A. (1983). Socialization in the context of the family: Parent–child interactions. In P. H. Mussen (Ed.), *Handbook of child psychology* (4th ed., Vol. 4). New York: Wiley.

Mavrogenes, N. A. (1990). Helping parents help their children become literate. *Young Children, 45,* 4–9.

Menyuk, P. (1969). *Language and maturation*. Cambridge, MA: MIT Press.

Morrison, G. S. (1988). *Education and development of infants, toddlers, and preschoolers*. Glenview, IL: Scott, Foresman.

Morrow, L. M. (1989). *Literacy development in the early years*. Englewood Cliffs, NJ: Prentice–Hall.

O'Brien, S. (1991). How do you raise respectful children in a disrespectful world? *Childhood Education, 67,* 183–184.

Piaget, J. (1963). *The origins of intelligence in children* (M. Cook, Trans.). New York: Norton.

Quintero, E., & Huerta–Macias, A. (1990). All in the family: Bilingualism and biliteracy. *The Reading Teacher, 44,* 304–309.

Santrock, J. W. (1990). *Children*. Dubuque, IA: Wm. C. Brown.

Schickedanz, J. A., Hansen, K., & Forsyth, P. D. (1990). *Understanding children*. Mountain View, CA: Mayfield.

Schwartz, S. L., & Robison, H. F. (1982). *Designing curriculum for early childhood*. Boston: Allyn & Bacon.

Seefeldt, C., & Barbour, N. (1990). *Early childhood education: An introduction*. Columbus, OH: Merrill.

Skinner, B. F. (1953). *Science and human behavior*. New York: Macmillan.

Soderman, A. K. (1985). Dealing with difficult young children. *Young Children, 40,* 15–20.

Sulzby, E. (1985). Kindergartners as writers and readers. In M. Farr (Ed.), *Advances in writing research* (Vol. 1). Norwood, NJ: Ablex.

Teale, W. H. (1986). Home background and young children's literacy development. In W. H. Teale & E. Sulzby (Eds.), *Emergent literacy: Reading and writing* (pp. 173–206). Norwood, NJ: Ablex.

Thomas, A., Chess, S., & Birch, H. (1970, August). The origin of personality. *Scientific American, 223,* 102–109.

Troy, M., & Sroufe, L. A. (1987). Victimization among preschoolers: Role of attachment relationship history. *Journal of the American Academy of Child and Adolescent Psychiatry, 26,* 166–172.

Weber, E. (1984). *Ideas influencing early childhood education*. New York: Teachers College Press.

Weiser, M. G. (1982). *Group care and education of infants and toddlers*. St. Louis: C. V. Mosby.

White, B. L., & Watts, J. C. (1973). *Experience and environment: Major influences on the development of the young child* (Vol. 1). Englewood Cliffs, NJ: Prentice–Hall.

Wortham, S. (1984). *Organizing instruction in early childhood*. Boston: Allyn & Bacon.

CHAPTER FOUR

Organizing Infant–Toddler Programs

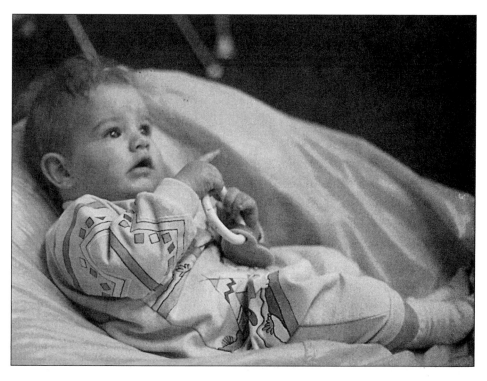

The idea that very young infants are alert learners is still new to many adults, even some of those who care for children. Not only have we learned that infants are sponges for learning about the people and things in their environment, we also know that they in turn affect those who care for them. We have come a long way from the days when babies were considered to be passive and helpless. The vast amount of information we have learned about early development in this century has been vital in understanding how we can develop programs for the very young. The contributions from extensive research into infant development combined with the growing need for infant and toddler care and programs have stimulated the development of models for quality programs for infants and toddlers. In this chapter, we will trace the roots of these programs and the theories and contexts that have supported advances in infant–toddler care and learning. We will also describe a model for an infant–toddler program and discuss how such a program can enforce quality developmental experiences for very young children.

THE EVOLUTION OF INFANT–TODDLER PROGRAMS

The evolution of infant–toddler nurture and care parallels that of early childhood education in general; however, until recent years, the strongest trend for infants and toddlers has been custodial care. From the beginning, early childhood education for the preschool child from three to five years of age included some sort of educational program in kindergartens, nursery schools, and private preschools. But infant and toddler care has been closely related to the evolution of the child care movement; therefore, until the 1970s, care was the most significant service provided to infants and toddlers. The transition from an emphasis on care to care plus attention to developmental experiences has become more important since that time. In the discussion that follows, we will trace how our understanding about the development of infants and toddlers has merged with the programs that have been developed for their care and learning.

Infants and Toddlers Prior to the Twentieth Century

Prior to the first decades of the twentieth century, infant mortality was the most significant concern regarding infants and toddlers. In the eighteenth century, infants and young children of families emigrating to the United States rarely survived the voyage from their homeland. Physicians knew little about hygiene and how to avoid the spread of disease that contributed to the high mortality rate among infants and children under the age of seven. Parents likewise were ignorant about child-rearing practices and proper nutrition. Midwives who delivered the infants of the poor commonly dressed the umbilical cord with snuff, and, for medication, they fed infants a mixture of molasses and the child's urine (Public Health Service, 1976).

In the early years of the republic, children were considered either chattels or the property of their parents. Furthermore, they were perceived as innately bad by nineteenth-century philosophers and evangelical Christians. Evangelical parents saw it as their responsibility to impose their will and enforce the child's unquestioning obedience, beginning in the child's first year. Greven (1977) explained further:

> From the earliest months of life through the subsequent years of childhood, evangelical parents acted upon the assumption that parental authority was unlimited and incontrovertible. Parents systematically imposed their own wills upon their infants and small children without interference from servants or grandparents. Total power of parents, total dependency and obedience of children—this was the persistent polarity (p. 34).

In 1874, a nine-year-old child who had been whipped daily, stabbed with scissors, and tied to a bed was rescued from the brutal treatment of her guardians. Because there were no laws protecting children at that time, the Society for the Prevention of Cruelty to Animals (SPCA) finally intervened to remove the child from

the home where she was an indentured servant. In the following year, 1875, the New York Society for the Prevention of Cruelty to Children was established to protect children from inhumane treatment (Maxim, 1989).

At the turn of the century, conditions for infants and young children were still discouraging. Health experts were concerned about the ignorance concerning the health and safety of infants and toddlers. The high infant mortality rate was attributed partially to the distribution of contaminated milk from dirty sources of the milk supply. Another source of infant and toddler deaths was the ignorance of mothers. A 1904 edition of the *Ladies' Home Journal* described the practice of many mothers who gave their babies patent medicine that contained 44 percent alcohol, opium, or cocaine. Regulated milk stations were then set up to ensure the distribution of safe milk, and the Children's Bureau battled parental ignorance through the publication of pamphlets designed to inform parents about the care of their infants. The first edition of *Infant Care* was published in 1914; subsequent editions have been published continuously since then (Public Health Service, 1976).

Some of the worst treatment of infants and young children declined during the second half of the nineteenth century. Jean-Jacques Rousseau's view of childhood was one influence that changed parenting and education in Europe and the United States. Rousseau felt that children were innately good. He proposed that babies were born with only goodness in their hearts, and if they were reared in an environment of regulated liberty they would flower, or unfold. Parents and educators responded to Rousseau's influence by replacing repressive parenting and teaching with loving and nurturing environments for infants (Maxim, 1989).

Further concerns for the health, safety, and nurturance of infants and young children emerged at the end of the nineteenth century. At the same time that Rousseau's perceptions of the needs of young children were changing attitudes about the rearing of infants and toddlers, waves of immigrants were entering the United States and settling in urban areas. Widows and abandoned mothers and some wives with large families found it necessary to go to work if they and their families were to survive. With no one to care for their children, some women sent them to orphanages or foster homes or were forced to leave them unattended when they were at work. Wealthy philanthropists responded to the dilemma by opening day nurseries for unattended infants and young children. The first day-care programs provided custodial care: a safe place, nutritious meals, and places for the children to rest for twelve hours a day while their mothers were at work (Maxim, 1989).

At the beginning of the twentieth century, conditions were still very poor for infants and toddlers; in the first decade, one-fifth of the deaths in New York City were of babies less than one year old (Public Health Service, 1976). However, further changes were occurring. Improvements in health services and medical services, the advent of the child-study movement with its new knowledge about child development, and growing interest in programs for the very young led to improvements in conditions for infants and toddlers in the decades that followed.

Infants and Toddlers in the Twentieth Century

The work of researchers in the child study movement that was begun at the turn of the century had implications for the perception and understanding of the importance of the first two years of a child's development. Early studies of infants and toddlers were used to describe how development progresses during the first two years. Arnold Gesell established developmental norms that were the first to sequence biological development in children. His developmental schedules (Gesell, 1925) were subsequently used to construct scales to measure development and developmental delay in infants and toddlers; these were, specifically, the Bayley Test of Infant Development, the Cattell Test, and the Denver Developmental Test (Weiser, 1991). During the same period, H. M. Skeels was studying the development of institutionalized infants as compared with babies placed with older girls in a home for retarded children. The significant developmental difference in the babies showered with attention by the retarded girls projected the concept that environment and attention in the first three years affects the course of development (Skeels, 1966). Sigmund Freud's work describing the effects of the early years on the development of personality made people further aware of the nature of emotional development and the importance of positive child–adult relationships in the early years (Hall & Lindzey, 1970).

The interest in a program that provided more than custodial care for very young children emerged in the first decades of the century as a result of Margaret McMillan's work in England. McMillan had observed that although the majority of babies were born healthy in England, only 20 percent entered school in good health. To counter neglect during the preschool years, she opened nursery schools for children younger than school age that provided for emotional, social, and educational growth. In addition to being given physical care and nutrition, the children were taught self-care and hygiene skills. The program included outdoor play, sensory experiences, and creative self-expression activities. Abigail Eliot transported McMillan's ideas to the United States and transformed the Ruggles Street Day Nursery in Boston into a nursery school in 1922 (Eliot, 1972). The Ruggles Street Nursery School, the first to establish a learning program in addition to providing care, was soon followed by other such schools. Also in the 1920s, other professional educators were addressing programs for infants and toddlers. Harriet Johnson wrote *Children in the "Nursery School"* (1928) and later *School Begins at Two* (1936), both of which describe programs for children under the age of three.

During the Great Depression of the 1930s, nursery schools expanded through the Works Progress Administration (WPA) project that funded nursery schools to create jobs for unemployed teachers and to provide care so that mothers could contribute to family incomes. These nursery schools tended to be custodial in nature; however, training for nursery school teachers was becoming available in university home economics departments, the first having been established in 1924 at Iowa State University (Maxim, 1989).

As the WPA nursery schools were phased out at the end of the 1930s, the advent of World War II initiated a new need for child care during the war effort. Women went to work in large numbers in factories that produced equipment and materials for the war effort twenty-four hours a day, and the federal government recognized that child care was thus needed. Child-care facilities were established through passage of the Lanham Act, which provided children with food, rest, shelter, and caregivers. Infants and toddlers were served with predominantly custodial care. Exceptions were the Kaiser Child Service Centers, established at the Kaiser shipyards, which contained special innovative features that included constructive play, trained teachers, and an educational program (Braun & Edwards, 1972). Also, under the leadership of James Hymes, two outstanding centers were established that provided twenty-four-hour-a-day care for one thousand children of ages eighteen months to six years (Dickerson, 1992). Hymes later attributed the excellent program to trained staff and adequate funding (Hymes & Stolz, 1978).

After the end of World War II, programs for infants and toddlers were affected by growth in the child-care industry as higher percentages of mothers with children under the age of six entered the work force in each decade between 1950 and 1990. For infants and toddlers, custodial child care was still more common than educational programs; nevertheless, studies and theories that emerged in the 1950s and 1960s were the foundation for experimental programs for infants and toddlers from families who were minorities or poor or both. The innovative programs that developed during those years changed the perception of the developmental potential of the very young child and gave new emphasis to developmental and educational components in settings that served infants and toddlers. A major concern in the 1950s and 1960s was whether preschool children, particularly infants and toddlers, should be put into caregiving settings while their mothers worked. Finding good care for babies during the day was a major problem for working mothers.

The focus on the effects of poverty on preschool children had implications for infants and toddlers. The importance of the early years for development and learning was reported in research done by J. McVicker Hunt (1961), who reported that expe-

riences in the first years of life affect the child's intelligence. Benjamin Bloom likewise reported similar information that reinforced the idea that the early years are significant for the development of intelligence (Bloom, 1964). The relationship between socioeconomic status and intelligence before three years of age was reported by Kagan (1971) and White and Watts (1973). These and other studies reinforced the proposition that deprivation during the first three years has measurable effects. When federal intervention efforts for children from low-income homes were funded in the 1960s, the issues of the effects of care on infants and toddlers and the efficacy of early intervention programs for children under the age of three could both be addressed. The advances accomplished through the various types of infant intervention projects in the 1960s and 1970s laid the groundwork for the infant–toddler programs that serve very young children in the 1990s.

The first infant intervention programs focused upon the child. The model for infant–toddler care and education established by Bettye Caldwell and Julius Richmond in the Children's Center at Syracuse University in 1968 established a positive approach to center-based care as opposed to home care. Two additional infant–toddler programs were established by Mary Elizabeth Keister at the University of North Carolina at Greenboro (Keister, 1970) and by Willis and Ricciuti (1975) at Cornell University.

Later model programs focused on parents as well as children. These programs emphasized the importance of the mother in the child's growth and development and addressed different approaches to working with parents and babies to enhance the child's development. Some of these parent–infant–toddler projects included the Gordon Parent Education Program in Florida, the Karnes Home Intervention Program, the Family Development Research Program developed by Lally and Honig, Levenstein's Mother–Child Program, and Schaefer's Infant Education Research Project (Cataldo, 1983; Day & Parker, 1977). These programs reinforced the understanding that parent involvement with infant care and learning is essential for the child's development. Intervention with infants alone is not effective; moreover, intervention with the low-income parent is the key to permanent enhancement of the child's environment in the years before age three.

In the 1970s and 1980s, it became apparent that larger numbers of infants and toddlers were in need of care during the day. Working wives, single parents, teenage mothers, and women in other categories of low socioeconomic families needed care for their very young children. The rapid expansion of the child-care industry led to national concerns about the quality of child care and the need for establishing standards for caregiving programs. The National Association for the Education of Young Children (NAEYC) took a leadership role in establishing a national accreditation system for preschool and child-care settings. The NAEYC National Academy of Early Childhood Programs was established in 1987 to accredit quality programs. Standards for accreditation included characteristics of quality infant and toddler programs (Recken, 1989).

Similar efforts were made to provide quality training for teachers and caregivers in early childhood programs that were not a part of the public schools that required certified teachers. A consortium of organizations that included the American Association of Elementary/Kindergarten/Nursery Educators, the Association for Childhood Education International, and the National Association for the Education of Young Children began work on a credentialing system in 1972 named the Child Development Associate Program. This program involved training in the care of infants and toddlers. In 1975 the first credential was awarded, and by 1990 more than thirty thousand teachers and caregivers had been credentialed (Phillips, 1990).

By 1990, new programs were available for intervention with high-risk infants and toddlers. One priority was for early intervention with very young children with disabilities; such a program was initiated with the passage of PL 99-457 in 1986 that included services for infants and toddlers. The intention of the federal legislation was to include provision of services to infant and toddlers who have a developmental delay or have a condition that is likely to result in a developmental delay (Silverstein, 1989). The federal government proposed that the funding would encourage states to develop comprehensive plans for intervention programs for infants and toddlers with disabilities and their families (Weiser, 1991).

Those who were involved with Project Head Start were focusing on intervention with infants and toddlers who were at risk because of the low socioeconomic status of their families. Head Start, originally established to serve children from age three to five, took on a new role in 1990 when the Human Services Reauthorization Act of 1990 made it possible to double the number of Head Start parent–child centers. In addition, consideration was given to extending Head Start programs to serve infants and toddlers and their families. Goals for the infant–toddler programs included parent education and training (Pizzo, 1990).

As the decade of the 1990s opened, the concept that infants and toddlers need both education and care was well established. *Educare* had been proposed as the appropriate term for programs that included child care for infants, toddlers, and preschoolers (Caldwell, 1986, 1989; Gerber, 1981; Weiser, 1991). Models for nurturing development and learning were available; moreover, standards for developmentally appropriate care for infants and toddlers had been established by the NAEYC (Bredekamp, 1987). Programs with different goals and purposes had become available for infants and toddlers from all types of families.

Infants and toddlers in caregiving programs in the 1990s represent the diversity of families in the total population. The babies are of all ethnic and racial groups. They come from families with a variety of cultural traditions and languages. They may be from a family of the unemployed poor or they may be the children of professional parents. Some of these infants and toddlers have disabilities or developmental delays. Others may be exceptional in that they have high intellectual abilities.

Some of the babies live in families that are new to this country. Not only are the infants trying to adjust to a new community, a new language, and new customs, but they may be frightened at the prospect of leaving the security of familiar family members to enter a caregiving situation with strangers who cannot communicate with them in their home language (Packer, Milner, & Hong, 1992).

Adults in caregiving settings are challenged to understand the multiple factors that affect the infants and toddlers in their care, as well as to guide them in understanding each other. Because very young children begin to understand gender, race, and physical characteristics by the age of two, their experiences in caregiving programs are important for the attitudes they are developing about themselves and others (Honig, 1983; Katz, 1982). Toddlers are capable of developing stereotypes and prejudices at a very young age; therefore, caregivers and parents have an important role in guiding their acceptance and empathy for all the children in their world. To accomplish this goal, adults also must work to accept diversity among the babies in their care. They will need to overcome their own prejudices and biases that limit their abilities to nurture each of the children they care for. They must also work at relating and responding to the uniqueness that each infant and toddler and their families bring to the program.

Infant–Toddler Programs Today

The two major categories of settings serving infants and toddlers today are child-care and intervention programs. Parenting programs are also part of infant intervention projects, serving populations of parents and children from all socioeconomic categories. Some infant–toddler programs focus only on babies from more affluent families. The purpose of all these programs is to accelerate or facilitate development and learning or to provide enrichment for infants and toddlers. Yet the individual goals of these programs can be very diverse—they might have contrasting views of the developmental needs of infants and toddlers and the kinds of educational approaches that are most appropriate.

Infant–Toddler Child Care. There are still concerns about infants being placed in group child care before their first birthday. The basic issue has been whether out-of-home care during the first year negatively affects young infants' intellectual or emotional development (Howes, 1989). Belsky and Steinberg (1978) proposed that infants placed in nonmaternal care for more than twenty hours a week before their first birthday are at risk for later development. Bernstein (1982) pointed out that parents are likely to perceive group care as better than in-home or family day home care because centers are regulated through licensing and periodic inspections. There are still no definitive answers to these issues about out-of-home care (Kelley & Surbeck, 1990). In the meantime, large numbers of infants are in some type of caregiving setting: in their own homes, family day-care homes, child-care centers, infant-care centers, public school centers, and child development centers.

In-Home Care. The largest percentage of infants in child care receive in-home care (48 percent in 1985) (Kelley & Surbeck, 1990). Such care is provided by a relative, a paid baby-sitter or housekeeper, a live-in nanny, or another individual who provides care in the baby's home.

Family Day Care. Family day care is the main source of out-of-home care for infants and toddlers (Eheart & Leavitt, 1989). In this arrangement, child care is provided in the home of the caregiver, who serves a small number of children in her (or his) home. The number of children served varies with licensing laws in different states; however, not all family day-care homes are licensed (Kelley & Surbeck, 1990). If the home is licensed, it must maintain health and safety standards set by the state licensing agency (Maxim, 1989).

Child-Care Centers.   The number of infants and toddlers attending child-care centers is growing. Center care is expensive because of the high teacher-to-child ratio and because infants require more time and attention from caregivers (Bernstein, 1982). The adult-to-child ratio varies from state to state, ranging as high as one to eight. In addition, some centers group caregivers and infants in a single large room, a practice that Kelley and Surbeck (1990) suggest depersonalizes the care and increases illnesses, injuries, and poor caregiving practices. Some centers, however, serve only infants and seek to provide quality care by adhering to small adult-to-child ratios of one adult to three infants. The building, equipment, and materials are focused on infant and toddler care (Maxim, 1989).

Public School Centers.   Public school child-care centers are being established in more and more high schools, partly in an effort to provide high school students in vocational homemaking programs with experience in a child-care program. More significant is that such programs are being implemented to help teenage mothers continue their education and provide young parents with parenting training.

School-based child care is also located in elementary schools to meet community needs. Following the example of the Kramer Project in Little Rock, Arkansas, where child care and education was provided for babies as young as six months of age (Elardo & Caldwell, 1974), child-care facilities located at an elementary school can be convenient for parents who have older children at the school and for teachers who can bring their infants and toddlers to school with them.

Intervention Programs for Infants and Toddlers.   As more has become known about the benefits of early intervention for children who are at risk for development and learning, programs for intervention with infants and toddlers have been added to existing intervention programs for preschool children. As was reported earlier, both Head Start and PL 94-142 funding serviced children with disabilities who were as young as age three; PL 99-457 amended PL 94-142 to include infants and toddlers. Part H of PL 99-457, passed in 1986, gave states five years to develop and implement statewide plans to provide multidisciplinary, multiagency intervention services for infants and toddlers with disabilities and their families. The programs for at-risk infants and toddlers should be provided in the type of settings where infants and toddlers without disabilities are also served. In other words, the intent is that infants and toddlers with disabilities will be served in integrated child-care, nursery school, and family day home environments along with children without disabilities and their families (Sexton, 1990). Existing infant–toddler programs are to be adapted to serve babies with disabilities and their families.

The disabilities to be served are the conditions of the following groups: children with a known disabling condition, such as Down's syndrome, children who exhibit delay in one or more developmental areas, and infants at risk to develop a disability because of biological factors. Although most states plan to serve children with established disabilities, fewer will serve at-risk infants. If at-risk infants are to be served, prevention of disabling conditions will be addressed in addition to intervention with existing disabilities (Graham & Scott, 1988). However, attempts to serve the large numbers of infants who could be identified with criteria for environmental and biological disabilities are cost prohibitive (Sexton, 1990).

An important component of intervention programs for infants and toddlers is the inclusive role of the family. PL 99-457 requires an Individualized Family Service Plan (IFSP), which identifies infant needs within the context of the family. The IFSP offers a family-centered approach in the services provided by the program. Intervention programs for economically deprived children, such as Head Start, also include family training and services. Indeed, many of the earlier models for infant and toddler programs were designed to counteract familial problems and include goals for both child and parent. Levenstein's Verbal Interaction Project used the family as the child's primary teacher, and the Milwaukee Project sought to prevent retardation in infants through family rehabilitation. The parent education program developed by Ira Gordon at the University of Florida was devised for parents to achieve better learning experiences for at-risk infants (Cataldo, 1983).

Infant–Toddler Enrichment Programs. Not all infant–toddler programs are for babies needing care or intervention. There are many parents who are interested in learning more about how the child is developing and how they can provide learning experiences. At the same time, they may need help with parenting skills. Programs designed for meeting these parental needs are available. Some have been described as enrichment programs (Cataldo, 1983); others are considered formal education (Maxim, 1989).

Enrichment programs assume that the family and infant are functioning in a normal manner. The program can enhance the child's development through enrichment experiences. Program developers have used varied approaches to informing parents how to interact with their children. Two such programs are the Nova University Play and Learn Program and the Toy Lending Library. The Nova University program offers parent manuals with suggestions for activities (Segal & Adcock, 1979), and the Toy Lending Library offers a collection of infant and preschool materials and toys that parents can use for their children's learning and development (Nimnicht, Arango, & Adcock, 1977).

Early academic programs are more formal programs for early developmental stimulation and learning. Suzuki music lessons, swimming programs for babies, and toddler physical development classes are examples of programs some parents want their infants to participate in as early as three or four months. The best-known infant-stimulation program, developed by Glen Doman, is implemented through Doman's Better Baby Institute. Parents are offered methods and materials to promote infant intelligence. Although the formal academic approach is questioned as being developmentally inappropriate for infants and toddlers (Brazelton, 1985; Elkind, 1986), Doman proposes that infants love the mental stimulation and are not pushed beyond their abilities. The services provided through the Better Baby Institute are attractive to parents who wish to accelerate their child's development and learning; nevertheless, many child development specialists caution parents to consider how appropriate the program is for the developmental characteristics and needs of infants and toddlers (Maxim, 1989).

CONSIDERATIONS FOR DEVELOPING MODELS FOR INFANT–TODDLER PROGRAMS

When developing a program for infants and toddlers, there are several considerations that must be taken into account. One issue is the theoretical bases that are to be included in the model to be used. The populations of infants and toddlers to be served are considered, as well as is the way in which parents are to be involved.

Theoretical Bases for Infant–Toddler Programs

Theories of development and learning were discussed in chapter 3. Now we want to review them as they apply to infants and toddlers.

Erikson described affective development in terms of stages. Very young children between birth and age two work through the first of Erikson's stages (trust versus mistrust) and proceed into the second stage (autonomy versus doubt and shame). Erikson's stages are important in terms of development of a sense of identity. The infant gradually understands that he or she has an identity that is separate from others. The infant's attachment to another moves from a relationship based on need to one based on love. If infants develop a secure attachment to caregivers, they will achieve a positive adjustment in an infant program. Further, if caregivers can interact well with the infants and toddlers in their care, the babies can also make positive multiple attachments to them.

Arnold Gesell's maturational theory has implications for infant–toddler programs in terms of his age norms for development. The concept that certain behaviors and abilities tend to emerge within a time range and within a sequence helps parents and caregivers have realistic expectations about the child's development. However, nor-

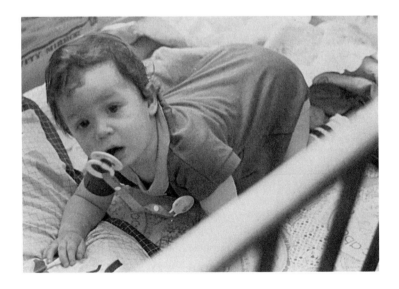

mal variations in development, particularly during the first two years, mean that programs for these youngest children should respond to individual development, rather than on group expectations.

Jean Piaget's cognitive-developmental theory helped us to reevaluate Gesell's proposal that we should wait for a child to mature or become ready for learning experiences. Piaget's position on the child's reconstruction of knowledge suggests that infant and toddler caregivers and parents can promote development and learning through a variety of methods and materials that will build upon the child's previous experiences (Kamii & DeVries, 1978). Piaget believed that developmental progress depended upon both maturation and the individual's active experiences, and he thus proposed that the child's utilization of feedback from active experiences combined with maturation to further intellectual, physical, and social development (Weiser, 1991).

During the first two years, the infant and toddler are in what Piaget termed the sensorimotor stage of development. The child's thinking is dependent upon his or her senses and physical actions. Babies use their senses and emerging motor abilities to discover and explore within their immediate environment to learn and understand. As they become mobile, their world for learning expands, depending on how much encouragement, materials, and experiences are available to them. Teachers, parents, and caregivers who understand the cognitive-developmental process can interact with the babies and provide the kinds of opportunities that are optimal in encouraging development.

The behaviorist theory, particularly Bandura's social learning theory, has a role to play when planning a program for infants and toddlers. Skinner's behaviorist theory, which proposes that learning occurs as a result of reinforcement and reward systems, is not seen by some child specialists as compatible with Piaget's position that learning is intrinsic. The social learning theory, on the other hand, has relevance for infant and toddler programs in that Bandura proposes that much behavior is learned through observation. Babies observe how new behaviors are performed and make adjustments following their own attempts at the modeled behavior. The child engages in self-regulation rather than just responding to a stimulus or a reward. Parents and teachers find the behavioral approach combined with social learning helpful in management of behavior. Adults and older children have a major role in providing modeling behaviors for infants and toddlers. Babies can observe others playing with toys and putting on and removing clothing, as well as many other aspects of daily routines and play that they will learn through experience.

The theories mentioned above interact when programs for infants and toddlers are implemented. Although each has strengths and weaknesses, they are helpful in understanding how to promote development and learning. The purposes of an individual program and the population of children served will have an effect on how the theories are included; nevertheless, all can contribute to the design of quality programs.

Approaches for Infant–Toddler Programs

Programs designed for infants and toddlers can be derived from the developmental theories discussed above. Task analysis and modeling approaches follow the behav-

iorist and social learning theories, respectively. In task analysis, the component skills of a task are determined. Children learn one step of a skill at a time and are reinforced for successful mastery of the skills and ultimate behavior. Modeling is used to demonstrate the desired behaviors so that the child can imitate them (Morrison, 1988). This specific skills approach is very useful for use with children with disabling conditions. Children who have a disability may need a carefully prescribed set of activities to respond to the diagnosis of the disability. Particular skills must be developed. Teachers and caregivers use reinforcement strategies to promote development or provide intervention in tasks designed to overcome delays or disabilities (Cataldo, 1983).

Programs that follow a Piagetian model utilizing intrinsic learning can be described as following a discovery, or interpersonal–environmental, approach. In these types of programs, the adult–child interactions and environment are significant. Developmental experiences, teacher and caregiver activities, and the environment are organized to support the child's experiences that will broaden their active exploration. A prepared environment and opportunities to play are essential elements of the approach. Discovery-learning opportunities are provided in all areas of development—physical, social-emotional, and cognitive and language. Caregivers interact with the babies by asking questions, modeling, and making suggestions or comments that provide ongoing feedback. Direct instruction is used when there are specific behaviors or skills that need to be learned; nevertheless, responsive strategies predominate as caregivers and teachers interact with individual schedules, interests, and progress of infants and toddlers (Cataldo, 1983; Morrison, 1988).

CHARACTERISTICS OF A QUALITY INFANT–TODDLER MODEL

A quality program for infants and toddlers attends to the physical, social-emotional, and cognitive needs of the very young child. To provide for these developmental needs the program must include quality caregivers, a responsive environment, a developmentally appropriate program, and active parental involvement. The program includes individualized experiences and opportunities for exploration and play. Each characteristic must be present if infants and toddlers are to be nurtured appropriately, whether they are in the home or in out-of-home care.

The Role of Quality Caregivers

It is impossible to overstress the importance of the adults who provide care to infants and toddlers. Caregivers are the most important element of a quality program for babies. Honig (1989) described their role as the primary ingredient in quality caregiving: "The primary ingredient to help young children flourish consists of *loving, responsive* caregivers, generously committing *energy, body-loving,* and *tuned-in attentiveness* to their child's well-being" (p. 4). The infant–toddler caregiver is able to provide intensive personal interactions with each baby in his or her care. The caregiver understands that very young children have individual temperaments and

schedules and the adult has the major responsibility to initiate interactions with each infant and toddler. Some of the behaviors the quality caregiver exhibits include cuddling and carrying the baby and using loving looks and positive voice tones. Weiser (1991, p. 21) described six goals for loving adults who care for infants and toddlers:

1. Respect uniqueness in temperament, state, and developmental stage.
2. Meet dependency needs, both social and physical, as well as encourage increasing independence.
3. Frequently initiate physical, social, and verbal contacts with the child.
4. Respond to and reinforce the child's physical, social, and verbal behavior most of the time (always would be ideal).
5. "Program" experiences, interactions, and materials appropriate to child's individual current levels of functioning.
6. Be consistent and predictable.

The Role of the Environment

The environment also is responsive to the individual needs of infants and toddlers. Basic components of an infant–toddler indoor environment include areas for diapering, feeding, sleeping, and playing. Carpeting for the floor is a must, as well as open areas where a variety of play activities may take place. The indoor environment may divided into separate areas using low shelving or partitions. The caregiver should be able to see every child at all times. Weiser (1991, p. 21) suggested that the environment be

- physically safe, clean, and healthful (including providing nutritious food)
- emotionally warm and supportive (trust-supporting)
- comfortable and functional
- rich in sensorimotor and social experiences
- available for extensive exploration, manipulation, and discovery of objects
- available for social relationships with adults and other children
- consistent and predictable.

Cataldo (1983) suggested that the activity area be organized into a number of centers. She described thirty possible interest areas for infants and toddlers, such as the reading center, manipulative area, creative corner, and puppet and doll house. Centers could be used on a rotating basis with toys and materials stored when not in use. Cataldo also proposed that more independent activity takes place in the center that is organized. Interest centers provide toddlers with many choices of toys to explore and master.

Developmentally appropriate environments for both infants and toddlers are described in *Developmentally Appropriate Practice in Early Childhood Programs Serving Children from Birth Through Age 8* (Bredekamp, 1987). See Figures 4.1 and 4.2 for examples of quality infant and toddler environments.

The Role of Play

Infants and toddlers spend their waking hours in some form of play. They play in interaction with adults, by themselves, near other babies, or alongside each other in first attempts to be involved with other children. The play that infants and toddlers engage in parallels their development; therefore, it is useful to discuss the role of play in terms of physical development, cognitive development, and social development. Since infants are in what Piaget called the sensorimotor stage of development and

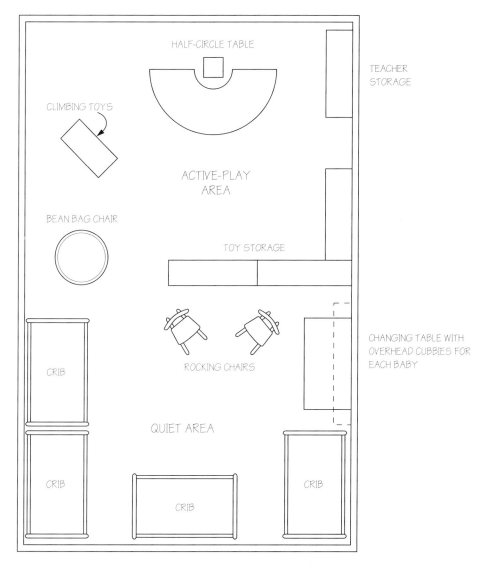

Figure 4.1   Indoor Infant Environment—Six to Twelve Months

toddlers are progressing from the sensorimotor to the preoperational stage of development, play reflects their developmental progress.

Physical Play.   Physical play begins at birth, when newborns use the limited resources they have. They use mouth play such as bubbling saliva or mouthing a nipple (Muenchow & Seitz, 1980). As they develop more physical control over their bodies they extend physical play to their hands, feet, and other body parts. Adults

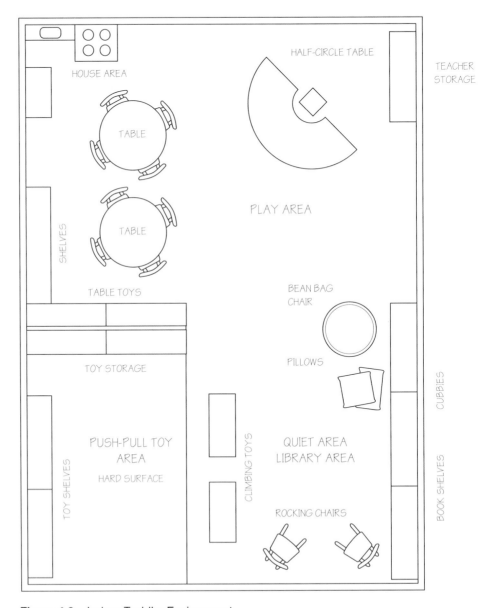

Figure 4.2   Indoor Toddler Environment

extend physical play experiences as they rock and use other movements to jiggle or swing the baby about. When the infant can grasp a toy, play is extended to objects in the environment (Wortham & Wortham, 1989).

Physical or motor play expands widely when the child achieves mobility and becomes a toddler. Now the child is able to extend physical play to explore the environment. The baby learns to walk and run and begins to develop better eye–hand coordination. Continual practice in physical play enables gross and fine motor skills to develop.

Cognitive Play.   Cognitive development enables the infant to combine emerging physical abilities with cognitive competencies to learn about the world. Play with objects and exploration of the environment facilitate infant cognitive development. The infant between six and twelve months explores the properties of toys. The child has to use sensory and motor skills to play with toys (McCune, 1986). Typically, infants mouth and visually explore toys. They may turn a toy over to examine all sides. They bang objects and focus on specific characteristics to better understand the toy. Later, infants are able to use the objects in play because they have mastered an understanding of what the toys can do.

As the older infant achieves object permanence and develops the ability to evoke images and use imitative activities, symbolic, or pretend, play emerges. The toddler can pretend one object is symbolized by another and uses this ability in make-believe play (Johnson, Christie, & Yawkey, 1987). The infant can now pretend to be drinking from a cup. When the older toddler can pretend that a doll is drinking from a cup, genuine symbolic play is part of the cognitive repertoire. Pretend play activities become more complex and sophisticated as the child is provided opportunities for play with objects and materials.

Social Play.   Play has an important role in social development. The infant's and toddler's individual social world has a strong influence on how they can engage in social play. The infant's first social play involves interactions with adult caregivers. The accommodating play partner engages the infant in social activities such as peek-aboo or tummy tickling. The infant learns social taking of turns in interactions and communicating; through attending to and responding to social games, the infant waits for a turn and reciprocates in the give and take of the experience. Infants use these same social skills to initiate others in socialization. Smiling and vocalizations are used to attract another to interact with them.

Toddlers can use objects to engage in social play with adults and peers. Johnson, Christie, and Yawkey (1987) propose that toys serve as "social butter" for mediating play between toddlers. The emergence of symbolic play enables toddlers to use pretend play with other babies.

Erikson (1950) characterized the stages of social play as autocosmic, microspheric, and macrospheric. Infant play is autocosmic because the infant's attention is focused on his or her own body. The microspheric stage evolves when the child can extend play to include toys and objects; a few significant others in the infant's environment can be included in the infant's play. Social play improves in the macrospheric stage when the child can engage in the play of others; play structures that facilitate shared play, such as wide slides, rocking boats, and large sand boxes, encourage social interactions among toddlers.

The Outdoor Play Environment. In addition to initiating and encouraging social interactions with infants and toddlers, adults also have the responsibility of organizing the environment to facilitate physical, social, and cognitive development through play. Earlier in the chapter the characteristics of a quality environment were explored. Examples of indoor environments for both infants and toddlers were

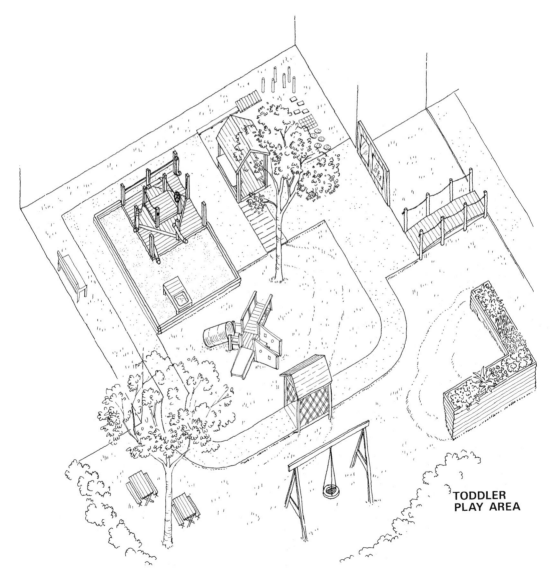

TODDLER
PLAY AREA

Figure 4.3 Outdoor Play Environment

described to include materials and toys that are developmentally appropriate for the two age groups. The equipment and toys recommended for infants and toddlers are related to the developmental progress from one age to the other that is reflected in play experiences and materials that are beneficial and enjoyable.

The outdoor play environment likewise provides play experiences that enhance infant and toddler development and play. Like the indoor environment, the outdoor playscape should be designed with the unique developmental needs of infants and toddlers in mind. For infants, a secure, enclosed area outdoors can provide them with opportunities to experience climate changes, landscape elements, and sensory experiences involving sun, shadows, wind, textures, and wildlife (Greenman, 1985; Miller, 1989). Infants need areas for crawling and provisions for practicing standing, cruising, and walking. Wind chimes and colored banners, hanging plants, and other natural environment features provide sensory experiences. The environment should also include toys for object play and swing sets where adults and infants can engage in social interactions during outdoor play (Wortham, 1990).

Provisions for toddler outdoor play expand the possibilities for social, physical, and cognitive play compatible with the toddler's emerging skills and development. Pathways with different surfaces and textures; simple climbing structures that provide a slide board, steps, and a crawl-through experience; and elements that can be acted upon, such as bells, steering wheels, and chutes, challenge toddlers' physical and cognitive growth. Greenman (1985) suggests that toddlers need outdoor spaces for developing motor skills for swinging, sliding, rolling, climbing, jumping, running, kicking, traveling, riding, and transporting. A vehicle trail provides opportunities for playing with push and pull toys and wheeled vehicles.

Both small and large toys facilitate social and cognitive development. Objects that facilitate exploratory, symbolic, social, and cognitive play should be included. Toddlers are ready for materials that enhance pretend play, such as toy lawnmowers, trucks, cardboard boxes, and playhouse structures and equipment. Creative play is enhanced with facilities for sand and water play and outdoor art experiences. Figure 4.3 shows an example of the components of an outdoor infant and toddler play environment.

The Role of Routines

Adults are the primary source of care and learning for infants and toddlers. Routines are the elements of the very young child's day, whether care is provided in or out of the home. The experiences that babies have when being diapered, bathed, dressed, and fed are the opportunities for adult–child interactions that form the infant–toddler curriculum. The affectionate care and responsiveness to each individual child during the day's routines are the sources of the baby's learning.

During the first year, the adult caregiver individualizes interactive opportunities for socializing, feeding, and playing to be in tune with the infant's individual schedule, which Honig (1989) describes as the child's tempo. During the second year, toddlers in group care can follow scheduled times for playing, eating, and performing other brief activities with flexibility for individual needs for attention and rest. Some routines, such as diapering, are still done on an individual schedule; however, caregivers can plan for group activity and play periods and can establish times for feeding and napping for the group as a whole.

The routines followed when babies arrive and leave are also important parts of the day. The smooth transition from home to the care facility at the beginning of the day and then the change at the end of the day promote security and calm for babies and their families. Other transitions in routines for toddlers—for example, changing from one activity to another or washing hands before a meal—provide predictability and consistency for the daily schedule. Caregivers help toddlers anticipate changes in the routine by giving signals that help toddlers move from one activity to another. Conversations, stories, and fingerplays are also used to engage toddlers in transitions from one activity or routine to another (Morrison, 1988).

The Role of Parents

Quality infant–toddler programs support the family. Because parents are the prime adults in the child's life, close communication between caregivers and parents is particularly important. The relationship between the parents and caregivers should be a partnership; consistency between routines and child-rearing practices at home and at the caregiving setting is critical for the baby's security and development. Parents and caregivers are sharing in the child's life, and thus it is important that they discuss their roles and expectations (Bredekamp, 1987; Powell, 1989).

Parents have different needs in their relationships with staff members and caregivers in infant–toddler programs. Working parents may feel guilty and anxious about leaving their child in out-of-home care. They need reassurance about the child's daily routines and experiences, which help them keep in touch with what the child's progress is and how the day went for the child and the caregiver. Parents of infants and toddlers with disabling conditions who are in early intervention programs need ongoing progress reports and instruction on how they can contribute to the efforts being made in the child's individual program. Many parents, particularly single, teenage mothers, need supportive guidance in parenting skills.

If caregivers and other staff members in caregiving settings for infants and toddlers are responsive to cultural and language differences among the children and their families, they can learn to respond to the individual needs of parents, as well as to support the diversity of the children. Non-English-speaking parents need support and encouragement as much as their children need understanding and security (Miller, 1992). These parents may be unable to communicate their desires for their child's care or hesitant about using their limited English. Sensitive caregivers make efforts to help parents explain their caregiving practices. Likewise, staff members seek to learn about the child's family and background.

Parents of biracial children may have concerns about their children's acceptance and identity. Single parents and teenage mothers may have questions about parenting skills. Parents of children with disabilities may have information about their children's care that needs to be shared. Others, such as parents of children with fetal alcohol syndrome, may have feelings of guilt about their involvement in their children's impediment. These parents, too, need to be accepted and involved in the program (Gargiulo & Graves, 1991).

When serving children from diverse families representing many cultures, caregivers will want to be perceptive about differences in caregiving, feeding, and other practices used in the care of babies. Parents can be asked about how they dress the baby, what sleeping patterns they expect, and what kinds of foods they prefer for their child. There are both subtle and obvious variations in caregiving among different cultures. The parents as well as the caregivers will feel comfortable about the child who receives care outside the home if these practices are understood and followed.

The caregiver in the infant–toddler program can provide ongoing support and information that can facilitate the parents' role as primary caregivers and teachers of their child. A daily report to all parents of infants and toddlers about how the child ate, slept, and played is important to provide consistency in the child's routines and planning between home and the program. The Integrated Components of Appropriate and Inappropriate Practice for Infants and the Integrated Components of Appropriate Practice for Toddlers (Bredekamp, 1987, p. 38) include the following characteristics of appropriate practices in staff–parent interactions:

- Parents are viewed as the child's primary source of affection and care. Staff support parents and work with them to help them feel confident as parents.
- Parents and staff talk daily to share pertinent information about the child.
- Staff help parents anticipate the child's next areas of development and prepare them to support the child.

Planning and Managing Infant–Toddler Developmental Experiences

Infants and toddlers learn through their own experience, trial and error, repetition, imitation, and identification. Adults guide and encourage this learning by ensuring that the environment is safe and emotionally supportive. An appropriate program for children younger than 3 invites play, active exploration, and movement. It provides a broad array of stimulating experiences within a reliable framework of routines and protection from excessive stress. Relationships with people are emphasized as an essential contribution to the quality of children's experiences (Lally, Provence, Szanton, & Weissbourd, 1987, p. 29).

The above summary of good programs for children under the age of three describes the infant–toddler model that adheres to an interpersonal–environmental approach. The environment prepared for discovery and exploration through play provides experiences and adult–child interactions through daily routines. The flexible routines and activities that are initiated by the adult follow the needs of individual children. The curriculum is developmental in that adult–child interactions and experiences promote physical, social-emotional, and cognitive development matched to the infant's or toddler's current level of development. Therefore, the model for planning and managing developmental experiences centers on the behaviors of the caregivers and the types of activities and interactions they present to the babies (Cataldo, 1983).

Interactions and Experiences for Physical Development. During the first three years, infants and toddlers learn the skills of movement. The movement education curriculum provides guidance on interactions and experiences that promote the development of gross and fine motor skills. The caregiver plans and initiates activities designed to encourage practice of physical skills. (In this and all descriptions of interactions the reader should be aware of how caregivers include experiences as part of daily routines as well as provide planned activities.) Caregivers who perform behaviors that promote physical mastery and manipulation listed by Cataldo (1983, pp. 81–82) do the following:

- Attempt to get young infants to look at, reach for, and kick at objects.
- Encourage young infants to hold, mouth, bang together, and examine rattles and other safe objects.
- Try to arrange toys for infants to see and to manipulate with fingers, hands, or feet when they are in a quiet state.
- Use a variety of objects and toys as playthings for exploration and manipulation; check to be certain that objects are "childproof."
- Encourage rolling over, sitting, and creeping, providing both a safe, nonrestrictive area for practice and physical support and verbal encouragement.
- Arrange soft, sturdy objects so that older babies can practice standing and pulling to stand; encourage the children.
- Provide tiny, soft food objects to facilitate use of fingers and promote self-feeding by older babies.
- Use chairs, hassocks, or pushcarts, as well as abundant praise and encouragement, with toddlers learning to walk independently.
- Demonstrate to toddlers and assist them in gaining independent dressing and undressing skills.

Interactions and Experiences for Social and Emotional Development. Infants and toddlers have a basic need to develop social competency and a positive concept of self. The very young child has the dual task of understanding him- or herself as an individual, unique person separate from others and becoming a social being in the company of others. The adult caregiver nurtures social and emotional development through interactions that will support the development of a positive sense of self and guidance in the development of appropriate social behaviors. Cataldo (1983) described these important developmental accomplishments in terms of social interactions; such accomplishments include adult behaviors that will foster interactions with the baby. The adult approach to establishing an environment that provides emotional security includes the understanding that infants and toddlers must be able to develop a sense of trust. Adult–child interactions also reflect an understanding of different temperaments in infants and toddlers, which require alternative responses from adults. Some appropriate adult behaviors that facilitate social development are described here (Cataldo, 1983, p. 81):

- Regularly providing babies with moderately stimulating experiences, such as comforting, talking, playing music, and moving mobiles, even though very young infants may respond little.
- Attempting to achieve smiling and cooing in young infants with animated and frequent face-to-face interactions.

- Paying attention to infants when they actively seek attention or comfort.
- Engaging babies in frolic and imitation play, such as rattle shaking, patting, arm waving, tickling, and laughing.
- Playing cooperative interaction games, such as peekaboo and pattycake.
- Responding positively to toddlers' requests for help and guidance with toys, games, and play involvement with other children, even when problematic.
- Handling frequent management or discipline problems in toddlers with consistency, affection, and a view toward learning from conflict and challenge.
- Demonstrating realistic expectations and flexibility regarding toddlers' beginning skills in taking turns, sharing, and waiting for assistance.

Interactions and Experiences for Cognitive and Language Development. The experiences provided for cognitive and language development build upon what we understand about the child's role in initiating language and the internal mechanisms the child has for constructing language in increasingly complex form and content that come from continued practice with communication. The adult models new language forms and expands and extends the child's efforts at communication, thus providing vocabulary that the child can incorporate into future verbalizations. Verbal interactions initiated by the caregiver respond to the baby's interests in exploring the environment and engaging in communication episodes with the caregiver. The caregiver initiates conversations with infants and toddlers that may seem one-sided in the early months. During caregiving routines and play activities the caregiver describes, explains, and encourages responses from the infant, even though the baby is still unable to respond using words. Later, the caregiver responds to the toddler's attempts to combine words to form communication with the adult and initiates communication experiences that will encourage the toddler to use more language.

In cognitive interactions, the adult also uses language to point out concepts and features of toys and the environment. Physical demonstration is used to show how objects and toys work. Ongoing verbalizations provide the infant and toddler with contextual explanations of activities and experiences throughout the day's routines and times for play. Examples of appropriate interactions as described by Cataldo (1983, p. 84) include the following:

- Recognizing the need to talk and sing to young infants regardless of their minimal ability to respond.
- Encouraging vocalizing, smiling, and exaggerated imitative mouth movement responses in young infants.
- Planning for crib or change table "talk time" so that babies can listen to themselves, try out sounds, and repeat expressions before going on to other routines.
- Speaking several simple words to babies before and during routines and repeating these frequently so that they will recognize them.
- Praising all sounds that stand for certain objects and realizing that these are forms of early words.
- Teaching the words for body parts, foods, and diapering materials.
- Using picture books and repeating the words for objects that toddlers point to; naming details.

- Occasionally withholding objects desired by toddlers and coaxing them to attempt to use the words or sounds that seem appropriate for them.
- Using language to animate puppets or little toy people for toddlers, pretending and describing where they are going and what they will do.
- Using phrases and simple commands for toddlers to respond to, such as "get the ball," "pat the doggy," or "put the spoon in the cup."
- Repeating and expanding the utterances of toddlers.

The Role of Thematic Curriculum for Infants and Toddlers

Is it appropriate to design developmental learning experiences for infants and toddlers that are based on themes? If done carefully, an organized, thematic approach can be useful in helping caregivers focus on interesting experiences to share with very young children. For example, a unit on spring could easily be designed to include excursions outside to view signs of flowers and budding plants and trees during the early weeks of spring. Laminated pictures showing spring scenes could be mounted at infant–toddler eye level. Appropriate picture books could be shared with the children. Flowering, nontoxic plants could be displayed in the room and made available for careful touching and smelling.

Teachers and caregivers contemplating thematic experiences for very young toddlers should be cautious that the activities are child centered and appropriate. The activities selected should be responsive to individual development and schedules. Art products and other activities that are beyond the child's capabilities should not be included. The guidelines for quality caregiver and child interactions should be followed; nevertheless, a thematic approach can provide an opportunity to design interesting experiences and new materials that caregivers and babies can enjoy together.

(In chapter 5, the infant–toddler curriculum will be described more specifically in terms of how caregivers and parents can design experiences to use with babies. Following an interpersonal–environmental approach, the experiences will be discussed in developmental categories that support the progress of the child's growth and learning.)

The Role of Evaluation in Infant–Toddler Programs

A quality program for infants and toddlers includes provisions for evaluation. Evaluation facilitates assessment and improvement. It allows program planners and staff to look at what has been accomplished and what components need to be strengthened or perhaps removed from the program. In this section, two types of evaluation will be discussed. First, the child's developmental progress will be described. Evaluation of the program itself will be discussed to include the environment, experiences and activities provided for infants and toddlers, and the actions of caregivers. In addition, attention will be given to evaluation of parental involvement in the program and considerations that have to be made when evaluating infants and toddlers with special needs who are served in programs for early intervention.

Evaluation of Infant–Toddler Development and Competencies. Observation of infants and toddlers takes place daily as caregivers note them eating, sleeping, and eliminating during the course of the day. In good programs, evaluation of the infant's and toddler's progress during the day is reported to parents each afternoon when they arrive to take the child home. Assessment in this context is made to monitor the child's well-being and health each day. The caregiver can also comment on the day's activities and the child's participation.

A less frequent but equally important evaluation with infants and toddlers is that of developmental progress. Because growth and development is so rapid during the first two years, caregivers and parents are especially aware of the baby's developmental achievements. If infants and toddlers are in out-of-home care during the day, parents look to caregivers to provide indicators of developmental progress in their absence.

Developmental charts or checklists similar to the ones provided in chapter 3 are frequently used by parents and caregivers to track individual development. The infant or toddler is observed weekly or biweekly using the checklist. When a new behavior or skill is observed during the scheduled period or incidentally during the day, the achievement is noted on the child's individual checklist record, as well as is the date it was observed. Frequent reports are shared with parents; parents in turn share similar information with caregivers. Sources of developmental indicators are easily located: in addition to the Wortham Developmental Checklist for Infants and Toddlers found in chapter 3, *Developmentally Appropriate Practice in Early Childhood Programs Serving Children from Birth Through Age 8* (Bredekamp, 1987, pp. 30–31) contains a list titled Developmental Milestones of Children from Birth to Age 3 (Lally, Provence, Szanton, & Weissbourd, 1987). Weiser (1991) likewise includes the same Developmental Milestones of Children from Birth to Age 3 in Appendix B of *Infant/Toddler Care and Education*.

Evaluation of Program Components. All aspects of the infant–toddler program benefit from evaluation procedures. Among the components that are assessed are the environment, the experiences of and activities performed with the children, and the behavior of the adult caregiver.

Evaluation of the Environment. As was described earlier, the environment planned for the infant and toddler program is organized for the specific needs of infants and toddlers. The equipment, toys, materials, and arrangement are focused on unique developmental characteristics of children younger than three years of age. The resulting environment is evaluated to determine whether the developmental characteristics of infants and toddlers are addressed in the room established for their care. For example, the furnishings in an infant room should include tables, infant seats, shelving, and toys that are suited to infants (Harms & Clifford, 1980). Staff members can use the indicators of an appropriate environment for infants and toddlers that are part of the Integrated Components of Developmentally Appropriate Practice for Infants and Toddlers (Lally, Provence, Szanton, & Weissbourd, 1987) reproduced in Figure 4.4. A rating scale with a range of indicators for the quality infant and toddler environment is available in the Infant/Toddler Environment Rating Scale (Harms, Cryer, & Clifford, 1990).

APPROPRIATE PRACTICE	INAPPROPRIATE PRACTICE
• The diapering/toileting, sleeping, feeding, and play areas are separate, both for sanitation and to ensure quiet, restful areas.	• Areas are combined, very noisy, and distracting.
• The environment contains both soft (pillows, padded walls, carpeting) and hard (rocking chairs, mirrors) elements.	• The environment is dominated by hard surfaces because they are easier to keep clean.
• The environment contains private spaces with room for no more than two children.	• The environment provides no private spaces.
• Children have their own cribs or cots, bedding, feeding utensils, clothing, and other special comforting objects. Toddlers' names are used to label every personal item.	• Children share sleeping quarters in shifts, or otherwise do not have their own special supplies. Favored objects are not permitted.
• Children have many opportunities for active, large muscle play both indoors and outdoors. The environment includes ramps and steps that are the correct size for children to practice newly acquired skills. Toddlers' outdoor play space is separate from that of older children. Outdoor play equipment for toddlers includes small climbing equipment that they can go around, in, and out of, and solitary play equipment requiring supervision such as swings and low slides.	• Toddlers' indoor space is cramped and unsafe for children who are just learning how to move their bodies and need to run more than walk. Toddlers share outdoor space and unsafe equipment designed for older children.

Figure 4.4 Characteristics of a Toddler Environment
S. Bredekamp, *Developmentally Appropriate Practice in Early Childhood Programs Serving Children from Birth through Age 8.* (National Association for the Education of Young Children, 1987), pp. 43–44. Used by permission of the publisher.

Evaluation of Infant–Toddler Experiences and Activities.   The types of activities and experiences planned and implemented for infants and toddlers are also assessed. The criteria for developmentally appropriate experiences has been discussed previously. These same criteria are used to evaluate the effectiveness of the activities, which should be evaluated immediately after use to determine if they have met the child's needs and interests. Likewise, activities should be assessed to determine if they have met the purpose for which they were intended. Should an activity be used again? Does the experience need to be modified to make it more interesting or use-

APPROPRIATE PRACTICE	INAPPROPRIATE PRACTICE
• The room is cheerful and decorated at the children's eye level with pictures of faces of people, friendly animals, and other familiar objects. Pictures of children and their families are encouraged.	• Areas are dingy and dark. Decorations are at adult eye levels, or are too syrupy and cute. No evidence exists of personal involvement for families.
• Sturdy picture books are provided. Pictures depict a variety of ages and ethnic groups in a positive way.	• Books are not available because they get torn or soiled. Pictures are cartoons or other stereotypes.
• Toys are available on open shelves so children can make their own selections. Toys can be carried and moved about in the environments as children choose.	• Toys are dumped in a box or kept away from children's reach so they are at the mercy of adult's selection. Adults attempt to restrict the use of toys to certain areas, like housekeeping or block-play areas.
• Climbing structures and steps are low, well padded, and safe for exploration.	• No provisions are made for children to climb; or, structures are safe only for older, more mobile children.

ful? Because many experiences involve adult interaction with the child, evaluation must include assessment of the adult's behaviors as well.

Evaluation of the Behavior of Adult Caregivers. Two categories of adult interactions can be evaluated. The first relates to the interactions and experiences the adult initiates with the child that promote development and learning. The second category concerns the personal care routines the adult engages in with each child that concern the health, safety, and nutrition of infants and toddlers.

The Integrated Components of Developmentally Appropriate Practice for Infants and Toddlers (Lally, Provence, Szanton, & Weissbourd, 1987) contain the contrasting indicators between appropriate and inappropriate practices used by infant–toddler caregivers in interactions and routines with babies. The caregiver's behaviors can be evaluated using the indicators related to these characteristics. The caregiver can also use the same indicators for self-evaluation and likewise study the characteristics of appropriate routines used with infants and toddlers to ensure that personal care routines and health, safety, and nutrition practices are being properly observed or carried out on a daily basis. Personal care routines and appropriate interactions and experiences can also be evaluated through use of the scales on the Infant/Toddler Environment Rating Scale (Harms, Cryer, & Clifford, 1990). Interactions and activities that include language, physical skills, creative activities, social play, and cognitive skills can be evaluated using this scale.

Personal care routines used with infants and toddlers are especially important to prevent or reduce illness in very young children in out-of-home care. Staff members in locations that provide infant and toddler care will want to be very familiar with appropriate health and safety practices that are also part of personal care routines. Caregivers will want to review their practices and compare them with standards or recommended practices frequently to be sure that they are protecting the children from unsafe and unhealthy experiences. Personal care routines, especially, need ongoing attention to prevent disease and danger. Evaluators can review the indicators of appropriate practice for infants and toddlers found in the infant and toddler section (Lally, Provence, Szanton, & Weissbourd, 1987) of *Developmentally Appropriate Practice in Early Childhood Programs Serving Children from Birth Through Age 8* (Bredekamp, 1987) or use the appropriate rating scales in the Infant/Toddler Environment Rating Scale (Harms, Cryer, & Clifford, 1990).

Evaluation of Infants and Toddlers with Special Needs.   According to PL 99-457, Education of the Handicapped Act Amendments of 1986, Part H, infants and toddlers (from birth to age two) with disabilities will be served with an individualized family service plan (IFSP) that includes the specific early intervention services that are necessary to meet the individual needs of the child and the family. The plan involves the infant's or toddler's present levels of physical, cognitive, language, and psychosocial development, self-help skills, and major outcomes that are expected to be achieved for the infant and family. Included with the outcomes or objectives for the child's progress as a result of intervention are the objective criteria that will be used to measure the child's progress. Periodically, within the course of intervention services, the child's progress is evaluated and decisions made whether to continue the original plan as designed or to make needed modifications to better serve the child's intervention needs.

Evaluation of Parental Involvement in Infant–Toddler Programs.   If an infant–toddler program is serving children with special needs with individualized early intervention plans, the plan includes the family as well as the affected child. When the intervention program is evaluated, the parental aspect of the plan is also evaluated. A similar process should occur with programs for normal infants and toddlers who are in out-of-home care. When parental components are included in the infant–toddler program, provisions should also be made to evaluate and improve the parent and center relationships. If parents are involved in volunteer work at the center or in an evening parenting program, they should be given an opportunity to provide feedback on their experiences and changes they believe would be beneficial to the program. Staff members should engage in a similar process to determine how effective are interactions with parents and how well they are meeting parental needs. Are the content and approach of parenting sessions meeting the parents' interests and needs? Do parents find the newsletter helpful? These and many other questions should be reviewed to assess the overall effectiveness of parental relationships and to plan future changes and additions.

Summary

Programs designed for infants and toddlers are associated with the advent of child care in this country. Although newer than preschool programs, infant–toddler programs have increased in number and have become of higher quality with the rapid growth in out-of-home care for very young children in recent years. Specialized infant–toddler programs have also emerged in the form of intervention programs for children from low-income homes and infants and toddlers born with a disabling condition or who are at risk to develop a disabling condition.

Like programs for older children, infant and toddler programs are developed from theoretical bases. Theories of learning and development, particularly recent ones that emphasize the importance of the first three years for optimal development, form the foundations upon which infant and toddler programs are organized. The purposes for the program evolve from the needs of the parents as well as the children. Some programs are used primarily for care, although experiences for development and learning are increasingly becoming a part of care. Intervention programs may serve babies of unmarried teenage mothers, low-income children who need basic experiences for language and cognitive development, and very young children who have special needs. Middle- and upper-class parents are interested in general enrichment programs that will enhance their baby's development. Motor skills programs for infants and toddlers and accelerated literacy programs are frequently sought out by these parents.

Regardless of the type of program implemented for infants and toddlers, the child's developmental characteristics usually form the background for the choices of curriculum, activities, and experiences provided. Because physical, social-emotional, and cognitive development are so important in the early years, programs for infants and toddlers focus on experiences and activities that promote development in these areas.

Adult caregivers have a key role in infant–toddler programs. Adult–child interactions are the forum for the activities conducted with the child. The interactions may occur naturally during caregiving routines and play episodes throughout the day. Because of the central nature of the adult's behavior with the child, much of the quality of the program and success of interactions and experiences depends upon the qualities of the caregiver. The caregiver must be cognizant of the desired caregiving characteristics and behaviors that affect the child's experiences during the day. The caregiver needs to understand the match between experiences and interactions and the infant's or toddler's current stage of development and personality. The congruence between the child's current abilities and interests and the caregiver's choices of behaviors and activities to be used with the child form the curricular part of the infant–toddler program.

Although there is a place in infant–toddler programs for learning through imitation that follows the behaviorist and social learning models of learning, the Piagetian description of cognitive development is most closely related to the model used in this chapter. The model, described as an interpersonal–environmental approach to infant–toddler programs, is based on the Piagetian belief that learning is intrinsic. The very young child learns through discovery and interaction with the environment. For infants and toddlers, exploration of the environment and interactions with adults with appropriate materials and activities on an individual basis form the framework for their program. Although caregivers plan and initiate many of the experiences that occur with infants and toddlers each day, they also respond to the child's interest in activities with language, modeling, and encouragement. These responsive strategies reflect the caregiver's careful observations of the child and keen awareness of the kinds of interactions and experiences that will facilitate the child's development at the current stage.

The environment likewise is organized to promote the child's exploration and play. Equipment, furnishings, and toys are selected to fit the very young child's ability to explore and play. Room arrangement encourages emerging physical and cognitive abilities at the same time that it nurtures security and confidence. The caregiver makes appropriate experiences available and removes, adds, or rearranges toys and materials in a flexible manner to suit the changing needs of the rapidly growing child.

Parents are another key element in infant–toddler programs. Intervention programs seek to serve parental as well as child needs. The aim of child-care programs is to build a close partnership between parents and caregiver as they all share the infant's and toddler's daily life. Programs of all types may include opportunities for parents to develop parenting skills. In addition, parental involvement with the program, when included, strengthens the relationship between caregivers and parents and the overall quality of the program.

Evaluation is important to the continued growth of both children and programs. Evaluation of the child's developmental progress keeps parents and caregivers aware of the child's changing developmental characteristics. Awareness of developmental progress provides information that affects the nature of the program during the year as the caregiver and parents seek to respond to the child's changing developmental needs. For children with developmental delays or special needs, the intervention program based on the child's current developmental status is also evaluated based on the child's progress on the same criteria.

Other aspects of the program that benefit from evaluation are the caregiver's qualities and behaviors, the quality of the parental involvement program, and the quality of the environment. With periodic assessments of all components of the programs, ongoing improvement continues the trend toward the development of a quality program for infants and toddlers.

Summary Statements

1. Infant–toddler programs have emerged as a result of the growing numbers of infants and toddlers in out-of-home care and funding of programs for infants and toddlers who have special needs because of disabling conditions.
2. Early infant–toddler programs focused on health, safety, and care parallel to the history of the child-care industry. However, the programmatic element is now important to infant–toddler care.
3. Our understanding of the needs and potential of infants and toddlers has been based on the information that came from the child-study movement that related to infant–toddler development.
4. Much of the growth in infant and child care was stimulated by the need for out-of-home care for babies during the Great Depression and World War II. More recently, employment by both parents or single parents has led to expansion of the child-care industry and other settings that provide care during the working day.
5. The work of psychologists during the 1950s and 1960s led to a new awareness of the importance of the first three years of life to learning potential.
6. The emphasis upon learning in the early years led to intervention programs for children who were at risk because of socioeconomic circumstances.
7. Intervention programs for infants and toddlers in the 1960s and 1970s were part of the funding that also involved Head Start and Follow Through programs to help children from homes with low incomes.

8. Intervention programs for infants and toddlers with disabling conditions were funded because of the success with similar programs for preschool children.

9. In addition to programs for child care and intervention, there are enrichment programs for infants and toddlers that focus particularly on middle- and upper-class families.

10. The purpose of enrichment programs is to accelerate academic or developmental skills in motor, language, and cognitive development.

11. Infant–toddler programs are based on the developmental needs of the very young child as explained by theories of development.

12. Characteristics of stages of development as described by Gesell, Erikson, and Piaget form the foundation for program goals for cognitive, physical, and social-emotional development.

13. The approach for the interpersonal–environmental model recognizes that the interactions between the adult and child in a well-planned environment provide the elements essential to a quality infant–toddler program.

14. The quality of the caregiver's behavior, the environment, and planned experiences and interactions determines the overall effectiveness of the infant–toddler program.

15. Parental interaction and involvement with the caregiver and other staff members of the infant–toddler program are essential for a successful experience for the child.

16. Evaluation of all program components is likewise essential if the program is to improve services to the child and family.

17. Evaluation of the child's progress is a vital element for tracking the child's developmental progress and obtaining feedback for ongoing program development.

18. Daily observation of the infant and toddler facilitates communication between the child-care setting and the home.

19. Ongoing assessment of caregiver behaviors and skills helps staff members sharpen their understanding of their role in the child's routines and learning.

20. Evaluation of caregiver characteristics can be used to effect improvement in the caregiver's skills.

21. Evaluation of the environment and activities can provide clues as to where improvement is needed in the learning program.

22. Evaluation of parental involvement should include parents' input so that their needs and perceptions are used in developing the direction of parent–teacher relationships and activities.

23. Evaluation of individual progress in intervention programs can also be used to determine future plans for the child; moreover, success of the individual plans and overall quality of the intervention program can be indicated by individual progress reports.

24. Intervention programs must also be evaluated in terms of services to parents, because parental services cannot be separated from services to the child.

25. With increased funding for intervention programs, including Head Start, and further growth in other types of infant–toddler programs, larger numbers of infants and toddlers should be served by some type of service throughout the rest of the 1990s.

Study Questions

1. Why has custodial care always been a factor in many programs for infants and toddlers, even at the end of the nineteenth century?

2. Why did infant mortality remain high into the first decades of the twentieth century?

3. What were some of the factors that led to the improvement of infant life and welfare after the turn of the century?

4. How did Jean-Jacques Rousseau see childhood differently than the philosophers who preceded him?

5. What specific findings in the child-study movement have affected our perception of infants and toddlers?

6. Why did the first major developments in infant–toddler programming take place after World War II?

7. A major issue since the 1950s has been whether infants should be in out-of-home care. Why is this issue still a concern today?

8. What were the contributions of the infant–toddler programs funded in the 1960s? Why were these contributions important?

9. Why are standards for infant–toddler programs and standards for the preparation of teachers and caregivers for these programs critical at this time?

10. What is the appeal of infant–toddler programs focused on enrichment or accelerated development? What are some possible problems with these programs?

11. Is there a best type of care setting for infants and toddlers? Why or why not?

12. What is the rationale for the implementation of intervention programs for infants with disabilities and their families?

13. What is meant by the interpersonal-environmental infant–toddler model? What is implied by the name of the model?

14. How and why do the caregiver's abilities control the quality of the infant–toddler program?

15. How and why is the environment of an infant–toddler program important to how the program is conducted during the whole day?

16. Why do parents need to be considered as partners in the infant–toddler program?

17. How can the infant–toddler program be affected by the quality of communication between the home and the program?

18. Why do parents of infants and toddlers in out-of-home care need a daily report on the child's progress?

19. How can caregivers assess and evaluate their behaviors to improve the infant–toddler program?

20. Why do infant–toddler intervention programs need to consider the needs of the family?

References

Belsky, J., & Steinberg, L. (1978). The effects of day care: A critical review. *Child Development, 49*, 929–949.

Bernstein, N. (1982, April 16). Infant day care: Controversial, expensive, and scarce. *Milwaukee Journal*.

Bloom, B. S. (1964). *Stability and change in human characteristics*. New York: John Wiley & Sons.

Braun, S. J., & Edwards, E. P. (1972). *History and theory of early childhood education*. Belmont, CA: Wadsworth.

Brazelton, T. B. (1985, December). Do you really want a superkid? *Family Circle*, p. 75.

Bredekamp, S. (Ed.). (1987). *Developmentally appropriate practice in early childhood programs serving children from birth through age 8*. Washington, DC: National Association for the Education of Young Children.

Caldwell, B. (1986). Day care and the public schools—Natural allies, natural enemies. *Educational Leadership, 44*, 34–39.

Caldwell, B. (1989). A comprehensive model for integrating child care and early childhood education. *Teacher's College Record, 90*, 404–414.

Cataldo, C. Z. (1983). *Infant and toddler programs: A guide to very early childhood education*. Reading, MA: Addison–Wesley.

Day, M. C., & Parker, R. K. (Eds.). (1977). *The preschool in action* (2nd ed.). Boston: Allyn & Bacon.

Dickerson, M. (1992). James L. Hymes, Jr. In Association for Childhood Education International, *Profiles in childhood education 1931–1960* (pp. 82–90). Wheaton, MD: Author.

Eheart, B. K., & Leavitt, R. L. (1989). Family day care: Discrepancies between intended and observed child care practices. *Early Childhood Research Quarterly, 4*, 145–162.

Elardo, P., & Caldwell, B. (1974). The Kramer adventure: A school for the future? *Childhood Education, 50*, 143–152.

Elkind, D. (1986). Formal education and early childhood education: An essential difference. *Phi Delta Kappan, 67*, 631–636.

Eliot, A. A. (1972). Nursery schools fifty years ago. *Young Children, 27*, 210–214.

Erikson, E. H. (1950). *Childhood and society*. New York: Norton.

Gargiulo, R. M., & Graves, S. B. (1991). Parental feelings: The forgotten component when working with parents of handicapped preschool children. *Childhood Education, 67*, 176–178.

Gerber, M. (1981). What is appropriate curriculum for infants and toddlers? In B. Weissbourd & J.

Musick (Eds.), *Infants: Their social environments* (pp. 77–85). Washington, DC: National Association for the Education of Young Children.

Gesell, A. (1925). *The mental growth of the preschool child.* New York: Macmillan.

Graham, M. S., & Scott, K. G. (1988). The impact of definitions of high risk on services to infants and toddlers. *Topics in Early Childhood Special Education, 8,* 23–38.

Greenman, J. (1985, Summer). Babies get out: Outdoor settings for infant toddler play. *Beginnings,* pp. 7–10.

Greven, P. (1977). *The protestant temperament.* New York: Alfred A. Knopf.

Hall. C. S., & Lindzey, G. (1970). *Theories of personality* (2nd ed.). New York: Wiley.

Harms, T., & Clifford, R. M. (1980). *Early Childhood Environment Rating Scale.* New York: Teacher's College Press.

Harms, T., Cryer, D., & Clifford, R. M. (1990). *Infant/Toddler Environment Rating Scale.* New York: Teacher's College Press.

Honig, A. S. (1983). Sex role socialization in early childhood. *Young Children, 38,* 57–70.

Honig, A. S. (1989). Quality infant/toddler caregiving: Are there magic recipes? *Young Children, 44,* 4–10.

Howes, C. (1989). Infant child care. *Young Children, 44,* 24–28.

Hunt, J. McV. (1961). *Intelligence and experience.* New York: Ronald.

Hymes, J., & Stolz, L. M. (1978). The Kaiser Child Service Centers. In J. L. Hymes (Ed.), *Living history interviews. Book 2: Care of the children of working mothers* (pp. 26–56). Carmel, CA: Hacienda Press.

Johnson, H. M. (1928). *Children in "the nursery school."* New York: Agathon.

Johnson, H. M. (1936). *School begins at two.* New York: New Republic.

Johnson, J. E., Christie, J. F., & Yawkey, T. D. (1987). *Play and early childhood development.* Glenview, IL: Scott, Foresman.

Kagan, J. (1971). *Change and continuity in infants.* New York: John Wiley & Sons.

Kamii, C., & DeVries, R. (1978). *Physical knowledge in preschool education.* Englewood Cliffs, NJ: Prentice–Hall.

Katz, P. (1982). Development of children's racial awareness and intergroup attitudes. In L. Katz (Ed.), *Current topics in early childhood education* (Vol. 4, pp. 17–54). Norwood, NJ: Ablex.

Keister, M. E. (1970). *"The good life" for infants and toddlers.* Washington, DC: National Association for the Education of Young Children.

Kelley, M. F., & Surbeck, E. (1990). Infant day care. In E. Surbeck & M. F. Kelly (Eds.), *Personalizing care with infants, toddlers, and families* (pp. 62–70). Wheaton, MD: Association for Childhood Education International.

Krogh, S. (1990). *The integrated early childhood curriculum.* New York: McGraw-Hill.

Lally, J. R., Provence, S., Szanton, E., & Weissbourd, B. (1987). Developmentally appropriate care for children from birth to age 3. In S. Bredekamp (Ed.), *Developmentally appropriate practice in early childhood programs serving children from birth through age 8* (pp. 17–33). Washington, DC: National Association for the Education of Young Children.

Maxim, G. W. (1989). *The very young* (3rd ed.). Columbus, OH: Merrill.

McCune, L. (1986). Symbolic development in normal and atypical infants. In G. Fein & M. Rivkin (Eds.), *The young child at play* (pp. 45–62). Washington, DC: National Association for the Education of Young Children.

Miller, K. (1989, Summer). Infants and toddlers outside. *Texas Child Care Quarterly,* 20–29.

Miller, K. (1992). Guidelines for helping non–English–speaking children adjust and communicate. In B. Neugebauer (Ed.), *Alike and different: Exploring our humanity with young children* (pp. 50–53). Washington, DC: National Association for the Education of Young Children.

Morrison, G. S. (1988). *Education and development of infants, toddlers, and preschoolers.* Glenview, IL: Scott, Foresman.

Muenchow, S., & Seitz, V. (1980, September). How play begins. *Parents,* pp. 61–64.

Nimnicht, G., Arango, M., & Adcock, D. (1977). The parent/child toy library. In M. Day & R. Parker (Eds.), *The preschool in action* (2nd ed.) (pp. 129–148). Boston: Allyn & Bacon.

Packer, A. B., Milner, S. C., & Hong, M. H. (1992). Lost in a distant land: The foreign child's dilemma in child care. In B. Neugebauer (Ed.), *Alike and different: Exploring our humanity with young children* (pp. 42–49). Washington, DC: National Association for the Education of Young Children.

Phillips, C. B. (1990). The Child Development Associate Program: Entering a new era. *Young Children, 45*, 24–27.

Pizzo, P. D. (1990). Family–centered Head Start for infants and toddlers: A renewed direction for Project Head Start. *Young Children, 45*, 30–35.

Powell, D. R. (1989). *Families and early childhood programs*. Washington, DC: National Association for the Education of Young Children.

Public Health Service (1976). 200 years of child health in America. In E. H. Grotberg (Ed.), *200 years of children* (pp. 61–122). Washington, DC: U.S. Government Printing Office.

Recken, R. (1989). Accreditation update: Who gets accredited? *Young Children, 44*, 11–12.

Segal, M., & Adcock, D. (1979). *From birth to one year/From one to two years*. Rolling Hills Estates, CA: B. L. Winch and Associates.

Sexton, D. (1990). Quality integrated programs for infants and toddlers with special needs. In E. Surbeck & M. F. Kelley (Eds.), *Personalizing care with infants, toddlers, and families* (pp. 41–51). Wheaton, MD: Association for Childhood Education International.

Silverstein, R. (1989). A window of opportunity: P. L. 99-457. In C. Berman & E. Szanton (Eds.), *The intent and spirit of P. L. 99-457: A sourcebook*. Washington, DC: National Center for Clinical Infant Programs.

Skeels, H. M. (1966). Adult status of children with contrasting early life experiences. *Monographs of the Society for Research in Child Development, 31*(Serial No. 105).

Weiser, M. G. (1991). *Infant/toddler care and education* (2nd ed.). Columbus, OH: Merrill.

White, B. L., & Watts, J. C. (1973). *Experience and environment: Major influences in the development of the young child* (Vol. 1). Englewood Cliffs, NJ: Prentice–Hall.

Willis, A., & Ricciuti, H. (1975). *A good beginning for babies: Guidelines for group care*. Washington, DC: National Association for the Education of Young Children.

Wortham, S. C. (1990). Infant–toddler playgrounds. In S. C. Wortham and J. L. Frost (Eds.), *Playgrounds for young children: National survey and perspectives* (pp. 69–88). Reston, VA: American Alliance for Health, Physical Education, Recreation and Dance.

Wortham, S., & Wortham, M. (1989). Infant/toddler development and play: Designing creative play environments. *Childhood Education, 65*, 295–299.

CHAPTER FIVE

Infant–Toddler Curriculum: Birth to Age Two

In chapter 4 we discussed the evolution of educational programs for infants and toddlers. Infant–toddler child care of the past was described as having been expanded and developed into today's programs, which serve all types of very young children through educational care, intervention, and enrichment. The important role played by caregivers and the environment in providing developmental experiences for infants and toddlers was also described; play and adult-child interactions are very significant in infant–toddler programs. The curriculum for infants and toddlers was explained in terms of physical, social-emotional, and cognitive development. We described a developmental curriculum based on themes for toddlers, introducing the concept of an integrated curriculum that will be further developed for preschool and primary-age children in early childhood programs discussed throughout this text.

In this chapter, we will focus on the activities and experiences that can be planned for the developmental curriculum for infants and toddlers. The curriculum for physical development, cognitive development, language development, social development, and the expressive arts will be discussed in terms of how infants and toddlers acquire each category of development. We provide examples of activities that are appropriate for infants and toddlers. The activities described within the developmental curriculum will be matched to the developmental characteristics listed in chapter 3 in the Wortham Developmental Checklist for Infants and Toddlers, for babies from birth to twenty-four months.

CURRICULUM FOR PHYSICAL DEVELOPMENT

Nurturing Physical Development in Infants and Toddlers

During the first eighteen months the infant and toddler are in what Piaget termed the sensorimotor stage of development. The individual learns about the environment through his or her senses and by performing physical activities. As motor skills develop, so do the possibilities for experiencing the environment. The physical abilities of newborn infants are very limited; initially, they use reflexive movements such as blinking, swallowing, and alternately kicking the legs. These reflexes either are precursors of later skills or are protective. At about eight months, movements become more voluntary—they are no longer automatic. Voluntary physical movements are categorized as gross motor, involving the large muscles, and fine motor, involving the small muscles (Gonzalez-Mena & Eyer, 1980).

Motor skill development occurs through movement. Much of the development in gross and fine motor skills occurs naturally as the infant and toddler use emerging physical skills to extend their possibilities to experience their surroundings. Physical actions are the first medium that infants and toddlers have for communication and expression. They use movement to express their state of being and their feelings, to communicate their needs in concert with vocalizations, such as cooing or crying (Weiser, 1991).

Motor skill development also occurs through the acquisition of body management skills, or body control. Body control begins with the head and neck and progresses downward along the spine in the cephalocaudal process. Body management skills are acquired from the center of the body out to the limbs in a proximodistal process. The infant is able to control the center of the body first and the hands and fingers last. In this sequence, gross motor skills precede fine motor skills (Gober & Franks, 1988).

Motor skills are acquired very rapidly. Much of the energy expended by infants during their waking hours involves physical activity. In the following section, experiences for infants and toddlers that will promote physical development are described. The activities are coded to the Wortham developmental checklists in chapter 3 (Figures 3.3, 3.4, and 3.5).

Experiences for Physical Development in Infants

Practicing Eye Movement

Age: Birth to six months

Checklist skill (3) Follows a moving person or object with eyes
Hold the baby in your arms or in your lap. Introduce a new toy by holding it in front of the baby's eyes. Slowly move the toy back and forth and allow the baby to follow

the movement. When the baby tires, stop the activity. If the activity is resumed, introduce a new toy or object.

Materials needed: Infant toys

Patterns and Faces

Age: Birth to six months

Checklist skill (4) Looks at suspended object
Very young infants prefer looking at patterns or faces to bright colors. Patterns can be placed on the side of the crib or held for the infant to look at while he or she is lying in a caretaker's lap. Checkerboard and bull's-eye designs, simple geometric shapes, and large, simple faces attract the baby's visual attention.

Materials needed: Checkerboard and bull's-eye designs; geometric shapes; drawings of simple faces

Suspended Crib Toy

Age: Birth to six months

Checklist skill (6) Moves arms and legs actively
Hang a toy on the crib that will move when the baby moves his or her arms or legs. The more the baby moves, the more he or she will be rewarded by the movement of the toy. Babies also enjoy being able to activate a toy by hitting at it or kicking it.

Materials needed: Crib toy that moves easily; brightly colored pictures suspended across the crib

Rolling Over

Age: Birth to six months

Checklist skill (9) Learns to roll over
As the baby begins to gain control of his or her arms and legs, the baby will begin trying to roll over. Daily opportunities to play on a pad or blanket on the floor will encourage learning to roll over. Alternately place baby on tummy and then on back. To encourage rolling from back to tummy, introduce a toy so that the baby must reach for it. Gradually move the toy farther away until the baby must roll to grasp it. Praise all efforts.

Materials needed: Small toys to grasp

Grab It

Age: **Birth to six months**

Checklist skill (11) Uses eye–hand coordination in reaching
As you observe the baby during the first few months, you will notice that he or she is trying to reach for a toy. To accomplish this skill, eyes and hands have to be coordinated. To encourage reaching skills, hold or suspend a toy or object over the baby lying in a prone position. At first, the toy should be placed very close to the baby. As reaching skills improve, move the toy farther away.

Materials needed: Small toy; yarn

Another Toy

Age: **Six to twelve months**

Checklist skill (2) Transfers object from one hand to another
Babies will naturally learn to transfer an object from one hand to another. Offer the baby a toy. Then offer a second toy. At first, the first toy will be dropped. Show the baby how to transfer the toy. Repeat.

Materials needed: Small toys

Cereal Snack

Age: **Six to twelve months**

Checklist skill (4) Picks up small things with thumb and forefinger
Place a few pieces of cereal, such as Cheerios, on the high-chair tray. Show the baby how to pick up one. When all have been grasped and eaten, place a few more on the tray.

Materials needed: Cereal pieces

Getting Around

Age: **Six to twelve months**

Checklist skill (9) Creeps or gets from one place to another
To encourage creeping and crawling, provide the baby with opportunities to play on the floor or outside on a pad or quilt. Place a popular toy just out of reach and encourage baby to try to reach for the toy. Reward all attempts with smiles and approving language.

Materials needed: Blanket; toys

Hit It

Age: Six to twelve months

Checklist skill (11) Stands holding on
Once the baby has learned to pull up to a standing position, he or she enjoys the opportunity to practice the new skill. To make standing fun, place two chairs facing each other. Suspend a rope between the chairs and hang toys or household items from the rope. Encourage the baby to stand holding on to the chair and hit at the objects.

Materials needed: Two sturdy chairs; rope; small toys or household items; yarn to attach objects to the rope

Walk the Maze

Age: Six to twelve months

Checklist skill (12) Walks holding on
Set up chairs, soft forms, or other infant furniture into a maze so that the baby can walk continuously holding on in a complete pattern. On other occasions, make different arrangements so that there will be a variety of "mazes" to experience.

Materials needed: Sturdy furniture or plastic-covered foam shapes that can be arranged into an enclosure

Drop It

Age: Six to twelve months

Checklist skill (13) Drops or places objects into a container
When the baby is able to grasp and hold objects, he or she soon learns to drop them with some control. The adult can encourage hand control by playing a dropping game with the baby. Using small objects such as cubes and a container, the adult picks up an object and drops it in the container. The baby is then given an object and encouraged to drop it in the container. The baby should be praised for all efforts.

Materials needed: Container such as a basket, pan, or bowl; small blocks, cubes, or toys to drop into the container

Surprise Box

Age: Six to twelve months

Checklist skill (13) Drops or places objects into a container

Use a shoe box or other container with a lid. Place small toys in the box. Show the baby how to remove the lid and "find" the objects. Show how to put the objects back into the container and replace the lid. Repeat with different toys.

Materials needed: Box or large can with lid; small toys

Experiences for Physical Development in Toddlers

Throw It!

Age: Twelve to eighteen months

Checklist skill (1) Throws ball
Toddlers love to throw, and balls are a favorite toy. Provide the toddler with a soft sponge or rubber ball that can easily be held in one hand. Take turns throwing the ball back and forth for a short distance. As the toddler gains competence, lengthen the distance. Use a larger ball requiring the toddler to use both hands for a different throwing experience.

Materials needed: Sponge or rubber ball

I Can Build

Age: Twelve to eighteen months

Checklist skill (2) Builds two-block tower
Use a set of traditional wooden blocks or plastic blocks that are about two inches square. Demonstrate how to line them in a row and how to stack them. Larger, light-weight cardboard blocks can also be used to build a tower.

Materials needed: Small wooden or plastic blocks or large cardboard blocks

What Can You Make?

Age: Twelve to eighteen months

Checklist skill (2) Builds two-block tower
Gather a collection of small, sturdy cardboard boxes and other stackable containers. Cover them with Con-Tact paper. Help the toddler stack the containers. Encourage the toddler to try his or her own system of arranging and stacking. Round containers such as coffee cans and oatmeal boxes can also be covered and used for stacking.

Materials needed: Empty containers covered with Con-Tact paper

Walking Here, Walking There

Age: Twelve to eighteen months

Checklist skill (3) Walks well
Take the toddler outdoors for a walk. Find different types of walking surfaces to experience. Practice walking on sidewalks and uneven ground. Find different kinds of paved surfaces and walk up gradually sloping grassy surfaces and natural paths.

Materials needed: None

Big Steps, Little Steps

Age: Twelve to eighteen months

Checklist skill (3) Walks well
Walk with the toddler in an open area. Show the child how to take big steps and little steps. Practice running on tiptoe and taking running steps. Make taking the different kinds of steps into a game. Talk about the kinds of steps you are taking.

Materials needed: None

A Little Dance

Age: Twelve to eighteen months

Checklist skill (4) Walks backward
Put on a record or tape of slow music and try a simple dance. First take forward steps with the toddler. Occasionally take a backward step. Alert the toddler some time before a backward step is taken.

Materials needed: Music

Learning About Spoons

Age: Twelve to eighteen months

Checklist skill (8) Uses spoon with little help
Put dried beans such as pinto or large navy beans into a shallow dish. Show the toddler how to use a spoon to transfer the beans to a second dish. Start with a few beans at first and increase as dexterity is acquired.

Materials needed: Spoon; beans; shallow dishes

Scribbling

Age: Twelve to eighteen months

Checklist skill (11) Scribbles
Give the toddler large pieces of paper and a large crayon. Show the child how to make marks on the paper. Offer a different color. Name the colors as they are used. Praise all efforts. Put the completed "pictures" where they can be admired.

Materials needed: Large paper; large crayons

Kick It Back!

Age: Eighteen to twenty-four months

Checklist skill (3) Kicks ball forward
Engage the toddler in a game of kicking a ball back and forth. Start with a short distance and gradually move farther away. Encourage the toddler to use both feet, rather than kicking with one foot every time.

Materials needed: Large rubber ball

Balls and Balls

Age: Eighteen to twenty-four months

Checklist skill (4) Throws ball overhand
Gather several different balls that can easily be held in one hand. Demonstrate how to throw the ball using an overhand motion. Enjoy taking turns throwing the different balls with the toddler.

Materials needed: An assortment of small balls

Follow Me

Age: Eighteen to twenty-four months

Checklist skill (5) Walks up steps
Cut footprints the size of the toddler's feet in various bright colors. Attach them to the floor and up a three-stair climber. Have the child step on the patterns as he or she climbs up and down the stairs using alternating feet. Don't push if the toddler is not ready.

Materials needed: Cut-outs of foot shapes on colored paper; tape; low set of stairs

Run! Run! Run!

Age: Eighteen to twenty-four months

Checklist skill (6) Runs
Mark three large circles with rope in an open area. With a toddler or group of toddlers, start in a circle and run to another circle. Pause, and then run to the third circle. Later, widen the distance between the circles. If a wooded area is available, toddlers can run to marked trees. On a playground, they can run from one piece of equipment to another.

Materials needed: Lengths of rope or other materials to mark goals

Running Like the Wind

Age: Eighteen to twenty-four months

Checklist skill (6) Runs
Give each toddler a paper streamer or a scarf. Show them how to run holding the streamer. Use an open, grassy area for running and observing the streamer as it flutters behind.

Materials needed: Paper streamers or scarves

Pouring Rice

Age: Eighteen to twenty-four months

Checklist skill (10) Drinks from cup or glass
To improve motor skills used to drink from a cup or glass, let the toddler pour from various types of cups and glasses. Fill a plastic dishtub half full of rice. Show the toddler how to pour the rice from one container to another. For a group of toddlers, spread an old bed sheet on the floor and provide each toddler with a plastic tub, rice, and plastic cups and glasses.

Materials needed: Plastic dishtubs; rice; plastic cups and glasses of various sizes

CURRICULUM FOR COGNITIVE DEVELOPMENT

Nurturing Cognitive Development in Infants and Toddlers

In the section on physical development, we described infant development as involving the senses and physical actions to learn about the world. Physical movement and development of body control facilitates learning; likewise, the senses are used to take information that leads to cognitive development. Because infants use their senses and physical actions simultaneously, the two cannot be separated. The senses cannot be used without physical action.

Cognitive development is the means for learning. Through the acquisition of cognition, infants and toddlers learn and become intelligent beings. Learning leads to understanding. Weiser (1991) proposes that understanding involves three steps: infants (1) take in information with their senses, (2) process it, and (3) use it to understand.

Caregivers and parents have a significant role in nurturing cognitive development because there are affective dimensions to learning. Infants and toddlers not only need to have the capacity to learn—they also need to be motivated to want to find out about the world. They need to have the disposition to acquire knowledge (Katz, 1988). The goal for parents and caregivers is not only to help infants and toddlers be exposed to experiences that will develop cognition but also to guide them to perceiving that learning is an enjoyable process.

In the following pages, activities that will provide cognitive experiences are explained. The activities are matched to checklist characteristics described in the Wortham developmental checklists in chapter 3 (Figures 3.3, 3.4, and 3.5).

Experiences for Cognitive Development in Infants

Propping Up Baby

Age: Birth to six months

Checklist skills (3) Follows a moving person or object with eyes; (10) Looks at objects and realistic pictures
Just as babies need to be held in different positions, they also need to be placed in different positions so that they can observe their surroundings from different perspectives. Babies can be seated in an infant seat or on a beanbag chair or propped up in a seated position with pillows. They can observe the movement and activities of others, view pictures, and observe natural features of the outdoor environment.

Materials needed: Beanbag chair; pillows

Looking and Finding

Age: Birth to six months

Checklist skill (3) Follows a moving person or object with eyes
Babies love to watch the movements of their caretaker. As they gain experience, they are able to locate adults by the location of their voice. Play a game by calling to the baby from different locations. When the baby turns his or her head to locate your voice, reward the baby with hugs and praise. The baby should be placed in different positions—on the back and tummy and in seated positions—to stimulate different kinds of movement to locate the adult playing the game.

Materials needed: None

Crib Mobiles

Age: Birth to six months

Checklist skill (4) Looks at suspended object
At a very young age, babies are able to focus visually on items hanging from the crib. Interesting household items can be suspended over the baby's crib. It is important that the objects are beyond the infant's ability to grasp if they can possibly be harmful. Because infants need moderate variety to maintain interest, new materials can be introduced when the baby appears to be bored with the existing objects.

Materials needed: Strap to attach across the crib; yarn; rubber kitchen tools or toys to suspend

Looking, Looking

Age: Birth to six months

Checklist skill (10) Looks at objects and realistic pictures
Babies are interested in looking at objects and pictures in their environment. When they are sitting in the caregiver's lap, they can be introduced to pictures in a magazine or picture book. They also enjoy being carried about and shown plants, grass, flowers, pets, and interesting objects. Looking activities should be accompanied by conversation about the things observed.

Materials needed: Objects, animals, plants, etc., from the indoor and outdoor environment; pictures; picture books

What Do You Hear?

Age: Birth to six months

Checklist skill (12) Turns head to sound of bell or rattle
Infants are attentive to new sounds. To give the baby practice in hearing and listening, use a rattle or bell in a listening game. Seat the baby in the parent's or caretaker's lap. Come from behind the baby and ring the bell. The baby will soon turn toward the new sound. Reward the baby by offering the toy to be held and explored.

Materials needed: Bell, rattle, or other toy that makes noise

Find It

Age: Six to twelve months

Checklist skill (5) Uncovers hidden toy

Between six and twelve months, most babies learn object permanence. To nurture this developmental milestone, tie brightly colored ribbons to small toys. Hide the toys with the ribbon showing. Show the baby how to pull the ribbon to find the toy. Praise all efforts.

Materials needed: Ribbons of several colors; small toys

Texture Fun

Age: Six to twelve months

Checklist skill (14) Manipulates objects

Babies love to experiment with materials that have different surfaces, textures, and sounds. Give babies wax paper, cellophane wrap, newspaper, a soft towel, or gift-wrapping paper. Supervise carefully because the materials may end up in their mouths.

Materials needed: Cellophane wrap; paper of various colors and textures; etc.

Nesting Cups

Age: Six to twelve months

Checklist skill (14) Manipulates objects

Give the baby a set of measuring cups or toy nesting cups to explore. Show the child how to place a smaller cup into a larger one. Praise all efforts. Measuring spoons will add to the interest in the activity.

Materials needed: Nested measuring cups or toys; measuring spoons

Simon Says

Age: Six to twelve months

Checklist skill (16) Imitates actions

In this simplified version of "Simon Says," the adult initiates activities such as clapping hands for the baby to imitate. "Pat-a-Cake" is also an example of an imitating game. The adult first models the actions and encourages the baby to do it also. Touching and naming nose, knees, etc. can be imitated. Traditional imitating activities taught to babies include giving a kiss, throwing a kiss, and waving bye-bye.

Materials Needed: None

Experiences for Cognitive Development in Toddlers

Egg Hunt

Age: Twelve to eighteen months

Checklist skill (1) Pursues and retrieves a toy that is out of sight
Hide plastic Easter eggs so that only part of each one is hidden. Show the toddlers how to find the eggs. At first, make the eggs fairly obvious. After more experience, leave less and less of the egg in sight.

Materials needed: Large plastic Easter eggs or hosiery containers shaped like eggs

Mailman

Age: Twelve to eighteen months

Checklist skill (1) Pursues and retrieves a toy that is out of sight
Put toys or other interesting objects in letter envelopes or manila mailing envelopes. Put the "mail" in a large box. Invite the toddler to pick out an envelope and find what is inside. After the game has been repeated several times, change the items in the envelopes.

Materials needed: Small and large envelopes; toys and other items to be put into the envelopes

Clothespins in the Can

Age: Twelve to eighteen months

Checklist skill (2) Puts objects in and out of container
Cover a coffee can with Con-Tact paper. Cut a round hole larger than a clothespin in the plastic lid. Show the toddler how to put clothespins (try to use round clothespins) through the hole. Count the clothespins as they are placed through the hole. When all of the clothespins are in the can, show the toddler how to take off the lid and dump them out. Repeat.

Materials needed: Coffee can or other container with a plastic lid; clothespins

Ring, Ring

Age: Twelve to eighteen months

Checklist skill (3) Role plays with familiar objects
Provide toddlers with old telephones or play telephones. Show them how to dial the number and "talk" on the telephone. Encourage them to call someone in their fam-

ily. Become involved in the role play by pretending you are talking to someone on the telephone.

Materials needed: Toy telephones or discarded telephones

Going Shopping

Age: Twelve to eighteen months

Checklist skill (3) Role plays with familiar objects
Collect empty food containers. Put the containers on a low table or shelf. Show the toddler how to go shopping using a large basket, bag, or play grocery cart. Talk about what the toddler is going to buy. After items have been selected, name each one and encourage the toddler to take out the named item. Change items to provide variety and new vocabulary opportunities.

Materials needed: Empty food containers; bag, basket, or cart for shopping

Hat Game

Age: Twelve to eighteen months

Checklist skill (4) Recognizes and responds to self in mirror
Make a collection of old hats, the more outrageous the better. Show the toddler how to try on the hats and look in the mirror. Enjoy taking turns and recognizing each other in the funny hats. Be sure to have hats for both males and females and encourage the toddler to try on all types of hats.

Materials needed: A collection of hats

Puzzle Play

Age: Twelve to eighteen months

Checklist skill (5) Solves simple puzzles or constructions
Purchase simple puzzles with two or three parts or make puzzles by mounting a picture on cardboard and cutting it into two or three pieces. Wooden puzzles should have knobs for picking up the pieces. Show toddlers how to assemble the puzzle. Praise all efforts. When the puzzles are too easy, increase the number of pieces. An endless supply of puzzles may be made from empty food boxes.

Materials needed: Puzzles with two or three pieces, either purchased or hand constructed

Mechanical Toys

Age: Eighteen to twenty-four months

Checklist skill (1) Demonstrates perception of correct function of toy
There are many toys available that require the toddler to push buttons, pull levers, or perform some other physical action to activate the toy. Introduce the toddler to such a toy and demonstrate its function. When interest lags, put the toy away for a while and substitute another toy.

Materials needed: Toys with mechanical function

Outside Toys

Age: Eighteen to twenty-four months

Checklist skill (1) Demonstrates perception of correct function of toy
Make available a variety of outdoor push and pull toys. Show the child how to "cut the grass" with a toy lawnmower, or to push a doll in a doll carriage. When the toddler is playing with a toy, talk to him or her about the activity and the use of the toy.

Materials needed: Push and pull toys

More Shapes

Age: Eighteen to twenty-four months

Checklist skill (3) Places correct shape in shape box
Make or acquire a "shape box" with five different shapes. Invite the toddler to experiment with putting shapes into the correct holes. If the toddler finds the task too difficult, show how the shaped pieces fit.

Materials needed: Shape toy with five or more pieces

Soap Bubbles

Age: Eighteen to twenty-four months

Checklist skill (4) Uses housekeeping toys
Fill a plastic dishpan about half full of water. Add liquid detergent. Show the toddler how to use a whisk or eggbeater to make soap bubbles. Toddlers may be more interested in playing in the soapsuds with their hands. A large piece of plastic may be needed to protect surfaces. A child's apron will protect the toddler's clothing. A water play table may be used for a group of toddlers.

Materials needed: Dishpan; detergent; eggbeater or whisk; plastic sheeting; aprons

Playhouse

Age: Eighteen to twenty-four months

Checklist skill (4) Uses housekeeping toys
Make a playhouse by putting an old sheet over a table. Cut an opening for a door. Put play dishes, child's sleeping bag, or other dramatic play toys in the playhouse. Invite the toddler to enjoy pretending in the house.

Materials needed: Table; old sheet; playhouse toys

Here I Am

Age: Eighteen to twenty-four months

Checklist skill (5) Recognizes self in photograph
Make a book of individual and group photographs that include pictures of the toddlers. As you look through the book together, ask toddlers to find themselves or identify another in the pictures.

Materials needed: A collection of photographs or photograph book

Find Another One

Age: Eighteen to twenty-four months

Checklist skill (6) Matches familiar objects by color
Select six wooden cubes or other objects: two red, two yellow, and two blue. Put one of each color in front of the toddler. Select one of the other three cubes and show the toddler how to match it with the same color. Repeat with each of the cubes. Reward all efforts. Discuss the colors of the objects as they are matched.

Materials needed: Two cubes or other objects of each color: red, yellow, blue

One More

Age: Eighteen to twenty-four months

Checklist skill (8) Understands "one more"
Engage in a game counting objects with the toddler. Stop after counting to three or four. Add one more to the group of objects and say, "One more." After repeating the activity several times, ask the toddler to give you "one more."

Materials needed: Toys or objects to count

Put It Away

Age: Eighteen to twenty-four months

Checklist skill (9) Returns toy to correct place
Divide a toy shelf into three or four spaces with colored tape. Choose four toys to arrange in the spaces. Find a picture of the toy in a catalog. If no picture is available, draw a simple picture to represent the toy. Play a game of putting toys on the shelf to match the picture. At the end of play times, help toddlers replace toys in the correct spot. When one shelf has been mastered, add another shelf of toys.

Materials needed: Storage shelf; toys; pictures or drawings of toys

Feeling

Age: Eighteen to twenty-four months

Checklist skill (Social-Emotional Development) (5) Shows interest in exploring new places
Take toddlers on a feeling expedition outdoors. Show them different elements in the playscape such as grass, sand, tree bark, etc. Help them to touch and experience the texture and verbally describe it for them.

Materials needed: None

Bug Hunt

Age: Eighteen to twenty-four months

Checklist skill (Social-Emotional Development) (5) Shows interest in exploring new places
Help toddlers be on the alert for insects in the outdoor environment. Show them how to look for bugs on the ground, on trees and flowers, or on fences. If possible, collect the bugs for them and put them in a jar for them to observe with adult supervision.

Materials needed: Bug nets and cages or glass jar with lid and air holes

CURRICULUM FOR LANGUAGE DEVELOPMENT

Nurturing Language Development in Infants and Toddlers

Although true vocalizations and communication using language do not generally occur before the end of the first year, the process of acquiring language begins at birth, or even before birth. The tremendous task of learning to use language to communicate with others begins with the infant's using the sense of hearing to understand sounds and language in his or her environment. Infants and toddlers must learn the sounds, or phonology, of the language; the semantics, or meaning, of the language; the formation of words, or the syntax and grammar, in the language; and the actual logistics of communication, or pragmatics, of the language (Weiser, 1991). The process of learning all of these language components begins in the early months of the first year and continues throughout life, although the basic systems of the language are mastered by the time the young child enters school.

Theorists have different perspectives about how language is acquired. Skinner (1957) proposed that adults provide the language model that children acquire through imitation. Language and thought are initiated through interactions between adult and child. Innatists (Chomsky, 1965; Lennenberg, 1967; McNeil, 1970) believe children have an internal ability to learn language; as the child matures, language expands. Piaget (Piaget & Inhelder, 1969) proposed that language results from children's experiences with language in their world; early language reflects the child's sensory experiences. Vygotsky (1978) believed that social relationships affect the child's speech in that adult language and encouragement for the child's language match the child's need for help with language.

Infants and toddlers are encouraged to speak when they are reinforced by adults for their efforts. Likewise, they use language, once they are able to verbally communicate, to describe their actions and cognitive progress. They learn vocabulary by imitating the words they hear, although they impose their own level of syntax upon the words they use. In effect, the complex nature of language acquisition is explained in part by each of the theories, although none of them provides a complete understanding of the process.

The role of adults is significant in the development of language in infants and toddlers. The verbal environment provided by adults and supporting interactions that include verbal communication are necessary if the child is to hear and attempt to use language. Literacy is also part of language development. The use of books and stories with infants and toddlers is part of the continuum in becoming able to read and write, in addition to being able to listen and speak (Morrow, 1989).

Very young children who come from homes where a language other than English is spoken have special needs in language development. These infants and toddlers are encountering a different language in the caregiving setting than in the home. They are being exposed to and learning two languages. Miller (1992) suggests that adults in the caregiving setting can help their non-English-speaking children to adjust to the new language and learn to use it by following the following guidelines:

1. Build trust by helping the child feel safe and secure. To make the child feel comfortable, hold and otherwise touch the child, use eye contact, and smile at the child.
2. Use key words in the child's language. Find out from the parents how the child communicates his or her needs.
3. Be a good model by speaking slowly and clearly. Model the use of complete sentences and extend the child's single-word utterances.

4. Build receptive language through talking about what is happening. Talk to the child about what he or she is doing and the sequence of routines and events in the classroom.
5. Encourage productive language by encouraging the child to use key social words such as "thank you," "yes," "no," and "okay."
6. Try to understand nonverbal communication by observing the child's efforts to communicate through gestures and sounds and using verbalizations to interpret for the child.
7. Encourage the child to interact with other children in the classroom. Social interactions will help in socialization and provide experiences with language.

In the following section we present activities that caregivers can use to implement a curriculum for language development. The activities are related to the Wortham developmental checklists in chapter 3 (Figures 3.3, 3.4, and 3.5). For infants under six months, the checklist items are found in the "Social-Emotional Development" section; for children six to twelve months they are part of the "Physical-Cognitive Development" section; for those who are older than twelve months, checklist items are in the "Language Development" section.

Experiences for Language Development in Infants

Little Talks

Age: Birth to six months

Checklist skills (3) Responds to talking, smiling, or touching; (6) Vocalizes in association with pleasure, displeasure, eagerness, and satisfaction
Provide frequent opportunities when the baby is rested and fed to hold and talk to him or her. The baby should be held close enough to view your face as you talk and smile. If the baby vocalizes, smile and reflect the vocalization. Both the infant and adult reinforce their loving attachment from positive "conversations" with each other.

Materials needed: None

Body Parts

Age: Birth to six months

Checklist skill (3) Responds to talking, smiling, or touching
Place the baby in your lap or on the floor on a blanket. Touch and pat the baby on different parts of the body as you name them. All vocal conversation should be accompanied by smiles. If the baby also vocalizes, these should be rewarded with more smiling and talk.

Materials needed: None

Communicating Feelings

Age: Birth to six months

Checklist skill (6) Vocalizes in association with pleasure, displeasure, eagerness, and satisfaction
During the first six months the infant begins to communicate different kinds of feelings through vocalizations. On some occasions babies will coo when interacting with an adult. When tired, hungry, or frustrated, fretting vocalizations or crying will occur. Respond to different kinds of communication with understanding. Talk to the baby concerning your understanding about how he or she feels.

Materials needed: None

Laugh with Me

Age: Birth to six months

Checklist skill (9) Chuckles and laughs
Babies love to "talk" with familiar people. As they gain experience with communicating, they first coo and soon chuckle or laugh. Lay baby in your lap facing you when he or she seems to be in a mood to "chat." Talk to baby, smiling and laughing. The infant will let you know if he or she wants to escalate the fun. You will soon know which kinds of conversation or physical movement on your part will bring forth chuckles and laughs. When baby tires of the activity, change to something quieter.

Materials needed: None

Talking with Baby

Age: Six to twelve months

Checklist skill (8) Imitates speech sounds
Although infants cannot vocalize true words at this age, they are able to vocalize and imitate sounds. You can initiate a "conversation" or respond to the infant's efforts to use sound to communicate. Hold the baby in your lap facing you, and acknowledge a sound made by the baby and imitate it. You can then initiate a sound such as "ba-ba-ba" and encourage the baby to make the same sound. All efforts should be rewarded.

Materials needed: None

Learning New Words

Age: Six to twelve months

Checklist skill (8) Imitates speech sounds

The infant can begin to learn names of things in the environment, although the names cannot be verbalized. While the baby is playing, introduce or name things in nearby areas. If the baby responds or tries to imitate your speech, praise and reinforce the efforts and repeat the names of the objects. Repeat the activity with the same and different items.

Materials needed: Toys and other items in the environment

Hi and Bye-Bye

Age: Six to twelve months

Checklist skill (15) Says single words such as "mama" and "dada"
One of baby's first ways to communicate is to say "hi" and "bye-bye." Wave to the baby, saying these words, and encourage baby to imitate you. Use other familiar words, such as names of pets, siblings, etc. Praise all efforts.

Materials needed: None

Encouraging Language for Communication

Age: Six to twelve months

Checklist skill (Social-Emotional Development) (8) Uses motions or gestures to communicate (holds out arms to be picked up)
Before infants are able to talk, they use gestures to let the caretaker know what is wanted. The baby will gesture or point, or perhaps whine. To encourage positive communication, ask the baby what he or she wants. "Do you want a banana?" "Can you say, 'banana'?" Praise efforts to verbalize. "Good. You said 'banana.' Here is the banana." Repeat for different gestures, each time modeling for the baby how to use words or positive verbalization rather than gestures or whining.

Materials needed: None

Experiences for Language Development in Toddlers

Talk to Me

Age: Twelve to eighteen months

Checklist skill (1) Says single words (may add two and three words)
Before the baby can say words, he or she babbles, using vocalizations that sound like words. Because the baby's first words stand for a complete thought, the adult tries to determine what the baby is expressing and reflect the communication. For example, if the baby says, "light," the adult may say, "Yes, that is a light." Praise all the efforts to communicate by responding to the baby's utterances.

Where Are Your Eyes?

Age: Twelve to eighteen months

Checklist skill (2) Points to a body part on request
Before the toddler can name things, he or she can point to them. Toddlers are interested in their body and respond to learning the names of body parts. Adults can help toddlers learn the names by pointing to each body part and naming them. Later they can play a question game such as "Where are your eyes?" or "Show me your mouth." When the toddler has mastered pointing to major body parts, add others. When the names of the body parts can be verbalized, ask the toddler to name them as you point to them.

Materials needed: None

Body Puzzle

Age: Twelve to eighteen months

Checklist skill (2) Points to a body part on request
Make a puzzle by gluing a simple doll picture on cardboard and cutting out the body parts or gluing the picture on flannel and using it on a flannel board. Show the toddler how to assemble the puzzle. Ask the toddler to put on the arms, legs, etc. Name the body parts and have the toddler point to each one.

Materials needed: Body puzzle made from a picture of a doll or human figure glued to cardboard or flannel and cut out by body parts

Names in Books

Age: Twelve to eighteen months

Checklist skill (3) Imitates words
Select beginner books that feature objects, toys, or animals that are familiar to the baby. As you and the toddler look at the book, name each picture. Encourage the baby to say the name of the picture after you. Repeat many times with many books.

Materials needed: Simple picture books

Where, Oh Where?

Age: Twelve to eighteen months

Checklist skill (4) Responds to a single request
Sing the song, "Where, oh where is dear little _____?" The toddler points to him- or herself when requested. The song can be expanded to other children, pets, etc. The toddler points to the things named in the tune. In a group setting, the toddlers

can point to the person named in the tune. This activity teaches vocabulary, as well as how to follow a request.

Materials needed: None

Old MacDonald

Age: Twelve to eighteen months

Checklist skill (5) Says the names of at least five things
Make of book of pictures of animals or select an animal picture book. Adapt the song "Old MacDonald" to fit the pictures in the book. As you look at the book with the toddler, sing the song, leaving out the name of the animal in the pictures. Encourage the toddler to supply the missing name. Provide help when needed.

Materials needed: Picture book of farm animals

Outside Talk

Age: Twelve to eighteen months

Checklist skill (5) Says the names of at least five things
When outdoors with toddlers be alert for things in the environment they can observe. Point to a bird flying overhead and name it for the toddlers. Repeat with other elements in the environment. After many experiences, ask the toddlers to name the things that are seen.

Materials needed: None

What Am I Doing?

Age: Eighteen to twenty-four months

Checklist skill (1) Combines two to three different words
Pantomime familiar activities. Ask the child to tell you what you are doing. For example, do the motions for washing your face, putting on clothing, drinking from a glass, etc. Show the toddler how to pantomime an action. Tell what he or she is doing. Repeat, using other activities.

Tell Me About Food

Age: Eighteen to twenty-four months

Checklist skill (1) Combines two to three different words
During mealtime or snacks, talk to the toddler about the food being eaten. Talk about the name of the foods, their color, how they taste, etc. Ask the toddler about

the foods. Praise all responses and voluntary statements. (This process for eliciting language can be used in many everyday activities.)

Materials needed: Mealtime foods or snacks

Here's a Ball

Age: Eighteen to twenty-four months

Checklist skill (1) Combines two to three different words
Learning simple fingerplays helps children to develop language. An example of a simple fingerplay is "Here's a Ball." The adult says the fingerplay and models the actions. Encourage the toddler to imitate the actions and say the words with you.

> *Here's a Ball*
> Here's a ball [make circle with thumb and forefinger],
> And here's a ball [make circle with both hands],
> And a great big ball I see [make circle with both arms].
> Can you count them? Are you ready?
> One [make circle with thumb and forefinger],
> Two [make circle with both hands],
> Three [make circle with both arms]!"

Repeat fingerplays frequently. As toddlers become familiar with them, they enjoy being able to participate in the activity.

Materials needed: Simple fingerplays

Play Talk

Age: Eighteen to twenty-four months

Checklist skill (1) Combines two to three different words
When outdoors talk to the toddlers about different play activities. Encourage them to talk to you about what they are doing. For example, if toddlers are digging in the sand with shovels and pails, make comments about the activity and ask the children to tell you about it. Encourage attempts to share information about the activity.

Materials needed: None

Names, Names

Age: Eighteen to twenty-four months

Checklist skill (3) Names pictures
Construct or collect sets of pictures of categories of things such as animals, foods, furniture, toys, etc. Using one category of pictures, name each picture for the toddler.

Ask the toddler to name them. When possible, relate the picture to the actual item. After many naming activities, go through a set of pictures and see how many the toddler can name without prompting. Praise all efforts.

Materials needed: Sets of pictures of familiar categories of things

Stories

Age: Eighteen to twenty-four months

Checklist skill (3) Names pictures
Read simple storybooks frequently. When the toddler is familiar with the story, look at the pictures and encourage the child to name things in the pictures. Ask the toddler to tell you what is happening in the picture.

Materials needed: Storybooks

Puppets

Age: Eighteen to twenty-four months

Checklist skill (4) Imitates adult speech without prompting
Engage in puppet play with toddlers. Have the puppet "talk" to the child. After the toddler is familiar with the puppet, invite the toddler to make the puppet "talk" to you. Don't push if the toddler is apprehensive.

Materials needed: Familiar puppets

CURRICULUM FOR SOCIAL DEVELOPMENT

Nurturing Social Development in Infants and Toddlers

Social development begins as soon as the neonate engages in the first interactions with the people in his or her environment. Immediately after birth, the infant may be placed on the mother's abdomen and held by the father. These early interactions begin the process of bonding between the parents and the infant. Social interactions that occur in the neonate's times of wakefulness and alertness continue the process of social and emotionaldevelopment.

During the first eighteen months, infants are in what Erikson (1950) said was the first stage of psychosocial development: trust versus mistrust. The dependability and consistency of adult attention to the infant's needs are the basis for positive social and emotional development. The toddler then enters the stage of autonomy versus shame and doubt, when the need to develop a sense of self as an individual emerges. Adult support for exploration and independence facilitate the now mobile individual's quest for affirmation of autonomy.

Many of the activities that are a part of daily routines nurture social and emotional development in infants and toddlers; however, adult caregivers may not be aware of the importance of social interactions that occur as a part of the activities. In a previous section, it was stressed that caregiver verbalizations and communications with infants and toddlers encourage language development. Social interactions likewise nurture social and emotional development. In the activities described below, attention is given to how adult interactions with infants and toddlers can support social development.

Experiences for Social Development in Infants

Ride a Cock-horse

Age: Birth to six months

Checklist skill (1) Looks attentively at an adult
All babies love this game. It gives them an opportunity to gaze directly at the adult's face and interact through vocalizing as the game progresses. Place the baby in your lap facing you, and bounce the baby gently as you repeat the poem. The baby is

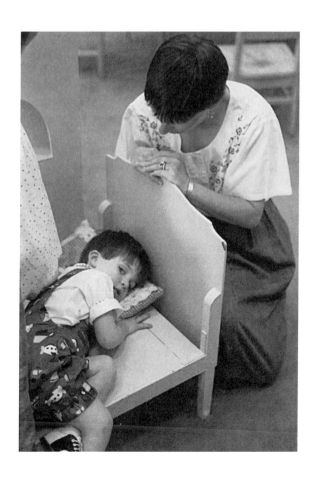

bounced higher on the final word, "goes." Both adult and baby will enjoy the anticipation of the end of the rhyme.

> *Ride a Cock-horse*
> Ride a cock-horse to Banbury Cross
> To see a fine lady upon a white horse;
> Rings on her fingers, and bells on her toes,
> She shall make music wherever she goes.

Holding Baby

Age: Birth to six months

Checklist skill (2) Adjusts body to the way the adult holds him/her
Hold the baby in various positions: on your shoulder, cradling in your arms, etc. Place picture, patterns, etc., within the baby's line of vision. Vary where you stand or sit so that the baby will have a variety of things to see. The baby learns trust and love by being held and cuddled. Talking to the baby reinforces the communication felt through bodily contact.

Materials needed: Colorful patterns, pictures, or objects for the infant to see

Up and Down

Age: Birth to six months
Checklist skill (3) Responds to talking, smiling, touching
The baby enjoys the play of being lifted up and down gently as the adult smiles and talks. Trust in the adult develops as the enjoyment of physical action reinforces the bond of attachment between the baby and adult. The adult should maintain eye contact with the baby as the baby is lifted gently or raised up over the adult's head in a playful gesture. The baby will respond to the adult's pleasure in the activity.

Materials needed: None

Hold Me

Age: Birth to six months

Checklist skill (4) Quiets when picked up
When an infant is upset, he or she wants to be held. Very young babies are still adjusting to a new environment. Knowing that he or she will be held builds a feeling of security and trust. When the baby is upset, hold it close as you talk in a soothing voice. Touching, patting, and stroking also help to reassure a fretful baby. The baby is also reassured by the tactile feeling of being enclosed securely in a warm blanket.

Materials needed: None

Baby Wants Attention

Age: Birth to six months

Checklist skill (5) Stops crying when someone plays with him/her
It used to be thought that picking up a young infant when he or she was crying would spoil the baby. Research now shows that when a baby's need for security and holding are met in the early months, the baby will demand less attention later.

When the infant cries for attention, instead of always picking the baby up, stop to play. Talk, touch, or offer a toy, letting the baby know you are there, if needed.

Materials needed: Toy

Where Am I?

Age: Birth to six months

Checklist skill (8) Knows familiar people or things by sight or voice
Soon after birth, infants learn to discriminate between their mother or primary caregiver and less familiar adults. Play a recognition game by calling to the infant when out of sight. When the infant begins to look for you, reward the baby by appearing and engaging in talking, holding, or playing.

Materials needed: None

Mirror Fun

Age: Six to twelve months

Checklist skill (2) Plays with image in mirror
Place a mirror in front of the infant while he or she is being held in an adult's lap. Allow the baby to view his or her image in the mirror. Encourage the baby to interact with the image in the mirror. As an alternative, place the baby on its tummy on the floor in front of a free-standing mirror.

Materials needed: Hand mirror or large mirror at floor level

The Hat Game

Age: Six to twelve months

Checklist skill (2) Plays with image in mirror
Babies love to put on hats. Seat baby in front of a mirror beside you. Show the baby how to put on the hat and admire him- or herself in the mirror. Take turns putting on hats and enjoying and admiring each other.

Materials needed: An assortment of interesting hats

A New Friend

Age: Six to twelve months

Checklist skill (4) Responds to presence of a new person
When infants are in a period of "stranger anxiety," caution is needed when introducing a new person. Allow the baby to become familiar with the person from a secure position such as the lap of a family member or caregiver. Only when the infant indicates an interest in approaching the "new friend" should social interactions be initiated. When the baby feels comfortable with the new person, he or she will indicate readiness for including that person in interactions.

Materials needed: None

Experiences for Social Development in Toddlers

See My Toy?

Age: Twelve to eighteen months

Checklist skill (2) Offers object to another person
One of the first ways a toddler shows an awareness of social interactions is by approaching someone with a toy or object. The baby may want to show the toy or offer it to be held. The adult responding to the action should accept the toy and thank the baby. The gesture is usually temporary, and the baby soon expects the toy to be handed back. Often one toy after another is offered as the baby makes a game of the activity.

Materials needed: Toys or other objects

By Myself

Age: Twelve to eighteen months

Checklist skill (3) Plays independently or in parallel play
Toddlers who receive adequate attention do not always have to have an adult to engage in play with them. When the adult notices that the baby is happy playing by him- or herself, the adult can refrain from interrupting and keep an eye on the baby from a distance. The adult can encourage or check on the activity after a short period of time.

Materials needed: None

Setting the Table

Age: Twelve to eighteen months

Checklist skill (4) Helps with simple tasks

The toddler is aware of tasks that are performed in the home or in a center setting. One of the tasks that the toddler can help with is setting the table. An adult can show the toddler how to put a napkin out at each place setting. The toddler may be able to put a cup beside each napkin with adult guidance. Show appreciation for the help, even if it is time consuming!

Materials needed: Napkins; cups

Love the Baby

Age: Twelve to eighteen months

Checklist skill (7) Carries, hugs toys

Toddlers who receive plenty of affection soon learn how to express love. Parents and caregivers can model loving behavior with a toy and show approval when the baby demonstrates affection. The adult may suggest, "Pat the baby," or, "Love the monkey."

Materials needed: Toy doll or animal

How Are You Feeling?

Age: Eighteen to twenty-four months

Checklist skill (1) Uses words to make wants known or express feelings

Toddlers can learn to identify and express their feelings. Adults can facilitate the expression of feelings. When the child is happy, angry, or afraid, the adult can reflect the feeling in conversation by saying, for instance, "_____ is very happy." Or a question can be asked, "Are you feeling mad? Sometimes Mommy feels mad, too." If the toddler's feelings are discussed frequently, the toddler will come to understand that he or she has different feelings and that they are a normal part of living.

Let's Put Toys Away

Age: Eighteen to twenty-four months

Checklist skill (2) Puts toys away on request

Older toddlers are pleased to be able to respond to requests. A task in which they can easily cooperate is in putting toys away. The toys should have specific locations where they are stored. Adults can talk about where the toys belong and model how to put them away. Although the toddler is not likely to complete the task alone, he or she will enjoy participating in the task. Help and continued praise are essential elements of the activity.

Materials needed: Toys

Loving You

Age: Eighteen to twenty-four months

Checklist skill (3) Engages in affectionate interchanges with adults and children
The toddler is developing social skills as a part of a group. Adults can encourage affection in the toddler by being loving and affectionate themselves. Toddlers need opportunities to participate in group activities. Adults can encourage affectionate interchanges among toddlers. When adults observe a child being loving toward another, they can praise the child and reward him or her with an affectionate gesture.

Materials needed: None

Outings

Age: Eighteen to twenty-four months

Checklist skill (5) Shows interest in exploring new places
As toddlers overcome their hesitation in the presence of strangers or new places, they enjoy a variety of experiences. They are avid learners and show a continued awareness of new people and places. Take toddlers to parks, puppet shows, informal musical events, and other locations where they can observe and experience. Talk about where you are and what is happening.

Materials needed: None

CURRICULUM FOR THE EXPRESSIVE ARTS

Nurturing Expressive Arts in Infants and Toddlers

Is it possible for infants and toddlers to develop an appreciation for the expressive arts? Can infants and toddlers participate in expressive activities? Although their limitations are obvious, these very young children can use the competencies they do possess to develop an awareness of the aesthetic quality of the natural world and manmade expressions of the expressive arts.

Infants and toddlers use their senses and physical actions to experience and understand their world. Adults can foster their awareness of sensory characteristics of their environment by providing activities that introduce them to music, beautiful elements of the natural environment, sculpture that can be touched and felt, pictures that are representative of the work of great artists, and other activities that allow them to interact with quality aesthetic examples of the fine arts.

Infants and toddlers are introduced to music and songs through nursery rhymes and other singing activities that are made a part of their daily activities. They can also be exposed to fine music when riding in the car, playing with toys, and other quiet times of the day. Parents and caregivers can rock or move about with babies in their arms to classical music pieces that are examples of different tempos and moods. Outdoor concerts can be enjoyed with the family when there are also other play opportunities available to provide diversions for short attention spans.

The value of books and story experiences can be extended to aesthetic appreciation. Adults can be selective in the kinds of books to share with infants and toddlers. In addition to concern for durability, as the toddler gains experience in caring for books, adults can look for books with quality illustrations. Picture books that contain reproductions of well-known art can be introduced with an eye to using pictures that will appeal to the very young viewer.

Nursery rhymes and finger plays introduce the very young child to poetry. Singing and telling nursery rhymes and singing songs with the babies permit them to both experience and participate in examples of interesting, melodic language. Repeated experiences with action rhymes such as "Ride a Cock-horse" and "This Little Piggy Went to Market" allow the child to hear the rhythm and melody of language and the anticipation of physical actions that accompany the rhymes.

Aesthetic appreciation is fostered particularly through the presence of examples of beautiful living things from the natural environment. Fish in an aquarium, flowers, colorful plants, and interesting animals and birds provide infants and toddlers the opportunity to experience beautiful colors and striking combinations of color and shape. The infinite variety in flowers and plants can be viewed and often touched and smelled. Babies' sensory capabilities are stimulated and extended through many experiences with elements of nature.

Although there are no developmental characteristics on a checklist specifically related to appreciation for the expressive arts, there are activities that can be planned with attention to the inclusion of aesthetic experiences. The activities that follow can be selected for a developmental objective; however, they can also be planned with the intention of fostering aesthetic appreciation or expression.

Experiences for Aesthetic Appreciation and Expression in Infants and Toddlers

Looking and Listening

Age: Birth to six months

Checklist skill (Physical-Cognitive Development) (4) Looks at suspended object
Babies enjoy viewing and experiencing suspended objects that move and possibly make sounds. Wind chimes, colorful banners, flags, wind socks, and trees moving in a breeze are possibilities for young infants to experience the movement of suspended objects and living things.

Materials needed: Natural elements or suspended objects that move

Looking and Listening II

Age: Birth to six months

Checklist skill (Physical-Cognitive Development) (10) Looks at objects and realistic pictures
In this activity the baby is active and objects or natural elements are acted upon. The baby is taken to or shown flowers, pets, interesting objects, and other elements in the surrounding environment. Interesting pictures on the walls or in books are viewed and discussed by the adult caregiver.

Materials needed: Objects, pictures, and animals in the child's environment

Looking at Beautiful Books

Age: Six to twelve months

Checklist skill (Physical-Cognitive Development) (6) Looks at picture book
Select books with quality illustrations. When viewing the pages and naming items, attention is given to aesthetic qualities in the pictures.

Materials needed: Picture books selected for the quality of the illustrations

Moving to Music

Age: Six to twelve months

Checklist skill (Physical-Cognitive Development) (16) Imitates actions
Play a piece of music that has a distinctive tempo, such as a march. Carry the infant as you move to the tempo. Clap to the tempo, encouraging the baby to clap. Engage babies in this activity frequently, using different types of quality music with various tempos and moods.

Pat-a-Cake

Age: Six to twelve months

Checklist skill (Social-Emotional Development) (7) Enjoys and plays games with others
Babies enjoy playing games, particularly games that include rhyming and physical actions. "Pat-a-Cake" is a favorite that has been handed down for many generations.

> *Pat-a-Cake*
> Pat-a-cake, pat-a-cake, baker's man [clap baby's hands together].
> Bake me a cake as fast as you can [make whirring motion with baby's hands].
> Roll it out, cut it, and mark it with a "B" [make rolling, cutting motions].
> And put it in the oven for Baby and me [Push baby's hands gently in his or her tummy]!

Materials needed: None

Watch Me Color!

Age: Twelve to eighteen months

Checklist skill (Physical-Cognitive Development) (11) Scribbles
Felt-tipped markers make exciting strokes in bright colors. Offer the toddler a marker and a piece of paper. Let the toddler experiment with one marker at a time. Or,

alternatively, put a newspaper page on the wall and encourage the toddler to color on it. Supervision is very important. Toddlers may enjoy working in a group situation with a large piece of butcher's paper. The resulting "mural" can be mounted on the wall to be enjoyed by all.

Materials needed: Paper; newsprint; butcher's paper; nontoxic, washable marking pens

Finger Play Fun

Age: Twelve to eighteen months

Checklist skill (Physical-Cognitive Development) (11) Scribbles
Place a small amount of pudding on a formica-topped table in front of the toddler. Show the toddler how to experiment with scribbling with the pudding. Tasting is allowed. With older toddlers, use aerosol shaving cream and combine touching and smelling it.

Materials needed: Pudding; shaving cream; aprons to protect clothing

Roll It Out

Age: Eighteen to twenty-four months

Checklist skill (Physical-Cognitive Development) (7) Pounds and rolls clay
Older toddlers enjoy experimenting with various forms of clay or dough. Introduce them to soft, homemade dough, which is easier to use at first than commercial dough. Let the toddler first experiment with the dough to learn how it feels and is manipulated. Later, introduce a small rolling pin or cylindrical block to roll the dough. Simple cookie cutters are fun, as well as shells, stones, toys, and objects with interesting shapes and surfaces to make prints in the dough.

Materials needed: Dough; wet clay; cylinders or small rolling pins; cookie cutters; toys and objects for printing

Nursery Rhymes

Age: Eighteen to twenty-four months

Checklist skill (Language Development) (4) Imitates adult speech without prompting
Look at a nursery rhyme book with the toddler. Say the nursery rhymes until they are familiar. After the toddler knows a rhyme, say it, leaving off the last word of each line. Help the toddler supply the missing word. Encourage the toddler to say more of the rhyme with you.

Materials needed: Nursery rhymes and rhyming storybooks

Sing Along with Me

Age: Eighteen to twenty-four months

Checklist skill (Social-Emotional Development) (4) Sings with adults or other children

Introduce toddlers to simple songs such as "Row, Row, Row Your Boat," "Mary Had a Little Lamb," and "Jack and Jill." Encourage toddlers to sing along, clap, and dance to the songs. Praise all efforts to participate.

Play simple recorded songs. Sing along with the records and praise the toddler for any attempts to sing along.

Materials needed: Recorded songs

Rhythm Band

Age: Eighteen to twenty-four months

Checklist skill: None

Provide toddlers with simple rhythm band instruments such as drums, bells, or sticks. Kitchen utensils such as metal pans and wooden spoons can be substituted. Play recorded music that has a definite beat. Encourage the toddlers to match the beat of the music. Alternate with music with a different type of beat.

Materials Needed: Rhythm band instruments; pots; wooden spoons; recorded music

Summary: A Word of Caution

Infants and toddlers are active learners. They use their physical and sensory capacity to explore and understand their environment. Parents and other adults can encourage the learning and development process by responding to the child's emerging abilities expressed in interesting and appropriate activities. An understanding of the developmental characteristics of infants and toddlers provides adults with clues to the types of activities the child will enjoy and are beneficial. This chapter has described the types of experiences that can be enjoyed by adults and infants and toddlers together. Suggested activities have been included for each age from the neonate to two years of age.

The nature of the very young child's approach to exploring also makes it necessary to be very alert to possible dangers in materials and places used for infant and toddler activities. Because babies rely on their senses and physical abilities to explore the toys and locations in their environment, adults need to use caution and careful planning for experiences and activities. Children under the age of two, and often older preschool children, put everything in their mouth. This includes bugs, pebbles, paper clips, and anything else that comes their way. They require constant supervision as soon as they develop the ability to grasp. When they are mobile, new dangers are possible. They can pull things off of tables and beds, climb up the most unlikely places, and get themselves stuck in very small spaces.

Teachers, caregivers, and parents must plan all activities and experiences with these cautions in mind. The infant who enjoys a crib toy dangling overhead becomes the infant who can reach the same toy and choke on it two months later. Toddlers are capable of climbing a play structure meant for preschool children and being injured in a fall, or entrapping their head between railings that are too far apart to prevent such a disaster. When planning all activities and selecting materials, adults must consider possible dangers from the materials themselves and from improper use of the materials. Materials with toxic paint or other possibly poisonous elements should not be used. No objects that have parts that can be dislodged and swallowed should be placed within the reach of small children. Infants and toddlers use their sensory abilities to explore, but these same capacities combined with extreme limitations in their understanding of danger make it necessary for adults to plan experiences and activities with the safety and health of the child in mind.

References

Chomsky, C. (1972). Stages in language development and reading. *Harvard Educational Review, 42*, 1–33.

Erikson, E. H. (1950). *Childhood and society*. New York: Norton.

Gober, B. E., & Franks, B. D. (1988, September). Physical and fitness education of young children. *Journal of Physical Education, Recreation and Dance*, 57–61.

Gonzalez–Mena, J., & Eyer, D. W. (1980). *Infancy and caregiving*. Palo Alto, CA: Mayfield.

Katz, L. (1988). What should young children be doing? *American Educator, 12*, 28–33, 44.

Lennenberg, E. (1967). *Biological foundations of language*. New York: Wiley.

McNeil, D. (1970). *The acquisition of language: The study of developmental psycholinguistics*. New York: Harper & Row.

Miller, K. (1992). Guidelines for helping non–English–speaking children adjust and communicate. In B. Neugebauer (Ed.), *Alike and different: Exploring our humanity with young children*. (pp. 50–53). Washington, DC: National Association for the Education of Young Children.

Morrow, L. M. (1989). *Literacy development in the early years*. Englewood Cliffs, NJ: Prentice-Hall.

Piaget, J., & Inhelder, B. (1969). *The psychology of the child*. New York: Basic Books.

Skinner, B. F. (1957). *Verbal behavior*. Boston: Appleton–Century–Crofts.

Vygotsky, L. S. (1978). *Mind in society: The development of psychological processes*. Cambridge, MA: Harvard University Press.

Weiser, M. (1991). *Infant/toddler care and education*. New York: Merrill.

CHAPTER SIX

A Developmental Model
for Preschool Programs

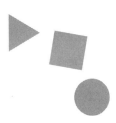

In this chapter we explore how teachers and caregivers can develop a quality program for preschool children. More specifically, we discuss the process whereby a model for a quality preschool program is developed and the way in which the model is affected by various influences. Within this broad outline we address how models and programs evolve, what the characteristics of a quality program are, how the professional educator plans and manages instruction for a developmental program, and how all the factors of program development come together when the program is implemented with children.

Before we look at one example of a cognitive-developmental model and the way in which it is put together, we review the heritage of early childhood education and the accumulated influences that continue to help us make decisions about programs and curriculum.

HOW DOES A MODEL OF EARLY CHILDHOOD EDUCATION EVOLVE?

The Historical Heritage

Early childhood education in the United States and other countries has been influenced by many sources. As was discussed in chapter 2, certain sources of influence came from Europe and England in the nineteenth century. The first movement to serve children under the age of six introduced the kindergarten to the United States, which initially was an adaptation of Froebel's kindergarten in Germany. The influence for the nursery school movement came from the nursery schools established by the McMillan sisters in Great Britain. To move back even further in history, our attitudes toward children and their early needs originally came from the eighteenth-century writings of Rousseau about the growth and learning of children and from the early-nineteenth-century work of Pestalozzi in establishing schools for children (Weber, 1984).

In earlier chapters we discussed the contributions of theorists such as Freud, Erikson, Piaget, Gesell, and Skinner in the twentieth century. These theorists are reviewed again in this chapter because their individual and collective views on development and learning have had a continuing influence on how educators structure and implement curriculum and instruction in early childhood programs today.

Freud and Erikson were concerned with the child's emotional development. Erikson translated the child's psychosocial development into life stages. His description of the child's resolution of these stages during the process of personality development helped parents and teachers understand the factors that influence the child's emotional status. Gesell established norms for child development that served as guidelines for developing realistic expectations for children at different ages. The norms also served as guides in program and curriculum development (Santrock, 1990). Skinner's learning theory (1953) emphasized the role of both the adult and the environment. Skinner brought an awareness of how the child is influenced by adult behavior and how those behaviors can in turn be used to meaningfully direct the child's own learning and social behaviors.

Maria Montessori was a leader in early childhood education. In addition to being the first female physician in Italy, she developed an educational program for poor children and children with disabilities. Montessori believed in the importance of a child-directed form of instruction (Montessori, 1964). She also believed that young children could learn more effectively and at a younger age if the curriculum was carefully sequenced and utilized the child's senses. Her curriculum materials were manipulative in nature and self-correcting, so that the child could assume the major responsibility for learning rather than depend on the teacher (Weber, 1969).

Jean Piaget believed in the child's intrinsic ability to learn. Unlike Skinner, he believed that the child, rather than the adult, initiates learning. He defined stages of cognitive development that described qualitative changes in the child's styles of thinking and learning at different developmental periods (Piaget, 1952).

These and many other theorists and leaders influenced the field of childhood education over the years. How can we remember the many ways we have been influenced about how children are taught? How do we retain an understanding of the impact that the theories of learning and development have as separate constructs? How can we yet understand how the influences both past and present have affected early childhood programs during different periods of educational history? One way of organizing movements and influences to gain perspective about the connections among them is to put them into a historical framework. In the context of early childhood education in this country, these periods and movements frequently are organized as follows:

- The kindergarten movement of the second half of the nineteenth century
- The progressive education era, which developed at the turn of the twentieth century and lasted until the 1950s
- The Great Society efforts of the 1960s
- The back-to-basics movement of the 1970s and 1980s

The kindergarten movement that occurred during the nineteenth century had a major influence on preschool education between the end of the Civil War and the beginning of the twentieth century. The Froebelian method for the education of young children, particularly young poor children, was an exciting concept during a time when women in philanthropic and religious organizations were trying to help the children of massive numbers of immigrants who were seeking new opportunities in the United States. Teachers were enthusiastic in their implementation of Froebelian techniques in the early kindergartens, which were established for preschool children too young to attend school and who needed supervision during the day while their parents worked (Cremin, 1961, 1988). After kindergartens became part of the public schools, they served only five-year-olds, and philanthropic kindergartens gradually declined in number.

The Progressive Era at the turn of the century was marked by an economic shift from an agrarian to an industrial society; population shifts from rural to urban areas led to extensive growth in cities where factories were established. The growth of industry led to the development of a large middle class, which replaced the wealthy few who had previously conducted the business of the nation. A spurt of inventions revolutionized both methods of production and styles of living (Henretta, Brownlee, Brody, & Ware, 1987). The Progressive Era also involved an educational movement. At the same time that large cities were being built, expansion of public school systems and enactment of laws mandating school attendance and outlawing child labor led to large enrollments in the nation's schools. Control of education shifted from local to centralized authority at the city and state level. Curriculum decisions were made by boards of education, state education agencies, and the commercial companies that produced curriculum materials. It was a period of reform during which educational leaders sought to construct an educational program that fit the needs of students from all types of populations rather than only children from predominantly middle- and upper-class homes (Cremin, 1961; Curti, 1959).

Several elements of the progressive education movement had an impact on early childhood education. The kindergarten went through a period of reconstruction—from dependency upon Froebelian techniques to the incorporation of ideas evolving from child-study results, the testing and measurement movement, and the ideals of progressive education espoused by John Dewey and others. Reformers who were expanding teacher preparation programs tried to incorporate the information produced by these new influences into textbooks and courses for future teachers. Experimental schools based on the work of Dewey, William Heard Kilpatrick, Freud, Montessori, and G. Stanley Hall's connectionism were established in different locations around the nation. Programs based on Gesell's maturational theory became firmly entrenched in public school systems. The progressive education era was a period of innovation and experimentation that peaked in the 1920s and was influential through the 1930s and 1940s (Cremin, 1988; Snyder, 1972; Weber, 1984).

The next significant period occurred in the 1950s and 1960s when progressive education gave way to another reform movement. After the Soviet launching of *Sputnik*, the United States entered a period of self-appraisal that involved social, economic, and educational reform. These decades are commonly referred to as the Great Society years. The intention of the movement was to improve education, particularly in mathematics and science, and to make it possible for all populations in the nation to achieve equal opportunities for education, work, and living conditions. Early childhood education was seen as one route by which children of the poor could achieve an educational level that had been denied them previously. In 1965, laws were enacted by the federal government authorizing the Head Start program to provide enriched early childhood programs for young poor children who were at risk to succeed in school (Cremin, 1961). Head Start was unique because it went beyond educational programs designed for such children. In addition to providing enrichment activities to better prepare preschool children to succeed when they entered elementary school, services included parent involvement and training and medical and dental care; attention to health and nutrition, whereby meals and snacks were provided to the children each day; provision of social services to the families of Head

Start children; and opportunities for parents in the Head Start projects to work as employees and volunteers (Greenberg, 1990; Mallory & Goldsmith, 1990; Pizzo, 1990). Today, Head Start programs also serve preschool children with disabilities and infants and toddlers and their families. Planners are working toward offering full-day services and further expanding the program to reach more children and families (Lombardi, 1990).

The influences of the Head Start movement on early childhood education during the 1960s and 1970s were significant. In addition to funding being available for preschool classrooms, large amounts of money were awarded to universities, consortia, and other agencies to develop models of early childhood education with provisions for measuring the comparative successes of the different approaches. Groups of early childhood specialists studied theories of learning and development and designed a variety of models; some were based on single theories and others were based on a combination of theories and approaches. Head Start models were based on influences dating back to the child-study movement of the early 1900s but were more heavily structured on models proposed by the new leaders of the 1950s. Some models were behaviorist, with influences from Skinner. Others were based on Piaget's research and theory on the child's intellectual development. Still others were derived from Montessori's concepts, the nursery school movement, and research in language development.

Today we are immersed in a back-to-basics movement that emerged in the 1980s. This movement had as its impetus the notion that American schools were too lax and did not have the rigorous curriculum required to challenge the nation's students; it seemed that our graduates could not compete with those from countries perceived as successful competitors of the United States in technology and business. Early childhood education was affected by a downward extension of accelerated requirements for curriculum and increased expectations for achievement. The "push-down" curriculum and practices of retention and exclusion from early childhood classrooms on the basis of assessments of maturity and readiness was countered by a movement for developmentally appropriate curriculum and instruction. In the 1990s, creators of early childhood programs are continuing their efforts to develop the most appropriate types of activities for preschool children. Teachers at early childhood centers and public preschools are continuing their efforts to provide quality programs that maximize learning and also meet the developmental needs of children age five and younger.

The Differences between Theory and Practice

In discussing the differences between theory and practice in early childhood education, one can describe the main points of major theorists and the implications for how their ideas should influence practice in the classroom. It is also plausible to cogently describe past educational movements and the ways in which schools and early childhood programs implemented the curriculum indicated by certain theories and movements.

However, one is much more tentative when discussing what actually happens in the classroom. Individual understanding, acceptance, and implementation of theories, educational movements, and innovative approaches to instruction are difficult to see in practice in many settings. Teachers are not only bombarded with current trends and fads in education, they also have been influenced by their own experiences and thus function according to how they perceive appropriate education should progress. It is said that we often "parent as we were parented"; we also often "teach the way we were taught," not the way we were taught to teach. The individual teacher's idea of what constitutes a quality early childhood program is strongly affected by his or her own beliefs and experiences. Although education movements are described in general terms of the major influences of a period, implementation of practices has ranged from one extreme to another—from quite innovative to very traditional. Regardless of the theories or innovations made available to them, teachers in all periods of schooling in the United States have varied in their conscious and unconscious decisions about how they would teach young children. There continues to be a significant discrepancy between the current theories and models and the way in which those ideas are transformed into practice.

During the progressive period many primary-grade teachers continued the practice of rote learning and rigid drills. Some kindergarten teachers used Froebelian methods in spite of new progressive ideas about classroom democracy and learning centers. In the decade of the 1970s when elementary classroom teachers were trying open concept methods and team teaching, others continued round robin reading and spelling drills (Weber, 1969).

It is therefore not surprising that there are wide variations in how early childhood programs are designed and implemented today. There is a multitude of theories and practices that affect current thinking. Teachers, administrators, and other early childhood advocates vary widely in their understanding, acceptance, and willingness to implement programs that are of the best quality for young children. The model proposed in this text reflects the current thinking that curriculum and instruction must be compatible with the developmental abilities of young children. Moreover, the cognitive-developmental theory of Jean Piaget, which perceives the child as an active learner with intrinsic potential to engage in learning, is the major theoretical influence for the model to be described. However, pure models following one theory rarely exist; thus, an eclectic approach that builds upon various effective innovations and possibilities will be incorporated. Finally, although the possibilities for a quality model can be advocated in a textbook, the practices that might be followed in individual classrooms by future teachers will also be different and will evolve continually, depending upon the experiences, influences, and individual efforts of teachers to continue to sort out, interpret, and incorporate past experiences into future innovations and possibilities. Adults and teachers, like children, continue to develop; moreover, the progress of their growth as teachers will depend upon their motivation to continue to search for the best ways to facilitate the learning of preschool children.

CONSIDERATIONS FOR DEVELOPING A MODEL FOR PRESCHOOL EDUCATION

In this chapter, a model for early childhood preschool classrooms is described that addresses issues and problems educators are facing in the 1990s. Because the model is founded on Piaget's work on children's cognitive development, it is important to review the basic understanding of how young children learn that we have acquired from Piaget's cognitive-developmental theory. The key elements of the theory and the way in which they relate to practice include the notion of reconstruction of knowledge, the learning process, and the implications of the understanding that the child is an active learner.

The Process of Cognitive Development Revisited

Much of what is espoused for classrooms that follow the cognitive-developmental theory is based on the idea that the child reconstructs knowledge. The child takes in information as a result of interactions with his or her world and tries to make sense of the new information in the context of what is already known from previous experiences. The child is continually engaged in the process of constructing knowledge for him- or herself through fitting new input into existing information. For this reconstruction to happen the child has to have the opportunity to encounter new experiences, be provided with additional activities to contemplate the connections the new information brings, and integrate the new information into a broader understanding of the underlying concepts. Each child brings different past experiences to the newly acquired knowledge and will construct further knowledge within an individual perspective. It is not a matter of providing children with a body of common knowledge but rather providing a range of activities related to knowledge that will permit each child to process the new information (Katz & Chard, 1990).

Piaget (1952) provided a framework for understanding the process of learning that takes place within the child. The framework is based on the interaction of schema; the process of assimilation, accommodation, and equilibration; and the way in which knowledge is reconstructed using this process of learning. *Schema* refers to the child's current concept or available knowledge about a concept. When new information is encountered related to the schema, the child simultaneously takes in the new information (assimilation), incorporates it into the existing schema, and in the process expands the schema or the available knowledge (accommodation). Equilibration occurs when the process is completed; when new information again is encountered, the process continues (Morrison, 1988).

The process of learning occurs at all stages of development. The process is engaged in differently according to the child's cognitive thinking style within a developmental stage; nevertheless, the process itself does not vary. We have previously discussed how the quality of thinking was described by Piaget in the sensorimotor, preoperational, concrete operational, and formal operational periods. The child uses the available thinking skills to reconstruct knowledge at each developmental stage; in addition, the more opportunities the child has to experience new concepts and information, the better the child will be equipped to utilize the knowledge and make it part of his or her schematic repertoire.

Piaget's description of the process of learning leads to a better understanding of the idea of the child as an active learner. The term *child-centered instruction* has a richer meaning if we incorporate the concept of the child as actively reconstructing knowledge with the concept of how the teacher implements instruction to facilitate the process of learning. The description of the child as an active learner includes the understanding that the teacher will prepare learning activities and materials that will focus on the child's opportunity and ability to interact with the knowledge and "learn" it through his or her own available thinking skills. The teacher implements child-centered instruction by structuring the environment and learning activities to permit the child to take the initiative for interacting with, rather than being a passive recipient of, new information. A quality developmental model for preschool education builds upon a belief in child-centered, active learning and reconstruction of knowledge when organizing the program of curriculum and instruction (Hohmann, Banet, & Weikart, 1979).

Characteristics of a Quality Developmental Model

A quality preschool program provides the kinds of experiences that promote learning for children in the preoperational period. Further, the types of activities selected or constructed are compatible with the developmental levels of the students. Because there is acceptance of a normal variability in development among children of the same chronological age, the activities must accommodate for successful learning within those variations. Moreover, preschool programs based on developmental criteria can be designed either for a single age group or for multiage groups.

Developmentally Appropriate Practices. The National Association for the Education of Young Children (NAEYC) describes quality preschool programs that provide curriculum that matches young children's development as developmentally appropriate practices. In the publication *Developmentally Appropriate Practice in Early Childhood Programs Serving Children from Birth through Age 8* (Bredekamp, 1987), the NAEYC not only defined what is meant by *developmental appropriateness* but provided guidelines for developmentally appropriate practice. The section titled "Guidelines for Developmentally Appropriate Practice" introduces the discussion on curriculum with the following statement:

> A developmentally appropriate curriculum for young children is planned to be appropriate for the age span of the children within the group and is implemented with attention to the different needs, interests, and developmental levels of those individual children (Bredekamp, 1987, p. 3).

Specific descriptors for appropriate and inappropriate practice for programs for four- and five-year-olds provide further information on curriculum and teaching strategies. In Figure 6.1, appropriate practices are contrasted with inappropriate practices in curriculum goals and teaching strategies used with four- and five-year-olds. The curriculum is based on child development and includes learning for physical, social, emotional, and cognitive development. Students are given the opportunity to select many of their own activities and are expected to be active participants in their learning.

The process of the child's learning is further described in Figure 6.1. Under the topic of cognitive learning, appropriate activities are described; moreover, the point is made that learning is integrated so that children can make connections between

COMPONENT	APPROPRIATE PRACTICE	INAPPROPRIATE PRACTICE
Curriculum goals	• Experiences are provided that meet children's needs and stimulate learning in all developmental areas—physical, social, emotional, and intellectual.	• Experiences are narrowly focused on the child's intellectual development without recognition that all areas of a child's development are interrelated.
	• Each child is viewed as a unique person with an individual pattern and timing of growth and development. The curriculum and adults' interaction are responsive to individual differences in ability and interests. Different levels of ability, development, and learning styles are expected, accepted, and used to design appropriate activities.	• Children are evaluated only against a predetermined measure, such as a standardized group norm or adult standard of behavior. All are expected to perform the same tasks and achieve the same narrowly defined, easily measured skills.
	• Interactions and activities are designed to develop children's self-esteem and positive feelings toward learning.	• Children's worth is measured by how well they conform to rigid expectations and perform on standardized tests.
Teaching strategies	• Teachers prepare the environment for children to learn through active exploration and interaction with adults, other children, and materials.	• Teachers use highly structured, teacher-directed lessons almost exclusively.
	• Children select many of their own activities from among a variety of learning areas the teacher prepares, including dramatic play, blocks, science, math, games and puzzles, books, recordings, art, and music.	• The teacher directs all the activity, deciding what children will do and when. The teacher does most of the activity for the children, such as cutting shapes and performing steps in an experiment.

Figure 6.1 Integrated Components of Appropriate and Inappropriate Practice for Four- and Five-Year-Old Children (pp. 183-188)

S. Bredekamp, *Developmentally Appropriate Practice in Early Childhood Programs Serving Children from Birth Through Age 8.* (National Association for the Education of Young Children, 1987). pp. 54-55, 56-57. Used by permission of the Publisher.

	APPROPRIATE PRACTICE	INAPPROPRIATE PRACTICE
strategies *(continued)*	• Children are expected to be physically and mentally active. Children choose from among activities the teacher has set up or the children spontaneously initiate.	• Children are expected to sit down, watch, be quiet, and listen or do paper-and-pencil tasks for inappropriately long periods of time. A major portion of time is spent passively sitting, listening, and waiting.
	• Children work individually or in small informal groups most of the time.	• Large-group, teacher-directed instruction is used most of the time.
	• Children are provided concrete learning activities with materials and people relevant to their own life experiences.	• Workbooks, ditto sheets, flashcards, and other similarly structured abstract materials dominate the curriculum.
	• Teachers move among groups and individuals to facilitate children's involvement with materials and activities by asking questions, offering suggestions, or adding more complex materials or ideas to a situation.	• Teachers dominate the environment by talking to the whole group most of the time and telling children what to do.
	• Teachers accept that there is often more than one right answer. Teachers recognize that children learn from self-directed problem solving and experimentation.	• Children are expected to respond correctly with one right answer. Rote memorization and drill are emphasized.
Guidance of social-emotional development	• Teachers facilitate the development of self-control in children by using positive guidance techniques such as modeling and encouraging expected behavior, redirecting children to a more acceptable activity, and setting clear limits. Teachers' expectations match and respect children's developing capabilities.	• Teachers spend a great deal of time enforcing rules, punishing unacceptable behavior, demeaning children who misbehave, making children sit and be quiet, or refereeing disagreements.

Figure 6.1 Integrated Components of Appropriate and Inappropriate Practice for Four- and Five-Year-Old Children *(continued)*

COMPONENT	APPROPRIATE PRACTICE	INAPPROPRIATE PRACTICE
Guidance of social-emotional development *(continued)*	• Children are provided many opportunities to develop social skills such as cooperating, helping, negotiating, and talking with the person involved to solve interpersonal problems. Teachers facilitate the development of these positive social skills at all times.	• Children work individually at desks or tables most of the time or listen to teacher directions in the total group. Teachers intervene to resolve disputes or enforce classroom rules and schedules.
Language development and literacy	• Children are provided many opportunities to see how reading and writing are useful before they are instructed in letter names, sounds, and word identification. Basic skills develop when they are meaningful to children. An abundance of these types of activities is provided to develop language and literacy through meaningful experience: listening to and reading stories and poems; taking field trips; dictating stories; seeing classroom charts and other print in use; participating in dramatic play and other experiences requiring communication; talking informally with other children and adults; and experimenting with writing by drawing, copying, and inventing their own spelling.	• Reading and writing instruction stresses isolated skill development such as recognizing single letters, reciting the alphabet, singing the alphabet song, coloring within predefined lines, or being instructed in correct formation of letters on a printed line.

COMPONENT	APPROPRIATE PRACTICE	INAPPROPRIATE PRACTICE
Cognitive development	• Children develop understanding of concepts about themselves, others, and the world around them through observation, interacting with people and real objects, and seeking solutions to concrete problems. Learnings about math, science, social studies, health, and other content areas are all integrated through meaningful activities such as those when children build with blocks; measure sand, water, or ingredients for cooking; observe changes in the environment; work with wood and tools; sort objects for a purpose; explore animals, plants, water, wheels and gears, sing and listen to music from various cultures; and draw, paint, and work with clay. Routines are followed that help children keep themselves healthy and safe.	• Instruction stresses isolated skill development through memorization and rote, such as counting, circling an item on a worksheet, memorizing facts, watching demonstrations, drilling with flashcards, or looking at maps. Children's cognitive development is seen as fragmented in content areas such as math, science, or social studies, and times are set aside to concentrate on each area.
Physical development	• Children have daily opportunities to use large muscles, including running, jumping, and balancing. Outdoor activity is planned daily so children can develop large muscle skills, learn about outdoor environments, and express themselves freely and loudly. • Children have daily opportunities to develop small muscle skills through play activities such as pegboards, puzzles, painting, cutting, and other similar activities.	• Opportunity for large muscle activity is limited. Outdoor time is limited because it is viewed as interfering with instructional time or, if provided, is viewed as recess (a way to get children to use up excess energy), rather than an integral part of children's learning environment. • Small motor activity is limited to writing with pencils, coloring predrawn forms, or performing similar structured lessons.

Figure 6.1 Integrated Components of Appropriate and Inappropriate Practice for Four- and Five-Year-Old Children *(continued)*

COMPONENT	APPROPRIATE PRACTICE	INAPPROPRIATE PRACTICE
Aesthetic development	• Children have daily opportunities for aesthetic expression and appreciation through art and music. Children experiment and enjoy various forms of music. A variety of art media is available for creative expression, such as easel, and finger paints and clay.	• Art and music are provided only when time permits. Art consists of coloring predrawn forms, copying an adult-made model of a product, or following other adult-prescribed directions.
Motivation	• Children's natural curiosity and desire to make sense of their world are used to motivate them to become involved in learning activities.	• Children are required to participate in all activities to obtain the teacher's approval, to obtain extrinsic rewards like stickers or privileges, or to avoid punishment.
Parent–teacher relations	• Teachers work in partnership with parent, communicating regularly to build mutual understanding and greater consistency for children.	• Teachers communicate with parents only about problems or conflicts. Parents view teachers as experts and feel isolated from their child's experiences.
Assessment of children	• Decisions that have a major impact on children (such as enrollment, retention, assignment to remedial classes) are based primarily on information obtained from observations by teachers and parents, not on the basis of a single test score. Developmental assessment of children's progress and achievement is used to plan curriculum, identify children with special needs, communicate with parents, and evaluate the program's effectiveness.	• Psychometric tests are used as the sole criterion to prohibit entrance to the program or to recommend that children be retained or placed in remedial classrooms.

COMPONENT	APPROPRIATE PRACTICE	INAPPROPRIATE PRACTICE
Program entry	• In public schools, there is a place for every child of legal entry age, regardless of the developmental level of the child. No public school program should deny access to children on the basis of results of screening or other arbitrary determination of the child's lack of readiness. The educational system adjusts to the developmental needs and levels of the children it serves; children are not expected to adapt to an inappropriate system.	• Eligible-age children are denied entry to kindergarten or retained in kindergarten because they are judged not ready on the basis of inappropriate and inflexible expectations.
Teacher qualifications	• Teachers are qualified to work with four- and five-year-olds through college-level preparation in Early Childhood Education or Child Development and supervised experience with this age group.	• Teachers with no specialized training or supervised experience working with four- and five-year-olds are viewed as qualified because they are state certified, regardless of the level of certification.
Staffing	• The group size and ratio of teachers to children is limited to enable individualized and age-appropriate programming. Four- and five-year-olds are in groups of no more than twenty children with two adults.	• Because older children can function reasonably well in large groups, it is assumed that group size and number of adults can be the same for four- and five-year-olds as for elementary grades.

Figure 6.1 Integrated Components of Appropriate and Inappropriate Practice for Four- and Five-Year-Old Children *(continued)*

content areas in the curriculum. In other words, the child's learning takes place in a meaningful, purposeful context rather than through isolated skills acquisition. Figure 6.1 also refers to activities for physical and aesthetic development. Physical development occurs through unstructured play, whereas aesthetic development results from daily opportunities for creative expression through art and music.

The Teacher's Role.   The teacher's role is to use the environment and teaching activities to facilitate learning. The teacher has a major role in planning and implementing instruction; however, rather than instruction being primarily teacher directed, the focus is on possibilities for the child to take the initiative, make selections, and assume active responsibility for learning.

The teacher is a designer of curriculum. Instead of total dependence on commercial, preplanned curriculum kits and teacher guides, such manuals are used as resources when needed as the teacher organizes learning activities for the children. Using an integrated approach to curriculum development that evolves from a topic or theme, the teacher designs activities that will comprise both teacher-guided lessons and child-centered and -selected activities.

Using Piaget's concept of the child's process of learning in the preoperational stage of development, the teacher makes available a variety of activities to help the child learn new concepts or information. If the child is to assimilate and accommodate new knowledge into a schema, there must be opportunities to actively explore the information; the child must have concrete experiences with the information. Hohman, Banet, and Weikart (1979) described progressions that explain active reconstruction of knowledge. Three of these progressions include concrete to abstract, simple to complex, and experiencing to representing.

The progression of concrete to abstract indicates that early experiences with new information should begin with concrete materials and real experiences. Active learning includes manipulation and physical activity. As familiarity with the concept proceeds, more abstract or symbolic materials and activities are introduced. For example, to learn about fruits, the teacher might begin with opportunities for children to examine, discuss, and sample different fruits. After the children become familiar with the fruits that were introduced, plastic fruits, pictures, films, videos, and books about the fruits might be experienced for further exploration and discussion.

The progression of simple to complex implies that learning experiences should begin with simple concepts and progress to more complex ones. For example, in learning shapes, one shape at a time would be introduced initially, with combinations of shapes utilized after enough experiences have made it possible to work confidently with several different shapes. The increasing complexity of physical actions can also be used to explain simple to complex in active learning. Opportunities to make paintings using large brushes can be followed by later activities with pencils and marking pens requiring more precise fine motor skills.

These progressions are actualized in the child's understanding by structuring learning activities to include an additional sequence: experiencing to representing. The learning opportunities provide activities to experience new information in various ways. Field trips, physical manipulation, and exploration provide the experiences at a concrete level. The child is given opportunities to express understanding of the new knowledge through activities that will permit representation of what is being learned. Through dictating stories, creating paintings, making clay models, singing songs, and performing other representations, the child is able to make the connections and relationships that expand the schema or available store of knowledge. As a result of making representations, the child uses concrete and more abstract creations to better internalize knowledge; at the same time, the child demonstrates his or her understanding to others. Because representations are creative, further connections in understanding can be made through the activity itself.

The teacher consciously considers the progressions when organizing activities for cognitive learning. When studying a new topic or concept, the teacher will commence with a real activity. If, for example, the children are studying pets, a pet might be introduced to the classroom in the science center or an outdoor cage. Children might be given the opportunity to represent their understanding of pets by making play dough models, writing stories, or drawing pictures.

The Role of the Environment. The preschool classroom is arranged into learning or activity centers or areas. Learning areas should allow the children to be able to make choices and carry them out. The materials in each area are organized to support the curriculum; therefore, the child-initiated activities that are possible in each learning center facilitate self-directed learning and independence. There are many ways to arrange the classroom into centers or areas. For the model we are describing, we will use the dramatic play center, language center, science and mathematics center, art center, and music and movement center.

The dramatic play center includes housekeeping equipment, an area with blocks and trucks, and provisions for puppetry and dramatic productions. The purpose of the center is to provide combinations of opportunities for sociodramatic play. Prop boxes for changing themes and other rotating materials should be available, along with toys and blocks that are permanently located in the center.

The language center is the location for language and literacy development. It includes the library, listening center, materials for writing, and possibly a computer or typewriter. Language experience charts, individual slates, and various sizes of paper are just some of the items to be found in the center.

The science and mathematics center can incorporate equipment for sand and water play; animals and plants; materials for counting and working with other mathematical concepts; and temporary projects related to topics of study. It can also house a manipulative area for materials such as puzzles and fine motor construction materials.

The art center includes easels and a variety of materials for art activities. Painting supplies, crayons, marking pens, and ample paper supplies are always available, whereas specific activities requiring particular supplies and materials are placed in the center when needed for a few days.

The music and movement center can share an area with a classroom space used for large-group activities. Record and cassette players, musical instruments, and other props for activities are located adjacent to a large rug area with ample space for physical activities.

Room arrangement is fluid and modifiable. As activities warrant, some areas may be expanded and others reduced or eliminated for a time. Teacher observation of center activities may discern a need for more extensive rearrangement because children are actually using space differently than anticipated. The main point is that the environment should support the children's choices and activities, not dictate them. Because the purpose of the room environment is to facilitate active learning with materials available to encourage the child's participation in self-initiated learning, the work or learning center areas are not meant for free play or to be used as a reward. The environment is a key to active learning; the teacher, as facilitator and resource person, uses the learning areas to implement the progressions in the child's reconstruction of knowledge.

The Role of Play. The role of play seems to be one of the most difficult aspects of young children's development and learning for many educators and parents to understand. Play is sometimes perceived as idleness or useless activity when contrasted with learning. For many parents and teachers, learning is associated with sitting quietly and listening to the teacher or working preschool workbook pages. To the contrary, play provides opportunities for active exploration of information, social interactions, and physical activity essential to learning and development.

Furthermore, a growing body of research supports the role of play in various types of development. A few examples of activities that demonstrate the relationships between play and learning are described next.

In cognitive development, sociodramatic play and construction play may have positive relationships to IQ scores (Johnson, Ershler, & Lawton, 1982). It is also proposed that the problem-solving behaviors used in play influence general problem-solving abilities (Bruner, 1972; Simon & Smith, 1983).

There is also a relationship between creativity and play. Lieberman (1965) conducted research that showed a possible link between play, creativity, and intelligence. Lieberman (1977) further linked creativity with early playfulness. Divergent thinking has also been linked with imaginary play (Hutt & Bhavnani, 1976; Lieberman, 1965).

Play has an important role in the development of language. As the child engages in object play, language is attached to meanings and relationships (Frost, 1992). Language is used during play to imitate adult speech, for sociodramatic play, and to organize and manage play (Smilansky, 1968). Young children also play with the language itself (Garvey, 1977). For example, babies sometimes sing themselves to sleep with rhyming utterances; preschoolers make up words and names and try to outdo each other with outrageous verbalizations.

Play facilitates social development. Group dramatic play requires that children plan and interact if they are to engage successfully in pretend or make-believe play episodes. As a result, sociodramatic play helps children to practice and perfect their social skills (Johnson, Christie, & Yawkey, 1987).

More obviously, play facilitates physical development. The basic locomotor skills that are refined during the preschool years are acquired through daily activities involved in indoor and outdoor play. Larger and fine motor skills are also practiced through play activities (Jambor, 1990).

Play provides the experiences that enable the child to integrate and make sense of the vast amounts of information to which he or she is exposed each day. Because the child is in charge of play events, he or she is able to use sociodramatic, physical, and aesthetic play activities to process and understand new knowledge, as well as practice physical, social, and language skills. The teacher will want to use indoor and outdoor play periods to support development and learning. Centers in the classroom are organized for sociodramatic play, construction play, fine motor play, and aesthetic play. Outdoor play environments can offer more than physical and social play opportunities by including sociodramatic play props and aesthetic and creative activities. Cognitive development can be encouraged through gardening, pet observation and care, and provisions for group dramatic and literacy activities. Science experiments and natural science activities can be easily engaged in outdoors. If young children are to understand their world, the teacher needs to use the natural environment that is accessible nearby.

The Role of the Daily Schedule. As recommended in the teaching strategies listed in Figure 6.1, children should work individually or in small groups most of the time. Nevertheless, there will be times during the day when teachers will find that whole-group activities are useful and appropriate. The daily schedule will provide opportunities for children to plan and carry out projects and other learning and play activities, for the teacher to conduct small-group and whole-group activities, and for groups to enjoy both indoor and outdoor activities. When planning the daily schedule, the teacher will want to achieve a balance between teacher-directed and child-directed or child-initiated activities. Various combinations of schedule components can be used. In this model we will describe schedule components as large-group time, center time, small-group time, and outdoor time.

Large-group time provides opportunities for activities in which the whole group of children can participate. It may occur several times during the day, especially early in the day and after the completion of center and lesson activities. Large-group time can be used for sharing experiences, discussing plans for the day, reviewing concepts learned earlier in the year, performing music and movement activities, telling stories, and reviewing what has been accomplished, as well as a time for transition between activities.

Center time occurs so that children may work in learning centers. This time is preceded by a period of planning, during which individuals or small groups of children describe what they will accomplish in the center. The teacher may prepare the children for center time by introducing the activities that are available and their purposes. The teacher may also want to give instructions on the proper use of a new toy, for example, or on material that has been placed in the center for the first time. Some center activities may be expected to be used by all children; others can be the child's choice. The teacher also uses preparation for center time to guide children who have difficulty in making choices. During the center time period, the teacher interacts with the children and assists them in making the best use of their activities. The teacher may work in a center with a small group if assistance is warranted. After center time, there is a period for cleaning up and restoring center materials to their proper location. A large-group activity can follow center time to review what the children did and how they implemented their plans.

Small-group time offers an opportunity for the teacher to guide a learning activity or engage in direct instruction. Working with a group of four or five children at a time, the teacher engages in work with concepts, discusses theme topics, conducts hands-on activities such as cooking or special art projects, and teaches lessons. Small-group times can be scheduled during center times, with the teacher alternating between facilitating center activities and conducting small-group activities.

Outdoor time provides an opportunity to play or work outdoors. If the outdoor environment is perceived as a classroom, some outdoor periods may be used for large- and small-group instruction and others for free play. Physical activities, both structured and unstructured, are planned for outdoor periods, as are field trips, neighborhood walks, and other curriculum-related activities.

PLANNING AND MANAGING INSTRUCTION

In this section we will discuss how to plan and implement developmentally appropriate instruction. Using the approach that children learn best when learning is purposeful and meaningful, we will describe how to plan thematic or integrated curriculum that will maximize the possibilities for children to make connections between new information and knowledge that they already understand. We will further discuss how the daily schedule is used to implement integrated learning.

How does the teacher plan and implement developmentally appropriate instruction? We have studied the indicators of developmentally appropriate instruction provided by the NAEYC (Bredekamp, 1987). Likewise, we have described the characteristics of a program designed for the early childhood years. Now we want to explore how the classroom teacher designs and implements developmentally appropriate curriculum for preschool students. Teachers not only must consider the general developmental characteristics of their students as a group, but they must also consider the unique qualities of each individual student. Teachers analyze the diversity represented among their students in terms of cultural and economic backgrounds, as well as in terms of individual differences in interests and abilities. If children with special needs are assigned to the classroom, their individual limitations and potential are considered in planning appropriate activities.

There are many available resources for determining goals and objectives for curriculum in early childhood classrooms. Sources for curriculum development can include developmental checklists, state-mandated curriculum objectives, commercial curriculum objectives related to adopted basal materials, and locally determined curriculum goals. All these resources help the teacher understand which curriculum goals are appropriate or expected in the educational setting where he or she teaches (Seefeldt, 1989).

The way in which one plans and manages the curriculum to achieve the desired goal can take various forms. If the program is to be developmentally appropriate, however, the curriculum design must facilitate successful learning that accommodates developmental differences within a child-centered or child-initiated approach. If learning is to be integrated and purposeful for the child, the approach for curriculum design must incorporate those characteristics. In this text, *developmental-thematic* is the term used to describe a curriculum that meets the characteristics introduced above.

Understanding Developmental-Thematic Curriculum

We have been designing curriculum based on themes for a long time. Every college student can remember studying Indians, community helpers, or some other topic during his or her elementary school years. John Dewey introduced thematic curriculum with his project approach during the Progressive Era. He felt that the classroom should be a miniature democracy and children should be engaged in projects that would help them understand their role in their community (Cremin, 1961). Themes were used for the meaningful projects that Dewey believed would engage children in learning for a purpose. Projects were activities planned by the students with a practical purpose, and problem solving was the process used to conduct projects. For example, in making plans for a garden, students were required to make their own decisions regarding how to design the layout and plant the seeds (Parker & Temple, 1925). Later, Dewey lamented that his project approach had been reduced to a collection of activities rather than useful experiences that would have a real purpose for the child's understanding. He described the contrast between, on the one hand, aimless utilization of activities collected by teachers and, on the other hand, working with problems that emerged from the children's experience and were within their capacity to understand the relation of means and ends (Dewey, 1938).

Recently, Dewey's ideas have resurfaced with the new understanding of the child's role in the learning process that we have gained from Piaget. It has been called the Project Approach (Katz & Chard, 1990), Integrated Learning (Krogh, 1990), and the concept of thematic curriculum (Seefeldt, 1989), among other variations of names. The new advocates of this type of curriculum stress not only the interrelated nature of learning but also the importance of child involvement in planning and implementation of the themes that are developed. Moreover, the format for theme planning facilitates an understanding on the part of both teacher and students about how different content areas are related to each other and how individual activities can support learning in several areas of development and content areas.

What then is thematic curriculum? Essentially, it is a curriculum that is planned around a theme that the teacher has selected or the students have identified as a learning topic. The learning activities selected for the theme are reflective of how the students want to explore the topic or the kinds of activities they have identified that will help them acquire the knowledge or skills related to the theme (Krogh, 1990). As an alternative, the teacher might do some initial brainstorming about unit activities and the students would either select which activities are most desirable or expand upon the teacher's ideas. As planning proceeds, the teacher and students use a process called webbing, which involves brainstorming about the possible activities and analyzing the ways in which content areas of the curriculum are being utilized or incorporated into the theme or unit plans.

In the context of the early childhood years, the curriculum has also been identified as developmental. By now the implications of the developmental nature of thematic curriculum should be obvious. The curriculum will not only provide for integrated, purposeful learning but will also provide for the development of the students (Bredekamp, 1987). In choosing the kinds of activities to design for the unit or theme, the teacher will consider how learning is furthered in content areas of the curriculum; more important, however, is that the focus should be on how physical, social, and cognitive development are involved in the activities. In addition, the activities selected and developed will be planned to accommodate a range of developmental levels so that all students will have successful experiences as a result of being actively involved in the unit projects (Katz & Chard, 1990). Consideration of development is an integral part of the planning and implementation process.

Roles of Developmental-Thematic Curriculum

How does developmental-thematic curriculum fit into school routines? Ideally, it could be the organizational pattern for the entire school program. It is easy to conceptualize how such a curriculum could be used in a developmentally appropriate setting for the total program—in effect, it could be used to determine the environmental arrangement, daily schedule or routines, and learning activities that will be provided in a series of units or themes throughout the year.

Many early childhood teachers, particularly those in public school settings, lack the flexibility to fully determine their schedules. For them, incorporation of the thematic-developmental curriculum into their program might take different forms. To explore several possibilities, we will discuss the developmental-thematic curriculum in terms of a primary framework for curriculum; as one of several instructional methods; and as an occasional resource for exploring special topics.

Developmental-Thematic Curriculum as the Basic Framework.   When themes can be used to design the total curriculum for a preschool program, they become the framework, or scaffold, for the program. The teacher studies the educational goals or objectives for the program and correlates them with the units or themes that are developed during the course of the year. Planning is carried out with the students providing their ideas and input; however, the teacher also studies the overall plan and incorporates or modifies activities to ensure that desired goals are accomplished. The daily schedule for a block of days and, more probably, weeks is devoted to implementation of theme projects and activities. The time allotted in the yearly calendar is flexible and can be modified according to student interest and possible additional projects or activities that might arise during the course of the theme. While one theme is reaching closure, the planning process can begin for the next theme. Teachers and children can be gathering resources in anticipation of the initiation of the new theme as the planning stage comes closer to the implementation stage. In this approach, cycles of planning, implementation, and evaluation of completed themes and projects are ongoing throughout the year.

Developmental-Thematic Curriculum as One of Several Approaches.   Some teachers may find themselves in a situation where a schedule for preschool already exists and must be followed. The teacher does not have the opportunity to totally determine the instructional methods that can be used. There may be predetermined curriculum materials that must be used to provide consistency within a school or school district. Perhaps the teacher may plan and modify the schedule and curriculum within limits but may not abandon district expectations entirely.

In this type of program, the teacher tries to fit themes or units within existing instructional practices. Project or theme curriculum is planned and organized to integrate the curriculum; however, some elements will alternate with other required work. Likewise, activities or projects might have to be accomplished during scheduled times devoted to particular content areas. The teacher and students would be working on projects and theme activities in an ongoing, consistent manner, but theme units would complement rather than replace existing instructional practices in the school. Given time constraints in many schools, scheduling would have to be carefully planned in order to accomplish both theme and separate learning objectives. This approach of including themes into the curriculum might be more difficult than the first total approach; nevertheless, teachers have found that with some initial effort, they can comfortably include thematic instruction and increase its use as they become more perceptive to how it can be implemented in a variety of combinations within the daily schedule.

Developmental-Thematic Curriculum as an Occasional Resource.   Some teachers, particularly beginning teachers, may find it easier to plan only occasional units until they become more secure in managing children and curriculum. In this context, the teacher follows the routines and curriculum in the school setting and plans a thematic unit for a special occasion or topic. A holiday or social studies topic is used as the theme. An integrated, developmental curriculum is planned around the theme, but projects and activities occur in conjunction with a subject area each day until the unit is completed. Once a unit has been completed, there may be a period of time before another unit is planned and implemented. This approach might be considered similar to existing models of unit planning; to the contrary, it differs in the conscious inclusion of interrelated learning activities and accommodation for variations in development among the students. Another difference is the emphasis on child-planned and -initiated projects and opportunities for purposeful problem solving.

Each of these approaches has merit. Regardless of which approach a teacher decides to use, the principles of developmentally appropriate learning can be maintained. However, implementing developmental-thematic curriculum as one of several approaches or as an occasional resource rather than as the basic framework provides fewer opportunities for the children to see relationships or connections in learning. The teacher will want to begin using developmental-thematic curriculum at a level that is comfortable; then, as experience makes it possible to see new avenues for integrated instruction, the teacher can increase the number of times themes are used and improve the way in which themes are planned and used in the classroom.

Designing Developmental-Thematic Curriculum Units

How, then, do the teacher and students go about planning a developmental-thematic curriculum that meets all the goals of an integrated approach to learning? Designing such a unit of work can be accomplished by following a sequence of activities from planning to implementation. The sequence begins with selection of the topic and proceeds through brainstorming, organizing ideas into a web, selecting objectives or outcomes and activities for a balanced curriculum, describing the interrelatedness of the developmental activities in the curriculum, and, finally, planning and scheduling for curriculum activities.

Selecting a Theme Topic.   There are many ways to select a theme for study. In past decades, it was common for the social studies curriculum in elementary schools to be organized into themes or units. In some school systems, teachers designed the thematic curriculum to be used at each grade level.

In this context, theme topic selection is intended to be more relevant to the teacher's and students' interests and needs within the individual classroom. If the teacher selects the topic, he or she may determine it from some aspect of the curriculum that needs to be covered. The topic is planned to include and interrelate developmental areas in the projects and activities that are to take place. The teacher might also initiate a topic as a result of some event that has occurred that has meaning for the students. For example, the teacher of a class of four-year-olds planned to bring a new pet, a gerbil, into the classroom. She initiated the topic of gerbils as a theme, and with her students she planned the unit based on learning about gerbils and their care.

Topics should have relevance for the population of students in an individual classroom and the area in which they live. Children in southern locations of the United States or in the state of Hawaii would have a different understanding of winter than would children living in northern continental states, especially Alaska. The cultural diversity of children in a classroom would affect the study of many topics; in addition, family differences would have a bearing on how units that involved family traditions were planned.

The children also can be the source of the topic. Students might share a bit of news that is of interest to the entire class. For example, Kevin, a student in a kindergarten classroom, brought a brightly painted clay piggy bank to school to share with the class. A general discussion about banks that other children had at home led to a unit on saving money in small and large banks.

Brainstorming a Topic.   Once the topic has been selected, the teacher and students are ready to explore the information and activities that can expand their knowledge. In the case of preschool children, such a discussion might be very general, with the teacher culling suggestions from comments made by the children about the topic or guiding the discussion with ideas of his or her own. After gaining input from the children, the teacher can continue the brainstorming process him- or herself.

The focus of the brainstorming should be on creating ideas for working with the topic and developing or identifying resources that will support the theme. Both teacher and students will discuss what the children want to learn about the topic; also, the teacher will try to expand the brainstorming session to include information that might be acquired as part of unit activities. The teacher will list all of the possible activities that relate to the topic. Katz and Chard (1990) suggest that each of the possibilities be written on slips of paper. Whatever the method used, once the possible activities have been identified, it is time to develop a web.

A thematic unit on the topic of leaves can be used as an example. The unit was developed by Lisa, a student teacher, in response to students' curiosity about fall leaves that they were collecting on the playground. Lisa and her students live in New England, where the fall season is highly characterized by leaves turning colors and falling from the trees. (If the children lived in Hawaii or Arizona, a different element of nature might have been chosen for the unit topic.) In designing her unit, Lisa was required to follow a unit plan format that included the following components:

UNIT TOPIC:

OVERVIEW OR RATIONALE FOR THE UNIT:

DEVELOPMENTAL STAGE:

BRAINSTORMING WEB:

LIST OF ACTIVITIES (categorized as teacher directed, teacher–child initiated, or child initiated):

UNIT OBJECTIVES:

SUMMARY OF INTEGRATED ACTIVITIES:

Lisa first listed some ideas that she and the students generated about things they could do to learn about leaves. In her initial discussion with the children, they were able to make a list of the following activities:

take a nature walk to find leaves

visit botanical garden

draw leaves

rake leaves

make pictures with leaves

compare leaves

"write" stories about leaves

Lisa studied the original ideas and continued the brainstorming process to expand the thematic unit possibilities. She further organized activity ideas into activities using leaves and activities about leaves. Her expanded list of possible activities included the following:

take a nature walk

visit botanical garden

Activities using leaves

create leaf rubbings

describe characteristics of leaves

count sets of leaves

make leaf collages

measure leaves

group leaves by common characteristics

Activities about leaves

dictate stories about leaves

dictate stories about nature walk and visit to botanical garden

make sponge-print pictures of trees

discuss leaves that are food sources

sing songs about leaves

listen to stories about leaves

participate in music/movement activity (e.g., pretending to be fall leaves)

Developing a Brainstorming Web.   Lisa was now ready to make a brainstorming web (see Figure 6.2). She focused on developmental areas of the curriculum and placed all of the ideas in the appropriate categories of the web. Most of the activities fit into two or more categories because developmental areas were integrated in the activity. Lisa had not yet determined which of the activities would be developed for the unit. She was looking for a balance in developmental areas and was considering which activities had the most merit and the highest potential for providing meaningful, purposeful experiences that were developmentally appropriate for her students.

Selecting Unit Activities.   The next step in planning the thematic curriculum is to select the activities that will be used for the unit. The ideas and activities that were developed during the brainstorming activity and located on the brainstorming web

Figure 6.2   Brainstorming Web

are considered for inclusion in the final unit design. In addition, possible combinations of activities or expansion of original activity ideas is contemplated as the teacher begins to consider how the activities will be scheduled and implemented.

Lisa decided that the leaves unit would be appropriate for a week of study. She decided that taking a field trip to the botanical garden was beyond the scope of her possibilities for activities, but taking a nature walk to find and gather leaves on the school grounds and nearby park would be a suitable way to initiate unit activities and projects. She also decided to focus unit activities around the fall leaves themselves rather than to broaden the unit to include more about leaves in general. She narrowed the activities to twelve and made a final list. In the process of planning at this stage, she decided that making a book of unit activities would be a good project. The tree sponge-print pictures could be used for the cover of individual books. She then determined whether the activities were teacher directed, child initiated, or a combination of teacher and child initiated. She wanted to ensure that there was a balance between teacher- and child-directed activities. Lisa's final list was as follows:

1. Take a nature walk, then dictate stories about the walk (teacher–child initiated)
2. Discuss the characteristics of leaves (teacher directed)
3. Count, measure, and group leaves by common characteristics (teacher–child initiated)
4. "Write" stories about leaves (child initiated with teacher assistance)
5. Participate in movement to music (teacher directed)
6. Sing songs about leaves (teacher directed)
7. Rake leaves (teacher–child initiated)
8. Draw pictures of leaves (child initiated)
9. Create leaf rubbings (child initiated)
10. Make leaf collages (child initiated)
11. Make sponge-print pictures of trees (teacher–child initiated)
12. Make individual unit booklets (teacher directed)

Describing Developmental-Thematic Unit Objectives.   Once the teacher has determined which activities and projects will be incorporated into the unit to accomplish what both students and teacher want to learn about a topic, the activities are studied to identify more specifically what will be learned. The teacher has a major decision to make: what type of objective should be used to describe the purpose for the desired learning? Traditionally, preservice students have been taught to use performance objectives (Mager, 1975). The performance objective has three elements: the behavior that the learner will exhibit, the conditions under which the behavior will occur, and the standard of performance that is minimally acceptable. For example, one of Lisa's activities for the unit on leaves was to count groups of leaves. Lisa could write an objective for the activity as follows: "As a result of a lesson using leaves for counting, the student will be able to count sets up to five with 100 percent accuracy." In this example the behavior is the student's ability to count, the condition is the use of leaves in a counting activity, and the level of desired performance is 100 percent accuracy.

There is disagreement in the field of education, particularly in early childhood education, as to whether performance objectives are always appropriate for describing learning objectives for young children. Critics of performance objectives propose that they are too specific and result in breaking curriculum into fragmented elements that can be meaningless. Furthermore, integrated curriculum that emphasizes the child's opportunity to initiate and conduct learning activities does not lend itself to description by performance objectives (Seefeldt, 1989). Proponents of the use of performance objectives point out that many schools are predominantly teacher directed; furthermore, school districts and state education agencies might require the use of performance objectives. Schools that adopt Madeline Hunter's Instructional Theory into Practice (ITIP) (Hunter, 1979) model are examples of settings where performance objectives are required. Individual Education Plans (IEPs) that are used to plan curriculum objectives for special-needs children also require the use of performance objectives (Orlich et al., 1990).

In this text, we propose that a compromise between the two positions be used in writing learning objectives. The standard of performance will be omitted because learning processes are more important than achieving a specific level of performance; however, the condition and desired behavior will be retained. The circumstances under which the learning occurs can be derived from the planned activities. The behaviors will be those that the child can exhibit as a result of engaging in the planned activities.

Lisa determined that as a result of engaging in unit activities in the leaves unit her students would acquire specific concepts and abilities. The items in the behavior component of her objectives could be categorized as what the students could understand and what they would be able to do. She listed them as follows:

1. As a result of taking a nature walk to find leaves, students will understand that leaves change color and fall from trees in the fall.
2. As a result of taking a nature walk to find leaves, students will understand that there are many kinds of trees and leaves.
3. Following an activity to examine and discuss the characteristics of leaves, students will understand that leaves are different colors, shapes, and sizes.
4. As a result of participating in an activity to examine and discuss the characteristics of leaves and opportunities to group leaves by a student-identified characteristic, students will understand that leaves can be organized by common characteristics.
5. As a result of participating in an activity to examine and discuss the characteristics of leaves, students will be able to describe comparative characteristics of leaves.
6. As a result of participating in group activities with fall leaves, students will be able to "write" (emergent writing) stories about leaves.
7. As a result of participating in teacher-directed and center activities with fall leaves, students will be able to count, measure, and group leaves using their own criteria.
8. As a result of working with leaves, paper, and paste in the art center, students will be able to create leaf collages.

9. As a result of working with leaves, paper, and crayons in the art center, students will be able to create leaf rubbings.
10. As a result of working with sponges cut into the shape of leaves, tempera paint, and paper, students will be able to create sponge-print pictures.
11. As a result of completing art activities, students will be able to make a book of unit activities about fall leaves.
12. Students will be able to work cooperatively in groups to rake leaves on the playground.
13. Students will be able to use appropriate behaviors during the nature walk.

Describing Integrated Unit Activities.   The final step in formulating a unit plan is to write a summary of the activities that will be included in unit experiences. There are two purposes for briefly explaining the activity: to preview what will happen during the activity and to understand how the activity provides for integration of learning.

Lisa wrote such an explanation for her unit activities. Two of those activities were described as follows:

Nature Walk
The students will be given large grocery bags and will take a walk on the playground and in the park next to the school. We will observe the different types of trees we see, the variety of leaves on the ground, and other natural characteristics that might be seen. Students will collect leaves in their bags to be used in later activities. They will also be encouraged to collect seeds and other items they might find. The teacher will have hand magnifiers available to examine interesting aspects of the environment. The activity involves cognitive development, using concepts in science. It integrates language development in the discussions that take place during the activity and social development in the use of appropriate behavior on the walking tour and social interactions used during the experience. Large and fine motor skills are used in the process of taking the walk and collecting leaves and other objects. Safety must be observed. Aesthetic development is integrated within the discussions during the walk.

Leaf Collages
Leaves and other natural items collected on the nature walk will be located in the art center. Students will be instructed on how they can create their own collage using glue to paste items on a piece of paper. The activity provides for aesthetic development as the children construct their creation. Fine motor skills are integrated when the children manipulate the materials and use the glue.

After Lisa had completed the steps in her unit design, she was ready to write her final unit plan using the format mentioned earlier. She described her rationale for developing the unit and the general developmental level (preoperational) of the students.

Planning Lesson Activities.   Once the final unit design is completed, the teacher needs to plan the activities in detail. The unit objectives addressed by the activity, a description of the procedures for the activity, the materials needed to conduct the activity, and plans for evaluation are all considered. Students who are preparing to be teachers might be required to develop activities into lesson plans.

Lisa was required to use lesson plans for her unit on leaves. She followed a lesson plan format that included the following:

TITLE OF PLAN:
OBJECTIVES ADDRESSED:
ACTIVITY PROCEDURES:
    Large-Group Activity (teacher directed):
    Small-Group Activity (teacher–child initiated):
    Center Activities (child selected and initiated):
MATERIALS/RESOURCES NEEDED:
EVALUATION:
    Teacher Evaluation:
    Activity Evaluation:
    Student Evaluation:

When planning a lesson, the teacher first identifies the activity by giving it a title. If more than one activity is incorporated into a plan, the title would be broader to reflect activities and objectives addressed.

Under the category of objectives addressed, the teacher takes the unit objectives that relate to each individual lesson and cites them in this context.

The activity procedures describe in detail the activities to be undertaken. The teacher first determines which types of activities the lesson will include. Large-group activities are used with the whole class. This type of activity can be used for field trips, class discussions, and other experiences that benefit all children. Small-group activities are selected when lesson activities warrant including about five children at a time so that all can be equally involved and given individual attention. Center activities are chosen when opportunities for child-selected experiences are indicated. Most center activities should be possible for the child to engage in individually or with other children with some prior direction from the teacher. At times, the teacher or another adult is present to guide activities in a center.

Whichever type of activity is chosen, the procedures are planned and described in three parts: (1) introduction, or planning; (2) development of lesson or activity; and (3) summary, or review. The introduction, or planning, procedure is the beginning of the activity. If the activity is teacher directed, the teacher plans how the lesson will be introduced. If it is the first step for an activity that includes child planning, plans are made to solicit input from individual children or the group. If the activity is a center activity, the teacher uses this opportunity to give instructions for use of centers, and children are enabled to make their plans for selection and use of centers.

The development of the lesson or activity follows the beginning step of the learning experience. In this part of the lesson plan, the teacher describes plans for the main content of the lesson. The sequence of the lesson is explained, including questions and procedures. If a center activity is implemented, the teacher serves as a facilitator as children engage in their selected activities.

The last step of the learning experience, the summary, or review, is used to conclude the activity or reach closure. If the teacher is conducting an activity, the last step is a process for summarizing the lesson. More important, it is an opportunity for the children to review and provide feedback on their understanding and reaction to the lesson. If center experiences are the type of activity used, this is the time when students conclude their activity and put materials away. Then they meet with the teacher and discuss how they carried out their plans for the centers and review the experience.

In addition to planning for the body of the lesson, the teacher needs to anticipate what will be needed for successful implementation of the selected activities. In the materials/resources section of the plan, the teacher identifies what will be needed in the way of human, technological, and other materials for the lesson. Books, art materials, adult assistants, cassette tapes, videotapes, and food items are just a few of the items that would be listed as materials or resources. Needed equipment such as cooking utensils, projectors, and computers are listed.

The last component of the lesson plan is evaluation. The teacher plans how the lesson is to be appraised. Within the plan for assessment, a description is given of how the teacher's role, the activity itself, and the children's learning will be evaluated. More information on the role of evaluation and how it can be conducted follows.

Planning for Evaluation.   In this section, we will address how curriculum and instruction are evaluated as they relate to individual lesson plans. In keeping with the evaluation purposes of the lesson plan just discussed, we will describe the process of evaluation of the teacher's effectiveness, the activity itself, and the children's learning.

Evaluation of the Teacher.   Teachers will want to conduct ongoing evaluation of their effectiveness in working with the children and facilitating the desired learning. Reflection following small-group and large-group instruction can be conducted to determine success in group management, student interest in the activity, effectiveness of the materials used, and appropriate timing of the length of the activity. The teacher can note positive and negative aspects of teaching activities to constantly improve teaching and management behaviors.

Regarding Lisa's lessons, she determined how she would evaluate her effectiveness by asking herself specific questions. Did she adequately prepare the children to engage in the activity to make leaf collages? In talking about the leaves, did the manner in which she guided the discussion enable the children to understand how to use descriptive words to discuss the leaves?

Evaluation of the Activity.   Activity and curriculum evaluation in preschool programs should be ongoing whether the learning experiences are part of a thematic unit or included as a separate component of instruction. The teacher should reflect on how developmentally appropriate his or her curriculum choices are prior to using them in the preschool classroom. Following the use of a commercially designed material or participation in a teacher-designed activity, the teacher should reflect upon the effectiveness of the material and activity in accomplishing objectives. Also to be considered is student interest in the activity. Decisions to use the material or activity in the future should be based on an evaluation after the activity has been completed.

In Lisa's sample lessons, she wanted to know if the children enjoyed making leaf collages. She also wanted to know if the activity was appropriate for her preschool children. In the lesson on describing leaves, she wanted to evaluate whether her plan for conducting the lesson was effective with her students. She also wanted to find out if the leaves she used were good samples for the children to describe, as well as whether her questions to guide the children resulted in productive descriptions in their responses. Figures 6.3 and 6.4 represent two of Lisa's lesson plans.

Evaluation of Student Learning.   The teacher will also want to determine if students successfully mastered the learning objectives of the unit or other developmentally

---

TITLE OF PLAN: Leaf Collages

OBJECTIVES ADDRESSED
　　As a result of working with leaves, paper, and glue in the art center, students will
　　be able to create leaf collages.

ACTIVITY PROCEDURES: Art Center Activity
Introduction
　　The activity will be explained during large-group time. The teacher will describe
　　how leaves and other objects collected on the nature walk can be used to create
　　a picture. Instructions for using glue and putting away materials will be reviewed.

Development of Lesson or Activity
　　Students will construct their collages during center time. A volunteer parent will
　　be present to provide assistance and display the finished pictures.

Summary or Review
　　At large-group time following center time the teacher and children will discuss
　　the pictures. Children will be encouraged to explain or describe their selections
　　and the process they used to create their picture.

MATERIALS/RESOURCES NEEDED
　　Volunteer parent
　　Large construction paper of assorted colors
　　Paste or glue
　　Collection of leaves and other found objects

EVALUATION
Teacher Evaluation
　　Did the children understand the activity from the explanation given?
　　Were materials appropriate and adequate?

Activity Evaluation
　　Did the children enjoy the activity?
　　Were the children able to carry out the activity with little assistance?

Student Evaluation
　　Did all students participate?
　　Was descriptive language used to discuss the completed pictures?

Figure 6.3   Example of a Child-Initiated Lesson Plan

TITLE OF PLAN: Describing Leaves

OBJECTIVES ADDRESSED

As a result of participating in an activity to examine and discuss the characteristics of leaves, students will be able to describe comparative characteristics of leaves.

ACTIVITY PROCEDURES: Small-Group Lesson

Introduction

After getting the students settled around the table in the science–math center, the teacher will hold up two leaves from the collection and describe them for the children. Likenesses and differences will be discussed in terms of colors, shapes, and unique characteristics.

Development of Lesson or Activity

The students will be invited to find two leaves in the collection that are interesting to them. Each is given a turn to describe their leaves and guided to look at color and shape, as well as other unique qualities. Other students will be invited to add comments after individual children have completed their descriptions.

Summary or Review

Students will be guided in summarizing what descriptive words they used to tell about their leaves. A list of words can be made on the chalk board or a language experience chart. When the list is completed, the teacher and children will read the words together. The chart can be retained for follow-up activities.

MATERIALS/RESOURCES NEEDED

Collection of leaves

Experience chart

Marking pen

EVALUATION

Teacher Evaluation

Did the lesson proceed smoothly?

Did the lesson take an appropriate amount of time?

Were the teacher's questions effective?

Did the students understand the purpose of the activity?

Activity Evaluation

Was the activity appropriate for the students?

Did the students participate in the lesson?

Were the leaves appropriate for the discussions?

Student Evaluation

Were the students able to understand how to describe the leaves?

Were the students able to use descriptive words to describe the leaves?

Were new descriptive words used?

Figure 6.4   Example of a Teacher-Directed and Child-Initiated Lesson Plan

based curriculum. After working on activities with the new concepts or sk
teacher will want to conduct an assessment of individual understanding; the teach
will thus observe independent activities or tasks during a small-group time after having provided the children with sufficient opportunities with the materials.

The teacher will need to determine if student learning is expected to reach some
level of mastery or if the focus is on evaluating the learning process. If specific information is desired, the teacher will design a task or lesson activity that will give that
kind of information about the child's achievement. For example, if the teacher wants
to know that the child understands number concepts up to five, then a task would be
used with the child that would allow the child to demonstrate that understanding. A
certain level of performance is required of the child under those circumstances.
Likewise, some type of record keeping would be needed to maintain information on
student progress.

In the preschool curriculum described in this chapter, level of performance has
not been required; rather, the teacher is more interested in the child's ability to problem solve or use divergent thinking to engage in integrated activities. The teacher is
using evaluation to understand the child's developmental growth instead of mastery
of skills as such. In Lisa's sample lesson plans, she was evaluating the process of
learning. There was no student evaluation component of the aesthetic activity in
making leaf collages. In the lesson on the description of leaves, she was interested in
ascertaining how the children approached the process of describing characteristics of
leaves, not in determining some level of skill development in being able to characterize similarities and differences in the leaves.

Scheduling Unit Activities.   The final step in thematic unit planning is to determine
how the activities will be scheduled. This step will involve making decisions about
what components of the daily schedule are best suited for the activity. The teacher
will need to consider whether the activity requires teacher facilitation and assistance
or whether the students can conduct the activities independently with some prior
preparation and planning. In addition, if the activity needs teacher instruction or
direction, the teacher must decide whether it is best suited to whole-group participation or if alternating small groups would be more appropriate for all students to get
the most from the experience. Once these decisions are made, the teacher can complete a schedule for the period of time that the unit will be in progress.

Lisa was student teaching in a classroom that incorporated the developmental-
thematic approach to curriculum development and implementation. In charting her
unit for a period of a week she incorporated schedule components of the approach
as well as other elements of the preschool model. Figure 6.5 represents how Lisa's
unit was implemented in a preschool classroom in a five-day period. Some of her
activities were scheduled for large-group time so that the whole class could participate in planning, reviewing, and learning information. Some activities were implemented in small-group time, giving the teacher an opportunity to facilitate an activity
or engage in some direct instruction. Centers were used extensively for creative and
exploratory activities. Visits to the language center were included daily to encourage
the children to browse through the books related to fall leaves.

Schedule Component	Day 1	Day 2	Day 3	Day 4	Day 5
Large-Group Time	Plan nature walk	Plan for center time	Plan for center time	Plan for center time Songs about leaves	
Small-Group Time		Discuss characteristics of leaves	Count, measure, classify leaves	Pressed-leaf arrangements	Make unit booklet.
Center Time	*Library* Books about fall	*Art* Collages *Library* Books about fall Write leaf stories	*Art* Leaf rubbings *Library* Books about fall	*Art* Sponge rubbings *Science–Math* Count, measure, classify leaves	*Science–Math* Count, measure, classify leaves *Library* Books about fall
Large-Group Time	Songs about leaves	Reread dictated stories	Movement to music using leaves	Read book about leaves Plan for raking leaves	Movement to music
Summary and Review	Review nature walk Dictate story	Review center time activities Discuss leaves in individual collages	Review center time activities		
Outside Time	Nature walk			Rake leaves	
Individual		Review individual stories about leaves		Dictate leaf stories	Review unit booklets Discuss individual pictures and stories

Figure 6.5 Unit on Leaves: Schedule for One Week

Implementing Developmental-Thematic Curriculum

Before a teacher is ready to begin a new unit, some final preparations are in order. Resources must be gathered, the environment must be arranged to accommodate the activities unique to the unit, and further planning takes place with the children to involve them in preparations to begin the new topic for learning.

Gathering Resources.   If the teacher has planned carefully, needed materials and resources were listed as the thematic unit was being designed. Now it is time to study the list and determine which materials are already on hand and which need to be acquired. The art materials must be organized in preparation for the center and small-group activities that will occur during the week of the unit. A trip to the school library and other facilities is in order to find books that relate to the fall season and changes in leaves. Books that have illustrations of fall leaves can also be included in the classroom library. The teacher will want to determine which books to share with the children and which to place in the library area for browsing.

Students may be able to bring some unit materials from home. If materials for some of the activities represent items from home that can be recycled, the teacher can discuss the needs with the children and send a note home requesting that parents send the needed items. In some schools where parents have an active volunteer program, the parents will take the responsibility to help find needed resources without having to resort to purchasing materials. When purchase of some items is unavoidable, parents sometimes are enthusiastic errand runners and offer to conserve the teacher's time. Acquired resources can be organized so that they are readily available for unit activities before the unit is initiated.

The parents themselves may be needed resources during the course of the thematic unit. If the teacher needs assistance with activities during small-group time or center time, the presence of a parent volunteer can assure that activities go smoothly. If the preschool teacher is fortunate enough to have a teaching assistant for the classroom, parental help may not be as essential; nevertheless, with young children an additional adult supporter is always welcome when many active projects are under way.

Planning with the Children.   As was mentioned earlier, additional planning with children is important prior to initiation of a new unit. In addition to being involved in locating relevant resources, they will be enthusiastic supporters of activities to prepare the classroom. Children can organize the library center or other classroom areas that will be rearranged or organized for unit activities. They can also be involved in last-minute discussions about the activities that are being planned for the new theme.

Arranging the Environment.   Although learning centers or areas in the preschool classroom are rearranged frequently to provide variety and maintain interest, the beginning of a new thematic unit is also a time when room arrangement is reevaluated. The teacher consults the plan to determine which centers will be affected and need reorganization. Existing materials might be replaced with items required for the new unit. Art materials, prop boxes, artifacts, and other relevant resources are located in the appropriate centers or learning areas. In some cases centers may be relocated in the classroom to better facilitate unit activities.

In the case of Lisa's unit, the theme of leaves led her to enhance a science–mathematics area in the classroom. A large table was introduced where children could measure, count, and group leaves. Small-group time to introduce the activity would be conducted at the table. Later during the week the children could continue the activity independently during center time.

Lisa likewise rearranged the art area to facilitate the various creative activities using leaves. Art materials unrelated to the thematic unit remained in the area to provide choices; nevertheless, an additional space was reserved for unit-specific activities.

THE ROLE OF EVALUATION IN PRESCHOOL PROGRAMS

In the descriptions of the process of developing unit and lesson plans presented earlier in the chapter, there were provisions for evaluation. In the lesson plan description, possibilities for evaluating teacher effectiveness, lesson activities, and student learning were discussed. In this section of the chapter, we will discuss the broader purpose of evaluation in preschool programs, the measurement of child development and learning, and the evaluation of program components of preschool programs.

Evaluation of Child Development and Learning

Purposes for Evaluation.   In chapter 4, information was shared on how adults can monitor the development of infants and toddlers. During those years of rapid growth and development, frequent assessment of development permits monitoring of developmental progress in very young children. During the preschool years, development is slower, but awareness of developmental progress is still important. The preschool years are a significant period of development of potential for learning, as well as of physical, intellectual, and social development; therefore, information about the individual child's development is important for assessing developmental competencies, screening for delayed development, and determining possible placement in intervention programs.

Assessment of developmental competencies in the preschool years is done by parents, medical personnel, and personnel in school and child-care settings. Using developmental checklists and other instruments, the child's developmental characteristics are measured against the norms for that age. Competencies in language, motor skills, and social and cognitive development are assessed using indicators of the normal range of development. Pediatricians frequently use an instrument such as the Denver Developmental Test for a quick developmental evaluation. School and child-care center personnel might use a checklist similar to the Frost-Wortham developmental checklists found in chapter 3. Other sources include developmental indicators used by child development centers and public schools that are locally devised or obtained from books or other texts (Beaty, 1992; Wortham, 1990).

An important purpose for developmental assessment in the preschool years is to identify developmental delays. Children who are experiencing difficulties in hearing, vision, motor, language, or cognitive development or other types of developmental delays benefit from early identification and intervention. Screening for developmental problems can be conducted with a variety of standardized instruments, such as the Early Screening Inventory (Meisels & Wiske, 1983) and the Developmental Indicators for the Assessment of Learning-Revised (DIAL-R) (Mardell-Czudnowski & Goldenberg, 1983). If indicators of delayed development are identified through use of a screening instrument, more intensive testing can be conducted by medical or psychological professionals to diagnose the delay more specifically and refer the child to the appropriate program for intervention services.

Standardized tests are frequently used with preschool children in the early childhood years for various purposes. Developmental screening tests, readiness tests, IQ tests, and other standardized instruments are used to determine if young children should be withheld from preschool programs or retained at the preschool level instead of promoted to first grade. Because of the inaccuracy of standardized test results in the preschool years and the national concern about using this kind of testing for tracking or school placement, there are many testing specialists, early childhood specialists, and organizations serving as advocates opposed to inappropriate testing of children in the early childhood years, particularly children in preschool programs. The National Association for the Education of Young Children and the National Association of Early Childhood Specialists in State Departments of Education published its "Guidelines for Appropriate Curriculum Content and Assessment in Programs Serving Children Ages 3 through 8" (1991), and the Association for Childhood Education International published a position paper, "On Standardized Testing" (Perrone, 1991). Additional efforts have been made to provide information on alternatives to standardized testing for assessment and evaluation purposes (Fair Test, 1990; Grace & Shores, 1991; Wortham, 1990).

Evaluation of Children in Preschool Programs

There are several strategies recommended for adults who are evaluating development and learning in the preschool years. Teacher observation, hands-on tasks and activities, work samples, and portfolios are informal assessment tools that can be used to determine the child's progress in development and learning.

Preschool children demonstrate growth and learning through activity. Because they learn through active work and play, observation is a primary method for understanding the child's progress and the way in which the child thinks or behaves. Teachers can schedule systematic observations of individual children at regular intervals to update information on language development or fine and gross motor skills or to conduct observations for a specific purpose, such as identifying causes of inappropriate behavior. Checklists can be used for assessing developmental characteristics. Different types of observation tools, such as anecdotal records or time sampling, can be employed to obtain the desired information (Beaty, 1986; Grace & Shores, 1991; Wortham, 1990).

A more structured process for measuring learning can be accomplished through teacher-designed tasks or other hands-on tasks and activities for the children to complete. Within the context of a teacher-conducted small group or individual lesson or activity, the teacher can ask the child to do a task and observe the child's verbal and physical responses to determine the desired information. In a similar manner, the teacher can use discussions with children to determine ability to use language to demonstrate understanding of concepts. The teacher can also observe the child using materials in center activities for evaluation purposes (Wortham, 1990).

Teachers are increasingly using portfolios to collect materials to use for evaluation purposes. A large folder or box is designated for each child in the classroom. Grace and Shores (1991) recommend a large pizza box or similar type of container for the portfolio. The portfolio can contain samples of art work, emergent writing, checklists, and any other relevant materials that can document the child's progress over a period of time that can be shared with parents (Fair Test, 1990; Grace & Shores, 1991).

Teachers serving children with special needs have specific requirements for design of intervention activities and evaluation of progress. Diagnostic assessment of the child before he or she enters a program identifies the characteristics and needs for intervention that are specified and addressed through an Individual Education Plan. The plan identifies the strategies that will be used for intervention. Ongoing assessment is conducted to determine the effectiveness of the intervention activities and the child's developmental progress. Although there are concerns about the effectiveness of available standardized measures for diagnosis and ongoing assessment of children with disabling conditions (Fewell, 1983), Gautt (1990) recommends the Carolina Record of Individual Behavior (Simeonsson, Huntington, Shore, & Ware, 1982) as an effective observational instrument to be used with young children.

Evaluation of Program Components

Program evaluation is an important part of the total evaluation picture in preschool classrooms. The program is evaluated by paying attention to the indoor and outdoor environments, the curriculum, and the teacher.

The learning environment is essential to the development and learning of preschool children. Because learning is active and physical activities are part of the child's overall development, the environment is designed and arranged to facilitate learning through play and child-centered activities. Both the indoor and outdoor environments are planned to promote physical, social-emotional, language, and cognitive development. When assessing the quality of the environment, the observer looks for characteristics of the environment that promote all categories of development. Some of the specific characteristics that are essential include plans for a variety of activities, accommodations for large- and small-group activities, and age-appropriate and developmentally appropriate materials and equipment as described in the *Guide to Accreditation* provided by the National Academy of Early Childhood Programs (1991).

The outdoor environment should also meet the criteria described above. In addition, criteria for safety should be met. Information for evaluation of a quality outdoor environment is also described in the *Guide to Accreditation* (National Academy of Early Childhood Programs, 1991). More comprehensive information about quality outdoor playgrounds and the way in which to evaluate a quality, safe play environment for preschool children is available in *Playgrounds for Young Children: National Survey and Perspectives* (Wortham & Frost, 1990) and *Play and Playscapes* (Frost, 1992).

The effectiveness of the curriculum is also evaluated as part of the assessment of overall program quality. Teachers will want to have feedback on how well the curriculum fits the learning needs of children in preschool classrooms. The *Guide to Accreditation* suggests that materials, activities, and the daily schedule are among the factors that indicate an appropriate curriculum. The daily schedule ensures a balance between active and quiet activities, as well as periods for outdoor play. There is also a balance between small-group and large-group experiences. Materials that are used have multiracial and nonsexist elements; developmentally appropriate materials include manipulatives, blocks, art materials, dramatic play materials, and sand and water toys.

Finally, evaluation of the teacher and the teaching role are part of the assessment of program quality. The quality of adult interactions with children is a key to teaching effectiveness. The manner in which teachers and caregivers manage learning experiences, arrange the environment, and engage in working with the children forms the types of interactions that can be evaluated. The opportunities they provide for children and the manner in which they guide language, social behaviors, routines, and work and play experiences are important indicators of the quality of the teaching role. The qualifications the teacher brings to the teaching role are equally important for evaluating the teacher (National Association for the Education of Young Children & National Association of Early Childhood Specialists in State Departments of Education, 1991). The appropriate training in early childhood education that was obtained as a prerequisite for employment should be nurtured with opportunities for further ongoing training throughout each school year.

Summary

Preschool early childhood programs have both a historical and a theoretical heritage. The various types of preschool settings that are currently in operation reflect a combination of many influences that affect the type of instructional program used. In addition, individual teachers also reflect the various influences and experiences that have shaped their perception of how to organize an early childhood classroom.

When designing a model for a preschool program of the highest quality, developers also consider the historical heritage and current knowledge based on research in development and learning. The best of the influences are retained and incorporated into the new model that is conceptualized and implemented with today's young children.

No model can be transferred intact into all preschool settings. In addition, teachers are likely to incorporate other influences into their teaching practices. To enable teachers to plan and manage instruction in a variety of settings, suggestions were made as to how to plan and manage instruction using a developmental-thematic curriculum, as well as to how to adapt the process in a variety of types of preschool settings.

There are logical steps in planning thematic or integrated curriculum. Moreover, there are different ways that the curriculum can be incorporated into a daily schedule. Preschool teachers must carefully plan what activities will best meet their objectives for the unit, as well as what resources they will need to carry out the learning activities. Planning with children for unit activities is a must, as is rearrangement of the classroom environment to accommodate materials, activities, and long-term projects that will be accomplished over a period of days or weeks.

Specialists in early childhood education in the preschool years believe that young children learn best when they can see the purpose and connections in learning. The learning experiences provided for them in preschool classrooms should provide opportunities for the cognitive connections to be made through active interaction with new concepts. Developmental-thematic learning facilitates reconstruction of knowledge by young children in various types of learning settings that are developmentally appropriate. Ongoing evaluation of the curriculum, of student learning, and of teaching strategies helps the teacher to further improve and refine instructional activities for future students.

Evaluation is further conducted for the preschool program as a whole. Strategies for evaluation of overall development and learning of children throughout the year help guide program planning and communication with parents. Evaluation of the environment provides feedback on how well the environment, both indoors and outdoors, supports the child's development and learning. The teacher and teaching role are also part of program evaluation. The teacher's ability to provide developmentally appropriate equipment, materials, and activities is an indicator of teaching effectiveness. The curriculum used in the classroom should reflect effective use of developmentally appropriate activities and materials with students. The teacher's training in preparation to teach young children should also reflect a solid foundation in child development and the components of a quality educational program for preschool children.

Summary Statements

1. Historical periods in this country have affected the field of early childhood education.
2. Evolving theories of development and learning have also affected how children are taught in preschool early childhood classrooms.
3. Piaget's cognitive-developmental theory has important implications for developing quality educational programs for today's young children.

4. An early childhood model based on a developmental-thematic curriculum provides one framework for a quality preschool program.
5. A developmental-thematic curriculum can be planned and implemented in a variety of preschool settings, making it a flexible method for designing and implementing a developmentally appropriate curriculum.
6. A curriculum based on themes can be used in various ways to integrate development and content areas to help children understand the connections among learning experiences.
7. Steps in planning a developmental-thematic curriculum permit the teacher to analyze the relationships between content areas of the curriculum and developmental categories of growth.
8. When the planning process for a unit of thematic curriculum is completed, the teacher and children then plan how to acquire materials and other needed resources to begin unit experiences.
9. The classroom environment must also be organized prior to beginning a new unit so that general space and certain areas or centers are arranged to accommodate the hands-on activities that will be conducted by the teacher and children.
10. Evaluation of unit activities, teaching strategies, and student learning help the teacher assess the effectiveness of the accomplishment of unit objectives.

Study Questions

1. How have historical influences affected the nature of today's early childhood programs?
2. Which two theorists do you believe have the most influence on the development of programs for preschool classrooms? Explain your choices.
3. Why is it difficult to determine the sources of influences in many early childhood preschool classrooms?
4. Why do individual teachers vary in their perception of what constitutes a good early childhood program?
5. How has the current reform movement affected early childhood programs and curriculum?
6. How has the back-to-basics approach to instruction resulted in a conflict between theories of learning and development?
7. Why do classroom teachers find it difficult to implement new approaches to instruction in their own teaching?
8. How does Piaget's theory of cognitive development influence current programs that are developmentally appropriate?
9. Why does the Piagetian construct of the learning process in young children support integrated curriculum development?
10. How does a preschool developmental curriculum model exemplify child-centered instruction?
11. What is meant by meaningful or purposeful learning?
12. What is the process used to design and implement a cognitive-developmental curriculum?
13. Regarding the concept of active reconstruction of knowledge, what is the relationship between the progression of concrete to abstract and experiencing to representing?
14. Why does the learning environment in the preschool classroom need to be flexible in arrangement?
15. How does the daily schedule support child-centered learning?
16. How does the cycle of plan, do, and review facilitate the child's reconstruction of knowledge?
17. What is the origin of thematic curriculum?
18. How does the developmental-thematic curriculum incorporate an integrated approach?
19. How can a developmental-thematic curriculum be used in different types of early childhood programs?
20. Why is it helpful to use a webbing process that includes both developmental and content area categories of integrated curriculum?
21. How is student input included in the planning process of a developmental-thematic curriculum?
22. How can a brainstorming web be a vehicle for organizing early childhood curriculum?
23. Why is it important to carefully plan activities and room arrangement before beginning a thematic unit?
24. What is the role of evaluation in a developmental-thematic curriculum?

References

Beaty, J. J. (1986). *Observing development of the young child*. Columbus, OH: Merrill.

Beaty, J. J. (1992). *Skills for preschool teachers*. New York: Merrill.

Bredekamp, S. (Ed.). (1987). *Developmentally appropriate practice in early childhood programs serving children from birth through age 8*. Washington, DC: National Association for the Education of Young Children.

Bruner, J. S. (1972). The nature and uses of immaturity. *American Psychologist, 27*, 687–708.

Cremin, L. A. (1961). *The transformation of the school*. New York: Alfred A. Knopf.

Cremin, L. A. (1988). *American education: The metropolitan experience 1876–1980*. New York: Harper & Row.

Curti, M. (1959). *The social ideas of American educators*. Totowa, NJ: Littlefield, Adams.

DeVries, R., & Kohlberg, L. (1990). *Constructivist early education: Overview and comparison with other programs*. Washington, DC: National Association for the Education of Young Children.

Dewey, J. (1938). *Experience and education*. New York: Macmillan.

Fair Test. (1990). *Standardized tests and our children: A guide to testing reform*. Cambridge, MA: The National Center for Fair & Open Testing.

Fewell, R. (1983). Assessing handicapped infants. In S. G. Garwood & R. R. Fewell (Eds.), *Educating handicapped infants: Issues in development and intervention* (pp. 257–297). Rockville, MD: Aspen.

Frost, J. L. (1992). *Play and playscapes*. Albany, NY: Delmar.

Garvey, C. (1977). *Play*. Cambridge, MA: Harvard University Press.

Gautt, S. W. (1990). Early childhood special education. In E. L. Meyen (Ed.), *Exceptional children in today's schools* (2nd. ed.) (pp. 131–170). Denver: Love Publishing.

Grace, C., & Shores, E. F. (1991). *The portfolio and its use*. Little Rock: Southern Association on Children Under Six.

Greenberg, P. (1990). Head Start—Part of a multi–pronged anti–poverty effort for children and their families . . .Before the beginning: A participant's view. *Young Children, 45*, 40–52.

Henretta, J. A., Brownlee, W. E., Brody, D., & Ware, S. (1987). *American history since 1865*. Chicago: Dorsey Press.

Hohmann, M., Banet, B., & Weikart, D. (1979). *Young children in action*. Ypsilanti: High/Scope Press.

Hunter, M. (1979). Teaching is decision–making. *Educational Leadership, 37*, 62–64, 67.

Hutt, C., & Bhavnani, R. (1976). Predictions from play. In J. S. Bruner, A. Jolly, & K. Sylva (Eds.), *Play: Its role in development and evolution* (pp. 216–221). Englewood Cliffs, NJ: Prentice-Hall.

Jambor, T. (1990). Promoting perceptual-motor development in young children's play. In S. C. Wortham & J. L. Frost (Eds.), *Playgrounds for young children: National survey and perspectives* (pp. 147–166). Reston, VA: American Alliance for Health, Physical Education, Recreation and Dance.

Johnson, J. E., Christie, J. F., & Yawkey, T. D. (1987). *Play and early childhood development*. Glenview, IL: Scott, Foresman.

Johnson, J. E., Ershler, J., & Lawton, J. T. (1982). Intellective correlates of preschoolers' spontaneous play. *Journal of General Psychology, 106*, 115–122.

Katz, L. G., & Chard, S. C. (1990). *Engaging children's minds*. Norwood, NJ: Ablex.

Krogh, S. (1990). *The integrated early childhood curriculum*. New York: McGraw–Hill.

Lieberman, J. N. (1965). Playfulness and divergent thinking: An investigation of their relationship at the kindergarten level. *Journal of Genetic Psychology, 107*, 219–224.

Lieberman, J. N. (1977). *Playfulness: Its relationship to imagination and creativity*. New York: Academic Press.

Lombardi, J. (1990). Head Start: The nation's pride, a nation's challenge. Recommendations for Head Start in the 1990s. *Young Children, 45*, 22–29.

Mager, R. F. (1975). *Preparing instructional objectives* (2nd ed.). Belmont, CA: Fearon.

Mallory, N. J., & Goldsmith, N. A. (1990). Head Start works! Two Head Start veterans share their views. *Young Children, 45*, 36–39.

Mardell–Czudnowski, C. D., & Goldenberg, D. S. (1983). *Developmental Indicators for the*

Assessment of Learning–Revised (DIAL–R). Edison, NJ: Childcraft Education Corp.

Meisels, S. J., & Wiske, M. S. (1983). *The Early Screening Inventory.* New York: Teacher's College Press.

Montessori, M. (1964). *The Montessori method.* New York: Schocken Books.

Morrison, G. S. (1988). *Education and development of infants, toddlers, and preschoolers.* Glenview, IL: Scott, Foresman.

National Academy of Early Childhood Programs. (1991). *Guide to accreditation.* Washington, DC: National Association for the Education of Young Children.

National Association for the Education of Young Children & National Association of Early Childhood Specialists in State Departments of Education. (1991). Guidelines for appropriate curriculum content and assessment in programs serving children ages 3 through 8. Washington, DC: Author # 725.

Orlich, D. C., Harder, R. J., Callahan, R. C., Kauchak, D. P., Pendergrass, R. A., & Keogh, A. J. (1990). *Teaching strategies: A guide to better instruction.* Lexington, MA: D. C. Heath.

Parker, S. C., & Temple, A. (1925). *Unified kindergarten and first grade teaching.* Boston: Ginn.

Perrone, V. (1991). On standardized testing. *Childhood Education, 67*, 131–142.

Piaget, J. (1952). *The origins of intelligence in children.* New York: International Universities Press.

Pizzo, P. D. (1990). Family–centered Head Start for infants and toddlers: A renewed direction for Project Head Start. *Young Children, 45*, 30–35.

Santrock, J. W. (1990). *Children.* Dubuque, IA: Wm. C. Brown.

Schickedanz, J. A., Hansen, K., & Forsyth, P. D. (1990). *Understanding children.* Mountain View, CA: Mayfield.

Seefeldt, C. (1989). *Social studies for the preschool-primary child.* Columbus, OH: Merrill.

Simeonsson, R., Huntington, G., Short, R., & Ware, W. (1982). The Carolina record of individual behavior: Characteristics of handicapped infants and children. *Topics in Early Childhood Special Education, 2*, 114–136.

Simon, T., & Smith, P. K. (1983). The study of play and problemsolving in preschool children: Have experimenter effects been responsible for previous results? *British Journal of Developmental Psychology, 1*, 289–297.

Skinner, B. F. (1953). *Science and human behavior.* New York: Macmillan.

Smilansky, S. (1968). *The effects of sociodramatic play on disadvantaged preschool children.* New York: Wiley.

Snyder, A. (1972). *Dauntless women in childhood education 1856–1931.* Washington, DC: Association for Childhood Education International.

Weber, E. (1969). *The kindergarten.* New York: Teacher's College Press.

Weber, E. (1984). *Ideas influencing early childhood education: A theoretical analysis.* New York: Teacher's College Press.

Wortham, S. C. (1990). *Tests and measurement in early childhood education.* Columbus, OH: Merrill.

Wortham, S. C., & Frost, J. L. (Eds.). (1990). *Playgrounds for young children: National survey and perspectives.* Reston, VA: American Alliance for Health, Physical Education, Recreation and Dance.

CHAPTER SEVEN

Preschool Curriculum:
Ages Three to Five

Language and Cognitive Development

CURRICULUM FOR LANGUAGE DEVELOPMENT

In chapter 5 we discussed the nature of language development—how theorists and researchers who study the way in which humans acquire language have described the process babies and young children go through in learning to talk. We also discussed how infants and toddlers accomplish the first steps in learning to talk and what parents and other caregivers do to encourage the use of language. In this chapter we again emphasize why it is important to understand how language develops, not only for designing a program for language development but also for extending or expanding the process to include literacy.

There was a period in early childhood education from the 1930s to the 1950s when educators believed that the process of learning to read began in the first grade. Using Gesell's maturational theory (Gesell, 1925) as a guide, it was determined that children were ready to learn to read when they were six years old. Preschool and kindergarten teachers were advised not to introduce formal reading instruction before the students were mature or ready. The role of preschool teachers was to provide activities that would help children develop the readiness skills that were thought to prepare them to begin formal reading instruction. At the same time, standardized tests such as the Metropolitan Reading Readiness test were developed to determine if the child had developed the maturity and skills required for beginning reading instruction. Companies that produced basal reading programs prepared materials for preschool and kindergarten based on readiness skills. Skills such as auditory discrimination, visual discrimination, left-to-right eye progression, visual motor skills, and fine motor skills appeared both in reading readiness materials and reading readiness tests (Morrow, 1989). The concept that teachers should help children develop readiness for reading by teaching skills strongly influenced teaching practices for several decades.

Newer theories of child development and learning and, more specifically, results of studies conducted in the 1950s and 1960s of how children acquire oral language began to cast doubt on the skills approach to beginning reading. Studies demonstrated that children play an active role in oral language acquisition. Language development is similar to cognitive development as proposed by Piaget (1955). The child constructs language just as the child constructs knowledge (Bloom, 1972; Brown, 1973; Cazden, 1972; Chomsky, 1965). Further research extended this theory to involve acquisition of reading. As researchers studied acquisition of literacy, they determined that young children also learn written language through constructing their own rules and relationships.

Understanding how young children learn to talk helps us to also understand how they learn to write and read (Dyson, 1985; Goodman, 1986; Sulzby, Barnhart, & Hieshima, 1989). Consequently, as part of our discussion of the design of curriculum for language development we will further explore how young children develop language in the preschool years and how one plans a program for language development that complements how children acquire language and literacy.

How Young Children Develop Language

As was discussed in chapter 5, there are various theories of how children acquire language. The behaviorist position is that language is learned through reinforcement (Skinner, 1957). Adults selectively reinforce the child's utterances; moreover, behaviorists propose that the child learns language through imitation. Speech is learned first, followed by grammar.

Researchers such as Slobin (1966), McNeil (1966), and Chomsky (1968) support a different theory, which proposes that humans are biologically equipped for language acquisition; we have an innate capacity to learn language. Proponents of this view believe that children do not imitate nor reproduce what they hear. Instead, children learn a set of rules that they use to create their own utterances. They continue to try out their language and use this process to refine the rules and elaborate their language. The rules for the language are finite, but children can generate an infinite number of sentences using the rules (Jewell & Zintz, 1986; Spodek, 1985).

The interactionist or constructivist approach to language acquisition is based on both maturation and interaction with language. Proponents of this theory believe children develop the ability to speak as they mature and respond to the language in their environment. Interaction with language enables them to hypothesize and try rules for communicating. Piaget (1955) believed language development paralleled the child's ability to use thought. As children progress through the sensorimotor, preoperational, concrete operational, and formal operational stages, they use their own style of thinking and language interactions to learn language.

Vygotsky also agreed that language and thought are related in the child's acquisition of language; however, he proposed that language precedes thought (Vygotsky, 1962). Children first become conscious that they can communicate through speech. According to Vygotsky, human consciousness is developed through words. He stressed the importance of the adult's role in determining the directions for the child's concept and language acquisition. Through interactions with adults, children develop their understanding of the rules and functions of language. Verbal discourse with adults supplies the context for concepts.

It does not matter whether one advocates a single view or a combination of theories of language acquisition—all views have a role in our understanding of the child's ability to learn language. Research in this field continues to contribute to our understanding of the process. The three basic principles of language development that are agreed upon are as follows (Clark, 1983):

1. Young children generally have acquired the rules of their language by the time they enter school at age four or five.
2. The acquisition of language is a gradual process that has a predictable order.
3. Adults in the child's environment have an important influence on the acquisition of vocabulary, concepts, and fluency.

Forms of Language. Although much about the nature of language acquisition remains a mystery, we know that there are certain elements of language that all children acquire: phonology, syntax, and semantics. Jewell and Zintz have charted these three forms of language (see Figure 7.1). The phonology of the language is the sound system. The individual sound units are phonemes that are combined into

Phonology	Syntax	Semantics
Phonology is the study of the distinctive sounds of language.	Syntax, the grammar of the language, is the set of rules governing how morphemes are combined into sentences.	Semantics is the study of the meanings communicated through language.
1. There are forty-four distinctive sounds, called phonemes, in the English language.	1. Word order is an important distinctive feature of English. *Correct:* I see a bird. *Incorrect:* See I bird a.	1. The listener or the reader must rely on context clues; meanings depend upon context.
2. The alphabet is an imperfect representation of these sounds.	2. There are only a few basic "kernel" sentence patterns:	2. The English language contains many figures of speech, idiomatic expressions, slang expressions, antonyms, homonyms, homographs, and synonyms.

3. Phonemes combine into meaningful units of language called morphemes.	a. Noun, verb
	   b. Noun, transitive verb, object
	   c. Noun, linking verb, predicate noun or predicate adjective
	   d. Noun, verb, prepositional phrase
		3. English contains many words borrowed from other languages.

4. Stress, pitch, and juncture (called suprasegmentals) are distinctive features of English that *change meaning.*	3. Transformations:
	   a. Passive voice
	   b. Questions
	   c. Negatives
	   d. Imperatives
	   e. Using *it* and *there*
		4. The suprasegmentals — pitch, stress, and juncture — are phonemic because they change meanings, *but they are also* semantic because they communicate meaning changes.

5. Phoneme–grapheme relationships are often confusing because the same sound can have many variant spellings, and different sounds may have the same spelling.		

Figure 7.1 Three Forms of Language

M. G. Jewell & M. V. Zintz, *Learning to Read Naturally.* (Kendall/Hunt Publishing Company, 1986), p. 31.

meaningful utterances. The syntax of the language is the grammar. The child must learn the rules for how morphemes (the smallest units of meaning) can be combined in a sentence. The semantics of the language transmit the meaning of the communication. The child learns the cues in language that bring meaning to its spoken and written form. Every child lives in a unique community where language is used as a tool for communicating. Regardless of the variations in children's language communities, whether they are slight differences in a local English dialect or more significant, non-English-language, differences, the order in which children learn the forms of language remains the same.

Language Differences in the Preschool Years.   By the age of four or five the young child has acquired a basic mastery of the language spoken in the home. Although complete mastery is still to be developed, children are well on their way to using fully grammatical sentences and pronouncing words correctly. In spite of the common characteristics that children show in language development, there are also differences. The home and community language environments where the child learns to speak influence the kind of language that the child learns. Because adults in the child's home environment influence the child's opportunity to learn to speak, the type and frequency of language interactions between adults and children affect the course of the child's language development. Children who live in a family where the adults talk extensively to them and use opportunities for conversations to extend and expand language will develop a large vocabulary and be able to express fully formed sentences. On the other hand, children who live the preschool years in a home where the adults spend little time talking to them or use limited language when speaking to them will enter school with a more limited vocabulary and less developed sentence structures.

Some children live in homes where a language or dialect different from Standard English, the language used at school, is spoken. Children may thus come to school speaking a different dialect, such as Black English, which has a different structure than Standard English. Once thought to be an inferior form of Standard English, Black English has been found to have a sophisticated grammatical structure (Labov, 1970). Speakers of Black English use verbal games of wit and humor that are not part of Standard English (Hendrick, 1990). Teachers of children who speak Black English need to accept it as another fully developed language that is different from, but not inferior to, Standard English. Black children need to also acquire Standard English as a second language, as do other children who may speak a regional or subculture dialect of English. These children can maintain their home dialect and learn to determine when it is appropriate to switch to Standard English.

Children who come from a home where a language other than English is spoken will also need to learn Standard English. The most common non-English language spoken in the United States is Spanish. Other languages are spoken as well. It is not uncommon for elementary schools in urban and rural areas to have students who speak five or more different languages; moreover, they may speak different dialects of the languages. Teachers of young children who speak a language other than English will want to assist the child in learning English, while accepting and valuing the child's home language. In bilingual programs, adults who speak the child's home language work with the child using the first language as necessary to help them acquire English. Bilingual programs currently focus on a transition into English, although there are also maintenance bilingual programs in which equal emphasis is given to development and acquisition of literacy in both languages.

A more complex challenge for the teacher is the child who is limited in verbal skills and is not fluent in any language. Such a child may come from a home where adult–child interactions are very restricted. Bilingual children may be limited in the home language, as well as in English. Children who are lacking in speaking skills need special consideration, first to determine the cause of their limited language and then to provide special activities to help them develop language. The lack of language also might be traced to social immaturity, difficulty in feeling secure and comfortable in school, a hearing impairment, or a developmental delay. Whatever the source of the problem, an appropriate preschool program is begun as early as possible to provide intervention and remediation.

Children who come from diverse language backgrounds may have special needs for opportunities to learn Standard English. They will need to acquire the same skills in Standard English that they may be able to use in their home language or non–Standard English dialect. They must develop the ability to understand what is said to them, to organize and express their thoughts, and to communicate information to others (Schickedanz, York, Stewart, & White, 1990). The program for language development in the preschool years facilitates these abilities in children with various types of language differences and refines the same skills in children who have already developed a rich language prior to entering school.

PLANNING FOR LANGUAGE DEVELOPMENT

The curriculum for language development has as its first purpose to extend the child's acquisition of oral language. The most active period of development of the ability to communicate through speech occurs from the age of three to the age of five. The child at this period is also proceeding through the first steps of acquisition of written language. In planning for language development, the teacher conceptualizes a program that encompasses both oral and written literacy.

Goals for Language Development

There are four components of language that traditionally have formed the curriculum for language arts: listening, speaking, reading, and writing. The widely held belief for many years was that these language components were acquired in the order listed here. But research that has explicated the cognitive development view of cognition and the interactionist or constructivist view of language acquisition has influenced a revision of the sequential approach to language arts instruction. It is now proposed that these components of language should be integrated into a holistic approach without trying to separate categories or skills (Seefeldt & Barbour, 1990). Different components of the program are emphasized, depending on the context of the learning experiences; however, the teacher recognizes that progress in the various facets of language development results from interdependent experiences among the skills. The more the goals of language development are interrelated, the more meaningful the overall development of oral and written language.

Listening.   Children use different strategies for listening in varied contexts. Children who have been exposed to television tend to "tune out" distracting aural events. In school they need to know when to attend to classroom activities and when to screen out distracting noises. They need to be able to listen for instructions and develop an appreciation of language and environmental sounds. Spodek (1985) describes this listening ability as aesthetic appreciation of language.

Speaking.   Children acquire the basic elements of language through listening and speaking. Speaking facilitates the development of verbal communication skills, a rich language repertoire, and the ability to use language to influence and be influenced (Spodek, 1985). Children also learn to differentiate between when to use formal language or Standard English and when to use their community language, a dialect, or an informal language.

Writing.   Researchers of emergent literacy propose that reading does not precede writing. Rather, writing and reading play an interactive role as the child makes a transition from oral literacy to written literacy. As this development proceeds, children use writing to share information, show appreciation, or ask for information (Seefeldt & Barbour, 1990). As they experience opportunities to write, they will be able to move through more sophisticated forms of writing, from scribbling to formed letters and from invented spelling to correct spelling of words.

Reading.   In reading, children move from the simple to the complex, similar to the process of acquiring skills in writing. They reconstruct the ability to read as they discover how to decode and comprehend written material by learning to recognize letters and words, developing sound-to-symbol relationships, and understanding the relationships between letters grouped to form words and their meanings. They develop a process for using context to understand increasingly difficult content.

The Role of Play in Language Development

We understand that play is the vehicle for the young child's development and learning. This is particularly true for the development of language. Children use oral language in all facets of play as they communicate with each other and with adults and use language to express themselves in play. Younger children may verbalize their activities to themselves in solitary play. While engaged in social play, they may use metacommunication or talk about a play event interpersonally with others to negotiate or revise a play theme (Rogers & Sawyers, 1988). In her research of sociodramatic differences in dramatic play, Smilansky (1968) found that children from higher-income homes played a richer form of dramatic play that resulted in more successful learning later in school. She also found that adult involvement in play could extend and expand the fantasy play of children from families of low socioeconomic status (Johnson, Christie, & Yawkey, 1987).

Frost (1992) proposes that language has an important role for play but that play has an equally important role in the development of language. Language is used for make-believe, as an imitation of adult speech, and for management of play activities. Frost (1992, p. 40) cited Levy's research (1984) on the role of play in language and cognitive development as follows:

1. Play stimulates innovation in language (Bruner, 1983; Garvey, 1977)
2. Play introduces and clarifies new words and concepts (Chukovsky, 1971; Smilansky, 1968)
3. Play motivates language use and practice (Bruner, 1983; Garvey, 1977; Garvey & Hogan, 1973; Smilansky, 1968; Vygotsky, 1962)
4. Play develops metalinguistic awareness (Cazden, 1976)
5. Play encourages verbal thinking (Vygotsky, 1962)

The Role of the Teacher in Language Development

The teacher acts as facilitator, instructor, and model for language development. The teacher facilitates language development through setting up the indoor and outdoor environments to support children's play. Opportunities to develop oral and written literacy are encouraged through the availability of materials for creative expression, construction play, motor play, and dramatic play. The teacher serves as an instructor through teacher-directed activities and structured experiences that incorporate concept and vocabulary development and provide opportunities for written language. The teacher is a model for language development through all verbal interactions with children. Opportunities to extend play and language are afforded through observation of children's language during play. The teacher suggests ways to extend dramatic play themes and models how to increase language and written literacy experiences into play episodes (Johnson, Christie, & Yawkey, 1987; Morrow & Rand, 1991). The teacher plays alongside children in play episodes and models written language through reading, writing, and taking dictation from children within the play experience (Fields & Hillstead, 1990). The teacher provides a variety of meaningful activities that will promote both oral and written literacy (Fields, Spangler, & Lee, 1991).

DESIGNING CURRICULUM FOR LANGUAGE DEVELOPMENT

When planning the curriculum for language development in the preschool classroom, although the teacher is interested primarily in oral language development, he or she is also keenly aware of activities that will facilitate the transition into written language. The curriculum for oral language development can be organized into activities that will promote the child's expressive and receptive language. Expressive language is a combination of the phonetic, syntactic, and semantic elements that the child is able to use when speaking. Receptive language includes elements that the child has heard and understood but cannot yet use in his or her expressive language.

Literacy is developed when the child is able to use written language that includes writing and reading. In the preschool years, the language development program provides activities that will form the foundations for literacy. The teacher provides activities that encourage children to be actively involved in reconstructing their understanding of literacy. Children begin the process of becoming readers and writers through child-initiated and teacher-directed activities that lead to their making sense of how spoken language can be written and read. This approach to literacy is called emergent literacy by some language experts because the process emerges within the child rather than being taught by the teacher.

Experiences That Promote Expressive Language

Expressive language development is promoted through activities that motivate the child to use oral language. When the child is engaged in play and work activities that necessitate using descriptive language and communicating with adults and other chil-

dren, expressive language is being expanded and extended. Morrow (1989, p. 51–52) has developed objectives for the development of expressive language as follows:

1. Children will be given opportunities to use their own language freely at any stage of development. Their desire to communicate will be encouraged, accepted, and respected.
2. Children will be encouraged to pronounce words correctly.
3. Children will be given opportunities to increase their speaking vocabularies.
4. Children will be encouraged to speak in complete sentences at appropriate stages in their development.
5. Children will be given opportunities to expand their use of various syntactic structures, such as adjectives, adverbs, prepositional phrases, dependent clauses, plurals, the past tense, and possessives.
6. Children will be encouraged to communicate in such a way that allows them to be understood by others.
7. Children will be given opportunities to use language socially and psychologically by interpreting feelings, points of view, and motivation and by solving problems by generating hypotheses, summarizing events, and predicting outcomes.
8. Children will be given opportunities to develop language that involves mathematical and logical relations, such as describing size and amount, making comparisons, defining sets and classes, and reasoning deductively.

Arranging the classroom environment into centers for learning and play and providing generous blocks of time to engage in center activities are fundamental tasks for teachers involved in oral language development. Children use expressive language to discuss activities with their peers and the teacher and to plan and engage in play themes in the housekeeping or block center. Experiences in the art center, such as painting or working with clay, lead to expressive language, as children share their ideas or reflect on the process they are using to create a piece of art. Expressive communication occurs when children interact in the manipulative or math and science centers asking for directions, giving suggestions, and describing activities. The teacher is a major player in center activities as he or she asks questions, engages in dialogues with children who are working and playing in various centers, and offers suggestions about extending activities and thematic play.

> *Playing "Doctor"*
> "Let's play house."
> "Naw, I wanna play doctor."
> "OK, this is where the doctor lives."
> "Yeah, and the hospital's over here."
> "You be the mother."
> "I don't wanna be the mother. I'm the doctor."
> "Let's both be doctors!"
> "Yeah!" (Ishee & Goldhaber, 1990, p. 70–71)

Dramatic play within the housekeeping center or elsewhere offers possibly the most important opportunity for child-initiated expressive language. As children design and carry out play themes, language is used as the primary communication tool to facilitate the enactment of the fantasy or pretend play (Spodek, 1985). It should be remembered that outdoor play is essential as well. Although girls tend to engage in play focused on family themes indoors and outdoors, boys use more pretend play in outdoor environments, as they engage in their preferred play themes, which include superheroes (Johnson, Christie, & Yawkey, 1987).

Teacher-directed or -facilitated activities also stimulate expressive language. Class discussions during sharing times and conversations about planned or completed activities require expressive language. Teachers can encourage children to retell stories or tell about important events that have occurred. Reenactment of stories involves expressive language in dramatic play (Ishee & Goldhaber, 1990). Teacher-led discussions using wordless books likewise encourage children to use their own language to construct and describe stories to go with the pictures in the books (Raines & Isbell, 1988). Puppetry also provides a medium by which the teacher can encourage expressive oral language.

Experiences That Promote Receptive Language

If the child is to extend and expand language to more closely approximate adult language, opportunities to hear language modeled are also important. The child's receptive language will reflect the nature of the adult language that is heard. Parents and teachers who pronounce words carefully and spend time in dialogue and explanation will provide the child with models of language that can extend the child's current ability to express him- or herself verbally. Morrow (1989, p. 51) provided objectives for the development of receptive language as follows:

1. Children will be provided with an atmosphere in which they will hear language frequently.
2. Children will hear language associated with pleasure and enjoyment.
3. Children will be given opportunities to discriminate among sounds heard.
4. Children will be exposed to rich sources of new words.
5. Children will be given opportunities to listen and comprehend what others say.
6. Children will be given opportunities to learn to follow directions.

When children enter a school setting, they spend more time listening than they do in less structured environments. It is through listening that they will acquire additions to their receptive language that will also become part of their expressive language. There are many types of activities that teachers and parents can use to add to the child's language.

Telling and reading stories is a major activity used with young children to help them develop listening skills and receptive vocabulary. Not only are the children being exposed to new words, they are also acquiring new information. Opportunities to hear and "experience" stories can be enhanced through the use of cassette tapes and listening centers and videotapes of stories. Reading poetry exposes children to a rhythmic flow of words, and fingerplays add physical actions to poetry.

Teachers use conversation throughout the school day to inform, instruct, and share information with children. Language used as part of classroom routines adds to the opportunities to model language for children. Instructional activities led by the teacher add to oral language possibilities, as do dramatic play activities that involve the teacher as a player and director and informal interactions with children in indoor and outdoor play. Taking field trips to places that are informative and interesting to young children and listening to classroom guests who relate their experiences provide additional opportunities for children to hear language modeled by adults.

DEVELOPING FOUNDATIONS FOR LITERACY

What is literacy? When does it develop? Literacy is a continuous process that begins at birth and develops as children work on understanding and using oral and written language. Having an interest in books and stories and in using conversation to communicate is part of the process for developing literacy. Adults serve as facilitators for oral and written literacy when they talk to children, read to them, tell them stories, model the process of writing, point out environmental print, and encourage the children's interests and efforts (Fields, Spangler, & Lee, 1991).

Resolving the Conflict between Reading Readiness and Emergent Literacy

At the beginning of the chapter we described the instructional practices that were prevalent from the 1930s through the 1970s, when kindergarten children were taught readiness skills to get them ready for formal reading instruction in first grade. We also discussed how newer research into language and literacy acquisition has led to the development of emergent literacy programs to replace reading readiness instruction and a skills approach to beginning reading. Although many early childhood programs now emphasize emergent literacy or whole-language methods, there are still conflicts in early childhood programs between the two approaches to literacy.

When reading instruction is perceived as teaching a progression of skills, the process is thought of as incorporating a prereading, or readiness, stage. Acquisition of readiness skills is thought to be a necessary step toward reading. As the child progresses and begins to read, additional skills instruction assists in furthering reading competence. Letters and sounds are taught prior to using writing to communicate (Fields, Spangler, & Lee, 1991).

Emergent literacy, on the other hand, is based on the assumption that children construct an understanding of literacy as a result of their own experiences with language. Oral language, writing, and reading are developed as the child engages in writing letters and words, looking at books, hearing stories, and reading books. Just as children differ in their progress in oral language development depending on the type of language interactions they experience in the home environment, they also vary in their progress toward literacy. Some children come to school with a variety of literacy experiences and are well on their way to reading, whereas others have had few experiences and are just beginning the process of understanding written language (Baker & Raban, 1991). Proponents of early literacy focus on the child's effective development of language skills and steer away from preset skills and commercial readiness programs (Freeman & Hatch, 1989).

The conflict between the two perceptions of the beginning stages of reading has become significant because many preschool programs still tend to emphasize traditional reading readiness instruction tied to basal series and workbooks (Hatch & Freeman, 1988). Although professional organizations have expressed concerns about rigid, formal prereading programs (International Reading Association, 1985) the practice remained firmly entrenched in the 1980s (Teale & Sulzby, 1986). The more developmentally appropriate literacy approach is increasingly being used; nevertheless, many teachers have been hesitant to abandon teaching readiness skills. One reason for their reluctance has been that some parents have put pressure on schools to accelerate academic instruction in kindergarten (O'Brien, 1989). Another major concern is student performance on test scores when they enter public school. Many teachers are pressured to get the children to produce higher scores on standardized tests. Skills instruction leading to higher test scores takes precedence over the child's development of literacy in the more appropriate mode (Manning, Manning, & Kamii, 1988). This issue will be discussed again as it applies to curriculum in the primary grades in chapter 10.

In the years between three and five, the developmental approach to literacy is significant and meaningful. Relationships between the components of language and literacy development are experienced within the integrated curriculum; and the individual child's journey into literacy is reconstructed through experiences that promote child-initiated and teacher-directed activities in the curriculum for language development.

The Role of the Environment in Emergent Literacy

The preschool classroom has been described as an inviting environment for young children. It is arranged into learning or activity areas that provide for creative, construction, dramatic, and manipulative play. The centers are arranged with materials that permit children to work on projects, express themselves through art and writing materials, and engage in pretend or role play as well as in dramatic play, including puppetry and story reenactment. Some of the activities that can be experienced in learning centers are selected by children in their own planning for work and play. Other activities are planned by the teacher and may involve the teacher's direction or indirect facilitation.

When considering use of the environment for language development, steps are taken to make the total area "print rich." According to Freeman and Hatch (1989), the term *print rich environment* implies that print should be everywhere in the form of labels, lists, signs, charts, and posters. Print materials are available in play centers to support literacy in children's play. The dramatic play center includes literacy materials consistent with changing play themes. When the play or study theme involves a grocery store, for example, the center includes empty food containers with familiar labels and paper and pencils for making grocery lists and pricing items (Fields & Hillstead, 1990). A social studies theme on the post office includes mailboxes for the children, envelopes, stamps, and greeting cards (Hatch & Freeman, 1988). The art center has writing materials for writing or dictating stories about pictures and other art work.

The library or language center is obviously the major area to support literacy development. It contains materials for all components of the language curriculum, including listening, speaking, writing, and reading. The writing area of the center has a variety of writing materials, including paper, pencils, markers, crayons, and pens. The reading area has shelves to house a large supply of picture concept books, picture storybooks, realistic literature or real-life storybooks, easy-to-read books, informational books, books with fables and folktales, wordless books, and books of poetry. Some of the shelving can be used to store a large number of books, and other shelves are open-faced, allowing children to be attracted by the covers of the books (Morrow, 1989). At least one shelf is reserved for books specific to the theme of study. Big books previously read by the teacher are also available for rereading by the children.

A listening center with cassette tapes of recorded books and a copy of the book for each headset provides opportunities for children to listen to stories throughout center activity periods. The center might also house a rocking chair and include soft seating areas with cushions, carpeting, beanbag chairs, and other arrangements that invite individuals and groups of children to browse and read.

The language center is enhanced by language experience charts, typewriters, a computer, and materials for making books. An alphabet chart is useful for children who are beginning to recognize and use letters, and a message board hung at the child's eye level can have examples of functional messages related to the school.

The teacher's role in the environment is to read to the children, engage in conversations about topics being studied, involve children in dictating contributions for language experience charts, discuss and share books and stories, and use poetry and fingerplays with the children. The child's role in the environment is to write on a daily basis, explore new books, review familiar books, listen to stories, engage in pretend and dramatic play, dictate stories, and discuss work and play activities (Freeman & Hatch, 1989; Gothard & Russell, 1990; Teale, 1987). More about these activities and the language development curriculum is described in the following sections on emergent literacy.

Emergent Writing

We know that developing literacy is an ongoing process that begins at birth and continues throughout the early childhood years. Morrow (1989) explains that the developmental process begins with learning to communicate first nonverbally and then verbally. Symbolic play follows, and then drawing emerges.

The process of using written language begins with playing with it before it is used to communicate. First attempts at writing consist of making marks on paper without understanding that the alphabet is used to symbolize speech. Later, children under-

FORM	CHARACTERISTICS
Scribble	Random scribbles with no differentiation between drawing and writing.
Drawing	Illustrations tell a story.
Linear-repetitive	Linear, uniform in size, repetitious, symbolic. Has shape of writing.
Letterlike	Looks somewhat like letters. No more than two letters alike next to each other.
Imitating conventional print	Direct copying or memorized writing.
Letters—nonphonetic	Use of letters with no attempt at making sound–symbol relationship. May include reordering letters of memorized words.
Invented spelling	Nonstandard forms that adults may not easily recognize.
Beginning	Child uses hypothesis such as letter name as sounds or one letter per syllable.
Advanced	Child attempts to regularize sound–symbol relationships.
Standard spelling	Child compares own spelling with that in books and that done by adults. Self-correction to match models results in more standard spelling.

Figure 7.2   Emergent Writing Forms

M. V. Fields, K. L. Spangler, & D. L. Lee, *Let's Begin Reading Right* (2nd ed.). (Merrill, 1991), p. 132. Reprinted by permission.

stand that letters are used to encode speech and that writing represents language (Ferreiro & Teberosky, 1982).

Research is being conducted to establish how children move through stages of understanding and use writing to communicate. Two sets of researchers (Sulzby, Barnhart, & Hieshima, 1989; Fields, Spangler, & Lee, 1991) have characterized these stages in different ways; both characterizations of the development of written literacy are helpful in understanding how a child learns to write.

Sulzby, Barnhart, and Hieshima (1989) have established six categories of writing, rather than a developmental sequence, that demonstrate ways that children attempt to write:

1. drawing
2. scribbling
3. making letterlike forms
4. reproducing well-learned units (i.e., letter sequences that are familiar, such as those that spell the child's name)

5. invented spelling
6. conventional spelling

Although the sequences are not considered stages, the categories reveal the evolution of understanding written language and the way in which children use writing experiences to express themselves.

Fields, Spangler, and Lee (1991) describe the progression of written literacy in terms of written forms. Figure 7.2 is a list of these forms with explanations of their characteristics. The researchers explain the sequence as beginning with scribbling and evolving to advanced standard spelling in the elementary school years.

Activities for Promoting Emergent Writing.   Children between the ages of three and five are at different levels in their progress toward written literacy. Some will be engaged in scribbling, whereas others will be interested in copying words and using invented spelling. The teacher makes available activities that encompass levels of ability within the group, as well as materials that will appeal to individual interests. In addition to providing writing opportunities and materials in the environment, planning is conducted for teacher-directed and child-centered activities. There are specific strategies the teacher can use to demonstrate how to write and use writing to communicate. The teacher will model writing by using it in a meaningful context the children can observe several times each day on the chalkboard or an experience chart. Dictation is taken from the children daily, both individually and as a part of group activities. Some dictation can be in the form of writing down experience chart stories,

ildren in a small group take turns contributing items for the chart follow-
esting classroom discussion. The teacher can write notes to individual
l make the children aware when notes are being written to parents or
'Hayes, 1990; Morrow, 1989). In addition to ensuring that written lan-
g modeled in various contexts throughout the day, there are other activ-
ner can conduct with the children. Suggestions for some activities are
......cu in the following sections.

My Very Own Word

Each day, the child is invited to determine the important word of that day (Morrow,
1989). The teacher writes the important word at the top of a large piece of manila
paper. The child draws a picture about the word. The child then returns to the
teacher and dictates a story about the picture. The important word is also written on
a file card to be put in the child's favorite-word box or bank. When ten to fifteen
word pictures are completed, they are stapled into a book. Word cards are used for
reviewing favorite words, copying, or recoding on a word list on the computer. The
child can reread the dictated stories.

Today's Plans

Each morning during planning time the teacher writes the day's plans on an experience chart as the day's activities are discussed. The teacher and the children read
and reread the plans. Later, the experience chart is placed in a convenient place for
easy access by the children who might wish to use it for their own writing and reading. They might choose to copy words or rewrite the sentences on their own sheet of
paper.

Journals

This process is normally used with older students but is adaptable for younger children. Each child is given a booklet of blank pages of paper that form a journal. Every
day, children and teacher write in their journals. Over a period of time teachers and
children review their entries in their journals. Young children may start with drawings
and gradually develop writing skills and the use of letter forms and invented spelling.

Group Dictation

Children dictate ideas for an experience chart following a learning activity, a story, a
field trip, an art experience, or an unexpected event. The dictated contributions are
recorded on an experience chart using the following guidelines:

1. Each statement is recorded exactly as dictated by the child, without correction of errors.
2. Each new contribution is started on a new line.
3. Punctuation marks can be highlighted using a red marking pen.
4. For preschool children, the dictated story should be limited to five statements.
5. The teacher rereads the statement as it is being written to draw the students' attention to the relationship between the spoken and written word. When completed, the entire statement is reread with the teacher using a hand to guide the child's eye along the words from left to right.
6. When the story is completed, the entire text is reread, again with the teacher guiding the flow from left to right below the written words.

Class Books

Class books are a collection of writing and drawing efforts that are created as a result of a thematic study or special class event or project. The illustrated writing effort of each child is collected into a book and put into the library for all to enjoy. A title for the book is selected by the class to go on the book cover.

Thematic Prop Boxes

Collections of materials and objects for thematic play are organized into prop boxes. The boxes contain writing and reading materials needed for the particular dramatic play theme. Morrow and Rand (1991) suggest a newspaper office setting, with writing paper, newspaper, telephones, telephone directories, maps, typewriters, and pens and pencils to stimulate writing efforts in the dramatic play center.

Sentence Strips

Sentences from group and individual stories are written on a tagboard sentence strip. The strip is then cut apart. Children can reassemble the sentence and copy it. They can also write more sentences using the first sentence as a model.

Both teacher-planned and informal opportunities that occur during play are used for written language. Birthday cards and stories are used as part of the celebration of a birthday. Children can write or dictate thank-you notes after a special class event such as an outing or a party. Constructions or projects can be labeled, as can record keeping of work done as part of integrated learning activities (Hayes, 1990). The teacher and children are constantly alert to the possibilities for using writing during classroom routines and learning experiences.

Emergent Reading

How do three-, four-, and five-year-olds engage in the lifelong process of learning to read? From the time that an infant is propped up on his or her mother's lap to share a picture book, the reading process has begun. The young child engages in the problem-solving process of understanding the relationship between speaking and the symbols that appear on a page each time a book is read. Teale (1982) proposed that the child's involvement in reading activities in a social context with a significant person is a key to acquiring literacy. He also concluded that reading and writing are learned in real-life settings when the child participates in activities where reading and writing are used in a meaningful context (Teale, 1986). In the preschool years, the child observes parents reading, is read to daily, sees adults writing and reading notes and letters, and begins to understand the purpose for written language.

There is evidence that understanding the purpose for written symbols comes at an early age. Toddlers become fascinated with environmental symbols—they are able to identify the golden arches of McDonald's restaurants and the graphics on the package of their favorite cereal. Understanding of environmental print and symbols expands rapidly as children are bombarded with visual symbols both inside and outside the home. Investigators have determined that children as young as three are able to read common words in the environment (Hiebert, 1986; Mason, 1980).

Children who are read to frequently between the ages of three and five make significant progress in learning to read. In addition to understanding how print is organized and used, they learn about books and how they are used. Wiseman and Robeck (1983) described book knowledge that young children acquired from reading experiences as knowing what the difference is between the beginning and the end of the book, where to begin reading, how to turn pages, and what the difference is between pictures and print, in addition to having an awareness that print moves from left to right.

What do parents and teachers do that nurtures the acquisition of reading? Jewell and Zintz (1986) described factors that occur in the home and are associated with developing the ability to read. First, children were not only read to, but also mothers engaged in incidental reading and pointing out environmental print throughout the day; they drew the child's attention to food labels and to familiar products advertised on television. Second, there were reading materials for both parents and children in the home; books of all types—from storybooks to nursery rhymes and fairy tales— were read and reread to the children many times. Third, the parents served as reading models; parents read frequently, allowing children to observe that reading was an important, positive activity for them. Fourth, writing materials were readily available to the children; they learned to move between reading and writing as they progressed in their knowledge of letter forms and the use of letters to communicate ideas. Fifth, persons in the environment were responsive and encouraging with the child's attempts at reading and writing; parental help was provided not as a formal, systematic process but rather in response to incidental questions and requests for help.

The same types of experiences found in the home that nurture the acquisition of literacy are used with preschool children in group settings. The foundations for the acquisition of reading are developed through interactions with many types of books and stories and extensive experiences with environmental print.

Once the child has acquired basic knowledge about books and the ways in which they are used, how does the process evolve into recognition of words and meanings from printed materials? Three kinds of reading behavior develop concurrently (Goodman, 1984; Mason, 1984; Morrow, 1989):

1. The child learns to understand the functions of print (such as environmental print) and family and teacher use of print, as was discussed earlier.
2. The child learns about the forms of print. The child acquires information about names, sounds, and shapes of letters.
3. The child learns how to use the conventions of print, such as the organization of letters into words, left-to-right progression, punctuation, and use of upper- and lowercase letters.

The development of word identification is acquired in three steps (McCormick & Mason, 1981):

1. Words are identified in context.
2. Words are identified using letter sound cues.
3. Words are sounded out.

In spite of the descriptions characterizing the process of becoming a reader, all children progress by using their own sequence and system of interpretation of reading and by using their own reading experiences as a guide. Learning to read is a complex process that cannot be easily described in stages and categories. The kinds of classroom experiences planned for children from three to five are based on the knowledge we have about reading acquisition and accommodate individual differences in progress and interest.

Activities for Promoting Emergent Reading. Books and book reading form a central element of the journey into reading. Daily experiences with new and familiar books are the nucleus of the transition into literacy, with each child benefitting from the experiences according to his or her own current understanding of the reading process. Beyond the obvious need for sharing books with children, there are activities that will facilitate understanding and use of written language, which will develop into reading. The activities can be understood by recalling the categories of reading behavior introduced above.

Activities for Understanding the Functions of Print. From their experiences with storybooks and other types of books, children learn that print is used to tell a story. They also learn that written language is used for other kinds of communication. When they engage in writing letters and notes, writing stories for their "very own words," and dictating individual or group stories, they are developing an understanding of how print is used to communicate ideas or feelings. When environmental print in the form of posters, empty product containers, and labels and other printed information is used in the classroom to give instructions and information, children become aware of how people use print to convey information. When reading and writing are used in thematic unit activities, the usefulness of print is conveyed.

Activities for Learning to Use the Forms of Print.   Visual experiences with print facilitate the development of understanding of the forms and sounds of letters. Individual writing experiences, dictated stories, big-book experiences (where children can follow the print as a story is read), and follow-up experiences (where children work with individual letter sounds and symbols with a written communication) allow the child to understand and identify letters. This process can evolve from experiences with environmental print, book narratives, individual writing efforts, and other activities where there are opportunities to develop an awareness of letter forms and learn the associated sounds and names.

Activities for Learning to Use the Conventions of Print.   Again, the activities used to acquire the other reading behaviors apply also to the ability to use the conventions of print. Through activities in which these conventions are used, the child learns that reading progresses from left to right, that letters are combined into words, that written statements are punctuated, and that both uppercase and lowercase letters are used in print. Dictating stories, reading big books, writing individually, and other written communication activities can be used to develop an awareness of the functions of the conventions of print. The sentence strip activities described in the section on written literacy can be used for understanding words, punctuation, and the use of upper- and lowercase letters.

In addition to the strategies just described, there are activities that serve multiple purposes in facilitating the development of literacy. Four of these—story reenactments, dictated stories, big-book activities, and predictable stories—are discussed below.

Story Reenactments

Story reenactment is a form of retelling a story. Story dramatization encourages oral communication as children discuss the plot, the sequence of events, and the characters' roles. Listening skills are enhanced because the children must pay careful attention to the content of the story prior to planning the reenactment (Han, 1991). By acting out a story, children strengthen their comprehension and memory of the story. Reenactment is a form of sociodramatic play that includes guidance and direction from the teacher. The teacher thus should help the players use fantasy play in their reenactment of the story (Ishee & Goldhaber, 1990).

A familiar story is used with this form of thematic-fantasy play. "The Three Bears" and "The Three Little Pigs" are two familiar stories commonly suggested for reenactment. The teacher has an important role in making sure that the story has been shared frequently and is well understood by the children. Props and costumes are important. The teacher determines which props are important to the story narrative. The teacher and players review the sequence of the story. During the fantasy play experience, the teacher prompts and cues as the children are guided through the sequence of the story (Johnson, Christie, & Yawkey, 1987). Because children develop their reenactment skills through practice, the reenactment is repeated several times. The teacher continues in the role of director, narrator, and actor but modifies each role as the children become more accomplished in the process (Ishee & Goldhaber, 1990).

Story reenactment helps foster social skills because children must plan and act together. They have to take turns and negotiate their parts just as they do in self-initiated fantasy play. They learn how to cooperate and participate in a group effort (Han, 1991).

Big-Book Activities

Big books are enlarged versions of books that are appropriate for young children. They serve the same purposes as any storybook; however, because of their size they are especially suited to group activities because all children can see the pictures and print. After the text is read, the books can be used for follow-up activities similar to those applicable to dictated group stories. When the book is read and reread, the teacher follows the text with a hand, allowing the children to make the relationships between the story and the written words. As the story is reread frequently, the teacher can highlight different print conventions (such as punctuation), point out letter–sound relationships, refer to spoken and written word relationships, and test comprehension skills, such as the ability to predict what will happen next in the story. For example, when rereading a big-book story, the teacher might do one or more of the following:

1. Call attention to punctuation marks. Teacher and children can compare the use of periods, question marks, and exclamation points.
2. Identify letters and words. Given a file card with a letter or word written on it, the child can match it with the same letter or word on a page in the story.
3. Identify letter sounds in the story. The teacher can point out an important word on a page and help the children identify the beginning and ending sound of the word and the letters that make the sounds.
4. Develop book knowledge. Children can identify such things as where reading begins on a page, when to turn a page, and where the front and back of the book are (Cassady, 1988).
5. Identify upper- and lowercase letters. Given a card with both upper- and lowercase forms of a letter, the child can find each form on a page of the big book. Discussion of the uses of upper- and lowercase letters can be a part of the activity.

Dictated Stories

The same strategies that are used with big books can also be used with group dictated stories. Following rereadings of the dictated story, the teacher can select the print knowledge characteristics that are addressed in the story and conduct activities that will develop the child's awareness and understanding. Any activities that can be used with big books can also be used with dictated stories. Because both use a large-size format, they are useful for group activities.

Predictable Books

Predictable books and stories have a pattern that can be chanted by the children as the teacher reads the story. The predictable pattern can also be used by the children in their own story writing. Two examples of books with predictable patterns are *The Three Billy Goats Gruff* and *Chicken Soup with Rice* (Sendak, 1962). In the poem "Over in the Meadow" (Keats, 1971), the repetitive pattern includes the sequence of numbers from one to ten. Through repeated readings of such poems and stories, children learn the rhythm of the poem or sentence patterns and enjoy participating in the reading. When using a repetitive pattern for their own writing, they can exercise their creativity and vocabulary in making their own repetitive statements.

DESIGNING LANGUAGE CURRICULUM FOR CHILDREN WITH SPECIAL NEEDS

Emergent literacy is a process of literacy acquisition that is flexible and adaptable to various levels of development. Its flexible nature is applicable to children who have special needs for learning in the preschool years. Little modification is needed in many classroom experiences, because there is no set level of participation required. For example, Mills and Clyde (1991) describe a child with mental retardation in a preschool classroom who used paper and pencil in the housekeeping center to engage in pretend play about renting a house. He used his own level of writing skills to make an inventory of the contents of the house.

Adapting the curriculum for hearing-impaired and deaf children requires more planning and thought because sign language is different from oral language. The musical features of rhymes are lost when translated into sign language. Dowd (1991) recommends the substitution of physical actions and visual picture clues to help hearing-impaired children make sense of Mother Goose rhymes.

Children whose first language is not English or who are limited in their ability to speak English are in the process of learning English as a second language. Because research literature supports the theory that children use the same process to learn a second language as they do to learn the first, the same emergent process to achieve literacy can be used with them (Abramson, Seda, & Johnson, 1990). Activities that integrate reading, writing, and language development will help the child acquire language and literacy in a meaningful context. Dictated stories, journal writing, and the use of books and stories are equally important. The teacher needs to be sensitive to the child's limitations in language and accept the more limited vocabulary and syntax in the child's early efforts. Time is needed in oral conversations for the child to consider how to respond in the new language.

In a bilingual program in southern Texas, a family literacy project with young children utilized a similar, whole-language approach to achieving literacy in English. Parents who were Spanish speakers were engaged in an effort to achieve English and literacy simultaneously. The designers of the project used the same strategies that have been described in this chapter and included integrated themes in the learning process. Parents and children worked together in their writing of stories. The authors stressed the need for the acceptance of code switching (i.e., the use of both Spanish and English in language efforts) as this population of learners grew in their ability to write, speak, and read English. Code switching is a natural part of the process of mastering and using the English language (Quintero & Huerta-Macias, 1990).

The thematic curriculum used in the project follows a sequence. The theme study begins with a discussion of the topic. As part of the discussion, parents are given information on how to have meaningful conversations with the children and expand their use of the language. A learning activity following the discussion permits the parents and children to work together in a hands-on activity. Next, a language experience activity engages parent and child in writing projects. The child may dictate a story or write a message. The parent's own level of literacy will dictate how much support will be needed from the teacher. Story reading is a fourth activity, and an activity for parent and child to take and do at home ends the activities for the session. Because these activities are suitable for children who have limited use of English, they can also be used in preschool classrooms with special attention to adapting teacher language and expectations to the child's language ability. Abramson, Seda, and Johnson (1990) propose that the teacher must use caretaker speech similar to the simplified speech used with infants and toddlers to assist the developing speaker through labeling, clarifying, and extending efforts to speak.

With careful planning, teachers can use the language curriculum with all children. The child's level of participation will vary or may have to be modified for a specific language difference, but the process and philosophy remain the same. The teacher tunes in to the individual child's stage of learning and individual combinations of abilities and limitations and finds the activities that the child can take part in to achieve literacy.

CURRICULUM FOR COGNITIVE DEVELOPMENT

In the preschool years, young children are expanding their knowledge about the world. They construct their understanding through encounters with the world. Between the ages of three and five, the child's thinking process changes as the sensorimotor period proposed by Piaget is left behind and preoperational thought is used to understand experiences the child has in the world. In this section we will explore the nature of cognition between the ages of three and five and the way in which educators structure the environment, activities, and behaviors to foster cognitive development. We will study cognitive development as it applies to science and mathematics. (Social development, or cognitive development as it is reflected in the content area of social studies, will be discussed in chapter 8.) We will also consider an example of integrated, thematic curriculum that features language and cognitive development.

It is urgent that a quality cognitive curriculum is introduced to young children in the preschool years. Because students in the United States compare unfavorably in mathematics and science with students from other industrialized countries, there is a national effort to improve the curriculum in these areas. Moreover, the gap in learning appears as early as kindergarten and first grade (Price, 1989; Stevenson, Lee, & Stigler, 1986). The implication for educators of children in early childhood programs is that cognitive development, particularly the study of concepts in mathematics and science, should be a strong component of the preschool curriculum.

How Young Children Develop Concepts

In chapter 3 we described developmental progress in cognition in the early childhood years. The preoperational child has entered a period that includes symbolic thought—the child is able to mentally represent objects and events. Children are controlled by what they see or perceive. Because they focus on one characteristic or attribute of an object at a time (i.e., centration), they are unable to organize objects using true classification. For example, if a child is asked to study two sets of objects to determine if they are equivalent, the physical size or arrangement of the objects, rather than just the number of objects in the two sets, will affect the child's response (Dutton & Dutton, 1991). The child lacks the ability to process multiple comparisons and to conserve (Schultz, Colarusso, & Strawderman, 1992).

The process used by the child to construct understanding of concepts involves hands-on interactions with concrete materials. Between the ages of three and five, children develop their schema about concepts through repeated experiences with a variety of materials to explore the possibilities those materials present.

Mathematics experiences prepared for preschool children should take into account the child's cognitive limitations and present a minimum of perceptual difficulties. Dutton and Dutton (1991) advise that concrete materials must be made available to manipulate, act on, arrange, and classify. They propose that the available objects should be familiar from the child's daily life. Buttons, keys, bottle caps, marbles, and rocks are examples of objects from the child's environment that provide meaningful mathematical experiences.

Science concepts, likewise, are learned through discovery and exploration. Preoperational children develop a familiarity with the phenomenal world that builds a foundation for later scientific learning. As children explore and experiment with their environment, they acquire the processes of scientific thinking—forming concepts and problem solving—at the same time that they acquire knowledge about the products of science (biological and physical sciences) (Seefeldt & Barbour, 1990). To engage in this process, children need opportunities with the environment to see, hear, touch, taste, and smell. The teacher provides the environmental experiences that will facilitate the child's internal ability to construct an understanding of scientific phenomena. As a result of these interactions, the child can construct the cognitive framework for meaningful and useful concepts.

Planning for Cognitive Development

Extensive research has been conducted on how children acquire concepts in the preoperational period. In addition, we have information about the sequence of concept development in mathematics and science. In setting curriculum goals for cognitive development, we must become familiar with the nature of progress in cognitive development, the way in which this understanding helps us organize instruction for cognitive curriculum, and the goals and objectives for preschool children.

Children acquire concepts through manipulation, observation, and discovery. An understanding of concepts is acquired through physical knowledge—the child's physical interaction with information rather than social transmission from one child to another (Piaget & Inhelder, 1969). Children construct their own understanding from their own manipulations and discoveries. The individual child's schema of concepts varies in content and rate, depending on frequency and context of experience. The child's ability to understand concepts related to mathematics and science in the preoperational period is developed through discrimination, classification, and one-to-one correspondence. Although the child lacks the ability to conserve or process multiple comparisons, he or she can focus on attributes and make global comparisons. The child can use discrimination to compare shapes, sizes, and colors. Discrimination of characteristics can be used to group objects and to determine what belongs or does not belong to a group.

One-to-one correspondence is a prerequisite to being able to count, add, and subtract. Matching sets of objects precedes the understanding of numbers, whereas seriation leads to the ability to order by size, texture, quantity, and other attributes (Schultz, Colarusso, & Strawderman, 1989). Although the child is functioning at a perceptual level, skills are being developed for higher-order cognitive development in science and mathematics.

For preoperational children, learning how to count is a major step in understanding numbers. The child moves through a succession of steps or observes principles in learning to count. First, the child learns that he or she needs to use the same number of counting words or tags as there are objects, even if the counting word order is unconventional. Next, the child understands that the sequence of counting words always follows the same order. The child then can make the connection between numbers and the process of counting (Gelman & Gallistel, 1978).

Learning in science results from a store of concepts that can be used when thinking about or understanding relationships between objects, events, or situations. Through observing and discriminating, children begin to categorize their experiences. First, broad categories are developed, followed by subcategories. Thus, all four-legged animals may be identified as dogs before the child understands the category of animal and subcategories of dogs, cats, cows, horses, and so on. Through discrimination of similarities and differences, the child determines what does or does not belong in a category.

Once the child has a broad base of concepts and can see relationships among concepts, generalizations can be made. The three processes of forming concepts—differentiating, grouping, and labeling—enable children to make sense of the hands-on encounters with the environment. Daily encounters with the environment and concept-building experiences are the foundation for acquiring concepts in science (Seefeldt & Barbour, 1990).

Approaches to Organizing Instruction for Cognitive Development

If children construct knowledge through the process of developing concepts, and if that process results from manipulation, observation, and discovery, how should instruction be organized? In addition to the contributions of Piaget, Jerome Bruner and Robert Gagne broadened our understanding of how interactive, cognitive experiences can be provided for young children.

Cliatt and Shaw (1992, p. 11) reported on five factors in Piaget's research that promote learning. They summarized these factors as follows:

1. Physical experience: manipulation of real materials
2. Social experience: interaction with others, confronting the ideas and views of others
3. Logical-mathematical experience: activities involving comparing, grouping, taking apart and putting together, seriating, and counting
4. Equilibration: a mental state of balance in which people take in new information and organize it into both their existing and changing mental schemes
5. Maturation: the passing of time

These five factors are all part of the process of manipulation, observation, and discovery. Experiences with real events and materials enable the child to use the first four of Piaget's factors in learning. Piaget also introduced the notion that the child not only needs to begin with real, concrete experiences but that a progression from concrete to abstract is a logical sequence in the child's understanding.

Jerome Bruner extended this idea in suggesting that children organize information in a mode of learning through discovery. Hands-on, discovery learning facilitates learning through inquiry, problem solving, and decision making. Bruner explicated three modes of presentation for combining the discovery learning process with a progression from concrete to abstract. The **enactive** mode provides contact with real objects. The **ikonic** mode employs representations of objects through models, pictures, and diagrams. And the **symbolic,** or language, mode uses words or written symbols to promote learning through discovery (Cliatt & Shaw, 1992).

Robert Gagne proposed that the process of inquiry and problem solving is taught by teaching young children to observe, describe, classify, measure, and infer. Seefeldt and Barbour (1990) reported that available science curricula, such as *Science—A Process Approach* (produced by the American Association for the Advancement of Science) and the *Science Curriculum Improvement Study* (developed by Robert Karplus at the University of California), use these processes.

Goals for Cognitive Development

When planning curriculum for cognitive development in mathematics and science for children between the ages of three and five, the influence of Piaget, Bruner, and Gagne and the interrelated nature of learning is evident. In fact, it is impossible to clearly delineate between science and mathematics because the cognitive-developmental description of the learning–thinking process is the foundation for both of the content areas. The preoperational child's cognitive development is assessed through tasks based on Piaget's processes of classification, seriation, and discrimination. Goals for cognitive development in mathematics and science are also derived from these processes.

Beaty (1992, p.99) described preschool practices for mathematics to include the following categories:

- Classification: the ability to group objects that have common characteristics
- One-to-one correspondence: the ability to match objects with each other because they belong together
- Seriation: the ability to order objects by size, texture, taste, color, sound, etc., in ascending to descending order
- Counting: the ability to name numbers in a fixed sequence and apply this to one object at a time, arriving at a total

Similar categories have been used to organize science processes that are congruent with Gagne's scheme for planning for concept development: observing, communicating, ordering, classifying, predicting, and inferring (Cliatt & Shaw, 1992; Seefeldt & Barbour, 1990). Regardless of these similarities, there are unique characteristics that can be applied to mathematics and science when organizing curriculum.

Mathematics is a science of numbers and their operations. For preoperational children, working with math is a process of constructing knowledge about mathematical concepts and engaging in problem solving. Through exploring, grouping and sorting objects, and making comparisons, young children develop understanding of the concept of number and its relationship to measuring quantity. Although each specialist in early childhood education might describe the processes of mathematics differently, one approach to organization might be the following:

Number
  One-to-one correspondence
  Counting
  Numeration
  Number operations

Measurement
  Length
  Width
  Distance
  Time
  Money

Geometry
  Shapes
  Patterns

Mathematical Reasoning
  Seriating
  Classifying and comparing
  Estimating
  Problem solving

Cognitive development in science follows a slightly different process. Children construct a framework of understanding that is based on observing, thinking, and reflecting on experiences they have engaged in with phenomena in the environment. In the scientific process, children use their experiences to form hypotheses, collect data, make decisions about the hypotheses, and make generalizations about their information. The scientific process includes the following (Brewer, 1992; Seefeldt & Barbour, 1990):

- Observing: children look for actions or information.
- Classifying and comparing: children compare and contrast information and group or classify.
- Measuring: data is collected through some type of measurement.

- Communicating: children share their observations and data collections.
- Experimenting: children manipulate conditions (e.g., trying a new way to ride a tricycle or experimenting with ways to construct bristle blocks).
- Relating, inferring, and applying: children draw relationships or determine cause and effect.

Designing programs in science to utilize the scientific process with preschool children can include topics such as the following: animals, plants, space, water, air, and light. Science curriculum can also be organized by categories of science: biological, physical, and earth science. Whatever scheme is used to plan the curriculum, it is organized in a meaningful, child-centered context that encourages young children to discover, explore, reflect upon their experiences, and represent their understanding of what they are learning.

In summary, cognitive development does not occur in isolation. Just as mathematics and science cannot be separated, cognitive development cannot be separated from physical, social, and language development. Developmental learning is integrated; furthermore, cognitive development as reflected in science and mathematics is best learned within real-life experiences that also promote other skills and opportunities to represent and express relationships and learning.

The Role of the Teacher in Cognitive Development

The adult's role in facilitating cognitive development includes making plans for including both teacher-directed and child-directed activities and experiences. Using center time, small-group and large-group time, and other scheduled components of the day, opportunities are planned for children to engage in activities that will help them to develop and expand concepts. Keeping in mind the processes that young children use to learn, the teacher will consider how to include experiences that will permit observing, manipulating, hypotheses testing, inferring, and other procedures that will promote scientific thinking and exploration with mathematical concepts.

The teacher will also want to keep in mind the sequences of learning that are developmentally appropriate for children in the preschool years and are logical for curriculum planning. The sequence of concrete to abstract ensures that the child will begin exploring a concept using manipulative materials or real phenomena such as plants, animals, and food items. The sequence of simple to complex will be maintained so that learning experiences follow a logical hierarchy that will guide the child's understanding of new information. For example, in working with mathematical concepts, the teacher will first include many experiences with number before adding numeral names. Likewise, the children will need to have confidence in both number and numeral names before counting and combining sets of objects and using the correct numerals with the sets.

The teacher will want to include many opportunities for children to use the sequence of experiencing and representing, particularly in working with concepts in science. Experiencing is part of the scientific process of observing, manipulating, ordering, and classifying. The child first needs to directly experience the concept. Representing is the child's opportunity to reflect on what is being understood. In science terms, inferring from data or making a decision about a hypothesis are methods of using representation to reflect knowledge being acquired. The child can use representation in math activities to practice or apply what is being learned.

The teacher will also consider how best to organize learning experiences. When is it best to plan teacher-directed activities for exploration, and when can children freely explore on their own? How much teacher guidance is needed for children to experiment with a concept? For example, if children are learning about plants, how much adult guidance is needed in planting seeds and monitoring the watering cycle? Which teacher-directed learning activities are best for small groups, and when are large-group times more effective? The processes for child-centered learning that are developmentally appropriate are combined with the unique characteristics of concept development in science and mathematics to plan meaningful, interesting activities for the children.

The Role of the Environment and Play in Cognitive Development

If children are to actively explore concepts in science and mathematics, the environment is an essential element. The classroom needs to have a center for exploration of mathematical and scientific materials. The center needs to have a multitude of common objects for working with number. Collections of many different objects from the community can be used for work in mathematics. Earlier, buttons were suggested as a resource; bottle caps, dried beans, nuts, shells, and other natural objects can be used as sources for the math center.

The science center can include insect cages, small animal cages, magnifiers, a terrarium, microscopes, aquaria, rock and mineral collections, plants, and many other resources (Barufaldi, Ladd, & Moses, 1984). A changing array of additional items can be introduced as part of thematic units throughout the year.

Not to be forgotten is the significance of the outdoor environment. If science and mathematics are to be understood as part of the child's world, the outdoor environment should be an extended classroom where much of the work can take place. The nearby community can also be explored for materials that expand the child's encounters with concepts.

If children are to learn through free exploration, then play is an essential ingredient in cognitive development. Much of what is learned is not the result of planned experiences but of incidental circumstances that occur during play. A child learns about weather when she observes leaves blowing in the wind or rushes inside the building when a rain shower moves to the playground. A child playing at a water table indoors learns about the qualities of water and what objects will sink and float in water through experimentation during a play experience.

Guided discovery of concepts can also achieve a similar result. The teacher can guide water table play and discuss the concepts of floating and sinking as items with which to experiment are introduced and observed. Guided observation of the wind movement can be accomplished with a group activity using paper streamers on a windy day. The point is that not all concept development occurs as a result of teacher planning. Concepts are being learned through play in all indoor learning centers and

outdoors during unstructured play. The teacher can use serendipitous play opportunities to guide the child's awareness and understanding of nature and other components of science. More significant is that the outdoor environment should be perceived as the most important location for scientific knowledge to develop.

DESIGNING CURRICULUM FOR COGNITIVE DEVELOPMENT

Cognitive development has been described here within the content areas of mathematics and science. It was pointed out that these content areas overlap, particularly in the preschool years when cognitive experiences involve the same processes. When designing curriculum for preschool children, the interrelationships in cognitive experiences reflect the nature of the preoperational child's thinking.

The activities described below are representative of the possibilities for activities that promote active involvement and child initiation. They are categorized by level and category using the Frost-Wortham developmental checklists in chapter 3. Activities are designated as appropriate for Level III, IV, or V and related to quantitative and problem-solving, or concept, development (identification, discrimination, and classification skills). Activities are organized under mathematics and science but can be located in both checklist categories.

Mathematics Experiences That Promote Cognitive Development: Measurement

 ### Pretty Ribbons

Checklist skill: Level III, Quantitative and Problem Solving.   Objective (7)
Discriminates differences in the size of object (big/little, long/short)

Description of activity: Cut six to eight different ribbons into two lengths, one obviously shorter than the other. Introduce the activity to the child by identifying one ribbon as being long and the other as short. Ask the child to find another short or long ribbon. After experiences with finding short and long ribbons, ask the child to put all the long ribbons together and all the short ribbons together.

Materials needed: Six or eight ribbons cut to two lengths

 ### Lady Dolls

Checklist skill: Level IV, Quantitative and Problem Solving.   Objective (6)
Compares differences in dimension (taller/shorter, longer/shorter, thinner/wider)

Description of activity: Place five nesting dolls in random order in front of the child. Demonstrate how to order the dolls from tall to short. Help the child locate the tallest doll and shortest doll. Ask the child to find a taller doll than the shortest doll and a shorter doll than the tallest doll. Put the dolls in random order. Select a doll and ask the child to find a larger doll or shorter doll. Repeat with different dolls. Ask the child to order the dolls from tall to short or short to tall.

Materials needed: A set of nesting dolls

Measuring Hands

Checklist skill: Level IV, Quantitative and Problem Solving.   Objective (6) Compares differences in dimension (taller/shorter, longer/shorter, thinner/wider)

Description of activity: Make handprints of children using tempera paint or have the children trace an outline of their hand using crayons. Identify the handprints and have the children cut them out. Use the prints to compare widths of hand spans. Children can compare two or more handprints to determine which is the widest and thinnest. A group of handprints can be ordered from thin to wide (or narrow to wide). Handprints can be used to measure books or other classroom items.

Materials needed: Paper; tempera paint or crayons; scissors

Ruler Activity

Checklist skill: Level V, Quantitative and Problem Solving.   Objective (1) Compares distance (height, width, length) to an independent object

Description of activity: This activity is designed to acquaint children with measurement using a ruler. The ruler is introduced to the children and markings for measurement are discussed. A collection of items are compared with the ruler. The children must determine if each item is longer or shorter than the ruler.

Materials needed: Foot ruler; five to ten items that are longer or shorter than one foot (Tinkertoy sticks, pencils, lengths of string, paper strips, etc.)

Walking and Measuring

Checklist skill: Level V, Quantitative and Problem Solving.   Objective (11) Compares distance (height, width, length) to an
    independent object

Description of activity: Show the children how to make larger measurements using walking strides. On the playground have the children practice measuring distances between two objects such as two jump ropes or stones that have been placed several yards apart. Once the children are familiar with counting strides between two objects, have them compare distances. They can compare distances between trees, playground equipment, or other objects that have been placed different distances apart.

Materials needed: Items that can be measured using walking strides

Mathematics Experiences That Promote Cognitive Development: Number

Egg Counting

Checklist skill: Level III, Quantitative and Problem Solving.   Objective (2) Count by rote from one to five

Description of activity: Using plastic Easter eggs, place one to five small items in each egg. Have children take turns opening an egg and counting the number of items. As an alternative, give children a set of eggs up to five and have them count their eggs.

Materials needed: Plastic eggs; small items such as beans or dried corn to put inside the eggs

Matching Sets of Dishes

Checklist skill: Level IV, Quantitative and Problem Solving.   Objective (7) Demonstrates one-to-one correspondence

Description of activity: Using a collection of toy dishes, make sets of cups and saucers or knives, forks, and spoons. Show the child how to make sure there is a cup for each saucer. Next, vary the sets so that there are more cups or more saucers. Let the child determine which has more by putting the cups on the saucers. Repeat the activity using knives, forks, and spoons. Show the child how to use one-to-one correspondence to determine that there are the same numbers of each eating utensil. Next, vary the sets so that the children can use one-to-one correspondence to determine if there are more spoons, knives, forks, etc.

Materials needed: Play dishes to include cups and saucers, knives, forks, and spoons

Concentration

Checklist skill: Level IV, Quantitative and Problem Solving.   Objective (7) Demonstrates one-to-one correspondence

Description of activity: Use a set of cards that have pairs of pictures. Place them face down and let the children take turns trying to turn two cards over to match a pair.

Materials needed: Set of ten to twenty cards with pairs of identical pictures

Counting Steps

Checklist skill: Level IV, Quantitative and Problem Solving.   Objective (1)
Counts by rote from one to ten

Description of activity: As you climb a set of stairs, count each step with the children. Vary how many steps you climb or descend. Once the children are familiar with the process, place an item on one of the stairs and let the children take turns counting the number of steps to the item. Let the children take turns placing the item on a step for another child.

Materials needed: Stairs; large item such as a unit block to serve as a marker

Counting Outside

Checklist skill: Level V, Quantitative and Problem Solving.   Objective (1)
Counts to fifty

Description of activity: Take the children outside. As a group, count objects in the environment such swings, pieces of playground equipment, trees, windows, etc. Let individual children choose what they want to count.

Materials needed: None

Comparing Clothes

Checklist skill: Level V, Quantitative and Problem Solving.   Objective (7)
Compares elements of unequal sets (more than/fewer than)

Description of activity: This activity combines one-to-one correspondence, counting, and graphing. Select items of clothing to compare. Have all the children wearing blue pants to stand. Using beads and shoelaces, have a child string a bead for each blue pair of pants. Count the number of beads on the string. Repeat with other colors of pants, shirts, styles of shoes, etc. Use a different color of beads for each string. When each string is completed, hang them on a coat hanger or rod. Label each string. Let the children compare which string has the most, least, etc. The strings can be ordered to make a graph demonstrating the comparisons in number. A similar activity could be conducted using stacks of one-inch blocks of different colors.

Materials needed: Beads; strings; paper labels; marking pen; coat hanger or wooden rod

Egg Shake

Checklist skill: Level IV, Quantitative and Problem Solving.   Objective (3)
Orders the numerals one to five

Description of activity: Place numeral cards up to five in a plastic hosiery egg. Let children take turns shaking the egg, taking out the numerals, and ordering them.

Materials needed: Plastic hosiery egg; numeral cards up to five

Egg Carton Numbers

Checklist skill: Level V, Quantitative and Problem Solving.   Objective (2)
Demonstrates the concept of numbers through ten

Description of activity: Place numerals in random order in the bottom of an egg carton. Give the children beans, dried corn, or other small objects to count out for each number.

Materials needed: Egg carton with numerals to ten in random order; beans or other small counters

Two, Four, Six, Eight

Checklist skill: Level V, Quantitative and Problem Solving.   Objective (6)
Groups objects into sets of equal number

Description of activity: Organize objects into sets of equal number up to ten. Give the child one of the sets and ask the child to make two sets with the same number. Ask the child to count each set to make sure they both are the same. Repeat with other even-numbered sets.

Materials needed: Ten objects

Mathematics Experiences That Promote Cognitive Development: Geometry

Sorting Shapes

Checklist skill: Level III, Concept Development.   Objective (6) Discriminates differences in the shape of objects (round, square, triangular)

Description of activity: Make a collection of classroom toys, blocks, etc., that are round, square, and triangular. On pieces of construction paper, make a large drawing of each shape. Encourage the children to examine the objects and place them on the appropriate shape picture.

Materials needed: Classroom objects that are round, square, and triangular

My Shape Book

Checklist skill: Level IV, Concept Development.   Objective (1) Points to basic shapes (circle, square, rectangle, triangle) on request

Description of activity: Make each child a booklet in the shape of one of the shapes to be learned. Supply the children with magazine pictures that have the desired shape. Have the children cut out the shape pictures and put them in the appropriate book. As an alternative, let the children draw pictures that include the shape.

Materials needed: Shape books; scissors; paste; crayons

Bead Patterns

Checklist skill: Level V, Concept Development.   Objective (5) Identifies likenesses and differences in two or more objects (shape, size, color)

Description of activity: Have a string and collection of beads for each child. Demonstrate how to make a pattern of beads. Ask the children to duplicate your pattern. When the children are familiar with the process, let them take turns making the pattern to be copied.

Materials needed: Strings and large assortment of wooden beads of different shapes and colors

Experiences That Promote Cognitive Development: Mathematical Reasoning

Making Stairs

Checklist skill: Level V, Concept Development.   Objective (12) Seriates (arranges) objects by size

Description of activity: Give each child a handful of pieces of paper one inch square. Show them how to make a stair by making a series of lines of squares, each one longer than the one before. The same activity can be conducted using wooden cubes.

Materials needed: Pieces of paper cut into inch squares; wooden inch cubes

How Tall Are You?

Checklist skill: Level V, Concept Development.   Objective (12) Seriates (arranges) objects by size

Description of activity: Use a roll of adding machine paper to measure children. Have them lie on the floor or stand next to a wall to measure their height on the paper. Put the child's name on their strip. Tape the strips to the wall using masking tape with all strips even at the bottom. Determine who is tallest, shortest, etc. Have the children rearrange the strips in order from tallest to shortest.

Materials needed: Adding machine paper; marking pens; scissors; masking tape

Sorting Nuts

Checklist skill: Level V, Concept Development.   Objective (8) Classifies foods (fruits, vegetables, meats)

Description of activity: Make a collection of different types of nuts (walnuts, peanuts, pecans, etc.). Ask the child to sort the nuts by type (all the pecans, peanuts, etc.). Then ask the child to determine a criterion for sorting (size, texture, etc.) A similar classification activity can be conducted with a collection of shells with more complex possibilities for classification.

Materials needed: An assortment of nuts in the original shells

The Button Game

Checklist skill: Level V, Concept Development.   Objective (11) Identifies and classifies common objects by shape (circle, rectangle, triangle, oval, square)

Description of activity: Make a large collection of buttons. Begin the game by making a set of buttons based on shape, size, or color. Ask the children to guess the common characteristic of the set. Make another set using another criterion such as number of holes or texture of the buttons. Encourage the children to take turns making sets using different characteristics of the buttons.

Materials needed: Large collection of buttons

Science

The activities that follow are described using the categories of science processes described earlier (Seefeldt & Barbour, 1990) and are not coordinated with a checklist skill. In addition, they are suitable for preschool children from three to five with some adaptation.

Science Experiences That Promote Cognitive Development: Observing

Observing Fish

Description of activity: There are many things that young children can observe about fish in a classroom aquarium. They can observe the likenesses and differences in different types of fish in the container. Other characteristics they might be guided to notice are the processes the fish use to breathe, the parts of the body such as fins and gills, and the way in which the body parts function. The children might observe different swimming patterns and the spots where individual fish prefer to spend the most time. They can also learn the names of the different varieties of fish and describe unique characteristics of each type.

Materials needed: Classroom aquarium with a variety of fish

Mud Puddles

Description of activity: On a rainy day, take the children where they can observe puddles forming in the soil. Discuss why puddles form in some locations and not in others. If the rain continues for some time, the size of the puddles can be measured and compared. After the rain is over, the puddles can continue to be observed and measured as the water evaporates. The children can also be guided to observe the drying process of the ground, trees, etc.

Materials needed: Yardstick to measure length and width of puddles

Watching the Clouds Go By

Description of activity: Take the children outdoors to a location where they can lie down and watch the clouds go by. Let them observe the cloud movement on a fairly windy day so that they can see the clouds changing. They can repeat the observation several times and note differences in types of clouds, numbers of clouds, and the way clouds look when it rains. Names of types of clouds can be discussed with older children. If clouds are observed daily, a calendar might be used to record the type of clouds observed over a period of about two weeks.

Materials needed: None

Outdoor Sounds

Description of activity: Take the children for a walk outdoors. Draw their attention to the sounds that they can hear. Discuss the difference between types of sounds such as bird or natural sounds versus manmade sounds from vehicles, machinery, etc. After the walk let the children contribute to a group-dictated story or let each child draw a picture of something observed during the walk that made a sound and dictate a story about the picture.

Materials needed: Paper for dictated stories; marking pen; crayons

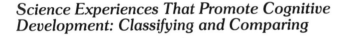

Science Experiences That Promote Cognitive Development: Classifying and Comparing

Comparing Leaves

Description of activity: If there are varieties of trees near the school, take children for a walk to gather as many different types of leaves as possible. Otherwise, take a collection of leaves for the children to use. Let each child select two leaves that are different and describe how they are alike and how they are different. They can then compare leaves by size, shape, texture, etc. Older children can sort leaves into two groups using their own characteristics for classification.

Materials needed: Large collection of leaves of many sizes and types

Sorting Types of Animals

Description of activity: Use a collection of pictures of different types of animals such as zoo animals, farm animals, and animals that are pets. For three-year-olds, discuss one type of animal. After discussing each animal in a group such as farm animals, mix a few farm animal pictures with zoo animal pictures. Encourage the children to decide which are farm animals and which are not farm animals. Repeat with more pictures.

For older children, three sets of animals may be compared. After discussing each set of animals separately, combine all of the pictures and ask the children to sort them into their appropriate group. Give them a picture clue of each type of animal to guide the classification.

Materials needed: Sets of animal pictures for zoo animals, farm animals, and animals that are pets

Science Experiences That Promote Cognitive Development: Measuring

Measuring Plants

Description of activity: Plant rapidly growing plants such as beans. Cut different colored strips of cardboard to measure three inches, six inches, nine inches, and a foot. After the plants have sprouted, measure the plants once a week. Chart the growth of the plants until they have grown to a foot. Individual plants can be compared as to rate of growth. Children can try the different size measures to determine which is the closest to the plant's height on the day it is measured.

Materials needed: Bean plants; measures for three inches, six inches, nine inches, and twelve inches

Measuring Popcorn

Description of activity: The children will compare the volume of popcorn before and after it is popped. Before popping the corn, discuss what happens when corn is popped. Encourage the children to describe what happens to the corn kernels and what causes them to expand. Place the unpopped kernels in a clear container such as a large glass or clear plastic jar or pitcher. Use a marking pen to measure how high the kernels reach in the container. After popping the corn, put it back in the container and measure the volume again. Encourage the children to describe why there is now more corn in the container.

Materials needed: Large, tall container; popcorn; popcorn popper; marking pen

Science Experiences That Promote Cognitive Development: Experimenting

Making New Colors

Description of activity: Place shallow containers of tempera paint of the three primary colors where the children can reach them. Give each child small clear plastic cups and a spoon. Show the children how two primary colors can be mixed to make a new color. Show them how to make different combinations in their cups.

Encourage them to observe and compare their color mixtures with the mixtures made by other children. Guide them to discuss why their colors are not the same. Follow up the activity with opportunities for the children to easel paint using the primary colors for further experimentation.

Materials needed: Three containers of paint in primary colors; small plastic cups; spoons

Tools and Gadgets

Description of activity: Collect discarded appliances, old clocks, or discarded telephones, etc. Give the children some pliers and screwdrivers and let them explore taking the items apart. Let them make an imaginary machine or invention with the loose parts. Discuss their observations and hypotheses about the purposes for the parts in the machinery of the objects they explore.

Materials needed: Old clocks, appliances, telephones, etc.; pliers; screwdrivers

Cooking Tools and Machines

Description of activity: Collect a hand electric mixer, blender, manual egg beater, and a potato masher. Explore what the children know about the use of these kitchen appliances and tools. Plan to make some scrambled eggs or mashed potatoes. Prepare some eggs in the blender or electric mixer and the manual egg beater. Discuss how each mixes the eggs and how the electric machines are the same as and different from the manual egg beater. A similar discussion can be conducted comparing the electric mixer, blender, and manual potato masher. If both foods are cooked, the children can observe and discuss why eggs are mixed or whipped before cooking and potatoes are mixed or whipped after cooking.

Materials needed: Hand electric mixer; blender; manual egg beater; potato masher; eggs; potatoes; facilities for cooking eggs and/or potatoes

The Food Grinder

Description of activity: Have available a piece of beef and ground beef. Discuss the texture of the two meats and discuss how ground beef is prepared before hamburgers are made. Help the children hypothesize how meat and other foods are ground as part of the process of preparing food. Show the children a manual food grinder that has not been assembled. Help the children assemble the grinder and predict the purpose of the different parts of the grinder. After the grinder has been assembled and attached to a surface, grind some cooked chicken or cheese to make sandwiches. Grind pickles or other ingredients as part of the grinding process. Let the children grind and mix the ground food with mayonnaise to make a sandwich spread.

Materials needed: Hand food grinder; cooked chicken or cheese to grind; mayonnaise; mixing bowl and spoon; crackers or bread slices to make small sandwiches for sampling

THE INTEGRATED CURRICULUM FOR LANGUAGE
AND COGNITIVE DEVELOPMENT

The activities that have been described thus far for language and cognitive development in mathematics and science are examples of developmentally appropriate activities for three-, four-, and five-year-old preschool children. They have also been offered to exemplify the content of language and cognitive development curriculum that forms the preschool program for preoperational children. These activities demonstrate the nature of experiences that young children can engage in to acquire new concepts. The activities require active interaction on the part of the child; moreover, they involve hands-on manipulative materials or experiences with realia or artifacts. Nevertheless, the activities as described are isolated or independent, with no necessary relationship to other components of the curriculum.

A more productive approach to developing curriculum is to place experiences into meaningful contexts. Opportunities to move from simple to complex, concrete to abstract, and experiencing to representing what has been learned result from a series of connected activities that permit the child to explore and reflect upon information through a variety of encounters. In this section, we will examine how interrelated experiences that focus on language and cognitive development can encourage children to explore and understand the connectedness in learning. Integration through children's literature and through a thematic unit are two processes for developing experiences in language and cognitive development connected with activities that promote all areas of development and expression.

Using Children's Literature as a Focus for Integrated Curriculum

Children's literature provides an abundant resource for curriculum that can be based on language development in partnership with cognitive development. Although a book for children automatically serves as a resource for language development and emergent literacy, it can also be the source from which cognitive curriculum can be developed.

Children's literature can lead to knowledge about science, mathematics, or other content areas. Thematic curriculum that includes activities in small and large groups and in interest centers can begin with a book or a story. Figure 7.3 provides an example of this process. The book *Air Is All Around You* by Franklyn M. Branley describes the properties of air and gives information about experiments that can be conducted to understand air. The authors of *Story Stretchers* (Raines & Canady, 1989), the source of this integrated curriculum, have taken the book and developed activities for the art and sci-

Circle Time Presentation

Talk with the children about how they know where air is. They will mention the wind blowing and some may mention blowing out air on a cold morning and seeing a little cloud. Read *Air Is All Around You*. Then discuss again how they know air is all around them after having heard the book. Assure the children that they will have a chance to do the science experiments. Tell the children you will place the book in the science center and during free play you will be there to help anyone who wants to do the experiments.

Story Stretcher

For Art: Fish Pictures

What the children will learn—
To recognize where the fish's gills are and to incorporate this into their picture

Materials you will need—
Brightly colored construction paper, scissors, easel, fluorescent tempera paints, variety of sizes of brushes

What to do—
1. Cut the construction paper into giant fish shapes.
2. Cut a half-circle flap where the fish's gills should be.
3. Encourage the children to use many different colors to paint their fish like the ones in the class aquarium.

Something to think about—
Children respond to new information and will incorporate their new learnings into their art work. If possible, display many pictures of fish near the art area and you will see more variety in the paintings.

Story Stretcher

For Cooking and Snack Time: Orange Air

What the children will learn—
To recall the analogy of how the peel of the orange is like the air around the earth

Materials you will need—
Whole oranges

What to do—
1. Read the analogy from the book: "Air is all around you, and it is all around the earth. Air covers the earth like peel covers an orange."
2. Cut thin stripes down the orange peel from top to bottom without cutting through to the inside of the orange. Cut stripes all around the orange so the children can peel their oranges more easily.
3. Let the children peel their own oranges.

Something to think about—
It is difficult to know when to provide assistance to children. Often volunteers in the classroom will quickly take over for the child and peel the orange. However, encourage them to wait and only provide assistance after the child is having a great deal of difficulty. Then, do not peel the entire orange, but get some of the sections started. Many children will persist and need more time to finish their snacks. Do not hurry them—let them enjoy peeling the orange and savor eating it.

Figure 7.3 Integrated Curriculum (pp. 266–268)
Shirley C. Raines & Robert J. Canady, *Story Stretchers*. (Gryphon House, 1989), pp. 104–105. Reprinted by permission.

Story Stretcher

For Housekeeping and Dress-up Corner: Astronauts

What the children will learn—
To pretend to be astronauts

Materials you will need—
Football helmets or bike riding helmets, large expandable hoses from a dryer connection, earphones from the listening station, down-filled jackets

What to do—
1. Show the picture of the astronaut in *Air Is All Around You.*
2. Ask the children how they might use the dress-up materials you have collected to dress up like astronauts. If possible, have several of each. If this is impossible, explain that there is only one astronaut outside the spaceship at a time and the others have their air supply inside the spaceship.

Something to think about—
Every time I see children playing astronauts, I am amazed at their inventiveness. The puffy down-filled coats reminded me of the air in the space suits; however, the idea of using the dryer air hose connection came from a child, as well as using the earphones for communication. Do not be concerned if you only have a few of the supplies, your astronauts will find what they need.

(Adapted from classroom at George Mason University's Project for the Study of Young Children.)

Story Stretcher

For Science and Nature Center: Inverted Glass Experiment

What the children will learn—
To follow directions of the experiment and observe what happens

Materials you will need—
Large clear mixing bowl, food coloring, paper napkins, glass

What to do—
1. Follow the directions in the book, which are:
   a. put water in a big bowl;
   b. color the water with a little bit of food coloring;
   c. stuff a paper napkin into the bottom of a glass;
   d. turn the glass upside down;
   e. keep the glass upside down, make sure it is straight up and down, do not tip it;
   f. push it all the way under the water;
   g. lift the glass out of the water; and
   h. turn it right side up and take out the napkin.
2. Have the children observe that the napkin is dry.
3. Let all the children who want to do the experiment have a turn.

Something to think about—
Remember that young children are hands-on learners. They will learn more if they do the experiment themselves. Many of the children will not understand what the experiment demonstrates, but they will enjoy following the directions and getting the same results as the teacher. Also, avoid referring to this experiment as magic or as a trick. While it may seem phenomenal, it is natural.

Another Story Stretcher

For Science and Nature Center: Fishy Water

What the children will learn—
To observe the air bubbling in an aquarium and the air bubbling in water

Materials you will need—
An aquarium, two glasses filled with water, magnifying glasses

What to do—
1. For the children who are interested, reread the section of the book about the air dissolved in the water for fish. Show the pictures of the fish and point out the fish's gills.
2. Have the children look at the fish in the aquarium with their magnifying glasses and see if they can see the fishes' gills moving as the water passes through them.

3. Do the science experiment where you will fill a glass with water, wait an hour and then look with the magnifying glasses for tiny bubbles of air.
4. After an hour, fill another glass with water, and have the children search for any air bubbles in this glass.

Something to think about—
While an aquarium requires a great deal of attention, it is worth it to have living things in the classroom. Before spending school supply money on an aquarium, check with parents; often there is one in storage or one in operation that a family will donate complete with fish. Get specific instructions about its operation from the owners.

Figure 7.3   Integrated Curriculum *(continued)*

ence center, as well as group activities such as a food- or circle-time experience. Note that the activity of observing fish described earlier as an individual activity is offered as a similar experience here in the context of learning about air.

Using Thematic Units as a Focus for Integrated Curriculum

Thematic units offer more comprehensive planning for integrated curriculum that include language and cognitive development. In a unit titled "Seeds," a science topic, nineteen activities were developed to provide a variety of experiences for children ages three to five. Younger children will not be able to be successful in some of the activities; nevertheless, more advanced experiences are provided to challenge more advanced students. Ten of these activities are described below. Study of the activities discloses that a wide range of experiences has been planned to include all areas of development. In addition, the teachers who planned the unit, Michelle and Cindy, have developed activities that provide a balance between those that are directed by the teacher and those that encourage children to take responsibility for directing their own plans. The complete unit, which includes unit and lesson plans, may be found in Appendix A.

Activities for a Unit on Seeds

1. The teacher begins each lesson with a series of books that introduce the topic of the lesson, which involves seeds. Through these readings and the discussions following them, language arts are integrated into every lesson in the unit.

2. The students will take an excursion around the school grounds and collect as many different kinds of seeds as they can find. The activity involves cognitive development using concepts in science. It also integrates language, aesthetic, and social development through discussions throughout the walk. Physical development, which includes fine and gross motor skills, is addressed through the process of walking and collecting leaves.

3. The teacher and students will discuss the characteristics of a variety of seeds. They will explore size, shape, color, and texture of the seeds. They will then dissect several seeds, taking note of the differences among them. This activity involves oral language, social skills through cooperative learning, and the use of fine motor skills for dissecting.

4. Students will be guided to use a variety of seeds to construct a seed collage using glue and construction paper. The activity provides for aesthetic development as the children construct their own collage. Fine motor skills are used in that the children must be able to manipulate materials to complete the collage.

5. The students are given a muffin tin labeled with numerals one through five or one through ten, depending upon their development in counting. They are then instructed to place the correct number of seeds in the appropriate tin cup. If children do not yet recognize numerals, the teacher will verbally ask them to count numbers of seeds. The children will use cognitive skills for counting and fine motor skills for placing seeds in the correct spaces.

6. The students will dictate a group story on the topic of seeds to the teacher, who will in turn write the contributions as a language experience story. Expressive language and emergent reading skills will be integrated through dictation and repeated readings of the story.

7. When provided with a series of pictures showing the growth of a plant at various stages, beginning with a seed, the students will place the pictures in appropriate order. Children will be using cognitive skills, as well as language and social skills in order to discuss the task and reach consensus in their cooperative learning groups.

8. The children will be asked to pretend to be a sprouting seed; background music should be played. The children will be using physical skills, pretending, and developing appreciation for music and its different tempos.

9. Children will be given an array of seeds to compare and contrast. They will be asked to describe likenesses and differences in the seeds. The activity requires students to use oral language and cognitive skills.

10. Seeds collected from the nature walk will be used to make rhythm instruments. Students will be given a selection of containers from which to choose. The completed instruments will be used in a musical activity. Students will

be developing an appreciation for tempo and music and creative and motor skills in constructing and using the instruments.

DESIGNING COGNITIVE CURRICULUM FOR CHILDREN WITH SPECIAL NEEDS

The nature of cognitive activities that are planned for preschool children makes them readily adaptable to a range of development levels. Because the activities are predominantly concrete experiences, children who are developmentally delayed can also benefit from interactions that permit them opportunities to use their senses and cognitive abilities to learn. The teacher must be sensitive, however, to adaptations that might be necessary for children who have special needs.

Children who have visual limitations must substitute touch for sight. When studying a concept such as shape, they need many opportunities to trace or use tactile skills to experience the physical configuration of different shapes. Developmentally delayed children will need to spend more time engaging in experiences focused on a single shape, whereas other children, particularly four- and five-year-olds, may be able to work with more than one shape and discriminate between them.

Children with language differences will need opportunities to build vocabulary that accompanies new concepts. Children whose first language is not English may need to use their home language vocabulary at first and add English when they demonstrate competence with the new knowledge. All children will need many opportunities to discuss information related to cognitive learning, but children with language differences benefit from the teacher's awareness of progress they are making in acquiring targeted vocabulary. Whatever special needs the individual child may have, the teacher can be alert to adaptations that will make an experience more accessible. Through an understanding of each child's strengths and learning style, the cognitive curriculum can be organized to be meaningful to all preschool children.

Summary

The curriculum for language and cognitive development in the preschool years is based on our understanding of how young children acquire concepts and language. Although educators used to believe that acquisition of literacy was based on the ability to master a sequence of readiness skills leading to beginning reading, the current understanding is that it is based on a cognitive developmental process within each child. The internal cognitive mechanism that facilitates acquisition of language and other forms of cognition also explains how the child achieves literacy.

There are contrasting theories of language acquisition. It is known that children develop the ability to use language by maturing and by receiving opportunities to hear and use language. They learn a set of rules that they use to create their own utterances. Within the first five years they master the forms of language that are used in their language community.

The acquisition of literacy follows a similar pattern. Literacy begins in infancy when the child is exposed to stories, books, and examples of written language. The child's progress into literacy is based on the language and literacy experiences that are available in the home environment.

By the time children enter preschool programs, they have acquired some level of language and literacy; however, they will differ because of the variations in circumstances in their home environment. The role of the teacher is to establish the school environment and curriculum to encourage further development. The teacher develops ongoing possibilities for children to use oral language and literature experiences. In addition, opportunities are provided and physical arrangements are made to encourage dramatic play, writing, art, and emergent reading activities.

The teacher uses similar planning processes to promote the child's cognitive development in science and mathematics. Piaget's cognitive development theory as it relates to the preoperational child is reflected in the categories of cognitive topics that are proposed for preschool children in mathematics and science.

The environment has an important role in the child's opportunities to learn about mathematics and science. Learning centers that offer a changing array of natural and man-made resources promote opportunities to explore, experiment, hypothesize, and reflect on phenomena and concepts in these two subjects. The outdoor area provides a natural learning center for planned and natural experiences. Weather, the path of the sun, and other elements of nature can be experienced on a regular basis.

The teacher organizes curriculum that includes a balance between child-planned and teacher-guided activities. Mathematics and science are explored within a milieu that includes a rich assortment of materials that incorporate all aspects of the curriculum.

Although individual activities that are developmentally appropriate are beneficial for learning, language and concept development experienced within an integrated approach is more meaningful. One approach to integrating curriculum involves using children's literature; another uses thematic topics as sources for curriculum development. If a book for young children serves as the stimulus for curriculum design, learning center activities and small and large group activities are planned as extensions or expansions of the content of the book. A thematic unit, on the other hand, originates with a topic to be explored. The activities selected for the topic not only center on the knowledge related to the topic but also incorporate meaningful activities in all areas of development that permit application of concepts and skills. Cognitive development in language, literacy, mathematics, and science is part of this comprehensive approach to learning, which can be accomplished through adhering to integrated thematic units.

Summary Statements

1. The understanding of the nature of language and literacy development has evolved during the last four decades as a result of research in the field.

2. Although all children acquire language during the preschool years, they have differences in language skills depending upon their early experiences in the home and their language community.

3. Many children learn a language or dialect other than Standard English in the home. They require special attention to ensure that they also are able to use Standard English.

4. In the preschool years, the major goal for the curriculum in language development is to extend the child's acquisition of oral language; however, literacy is an inherent component of the language arts program.

5. Play as a vehicle for development and learning is an essential element for language development.

6. The teacher's role in language development is as model, instructor, and facilitator of appropri-

ate activities that encourage oral language and emerging literacy skills.

7. Although many preschool programs still stress activities that develop readiness for reading, the emergent literacy or whole language approach is more compatible with the child's internal cognitive mechanisms.

8. The indoor learning environment, based on individual or group interests or on materials in learning centers, can be organized to facilitate language and literacy development.

9. Certain stages of emergent writing and reading are similar to stages in language acquisition.

10. Children with special needs, especially those who have language differences, benefit from the emergent literacy curriculum because it requires little or no adaptation to meet their language development needs.

11. Preschool children must have the opportunity to have many concrete experiences to be able to construct their understanding of the world.

12. Familiar objects should be used when preparing mathematics activities for young children.

13. Understanding of concepts is acquired through physical knowledge rather than social transmission.

14. Children need to manipulate materials, exchange information with others, and take part in logical-mathematical activities as part of the process of constructing knowledge.

15. Cognitive development in mathematics and science in the preschool years is described as a single category because similar processes are used as goals for curriculum development.

16. The teacher provides a balance between teacher-directed activities and opportunities for child-initiated exploration and experimentation in the cognitive curriculum.

17. The outdoor environment is an important learning center for cognitive development, particularly in science concepts.

18. The integrated curriculum is the most meaningful context for providing experiences leading to language and cognitive development.

Study Questions

1. How do young children become readers? Explain the process of emergent literacy.

2. How is emergent literacy related to the acquisition of language?

3. Why are there differences in children's abilities to speak in the preschool years?

4. What implications do these language differences have for the language curriculum in preschool programs?

5. What forms of emergent writing do preschool children use?

6. How is play an essential part of learning to speak? Describe the role of play in language development.

7. What kinds of roles can the teacher play in encouraging the use of expressive language? How does the teacher extend receptive language?

8. What kinds of language experiences lead to literacy in reading and writing?

9. What is the difference in philosophy between reading readiness and emergent literacy? What does each approach imply for the curriculum?

10. What is the difference between emergent writing activities in preschool classrooms and formal writing lessons?

11. How do toddlers acquire their first understanding of written language? What is environmental print?

12. What are the most significant activities in the home that promote literacy in the years between age one and age five?

13. What do children learn about print as part of the process of emergent literacy?

14. What is the nature of emergent literacy in bilingual children? Why do they have unique language and literacy needs?

15. What sequential process is involved in learning to count?

16. Why are physical experiences with manipulative material important in the cognitive curriculum designed for preoperational children?

17. What are the characteristics of the cognitive curriculum as described by Jerome Bruner and Robert Gagne?

18. Why are goals for mathematics similar to those for science in the preschool curriculum?

19. Why are both teacher-guided and child-planned activities important in the curriculum for cognitive development?

20. What materials can be placed in learning centers for cognitive development in science and mathematics? What activities can take place in learning centers for cognitive development in these subjects?

References

Abramson, S., Seda, I., & Johnson, C. (1990). Literacy development in a multilingual kindergarten classroom. *Childhood Education, 67,* 68–72.

Baker, P., & Raban, B. (1991). Reading before and after the early days of schooling. *Reading, 25,* 6–13.

Barufaldi, J. P., Ladd, G. T., & Moses, A. J. (1984). *Heath science* [Level K]. Lexington, MA: D. C. Heath.

Beaty, J. J. (1992). *Preschool appropriate practices.* Fort Worth: Harcourt Brace Jovanovich.

Bloom, B. (1972). *Language development: Form and function in emerging grammars.* Cambridge, MA: MIT Press.

Brewer, J. A. (1992). *Introduction to early childhood education.* Boston: Allyn & Bacon.

Brown, R. (1973). *A first language: The early stages.* Cambridge, MA: Harvard University Press.

Bruner, J. S. (1983). Play, thought, and language. *Peabody Journal of Education, 60,* 6–69.

Cassady, J. K. (1988). Beginning reading with big books. *Childhood Education, 65,* 18–23.

Cazden, C. (1972). *Child language and education.* New York: Holt, Rinehart & Winston.

Cazden, C. (1976). Play and language and metalinguistic awareness. In J. Bruner, A. Jolly, & K. Sylva (Eds.), *Play: Its development and evolution.* New York: Basic Books.

Chomsky, C. (1965). *Aspects of a theory of syntax.* Cambridge, MA: MIT Press.

Chomsky, N. (1968). *Language and mind.* New York: Harcourt Brace Jovanovich.

Chukovsky, K. (1971). *From two to five.* Los Angeles: University of California Press.

Clark, E. (1983). Meanings and concepts. In P. H. Mussen (Ed.), *Handbook of child psychology* (4th ed.). J. H. Flavell & E. Markman (Eds.), *Vol. 3. Cognitive development.* New York: John Wiley & Sons.

Cliatt, M. J. P., & Shaw, J. M. (1992). *Helping children explore science.* New York: Merrill.

Dowd, F. S. (1991). Mother Goose goes to school. *Childhood Education, 67,* 218–222.

Dutton, W. H., & Dutton, A. (1991). *Mathematics children use and understand.* Mountain View, CA: Mayfield.

Dyson, A. H. (1985). Individual differences in emerging writing. In M. Farr (Ed.), *Advances in writing research: Vol 1. Children's early writing development.* Norwood, NJ: Ablex.

Ferreiro, E., & Teberosky, A. (1982). *Literacy before schooling.* Exeter, NH: Heinemann.

Fields, M. V., & Hillstead, D. V. (1990). Whole language in the play store. *Young Children, 67,* 73–76.

Fields, M. V., Spangler, K. L., & Lee, D. L. (1991). *Let's begin reading right* (2nd ed.). New York: Merrill.

Freeman, E. B., & Hatch, J. A. (1989). Emergent literacy: Reconceptualizing kindergarten practice. *Childhood Education, 66,* 21–24.

Frost, J. L. (1992). *Play and playscapes.* Albany, NY: Delmar.

Garvey, C. (1977). *Play.* Cambridge, MA: Harvard University Press.

Garvey, C., & Hogan, R. (1973). Social speech and social interaction: Egocentrism revisited. *Child Development, 44,* 565–568.

Gelman, R., & Gallistel, C. R. (1978). *The child's understanding of number.* Cambridge, MA: Harvard University Press.

Gesell, A. (1925).*The mental growth of the preschool child.* New York: Macmillan.

Goodman, Y. (1984). The development of initial literacy. In H. Goelman, A. Oberg, & F. Smith (Eds.), *Awakening to literacy* (pp. 102–109). Exeter, NH: Heinemann.

Goodman, Y. (1986). Children coming to know literacy. In W. H. Teale & E. Sulzby (Eds.),

Emergent literacy: Writing and reading (pp. 1–14). Norwood, NJ: Ablex.

Gothard, H. M., & Russell, S. M. (1990). A tale of two teachers (or How our children led us into whole language). *Childhood Education, 66,* 214–218.

Han, E. P. (1991). "You be the baby bear." Story re–enactments by young children. *Dimensions, 19,* 14–21.

Hatch, J. A., & Freeman, E. B. (1988). Kindergarten philosophies and practices: Perspectives of teachers, principals, and supervisors. *Early Childhood Research Quarterly, 3,* 151–166.

Hayes, L. F. (1990). From scribbling to writing: Smoothing the way. *Young Children, 45,* 62–68.

Hendrick, J. (1990). *Total learning* (3rd ed.). Columbus, OH: Merrill.

Hiebert, E. H. (1986). Using environmental print in beginning reading instruction. In M. R. Sampson (Ed.), *The pursuit of literacy: Early reading and writing* (pp. 73–80). Dubuque, IA: Kendall/Hunt.

International Reading Association. (1985). *Literacy development and pre–first grade.* Newark, DE: Author.

Ishee, N., & Goldhaber, J. (1990). Story re–enactment: Let the play begin! *Young Children, 45,* 70–75.

Jewell, M. G., & Zintz, M. V. (1986). *Learning to read naturally.* Dubuque, IA: Kendall/Hunt.

Johnson, J. E., Christie, J. F., & Yawkey, T. (1987). *Play and early childhood development.* Glenview, IL: Scott, Foresman.

Keats, E. J. (1971). *Over in the meadow.* New York: Scholastic.

Labov, W. (1970). The logic of nonstandard English. In F. Williams (Ed.), *Language and poverty* (pp. 153–189). Chicago: Markham.

Levy, A. K. (1984). The language of play: The role of play in language development. *Early Childhood Development and Care, 17,* 49–62.

Lindfors, J. W. (1987). *Children's language and learning* (2nd ed.). Englewood Cliffs, NJ: Prentice–Hall.

Manning, M., Manning, G., & Kamii, C. (1988). Early phonics instruction: Its effect on literacy development. *Young Children, 44,* 4–8.

Mason, J. (1980). When do children begin to read: An exploration of four year old children's letter and word reading competencies. *Reading Research Quarterly, 15,* 203–227.

Mason, J. (1984). Early reading from a development perspective. In P. D. Pearson (Ed.), *Handbook of reading research* (pp. 505–543). New York: Longman.

McCormick, C., & Mason, J. (1981). What happens to kindergarten children's knowledge about reading after summer vacation? *The Reading Teacher, 35,* 164–172.

McNeil, D. (1966). Developmental psycholinguistics. In F. Smith & G. A. Miller (Eds.), *The genesis of language: A psycholinguistic approach* (pp. 15–82). Cambridge, MA: MIT Press.

Mills, H., & Clyde, J. A. (1991). For rent: The housekeeping area. *Dimensions, 19,* 26–27.

Morrow, L. M. (1989). *Literacy development in the early years.* Englewood Cliffs, NJ: Prentice–Hall.

Morrow, L. M., & Rand, M. K. (1991). Promoting literacy during play by designing early childhood classroom environments. *The Reading Teacher, 44,* 396–401.

O'Brien, S. J. (1989). But when is nap time? *Childhood Education, 65,* 163–164.

Piaget, J. (1955). *The language and thought of the child.* New York: Noonday.

Piaget, J., & Inhelder, B. (1969). *The psychology of the child.* New York: Basic Books.

Price, G. G. (1989). Mathematics in early childhood. *Young Children, 44,* 53–58.

Quintero, E., & Huerta–Macias, A. (1990). All in the family: Bilingualism and biliteracy. *The Reading Teacher, 44,* 306–312.

Raines, S. C., & Canady, R. J. (1989). *Story stretchers.* Mt. Rainier, MD: Gryphon House.

Raines, S. C., & Isbell, R. (1988). Tuck talking about wordless books into your classroom. *Young Children, 43,* 24–25.

Rogers, C. S., & Sawyers, J. K. (1988). *Play in the lives of children.* Washington, DC: National Association for the Education of Young Children.

Schickedanz, J. A., York, M. E., Stewart, I. S., & White, D. A. (1990). *Strategies for teaching young children* (3rd ed.). Englewood Cliffs, NJ: Prentice–Hall.

Schultz, K. A., Colarusso, R. P., & Strawderman, V. W. (1989). *Mathematics for every young child.* Columbus, OH: Merrill.

Seefeldt, C., & Barbour, N. (1990). *Early childhood education.* Columbus, OH: Merrill.

Sendak, M. (1962). *Chicken soup with rice.* New York: Harper & Row.

Skinner, B. F. (1957). *Verbal behavior.* New York: Appleton–Century–Crofts.

Slobin, D. I. (1966). Comments on developmental psycholinguistics. In F. Smith & G. A. Miller (Eds.), *The genesis of language: A psycholinguistic approach.* Cambridge, MA: MIT Press.

Smilansky, S. (1968). *The effects of sociodramatic play on disadvantaged preschool children.* New York: Wiley.

Spodek, B. (1985). *Teaching in the early years* (3rd ed.). Englewood Cliffs, NJ: Prentice–Hall.

Stevenson, H. W., Lee, S. Y., & Stigler, J. W. (1986). Mathematics achievement of Chinese, Japanese, and American children. *Science, 231,* 693–699.

Sulzby, E., Barnhart, J., & Hieshima, J. (1989). Forms of writing and rereading from writing: A preliminary report. In J. Mason (Ed.), *Reading and writing connections.* Boston: Allyn & Bacon.

Teale, W. H. (1982). Toward a theory of how children learn to read and write naturally. *Language Arts, 59,* 555–570.

Teale, W. H. (1986). The beginning of reading and writing: Written language development during the preschool and kindergarten years. In M. Sampson (Ed.), *The pursuit of literacy: Early reading and writing.* Dubuque, IA: Kendall/Hunt.

Teale, W. H. (1987). The emergent literacy classroom. *Reading Today, 7,* 14.

Teale, W. H., & Sulzby, E. (Eds.). (1986). *Emergent literacy: Reading and writing.* Norwood, NJ: Ablex.

Vygotsky, L. S. (1962). *Thought and language.* New York: Wiley.

Wiseman, D. E., & Robeck, C. P. (1983). The written language behavior of two socio–economic groups of preschool children. *Reading Psychology, 4,* 349–363.

CHAPTER EIGHT

Preschool Curriculum:
Ages Three to Five

Social and Physical Development

CURRICULUM FOR SOCIAL DEVELOPMENT

Understanding Social Development

The preschool years are very important ones for social development. This is the period during which young children make the transition to becoming social beings. As infants and toddlers, they were focused on themselves and viewed the world from that perspective. In the preschool years, young children enter the world of social interactions and learn to make a place for themselves in the social world. The first tentative steps that the toddler took toward interacting with others now evolve further as the child develops an interest in being with other children and being accepted into social groups.

During the preschool years, children are experiencing the stages that Erikson (1963) termed autonomy versus doubt and initiative versus guilt. As the child seeks autonomy, he or she learns self-control and self-assertion. At about age four or five, the child becomes more interested in reaching out to the world. The child wants to use initiative to formulate ideas for dramatic play and wants to be a part of a group in play activities. Four- and five-year-olds are developing leadership skills. They like to participate in making plans and decisions within a group, but they are more likely to use their enthusiasm to initiate a project than to seek satisfaction from its completion (Hendrick, 1990).

Because these children are in the preoperational period, their social development is related to their progress in cognitive development. The egocentric nature of their thinking affects their social interactions. They may be unaware of the effects their actions have on others; they are easily confused by misleading cues. For example, a young child may have difficulty in initiating a play activity with another child because he or she uses inappropriate behavior to get the other child's attention. The three-year-old child may be surprised to find out that changing another child's efforts to mold damp sand is not appreciated. As the child becomes less egocentric during the ages of four and five, he or she becomes more sensitive to the thoughts and feelings of others and can transfer this awareness into social successes (Schickedanz, York, Stewart, & White, 1990).

Social development is centered on the child's growing ability to become a part of group interactions; therefore, the use of the term *curriculum* for social development can seem awkward. Indeed, Hendrick (1990) reminds us that social development is not taught through artificially contrived group activities but emerges from the child's daily experiences with peers and adults. Development in social skills is the major goal for children between the ages of three and five; at this time they are also becoming able to understand the larger world in which they live. Curriculum for preschoolers can address both types of social development.

In this chapter we will address the means for fostering social development as well as the curriculum for social science. In the section that follows, these two aspects of the social science program will be described. Goals for planning for social development and for planning the social science curriculum will be discussed as separate parts of the program for social development.

Planning for Social Development

Social science is the study of people; through the study of the social sciences, children learn about other people (Jarolimek, 1986). However, before young children can understand and appreciate other people, they have to understand themselves. Thus, social development is a necessary prerequisite for appreciating social science.

> Unless children develop positive views of self, they are not likely to develop positive views of others; unless children appreciate their culture they are not likely to appreciate another's culture; unless children have self-respect, they are not likely to have respect for others; unless children experience success and self-worth, they are not likely to perceive others as worthy. As children look into the psychological looking glass, whatever they see in themselves, they tend to view a similar reflection of others. These mirroring effects emerge as children interact in the social world. . . .(Schickedanz, York, Stewart, & White, 1990, pp. 282–283).

Success in social development is critical in the preschool years; consequently, the plans made for social development in the program for three- to five-year-olds can have a significant role in the child's positive growth toward the development of autonomy and industry. The foundations established through experiences in social development in turn will make it possible for the developing child to appreciate other people in his or her expanding understanding of the world.

Goals for Social Development.   Preschool children are in the process of learning ways to live in harmony with others, both adults and other children. Social learning, then, is related to understanding how to get along with others. In planning for social development, the teacher has to keep in mind the relationship between development and learning. The goals for social development are based on children's developing social needs and might include self-concept, sex-role identity, socialization, and multicultural understandings and sensitivities.

Self-concept.   Young children need to develop a good self-image. If parents and teachers can nurture this characteristic in young children, many other kinds of development are enhanced. The child's positive concept of him- or herself results from successful encounters with the environment. The child who experiences success with people and events in life comes to value him- or herself as an important person. Supportive adults in a supportive environment are the ingredients needed for the establishment of self-concept.

Sex-Role Identity.   Between the ages of three and five, young children become very aware of their gender. Five-year-olds frequently discuss what boys or girls are "supposed to do." Although the process begins with parental behaviors that identify with the gender of the infant, during the preschool years children develop an awareness of the appropriate behaviors expected of males and females. There has been much effort expended in recent years to encourage nonsexist relationships by parents with their young children; nevertheless, the way that parents and other adults relate to the gender of their children affects personality and self-concept. The differentiated relationship that parents and teachers have with boys and girls results in different expectations and interactions.

Socialization.   Socialization, or the ability to get along with other people, begins very early in life. As children learn cooperating, sharing, and helping skills, they make progress in socialization. When the socialization the child has experienced is compatible with the expectations of the preschool group setting, the child finds the adjustment to school or early childhood center to be easily achieved. If the child's socialization does not conform to the group setting or school environment, he or she finds the expectations and adjustments very difficult. Successful socialization development in turn is dependent upon other developmental skills: controlling and expressing feelings appropriately; developing empathy; and developing prosocial skills.

Very young children must learn to control and express their feelings in an appropriate manner. Infants and toddlers begin this process and refine it in the preschool years. The child from age three to five has the difficult task of learning how to express anger in an appropriate manner and how to verbalize frustrating feelings to adults. In addition, the child must learn how to deal with another child's anger and frustration. Young children learn that they have many kinds of feelings: fear, happiness, anger, surprise, contentment. Being able to identify their feelings and act upon them appropriately is part of the process of socialization.

As children become less egocentric and more sensitive to others, they become aware that other children may be feeling and experiencing differently than they are. Awareness and sensitivity leads to empathy. Very young children begin to develop a positive regard for others. In the preschool years, empathy can lead to generosity, compassion, and concern. Children who develop empathy are able to react appropriately to another person's feelings or circumstances. Thus the preschooler can comfort a crying child or help a frustrated child complete a difficult puzzle. The child who can express and act upon empathy is developing socialization skills.

Socialization requires additional abilities, frequently described as prosocial skills. Prosocial skills are strategies that enable the young child to enter and successfully interact with a social group. The child must learn how to ask for a toy, engage in successful sharing, gain acceptance in a group play situation, and deal with inappropriate behavior on the part of other children. The process that begins with toddlers continues into the elementary school years; nevertheless, it is during the preschool years that the pattern of success or failure in prosocial skills becomes important (Hendrick, 1990; Maxim, 1989).

Multicultural Understandings and Sensitivities.   Racial bias and misunderstanding can begin at a very early age; conversely, understanding and acceptance of ethnic and cultural differences can also begin very early. Preschool children can become accustomed to differences in skin color, ethnicity, and language. They can be nurtured to accept these differences as normal and equally valued by the teacher, other children, and society at large. The preschool setting should offer dolls, books, and other materials and activities that reflect diversity in a positive manner. Children can become sensitive to and appreciative of similarities and differences in children and their families (Ramsey, 1987).

Goals for Social Science.   Earlier we mentioned that the goal for social development is for young children to develop the capability to understand and value themselves and get along with others. Social development is part of the foundation of understanding the social sciences. The major goal for social science in turn is to develop people who have self-respect and self-worth and who can become productive contributors to society. Achieving this broad goal is a life-long process that begins with the socialization of the very young child.

In the primary grades, social science is understood within a content field that includes psychology, history, geography, economics, sociology, and anthropology. These areas of study continue throughout the years of formal schooling. Although preschool children cannot comprehend the specialized fields that are grouped within social studies, they can develop the foundations for understanding them.

Psychology.   Psychology involves the understanding of human behavior. For the young child, understanding relates to self-concept. Children can understand them-

selves as unique individuals who are competent. They can also come to understand that there are individual and group similarities and differences. They can learn about others through study of similarities and differences in homes, families, and individuals.

History.   History is the study of the events of the past and the forces and changes that caused the events. Young children are not able to comprehend the passage of time, but they can understand their own history and past. They can learn about themselves and the changes they have gone through in their development, as well as interesting events in their family history. They are interested in hearing stories about the past and exploring artifacts from earlier times.

Geography.   Geography relates to characteristics of the earth's environment and the relationships among different environments and peoples. Young children cannot understand distant characteristics of geography, but they can relate to the more familiar and local characteristics. They can visit nearby environments and understand what is meant by geographic differences and what it means to travel from one location to another. They can become familiar with physical features and geographic differences in their community.

Economics.   Although young children cannot understand the comprehensive nature of a nation's economy and the role of goods, services, and the monetary system as a vehicle of exchange, they can address economic concepts that affect their own lives. Young children can begin to develop an awareness of the purposes of commercials on television and other advertising media in appealing to the desire to acquire foods, toys, and other goods. They can come to understand the differences between acquiring things that are needed and those that are wanted and the way in which choices must be made depending on how much money one has. They can also understand how people buy services and goods and how people are dependent upon each other to acquire money for their needs.

Sociology.   Sociology is the study of how people live in groups and communities. Although young children cannot comprehend how people organize themselves into groups, communities, and nations and develop social classes and institutions, they can understand the social groups that are closest to their own experience. They can understand the family as a social unit and extend the concept to relate to the school and immediate community near their home.

Anthropology.   Anthropology is the study of cultures and diverse life-styles; it is the study of the art, music, institutions, beliefs, dress, food, religion, and celebrations of different cultures. Although preschool children cannot address the cultural differences of unfamiliar cultures, they can relate to cultural diversities within their own community. They can learn about cultural variety by experiencing many ongoing activities. In addition, they can engage in an appreciation of cultural and social differences and the contributions of different cultural groups in their community. Teachers can promote multicultural understanding to address and prevent prejudices, discrimination, and stereotypes that are prevalent in our larger society today (Schickedanz, York, Stewart, & White, 1990; Seefeldt, 1989).

Ultimately, the goals for social development and social science are very similar. The first focuses on the child and his or her social world; the second focuses on social groups and how the world of social groups function. Because the young child first relates to his or her immediate world and social group, social development and the study of social sciences emerges from that environment and world. In the sections that follow, we will discuss the role of the teacher and the environment in promoting social development. The importance of play as a socialization tool in the child's environment will be described, especially those facets of play (such as dramatic play) that are vehicles for the child's social development and understanding of him- or herself within the family and other social groups.

The Role of Play in Social Development

Although infants and toddlers are more likely to play by themselves or engage in parallel play alongside another child, children between the ages of three and five enter the world of true social play. They try out social interactions in all types of play—for example, when involved in physical play on complex climbing structures, playing with wheel toys, or exploring sand and water. The richest opportunities for learning social skills, however, develop through dramatic play.

When very young children develop the ability to use pretense in their play, they can engage in dramatic play. As they move away from egocentricity and cooperate with others in pretend play, they can interact with other children in sociodramatic play. Studies of the benefits of sociodramatic play have revealed a correlation between sociodramatic play and social and cognitive competence (Garvey, 1977; Smilansky, 1968). Through fantasy play with peers, children learn social skills (Frost, 1992); moreover, the amount and frequency of fantasy play predicts social skills, popularity, and positive social activity (Connolly & Doyle, 1984; Johnson, Christie, & Yawkey, 1987).

Beaty (1992) described some specific benefits of sociodramatic play. When children are involved in dramatic play roles they are learning socialization skills. Fantasy play episodes involve peer pressure for appropriate social behaviors, as well as an understanding of the negative social effects of aggression. Children learn how to resolve interpersonal conflicts when observing other children using successful strategies. Role playing allows the child to try on different roles, such as that of mother, father, sibling, or friend. As a result of engaging in planning and implementation of fantasy play themes, children learn both leader and follower roles. As they use their imagination and creativity to develop themes and roles for sociodramatic play, they learn the difference between fantasy and reality. Sociodramatic play helps children deal with emotions. They are able to use fantasy or pretend play to gain control over fears and other negative emotions. Cathartic play helps resolve traumatic feelings as children reenact frightening experiences (Frost, 1992).

If teachers are to provide opportunities for sociodramatic play for preschool children, they will have to set up the environment to facilitate fantasy play themes and encourage appropriate social behaviors. In addition, they must become sensitive to their role in enabling children to develop social skills.

The Role of the Environment in Social Development.   Because play is an important component for social development, the preschool classroom environment also has an important role in social development and the social science curriculum. Before children engage in sociodramatic play, there must be space and materials available both indoors and outdoors. The homemaking or dramatic play center is the area most commonly thought of as the location for fantasy play themes; however, in reality, children engage in sociodramatic play in the block and truck center, art center, and other classroom areas. Outdoors, play themes can originate on the complex climbing structure or in a playhouse setting and then move to the playground as children act out the fantasy situation.

The arrangement of the environment can affect the development and use of social skills. If the classroom is organized so that children have access to play materials, positive social behaviors are more likely to be used. Children need time and space to be able to interact appropriately; in addition, play opportunities and materials must continually challenge and interest them. Beaty (1992, p. 206) suggests that the following factors in the learning environment can cause inappropriate social behaviors:

1. Too few activities and materials
2. Activities and materials not appropriate for developmental levels of children
3. Too much room to run around
4. Activity areas not clearly defined
5. Classroom geared for total group activities rather than individual and small-group activities
6. No duplicates of favorite toys or materials
7. No change in old materials, books, toys

The daily routine or schedule can also encourage the use of social skills. Young children need the security of predictability in the routines from day to day. They are comfortable when they know what will be happening during the day. When normal routines are changed for field trips, holiday celebrations, and other special occasions, children are likely to react with excitement and difficulty in following normal expectations for behavior. When changes are unavoidable, children will respond more positively if they are prepared for schedule differences beforehand.

The need for predictability extends to classroom rules and expectations for appropriate behavior. When children know the kinds of behaviors that are acceptable for different classroom and outdoor activities, they are better prepared to demonstrate their cooperation with appropriate social skills. They need to have a voice in establishing classroom rules and frequent feedback on whether the rules are being followed successfully. Children between the ages of three and five need many opportunities to learn classroom procedures and benefit from reminders before their behavior gets out of control and firm measures must be taken to restore order. Young children want to use appropriate behavior. When the classroom is arranged to maximize active involvement in challenging activities, and expectations for appropriate social behaviors are clearly understood, preschool children are more likely to respond positively with their developing social skills.

The Role of the Teacher in Social Development.   The teacher has a direct role in helping children acquire social skills and make progress in social development. The teacher must prepare the environment for sociodramatic play and appropriate social behaviors, but young children also need help in controlling their behavior. The teacher will need to develop strategies for helping children manage their behavior, develop activities for fostering and improving sociodramatic play, and plan the social science curriculum.

In spite of the teacher's best efforts to set the tone of the classroom to encourage prosocial skills, young children have difficulty in maintaining appropriate behaviors. As a result, the teacher is forced to intervene when unsocial impulses cause a child to misbehave. When children break rules for appropriate behavior, the teacher must take

steps to correct the situation. If a child attempts to use physical aggression to hurt another child, immediate steps must be taken to prohibit the child from making further attempts to use the behavior. To help the child acquire more long-term controls, the teacher can initiate steps that will lead toward the goal. The child can be reminded of the rule and the consequences for breaking it; redirected to a more appropriate activity; isolated and given the opportunity to discuss feelings; asked to indicate when he or she feels able to return to an activity and use appropriate behavior; or helped to choose another activity (Hendrick, 1990). Whatever strategies are established to guide children to appropriate behaviors, consistency is important. Children need to know what to expect when they lose control and feel assured that the teacher will take steps to help them stay within the limits for appropriate social behaviors.

Sometimes children use inappropriate behaviors because they don't know how to use prosocial skills. They don't know how to use positive alternatives to interact with other children. These children need direct suggestions for using successful behaviors. Children can be shown how to offer to contribute to a play group or play alongside a play activity until accepted into the group. They can be taught how to ask for a turn with a toy and to apologize when they are responsible for accidentally (or deliberately) hurting another child. The teacher shows approval and gives positive feedback when positive behaviors are used.

Similar direct and indirect teacher behaviors can be used to nurture and extend children's sociodramatic play. Although teachers should avoid excessive intervention in children's play, observation can indicate when children would benefit from adult involvement to extend and further develop their play. The teacher can join a play episode as a coplayer but can leave the children in charge of the play theme. Suggestions can be made about materials or equipment that could extend the play. The adult can model new approaches for dramatic play or tutor the children by demonstrating possibilities through questions or responding to children's actions and verbalizations. Most important, the teacher can encourage further sociodramatic play by showing approval of the play activity and demonstrating appreciation for the children's development of fantasy play themes (Johnson, Christie, & Yawkey, 1987).

The teacher's role in developing the social science curriculum is also significant. Many teachers believe that preschool children are too young to learn about social studies because they lack the experience and cognitive abilities to relate to the components of the curriculum. Teachers of young children can involve them in social science at their own level, which will not only further their development as members of their immediate social group but also add to their experiences in the social world in which they and their family live.

Designing Curriculum for Social Development

Fostering Social Development.   We have discussed the meaning of social development in the preschool years and the goals for social development in preschool children. We have also explained that the curriculum for social development is the social learning that young children acquire from daily experiences in their environment. There is not a written curriculum or curriculum topic that teachers organize into group activities so that children can learn how to get along with others. There are, however, categories of social development skills that teachers and children can address in the preschool classroom. Two major social accomplishments that young children must master in their social world are self-management skills and social participation skills. To this end, there are strategies teachers can use to develop these competencies in young children within group discussions and play experiences. Following are some activities teachers can use to foster social development in preschool children; these activities are based on research of preschool children's peer acceptance and social interaction (Kemple, 1991).

Activities for Fostering Social Interactions

Fostering Social Skills

Children who are lacking social skills can learn them from children who are socially competent. The teacher can organize special play sessions where less effective children are paired with children who have acquired effective social skills. Through play experiences, the less skilled child can learn to play more effectively.

Overcoming Social Isolation

Some children may understand social skills but are unable to use them. Sometimes pairing these children with a younger child will give them the confidence they need. When socially isolated children are exposed to play sessions with younger children, they may become more socially involved because they feel comfortable with younger children.

Learning Social Alternatives

Many children use aggression because they do not understand alternative strategies to resolve conflicts. Planned activities can be used to teach children alternative strategies that are more successful than aggression. The teacher can initiate skits, puppet activities, and group discussions involving hypothetical situations. Children can become involved in the problem and in determining alternative solutions. Children are encouraged to increase the number of appropriate strategies they might try.

Learning Prosocial and Empathic Behavior

Children who are popular are helpful and cooperative. Many children are not helpful because they do not recognize situations in which they can be of assistance. Through observation, teachers can determine whether students are empathic and how they can be helped to cooperate and offer assistance. The teacher can create opportunities for a child to demonstrate helpfulness or point out situations when the child can be helpful to another child who is in need or in distress.

Can I Play?

Many young children have difficulty entering a play group. One solution may be for the teacher to guide the isolated child to a smaller play group or a more cooperative group. The teacher can tutor the child identify the play theme and think of a role that can be played that would contribute to the group's play.

Improving Social Communication Skills

Children who have difficulty maintaining a play episode are unable to communicate effectively with playmates. Teachers can provide guidance on how to clarify communication within the play episode. The teacher can instruct a child to be more specific in an explanation. An unpopular child can be guided to be sensitive to the negative emotional cues that indicate that another child does not like the unpopular child's behavior or actions.

Helping Children Who Have No Friends

Peers should not be forced to play with a child; however, there are ways that teachers can facilitate the child's acceptance into the peer group. The teacher can interpret

the child's positive intentions to the other children and guide them toward helping the child successfully play with them. Teacher strategies can facilitate peer understanding and empathy for the child who has difficulty in making friends. The peer group can then help the child become more successful in play interactions.

Designing Curriculum for Social Science

In a previous section we discussed the components of the social science curriculum and the way in which it applies to young children of ages three to five. In this section we will describe how those components are implemented into learning experiences that are developmentally appropriate. Because children have their own limitations in cognition and experience, there are certain criteria for curriculum design: (1) the curriculum should emphasize direct activities, such as taking field trips, utilizing resource persons, and examining real things; and (2) the curriculum should focus on the children themselves.

Young children learn best about the social world in meaningful contexts; therefore, integrated curriculum is the best framework to use for planning. The teacher should plan units based on social science themes that permit young children to use their senses and receptive and expressive language to reflect upon the information they are encountering. If the curriculum is to be based on the children themselves, the units of study should center on their life histories, families, homes, and feelings. They can also extend their social world to include their peers, the school, and the society of the community. Schickedanz, York, Stewart, and White (1990) suggest that the social science curriculum be organized around two major categories: (1) understanding self and family and (2) understanding people and society. These two categories are further divided into major theme possibilities as follows:

Understanding Self and Family
   Understanding Self
   Each Individual Has Worth and Dignity
   Personal History
   Feelings Can Be Expressed in Acceptable Ways
   Death as a Part of Life
   Divorce and the Young Child
   Coping with Crisis Situations

Understanding People and Society
   The Family Unit Is Basic in a Society
   People Have Rights
   People Have Responsibilities
   People Have Needs and Desires

Rules Are Necessary When People Live in Groups

People Live in Communities

People Produce and Consume Goods and Services

People Do Different Types of Work

People Travel in Various Ways and Send Messages

People Represent Many Cultures

Important People of the Past and Present

Understanding Cultural Diversity

Values, Customs, and Traditions

These topics would have to be further simplified to make them applicable for preschool children age five and younger; nevertheless, they represent many of the significant topics in the social science curriculum that have been discussed earlier. When planning a unit, the teacher will plan unit activities with the children so that all may express their interest in the unit and the kinds of information they would like to find out from working on unit experiences and activities. In the activities described next, examples are given of some of the topics related to the social world of children that will extend their understanding of social science concepts. Then, an example of an integrated thematic topic will be described to demonstrate how social science activities can be enriched by being integrated with other areas of development using direct experiences.

Activities for Social Science

Understanding Historical Time

Preschoolers have a very limited understanding of past and future time. Because of their preoperational mode of thinking, they can understand past and future events only when they are described in relation to the present day. They can understand the passage of time based on the events of each day. Activities that include discussions of what happened earlier in the day and will happen later in the day help them to attend to the nature of passing time.

Celebrating birthdays and marking a monthly calendar can help older children build an awareness of the passage of days. Children can develop a foundation for historical perspective by taking part in activities that include the ages of different members of the family and their ranks based on time that has passed (Vukelich & Thornton, 1990).

Grandparents and Oral History

Children are interested in things that have happened in their family a long time ago. Children are fascinated by stories told of real-life experiences related to family history; resource people who can tell such stories are integral to this activity. If grandparents or surrogate grandparents can bring artifacts that represent their earlier life and share them with young children, the children gain a meaningful awareness of their social heritage. For example, a grandmother in Iowa brought a butter churn to the classroom. She demonstrated with the children how it was used to make butter. She showed a picture of the house she lived in when she was a little girl. The children were able to discuss how homes today compare with the grandmother's house; they could also compare the way we get butter today at a store with the way the grandmother had to churn her own butter when she was a child.

Death and the Life Cycle

Even young children need to understand that there is a cycle in life that ends in death. Many young children have experienced the death of a pet or seen a dead insect or plant. An experience with growing plants can help them to understand the life cycle. Teachers and children can plant seeds, nurture the growing plants, and enjoy the flowers that bloom when the plants are mature. Furman (1990) suggests that children need to experience the rest of the cycle, when the plant dies and decays. They can discuss what has happened to the plant and how seeds can be harvested from the flowers to make future plants. They can have a similar experience with a gourd or melon vine or a potato plant.

Understanding Transportation

All children notice different types of vehicles that pass their school, day-care center, or own home. They can learn the different transportation purposes that different kinds of vehicles serve. Children can discuss the different types of vehicles that pass a corner for a given period of time. The teacher can record the names of the vehicles or photograph them. The children can then study the photos and determine what was transported in the vehicle. They can decide whether the vehicle's purpose is to transport people or some type of goods or is used to perform a service.

Neighborhood Structures

A similar activity can be conducted with buildings in the neighborhood. Children can note the types of buildings they see on a brief walk and decide whether they are homes or stores or serve some other purpose. They can discuss the many kinds of buildings in a community. As a follow-up activity, they might construct their own community structures with blocks or make models out of cardboard boxes.

Understanding Change

One way to teach children what happens with the passage of time and how people live together in a community is to provide them with activities that show how things change. Children might take a walk near the school or center and note locations that are in the process of being built or changed. Next, they might search for places that indicate wear and aging, such as cracks or potholes in the street or paint that is peeling from a building. Areas being remodeled or renewed can be identified. The purpose is for the child to understand that change is a part of life.

Want and Need

Children need to differentiate between things that they want and things that they need. After a discussion of the difference, children might look through magazines for pictures and make a collage of things they would like to have on one side and things they need on the other side. As an alternative activity, a group mural could be constructed.

School Workers

Children can become aware of the different people who provide a service for them at their school or center. The teacher can take them to visit workers and observe what they do. The worker can then visit the classroom and discuss how the children are served through their efforts. The children can dictate stories about each worker and illustrate the story. A class book can be made of the stories.

Designing Integrated Curriculum in Social Science

Social science concepts are learned best in a meaningful context. Preschoolers need to be involved in real experiences if they are to understand concepts about their social world. It is recommended that social science activities for preschool children be closely related to their personal lives. One topic that is pertinent to young children is that of their own family. In the integrated social science curriculum described next, the unit on families can be related to the social science topic entitled "The Family Unit Is Basic in Society." The activities related to families center on the book *Daddy Makes the Best Spaghetti*, by Anna Grossnickle Hines. The book should be particularly appealing because Daddy does the cooking and shares in caring for his children. Since spaghetti is a favorite with young children, cooking and eating spaghetti will be an exciting event.

The family-life theme activities engaged in can center on such ideas as the way in which families eat together and the different types of family groups. The family-oriented activities that include favorite bedtime storybooks and pots, pans, and cooking spoons for a kitchen band experience are taken from *More Story Stretchers* (Raines & Canady, 1991). Figure 8.1 describes the activities and interest centers that can be incorporated into a thematic unit.

Integrated units in the preschool years can have their origin in any category of development; however, as has been pointed out several times, other types of development are also interfaced within integrated curriculum. This is especially true of physical development. Preschool children are physically involved when they are learning and playing. Nonetheless, the preschool program should include curriculum for physical development that extends beyond self-initiated or informal play activities to include activities that involve gross and fine motor skills. In the section that follows, we discuss the nature of physical development in the preschool years and appropriate curriculum to encourage physical activities.

Circle Time Presentation

Show the children the cover of Corey and Dad marching and making music with pots and pans. Ask the children to predict what they think the story is about. After reading the title, *Daddy Makes the Best Spaghetti,* ask if anyone wants to change their minds about what will happen in the story. Read *Daddy Makes the Best Spaghetti* and pause for the children to giggle at Dad's impersonations of "Bathman" and the delightful suspense as Corey tries to find Dad while almost losing his bath towel. At the end of the reading, several children probably will volunteer some descriptions of funny games their parents play. Encourage them to also talk about cooking with their dads.

Story Stretcher

For Cooking and Snack Time: Making the Best Spaghetti

What the children will learn—
To assist in making spaghetti

Materials you will need—
Prepared sauce or ingredients for your own sauce, range or hot plate, spaghetti, water, salt, butter, one large saucepan and one large pot, wooden spoons, colander, plates, silverware, brightly colored napkins and tablecloths

What to do—
1. Divide the children into four groups of chef's assistants. Discuss with each group what their task will include.
2. Make a rebus chart, a combination of words and symbols, for each group's instructions and the spaghetti recipe. Post the chart and refer to it throughout the cooking experience.
3. If possible, have a parent come to the classroom and prepare his or her favorite spaghetti sauce with the help of a small group of children acting as chef's assistants. If this is not possible, let this group help warm up the sauce in a large saucepan or place it in a microwave to heat.
4. Let another small group of children cook the spaghetti by boiling water, adding salt and butter, cooking the noodles, and, finally, draining them in a colander.
5. Have the third group of children set the table with brightly colored napkins and tablecloth.
6. Ask the fourth group of chef's assistants to serve the spaghetti to the rest of the class and parents.

Something to think about—
While cooking hot foods with young children takes extra preparation and caution, the pride of accomplishment the children feel and the valuable learning experiences are worth the extra efforts.

Figure 8.1   Integrated Social Studies Curriculum (pp. 293–295)

S. Raines & R. Canady, *More Story Stretchers.* (Gryphon House, 1989), pp. 40–41). Reprinted by permission of the publisher.

Another Story Stretcher

For Cooking and Snack Time: Families Setting the Table and Eating Together

What the children will learn—
To pretend to be families during snack time and how to set the table

Materials you will need—
If possible, real silverware, dishes, glassware, napkins and placemats or tablecloths

What to do—
1. Look again at the illustration of the family eating together in the book.
2. Ask the children to sit at the snack table; then at random ask children to pretend to be the father, mother, grandfather, grandmother, and children. At some tables there might not be a mother and at others there might not be a father. Discuss that we are still families even if one of our parents is not present.
3. Have these children sit together as families throughout the week during snack time.
4. Let different members of the family take turns setting the table.

Something to think about—
With older children, encourage table conversations with each person maintaining their role. With younger children, since snack time is not usually a pretending time, a teacher, aide, or volunteer may need to sit at the table to encourage conversation.

Story Stretcher

For Housekeeping and Dress-up Corner: Grocery Store

What the children will learn—
To set up the area, improvise props, play the roles involved

Materials you will need—
Canned and boxed foods, grocery bags, aprons, cash register, cents-off coupons, newspaper ads, scratch pads, pencils, posterboard, markers (optional—grocery carts)

What to do—
1. In the parent newsletter, announce the grocery store center and ask for empty cans and boxes.
2. After the cans and boxes have arrived, collect cents-off coupons and newspaper ads that correspond to the containers.
3. Give the players in the area the coupons, ads, scratch pads, pencils, posterboard, and markers. Ask them what they can do with these materials to make the area look like a real grocery store. Expect to see them make posters guiding the shoppers to the food displays and matching the cents-off coupons to the food. Eventually, as they shop, expect them to use the scratch pads to write checks for their groceries.
4. After the grocery store is set up, let the arrangers become the first customers, cashiers, produce managers, and baggers.

Figure 8.1   Integrated Social Studies Curriculum *(continued)*

Something to think about—
A grocery store is a wonderfully rich center for learning about community helpers, emergent literacy, nutrition, mathematics, and social studies as the children play the roles.

Story Stretcher

For Library Corner: Our Favorite Bedtime Books

What the children will learn—
To select a favorite bedtime book

Materials you will need—
Collection of books about bedtime, naptime, nighttime, or family experiences

What to do—
1. Show the illustration from *Daddy Makes the Best Spaghetti* where the little boy and his father are listening to his mother read a bedtime story.
2. Read one of your favorite bedtime or naptime books in a lowered, calm voice. Talk with the children about how it makes you relax when you read the book.
3. Ask the children to bring a copy of a book from home, one of their favorite books that helps them relax and go to sleep.
4. During the week, select bedtime books to read aloud in the library corner and at times during the day when a relaxing mood is needed.

Something to think about—
If some of your children have few books at home, let these children go with you to the school or city library and check out books for the rest of the class.

Story Stretcher

For Music and Movement: Pots and Pans for Our Kitchen Band

What the children will learn—
To march and keep the beat on their kitchen utensils and pots and pans

Materials you will need—
Large cardboard box, pots and pans, lids, coffee cans, large metal and wooden serving spoons, tablespoons, cassette recording of march music, tape player

What to do—
1. Collect all the instruments, pots and pans, and utensils for the kitchen band and place them in a large cardboard box.
2. During a second circle time of the day, play some march music and let the children parade around the edge of the circle time rug, marching and clapping their hands.
3. Have the children sit on the circle time rug again and at random; call out the names of the children to come up and select an instrument for the kitchen band.
4. March around the room, leading the kitchen band as they keep time with the march music.

Something to think about—
Banging around on pots and pans and coffee cans certainly is not real music; however, the improvised pretend band can enjoy the movement of the activity.

CURRICULUM FOR PHYSICAL DEVELOPMENT

Peter Paul and Amos
Peter Paul and Amos are sitting under a tree enjoying a glass of lemonade. They have been playing chase around the trees in the backyard of Peter Paul's house and are thirsty. They are munching on peanut butter cookies that Peter Paul's mother brought them for a snack. When Amos is finished, he pulls himself onto a low limb and looks for more limbs he can use to climb. "I can climb very high," he announces to Peter Paul. Not to be outdone, Peter Paul abandons his lemonade and runs to another nearby tree.

"I can, too," he calls to Amos.

"Not as high as I can," challenges Amos.

There is silence for a few minutes as each boy slowly makes his way up a few feet more. "I am high as a jet," Amos calls to Peter Paul.

"I am as high as the sky," Peter Paul responds.

The preschool years are significant for physical development. The emerging locomotor skills practiced by infants and toddlers are improved and refined during the

preschool years. Preschoolers spend many hours in active play that exercises gross and fine motor skills. They need abundant time for play, both indoors and outdoors. In this part of the chapter, we will study how physical development is part of the curriculum for three- to five-year-olds and how the teacher can prepare the environment and plan opportunities for children to exercise their bodies to develop physical abilities.

Understanding Physical Development

Physical development is referred to as motor development because the young child is using fine and gross motor movement in physical activities. It is also described as perceptual–motor development because there is interdependency between perception and motor skills. Motor behavior and changes in motor abilities follow perceptual actions (Williams, 1983).

In chapter 3 we described the characteristics of physical development in three- to five-year-olds. The Frost-Wortham developmental checklists describe major milestones in fine and gross motor skills at each developmental level. In this chapter we will address physical development as it involves perceptual–motor development. As the child develops the capacity to manage more complex sensory input, more skillful motor behavior follows (Jambor, 1990). The components of these interactive elements of sensory and physical actions constitute perceptual–motor development.

Components of Perceptual–Motor Development.   Fundamental movement skills are developed during the preschool years. Frost (1992, p. 46) describes these movement skills as follows:

> *Gross motor activities:* Throwing, catching, kicking, jumping, swinging
>
> *Fine motor activities:* Cutting lace, hammering, buttoning, pouring
>
> *Body awareness activities:* Naming, pointing, identifying, moving, and performing tasks using body parts
>
> *Spatial awareness activities:* Moving, exploring, locating, comparing, and identifying using walking, running, catching, rolling, and going through tunnels and mazes
>
> *Directional awareness activities:* Moving, stationing, pointing, identifying, and imitating using body objects and apparatuses
>
> *Balance activities:* Walking, bounding, and clapping using balance beams and boards, trampoline, and spring boards
>
> *Integrations activities:* Hitting moving ball, tracking moving objects, matching visual and motor responses, responding to auditory signals
>
> *Expressive activities:* Working with art, music, dance, and dramatic play

These categories of skills can be further explained as follows (Gallahue, 1976):

> *Gross motor skills:* Locomotor skills; movements using large motor abilities

Fine motor skills: Skills using fingers and hands that promote development of strength and flexibility in the fingers

Body awareness: The capacity to discriminate among the parts of the body and to understand how the body works—what parts of the body can do

Spatial awareness: Perceptual–motor development that permits children to orient themselves in space; includes understanding how much space their body occupies and how to locate themselves and objects in space

Directional awareness: Refers to directionality and laterality; the child is able to understand location and direction as it relates to the position of his or her body (left and right, up and down, front and back); also refers to the ability to see or understand direction in space; children must be able to perceive directionality of print on the page in the English language to be able to read

Temporal awareness: Refers to the relatedness between the body and time; related to physical coordination; rhythm, synchrony, and sequencing necessary for coordinated physical performance

Children's ability to control their bodies affects all other areas of development. The ability to use fine and gross motor skills affects the child's feeling of competence and is carried over to other areas of development. Self-image is related to mastery of physical skills. Children who perceive themselves as having good physical abilities can use their success for gaining confidence in addressing social and cognitive activities.

Planning for Physical Development

Children vary in their rate of physical development, just as they do in language, cognitive, and social development. Teachers need to be aware of these differences when planning environment arrangements and experiences for physical development. A range of experiences should be planned for perceptual–motor and movement activities that will promote physical development in young children.

Although children acquire many motor skills through normal working and playing activities in the indoor and outdoor environment, the teacher also plans for comprehensive physical development. The teacher identifies current levels of physical abilities in individual students and selects specific fine and gross motor skills that can be addressed in planned daily activities. Thus, the teacher might decide to put out boards, blocks, or a walking beam to help children develop balancing skills; or the teacher might plan a cutting activity to practice using scissors. Attention is given to both fine and gross motor skills that are developmentally appropriate for four- and five-year-olds as described by the National Association for the Education of Young Children in *Developmentally Appropriate Practice in Early Childhood Programs Serving Children from Birth through Age 8* (Bredekamp, 1987, p. 56.):

- Children have daily opportunities to use large muscles, including running, jumping, and balancing. Outdoor activity is planned daily so children can develop large muscle skills, learn about outdoor environments, and express themselves freely and loudly.

• Children have daily opportunities to develop small muscle skills through play activities such as playing with pegboards and puzzles, painting, cutting, and other similar activities.

When planning activities that provide for gross and fine motor skills, the teacher might make a choice from a list of activities such as the following (Beaty, 1992):

Large Motor Activities
    Walking
    Throwing, catching
    Balancing
    Hopping, jumping, leaping
    Running, galloping, skipping
    Climbing
    Crawling, creeping, scooting
    Using wheeled vehicles

Fine Motor Activities
    Zipping, buttoning, tying
    Twisting, turning
    Pouring
    Cutting
    Holding and printing, tracing, painting
    Inserting

Large motor skills activities for preschool children should be provided indoors as well as outdoors. Obstacle courses, indoor climbing equipment, and flexible motor skills apparatuses can be arranged for use in the activities to be included in the daily schedule. Other center activities, teacher-directed lessons, and small-group activities planned for the day or week can be analyzed for the type of fine and gross motor skills that will be used. Through a combination of planned activities and natural play opportunities during the day, children can have a balance of perceptual–motor experiences that permit them to refine and extend physical development (Hendrick, 1990).

The Role of Play in Physical Development

Play has an important role in all categories of development; however, its benefits for physical development may be more obvious for most teachers and parents. Physical exercise is associated with outdoor play, and traditional playground equipment used throughout most of the twentieth century has been designed to exercise motor skills.

For our concerns, the role of play for preschool children is more than that for providing gross motor exercise. Fine motor skills are considered as well within the understanding of the importance of play. Three- to five-year-olds spend much of their day in play. If they are in a caregiving or preschool setting, indoor and outdoor play periods should be alternated with more structured activities. During play opportunities, children combine language practice, socialization, and cognitive exploration with fine and gross motor activities. The child selects the play activities; thus, play events are self directed or group directed. Some children take leadership roles in play, and the physical activities engaged in are supportive to the child's purpose for the play activity.

The Role of the Environment in Physical Development.   The quality of the play environment affects the benefits of physical play. A primary concern is that the playscape is safe (Frost, 1990). Beyond consideration for safety of design and construction of equipment for physical play, the child's play activities are related to the type of space where the play takes place, the materials that are available for the play, and the way in which the place space is arranged (Johnson, Christie, & Yawkey, 1987).

Children play differently indoors than outdoors. Large motor play is more likely to occur outdoors, where there is more space and where play equipment encourages large motor activity. Construction play is more frequent indoors, where there is an abundance of blocks, manipulative materials, and art and writing activities (Henniger, 1985). Boys and girls play differently indoors and outdoors. Preschool boys prefer playing outdoors more than do girls; moreover, they engage in more make-believe play outdoors (Sanders & Harper, 1976). Girls, on the other hand, prefer to play indoors. They engage in more dramatic play indoors and are more likely to engage in fine motor activities than are boys (Johnson, Christie, & Yawkey, 1987).

The Indoor Environment.   A well-planned indoor environment is well stocked and arranged for both gross and fine motor activities. Materials and ideas for fine motor activities are always available in the art center, language center, and manipulative center.

In the art center, all activities will nurture fine motor skills. Painting, cutting, and pasting; molding play dough; constructing collages; and working with chalk and crayons are examples of expressive activities that nurture many fine motor movements. Hands and fingers are exercised and used differently for each of these activities.

The manipulative center also can facilitate varied fine motor actions. Puzzles, bristle blocks, Legos, and other such construction materials help develop fine motor coordination as children explore possibilities for working with the materials. The sensory nature of Montessori materials makes them particularly useful for fine motor experiences. Lacing, zipping, buttoning, and using snaps can be practiced in activities that teach dressing skills. The manipulative nature of Montessori materials for cognitive activities also incorporates physical manipulation of curriculum experiences.

The language center in a preschool classroom provides opportunities to use fine motor skills. Writing activities require fine motor exercise, as do emergent literacy games.

Large motor skills should also be nurtured indoors. In addition to the portable climbing equipment and temporary obstacle courses mentioned earlier, large motor activities can be engaged in through playing with sand and water and with different sizes of blocks and vehicles in the block center. Workbench activities also attract both girls and boys to opportunities for sawing, hammering, and drilling, using both gross and fine muscle skills.

Beaty (1992) recommends that the indoor classroom have a large motor center where activities can be planned for gross motor skills. She suggests that changing equipment arrangements be placed in the center to encourage specific gross motor exercise. Teacher-directed activities to promote large motor skills can supplement the options for child-initiated gross motor play.

The Outdoor Environment. Many large motor activities can be planned and encouraged indoors; nevertheless, the outdoor environment is where all gross motor actions can take place naturally. Outdoors, preschool children can run, jump, gallop, and so on most freely. The freedom of a large space permits many gross motor activities. In addition, equipment and design features provide more variety in physical activity opportunities.

A complex climbing structure, or superstructure, is a central feature of the playscape for physical exercise. The structure contains decks and attached apparatus that provide for a range of gross motor actions; such apparatus can include slides, firemen's poles, steps, clatter bridges, trapeze bars, and ramps (Frost, 1992). The opportunities offered by complex climbing structures include options for both upper torso and lower torso exercise. Swingsets are another standard piece of equipment that provides enjoyable gross motor activity. A path where vehicles can be ridden or pushed and pulled is also important on preschool playgrounds.

Natural features can also provide possibilities for climbing, running, sliding, balancing, and rolling. The site can be planned to include mounds, small hills, tree stumps and large dead trees; other natural features arranged in a large open area also encourage vigorous movement in play (Esbensen, 1990).

Preschool playscapes should also include opportunities for fine motor activities. Many art and craft activities are enjoyed in the outdoor environment. Outdoor sand and water activities promote both fine and gross motor movement, as do gardening and some dramatic play activities.

Both the indoor and outdoor environments for preschool children should include provisions for perceptual–motor development. Some activities will occur naturally as a result of having the facilities and materials available in the planned environment. Other experiences will require conscious planning on the teacher's part.

The Role of the Teacher in Physical Development. Perhaps the most important responsibility the teacher assumes when considering how to plan for physical development is for carefully planning how the learning environment and outdoor play area will nurture gross and fine motor skills. As described earlier, the teacher's understanding of the role of play in physical development and the effect the environment has for exercising emerging physical abilities must be translated into physical arrangements indoors and outdoors that will encourage the range of physical movement in preschool children.

A second important responsibility of the teacher is to be informed of the physical development needs of individual children. Through daily observation when children are at play, the teacher is alert to the physical skills the children are mastering. For example, the teacher may note that a child is having difficulty with play equipment or a locomotor skill; demonstration, modeling, and guided instruction can enable a child to try the fireman's pole or climb a ladder to the complex climbing structure. Likewise, the teacher can show a child how to hold a plastic bat to hit a sponge ball off a tee and can monitor the child's efforts to hit the ball successfully. The teacher needs to be actively involved in large and small motor activities to provide guidance and encouragement when needed.

The teacher's third responsibility is to plan curriculum activities. Some will be planned to be carried out indoors, whereas others will take place outdoors. Some activities will be planned for a motor activity period, and others will be integrated with activities in other developmental areas. The significant factor is that the teacher is sensitive to the importance of motor development and does not relegate outdoor free play periods as the only options for physical exercise. The preschool teacher who is enthusiastic about incorporating language, social, and cognitive experiences in integrated, thematic curriculum can be equally competent and interested in incorporating physical development into planned units. The section that follows discusses how the teacher can implement perceptual–motor experiences for preschool children.

DESIGNING CURRICULUM FOR PHYSICAL DEVELOPMENT

Teachers may be very familiar with the materials and equipment they need for cognitive and language development in the classroom. They may also be secure in their understanding of how the block and manipulative centers promote gross and fine motor skills. However, they may be less knowledgeable about how they can ensure that they have acquired the materials and equipment needed to implement a comprehensive program for physical development. Beaty (1992) suggests materials and activities that address the basic gross and fine motor skills that are part of the preschool physical curriculum; Figure 8.2 lists these suggestions. Although the majority of the activities described are more likely to be used indoors, many suggestions are also part of outdoor playground activities.

Jambor (1990) describes perceptual–motor activities for young children that are intended to promote kinesthetic and sensory development in outdoor experiences (see Figure 8.3, pp. 305–306). He described activities and equipment needed for locomotion, balance, body and space perception, rhythm and temporal awareness, rebound and airborne movement, and projections and reception movement. Although most of these suggestions for physical development are best conducted outdoors, many are also suitable for indoors.

The Integrated Curriculum for Physical Development

Preschool teachers can use Beaty's and Jambor's guides to develop a quality physical development program for preschool children; in addition, attention can be given to incorporating activities for physical development into the total curriculum. Many skills will be encouraged through ongoing center and teacher-directed activities in art,

Walking	Tires
Follow the leader	Swiss cheese board
Walk like an animal	Rowboat
Rocking boat	Tree stumps
Walking trail	Cable spools
Balancing	***Crawling, Creeping, Scooting***
Follow the leader	Spooky music
Hollow blocks	Tambourine
Be an animal	Tunnels of cardboard
Balance beam	Barrels
Block beam	Styrofoam tunnel
Con-Tact paper footprints	Masking tape obstacle course
Balance board	Scooter
Hopping, Jumping, Leaping	Wooden vehicles
Footprint trail	***Picking Up/Carrying***
Hopscotch	Large hollow blocks
Jump over the river	Boxes
Jumping jack period	Furniture
Running, Galloping, Skipping	Large toys
Follow the leader	***Throwing/Catching***
Relay race	Beanbags
Action chants	Ring toss
Climbing	Sponge balls
Jungle gym	Yarn balls
Rung ladder	Beach balls
Nesting climber	Rubber balls
Dome climber	

Figure 8.2   Equipment and Activities for Motor Development (pp. 303–304)

J. J. Beaty, *Skills for Preschool Teachers* (4th ed.). (Macmillan, 1992), pp. 90–91. Reprinted by permission of the publisher.

language, and mathematics and science. They naturally occur as part of the overall preschool curriculum. Other opportunities result from conscious attempts to correlate learning across developmental areas. The teacher deliberately uses physical activity options to help children integrate cognitive concepts; for example, perhaps an art activity is combined with emergent writing to address fine motor skills.

Trostle and Yawkey (1990) developed a handbook of integrated learning activities for young children. They classified integrated experiences into chapters and broad unit categories. One chapter, on transportation, provides particularly helpful advice for interrelating physical development with other curriculum components. Two integrated experiences in the chapter on transportation exemplify how physical development can be integrated with other areas of the curriculum. The activity titled "Wiggling Feet" (Figure 8.4, p. 307) describes how naming and moving body parts is part of language arts. Moving their bodies to songs and then having discussions helps

Wheeled Equipment
Tricycle
Big Wheel
Large wooden vehicles
Scooter
Conveyer belt trike path

Inserting
Shoe box collections
Egg carton
Wooden-knob puzzles
Legos
Pegboards
Golf tees
Geoboard
Frame puzzles
Photo puzzles

Zipping
Clothing with zippers
Zipper board

Twisting/Turning
Eggbeaters
Food mills
Can openers
Bottle and screw tops
Bolt boards
Orange squeezer

Pouring
Small pitchers
Rice, salt, sand

Cutting
Table knife and cooked vegetables
Paring knife and raw vegetables
Shredder
Grater
Melon baller

**Holding and
Printing/Tracing/Painting**
Pencil, crayon
Felt-tip pen

Figure 8.2   Equipment and Activities for Motor Development *(continued)*

children understand names of body parts, relationships between parts of the body, and the way in which the body moves.

The second activity, "Shape Jumping" (Figure 8.5, p. 308), combines playing with shapes with jumping activities. In order to engage in a hopscotch shape activity, children must also use skills in patterning and sequence. Children use fine motor skills to make the shapes used in the activities. In addition, the children must use listening skills to follow directions and use divergent thinking skills to develop a transportation story.

Motor skills activities can be planned for thematic units. Herr and Libby (1990) developed a handbook of thematic units for preschool classrooms. Some of the units provided for specific body movement activities. A unit titled "Music" focused on musical instruments. Activities are suggested for various areas of the curriculum, such as using water in crystal glasses to make music and constructing instruments out of vari-

Locomotion
- Rolling in various directions on flat and sloped grassy areas with arms in different positions
- Creeping, crawling, and walking on or across textured surfaces (to increase sensory input)
- Crawling through "space-holes": barrels, open-ended boxes, single mounted tires, tire tunnels, low playhouse windows
- Crawling across a wide plank
- Climbing on hills, ramps, stairs, platform levels, connected tire formations, rope nets, ladders, multipurpose structures, low limb tree branches, overhead and multidirectional ropes
- Stepping up on graduated levels: platforms, logs, tires, stumps, large wide blocks
- Jumping/bouncing on flat springboards, large flexible horizontal tires, inner tubes, mattresses (trampolines are considered dangerous and not recommended)
- Jumping from varying heights: tires, wooden platforms, stone/earth ledges, stumps, spring boards
- Hurdling over "natural" objects, objects prepared by adults (e.g., a horizontal bamboo pole between two adjustable vertical support points)
- Hopping in place with both feet, then with one foot at a time; hopping, back and forth over lines, between rungs of a wooden ladder on the ground
- Running and walking across bridges, up and down natural slopes and man-made ramps, in open grassy areas
- Chasing and "tag" games that utilize most play apparatus and available space
- Crossing "hand-over-hand" on overhead ladder
- Pumping a swing
- Pulling or pushing a wagon
- Wheel toys that coordinate alternate pumping and steering with feet and hands; obstacle course routes that challenge the coordination of perceptual and motor skills

Many of these actions and activities, as well as those that follow, can be controlled and enhanced by listening for music cues for stopping, starting, and intensity of action.

Balance
- Standing and balancing (both feet, then only one) on walking beam, vertical in-ground tire, moving bridge, suspended horizontal rope with overhead hand support; close eyes for added sensation
- Walking various heights, widths, and spans of wooden beams, vertical in-ground tires, large diameter rope and fire hose (with overhead supports to keep upright)
- Walking on wide beams with arms extended holding a weighted object in one hand or both

Figure 8.3   Outdoor Activities for Perceptual–Motor Development (pp. 305–306)

S. C. Wortham & J. L. Frost (Eds.), *Playgrounds for Young Children.* (American Alliance for Health, Physical Education, Recreation and Dance, 1990), pp. 159–162. Reprinted by permission of the publisher.

- Walking on a line or thin diameter rope configuration on ground
- Walking with one foot on and one off a ground-level beam, on a curb edge, on an edge of a ladder lying on ground, around the edge of a large-diameter horizontal tire
- Following the leader on a spontaneous or preplanned obstacle course throughout playground

Body and Space Perception
- Large mirror area for viewing self and specific body parts and experimenting with ways these parts can function
- Identifying body parts and relating them to a function of movement activity
- Responding to requests to use a body part(s) on climbing or balancing apparatus
- Coordinating body parts to perform physical feats of strength and agility in play spaces and on equipment
- Using arm and leg movements to create "snow/sand angels"
- Pushing someone on a swing
- Fitting into spaces; boxes, large tire opening, wagon, playhouse, play boat or car, across a bridge span, on a swivel tire, at top of a slide (number and size relationship concept)
- Coordinating running and movement activities within a limited space
- Climbing on, under, around, through, etc.; going to the left or to the right (body-objects relationships and directionality)
- Any activity requiring movement in space!

Rhythm and Temporal Awareness
- Recurring rhythm: swing (standard infant and strap seats, suspended tire or rope, swivel tire, vestibular platform, porch style); rocking boats, etc.; wheel toys
- Methodic, rhythmic bouncing on large tires, inner tubes, springboards
- Jumping over stationary rope or one swung in a quarter arc to a rhythmic beat
- Galloping, marching through playground to music, with rhythm instruments or hand claps
- Accelerating and decelerating physical movement to given tempo
- Running up or down diagonal ramps and hills
- Tossing, catching, kicking, dodging objects (e.g., various size balls, beanbags, balloons)

Rebound and Airborne Movement
- Bouncing on springboards, mattresses, large flexible tires, inner tubes (music varies the variety and tempo of action)
- Jumping onto a mattress or into sand, pea gravel, or other resilient ground base from varying heights
- Hanging by hands or legs from climbers, chinning bars, low tree branches, etc.
- Swinging on vertical rope; pushing off of objects to continue or vary movement

Figure 8.3   Outdoor Activities for Perceptual–Motor Development *(continued)*

WIGGLING FEET (Language Arts)

Overview: Children use body movements and practice movement as direction. In Target, they move parts of their bodies to soft and mood music. In Moving Ahead, they move their bodies to the rhythm of common, familiar songs.

Objective: Naming and moving parts of the body

Supplies: Audio recording of soft or mood music; audio recorder

Words You'll Like: *movement, body, body parts, direction, music, soft, practice, connect, opposite*

Getting Started

The children talk about and name their body parts, such as arms, toes, fingers, and so forth. After the discussion, the youngsters name several body parts of their choice and show how each part moves. The children invent and show new movements for each body part. For example, they shake their heads back and forth and swing their legs at the knees.

Target

The children lie on their backs on the floor and place their hands over their heads. The youngsters identify the body part opposite their heads. They wiggle their toes to show this point. The children think about the body part connected to their arms; then they move their shoulders. Repeat the questioning using different body parts as the youngsters demonstrate the appropriate movements. Try this activity while playing music. Introduce "Heads, Shoulders, Knees, and Toes," a favorite movement song among children everywhere.

Moving Ahead

The children sing and practice familiar songs involving movement, such as the "Hokey Pokey" or "The Farmer in the Dell." The children sing the song using the familiar body movements. Next, the children identify and practice several original movements to these songs using different body parts. Finally, the youngsters identify the new body parts they used in the movement songs. For example, using "Hokey Pokey" the youngsters might substitute thumbs, wrists, ankles, knees, calves, and necks for the traditional body parts.

Let's Talk

1. After the youngsters listen to and move their bodies to music or song, they describe their feelings as they performed these activities. Have them close their eyes as they perform. Compare differences in how they feel when their eyes are opened and closed.
2. Talk about fish and streams using nautical terms. If available, use a rocking boat (or use a rocking chair) for a fishing expedition. Provide poles and magnetic paper fish. As a variation, draw a body part on each fish. As children "catch" the fish, they name the body part drawn on it and move that body part. Others join in and "follow the leader" by also moving that body part.

Figure 8.4   Integrated Curriculum for Physical Development

S. L. Trostle & T. D. Yawkey, *Integrated Learning Activities for Young Children.* (Allyn & Bacon, 1990). Reprinted by permission of the publisher.

SHAPE JUMPING (Physical Education)

Overview: Children draw shapes and use them in hopping exercises to develop muscles, movements, and coordinations. First, the youngsters draw and color shapes and then use them in a hopping activity. Then they hop to shapes in circular and other arrangements. They discuss transportation as it relates to these activities.

Objective: Jumping to shapes in various arrangements.

Supplies: Poster board, oak tag, or other durable material; ruler; crayons; tape

Words You'll Like: *drawing, hopping, order, rectangle, circle, square, rhombus, elipse, triangle, pretend*

Getting Started

The children draw shapes, such as circles, triangles, squares, elipses, and rectangles on pieces of poster board, oak tag, or other durable paper. After coloring the shapes, the children place the shapes on the floor to make a straight path about one inch apart. They help tape down the shapes to secure them while the youngsters are hopping. Have the children hop forward and back on the shapes, stating the shape's names as the children go.

Target

Using more durable paper, the children draw two of each of the following: triangle, circle, square, rhombus, and elipse. After outlining and coloring these shapes, they tape the shapes on the floor making a straight path about eight inches apart in the following order: triangle, circle, square, elipse, rhombus, triangle, circle, square, elipse, rhombus. The children stand at one end of the path on the triangle. Call out a series of shapes indicating to the children where

Figure 8.5 Integrated Curriculum for Physical Development
S. L. Trostle & T. D. Yawkey, *Integrated Learning Activities for Young Children.* (Allyn & Bacon, 1990), pp. 268–269. Reprinted by permission of the publisher.

ous materials. For large muscle activities the authors suggest the following (Herr & Libby, 1990, p. 357):

Body Movement Rhythms

Introduce a simple body movement. Then have the children repeat it until they develop a rhythm. Examples include the following:

stamp foot, clap hands, stamp foot, clap hands

clap, clap, stamp, stamp

clap, stamp, clap, stamp

clap, clap, snap fingers

clap clap, stamp, clap clap, stamp

they jump next. For example, call "circle, elipse, rhombus." Continue by changing the patterns where the children are jumping. The children can also identify jumping patterns. As the youngsters become more skillful, add rectangles and increase the space between the shapes. Finally, the youngsters jump from shape to shape and, as they land, add a new line to a pretend story about traveling. As they tell their stories, they give characteristics of their transportation vehicles and destinations.

Moving Ahead

The children arrange and secure all their shapes in one large circle in a specified order. For example, the children arrange and jump from circle, to square, to rectangle, to elipse, to circle, to square, to rectangle, to elipse. Repeat each pattern several times. The children anticipate what shape comes next and identify jumping patterns. After they hop around a circle, try forming other shapes such as a large square or rectangle.

Let's Talk

1. The youngsters decide if they would like to always hop, jump, or fly rather than walk from one place to another. They talk about hopping, jumping, and flying forms of transportation. The children explain why they would or would not like to use these modes of transportation.
2. The children name several animals that primarily use hopping for transportation, such as the rabbit, frog, toad, grasshopper, and kangaroo. After naming the different animals, the children imitate the animal's movements. Try other types of animal movements and exercise, such as crawling, and follow the same steps.

Body Percussion

Instruct the children to stand in a circle. Repeat the following rhythmic speech:

We walk and we walk and we stop [rest].
We walk and we walk and we stop [rest].
We walk and we walk and we walk and we walk,
We walk and we walk and we stop [stop].

March

Play different rhythm beats of a piano or another instrument. Examples include beats that provoke hopping, skipping, gliding, walking, running, tiptoeing, galloping, etc. The children can move to the rhythm.

The thematic units developed for preschool classrooms in this text that include kindergarten also incorporate physical activity experiences. In the unit described in chapter 7 titled "Seeds," students make and use musical instruments using seeds they have collected in rhythm band activities (see Appendix A). In addition to fine motor activities related to art activities, the students also engage in a music and movement activity. Another preschool unit, "Farm Animals" (Appendix B), correlates mathematics and body movement in a duck walk game. Children are also taught a simple square dance that integrates music and movement. In addition, the students must coordinate different steps in the dance, follow directions, and move in time with the rest of the group.

DESIGNING PHYSICAL DEVELOPMENT ACTIVITIES FOR CHILDREN WITH SPECIAL NEEDS

Children with handicaps experience difficulty in engaging in motor activities, especially physical play. Children with physical handicaps have restricted abilities to participate in motor activities; consideration must be made to accommodate activities to match the physical characteristics of individual preschool children. The play environment likewise must be adapted to individual handicaps. The adult may need to prepare the child for physical activities.

Children with visual handicaps can be helped to orient themselves to space and time and participate in motor activities, with attention being paid to their visual impairment. The following are suggestions for planning activities for children with special needs (Frost, 1992; Wortham, 1992):

- Adults can assist by planning a play activity with the child in terms of what is available: play materials, other children, special equipment.
- The playground should offer sensory clues such as different textures on walking surfaces that will guide the child to play opportunities. The teacher can help the child orient him- or herself toward the equipment or materials the child wishes to use.
- Before play, the adult can help the child practice with materials or equipment that will be used.
- The adult supports and encourages the child during play activities.

Children with motor handicaps have difficulty participating in physical activities and using environments that have not been adapted for such handicaps. In spite of restrictions in movement, these children are able to participate in some activities. The play environment should be modified to allow the child access to play experiences, to allow the teacher to physically locate the immobile child in a play experience, and to allow the teacher to develop broadened opportunities for the physically limited child's physical development. The goal is to develop alternative ways for children with physically handicaps children to participate in activities that require mobility. The play environment should be studied for accessibility. Accessibility considerations are different for children who use a wheelchair for mobility and those who are able to use a walker. Accessibility to play equipment and activities is adapted differently depending on the child's physical limitations.

Summary

Preschool children are busy becoming social beings. They are learning how to live in a world of many people who have their own feelings and ideas. Young children are learning that some of the ways they use to interact with others are more successful than others. They want to be accepted into group play and are feeling their way in developing successful skills to get along with their peers and in behaving appropriately to meet adult expectations.

One goal for the preschool curriculum for social development is to help children become comfortable with themselves and others. The social development curriculum is based on an environmental setting and activities that assist children in living and playing in harmony.

The child's socialization involves the ability to control and express feelings appropriately, develop empathy, and use prosocial skills. Children must learn how to understand their own feelings and how to act upon those feelings in an acceptable manner. They learn to recognize similar feelings in other children and how to respond to those emotions. When they can respond to another child in a sympathetic way, they have begun to experience empathy.

The teacher has an important role in helping children develop social skills. There are certain strategies the teacher can use to make socialization easier. The classroom, routines, and daily activities can be organized to facilitate harmony and minimize conflicts among children. However, because young children are just learning successful behaviors, the teacher has to take an active role in guiding them. Children who are angry, aggressive, or otherwise behave inappropriately need adult intervention and redirection to learn the correct behaviors.

The teacher also has a role in guiding children to understand and accept multicultural differences. Because racial bias begins early in life, the teacher nurtures a sense of value toward different cultures. The preschool setting and social development curriculum reflect multicultural diversity in a positive manner.

Social development also encompasses the social sciences. Learning to get along with others is part of a larger goal of understanding and participating in the larger society. Foundations for later study of history, geography, economics, sociology, and anthropology are established through the social science curriculum in the preschool program. The social science curriculum is best learned in an integrated, meaningful context; therefore, experiences that are planned help extend the child's understanding of him- or herself and others and relate to the child's life and experiences. Learning about social science topics within thematic units enables children to understand their membership in society in more depth and breadth.

Great strides are made in physical development in the preschool years. Children between the ages of three and five are extremely active and energetic in exercising their bodies through play. Perceptual–motor development, which depends upon the interaction of sensory and physical advances, results in more complex sensory input accompanied by more skillful motor behaviors.

The child's physical development involves gross and fine motor skills, body awareness, locomotor skills, and body, spatial, temporal, and directional awareness. Both the indoor and outdoor environments should be planned and equipped for these kinds of perceptual–motor development to be encouraged. Also, the teacher plans activities to promote development, particularly in large and fine motor activities. In addition to ensuring that children have substantial time for indoor and outdoor play, a balance of large and fine motor activities is planned as part of the physical development curriculum.

The teacher must be aware of the individual needs of children for physical activities. Because children vary in level of physical development and opportunities they have for physical activities outside the group setting, the teacher provides opportunities for physical exercise and practice that meet individual differences. Opportunities for fine and gross motor activities occur naturally during the day through participation in ongoing preschool activities. Motor skills are developed through center activities, play periods, and teacher-planned activities. Activities can also be planned within thematic units.

Special consideration needs to be given to children who have physical limitations. Outdoor play equipment needs to be accessible to children who have no mobility or must use a walker or wheelchair.

Curriculum activities that require physical movement may need to be modified or adapted for children with physical handicaps. The teacher's goal should be to make it possible for the child with special needs to participate as much as possible in some capacity.

Summary Statements

1. The preschool years are important for the young child's socialization into group interactions.
2. Children between the ages of three and five are learning how to use prosocial skills in their efforts to get along with their peers.
3. Some objectives of the curriculum for social development are to guide children in understanding themselves and others, in developing social skills, and in understanding the larger world in which they live.
4. The teacher has an important role in guiding young children in the successful development of social skills.
5. When planning for social development the teacher considers the child's current level of social development and how socialization can be nurtured.
6. The preschool child's needs for social development include self-concept, sex-role identity, socialization, and multicultural understandings.
7. Cognitive maturity permits the child to develop empathy, including compassion for others.
8. Although young preschool children cannot comprehend the social studies as older students do, they can understand social science concepts that relate to their life experiences.
9. Play has an important role in social development because social interactions that take place within play events foster socialization.
10. Sociodramatic play facilitates socialization through role playing, participating in fantasy themes, and taking leader and follower roles.
11. The teacher's arrangement of the environment can either facilitate positive social interactions or contribute to conflict.
12. The teacher's classroom management skills can also affect behavior.
13. Teachers of preschool children must use direct intervention and redirection in guiding children's behavior.

14. Teachers can learn and use strategies to help individual children develop prosocial skills and empathic behavior.
15. The social science curriculum for preschool children can be organized under the two major topics of understanding self and understanding other people and society.
16. Social science experiences developed with regard to understanding self, other people, and society should have a direct relationship with the child's life experiences.
17. Social science concepts are more meaningful when they are taught in the context of real experiences within all areas of the preschool curriculum.
18. Significant growth is made in physical development in the preschool years as children master and extend their abilities in locomotor skills.
19. Development of motor skills is also referred to as perceptual–motor development because of the interrelatedness between sensory input and motor behavior.
20. Indoor and outdoor play are natural vehicles for gross and fine motor exercise; however, the teacher also has a responsibility to structure perceptual–motor activities.
21. Indoor and outdoor motor activities should reflect a balance between fine and gross motor development.
22. Although the indoor environment is most likely to offer fine motor activities and the outdoor environment gross motor activities, both environments should include opportunities for both fine and gross motor development.
23. The teacher's role in fostering the child's physical development begins with observation to understand each child's current level of physical development and the kinds of physical activities that are needed.

24. The teacher should give the same emphasis to the physical development curriculum as is given to other developmental areas.

25. Physical activities can support or be supported by other curriculum areas through planning for integrated experiences.

Study Questions

1. Why do preschool children need play experiences each day to help them develop social skills?
2. How do preschool children develop successful behaviors in interacting with others?
3. How does cognitive development help the child acquire empathy?
4. What is the nature of a "curriculum" for social development in the preschool program?
5. How does a good self-image affect development of socialization skills?
6. What kinds of behaviors does a child have to use for successful socialization?
7. What kinds of behaviors do children use when they have developed empathy?
8. How does the teacher nurture multicultural sensitivity in preschool children?
9. What are the goals for a social science curriculum in preschool classrooms?
10. Why is sociodramatic play important for both socialization and the social science curriculum?
11. How does inappropriate organization of the classroom environment result in inappropriate behaviors in young children?
12. What kinds of strategies can the teacher use to minimize or eliminate inappropriate behaviors?
13. What kinds of activities best help children understand social science concepts?
14. Why do social science experiences need to relate to the child's life experiences?
15. What is perceptual–motor development?
16. What kinds of activities promote perceptual–motor development?
17. Should the teacher consider daily outdoor play adequate for meeting physical development needs?
18. How can the indoor environment be arranged to foster gross motor skills?
19. What are some strategies that the teacher uses to develop a comprehensive perceptual–motor development program that achieves a balance between gross and fine motor skills?
20. What features need to be included in the outdoor environment to nurture both fine and gross motor development?
21. Why is teacher observation of children's play important when planning physical development experiences?
22. Can physical development activities be part of the integrated curriculum? Explain.
23. Should preschool teachers consider how to include children with physical handicaps in physical activities?
24. How should the outdoor playground be modified for children with physically handicaps?
25. Why do children's individual handicaps make a difference when the teacher is planning how to modify a playground for children with physical limitations?

References

Beaty, J. J. (1992). *Skills for preschool teachers* (4th ed.). New York: Macmillan.

Bredekamp, S. (Ed.). (1987). *Developmentally appropriate practice in early childhood programs serving children from birth through age 8.* Washington, DC: National Association for the Education of Young Children.

Connolly, J. A., & Doyle, A. B. (1984). Relation of social fantasy play to social competence in preschoolers. *Developmental Psychology, 20,* 797–806.

Erikson, E. H. (1963). *Childhood and society* (2nd ed.). New York: Norton.

Esbensen, S. B. (1990). Play environments for young children: Design perspectives. In S. C. Wortham

& J. L. Frost (Eds.), *Playgrounds for young children: National survey and perspectives* (pp. 49–68). Reston, VA: American Alliance for Health, Physical Education, Recreation and Dance.

Frost, J. L. (1990). Young children and playground safety. In S. C. Wortham & J. L. Frost (Eds.), *Playgrounds for young children: National survey and perspectives* (pp. 29–48). Reston, VA: American Alliance for Health, Physical Education, Recreation and Dance.

Frost, J. L. (1992). *Play and playscapes.* Albany, NY: Delmar.

Furman, E. (1990). Plant a potato—Learn about life (and death). *Young Children, 46,* 15–20.

Gallahue, D. L. (1976). *Motor development and movement experiences for young children (3–7).* New York: John Wiley & Sons.

Garvey, C. (1977). *Play.* Cambridge, MA: Harvard University Press.

Hendrick, J. (1990). *Total learning* (3rd ed.). Columbus, OH: Merrill.

Henniger, M. L. (1985). Preschool children's play behaviors in an indoor and outdoor environment. In J. L. Frost & S. Sunderlind (Eds.), *When children play* (pp. 145–150). Wheaton, MD: Association for Childhood Education International.

Herr, J., & Libby, Y. (1990). *Creative resources for the early childhood classroom.* Albany, NY: Delmar.

Jambor, T. (1990). Promoting perceptual–motor development in young children. In S. C. Wortham & J. L. Frost (Eds.), *Playgrounds for young children: National survey and perspectives* (pp. 147–166). Reston, VA: American Alliance for Health, Physical Education, Recreation and Dance.

Jarolimek, J. (1986). *Social studies in elementary education.* New York: Macmillan.

Johnson, J. E., Christie, J. F., & Yawkey, T. D. (1987). *Play and early childhood development.* Glenview, IL: Scott, Foresman.

Kemple, K. M. (1991). Preschool children's peer acceptance and social interaction. *Young Children, 46,* 47–54.

Maxim, G. W. (1989). *The very young: Guiding children from infancy through the early childhood years.* Columbus, OH: Merrill.

Raines, S., & Canady, R. S. (1991). *More story stretchers.* Mt. Rainier, MD: Gryphon House.

Ramsey, P. (1987). *Teaching and learning in a diverse world: Multicultural education for young children.* New York: Teacher's College Press.

Sanders, K. M., & Harper, L. V. (1976). Free–play fantasy behavior in preschool children: Relations among gender, age, season, and location. *Child Development, 47,* 1182–1185.

Schickedanz, J. A., York, M. E., Stewart, I. S., & White, D. A. (1990). *Strategies for teaching young children.* Englewood Cliffs, NJ: Prentice–Hall.

Seefeldt, C. (1989). *Social studies for the preschool-primary child* (3rd ed.). Columbus, OH: Merrill.

Smilansky, S. (1968). *The effects of sociodramatic play on disadvantaged preschool children.* New York: Wiley.

Trostle, S. L., & Yawkey, T. D. (1990). *Integrated learning activities for young children.* Boston: Allyn & Bacon.

Vukelich, R., & Thornton, S. J. (1990). Children's understanding of historical time: Implications for instruction. *Childhood Education, 67,* 22–25.

Williams, H. G. (1983). *Perceptual and motor development.* Englewood Cliffs, NJ: Prentice–Hall.

Wortham, S. C. (1992). Creating play opportunities for preschool children with special needs in child care settings. In press.

CHAPTER NINE

A Model for Programs for Children Age Five to Eight

In this chapter we will consider how to design and implement curriculum for students in the primary grades. It has been stressed throughout the book that development and learning are continuous, especially as children move from preschool into the primary grades. We have also considered how an understanding of the course of development in children is particularly important as we plan curriculum that is developmentally suitable for students in the latter years of early childhood. In chapter 3 we described these years as transitional because children are making important changes in areas of development, as well making the transition to a different level of schooling.

One might well question why the age of five is included in both preschool and primary grade curriculum. There is a need to establish bridges across the preschool and primary years and to emphasize the continuity through the years of early childhood. In addition, different early childhood settings use one organization or the other; that is, either they have programs for three-, four-, and five-year-olds or the program has five-year-olds in kindergarten before they enter first grade. Private and church-related settings frequently do not go beyond preschool. It is logical to place four- and five-year-old children together for those settings. Public schools, on the other hand, may have a variety of possibilities for organizing early childhood programs. For schools that do not have prekindergarten, kindergarten may be the level of entry into the school system. In this chapter, designing curriculum for the primary grades is considered as a continuum that begins in kindergarten. Although we want to understand how developmental changes permit children to use more sophisticated and complex thinking, we know that they are at the same time making a transition along a continuum in their development. Therefore, we also want to deepen our understanding of how developmental advances facilitate the use of broader possibilities for instructional strategies. We want to be able to design curriculum that will be adaptable for individual differences in development to ensure success for all students. We will explore how to provide a balance between systematic instruction and integrated, or thematic, curriculum. A model for a quality program in the primary grades, known as the ungraded primary, will be described; we will also describe how to design and implement curriculum within the model.

THE SIGNIFICANCE OF DEVELOPMENTAL CHANGES IN THE PRIMARY GRADES

Although overall growth and development occurs more slowly between the ages of five and eight than during earlier years, significant developmental changes occur that permit acquisition of reading and writing skills during the primary grades. Nevertheless, because of the normal variations in development, children's individual timetables have implications for how teachers build in flexibility for curriculum and instruction.

Physical Development

Children entering the primary grades continue the process of developing control over their bodies. They are able to sit and work at tasks for longer periods of time. They become skilled in many physical games requiring gross motor skills, such as Frisbee, baseball, and soccer. Fine motor skills are developed through working with crafts, building models, and playing a musical instrument (Schickedanz, Hansen, & Forsyth, 1990).

Because primary-age children are in the process of continuing their development of motor skills, they need to be physically active during the school day. They need frequent opportunities for physical activities if their gross motor skills are to be refined (Bredekamp, 1987). Daily participation in physical activities is essential for the development of motor coordination and body strength. In addition, physical activity helps in a general feeling of well-being. Current emphasis on academic skills has resulted in diminished attention to physical development (Ross & Gilbert, 1985). Schools in many parts of the country are restricting both physical education periods and unstructured free play or recess periods in favor of spending more time in reading and other categories of academic instruction.

Involvement in organized sports should be approached with caution during kindergarten and primary school years. Although children become interested and adept at physical games, their bones and muscles are immature. Extensive stress can cause strain and injury to developing bones and muscles. Prolonged use of one area of the body can lead to injuries such as sprains and stress fractures or result in accelerated bone growth (Harvey, 1982; Stoner, 1978). Participation in games and sports by all children is important; nevertheless, overemphasis upon competition in organized sports with extended practice periods can be damaging to gross motor development.

Cognitive Development

We have previously discussed how children gradually shift from preoperational to concrete operational thinking between the ages of five and seven. A major cognitive achievement in young children entering the concrete operational stage is the acquisition of the mental ability to think about and solve problems in their heads. As this mental ability, or metacognition, develops, children become able to develop systems to organize and remember information. When children are able to use metacognition they can plan strategies for games, understand riddles, and address how others think and feel. An appropriate primary-grade curriculum is designed with the understanding that cognitive change is gradual and subject to individual variations. These young students still need to actively reconstruct knowledge. The opportunity to engage in hands-on, manipulative materials permits them to have concrete reference points in their encounters with new information (Katz & Chard, 1990). Written assignments to supplement concrete materials should be designed for emerging writers in various stages.

The first years of school between kindergarten and third grade are also significant in the development of motivation to learn. Emerging cognitive abilities allow young children to assess and reflect upon whether they are successful or experiencing failure in school. Children become quite aware of whether they are proficient students and whether they are able to control their success (Rotter, 1954). Children vary in how they perceive their competence and are also affected both positively and negatively by parental and teacher feedback in response to their learning efforts.

Inappropriate curriculum materials and teaching strategies that assume all children in first grade have achieved concrete operations puts many students at risk for achieving success and perceiving themselves as being in control of their learning. The curriculum in kindergarten and first, second, and third grades should facilitate the shift from preoperational thinking; at the same time, opportunities to use manipulative materials should always be included as part of instruction to ensure that possibilities for successful learning are maximized for children who are making the transition at different rates in cognitive development (Schickedanz, Hansen, & Forsyth, 1990).

Social and Emotional Development

A major task for children in the primary grades is to be able to work and interact effectively with their peers. Children who are unsuccessful in establishing positive peer relationships tend to have low self-esteem and achieve less in school, and they may have more problems later in life. Teachers and parents play a major role in the child's development of self-control and social skills between the ages of five and eight. Research has demonstrated that adult intervention can be effective in helping children develop successful social relationships with their peers (Asher & Williams, 1987). Teachers who use positive guidance techniques can help children develop social competence (Katz, 1988). By modeling appropriate behaviors, involving children in developing classroom rules, and engaging students in cooperative group learning activities, teachers can have an active influence on student acceptance of self-control and responsibility.

Failure to develop a sense of competence because of inappropriate teaching practices can also affect social and emotional development. When children are expected to learn skills beyond their ability, they experience failure because they have not acquired a skill as quickly as have other students. Moreover, they may develop low self-esteem because they perceive themselves as unsuccessful learners (Elkind, 1987). According to Erikson's (1963) stages of psychosocial development described in chapter 3, the child will either develop a sense of industry or a sense of inferiority during these years. Just as teachers need to build in flexibility in the learning program to adjust for variations in cognitive and motor development, they also need to respond to individual differences in social and moral development. Sensitivity to differences in social and emotional development in the primary grades can result in teaching and management practices that will support social competence in young students.

THE ROLE OF PLAY IN THE PRIMARY GRADES

As children progress through kindergarten and the primary grades, their cognitive, social, and physical development results in a shift in their approach to play. In the preschool years sociodramatic play and preoperational thinking predominated. As children develop toward and into concrete operational thinking, their play interests gradually change. In earlier years, play on various structures supported physical activities and play themes. Mastery of physical skills was accomplished through play. As children move into the primary grades, games with rules and organized sports become more important.

There is a tendency in some elementary schools for teachers to perceive outdoor periods as a part of the daily curriculum. Structured physical education periods directed by an adult are considered enough for the child's physical development. However, teachers who share this perception ignore the purposes for play in a period of continuing development that goes beyond physical skills. Children's social and cognitive development during these years is also facilitated through play. Moreover, this is a period when peer relationships become increasingly important. Peer social groups develop and change as children participate in undirected play; in addition, such groups are the major socializing agent for children in the elementary grades (Hartup, 1983).

The peer culture is transmitted through play. Children learn from children. Physical and social skills that are necessary for group acceptance are learned through play. The more experienced children in a peer group teach slang expressions, jokes, stories, riddles, and group games to newer members of the group. Hughes (1991) reminds us that parents may teach their children how to ride a bicycle, but it is members of the peer group who teach them how to do "wheelies" or jump across a ditch.

Play can be a source of either positive or negative self-concept during these years. Children who do not excel in academic areas might be skilled in physical activities. Their emerging need for competence and acceptance might be fulfilled through outdoor play activities, where their proficiency can be acknowledged by peers. The sense of competence gained from proficiency in physical activities can carry over to mastery of more difficult academic skills in the classroom. On the other hand, social acceptance or rejection in outdoor play can be based on physical ability.

In a study of second-grade children, Barbour (1993) found that those with poor physical skills were not selected for teams in games organized by children. The importance of contribution to a group effort through physical skills needed for a sport or game had replaced acceptance based on social skills in the preschool years.

Adults working with children in the primary grades can take advantage of the emerging ability of children to teach each other through play, both indoors and out-doors. Opportunity to take leadership roles and work through cooperative planning can be nurtured through structured and unstructured play periods during the school day. Likewise, parents and teachers can be cognizant of the child's success or diffi-culty in play situations and facilitate improvement in peer acceptance. It should not be assumed that free play periods are no longer needed for the child's development. Physical, social, and cognitive development are changing in nature during the later early childhood years, but they are equally important. Play that results from peer groups and is not directed by adults during these years continues to be significant and important.

DESCRIBING DEVELOPMENTALLY APPROPRIATE CURRICULUM FOR CHILDREN AGE FIVE TO EIGHT

If we accept that variations in development in the period between five and eight years of age are normal, then schooling for children between kindergarten and third grade should reflect their developmental needs at those ages. More specifically, cur-riculum in first-, second-, and third-grade classrooms should accommodate develop-mental differences rather than describe achievement expectations within a narrow framework of required skills.

Teaching practices with children from ages five to eight allow for the unique background and level of development that each child brings to the classroom. The "Integrated Components of Appropriate and Inappropriate Practice in the Primary Grades" section of *Developmentally Appropriate Practice in Early Childhood Programs Serving Children from Birth through Age 8* (Bredekamp, 1987, p. 67) includes three curriculum goals toward achieving appropriate practice with children of ages five to eight. These goals emphasize that curriculum should include all areas of development and be responsive to individual differences in the pace of develop-ment as follows:

1. Curriculum is designed to develop children's knowledge and skills in all devel-opmental areas—physical, social, emotional, and intellectual—and to help children learn how to learn, to establish a foundation for lifelong learning.
2. Curriculum and instruction are designed to develop children's self-esteem, sense of competence, and positive feelings toward learning.
3. Each child is viewed as a unique person with an individual pattern and timing of growth. Curriculum and instruction are responsive to individual differences in ability and interest. Different levels of ability, development, and learning styles are expected, accepted, and used to design curriculum.

DESCRIBING CURRICULUM FOR CONTINUING DEVELOPMENTAL NEEDS

When describing developmental learning needs of the young child in the primary grades, one can point out many similarities among preschool children. These students are active learners who reconstruct knowledge through individual involvement with information. They come to school from various backgrounds and previous experiences. They vary in physical, social-emotional, and cognitive development. They have different learning and socialization styles. They may also have different cultural backgrounds and family experiences that affect their approach to schooling.

Most important, these children are moving through the last years of early childhood. They are in the latter stages of preoperational thinking and moving into concrete operational thinking. Although they are developing skills in reading and writing, their individual progress in the transition to literacy necessitates curriculum that ensures success for all. Children at this stage of development are eager to succeed in school and are becoming aware of limits in abilities. Their comparison of themselves with other children can be either favorable or unfavorable and in turn affects their motivation to learn (Hills, 1986).

Curriculum to meet continuing developmental needs in the primary grades accounts for a range in individual development. In addition, it facilitates child-initiated experiences to provide for reconstruction of knowledge. As was emphasized in the discussion about preschool children, connections and relationships in learning are stressed through meaningful and purposeful activities. The relationships in knowledge are developed through an integrated curriculum that provides a meaningful context for learning. At the same time, the integrated curriculum allows children to select activities that permit them to work cooperatively and independently so that their developmental differences are complementary rather than competitive.

Systematic instruction is also needed in the primary grades as a balance is achieved between child-initiated and teacher-directed instruction. Increasingly in the primary grades, it is necessary for children to acquire specific skills and knowledge (Seefeldt, 1993). Systematic instruction is composed of lessons planned by the teacher to introduce and practice specific skills and concepts. In some contexts, the skills and concepts are sequential or hierarchical; that is, there is an order in which they are learned. For example, children must have number and numeral concepts before they can address learning how to add. In other instances, the teacher is aware that children will need to understand a concept or skill as a tool to other learning. For example, in a third-grade social studies unit, students needed to be able to look up addresses in a phone book. The teacher conducted a series of lessons on alphabetical order using the telephone directory prior to implementation of the activity in the unit.

The teacher introduces systematic instruction to ensure that children are mastering skills that will enable them to progress. Through systematic teaching activities the teacher maintains meaningful instruction and teaches related skills when they are relevant to achieving proficiency (Katz & Chard, 1990). The primary-grade curriculum achieves a balance between informal child-initiated instruction and systematic teacher-designed instruction within a meaningful context.

Acquisition of skills through teacher-designed instruction can be achieved through integrated, or thematic, curriculum. The NAEYC handbook *Developmentally Appropriate Practice in Early Childhood Programs Serving Children from Birth through Age 8* (Bredekamp, 1987) describes how teachers blend systematic instruction within an integrated curriculum. Figure 9.1 lists two descriptors of appropriate teaching strategies, which provide examples of when and how primary-grade teachers determine to build skills instruction into the integrated curriculum.

Primary-grade teachers cannot assume that students can acquire all skills presented within thematic curriculum. The increasingly complex skills associated with reading and mathematics require specific planning and instruction on the part of the teacher. The teacher also continuously assesses student learning needs and teaches complex academic skills through teacher-selected tasks and instruction (Katz & Chard, 1990).

THE UNGRADED PRIMARY: A MODEL
FOR CHILDREN AGE FIVE TO EIGHT

Educators across the United States have been searching in recent years for alternatives to the present structure of three primary grades in the elementary school. The search for an alternative structure has resulted from the problems encountered by children within the school reform movement whereby schools have accelerated expectations for achievement in the primary grades. As higher percentages of children have been identified as being at risk for failing in the primary grades, particularly in first grade, efforts to better meet the needs of students have been launched.

A common practice that became popular in the mid-1980s was the pre-first-grade, or transitional, classroom, which provided an additional grade between kindergarten and first grade for children who were felt to be at risk, or not ready for first-grade curriculum. Children were evaluated during the kindergarten year using various types of standardized tests and/or more informal measures to determine whether they were developmentally ready to successfully complete first grade. This practice was implemented to a lesser extent with younger and older children in prekindergarten and pre-second-grade classrooms in some school districts.

The problems associated with these transitional programs soon became apparent. The tests used to identify "immature" students were questionable in terms of reliability and validity (Shepard & Smith, 1986). Accountability for accuracy in identification was lacking (Bredekamp & Shepard, 1989; Meisels, 1989). The focus on the child as being unready rather than on the curriculum as being inappropriate at these grade levels was also questioned. Instead of the curriculum being designed to fit the varied developmental levels of the students, children were expected to fit the curriculum (Day, 1988). Finally, the extra-year programs were a form of retention in themselves (Smith & Shepard, 1987). Although the transitional programs were designed to prevent failure, they added an extra year to the elementary school grades; in effect, many young students perceived that they were failures (National Association of Early Childhood Specialists in State Departments of Education, 1987).

COMPONENT	APPROPRIATE PRACTICE	INAPPROPRIATE PRACTICE
Teaching strategies	• The curriculum is integrated so that learning occurs primarily through projects, learning centers, and playful activities that reflect current interests of children. For example, a social studies project such as building and operating a store, or a science project such as furnishing and caring for an aquarium provide focused opportunities for children to plan, dictate, and/or write their plans (using invented and teacher-taught spelling), to draw and write about their activity, to discuss what they are doing, to read nonfiction books for needed information, to work cooperatively with other children, to learn facts in a meaningful context, and to enjoy learning. Skills are taught as needed to accomplish projects.	• Instructional strategies revolve around teacher-directed reading groups that take up most of every morning, lecturing to the whole group, total class discussion, and paper-and-pencil practice exercises or worksheets to be completed silently by children working individually at desks. Projects, learning centers, play, and outdoor time are seen as embellishments and are offered only if time permits or as reward for good behavior.
	• Teachers use much of their planning time to prepare the environment so children can learn through active involvement with each other, with adults and older children serving as informal tutors,	• Teachers use most of their planning time to prepare and correct worksheets and other seatwork. Little time is available to prepare enriching activities, such as those recommended in the teacher's edition of

Figure 9.1   Teaching Strategies for Children Ages Five to Eight (pp. 325-326)

Bredekamp (Ed.), *Developmentally Appropriate Practice in Early Childhood Programs Serving Children from Birth through Age 8*. (National Association for the Education of Young Children, 1987), p. 8. Used by permission of the publisher.

COMPONENT	APPROPRIATE PRACTICE	INAPPROPRIATE PRACTICE
Teaching strategies *(continued)*	and with materials. Many learning centers are available for children to choose from. Many centers include opportunities for writing and reading—for example, a tempting library area for browsing through books, reading silently, or sharing a book with a friend; a listening station; and places to practice writing stories and to play math or language games. Teachers encourage children to evaluate their own work and to determine where improvement is needed and assist children in figuring out for themselves how to improve their work. Some work is corrected in small groups where children take turns giving feedback to one another and correcting their own papers. Errors are viewed as a natural and necessary part of learning. Teachers analyze children's errors and use the information obtained to plan curriculum and instruction.	each textbook series. A few interest areas are available for children who finish their seatwork early, or children are assigned to a learning center to complete a prescribed sequence of teacher-directed activities within a controlled time period.

Figure 9.1 Teaching Strategies for Children Ages Five to Eight *(continued)*

The search for a better solution to the issue of preventing children from being at risk in the primary grades now focuses on effective ways to design curriculum and instruction between the ages of five and eight (ASCD Early Childhood Education Policy Panel, 1988). The early childhood unit that groups preschool and primary classrooms as separate wings in a building or separate schools in a district is one alternative that is being advocated. Such organizational patterns can group children together in the early childhood years. Teachers and administrators in these units can restructure curriculum to focus on the developmental nature of children in early childhood education and use developmentally appropriate curriculum materials (National Association for the Education of Young Children & National Association of Early Childhood Specialists in State Departments of Education, 1991; National Association of Elementary School Principals, 1990).

Another alternative is the ungraded primary, in which the age-related grade levels are removed and the school is restructured to provide developmentally appropriate curriculum and instruction (Day, 1988). It is this type of alternative structure that we will use to develop our model for primary-grade children. There is more than one possibility for restructuring the primary grades. Potential arrangements include a three-year experience with a single teacher or a team of teachers and some form of multiage grouping in an ungraded setting. None of these possibilities are new. All of the examples we will describe have been in use with elementary age children in the United States as well as in other countries. They are being reconsidered again as alternatives to the graded, academic approach that predominates in U.S. schools at the present time.

The British Infant School Model

British infant schools have had an ungraded structure for many years. Children enter school when they turn five and stay with the same teacher until they reach the age of seven. A teacher has students ranging across the three age levels, loses some older students each year, and gains others when they have their fifth birthday. The teacher plans the curriculum for the needs of individual students by responding to their individual interests, development, and level of achievement. Small-group and large-group instruction and activities are conducted, but children are also able to engage in individual projects for portions of the school day. Using a concept called the integrated day, teachers relate the subjects by integrating content areas through topics of study. Large blocks of the day are devoted to the integrated curriculum (Rothenberg, 1989).

For our purposes, an adaptation of this structure for an ungraded model in the primary grades would have students enter a classroom and stay with a teacher or a team of teachers for three years. The age range could be from five to seven or six to eight. Children would engage in thematic study for much of the curriculum, with activities designed for a range of development and achievement levels. Students would work on projects and theme activities individually and in groups as interests and the characteristics of theme experiences permitted. At the end of the three years, students would be evaluated for their achievement relative to typical expectations for students completing third-grade curriculum. If a school followed a practice of continuous progress or outcome-based education, all children would move to intermediate grades, with instruction adapted to their current level of achievement. Retention would be a reality in schools where a minimum level of achievement would have to be attained for promotion.

Systematic instruction, both group and individual, would be conducted to support the child's progress through required objectives of the curriculum. Additional planning requirements for teachers would be offset by possibilities for peer teaching by students and small cooperative learning groups of students with mixed achievement and abilities. Peer teaching could involve pairs of students discussing information and providing feedback about information being learned. Likewise, a student who is more advanced than other students could conduct study sessions to practice skills. Cooperative learning groups would be particularly useful in problem-solving activities, particularly for thematic experiences. Mixed groups of students could work together to find and report on information about a topic. Groups could plan and

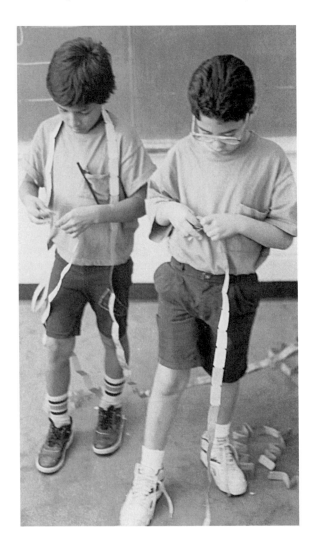

implement a unit project, with differentiated responsibilities determined under teacher guidance and supervision. There would be a strong emphasis on student-initiated experiences and student responsibility in attending to learning activities and managing the environment.

Team Teaching

Teams of teachers focusing on an ungraded primary class could organize a modification of the three-year experience. The same students would remain with each other for the span of three years; however, a multiple-class organization would prevail. Two or three classes would be grouped together according to the team organization desired. Teachers would share classroom environments and planning and teaching responsibilities for thematic and systematic instruction. Individual teachers could focus on specific content areas for systematic instruction.

Much of the curriculum would be designed through thematic units that would incorporate topics suitable for three grade levels. Topics selected and skills taught over the three-year period would incorporate overlapping objectives for the three grade levels that might be repeated in a traditional, separated primary-grade organization. In the ungraded primary, similar learning objectives in some content areas would be introduced to all of the students regardless of grade level. Objectives would be covered several times during the three-year span using different approaches. Application of the skills or concepts for different grade levels would be incorporated into thematic experiences, supplemented with systematic instruction when needed.

Team teaching, using integrated themes, and implementing systematic instruction that accommodated for different achievement and ability levels would be more time efficient than planning for separate grade levels. Teachers could plan for continuity of learning experiences rather than conceptualize instruction for a span of a single year. For example, in typical curriculum planning, instruction is planned for a single grade level. A theme in social studies might be designated for a particular grade level and taught only at that level. (In some school districts, topics for themes are designated for particular grade levels.) In an ungraded situation, a team of teachers could plan curriculum for a broad range of student abilities. Because the same children would be in the class for more than one year, a topic could be expanded and explored in more depth, building on experiences from the previous year.

Multiage Grouping

Multiage grouping in the ungraded primary would group children of more than one chronological age together for a single year (Nachbar, 1989). In this pattern of organization, students would be placed by developmental similarities rather than by chronological age. Curriculum would be flexibly designed to facilitate achievement in learning on a continuum for a three-grade range rather than for a single grade level. Students would be regrouped for each of the three years. The goal would be to move the children through the curriculum objectives taught through systematic instruction complemented by ongoing thematic instruction. Students would complete third-grade curriculum by the end of the third year; however, the emphasis would be upon matching the type of learning experiences selected with the shared developmental characteristics of the students. In any of the ungraded structures discussed, the issue of retention would not be totally solved. Although development is more stable and evened out by third grade, there would still be some students who would not complete the third-grade curriculum with their peers. The school system would need to determine what would be done with students who needed additional remediation or retention before moving into the intermediate elementary grades.

Team teaching could also be used for multiage grouping. Multiple classes could be combined or teachers could conduct cooperative teaching with separate classes. There would be combined thematic activities and exchanges of students for systematic instruction to match individual learning needs. Groups would be flexible, and frequent regrouping could assure that student progress was encouraged.

There is a precedent in United States education for both multiage classrooms and team teaching, in addition to multiage groupings found in British infant schools. One-room rural schools at the turn of the century had multiple ages learning together. In the 1970s, multiage grouping and team teaching were utilized in open classrooms and conventional school facilities. Some schools retained these practices into the 1990s.

Cooperative learning groups and peer teaching could be incorporated into multiage grouping. Class groups would not be organized by grade levels. The multiage groups would engage in a continuous curriculum that cut across grade levels. Thematic curriculum would be the source of cohesion of instruction during the school year.

CHARACTERISTICS OF THE UNGRADED PRIMARY MODEL

Regardless of the organizational pattern found in the ungraded primary model, such a restructuring of the primary grades would have common characteristics. One primary purpose of all styles of ungraded organizations would be to provide developmentally appropriate curriculum to adjust for the normal variations found in primary-age children moving from the preoperational stage in cognitive development to the concrete operational stage. All such models would adopt some form of continuity in curriculum that would eliminate traditional grade levels. These common characteristics are described more specifically in the next section.

Ungraded Classrooms

The ungraded primary model is characterized by the elimination of the traditional grade levels organized by chronological age. This type of restructuring of the primary grades is no more radical than the change from ungraded one-room rural schools to urban graded schools at the beginning of the twentieth century. Children would be grouped to permit flexibility in instruction to accommodate for variation in development between the ages of five and eight. How five-year-olds would be placed in the nongraded organization could vary. Whatever the organizational plan, the student would move through the three-year span without being assessed for promotion or failure from one level to another. Instead, curriculum and instruction would support individual achievement and development and be designed to provide experiences that allow for spurts and lags in developmental growth.

Developmental Curriculum

The ungraded primary model will be characterized by a developmental curriculum, which will take into account the abilities of students during the ages of five to eight. Learning experiences will include manipulatives, problem solving, creative activities, and other hands-on activities to facilitate the child's role as an active learner. At the same time, these active experiences will promote child-initiated learning and ensure success for children who vary in cognitive, motor, and social development. The learning experiences are open-ended and flexible enough that children at various stages in the acquisition of reading and writing can work together successfully.

Integrated Curriculum

The ungraded primary model curriculum is integrated. Thematic units that include all content areas of the curriculum—reading, mathematics, science, social studies, health and safety, fine arts, and physical education—in meaningful context form a large part of the overall curriculum. Because this type of curriculum involves planning on the part of the students, experiences and activities incorporate student interests and competencies. Children gain an understanding of the connections between content areas rather than assuming they are separate, unrelated categories. Likewise, the whole-language approach to the language arts enables students to use their own interests and ideas in reading and writing to develop their competencies in these areas. Activities completed within integrated curriculum minimize developmental differences between students and ensure successful involvement by all.

Systematic Instruction

The curriculum also includes instruction in the content areas taught separately from thematic units. Although there are opportunities in thematic curriculum to gain information and learn skills related to the topic being studied, comprehensive instruction may also be indicated in content areas that require planning for instruction of skills in a sequential manner, such as mathematics and, in some instances, reading. For example, in mathematics there is a sequential or hierarchical pattern to how concepts are acquired. The student must master the concept and skills related to addition before multiplication is introduced. The teacher uses systematic instruction to ensure that each concept is understood and practice provided for mastery. The ungraded primary model includes scheduling for systematic instruction—the teacher plans activities to introduce and work with identified concepts and skills in teacher-directed lessons and then provides opportunities for students to practice and achieve competence. Skills instruction will be incorporated into integrated thematic curriculum as much as possible; nevertheless, because of the increasing quantity of specific concepts and skills that are part of curriculum objectives in the primary school, systematic instruction is included to ensure steady progress. Organized instruction is matched to individual needs and progress. Skills instruction in mathematics and reading combines planned instruction in skills and concepts that is compatible with contextual instruction within thematic learning. Whole-group systematic instruction is infrequent. Small-group and one-to-one instruction are more relevant for individual learning needs.

Cooperative Learning Groups

Cooperative learning is a practice whereby small groups or committees of students engage in accomplishing learning activities. Students with a range of achievement, learning styles, and abilities work together in a cooperative effort to solve and report on a learning objective. The group engages in brainstorming and problem solving before reaching consensus on the solution. For example, in the first grade, cooperative learning groups could brainstorm to come up with as many words beginning with a consonant during a limited time period; in the third grade, groups could collaborate on finding locations on a map.

Students in the ungraded primary unit are capable of working together in learning activities. Because of the transitions occurring in their cognitive and social development, they are able to benefit from group interaction to enhance their own learning and to be of assistance to others. Differences in ability to read and write can be used in a cooperative rather than a competitive manner as students use their emerging abilities for different tasks within group activities. Students who are more advanced in reading and writing skills can take a leadership role in reading and recording information. Students who are moving more slowly in acquiring literacy skills might take a leadership role in art projects or activities requiring organization of materials. Students will facilitate the learning of others as they work together in solving problems and completing projects and assignments. The teacher guides planning and implementation of activities so that all students have leadership roles and achieve success in cooperative activities.

Peer Teaching

Students in the ungraded primary unit can develop leadership roles by engaging in teaching responsibilities. Because students of different ages and developmental stages will be grouped together, they can use their competencies to serve as peer teachers. All students can take leadership roles according to their individual strengths; nevertheless, older students or students with more advanced skills in reading, writing, and mathematics can serve as tutors or guides for younger or less advanced students. Age differences are minimized as all students are encouraged to take responsibility for activities and tasks within their ability to perform.

PLANNING AND MANAGING INSTRUCTION

Earlier in the chapter we discussed the need for both thematic and systematic instruction in the primary grades. In this section we will discuss how to plan and implement each type of instruction within an ungraded school structure. The roles of the teacher and students will be explained, as well as how both thematic and systemic instruction still maintain the approach that learning must involve the student as an active learner who needs opportunities for self-directed or child-initiated choices. We will also explore how the classroom environment is organized for developmentally appropriate instruction.

The Role of the Environment

The classrooms that serve children age five to eight or some combination of these age ranges must have materials and resources that facilitate learning at several developmental and academic levels. Because the environment will be used for both systematic learning and thematic curriculum, organization of space must include provisions for all types of activities—group projects, individual work, small-group instruction, and large-group experiences. Flexibility in arrangement will accommodate changing needs as thematic units are designed and implemented.

Room Arrangement.   There are various ways to describe the classroom environment. All of the descriptions have characteristics in common that help the teacher understand the possibilities for arrangement to provide for activities that reflect student interests. Just as in the preschool classroom, the primary classroom uses spaces for students to work, play, and engage in teacher-directed lessons. The classroom can be arranged to take into account certain areas of interest, or learning centers can be set up, so that various types of activities can occur simultaneously.

Seefeldt (1989) characterized the classroom as a small community or workshop. Although she perceived the classroom as an artificial environment as compared with the natural outdoor environment, she proposed that the room be arranged into clearly defined areas that would allow children to engage in meaningful learning in groups or individually. She also suggested that both preschool and primary classrooms should include areas that offer materials for sociodramatic play, mathematics, art, reading, manipulative play, sand and water play, woodworking, and music and writing.

Katz and Chard (1990) describe learning activities in terms of individual and group projects. They would see the room arranged to accommodate large projects that would be conducted to accomplish three types of activities: construction activities, investigation activities, and dramatic play. They would also support activities being engaged in by individual students, thus necessitating spaces in which one person could work at a time.

The concept of open and closed spaces was proposed by Day (1983). He believed that a balance between open space (which gives children freedom to move) and closed space (which provides security and privacy) should be met when arranging the classroom. Among the criteria Day proposed for evaluating the room environment with open and closed spaces were whether the learning areas supported the goals of the program; whether the arrangement provided for large-group, small-group, and individual activities; and whether the children used the areas as they were intended to be used.

One way to organize primary-grade interest areas could be to arrange a few centers to encompass a wide spectrum of activities. Thus, one large area could accommodate the language arts center. Within that interest area would be space for writing activities, a library, listening center equipment and resources, and other reading instruction materials. A similar center could house science, math, and manipulatives. Space for both group investigations and individual work could be included in that learning center.

Art and creative dramatics could occupy yet another center. Changing role-play materials, puppets, and other materials for dramatic play could share space with art materials and working surfaces for group and individual creative activities. Provisions for sand and water and blocks could extend creative and construction play (Seefeldt, 1989).

Ideally, tables of various sizes would replace the individual desks frequently found in primary classrooms. Students could work at various tables during the day and store their books and materials in individual cubbies. If desks must remain, they could be clustered in groups of four to six to provide for group efforts and larger working surfaces.

If the large combined center concept were to be used, three center areas could be located in each of three corners of the room. The center of the room could be used for large-group activities and larger project work. The fourth corner could house the teacher's desk and teaching materials and include arrangements for small-group and individual work and instruction. Student cubbies could be located adjacent to this area so that students could have access to their learning materials when needed.

Whatever arrangement is chosen, two additional factors need to be considered when organizing the environment. One is the inclusion of the students in planning for and implementing arrangement of the classroom environment. This is also important when the room is reorganized for each thematic unit. In addition, the use of the outdoor environment is an important factor. Because the indoor environment is artificial, students should be engaging in activities outdoors whenever it is relevant to do so. Noisy projects, science and art activities, creative dramatics, and many language arts activities can be done outdoors.

Designing Thematic Curriculum

Thematic curriculum is particularly appropriate for instruction in ungraded and multi-age classes in primary grades. Because a variety of projects and activities is included for a unit, certain activities are appropriate for students who vary widely in their developmental and academic progress. Students of different ages and abilities can work together on projects, with younger students learning from older classmates. Younger students and students working at less advanced academic levels will find activities that are motivating and can be accomplished successfully. Older and more advanced students will find challenging activities and will be able to plan experiences and projects that are of interest to them. The curriculum is planned by the teacher and students; consequently, consideration can be made for cultural diversity within the classroom or included because the theme lends itself to cultural differences and contributions.

Because thematic curriculum is completed over a period of time, there is opportunity for exploration, investigation, and representation of learning in an unhurried environment. The unhurried nature of the units makes it possible to include experiences for children with special needs. If children with handicaps or learning disabilities are mainstreamed into the class, the teacher can plan to adapt activities to address the special needs of the students, whether they have physical handicaps or are emotionally disturbed or gifted. The unit plans are analyzed to determine how each student can play a special role in the learning activities designed for the unit curriculum.

There are obvious similarities between preschool and primary thematic curriculum. Webbing is used to design the topic and its activities. Children are involved in planning, and the curriculum is integrated. Nevertheless, because of the advancing capabilities of the children, their active participation in the process is increased. Likewise, more complex concepts can be addressed, the unit can extend for a longer period of time, and more activities can be incorporated to match individual interests. Opportunities for children to work together can be ongoing, with children of varying abilities supporting and helping each other in project activities. The teacher has a major role in conceptualizing, planning, and managing unit work, but student contribution and initiative is more extensive, at both the planning stage and the implementation stage.

Selecting a Theme Topic.   As is true with preschool thematic units, there are different approaches to use for getting a starting point to identify a theme topic. Krogh (1990) uses a content area approach. The focus of the unit is on a content area of the curriculum such as science, mathematics, social studies, or language arts. The chosen topic has as its major focus that area of the curriculum, although all other content areas are integrated into the unit.

Another approach is to begin with an important event or celebration. The annual celebration of Valentine's Day could lead to a study of Valentine's Day cards or the origin of Valentine's Day. Also, many communities and states have annual celebrations that reflect their history and community characteristics. Some aspect of the celebration can be studied to help students understand and broaden their concepts about their local history and culture.

Incidental sources of interest can lead to a unit of study. A child's unique experience or discovery of a natural phenomenon can lead to a unit of interest to the whole class. Likewise, an interesting topic can occur to the teacher through professional reading, watching an interesting program on television, or another unexpected source. Katz and Chard (1990) suggest that criteria for selecting a topic should include whether the topic is relevant to the children's lives, whether the needed materials and equipment are available, and whether there is access to needed resources in the school and community. Dearden's (1983) criteria for topic selection include opportunities for children to make sense of their experiences, particularly in their own community; topics that give students opportunities to extend their knowledge and skills; and topics that are helpful in preparing them for later life. A common characteristic of all of the approaches to topic selection is that they provide the students with opportunities for meaningful and purposeful learning experiences in acquiring and extending knowledge and skills.

Brainstorming a Topic and Developing a Brainstorming Web.   Once the topic has been selected, the teacher is ready to begin the brainstorming stage for ideas for the unit. As with the preschool unit, the teacher uses his or her own brainstorming and incorporates the children's contributions as well. With primary-grade children, however, the teacher can engage them in the webbing process. The first brainstorming web will be an outgrowth of the brainstorming activity. The teacher might begin the initial generation of ideas him- or herself and include the children when ready to explore their ideas, which will include possibilities for projects. The teacher also considers topics that are relevant to the local community, preferably near the school.

An example of thematic curriculum developed for kindergarten through third grade is a unit developed by Mary Ann Roser, a teacher in an ungraded primary classroom. Her classroom is self-contained and arranged into flexible learning centers that are changed to reflect the unit being studied. She uses thematic curriculum throughout the year but also incorporates systematic instruction into the daily schedule. Mary Ann's unit plan format includes the following:

UNIT TOPIC:

OVERVIEW OR RATIONALE FOR THE UNIT:

DEVELOPMENTAL STAGE:

BRAINSTORMING WEBS:

LIST OF ACTIVITIES AND PROJECTS (categorized as teacher directed, teacher–child initiated, or child initiated)

UNIT OBJECTIVES:

CURRICULUM WEB:

SUMMARY OF INTEGRATED ACTIVITIES AND PROJECTS:

Mary Ann selected the topic of bakeries for a thematic unit focused on social studies. She considered the wide varieties in the types of bakeries the children might study. Because she taught in a large, urban community, she considered the types of baked goods that were available in local bakeries, which ranged from common sliced breads and rolls produced by commercial bakeries to ethnic foods such as pita bread, Italian bread sticks, bagels, and tortillas. A bakery, Trevino's, was located near the school; therefore, Mary Ann focused on the types of baked goods available in that bakery. Trevino's was located in a culturally diverse neighborhood with a strong Hispanic influence. In addition to typical American breads and pastries, items reflecting Hispanic traditions were sold. Mary Ann did some initial brainstorming and determined four subcategories that she would like for her students to learn about bakeries. In her initial brainstorming web she organized the four subtopics as follows: people who work in bakeries; products that are sold in bakeries; items that bakeries need to make and sell products; and people who buy bakery goods. Mary Ann's initial brainstorming web is pictured in Figure 9.2.

Next Mary Ann was ready to extend the brainstorming process with the students. She conducted a discussion of the cookies that had been served for lunch the previous day and explored the topic with the children. Once bakeries had been identified as a source for cookies and other baked products, the class was ready to work on the web. Included in the discussion was talk of baked goods from different cultures and bakeries

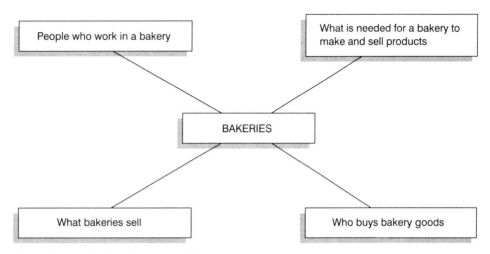

Figure 9.2   Initial Brainstorming Web

that specialized in breads and goods from different cultures. Each subtopic was discussed separately, with extension and expansion of the web as the conversation continued. Mary Ann wrote the children's contributions on a chalkboard so that the students could follow the progress of the web. When the web was completed, the students were ready to move to a discussion of the activities and projects they would like to pursue to learn more about bakeries. Figure 9.3 shows Mary Ann's final brainstorming web.

Planning with Students and Selecting Unit Activities.   As Mary Ann and the students talked about what they wanted to learn, they listed ways to find out more about bakeries and bakery products. As students suggested things they might like to pursue, Mary Ann made a list of activities and projects. The first list included the following:

  visit bakery
  find recipes for bakery products
  make bread, cookies, cupcakes, and pies
  find out about bakery jobs
  make a classroom bakery
  write stories about the visit to the bakery
  read books about bakeries and bakery products
  learn how different products are made
  make recipe books

Mary Ann later studied the list and refined and further organized it. She arranged the unit into projects and individual activities that did not fit into a project. She further categorized each item on the list to indicate whether it was teacher directed, teacher–child initiated, or child initiated. Her revised list was organized as follows:

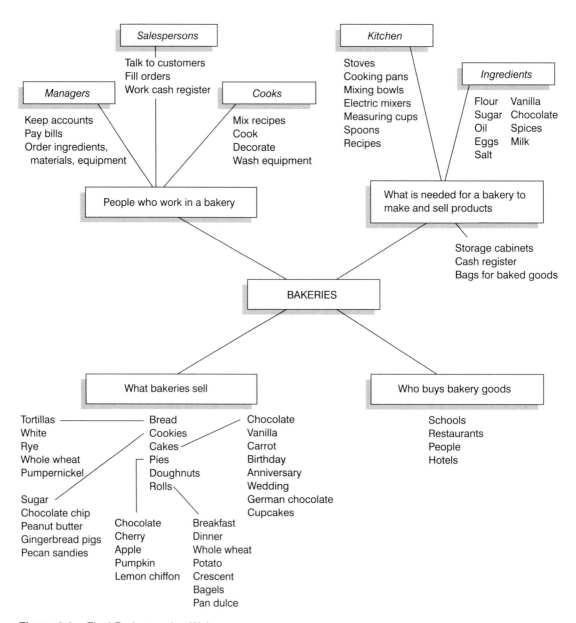

Figure 9.3   Final Brainstorming Web

Activities

visit bakery (teacher–child initiated)

write stories about the bakery visit (child initiated)

make a book of recipes (teacher–child initiated)

make a mural about bakery jobs (teacher–child initiated)

Projects

construct a classroom bakery (teacher–child initiated)

conduct a bakery day to sell products (teacher–child initiated)

bake cupcakes, cookies, and tortillas (teacher–child initiated)

 collect recipes

 collect equipment needed for baking

 make list of ingredients needed for baking each type of product

 shop for baking ingredients

 bake and package products

 sell products to school students on bakery day

In making her final list, Mary Ann determined which activities could accommodate her students' abilities; she included all of them in different parts of the curriculum. She also determined what was manageable for the students to bake. She selected cupcakes, cookies, and tortillas because they were easy to make and represented different types of ingredients and products. She included cookies that were traditional in certain cultures—gingerbread pigs from the Mexican culture, Chinese almond cookies, and Scotch shortbread recipes were solicited from parents. The cookies each had different textures and were mixed and prepared for baking differently.

Mary Ann added the activity that involved representing jobs in a bakery because she wanted to offer a creative way for all the students to participate in some capacity. To determine how the unit experiences would include a balanced, integrated curriculum, Mary Ann developed a curriculum web; it allowed her to organize the unit experiences into content and developmental categories. Figure 9.4 shows Mary Ann's curriculum web. She was pleased with the distribution of activities and felt that coverage of content areas and connections between the content and developmental areas were well defined. With decisions made about what and how the students would learn about bakeries, Mary Ann was able to transform the learning ideas into unit objectives.

Developing Unit Objectives. Because the thematic unit objectives were designed for students of varied ages and abilities, Mary Ann described them in general terms. She categorized the objectives according to what students would understand and what they would be able to do. The same process of describing the condition and the behavior as was used in chapter 6 was followed. Mary Ann's unit objectives were as follows:

1. As a result of visiting a bakery and observing bakery products, students will understand that a variety of baked goods are sold in a bakery.
2. As a result of visiting a bakery and observing bakery employees, students will understand that workers in a bakery have different responsibilities.
3. As a result of visiting a bakery and observing bakery operations, students will understand what equipment and materials are needed to run a bakery.

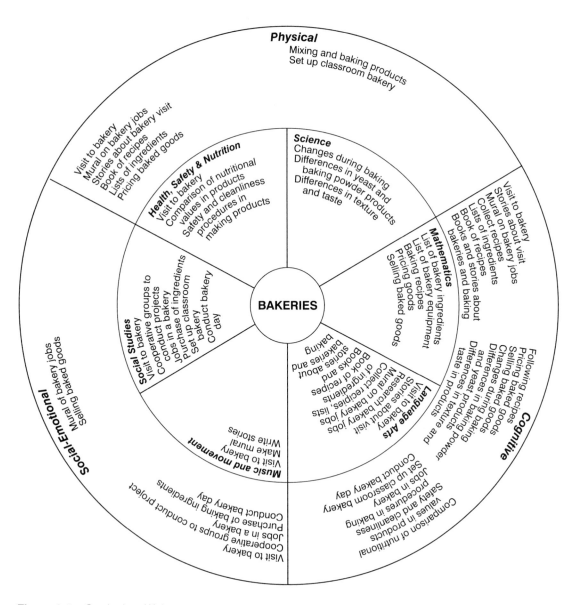

Figure 9.4 Curriculum Web

4. Following a visit to a bakery and discussions with bakery employees, students will be able to describe responsibilities of bakery workers.

5. As a result of visiting a bakery and studying recipes, students will be able to determine what ingredients and cooking equipment are needed to bake cookies and cupcakes.

6. Following a planning session with the teacher, students will be able to construct a classroom bakery and conduct bakery sales.

7. As a result of studying recipes and discussing how to interpret recipe terminology, students will be able to follow a recipe to make bakery products.

8. As a result of cooperatively planning unit projects, students will be able to work in groups to complete the planned projects.

9. As a result of practicing how to price baked products and make change, students will be able to conduct simple money transactions to sell bakery products.

10. After visiting a bakery, participating in discussions about bakeries, and reading stories about bakeries, students will be able to write stories about bakeries.

11. As a result of studying cookbooks and recipes donated by parents, students will be able to select recipes for cookies, cupcakes, and tortillas.

12. Following the baking of cookies, cupcakes, and tortillas and discussions about how much to charge for baked products, students will be able to package and price bakery products.

13. As a result of selecting and using recipes for cookies and cupcakes, students will be able to make a book of recipes.

14. After discussing bakery jobs and planning how to represent them, students will be able to make a mural describing the responsibilities of bakery workers.

15. After completing cooperative group projects to make a mural, construct a classroom bakery, and bake cookies, cupcakes, and tortillas, students will be able to participate in bakery day to sell baked products to students from other classrooms.

Planning Lesson Activities and Projects.   The planning process is not complete until the projects and activities are explored in more detail. The teacher will consider all of the procedures and materials needed for each activity and project. She will also determine when and how the activity will fit into the schedule. In the case of unit projects, the teacher will need to consider how much time should be set aside for the project and how the students can choose to be involved in planning and implementing the project. Activities will be described so that the teacher and students will understand specifically what will occur.

Mary Ann studied her unit activities and wrote a description of each one. Each activity was described and discussed in terms of how it incorporated different content areas of the curriculum. She described the visit to the bakery as follows:

Visit to Trevino's Bakery
After planning what to look for at the bakery, students, teacher, and volunteer parents will walk two blocks to the bakery. The manager will meet the group and explain how bakery goods are made in the kitchen and sold in the sales area. Students will be prepared to observe different equipment in the kitchen and the varied bakery products in

the sales shelves. Groups of students will have assignments to learn the different kinds of breads, cookies, cakes, and pies sold at the bakery. Some groups will be prepared to find out how different products are mixed, baked, and frosted or decorated by the cooks. The activity focuses on social studies; there will be discussion about the different roles people have in contributing to the needs of the community. Specifically, the contributions of the bakery to the local community are discussed. In addition, the activity includes language arts; oral discussions are conducted and students will record the types of products that are sold at this particular bakery.

Each of the activities was summarized in a similar fashion; projects, however, required more extensive planning. Mary Ann worked with the students in discussing each project and what would be necessary to complete each one. Students discussed their interests in being a part of certain projects. They were encouraged to select a project with which they would like to work. Because all of the students wanted to take part in cooking, the class was divided into groups to cook either cupcakes, rolls, or cookies. Other responsibilities for collecting recipes, mixing and baking equipment, and ingredients for baking were also divided among the groups. Students were given responsibilities according to their ability and interest. Students of different levels of achievement were grouped together, with group leaders selected to be responsible for helping to identify responsibilities for each of the group members.

When plans were completed for unit activities and projects, Mary Ann was able to complete the unit plan. The format used was the same general format used in the preschool unit plan. However, Mary Ann had the additional curriculum web to assist her in interpreting how she was relating and integrating experiences across the curriculum.

Mary Ann could also describe the final unit plans in terms of individual lessons. She included the lesson or project activities, a description of the procedures for the lesson, the materials needed to conduct the activity or project, and plans for evaluations. Mary Ann used the following format:

TITLE OF PLAN:
OBJECTIVES ADDRESSED:
ACTIVITY PROCEDURES:
    Large-Group Activity (teacher directed):
    Small-Group Activity (teacher–child initiated):
    Center Activities (child initiated):
MATERIALS/RESOURCES NEEDED:
EVALUATION:
    Teacher Evaluation:
    Activity Evaluation:
    Student Evaluation:

There were some differences between Mary Ann's plans for the primary grades and Lisa's plans for preschool children (refer to chapter 6 for a discussion of Lisa's plans). Mary Ann included systematic instruction lessons under small-group activities.

Projects and cooperative group activities could also be organized under the small-group category. Children could be more involved in evaluation procedures; students would be able to evaluate their own learning and assess the success of group projects with the group and the teacher.

Mary Ann's plans had many similarities to preschool plans. Within the activity category, three-part procedures could again be used to describe the sections of the lesson: (1) introduction, or planning; (2) development of lesson or activity; and (3) summary, or review. As was true in preschool lessons, each category could be adapted to fit the type of activity and the size of the group involved, as well as the flexible role of the teacher. A teacher-directed lesson would begin with a strategy to introduce the purpose for the lesson, continue with the procedures used to help children learn the lesson, and end with a summary of the main points of the lesson. A group project could begin with the teacher and the group planning the activity, followed by actual work on the project. At the end of the work period, the work area would be restored and materials put away; this would be followed by an opportunity to review and evaluate progress and make adjustments if needed. Figure 9.5 provides an example of Mary Ann's plan for a cooperative group lesson.

Planning for Evaluation.   As can be seen in Mary Ann's sample lesson, she conducted three types of evaluation to assess the effectiveness of curriculum and instruction in her classroom. She considered evaluation of the teaching role, evaluation of student learning, and evaluation of the quality of the activities used for the lesson.

Evaluation of the Teacher.   Mary Ann had a plan to assess her effectiveness in the teaching role as a part of every group activity or lesson. When conducting thematic experiences, she used the role of facilitator more frequently than she engaged in teacher-directed responsibilities. As facilitator and guide, she wanted to reflect upon how well she enabled the students to accomplish the objectives of the activity. She evaluated how well she was able to serve as a resource for ideas and processes to accomplish child-planned activities.

When she had a more directive role in systematic instruction, she evaluated herself in terms of student success in learning. She was sometimes interested in student mastery of specific skills. Teachers who are required to give grades would have to be very specific about how well students performed in acquiring information and skills. Evaluation of teaching effectiveness following systematic instruction would relate to how effective instructional experiences were in helping students achieve success in learning. In the example of Mary Ann's teaching described earlier, she was using evaluation to determine her success in helping students acquire the skills needed to engage in a unit cooking activity and at the same time was assessing the children's growth in working in groups to accomplish learning objectives.

Evaluation of Student Learning.   Mary Ann also wanted to determine how well students were learning. Again, her objectives for evaluation varied depending on the nature of the learning objective. In this lesson she wanted to assess how successful the students were in leadership, problem solving, and other processes involved in cooperative assignments requiring student collaboration.

TITLE OF PLAN: Understanding Recipes

OBJECTIVES ADDRESSED

As a result of studying recipes and discussing how to interpret recipe terminology, students will be able to follow a recipe to make bakery products.

ACTIVITY PROCEDURES

Large-group activity (teacher-initiated, small cooperative groups)

The lesson will be conducted with the class divided into cooperative groups to learn how to understand and follow a recipe.

Introduction

The teacher will write the recipe on a large chart tablet or overhead transparency. Rebus pictures will be used in addition to written measurements for young and less advanced readers.

Development of Lesson or Activity

Step 1

The teacher and students will read the recipe together

Peanut Butter Cookies

1 cup shortening
1 cup granulated sugar
1 cup brown sugar
2 eggs
1 teaspoon vanilla
1 cup peanut butter
3 cups enriched flour
2 teaspoons soda
1/2 teaspoon salt

Thoroughly cream together 1 cup shortening, 1 cup granulated sugar, 1 cup brown sugar, 2 eggs, and 1 teaspoon vanilla. Stir in 1 cup peanut butter.

Sift together 3 cups sifted enriched flour, 2 teaspoons soda, and 1/2 teaspoon salt. Stir into creamed mixture. Drop by rounded teaspoons on ungreased cookie sheet. Press with back of floured fork to make crisscross. Bake at 350° about 10 minutes or until light brown. Makes about 5 dozen cookies.

Step 2

Teachers and students will discuss the ingredients that they will need to make the cookies. Each cooperative group will make a list of ingredients that will be needed by studying the recipe. Their lists will be compared with the teacher's list.

Figure 9.5   Example of a Cooperative Group Lesson

Step 3

The recipe will be read again. Teacher and students will focus on what will need to be measured, sifted, etc. The cooperative groups will list the measuring, mixing, and baking utensils that will be needed.

Step 4

The recipe will now be studied for the processes that will be needed to make the cookie dough and bake the cookies. The teacher will underline the steps and processes to be followed. Cooperative groups then will list the processes and describe what each means. Individual lists will be compared with the teacher's list.

Summary or Review

The recipe will be read one final time. The teacher will guide the groups to identify kitchen items not specified in the recipe that will be needed to prepare the cookies (e.g., potholders, storage container, etc.).

MATERIALS/RESOURCES NEEDED

Recipe

Chart tablet or overhead transparencies and projector

Pencils and paper for student responses

EVALUATION

Teacher Evaluation

Could the students understand the recipe and procedures? Were they able to complete the group assignments with a minimum of teacher assistance? Could all students participate regardless of learning differences?

Student Evaluation

Did all students contribute to group activities? Were they interested in helping their group complete the assignments in an effective manner?

Activity Evaluation

Could the students understand the recipe and procedures? Were they able to complete the group assignments with a minimum of teacher assistance? Could all students participate, regardless of learning differences?

Mary Ann was also evaluating students' acquisition of specific knowledge and skills. She wanted to determine whether the students had adequately learned the information and skills presented. She wanted to evaluate how well the students learned the objective of the lesson.

Evaluation of the Curriculum.   Mary Ann had more than one type of curriculum to evaluate in her classroom. When she evaluated thematic curriculum, she assessed the effectiveness of the activities, materials, and equipment used for experiences and projects. She looked at the length of time needed for thematic activities and evaluated whether time and value of the activity were compatible.

When Mary Ann was engaged in systematic instruction, she assessed whether her teacher-designed or commercial materials were appropriate and whether she accomplished the objectives she had set for learning. Mary Ann wanted to know whether she had made good choices regarding the activities she used for children in their attempts to acquire specific knowledge or skills. She also wanted to know whether adequate time and activities had been planned for student learning.

Figure 9.5 describes Mary Ann's plans for evaluating her lesson. The strategies she used were representative of some of the purposes and processes for evaluation with primary-age students. More about evaluation in primary grades will be discussed at the end of the chapter.

Implementing Thematic Curriculum

Planning with Students and Parents.   Mary Ann extended planning with the students as she prepared to implement the unit on bakeries. At this point she contacted parent volunteers to help her in the final stages of decision making. Parents helped to identify where to acquire the resources needed to carry out the unit activities and projects. Individual parents accepted responsibilities for project activities or agreed to work in centers with children for art and language arts activities. Students were allowed to volunteer for leadership roles in projects, with parents acting as resources and supporters for facilitating successful completion of activities needing adult guidance.

Adults and children planned together how to get the room ready for the new unit. Mary Ann and the parents guided the children in discussing how to construct a bakery and the steps involved in setting up the bakery area. The students likewise discussed how to research recipes and make recipe books. Plans were made as to when and how needed resources for all of the projects and activities would be acquired. Arrangements were made to borrow the school's cooking cart and use the ovens in the school kitchen to bake in the afternoons when school cooks were finished for the day.

Scheduling.   Planning and carrying out the weekly and daily schedule required periodic times for planning and review. Mary Ann made a weekly plan that reflected her activities, including group projects, small-group instruction, and individual interaction and working with project groups. As was true in the preschool model, the sequence of planning activities and reviewing after activities were completed was incorporated into the schedule each day. Figure 9.6 shows Mary Ann's schedule for the first week of implementation of the unit on bakeries.

Schedule	Monday	Tuesday	Wednesday	Thursday	Friday	Learning Center Arts
8:00–8:15 Large group planning	Plan trip to bakery	Plans to begin group projects	Plans for the day	Plans for the day	Plans for the day	*Language Arts* Tuesday – Individual stories about trip to bakery *Recipe Group* Tuesday – Wednesday Research cookbooks Select and copy recipes on experience charts *Mural Group* Research bakery worker responsibilities
8:15–8:30 Group plans	Group plans for bakery information	1) Bakery construction group 2) Recipes group 3) Mural group	Problem solving for group projects	Meetings with project groups 4) Cooking committee	Cooking committees	Library books Books and stories about bakeries and bakery products
8:30–9:30 Small group instruction	Visit to bakery →	*Mathematics* / Systematic Instruction	*Mathematics* / Systematic Instruction	*Reading* / Systematic Instruction	*Reading* / Systematic Instruction	*Art /Creative Dramatics* *Classroom Bakery Group* Plan and construct bakery *Mural Group* Design mural panel for each bakery job List responsibilities in each panel Coordinate decoration of panels
9:30–10:00 Individual Help		Systematic Instruction	Systematic Instruction	Systematic Instruction	Systematic Instruction	
10:00–10:45 Project work	Write bakery stories	Monitor cooperative group activities	→	↑	Group reports on projects Review bakery stories	*Math/Science/Manipulatives* *Recipe Group* Select recipes Copy recipes Determine ingredients needed
10:45–11:15 Large group Review morning activities Plan for following day	Review trip Discuss plans for Tuesday	Review group projects	Review morning activities	Review morning activities	Plan for new and continued activities for following week	*Cooking Groups* Study recipe charts Determine cooking equipment needed

Figure 9.6 Weekly Schedule

Mary Ann scheduled the entire morning for unit work and instruction combined. Afternoons were reserved for instruction that could not fit into thematic work times and needed to continue in content areas. She started each morning with fifteen minutes for planning with the entire group. The next fifteen minutes was used for planning with the project groups. Each day for an hour she worked with small groups in systematic instruction, followed by an hour of interaction with individuals. She might spend the time conducting assessments, working on skills that were causing difficulties for individual students, or helping students complete work or try new methods to attack a problem. According to this week's schedule, she worked for two days in mathematics and then switched to reading for the following two days.

After the periods of systematic instruction, she spent forty-five minutes facilitating and working as a resource for the project groups. Students alternated among center activities, projects, and systematic instruction and related assignments during the morning. The children might work from contracts or follow group schedules put on the board during planning time. The project groups functioned as cooperative groups. Small-group instruction could likewise be conducted with cooperative groups working at different levels in the curriculum according to ability and achievement. These flexible groups could be reorganized when needed to meet individual needs or to allow children to progress at a different rate.

The section of the schedule devoted to learning center areas listed the activities that might take place on a daily or weekly basis. Some activities were for individual children to complete, whereas others were conducted by project groups. In the case of the recipe group, project research began in the library center and then moved to the mathematics–science–manipulatives area when it came time to use the recipes to get ready for cooking projects the following week.

The first day of the unit was used to plan and take the trip to the bakery. Students were prepared for the information they needed to find while touring the bakery. Upon returning from the bakery they were given time to begin their stories about the experience, which could be continued the following day in the language arts area.

At the end of the morning, the class completed a review session during large-group time to discuss the day's progress and make preliminary plans for the following day. At the end of Friday morning, the whole class reviewed the week's activities and discussed project progress with the respective committees. Before the review period ended on Friday, Mary Ann and the class made plans for the second week of the project, which would include baking cookies, cupcakes, and rolls and selling the products in the classroom bakery the following Friday.

This particular unit was planned for two weeks. Other thematic curriculum could be longer or shorter, depending upon the topic. It is obvious that this unit, although very interesting, would require a great deal of preparation on the part of the teacher, volunteer parents, and students. If the teacher wished to have ongoing units, he or she might want to plan less extensive units after the more demanding ones. This type of unit also might be planned infrequently, and then time could be provided for smaller projects until the teacher would be able to begin the planning process for the next theme. If a team of teachers was working together, they could alternate taking the major responsibility for planning a unit, with the other teachers acting as resource people. With this plan it would be possible to have a more continuous flow from one thematic unit to another, perhaps alternating among the content areas of the curriculum as the major focus.

Incorporating Systematic Instruction

When commercial producers began publishing curriculum materials around the turn of the century, they made it possible for state boards of education to set curriculum for school districts across the state. Prior to that, individual school districts and local boards of education had determined the curriculum for their children. With urbanization, consolidation, and construction of large school buildings with many classrooms, the purchase of curriculum materials that had been developed by specialists was a form of insurance for a centralized standard of instruction (Cremin, 1988).

Since the advent of commercial curriculum materials, the industry has grown; many large corporations now produce teaching resources for all grade levels, including preschool classrooms. Over the years, teachers have become very comfortable following the sequence of the curriculum as organized in the basal reader program, language arts text, mathematics series, and other content area resources. Unfortunately, the various texts and kits for each grade level were developed independently of each other and may have little in common in terms of content or approach to teaching.

Curriculum and instruction practices in early childhood classrooms were criticized earlier in this text because of accelerated content in the early grades that requires young children to perform in a manner that is not developmentally appropriate. If one studies the commercial resources available in a particular school for the primary grades, it will become readily apparent that at least some of the materials teach concepts and skills without any obvious connection to how the skills are applied for a purpose. Using thematic curriculum fills this gap by not only making connections between skills and how they are applied but also demonstrating the relationships among content and developmental areas. The problem is in how to incorporate basal texts for systematic instruction. The task can be difficult because the teacher may need to use the adopted textbooks for this type of instruction. Nevertheless, the same principles according to which young children learn must be applied to systematic instruction, and the teacher must be able to adapt existing resources so that students can reconstruct knowledge and have ample opportunities to work through acquisition of concepts with hands-on activities.

Managing Systematic Instruction.   When a teacher chooses to use systematic instruction, he or she knows there are some concepts or skills that need to be taught that have not or will not be covered in thematic curriculum. Perhaps the child has been having difficulty in decoding words or is not attending to endings on words. Some activities with the skills would strengthen the child's understanding and application of the needed skills. In mathematics, the teacher may be following a sequence of skills and through informal assessment has determined which students in the class need instruction on certain skills; the teacher organizes small groups in the class that he or she has identified and plans a series of lessons to help them acquire the math objective. Still another source of identification for systematic instruction would be thematic curriculum. In the course of carrying out unit activities, the teacher identified a student who was having difficulty in accomplishing a unit project that required a skill. The teacher would provide systematic instruction to facilitate the child's ability in the needed skill. In Mary Ann's unit, she might notice children were unable to understand the measurements in a recipe. She could plan lessons and let the children practice using measuring cups and spoons to help them acquire confidence in completing the correct measurements.

Regardless of the source of the need for systematic instruction, the teacher plans lessons to match the need for active learning and reconstruction of knowledge. This process is further explained in "Guidelines for Appropriate Curriculum Content and Assessment in Programs Serving Children Ages 3 through 8" (National Association for the Education of Young Children & National Association of Early Childhood Specialists in State Departments of Education, 1991, p. 25) as follows:

> Children need to form their own hypotheses and keep trying them out through mental actions and physical manipulations—observing what happens, comparing their findings, asking questions, and discovering answers. When objects and events resist the working model that the child has mentally constructed, the child is forced to adjust the model or alter the mental structures to account for the new information.

The guidelines further describe the learning process as a reoccurring cycle that includes awareness generated from experience, exploration of what is being learned, and utilization, whereby children are able to use or apply what they have learned. The cycle demonstrates how children use child-initiated learning to acquire new

knowledge. The point is that systematic instruction does not imply that the teacher is disseminating information for the child to absorb and master. There is a definite difference between systematic instruction and teacher-directed instruction. In teacher-directed instruction, the teacher directs and controls the process; in systematic instruction, the teacher plans the activities with a definite learning objective in mind, although the activities encourage the children to acquire the information using their own capacities for learning (Katz & Chard, 1990).

The teacher's responsibility, then, is to introduce the child to the concept or skill to be learned—to develop the child's awareness. Exploration with the skill or concept is promoted through hands-on and other sensory experiences so that it becomes personally meaningful. True understanding comes when the child is able to use the new concept or skill in various applications; the child is able to apply the learning to new situations. (National Association for the Education of Young Children & National Association of Early Childhood Specialists in State Departments of Education, 1991).

Whether the teacher is developing his or her own teaching strategies or using commercial materials for systematic instruction, he or she will want to provide experiences that meet the characteristics explained earlier. In both cases, the teacher will evaluate the activities being planned to determine how purposeful they are for the child. If the commercial resources do not provide a variety of hands-on exploratory activities to pursue the concept, the teacher must modify the lessons to include them. Likewise, if the learning activities include pencil-and-paper drill exercises but no meaningful application, opportunities for working with the skill or concept in a purposeful context should be provided.

Balancing Thematic and Systematic Instruction.   No matter how the teacher decides to employ thematic curriculum and systematic instruction in his or her classroom, there needs to be a balance established between the two approaches. If thematic curriculum is used as an ongoing part of the program, many of the skills in a state-mandated set of curriculum objectives will be covered through theme units. Systematic instruction will supplement thematic activities. The less often thematic curriculum is used, the more often systematic instruction will be incorporated into the program. If theme units are used only occasionally, systematic instruction will become the major source for instruction, whereas thematic curriculum will serve as the source for supplementary activities. Whichever combination is used, the teacher needs to keep firmly in mind the process by which young children learn, which is fostered through developmentally appropriate instruction that is child centered and meaningful.

THE ROLE OF EVALUATION IN KINDERGARTEN AND PRIMARY GRADES

The role of evaluation was discussed in chapter 6 in the context of preschool classrooms. Evaluations of thematic units, of the teacher's effectiveness, and of student learning were included as components of evaluation of the school program. The same elements remain when evaluating in the primary grades; however, evaluation of student learning becomes more significant as student achievement is measured for various purposes.

In chapter 2 we discussed the use of standardized tests with young children and the misuse of these tests for purposes of placing children in programs, excluding them from programs, and retaining them at certain levels. Standardized tests are also used to measure student learning in the primary grades; however, group achievement tests have limitations in measuring individual student learning. Other methods of assessment are more appropriate for measuring and reporting individual student achievement. As children enter the primary grades, evaluation may be used to assess and report student progress in learning, to evaluate and improve the instructional program, to identify and address learning problems, and to report to parents.

The Purposes of Evaluation in Kindergarten and Primary Grades

Evaluating and Reporting Progress in Learning.   Parents, teachers, and other school personnel must have information about students' progress in learning in kindergarten and primary grades. The information is needed to determine whether the individual child is progressing adequately in the instructional program, what individual and group instructional needs are, and how effectively the instructional program is serving to instruct the students. School districts commonly use standardized achievement tests to assess individual and group progress in learning; however, such tests are less effective for evaluating achievement in the primary grades, especially individual achievement. They can be an indicator of the quality of the instructional program in language arts and mathematics when comparing group achievement.

Informal types of assessment are more useful than standardized tests to measure student learning. They are available when needed, can be revised by the teacher when needed, and can be a natural part of ongoing instruction (Wortham, 1990). Informal assessment can stem from observation, representative work by the children, completion of tasks within small-group instruction, and other activities during the school day (Chittenden & Courtney, 1989; Teale, 1988). The teacher tries as often as possible to conduct assessment as an ongoing process within natural classroom routines rather than taking separate periods of time to conduct testing.

Informal strategies for assessment can include teacher-designed assessments, commercially designed assessments, and student portfolios.

Teacher-Designed Assessments.   In chapter 6, teacher-designed concrete tasks were described as developmentally appropriate for evaluating the learning progress of preschool children. This type of assessment activity continues to be appropriate for kindergarten and primary children. The teacher uses objects or pictures for the child to manipulate or otherwise indicate a response to a learning task. As children enter the primary grades, acquisition of reading and writing skills makes it possible for students to begin to respond to learning experiences with pencil-and-paper tasks. This transition is gradual and dependent on the child's competence in working with pictured, rather than real, objects. Likewise, the use of printed words is gradual, with prior orientation by the teacher to the written task. Children are asked to circle, make an X by, or underline the correct response (Wortham, 1990). Later they can fill in a missing word and move to more extensive written responses. Through the primary grades the use of written assessments is approached carefully; the teacher studies the design of written teacher assessments for specificity and appropriate level of written response on the part of the student.

Commercially Designed Assessments. Commercial instructional materials are frequently accompanied by written paper-and-pencil assessments to be used with the students. They may take various forms, such as end-of-unit assessments in science, assessments of mathematical skills, and tests at the end of a basal reader. Many of these assessments are well designed; nevertheless, others are neither useful nor appropriate. When deciding to administer a pencil-and-paper test to kindergarten and primary children, the teacher needs to determine whether it is the best method of assessment and whether it is appropriate for the information desired about the child's learning. A teacher-designed concrete task or written worksheet might be more specific for the objective to be assessed.

Student Portfolios. Student portfolios provide an opportunity to comprehensively evaluate student development and learning. The teacher begins collecting samples of the student's work early in the school year and continues adding materials throughout the year. Samples of writing, art, and classroom tests, as well as other representative materials, form a picture of the child's growth during the year. The teacher and student can review the materials periodically to evaluate progress and decide which samples to retain in the portfolio. The portfolio is used to assess student learning, but it also can provide the focus for student–teacher conferences for discussing ideas, plans, and difficulties the student might be having.

Reporting Progress to Parents. Although early childhood educators tend to be against giving grades, especially before third grade, progress reports have to be made to parents and administrators. If report cards are required, teachers are accountable for conducting periodic assessment for reporting purposes. If report cards are not used, assessment of learning is still important for planning appropriate instruction for individual students and measuring successful accomplishment in completing curriculum objectives. Progress reports to parents need to be accurate, whether or not report cards are used. Assessment is closely tied to instruction, whether thematic or systematic. If done in a developmentally appropriate manner, assessment will provide essential information about the student that will help guide plans for future learning experiences.

Effective reporting of student progress can include reports from teacher observation, informal teacher-designed assessments, or results of commercial tests. Student portfolios can be shared with parents and administrators who are interested in reports on student learning. Parents not only are interested in the child's work but also appreciate information about the child's learning through thematic units. Photographs taken during unit projects and group activities help parents visualize what their child participated in and learned about during unit experiences. Classroom displays of unit projects also add to the parents' appreciation of the benefits of thematic units.

The teacher will very likely be instructing children who come from different types of family backgrounds. As a result, the style of reporting may be different, depending on the interests and needs of the parents concerned. Parents with no ability or limited ability in English may need help in understanding how the child is learning and progressing. Professional parents may be more interested in results of standardized tests or the significance of integrated learning. Other parents may be most interested in the child's participation in class projects and the way in which it relates to academic progress. Many parents focus on the child's reading level and need information on the worth of other types of evaluation. The teacher will want to be prepared to respond to differences among parents in how they perceive the child's learning and achievement. All parents are interested primarily in knowing whether the child is learning successfully. The teacher has the responsibility to communicate the child's progress in a manner that is helpful to each parent.

Identifying and Addressing Learning Problems. In kindergarten and the primary grades, some students begin to encounter serious problems in learning, which will go beyond normal developmental differences during the latter early childhood years. As was mentioned earlier, attempts are made in infancy and the preschool years to identify and remediate handicaps resulting from birth defects and other handicapping conditions. Children with such handicaps are identified and referred to intervention programs as early as possible to obtain services that can minimize the handicaps and improve the children's chances of overcoming the problem or finding alternative avenues for learning.

In spite of these services, there are children who enter school in kindergarten or first grade who do not exhibit serious learning difficulties; however, after a few months in school, symptoms of difficulty begin to appear. Some children have trouble learning to read or are unable to comprehend concepts that most children are able to understand. When teachers begin to notice learning difficulties, there are steps that can be taken to assist the child. The teacher can begin by observing the child frequently to attempt to identify more specifically what difficulties the child is having and why they are present.

A next step is to have a specialist observe the child to confirm the symptoms of learning difficulties that the child is presenting. If more intensive diagnosis is indicated, the child is referred for individual testing through a series of standardized tests to identify the nature of the learning problem and the best strategies for assistance. If the child is to be served through the special education program funded under PL 94-142 explained earlier, services will be provided by both the classroom teacher and educational specialists (Meyen, 1990).

Summary

The philosophy of teaching children from ages five to eight is an extension of the philosophy regarding learning in the preschool years. Students in kindergarten through third grade are in the later early childhood years and are making the transition from the preoperational stage of thinking to the concrete operational stage. Developmental changes make it possible for them to acquire reading and writing skills at their own individual pace. Learning is centered within the child, who needs learning experiences that will extend his or her understanding of the world in a developmentally appropriate manner.

Because pace of development varies widely during these years from kindergarten through the primary grades, instruction must accommodate a range of abilities in students. The present structure of graded classrooms limits teachers' opportunities to be flexible in instructional planning that nurtures successful learning in students, regardless of their developmental variations. As a result, attention is being given to other options for school organization for children age five to eight; these options include ungraded classrooms and multiage grouping.

The model chosen for this text is based on the multiage organization first developed for British infant schools. A modified approach more suitable for schools in this country would group students from kindergarten through the primary grades in multiage classrooms. A teacher or team of teachers would plan and implement instruction that includes experiences at different levels of achievement to allow students to participate in learning activities based on individual development rather than chronological age.

Although thematic curriculum is used within the model to facilitate child-initiated learning and to accommodate developmental differences, systematic instruction is also appropriate at these grade levels to ensure that students are acquiring the necessary skills for continued academic progress in individual achievement. At the same time that the teacher plans for instruction for individual needs (which requires planning and assessment of individual progress), the age range within the classroom and the levels of social development make it possible for the students themselves to take active responsibility in the teaching and learning roles. Cooperative learning groups can be organized for group accomplishment of learning tasks. The cooperative groups can be selected to include a range of student abilities. The students use their individual strengths and talents to contribute to the group effort. Peer tutoring and matching older students (as leaders) with younger ones facilitates growth in confidence in more advanced students, while the younger children benefit from more sources of attention and instruction.

When planning for instructional design and implementation, the teacher must consider how to balance teacher-directed and child-initiated instruction. At the same time, decisions must be made as to how to manage thematic curriculum with systematic instruction. Developmental advances make it possible for the students to take a more active role in the development of thematic curriculum. Likewise, they can also assume more responsibility for gathering resources and arranging the classroom environment as the thematic topic moves from the planning stage to the implementation stage. The teacher or team of teachers must determine to what extent the two types of curriculum will be utilized in the classroom. School district requirements, personal teaching styles, and expectations about how instruction will be organized will affect how much teachers stress thematic curriculum or systematic instruction. Regardless of the emphasis, developmentally appropriate methods are used, which may necessitate adaptation of commercial curriculum resources for use in the program that has been designed for the various age groups represented in the classroom.

Scheduling the school day includes consideration of both types of curriculum and includes the various roles the teacher must play to manage a variety of activities interfaced with organized instruction for individuals, small groups, and the entire class. The teacher and students plan each day together to organize how thematic curriculum and systematic instruction will be managed within the schedule. Students are able to make choices for the activities and projects in which they wish to participate. At the same time, all must plan for how they will carry out their responsibilities for their own assignments and the activities where they will be working with and helping other students.

Summary Statements

1. Bridges between preschool and primary grades are necessary to provide developmentally appropriate curriculum to students of varied development in the latter stages of early childhood.

2. Developmental changes in children between the ages of five and eight result in a wide range of ability in children of the same chronological age.

3. Although overall development in the primary grades is slower than in preschool children, students make significant advances that permit the acquisition of reading and writing, as well as qualitative changes in thought processes.

4. The cognitive shift from preoperations to concrete operations permits metacognition and the ability for the student to assess whether he or she is competent as a student and as a member of a social group.

5. Curriculum designed for children ages five to eight should develop children's knowledge and skills in all developmental areas and facilitate self-esteem and a sense of competence.

6. Success or lack of success in learning can affect the student's motivation to learn.

7. Integrated, or thematic, curriculum provides a flexible structure for experiences that accommodate variations in ability and development.

8. Systematic instruction becomes important for children in the primary grades because it is necessary for these children to acquire more specific skills and knowledge.

9. Skills and knowledge are acquired through both thematic curriculum and systematic instruction.

10. Ungraded or multiage classrooms are seen as an improvement over graded classrooms when organizing instruction for students who are varied in development.

11. Curriculum for students ages five to eight is planned to include both thematic and systematic instruction, with the emphasis on each dependent upon variables that include teaching style and local expectations for curriculum structure and use of available resources.

12. Advances in social development make it possible for students to work cooperatively in group learning projects and to take more responsibility for planning and implementing thematic curriculum.

13. The ungraded or multiage classroom makes it possible for the teacher to incorporate peer teaching and matching of students of different ages so that older students can assist younger students.

14. The classroom environment for students ages five to eight is organized into learning centers and areas to accommodate a variety of activities, including individual work, theme projects, and other activities that support an integrated curriculum.

15. Thematic units planned for school-age students can be more extensive and complex than those organized for preschool classrooms.

16. Group projects planned for thematic curriculum permit students of different abilities to work cooperatively with different responsibilities to complete the required tasks.

17. Scheduling thematic and systematic curriculum requires careful planning between the teacher and the students.

18. The teacher's focus in the multiage classroom must be balanced between thematic curriculum and systematic instruction and between teacher-directed instruction and child-initiated activities.

19. The teacher will need to resist the temptation to reduce the emphasis on thematic curriculum in favor of systematic instruction.

20. Regardless of whether thematic curriculum or systematic instruction is being planned, the teacher will want to ensure that experiences and activities incorporate the principles of developmentally appropriate child-centered learning.

Study Questions

1. Why is it possible to include kindergarten children either with four-year-olds or with children in first, second, and third grades?

2. How can the significant developmental changes be characterized for children between the ages of five and eight?

3. Why is it important for teachers of children in these grades to understand that development is gradual and takes place on individual timetables?

4. What implications does the nature of development during these years have for the development of appropriate curriculum?

5. What kinds of problems emerge when inappropriate teaching methods are used with these children?

6. How do teaching practices affect the child's motivation to learn and the child's development of a sense of competence?

7. How does the teacher consider different levels of ability, development, and learning style when designing learning experiences for students between the ages of five and eight?
8. Why is it difficult to accommodate for these student differences in the typical graded classroom?
9. How are thematic curriculum and systematic instruction complementary?
10. What different approaches to planning and implementing instruction are required by teachers who work with thematic curriculum and systematic instruction?
11. Why is an alternative organization to graded classrooms needed for children in the primary grades?
12. How would an alternative structure of organization answer the problem of using transitional classrooms prior to kindergarten or first grade?
13. Why do the ungraded classroom or multiage grouping provide a positive alternative to graded classrooms?
14. How does thematic curriculum help bridge developmental differences in students in multiage classrooms?
15. Does the ungraded approach help solve the issue of retention in the early grades? If so, how?
16. How do cooperative learning groups and peer teaching help the teacher to improve the use of time for instruction?
17. How is the classroom environment that utilizes thematic curriculum similar to the preschool environment? How is it different?
18. What is the role of students in developing and implementing thematic curriculum?
19. How does student involvement in developing the brainstorming web facilitate their understanding of the connections between content areas in integrated curriculum?
20. How do student choices in selecting theme projects and activities enhance their social development and sense of responsibility?
21. Why does the teacher need to extensively involve students and parents in planning for implementation of unit projects?
22. What considerations must the teacher include when scheduling thematic curriculum and systematic instruction in the ungraded or multiage classroom?
23. What adaptations might the teacher consider to ensure that commercial material resources are developmentally appropriate?
24. How might commercial material resources be adapted for thematic curriculum units?
25. How can the teacher ensure that systematic instruction is included as needed, both within thematic curriculum and as a separate component of the daily schedule?
26. Why does assessment of individual progress become more important when planning and implementing instruction for children between the ages of five and eight?
27. How are assessment and teaching for individual needs related?

References

ASCD Early Childhood Education Policy Panel. (1988). Analysis of issues concerning public school involvement in early childhood education. In C. Warger (Ed.), *A resource guide to public school early childhood programs* (pp. 99–115). Alexandria, VA: Association for Supervision and Curriculum Development.

Asher, S. R., & Williams, G. A. (1987). Helping children without friends in home and school contexts. In *Children's social development: Information for teachers and parents* (pp. 1–26). Urbana, IL: ERIC Clearinghouse on Elementary and Early Childhood Education.

Barbour, A. (1993). *Physical competence and peer relations: Case studies of eight second–graders.* Unpublished dissertation, University of Texas at Austin.

Bredekamp, S. (Ed.). (1987). *Developmentally appropriate practice in early childhood programs serving children from birth through age 8.* Washington, DC: National Association for the Education of Young Children.

Bredekamp, S., & Shepard, L. (1989). How best to protect children from inappropriate school expectations, practices, and policies. *Young Children, 44,* 14–24.

Chittenden, E., & Courtney, R. (1989). Assessment of young children's reading: Documentation as an alternative to testing. In D. Strickland (Ed.), *Emerging literacy: Young children learn to read and write*. Newark, DE: International Reading Association.

Cremin, L. A. (1988). *American education. The metropolitan experience 1876–1980*. New York: Harper & Row.

Day, B. D. (1988). What's happening in early childhood programs across the United States. In C. Warger (Ed.), *A resource guide to public school early childhood programs* (pp. 3–31). Alexandria, VA: Association for Supervision and Curriculum Development.

Day, D. (1983). *Early childhood education: A human ecological approach*. Glenview, IL: Scott, Foresman.

Dearden, R. F. (1983). *Theory and practice in education*. London: Routledge & Kegan Paul.

Elkind, D. (1987). *Miseducation*. New York: Alfred A. Knopf.

Erikson, E. H. (1963). *Childhood and society*. New York: Norton.

Hartup, W. W. (1983). Peer relations. In P. H. Mussen (Ed.), *Handbook of child psychology* (4th ed., Vol. 4, pp. 103–196). New York: Wiley.

Harvey, J. H. (1982). Overuse syndromes in young athletes. *Pediatric Clinics of North America, 29*, 1369–1381.

Hills, T. (1986). Classroom motivation: Helping students want to learn and achieve in school. Trenton: New Jersey Department of Education.

Hughes, F. P. (1991). *Children, play, and development*. Boston: Allyn & Bacon.

Katz, L. G. (1988, Summer). What should young children be doing? *American Educator, 28–33*, 44–45.

Katz, L. G., & Chard, S. C. (1990). *Engaging children's minds*. Norwood, NJ: Ablex.

Krogh, S. (1990). *The integrated early childhood curriculum*. New York: McGraw-Hill.

Meisels, S. J. (1989). High–stakes testing in kindergarten. *Educational Leadership, 46*, 16–22.

Meyen, E. L. (1990). Educating exceptional children today. In E. L. Meyen (Ed.), *Exceptional children in today's schools* (pp. 15–46). Denver: Love Publishing.

Nachbar, R. R. (1989). A K/1 class can work—wonderfully! *Young Children, 44*, 67–71.

National Association for the Education of Young Children & National Association of Early Childhood Specialists in State Departments of Education. (1991). Guidelines for appropriate curriculum content and assessment in programs serving children ages 3 through 8: A position statement of the National Association for the Education of Young Children and the National Association of Early Childhood Specialists in State Departments of Education. *Young Children, 46*, 21–38.

National Association of Early Childhood Specialists in State Departments of Education. (1987). *Unacceptable trends in kindergarten entry and placement: A position statement*. (ERIC Document Reproduction Service No. 297–856).

National Association of Elementary School Principals. (1990). *Early childhood education and the elementary school principal*. Alexandria, VA: Author.

Ross, J. G., & Gilbert, G. G. (1985). The national children and youth fitness study: A summary of findings. *Journal of Physical Education, Recreation and Dance, 56*, 3–8, 45–50.

Rothenberg, T. (1989). The open classroom reconsidered, *The Elementary School Journal, 90*, 69–86.

Rotter, J. G. (1954). *Social learning and clinical psychology*. Englewood Cliffs, NJ: Prentice–Hall.

Schickedanz, J. A., Hansen, K., & Forsyth, P. D. (1990). *Understanding children*. Mountain View, CA: Mayfield.

Seefeldt, C. (1993). *Social studies for the preschool–primary child* (4th ed.). Columbus, OH: Merrill.

Shepard, L. A., & Smith, M. L. (1986). Synthesis of research on school readiness and kindergarten retention. *Educational Leadership, 44*, 78–86.

Smith, M. L., & Shepard, L. A. (1987). What doesn't work: Explaining policies of retention in the early grades. *Phi Delta Kappan, 69*, 129–134.

Stoner, L. J. (1978). Selecting physical activities for the young child, with an understanding of bone growth and development. *Research for Practitioners and Parents, 1*, 32–42.

Teale, W. H. (1988). Developmentally appropriate assessment of reading and writing in the early childhood classroom. *The Elementary School Journal, 89*, 173–184.

Wortham, S. C. (1990). *Tests and measurement in early childhood education*. Columbus, OH: Merrill.

CHAPTER TEN

The Transitional Curriculum:
Ages Five to Eight

Language Arts, Mathematics, and Science

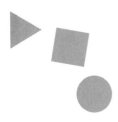

The ages between five and eight are exciting ones for children in the first years of school. We have described them as transitional years because at this time children make the transition from preoperational to concrete operational thinking. Children are also making the transition toward literacy. They will become true readers and writers during these years of kindergarten and the primary grades. In this chapter we will discuss language arts, mathematics, and science curriculum and instruction for children who are making the transition from preschool into the primary grades. The language arts curriculum will be discussed first, followed by mathematics, and then science.

CURRICULUM FOR LANGUAGE ARTS

In chapter 7 we discussed the acquisition of literacy in terms of language development. We described language skill as the ability to speak, listen, write, and read. The importance of understanding how language is acquired was discussed as a parallel to understanding how children acquire the ability to write and read. We explained the interrelated nature of language development, as well as the individual nature and pace of literacy acquisition. We also explored the issue of whether language development and literacy should be taught from a reading readiness or skills approach or as a natural, emerging process. Activities for promoting language development, including receptive and expressive oral language, writing, and reading, were suggested; in addition, integrated approaches, including that of thematic curriculum, were described.

In this chapter we will discuss the continuation of language development and literacy in the context of kindergarten and the primary grades and latter stages of early childhood education. The span of development that occurs between the ages of five and eight, or from kindergarten through third grade, as was described in chapter 6, is the range that will be included in our discussion. During these years, the child moves from preoperational to concrete operational thinking. In language arts, the movement is from emergent literacy to independent reading and writing.

In the first grades of primary school, beginning with kindergarten, the teaching of language changes from a developmental to a content-area approach. Therefore, whereas regarding preschool programs the acquisition of oral and written literacy was discussed in terms of language development, regarding the latter ages of early childhood it is described as the language arts.

Language arts includes listening, speaking, writing, and reading. The process of learning about these components is interrelated, just as it is in the preschool curriculum. Each component of the language arts curriculum is dependent upon and contributes to progress and growth in the others; therefore, experiences in the language arts program are described in holistic terms rather than as separate areas of study.

In the sections that follow, the language arts curriculum for students from five to eight is described as a transitional process. There is much similarity with the curriculum for the preschool years. The kinds of experiences that children need build on the foundations developed for three- and four-year-old children. Nevertheless, as students extend their abilities in literacy, competencies in reading and writing build rapidly. We can describe certain stages in the transition toward competence, as well as the kinds of experiences and activities that promote further progress in literacy.

Oral language and concept understanding continue to develop. We will therefore discuss the importance of addressing continuing acquisition of receptive and expressive language. The issue of a skills approach as opposed to a developmental approach to reading in the preschool years continues as an issue in the primary grades; we define it as a controversy between the whole-language approach and the skills approach in reading instruction. We will discuss the role of the teacher, the environment, and instructional materials, as well as appropriate activities for promoting development in writing skills. Finally, we will explore integrated curriculum in the language arts based on thematic units. We will include a description of the balance between thematic and systematic instruction as it applies to the language arts.

The Continuing Process of Language Development

Although much of the child's acquisition of the language of his or her home and community is acquired before kindergarten and first grade, children continue to add to their language ability. Five- to eight-year-olds have developed a good control of their language. They can use language creatively and generally are able to articulate well as they verbalize their thoughts, give directions, and ask questions. During the primary grades they will develop larger vocabularies, develop new meanings for words they already use, and use more complex language structure. As their cognitive abilities continue to expand, they will express more complex thought in their language (Seefeldt & Barbour, 1990).

Contrary to the practice in many elementary schools, the emphasis on reading instruction in the latter early childhood years does not preclude a need for further opportunities to develop oral language. No matter how well children are able to express themselves, language development should continue. Jewell and Zintz (1986) proposed that literacy is not the primary goal of schooling in kindergarten and first grade:

> The dominant goal is to enrich and expand children's knowledge and understanding of their world and to enable them to articulate more effectively those meanings through increased language skills. The richer children's conceptual store and language competence, the more meanings they bring to the world of print and the more natural literacy can be achieved (p. 140).

Children need to engage in many activities firsthand and need opportunities to talk about their experiences in their learning activities.

The rich experiences with language will lead to literacy. Children will respond to learning activities from their individual levels of development. Some will be able to express themselves in written form, whereas others will use mostly oral language at first to reflect upon what they have encountered. Regardless of the child's level, the opportunities to acquire concepts and language permit the child to move into literacy individually from a language base (Graves, 1983).

Addressing the Language Needs of Diverse Speakers

Children who are speakers of other languages or dialects especially need opportunities to further develop their oral language. Because these children learn language through communicating, they need daily activities that will facilitate the acquisition of language along with new information (Abramson, Seda, & Johnson, 1990).

The approach that guided bilingual students to learn English oral language skills prior to learning to read in English has been replaced with a whole-language or literacy approach. The more holistic method of literacy instruction assumes that students can acquire listening, speaking, and writing skills in the second language in an integrated fashion (Hudelson, 1984). Nevertheless, language acquisition cannot be left to chance with students who have diverse language differences. Special attention needs to be given to planning so that these students receive adequate opportunities to speak and use new language and vocabulary. Interactive experiences with other students encourage oral language usage. Oral collaboration between skilled English speakers and second-language or dialect speakers during literacy instruction helps many speakers acquire English (Enright & McCloskey, 1985). Likewise, when native speakers and bilingual students share their journals, this enhances the limited speaker's acquisition of new vocabulary and emergent writing (Urzua, 1987). Further, Hudelson (1984) found that these kinds of writing activities enabled students who were limited in English to read and write in English before expressing themselves orally.

Developers of an English literacy project that involved parents and preprimary and primary-age children assumed that social interactions were a vehicle for oral language development and literacy for limited-English speakers and second-language speakers. The researchers proposed the following assumptions, based on their review of the literature (Quintero & Velarde, 1990, p. 11):

1. Social context is of utmost importance in the child's learning in general and in literacy development specifically.
2. Use of oral language is an integral part of the literacy development process. Oral language is also strongly affected by social context.
3. Learners enter school knowing that written language has meaning, but they cannot understand print usage when it is presented to them as isolated letters and sounds.
4. Literacy behaviors are not restricted to the use of books but rather encompass many social and linguistic activities.

In the sections that follow, guidelines and examples are given of experiences that will promote oral language in all speakers in the latter early childhood years. The oral language curriculum follows the assumptions made by Quintero and Velarde (1990) that children developing oral language skills benefit from the social context of the kindergarten and primary-grade classroom.

Designing Curriculum for Language Development

Children develop their oral language by talking to their peers and to adults. The teacher's goal in designing curriculum for oral language development is to include speaking opportunities in learning activities. Although this may seem obvious, a visit to many elementary schools might demonstrate that verbal discussions are not the norm in primary classrooms. In a school where quiet classrooms are valued, children may have little opportunity to exchange ideas and participate in discussions. Further, reading instruction periods can be dominated by individual work, with more time spent on practicing reading skills in written form than on using conversational language. Daily oral discussions of many types are required for language competency to continue to expand and improve.

Following are some of the types of classroom (and outdoor) activities that foster oral language in kindergarten and primary-grade children. The length and form of the activities would vary depending on the age of the students, their prior experiences, and their confidence levels. Nevertheless, they can be used with some adaptation at all grade levels that serve children from five to eight years old.

Group Discussions.   There are many occasions when the entire class can engage in a group discussion. The discussion could follow a common group experience, an unusual local event that interests the children, or an opportunity to solve a problem. For example, an unexpected storm swept a local community without warning early one morning as the children were arriving at school. Soon after class began, the teacher gathered the children to discuss their experiences with the storm as they traveled to school. Having witnessed the unusual darkness of the sky, high winds, flooded streets, and other phenomena gave the children the opportunity to use descriptive language as the class discussed the storm and its effects on the community. In another instance, in a second-grade classroom, students had become careless with keeping the working areas organized. The teacher and students discussed the problem and decided which suggestions for improving the appearance and arrangement of classroom materials would be implemented.

Class Projects.   Projects related to unit or content study activities lend themselves to oral language experiences. Groups of students engaged in the projects can be asked to discuss and report the results of their project. Students might talk about the problems they encountered and solved in completing their project, the steps required to accomplish their goal, the reasons for choosing the project, and so on. The larger group can be encouraged to ask questions, make observations about the group's work, and reflect on what was learned about the topic studied.

Dramatic Productions.   Kindergarten and first-grade students enjoy acting out a familiar fairy tale or popular children's story. Older students in the second and third grades enjoy writing a play and presenting it to the rest of the class. Whichever form of production is used, students can plan the production, improvise costumes, practice parts, and otherwise engage in extensive language to prepare the dramatic production. The teacher may be needed to guide the process with younger children, but may serve only as a resource person for older students who have experience in initiating and carrying out activities in a small group. The dramatic activity requires extensive use of oral language as children develop dialogue and roles for the type of dramatic event they will present.

Field Trips.   Every field trip that focuses on a new experience—whether it be a walk outside the school or a trip a distance of many miles—is an opportunity to develop new vocabulary. Prior to the trip, the teacher can set the stage for important new words the children will be encountering. The children can be alerted to notice new information and words before the field trip begins. For example, a kindergarten class was studying trees. As part of the study of how trees are used, the children visited a lumber yard to see how lumber products are used in construction. The teacher asked the children to notice the products that are made of wood and to remember new words. After they returned from the lumber yard, children were asked to recall what they saw. They made a list of products made of wood, and then they told language experience stories. The teacher prompted the children to remember many new words, such as *lumber,* names of tools used to work with wood construction, and other words related to a lumber yard.

Children's Literature.   Children's books offer endless opportunities to develop and use oral language. One major goal for language development through children's literature is to appreciate the creative and aesthetic use of language in books. Glazer (1986) described the opportunities books offer for language development, including exposing children to mature language, listening to varied syntax, enjoying figurative language, hearing different dialects, introducing new vocabulary in context, presenting new words, sharing books that emphasize word meanings, and playing with language. Glazer used the stories *The Little Engine That Could* and *Millions of Cats* as examples of classic children's books that involve play with patterns of language.

Cooperative Learning Groups.   Cooperative learning group activities provide natural opportunities to use conversation and discussion. Because the students must interact to complete the activity, members of the group will be engaged in individual input as the problem or exercise is resolved. Mixing students who have varied language abilities will enhance the exchange of vocabulary and syntax during frequent verbal exchanges.

Curriculum for language development is not organized as a separate component of the language arts curriculum. Nor is it separate from activities in other content areas. In the suggestions put forth earlier, oral language activities are interwoven into ongoing classroom methods and strategies related to the total curriculum; the specific activities that are suggested next serve this purpose. They involve concept development, art, problem solving, science, and language arts. They are more likely to involve an individual student or a small group rather than large group efforts.

Activities That Promote Language Development

Memory Game

This memory game is frequently found in Montessori classrooms. The teacher assembles a number of objects or pictures related to a new concept. The objects are placed on a tray and the child is asked to study them. The objects are then covered and the child is asked to name them. More objects or pictures are added, a few at a time, and the exercise is repeated. Examples of objects that can be used include vegetables, articles of clothing, solid shapes, pictures of furniture items, etc.

Imaginary Creatures

Students are asked to make an imaginary creature using play dough, crayons and paper, or scraps of recycled materials. They are asked to describe to the rest of the group such things as what the creature looks like and where it lives.

What Is It?

This activity promotes divergent thinking and expressive language. The teacher finds objects that are interesting and unfamiliar to the children. Old household utensils such as coffee grinders or a rug beater are examples of objects that can be described. The children are asked to examine the object and describe its characteristics: how it is made, what materials it is made of, what its qualities are, etc. After the children have exhausted descriptive characteristics, they are asked to decide how the object could be used. They are not asked to identify the purpose of the object but rather to invent a use for it. At the end of the experience the teacher can tell the children the actual purpose and function of the object.

Explaining Recipes

Simple recipes offer rich opportunities for expressive language. After children engage in a cooking project, they can orally describe the cooking process and the changes in the foods that were prepared. Good examples of such activities include making butter, peanut butter, and popcorn. The children not only can explain what happens when popcorn pops or peanuts are put in the blender or food processor but they can also describe the steps involved in the process of preparation and the necessary equipment and ingredients needed.

Sequencing Stories

Oral comprehension and expressive language are used when retelling or sequencing a story. Kindergarten children enjoy retelling or sequencing by using flannel board pictures of a well-known story such as *The Three Little Pigs* or a nursery rhyme. The flannel pictures provide props for retelling the story. Older children can make up their own story or retell a story they have read. They enjoy making cartoon pictures of the story, perhaps including the dialogue, and sharing it with the other students.

The Continuing Process of Literacy Development

The Nature of Literacy Acquisition in Kindergarten and the Primary Grades.   What are the differences between the kinds of experiences that promote literacy in preschool and kindergarten and those that promote literacy in the primary grades? In some schools, a developmental approach to literacy is advocated for preschool classrooms for four-year-olds but is abandoned in kindergarten, when "serious learning" must begin. Language experience stories and big-book activities give way to basal reader lessons reinforced with workbooks and dittoed skills sheets.

The years between kindergarten and third grade are the most critical in determining whether the child will become a successful reader, will enjoy reading, and will be able to use the acquired reading and writing skills to become a competent and effective learner. The child crosses the bridge into literacy and continues to refine competence as a reader and writer. How successfully the child acquires literacy depends on the kinds of experiences that are provided and whether the child perceives him- or herself as a competent student. If a developmental philosophy prevails, the teacher will continue to provide literacy activities that facilitate the child's progress within an individual timeline. If a skills approach is advocated, much time may be spent in teacher-directed lessons using formal instruction in reading and writing. A problem that teachers in these grade levels must address is how to determine the best practices for their students. Should a whole-language approach be used in these critical grades? Or should a basal reader approach be used? When and how should skills be taught within a whole-language approach? If a basal reader program is followed, can emergent literacy also be part of the program? How can language arts be put into meaningful context? How can the teacher structure the curriculum to best ensure that kindergarten and primary-grade students will make a positive transition into literacy? There are many issues surrounding instruction for beginning readers and the role of language arts in the curriculum. We will first describe the current status of the controversy. Then we will define characteristics of the language arts program for students from ages five to eight and provide suggestions for addressing the questions asked above.

The Debate on Whole Language versus Phonics.   The controversy over how children should be taught beginning reading skills has a long history. The issues described in chapter 7 concerning emergent literacy and reading readiness skills is but a downward extension of a larger debate that dates back to the 1950s, when Rudolph Flesch criticized the then-popular method of teaching beginning reading skills through sight words or meaning-first methods (i.e., methods that stressed understanding the meaning of reading content) that had replaced letter-to-sound correspondence (Flesch, 1955). Flesch's book, *Why Johnny Can't Read,* triggered a decades-long controversy over how young children should be taught to read, or, more specifically, what is the best way to teach young children beginning reading skills. In 1967, Jeanne Chall completed a three-year study evaluating then-existing methods and materials and presented her results in *Learning to Read: The Great Debate.* Chall's findings suggested that the prevailing mood of the classroom was more significant than the approach of a particular program; nevertheless, she found a strong correlation between letter, or phonic, knowledge and reading achievement (Chall, 1983).

The growing popularity of the whole-language approach in the last decade renewed the debate over the role of phonics in beginning reading when Marilyn Jager Adams, at the Center for the Study of Reading at the University of Illinois (Urbana-Champaign), was asked to respond to a congressional request for an evaluation of phonics instruction. Adams studied what is known about the knowledge and skill required for acquiring literacy. The purpose in presenting the report of her research, *Beginning to Read: Thinking and Learning about Print* (1990), was to reconcile the debate. Instead, the book itself became controversial, as whole-language and other reading specialists debated Adams's interpretations of the role of phonics in reading instruction (Adams et al., 1991).

Although Adams's work focused on the efficacy of phonics, the concern is actually broader. The issue also involves whether the whole-language approach or basal reading methods should be used for reading instruction. More important, many kindergarten and primary-school teachers want to know what the role of skills instruction in beginning reading is and how such instruction, including phonics, fits into the language arts program between kindergarten and third grade.

One concern is whether basal programs overemphasize separate skills (Jewell & Zintz, 1986). Jewell and Zintz were concerned that beginning reading is often taught with the focus on the isolated components of reading rather than in a meaningful context. Using phonics, recognizing words, and other decoding skills are part of a systems approach to reading instruction in which the components of the system are more important than the acquisition of literacy as a whole.

Another issue concerns whether whole language includes structure, spelling, and grammar. Newman and Church (1990) propose that there are many myths about whole language, including the perception that it involves no instruction in phonics, it is limited to language arts, it is unsuitable for children with special needs, and it applies only to teaching in the early grades. The authors argue that whole-language teachers use a variety of teaching strategies and materials based on the individual learners in the classroom. It is possible, however, that whole-language teachers can fail to establish a balanced reading program because they have become preoccupied with the strategies of whole-language teaching. As whole-language books and materials flood the market, teachers can lose sight of how the most optimal language arts program can be devised for young beginning readers (Fountas & Hannigan, 1989).

One trend in the controversy between phonics and whole language seems to be to attempt to achieve a compromise between the two approaches. Whole-language teachers describe themselves as constantly growing and adapting their methods as they learn from their students. The issue concerns *how* skills instruction is taught, not *whether* it is taught. Freppon and Dahl (1991) point out that Adams (1990) discussed phonics instruction as research-based information about sound–symbol relations, spelling development, early reading, skilled reading, and instructional interventions. They counter that the context of the reading material, the learner's purposes and motivations, and sociolinguistic elements are among the factors that are more learner centered than those in Adams's analysis of the curriculum. These authors argue that children learn reading and writing by engaging in meaning-centered experiences with written language. Sound–symbol understanding develops with the teacher's guidance as children experiment with their own literacy efforts.

Increasingly, teachers are learning how to incorporate the best of both sides of the controversy. In achieving a balanced language arts program for their classroom from kindergarten to third grade, they have developed an understanding of the philosophy and practices of the whole-language approach and the way in which the strengths of basal resources can help establish the balance between skills instruction and child-initiated literacy efforts. Some teachers (Fountas & Hannigan, 1989) report using whole-language strategies to supplement their basal program, and others report moving away from the use of basals (Webb, Bowers, Hietpas, Lang, & McKinley, 1991). As developers of basal reading curricula move quickly to take a leadership role in designing programs based on whole-language and emergent literacy strategies, classroom teachers will enter a new era of curriculum design in language arts as they use these newest resources in their classrooms.

The Language Arts Program for Children Ages Five to Eight

In chapter 7 we described the curriculum for language development. We emphasized the importance of oral language development for literacy in the arrangement of the environment, the role of play, the role of the teacher, and the experiences that could be provided to facilitate language and literacy. We also discussed how meaningful experiences in book reading and storytelling, participating in integrated thematic units, and other daily experiences can promote the child's emerging literacy.

Earlier in this chapter we stressed the continuing importance of oral language and vocabulary as a foundation for competent readers and writers in the beginning elementary grades. In this section we will discuss the language arts program as it relates to reading and writing. The goal is to develop a balanced program that combines child-initiated and teacher-directed activities that will incorporate all of the experiences that are needed for a quality language arts curriculum. The balanced program also includes informal, contextual experiences, as well as regularly scheduled systematic instruction for students who need assistance in acquiring literacy skills. Within this curriculum framework, the teacher will provide formal and informal activities that will permit children to make progress toward literacy through both individual and group activities.

In keeping with the ungraded primary model described in chapter 9, we will not describe the process by age or grade levels; rather, the process is based on individual needs and progress based on reading and writing competencies usually acquired by the end of the primary grades. With these competencies in mind, we will describe a whole-language classroom with teacher behaviors, classroom environment, and learning experiences compatible with the whole-language philosophy but also incorporating systematic skills instruction when needed. As the stages of the program evolve to accommodate advancing reading and writing ability, the focus of the activities will change, as will the content of the curriculum.

The Role of the Environment.   In chapter 7 we described the classroom environment for emergent literacy, including center arrangements that foster listening, speaking, writing, and reading skills. In kindergarten and primary grades, a similar arrangement is appropriate. A large language arts center with collections of books of all types, including books written by the children, can be organized and displayed for easy perusal. Areas for listening to taped books, areas that are comfortable for reading, and quiet spaces for reading and thinking provide a relaxed ambience. An area for writing and illustrating written work contains writing materials; marking pens; crayons; a variety of art media such as chalk, watercolors, and tempera paints; and a selection of writing paper. Typewriters, computers, and book-making materials broaden opportunities for composing and reading.

The room might also accommodate a project, study, and planning and instruction center. The project center can contain materials for changing projects related to

thematic work. Book-making materials might also be located here, rather than in the library center. The study center is a quiet area where students can conduct individual work. A study table could seat several students who need to complete assignments or read. Individual desks can be transformed into carrels using cardboard dividers. The planning and instruction center is a larger area where the whole class can gather for planning and feedback sessions. Small-group instruction can also be conducted in this area (Jewell & Zintz, 1986).

The Role of the Teacher. The teacher in kindergarten and primary grades still serves as guide and facilitator of learning. In addition, the role of assessor and evaluator of the child's learning is expanded as the need to track the child's strengths and to instruct or guide the child in language arts skills becomes more evident. Much of the work is informal and incidental when the child asks for assistance or the teacher observes the child's progress during small-group instruction. At other times, the teacher will need to introduce a skill to some or all of the class or model forms in composition that the children are ready to use but which they have not developed through their individual reading and writing efforts.

The teacher will conduct much instruction informally within whole-language and integrated thematic activities. Periodic or regular systematic instruction will focus on specific objectives or skills. Jewell and Zintz (1986) offered some guidelines to the teacher's role as children move into literacy in a meaningful, enjoyable manner. The teacher's role would include the following adapted from their list (Jewell & Zintz, pp. 94–95):

1. Read to children that which they cannot read for themselves.
2. Read from a variety of materials with a high interest level.
3. Provide a reading environment by having an abundance of reading materials readily available in the classroom.
4. Have older, proficient readers tape stories and store the cassettes for children to use in the listening center.
5. Provide flannel boards with appropriate cutouts for children to use to tell stories to themselves or to others.
6. Have writing materials readily available: pencils, crayons, and paper.
7. Have a scrap or "attic" box filled with a collection of odds and ends for children to sort through, touch, and talk about in whatever way they choose.
8. Provide time to engage in all of the above activities.
9. Provide a multitude of hands-on activities for children to participate in and talk about.
10. With the emergence of reading behaviors, provide information and help as the child requests them.
11. Begin to prepare language experience stories by recording the child's talk about an experience in the classroom.
12. As children develop additional competencies and interests in reading, provide more time in frequently spaced periods for them to read.
13. Continue to share books with the whole group by reading daily.

The Role of Technology.   As more schools acquire computers for the classroom, educators have become interested in how computer technology can be useful in the language arts program. Much of the original software developed for kindergarten and primary-grade classrooms was meant for work with reading readiness and reading skills. Drill activities that replicated the same kinds of skill reinforcement found in reading workbooks prevailed. Although software of this type has been designed to be appealing to the user, the teacher will have to decide the merits of each software program available in relation to the type of language arts program being implemented in the classroom; the teacher must also decide when and if skills development or reinforcement is needed by individual students.

For teachers using a whole-language or emergent literacy approach to the language arts, the computer can be a useful tool for emergent writing. Simple word processing programs are available that can be used by younger children who are able to use the keyboard to write. As they become more proficient in the process of composing their writing, they can use editing features such as checking their spelling. An advantage of the computer for beginning writers is that mistakes or changes are much easier to make, thus minimizing frustration for the young writer. The main caution for teachers is to avoid getting caught up in the attractiveness of software; they should instead make purchases and decisions based on the usefulness of the program for the students in their classroom setting (Bullough & Beatty, 1991; Clements, 1985).

Stages of Literacy Acquisition.   The transition into literacy in the latter early childhood years is gradual and individual. If the teacher understands the nature of this accomplishment, developmentally appropriate materials and experiences can be planned to facilitate progress for each child. In the sections that follow, we will discuss literacy acquisition within three stages. Each stage has implications for the kinds of instruction and skills development that can complement natural experiences that nurture literacy.

The ages from five to eight are the years when most young children achieve literacy in reading and writing. Mastery of their home language is basically acquired by age five; likewise, the major steps into literacy are mastered between age five and eight. Literacy can be described as occurring in three overlapping stages: setting foundations for literacy, learning about print and understanding printed language, and becoming independent readers.

Stage One: Setting Foundations for Literacy.   The first stage, setting foundations for literacy, begins when the child is an infant and proceeds throughout the preschool years. Children acquire information about the processes of speaking, writing, and reading through activities in which they can experiment and express themselves in preliteracy steps of writing and reading. Through use of oral language and opportunities for emergent writing and reading, each child acquires many of the characteristics of literacy at an individual rate. By age five, as they enter kindergarten, children have progressed into literacy at their own individual rate. The first stage gradually becomes the second stage, learning about print and understanding printed language.

Stage Two: Learning about Print and Understanding Printed Language.   In stage two, the child masters the components of written language and becomes a reader and writer of English. Although the process of true mastery of reading and writing is a life-long task, understanding and using printed language is the major accomplishment in this stage.

To master literacy, the child must attend to features of printed language that include phonic elements, grammar, and punctuation. Major steps toward this goal were already made in the foundations stage, when the child developed an awareness of how letters are formed and put together into words to express thoughts. There is likewise an awareness of how punctuation is used to enable others to understand what one has expressed in written language. In this second stage, the child continues to learn about print and how it is used. Language experience stories used in stage one to develop awareness of printed language are continued in stage two to practice the elements of printed language. The skills used in relating to printed language that can be learned through language experience stories in stage two include the following:

1. Match letters, upper- and lowercase
2. Match words
3. Match sentences
4. Practice word recognition when the teacher frames individual words
5. Practice phonic, structural, and context clues to locate letters and words and identify them
6. Identify different types of punctuation
7. Reread stories and share reading with a buddy
8. Make similar sentences using the syntax model in a sentence

The specific reading skills that young children acquire in the primary grades can be categorized as recognizing sight words and understanding phonics, word analysis, context clues, and the mechanics of reading and writing (Fields, Spangler, & Lee, 1991). Although language experience stories are one vehicle for facilitating practice with the skills, the child's own reading and writing processes will incorporate others. The teacher can supplement these natural experiences for acquiring competence with the printed language with systematic instruction from basal materials or from his or her own design. Figure 10.1 lists the basic beginning reading skills; Figure 10.2

Sight Words—instantly recognizable words

Phonics—learning about letters and the sounds they represent

Word Analysis—learning parts of words
   compound words (bedroom)
   inflections–possessives ('s), plurals, endings (ed, s, ing)
   roots, prefixes (un), suffixes (ful, less, ly)

Context Clues—learning words from their location in a sentence

---

Figure 10.1   Beginning Reading Skills

Consonants | Vowels

Single Consonants	Consonant Combinations	Single Vowels	Vowel Combinations	Vowel–Consonant Combinations	The Schwa (ə)
Single consonants (one phoneme): b d f h i k l m n w y z	Consonant blends: bl br sc tw cl cr sk scr fl dr sm spr gl fr sn str pl gr sp shr sl pr st spl dw tr sw sch wr thr	Single vowels (may be long or short): a e i o u y (sometimes)	Vowel digraphs: ai in sail ay day ea beat ea head ea tea ee sleep ei receive ie believe ey key ey they oa boat oe toe ow show ou though	Vowels: a followed by "l" or "w": "aw" in bawl "al" in wall	pencil about beckon latent
Single consonants with two or more common sounds: "c" as "k" "c" as "s" "g" as "g" "g" as "j" "s" in hiss rose sugar "x" in six xylophone exact	Consonant digraphs: One sound: gh, ph, sh, ck, ng, nk Two or more sounds: th: this, thin wh: what, who ch: chin chalet choir		Vowel blends (dipthongs): oi in soil oy boy ue true ew in new ow now ou though oa goal	Vowels followed by "r": a in arm e fern i dirt o word u hurt y martyr q and u qu in quick squ squirrel	

Figure 10.2 Phonic Elements in Reading

M. V. Zintz, *Corrective Reading* (4th ed.). (Wm. C. Brown, 1981). Used by permission of the publisher.

lists the phonic elements that are acquired as part of beginning and independent reading between the ages of five and eight in kindergarten and the primary grades.

Although the child engages in activities that provide practice in the elements of printed language that will facilitate the ability to read, the transition into reading requires many experiences in reading. In the foundations stage, the children engaged in big-book and other read-along activities that led them to begin to put the pieces of the reading process into place. They learned that in English, print moves from left to right, and they became able to follow along and turn the pages when favorite stories were read. They contributed to group-dictated stories in addition to engaging in individual "reading" efforts with familiar books.

In stage two, children continue to advance in their ability to understand how to read print until they are able to read on their own. The transition into reading began in stage one, with repeated readings of big books or shared books (Holdaway, 1979), as described above. The process continues with assisted reading (Hoskisson, 1975). Hoskisson described three stages of assisted reading: (1) the child is asked to repeat a phrase or sentence after it has been read; (2) the child is asked to fill in a word that occurs repeatedly in a story; and (3) the child takes over more of the reading process and the adult prompts the words the child has trouble recognizing. In each step, the child takes over more of the reading process until the teacher assists only as needed.

After many activities with group and individual assisted readings with experience stories and shared books, basal materials can further growth in recognizing and understanding elements of print. When and how basal materials are introduced will

vary with practices used by individual teachers. Whole-language teachers are likely to use basal materials informally, while children are developing emergent reading and writing behaviors. After some proficiency has been achieved in reading, more formal activities can be used that target or reinforce specific elements or skills (Jewell & Zintz, 1986). The workbook is used sparingly for practice to supplement use of the skill in the child's own reading and writing efforts. In a similar manner, teacher-directed instruction taken from basal reading materials is selected based on learners' needs, rather than as routine lessons that are scheduled whether or not they are needed. Some teachers will use basal resources extensively, whereas others prefer to conduct all skill work independent of basal materials (Fields, Spangler, & Lee, 1991).

Stage Three: Becoming Independent Readers. Children need extensive reading experiences to master the reading and writing process. When they have developed competence in the beginning stages of literacy, they make the transition to independence in reading and writing. As they continue to use the features of written language, their competence and confidence also increase. Instruction in reading continues but is now based on individual needs. Whole-group instruction decreases, and small-group and individual instruction increases.

The teacher's role becomes more of that of facilitator, and the teacher is less focused on basic instruction. Books and reading materials are made available for all types of reading. Children need a balance between narrative and expository reading. The classroom library should include easy nonfiction as well as books about animals, places to visit, famous people, and nature (Sanacore, 1991). Books brought from trips to the school library and public library are supplemented with books brought from home. The teacher continues to read to the children but moves to longer books that are read in chapters. Reading in the content areas is used extensively as children study thematic units and seek out resources for developing class projects, assignments, and reports. Reading for problem solving is engaged in frequently, and skills for beginning research are developed as students search for information related to unit activities.

Organizing the Language Arts Program

How, then, do teachers determine how to organize the classroom for instruction as children move through the stages of literacy in the latter years of early childhood? In the pages that follow, examples are given of how some teachers decided to design their language arts program. In each of the examples, the teachers studied and analyzed what processes they believed would best provide their students with a language arts program that has a balance between whole-language, basal, and phonics instruction. The examples come from a first-grade classroom that was nonability grouped; a literature-based model; content-area grouping; and a reading workshop.

A Nonability-Grouped, Multilevel, First-Grade Classroom. Three teachers established a model for a first-grade classroom (Cunningham, Hall, & Defee, 1991). The children were grouped in three classrooms, with similar ranges of ability in each room. The teachers decided to include the four major approaches to reading: the basal approach, the phonics approach, implementing real books, and writing. They studied these approaches, determined that some children respond best to one particular approach, and built their program around four components, or blocks, based on the benefits of the four approaches. Children were told of the activities and were provided instruction in each of the four blocks.

In the basal block, children were given daily guided instruction in a basal reading series. The instruction included workbook activities, partner reading, whole-group instruction, and feedback activities at the end of the block.

A working-with-words block involved a "Word Wall" and "Making Words" activity. Each day, five words from the basal reading lessons were added to the Word Wall on a bulletin board. The children learned to read, spell, and alphabetize the words. A variety of group activities were conducted with the words each day. The Making Words activity involved making words from letters. The children were given a limited selection of letters at their desk. In some instances, the teacher called out the word to be made. In other activities, the children were told to make words out of some or all of the letters.

The writing block began with a short writing lesson modeled by the teacher. Next, the children engaged in their own individual writing activity. The teacher helped children edit and revise their work. The lesson ended with a brief period during which children could share their work with the class.

The fourth block, the real-books block, involved self-selected reading and reading aloud by the teacher. Children could select from a variety of books and could read alone or with a friend.

The three teachers combined whole-language and basal materials and activities for their reading program. They achieved a balance between teacher-directed and child-initiated work during the language arts period. They permitted students to develop literacy at their own rate, but at the same time they felt assured that they were working with beginning reading and writing skills in a systematic fashion.

Literature-Based Instruction.   A second-grade language arts classroom described by Fields, Spangler, and Lee (1991) was based on good books. The teacher conducted the program both to meet individual interests and to conduct group topics in science or social studies. He helped individual children select books that would support what they were trying to learn or do. He wanted the students to have control of their learning. His belief was that children learn and practice reading and writing through the study of content that they are interested in. He concentrated on the progress of each individual student and used responsive teaching to guide students in the development of reading and writing skills.

While reading and writing were conducted throughout the day, the teacher prepared skills instruction for small groups or individual children. He used basal materials or constructed his own activities to use with the children. Reports of student needs and progress were kept in individual folders. The folder contained daily journal and other written work, as well as projects the child had in progress or had completed. The teacher used the folders for planning with individual children and for assessing their instructional needs.

This classroom was offered reading and writing experiences through class projects and studies of topics in science and social studies. The class library became a source of reading material as the teacher, librarian, and students found resources that could be consulted for the topic being studied. Again, as the teacher identified reading and writing problems during topic activities, systematic instruction was planned to address needs of identified students.

Content-Area Grouping.   Content-area instruction and cooperative learning groups were used in a third-grade classroom to replace ability grouping and traditional reading instruction (Pardo & Raphael, 1991). The teacher was interested in developing independent learners who could extend their strategies for reading and learning. Reading and writing activities were used to study subject matter. Students selected the topics to be studied; developed a general concept about the topic; gathered, organized, synthesized, and reported information about the topic; and used their emerging reading and writing skills to share information about the topic.

Teacher-led whole-class discussions were used to introduce learning strategies and topic concepts and to develop background knowledge prior to exploring a topic. The teacher also used whole-group instruction to work with difficult text and conduct enrichment activities.

Small cooperative learning group activities afforded opportunities for students to practice and use new learning strategies and to work on topic activities. The groups gathered information and wrote reports on their findings. They generated and answered questions about the topic being studied or worked on a subtopic related to the larger class topic.

Individual work was undertaken to set individual goals and purposes related to study topics and to apply and practice reading and writing strategies. Students recorded their thoughts and reflections in dialogue journals. They responded to focus questions posed by the teacher and shared individual ideas, along with participating in other individual activities.

Because the students designed the topics to be studied, the teacher in this third-grade classroom maintained a role as facilitator and guide. She helped students map or web the information they wished to acquire from content-area topics. She introduced and modeled strategies that students needed to pursue and report on information developed through large-group and cooperative-group activities. She also was able to work extensively with individual students to extend their skills as independent readers and writers.

The Reading Workshop.   Teachers of the reading workshop in another third-grade classroom used a more directive approach to reading instruction (Reutzel & Cooter, 1991). They wished to achieve a balance between providing meaningful activities for the students and ensuring that instructional time was constructive and well managed. They used a seventy-minute reading workshop approach to organize their classroom. Through the workshop, they established a classroom environment that integrated reading with writing, speaking, and listening. Student-selected books were the focus of workshop activities, with regular demonstrations of reading and writing strategies.

The reading workshop consisted of periods for sharing (5–10 minutes), a mini lesson (5–10 minutes), state-of-the-class activities (5 minutes), and self-selected reading and responses (35-45 minutes). Sharing time was an introductory period used by the teacher to share new discoveries in literature. Mini lessons followed sharing time and were short, teacher-designed whole-group instructional sessions to demonstrate reading strategies. The mini lessons were derived from observed student needs or learning objectives from the school district reading curriculum objectives. State-of-the-class activities were used to update the teacher on individual student progress. The teacher could assess the effectiveness of the student's work and adaptations made when needed.

The major time period of the reading workshop was devoted to self-selected reading and responses. During this period the class engaged in sustained silent reading (SSR), some groups of children met with the teacher in literature response groups, and some participated in individual reading conferences. Students engaged in individual reading and writing activities with their self-selected reading materials if and when they were not meeting with the teacher in a group activity. Many different types of projects were planned and conducted by students within their reading and writing activities that had been planned previously with the teacher. At the end of the self-selected reading and response period, the whole class met for a few minutes to share their work as a culminating activity of the reading workshop.

The models just presented represent several approaches to language arts instruction in primary-grade classrooms that serve students in stages two and three discussed earlier. The models range from predominantly whole-language orientation to more structured combinations that incorporate both basal and whole-language strategies. In the sections that follow, we will present examples of activities suitable for beginning and independent readers. Many of the examples can be used in some or all of the models described.

Experiences That Promote Reading

Reading Buddies

Pairs composed of two students or a student and an adult are established for reading experiences. The buddies meet daily or on a regular basis to read together. They take turns reading from the same book or read from different books. Cross-age buddies can also be formed, whereby students from a higher grade have a buddy in kindergarten or the primary grades. The older buddy listens to the younger child read and reads books selected by the younger buddy. Writing activities can also be conducted. The younger child can dictate a story to the older buddy or receive help in writing a story. Same-age buddies can collaborate on a writing activity.

Read-Along Tapes

Tapes of familiar books are recorded. The child plays the tape as the book is read and reads along with the tape. The activity can be repeated many times until the student has mastered the story. Basal reader stories can be recorded. Many read-along tapes are also available from commercial resources.

Sustained Silent Reading (SSR)

A time is provided for all children to read on their own. Regardless of individual reading levels, all students participate. The book is usually self-selected, and the following guidelines are recommended (McCracken & McCracken, 1979, p. 35):

1. Begin with the whole class.
2. Each child selects one book.
3. Each child must read silently.
4. The teacher reads silently.
5. A timer is used.
6. There are absolutely no reports or records of any kind.

Poem Picture Books

Poem picture books can be used in a similar manner as are picture storybooks in the classroom. After they have been introduced and repeated with the children several times, they can, for example, be used as a read-along source; the poems can be chanted, accompanied by rhythm sticks or drums; or they can be illustrated. Children can make up similar poetry following the pattern of a poem and write their own poems (Glazer & Lamme, 1990).

Creating Nonsense Words

Provide the child with a selection of vowels and consonants. Ask the child to create nonsense words. Have the child "create" an animal or object to match the nonsense word.

Substitute Words

Select a word that is familiar to the children, such as *walk*. Ask the children to generate substitute words for the key word. Examples include *run, jump, tiptoe, creep,* etc. Use *walk* in a sentence. Substitute the word list in the sentence and have children read the sentence.

Word Games

Use a secret code by substituting numerals for letters in a message. Give the children the numeral code and have them "decode" the message. Another game uses palindromes, or words that are spelled the same frontward and backward (e.g., *wow*). See how many palindromes students can think of (Danielson, 1990).

Oral Reading to Share Information

Children can read together to share information. The following activities are suggested (Fields, Spangler, & Lee, 1991, p. 213):

1. Children can read the lunch menu, daily bulletin, and newspaper items.
2. Children can confirm an answer by reading it from a book.
3. One child (a good reader) can read out loud while others listen with their textbooks closed.
4. Children can read passages from reference books or trade books.

Experiences That Promote Writing

Journal Writing

Students write daily in a journal. The journal can be a part of the language arts program or used more broadly for the whole school day. The child records ideas, feelings, reactions to activities, etc. The teacher reads the journal and responds to the child. Mechanics of writing are not corrected. The teacher is interested in the child's expression of thoughts.

Story Starters

Children are given many opportunities to write their own stories and illustrate them. When they are stumped for ideas, story starters can be used. One form of a starter is a sentence that can be used as the first one in a story—for example, "The noise came closer and closer." Another way to spark a story is to have a collection of pictures and ask the child to select a picture and write a story about it.

Messages

Responding to messages can trigger interesting writing efforts. The teacher can give each child a mysterious message and ask the child to respond. Another type of message is curriculum related. The teacher can leave a message for the child to respond to a question that has been posed. For example, a small container of beans is placed in the mathematics center. The students are left a message to estimate the number of beans and record their name and estimate below the message. The next day, the students can respond to a message asking them to count the number of beans and again record their name and the number they counted.

Lists

There are all kinds of lists that can be generated. For example, students can be asked to write a list of foods they like the least or the best; or they can be asked to keep a list of the books they have read or the names of as many people in their family as they can remember.

Writing Workshop

Children in the primary grades who have become independent writers can use the processes of the writing workshop to improve their writing efforts. The student engages in a series of steps to initiate, improve, and evaluate the writing effort. The process is used each time students are asked to write a composition that will be edited and improved until the teacher and child are satisfied with the quality. Figure 10.3 lists the steps in the writing process (Fields, Spangler, & Lee, 1991, p. 187).

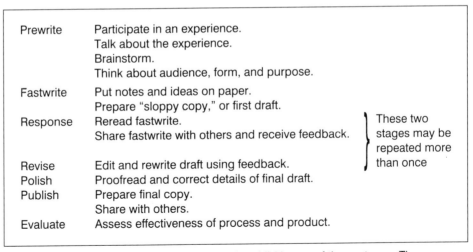

Prewrite	Participate in an experience.
	Talk about the experience.
	Brainstorm.
	Think about audience, form, and purpose.
Fastwrite	Put notes and ideas on paper.
	Prepare "sloppy copy," or first draft.
Response	Reread fastwrite.
	Share fastwrite with others and receive feedback.
Revise	Edit and rewrite draft using feedback.
Polish	Proofread and correct details of final draft.
Publish	Prepare final copy.
	Share with others.
Evaluate	Assess effectiveness of process and product.

} These two stages may be repeated more than once

Notes: The teacher may conference with the child in any of these stages. The writing process includes any or all of these stages.

Figure 10.3   Stages in Emergent Writing
M. V. Fields, K. L. Spangler, & D. Lee, *Let's Begin Reading Right.* (Merrill, 1991), p. 187. Used by permission of the publisher.

Accommodating the Learning Differences of Students with Special Needs

In spite of efforts to provide children in kindergarten and the primary grades with a quality language arts program, some children encounter difficulties in learning to read. It is important that these children be identified as soon as possible and efforts made to correct the problem.

Reading achievement in the first three years of school is critical for later achievement. If low-achieving students can be identified and brought up to grade level in the primary grades, they are more likely to remain at grade level than if remediation comes in later grades (Adams, 1990; Carter, 1984; Clay, 1979). The importance of the early years for later learning was also advocated in *Becoming a Nation of Readers* (Commission on Reading, National Academy of Education, 1985); ability to read determines the level of achievement in secondary education.

Prevention of reading difficulties through early intervention is a key to successfully assisting young students who are encountering problems in beginning to read. The students who are unable to progress in literacy are experiencing frustrations in processing print. They are unable to recognize words quickly and effortlessly and thus fall behind in reading comprehension (Adams, 1990; Gaskins, Gaskins, & Gaskins, 1991; Hill & Hale, 1991). Programs for early intervention focus on intensive instruction to help the student become successful as soon as possible.

Reading Recovery is an early intervention program designed for six-year-olds who are low achievers. The children receive intensive one-on-one instruction thirty minutes a day for twelve to twenty weeks. The purpose of the program is to help the child acquire the strategies used by good readers. Instruction includes reading activities using natural language and predictable texts. Writing activities are based on the child's experience or presented as an extension of text readings (Hill & Hale, 1991). The lowest-performing students are selected for the program; they are replaced with other students at the completion of the program, after they have begun performing comfortably with average children in the classroom. Reading Recovery does not replace regular classroom instruction in reading but rather complements the child's other language arts activities.

The Benchmark Word Identification Program is another method designed to identify students who have difficulty in processing print (Gaskins, Gaskins, & Gaskins, 1991). Originally designed at Benchmark, a school for poor readers, the program focuses on helping poor students with poor reading skills develop word identification skills. One strategy used with beginning readers is to immerse them in a rich language environment compatible with whole-language strategies. In addition, students are instructed in methods that will lead to effective decoding of words using sight vocabulary, phonological awareness, and word analysis. In the beginning program for nonreaders who are up to the second-grade level, word identification activities previously described for the nonability grouped, multilevel first-grade model (Cunningham, Hall, & Defee, 1991) are used.

The programs just described are but two intervention programs that have been developed to correct early reading problems. Both incorporate whole-language strategies that are child centered along with intensive work in specific reading skills that will assist the child in being able to process written language. Both are designed to achieve quick results before the child has experienced extensive failure; both methods have been successful in enabling students to reverse their low achievement in beginning reading.

CURRICULUM FOR MATHEMATICS

When cognitive development in the preschool years was discussed in chapter 7, concepts in mathematics and science were explained from a developmental perspective in terms of how the preoperational child learns. In this chapter, we will discuss mathematics and science as content areas approached with the child's development in mind.

Between the ages of five and eight, the child moves from the preoperational stage to the concrete operational stage of thinking. The child will move from thinking that is dominated by perceptual content to thinking that is logical, which allows them to use mental schema to make an operation that previously required concrete objects. Although the child needs concrete materials to understand new concepts, he or she no longer has to rely only on manipulating the objects; mental schema can also be used to classify, seriate, count, and perform other functions. In mathematics, this mental ability in the concrete operational stage is represented in conservation and reversibility. The ability to conserve and reverse operations allows the child to do mathematical problems using mental schema (Dutton & Dutton, 1991).

Curriculum in mathematics for children from age five to eight reflects this progression from preoperational to concrete operational thinking. Curriculum for five-year-olds is a continuation of the preschool curriculum. It is a continuum that becomes more complex as the child accumulates experience. The same categories of number, measurement, geometry, and mathematical reasoning used in the preschool years are still used to organize the curriculum. Moreover, repeated experiences with concepts previously introduced are required for the child to be able to internalize and apply mathematical principles. If one looks at mathematical curriculum from a grade-level point of view, mathematical concepts are reviewed and practiced at each level prior to moving to more complex applications. Mathematics is a continuum, but it is also hierarchical and sequential—complex concepts build on a foundation of prior concepts and skills. Thus, simple addition follows understanding of number, and more complex addition of several digits follows simple addition of one-digit numbers.

Trends and Issues in Mathematics

In the discussion of language arts, we explored current issues and trends, reflecting the national concern about literacy and about students who are poor readers in secondary schools. There are similar concerns and issues regarding mathematics curriculum and instruction. The concern of mathematics specialists has been that current mathematics curriculum is focused on basic skills that do not prepare students who will live and learn in the twenty-first century. More specifically, they take the position that much of the current emphasis on drill has become obsolete with the advent of calculators and computers. Workers of the future will need to be able to solve unconventional problems (Steen, 1990).

In 1989 the National Council of Teachers of Mathematics (NCTM) issued *Curriculum and Evaluation Standards for School Mathematics,* which proposed dramatic changes in mathematics curriculum and instruction. The standards specify that mathematics instruction should involve hands-on experiences, calculators and computers, manipulatives, and cooperative learning groups. The curriculum should emphasize making connections between math topics, problem solving, and communicating about mathematics (Willis, 1992). Five broad goals in the standards address children's future mathematical needs (Steen, 1990, pp. 21–22):

1. To value mathematics;
2. To reason mathematically;
3. To communicate mathematics;
4. To solve problems; and
5. To develop confidence.

Students in the primary grades should have a better balance between arithmetic, geometry, and statistics. The curriculum should include such topics as estimation, measurement, exploration of data, and symmetry. Students should be involved as active participants in their own learning. They should be able to apply mathematical concepts and skills in finding solutions to real problems and situations.

In the next section we present a mathematics program for children from five to eight years, which incorporates the guidelines advocated by the National Council of

Teachers of Mathematics. We will state the goals for a developmentally appropriate mathematics program for five- to eight-year-olds, and then we will discuss how the environment and teacher support curriculum and instruction. Next we describe the organization of the mathematics program, including components of the curriculum. Finally, we present examples of activities from a quality mathematics program that represent the new directions of the *Curriculum and Evaluation Standards for School Mathematics.*

Planning the Mathematics Program

Goals for the Mathematics Program.

> The goal of the math program is to enable children to use math through exploration, discovery, and solving meaningful problems. Math activities are integrated with other relevant projects, such as science and social studies. Math skills are acquired through spontaneous play, projects, and situations of daily living. Teachers use the teachers' edition of the math textbook as a guide to structure learning situations and to stimulate ideas about interesting math projects. Many math manipulatives are provided and used. Interesting board and card, paper-and-pencil, and other kinds of games are used daily. Noncompetitive, impromptu oral "math stumper" and number games are played for practice (Bredekamp, 1987, p. 71).

The developmentally appropriate mathematics curriculum for ages five to eight just cited is from *Developmentally Appropriate Practice in Early Childhood Programs Serving Children from Birth through Age 8.* It describes a program that is child centered and connected to real, problem-solving activities. Children are active participants in constructing math schema based on experiences that incorporate concrete to abstract thinking. Mathematical knowledge is reconstructed by experiencing and acting on objects in the environment and the process of reflection and, later, logical thinking (Kamii, 1982).

The key to a quality program in mathematics is to design experiences that bridge preoperational into concrete operational thinking. A present danger in kindergarten and the primary grades is that children are pushed into abstract functioning before they have the cognitive capacity. They are asked to use mental schema for operations in mathematics before they are able to do so. It is common to see children in primary classrooms counting on their fingers as they solve written addition problems. These students still require concrete referents for solving addition problems because they have not internalized the concepts of addition as a mental process. Children should be allowed to move at their own pace with concrete materials, followed by paper and pencil practice when they are ready (Charlesworth & Lind, 1990).

The goals for the mathematics program are based on both the child's cognitive development and the elements of mathematics that are part of the overall components recommended by the National Council of Supervisors of Mathematics (1988). The goals of the mathematics program in kindergarten and the primary grades lead to competence in the larger goals of society and adult living in the next century. The twelve goals are as follows (Dutton & Dutton, 1991):

1. Problem solving
2. Communicating mathematical ideas
3. Mathematical reasoning
4. Applying mathematics of everyday situations
5. Being alert to the reasonableness of results
6. Estimating
7. Using appropriate computational skills
8. Algebraic thinking
9. Measuring
10. Understanding geometry
11. Understanding statistics
12. Using probability to determine the likelihood of future events

The Role of the Environment and the Teacher.   The classroom environment is organized so that children can investigate mathematics through many types of hands-on experiences. The arrangement must be conducive to individual, small-group, and whole-group activities. The areas designed for these types of activities in the language arts program are also suitable for the mathematics program. An important requirement is a work and play area for mathematics activities and materials. The mathematics area, sometimes combined with the science area, contains the many materials needed for investigation and practice of mathematical concepts.

The math center should be organized so that children can participate in different types of activities. Items such as objects for counting, construction materials, unifix cubes, and other multipurpose materials are accessible for ongoing use. Other materials are placed in the center for a particular unit of study or for thematic projects. For example, balance scales and objects to weigh and compare could be placed in a learning station during the study of measurement of weight. Books related to time and different types of clocks (wind-up clocks, digital clocks, sand timer, stove timer, etc.) could be organized in an area with specific problems suggested for investigation during a unit on measuring time.

Whereas kindergarten teachers may find the use of a mathematics center easy to coordinate with mathematics curriculum, primary teachers unfamiliar with using centers may have to systematically plan how to include concrete, real-life activities to work with concepts if the adopted basal program focuses on whole-group instruction and workbook practice. Developmentally appropriate activities using materials in the mathematics center should be developed to ensure experiences that will facilitate the child's construction of new concepts.

The teacher has a key role in developing the kinds of mathematical experiences that will fulfill the goals of a developmentally appropriate mathematics program. Two basic considerations guide the learning experiences: the developmental characteristics of the students and inclusion of the new standards set forth by the National Council of Teachers of Mathematics. To design developmentally appropriate curriculum and instruction, the teacher follows the developmentally appropriate practices provided through the NAEYC. The twelve components of essential mathematics proposed by the National Council of Supervisors of Mathematics also serve as guidelines for the kinds of experiences that should be planned by the teacher.

An understanding of the progressions of concrete to abstract, simple to complex, and experiencing to representing introduced in chapter 6 is particularly useful when applied to mathematics instruction with students who are moving from preoperational to concrete operational thinking. Teachers will want to design activities that facilitate these progressions to accommodate the nature of the child's cognitive processes. Figure 10.4 provides a model of how these progressions are used for compatibility with the child's cognitive development. The model shows how activities move from concrete to abstract. The modes of information processing reflect how children experience activities through the receptive mode and represent them through the expressive mode.

The teacher also has a responsibility to make decisions as to when to use systematic instruction and when informal, integrated, or real-life, meaningful activities are the most appropriate. Some of the curriculum and instruction that is planned will attend to the scope and sequence of instruction. The teacher will plan to introduce concepts that will build upon concepts already acquired or lay the foundation for future units of work. Systematic, teacher-directed instruction to provide students with hands-on experiences with concepts will follow a sequential plan to make mathematical knowledge meaningful and logical.

In the primary grades, the teacher would consider how to include concrete activities before abstract practice within systematic instruction. For example, when learning place value, students can work with wooden cubes of different colors to represent tens and ones before moving to a flip book with pictured representations of place value and a pencil-and-paper exercise on place value.

Informal, practical experiences encourage the child to apply mathematical concepts when working with realistic problems. For example, children in a first-grade

Type of Cognitive Interaction	Learning Interaction	Mode of Information Processing	
		Receptive	Expressive
Type 1: Concrete	*Concrete manipulations and/or pictorial representations.* Emphasis is on manipulation of actual objects to problem solve.	Seeing Listening Touching	Sorting Speaking Drawing
Type 2: Transitional	*Manipulation of concrete objects and/or their pictorial representations* Emphasis is on matching the abstract symbols (numerals) with the objects in the problem-solving process.	Reading Seeing Listening Touching	Writing Sorting Speaking Drawing
Type 3: Abstract	*Problem solving using abstract symbols (numerals)*	Reading Listening	Writing Speaking

Figure 10.4 Hierarchy of Mathematical Learning Methods
K. A. Schultz, R. P. Colarusso, & V. W. Strawderman, *Mathematics for Every Young Child.* (Merrill, 1989), p. 8. Used by permission of the publisher.

classroom using an adding machine or a calculator to add up purchases in a grocery store set up in the mathematics area would be learning real-life purposes for math. At the same time, they would be using technology used for mathematical problem solving in today's world.

Integrated, thematic units would also provide opportunities for applying mathematical concepts for useful purposes. Kindergarten children could use measurement when following a simple recipe in a unit on cooking. In a unit on field games, second-grade students could use a stop watch to measure the time individual students required to run a measured distance; then they could graph the time recorded.

In the next section we will describe the components of mathematics for kindergarten and the primary grades; then we will present suggestions for activities that promote the development of mathematical concepts. The teacher can include these components when organizing systematic and informal instruction with students in a nongraded primary school or in a self-contained classroom serving students of a single grade or age.

The Role of Technology in the Mathematics Program.   Calculators and computers are part of the young child's world. They are now a given resource in learning mathematics. Children should be introduced to these technological resources in the preschool years, and this equipment should be integrated into the mathematics curriculum for children from ages five to eight.

At age five, children would learn the importance of calculators through free play and exploration. Dutton and Dutton (1991, p. 91) propose that five-year-olds can also engage in the following:

1. Learning to display numbers 1 through 9 and clearing the display after each entry
2. Increasing numbers such as 5 or 6 by adding one to each number
3. Subtracting by taking away one number from a previous number
4. Beginning to enter two-digit numbers—first 10, and then 10 and one more

Thereafter, children should be able to extend their use of the calculator with whatever skills and concepts they have learned. Once children have learned how to use an operation, they can use the calculator to increase their speed and accuracy. Educators must also learn to use the calculator appropriately with children. It is a tool that can enhance mathematical abilities; however, it is not meant to replace the child's understanding of mathematical processes and how to apply them.

Computers also have an important role in the mathematics curriculum because every young child needs to become computer literate beginning at age three or four (Schultz, Colarusso, & Strawderman, 1989). Computer software for teaching mathematics is being developed at a rapid rate. In addition to the materials being developed by commercial companies, the U.S. Department of Education helps schools learn about innovative programs through the National Diffusion Network (NDN) (Dutton & Dutton, 1991).

Seymour Papert has pioneered the use of computers in mathematical and language literacy with young children. Papert (1980) believes that children can become programmers and learn to communicate through computers. Using his background study at Piaget's Center for Genetic Epistemology in Geneva, Switzerland, Papert developed the LOGO computer language to enable children to communicate with computers. The use of the "Turtle" with LOGO enables children to use manipulation to give commands to the computer.

The National Science Foundation (NSF) advocated the use of computers in *Educating America for the 21st Century* (National Science Foundation, 1983). The NSF stated that children should learn through computers, learn with computers, and use computers to learn about computers.

Clements (1987) reviewed the efficacy of using computers with young children. Among his findings were that although computers can enhance learning, they are not a panacea; they have the same benefit as other valuable learning strategies and materials. Clements made two critical points about children using computers for mathematics and problem solving. He proposed that (1) children should understand concepts before they use computers for practice and (2) the teacher must play an active role in mediating the child's interaction with the computer.

Another caution regards the selection of developmentally appropriate software for young children. Haugland and Shade (1988) found that much of the available software does not reflect a developmental approach to teaching and learning. Teachers should review and evaluate software carefully prior to using it with young children.

Calculators and computers are part of the future in mathematics instruction. Teachers of young children need to become competent in the use of these resources. In addition, they need training in how to incorporate these tools effectively in the mathematics program designed for young children.

Organizing the Mathematics Program

The mathematics program for kindergarten and the primary grades includes the categories of number and numeration, operations of whole numbers, rational numbers, measurement, geometry, and problem solving/mathematical reasoning. If the subcategories are included, the components would be similar to the following framework:

Number and Numeration
    One-to-one correspondence
    Counting
    Using numerals
    Ordering numbers
    Ordinal numbers
    Place value
    Reading and writing numerals

Operations of Whole Numbers
    Addition

Subtraction

Multiplication

Division

Rational Numbers

Odd and even numbers

Multiples and factors

Prime numbers

Fractions

Decimals

Measurement

Length

Width

Height

Weight

Volume

Time

Money

Geometry

Shapes

Patterns

Problem Solving/Mathematical Reasoning

Sorting

Classifying

Similarities and differences

Part–whole relationships

Making problems

Estimating

Making predictions

Finding data

Making patterns

These components of the program can be described in even more detail. As was mentioned earlier, children encounter and review concepts before they are introduced to more complex concepts and skills. The child must understand certain elements if more advanced levels are to be meaningful. Figure 10.5 presents a sug-

	Number and Numeration	Operations of Whole Numbers	Rational Numbers	Measurement	Geometry	Problem Solving/ Mathematical Reasoning
Five-year-olds	One-to-one correspondence Equivalent sets More than, less than Using numerals 1–10 Ordering, writing First, second, middle, last	joining and separating	odd and even numbers	<u>Money</u> penney nickle dime dollar <u>Time</u> sequence of time clock time school time <u>Length</u> shortest, longest nonstandard and standard units — <u>Weight</u> thickness	<u>Shape</u> square bonding triangle curve circle (open and closed) cube <u>Patterns</u> matching completing making	Sorting and classifying, observing, predicting Sorting by property Finding a common property Forming subsets Making problems Estimating Making predictions
Six-year-olds	Set and subset Count 1–20 Write numerals to 10 Count by 2s, 5s, 10s to 100 Number lines Ordering numbers to 100 Place value up to 3 digits Ordinal numbers 1st through 5th	<u>Additions</u> addends up to 4 addends up to 6 addend double up to 10+10 associativity for addition <u>Subtraction</u> 1–5, 6–10, 11–18 two digits without regrouping Commutative property of multiplication Commutative property of division	multiples and factors primes and compounds with shapes fractions 1/2, 1/4, equal parts	<u>Length</u> ruler yardstick standard units <u>Time</u> clock faces hour, half hour kinds of clocks — <u>Money</u> coins bills <u>Measured Weight</u> balance beam scales <u>Capacity</u> liquid pint gallon dry quart	<u>Shape</u> converting areas finding shapes shapes in patterns perimeter around shapes <u>Patterns</u> figure patterns number patterns (row, column, diagonal)	Similarities and differences Identify attributes and nonattributes Use of more than one attribute Part–whole relations

Figure 10.5 Components of the Mathematics Program: Ages Five to Eight (pp.

	Number and Numeration	Operations of Whole Numbers	Rational Numbers	Measurement		Geometry	Problem Solving/ Mathematical Reasoning
Seven-year-olds	Ordering of numbers 1–1000 Place value up to 4 digits (ones, tens, hundreds) Odd and even numbers Ordinal numbers 1st through 10th Reading and writing numerals	Addition sums through 10 sums through 18 two digit three digit Column addition two digit and three digit with regrouping understand algorithm three and four digit columns	least common multiples greatest common factor fractions 1/2, 1/4, 1/3 decimals	Measurement length width height units of measuring weight Time hours, quarter hours, time intervals calendar	Money coins bills simple change adding and subtracting	Shape area: surface, closed corners, lines, space, plane figures symmetry Patterns number patterns rhythms practical uses	Cause and effect of changing numbers Explain answers Develop new strategies Find data, make word problems Make patterns

Figure 10.5 Components of the Mathematics Program: Ages Five to Eight *(continued)*

	Number and Numeration	Operations of Whole Numbers	Rational Numbers	Measurement	Geometry	Problem Solving/ Mathematical Reasoning
Eight-year-olds	Place value up to 5 digits Round off to nearest 10s, 100s, 1000s Estimation Ordinal numbers 1st through 12th Roman numerals	Subtraction from 10 from 18 two digit three digit two and three digit with regrouping three and four digit Multiplication multiples of 2, 3, 4, 5 factors in multiplying 2, 3, 4, 5 use of zero basic facts multiplying by 10s relation to addition two digit by one digit understanding algorithm Division basic facts by 2–3, 4–5, 6–9 relation to multiplication estimation quotients understanding algorithm	fractions 1/2, 1/4, 1/3, 1/8, 1/6 parts of regions, sets reading and writing decimals comparing decimals adding and subtracting with like denominations adding and subtracting with unlike denominations	Time hour, half hour, minute temperature linear: line segment, inches, feet volume-nonstandard capacity-unit of measure weight-unit of measure Money coins bills decimal for cents making change	Solids plane figures congruent shapes lines of symmetry	finding data estimating, checking two-step

gested mathematics program for kindergarten and primary-age children. It illustrates the spiral, or continuous, nature of the curriculum. More complexity is introduced at each succeeding age level, building on what is already known. It should be remembered that the age levels and sequential nature of the curriculum are guidelines only. The children may need to use a skill or mathematical strategy in a problem-solving situation where the teacher must introduce the relevant information and work with the students so that they can apply it for their purposes outside the order in which it might normally be introduced.

The mathematics program as described in Figure 10.5 is more of a guide to the hierarchical nature of mathematics than a prescriptive sequence that dictates what should be taught at an age or grade level. Teachers and children will progress through the curriculum based on the abilities and interests of the class. Moreover, in an ungraded or multilevel school organization pattern, children can work on the same objective at different age and ability levels through cooperative learning groups or paired student interactions. The teacher needs to understand the nature of the scope and sequence of the curriculum, however, so that planning for systematic and informal, integrated curriculum will include the content and types of experiences students will need to meet the NCTM standards.

Designing Curriculum for the Mathematics Program

When designing curriculum for kindergarten and primary classrooms, the teacher considers whether the activity will be a part of a teacher-directed lesson, a center opportunity, an assignment for a cooperative learning group, a whole-class investigation, or a game to be selected by a pair or small group of learners. The activities that follow are but a small representative example of some of the activities a teacher can design for young students. The activities are drawn from different components of the curriculum for different levels of complexity. Because some of the activities can be adapted for either more complexity or more simplicity, they are not identified by age or grade level.

Experiences That Promote Mathematics

Counting Games

Math component: Number and numeration

Description: Children can make games for game boards. Introduce them to a game that involves a spinner and numbered cards in a deck. Discuss how counting is used to play the game and determine the winner. Solicit suggestions for different themes that could be used for a counting game, as well as what will be needed for the game. Have pairs of students or cooperative groups come up with a game idea, make the game, and play it several times. Laminate the games to be put into the mathematics center.

Materials needed: Large sheets of paper or tagboard; marking pens; spinners or cards; game pieces

Domino Doubles Addition

Math component: Operations of whole numbers

Description: Teach the children how to play a simple version of dominoes, where they draw the dominoes and take turns attempting to make matches of number patterns. When they are able to make a match, have them make a larger set using the combined numbers with counting objects.

Materials needed: Dominoes; objects for making sets

Numeral Treasure Hunt

Math component: Number and numeration

Description: Divide the class into cooperative groups. Discuss how they can search for examples of numerals around the school and outdoors. Have each group tour the school environment and record as many examples of numerals as they can during a fifteen-minute period. When the activity has been completed, have each group report the numerals they found. The group with the most examples is the winner of the activity. Discuss why the numerals were needed in each example.

Materials needed: Pencils and notepads to record data

Number Bingo

Math component: Number and numeration

Description: Make assorted bingo cards with sixteen numerals ranging from 1 to 20 or higher. Use a set of cards with dots corresponding to all of the possible numerals on the cards. The game is played by having the students in a small group take turns drawing a card. They must determine which numeral matches their card and whether they have that numeral on their bingo card. The first player to make a horizontal or vertical line is the winner.

Odd and Even

Math component: Rational numbers

Description: Give pairs of students a small handful of counters, such as beans or poker chips. The goal of the activity is for the students to decide whether they have an odd or even number of objects. Ask the students to divide the objects between them. Then ask them to report whether they have an odd number or even number of items and justify why they came to the answer. They should be able to respond based on whether they have the same or different numbers of items.

Materials needed: Counting objects

Container Multiplication

Math component: Operations of whole numbers

Description: Collect a group of containers such as berry baskets or juice cans and counting objects such as sticks, crayons, cubes, or other objects. Select up to five cans. Ask a child to put the same number of items in each can, either two or three items. Demonstrate how the child can add the number of items in each can to get a total or multiply them to get the same total. For example, if four containers are used and three counters are put in the can, the child can add 3 plus 3 plus 3 plus 3 equals 12 or can multiply 4 times 3 equals 12. Repeat the activity several times using different combinations. Let the children make the addition and multiplication sentence for each combination. The activity can be made either simple or complex, depending on the abilities and experiences of the students.

Materials needed: Containers such as berry baskets or juice cans; counting objects

Egg Carton Division

Math component: Operation of whole numbers

Description: Use egg cartons with a dozen plastic eggs. The students will divide the eggs into equivalent groups and determine the appropriate division sentence. For example, the students might be asked to make the eggs into groups of three, four, or six. Ask them to determine how many groups of each total twelve. Demonstrate how a division expression can be written to describe the number of smaller sets in twelve. For example, 12 divided by 3 equals 4,etc.

Materials needed: Egg cartons; plastic eggs for each carton

Sand Buckets

Math component: Measuring

Description: Have students put varying amounts of sand in sand pails or other containers. Use measuring cups to measure how many cups of sand are in each container. Have the children measure fractions of a cup to the nearest half cup. As a follow-up have the students graph the measured amounts.

Materials needed: Sand buckets or other containers; measuring cups; pencils; paper; sand

Sorting Solid Shapes

Math components: Geometry; Problem solving

Description: Give students an array of solid shapes. Ask them to sort the shapes by some attribute. Have the students compare individual sorting criteria. Ask them to identify how the solid shapes are used for practical purposes in the environment.

Materials needed: Enough solid shapes for several children to have at least five

 Shape Symmetry

Math components: Shapes; Symmetry

Description: Give the students an array of two-dimensional shapes cut from paper, or have them trace a variety of common shapes, triangles, squares, circles, rectangles, ovals, etc. Ask the students to fold the shapes in half so that each shape has two equal sides. Define the term *symmetrical,* and ask the students to explain how their shapes are symmetrical. As a follow-up activity, ask the students to think of things in the environment that are symmetrical (e.g. butterflies, the human body, books, etc.).

Materials needed: Paper shapes; scissors

 Shape Fractions

Math components: Shapes; Rational numbers

Description: Use the same shapes as for the previous activity. Have the students determine how the shape has been divided into two equal parts, or into halves. Introduce the fraction one-half. Have the students divide the shapes once again so that there are four parts. Discuss the fraction one-quarter. Ask the students to show you one-half of the shape and one-quarter of the shape.

Materials needed: Paper shapes; scissors

Accommodating Learning Differences among Students

Special attention has been given to the need for curriculum and instruction that is developmentally appropriate in mathematics, especially in ensuring that learning experiences include the progression from concrete to abstract. This is especially relevant when working with children who are developmentally delayed or have cognitive-ability handicaps. Children who are delayed will not have made the transition from preoperational into concrete operational thinking. As a result, the teacher will need to assess the child's developmental status and design curriculum experiences based on development rather than on chronological grade or age.

Another difficulty children encounter occurs when asked to apply a concept without first having developed the necessary understanding of the concept. This can happen whether or not students have a learning disability. Students may be taught how to execute a mathematical operation without acquiring the underlying concept. The result is that when the child needs to use the concept in a real-life situation, problem-solving strategies cannot be applied to the concept. For example, a student may have learned the mechanics of simple division and completed many practice exercises. However, when asked how many loaves of bread can be purchased for $3.00, the child does not understand how division can be used to find the answer.

Children with learning differences may have difficulties in processing or expressing information about mathematics. Young children may have difficulty in expressing their mathematical understanding verbally because they lack the expressive vocabulary to describe the mathematical knowledge. Children whose first language is not English or who are otherwise limited in the ability to speak English may experience frustration when asked to use verbal responses. They need to have nonverbal opportunities to point to or manipulate objects to express their ability to use a concept.

A child may lack the motor skills to perform paper-and-pencil tasks to express mathematical knowledge or skills. The child may be delayed in fine motor skills or have difficulty with reversals. Instead of concluding that the child is unable to understand the mathematical process being studied, the teacher needs to determine whether the written expression required is causing the child's difficulty in responding appropriately.

Some young children experience receptive problems; that is, they cannot understand oral discussions of a concept or have difficulty in attending to printed information. Children may have difficulty discriminating between figure and ground on the printed page, which results in difficulty attending to and interpreting visual information.

Many children who experience receptive and expressive difficulties in mathematics will overcome the problem over time. They have a temporary delay that normal development will eliminate. For other young children, the difficulty is more permanent. The teacher will need to be alert to the child's learning differences and find alternative avenues to facilitate the child's ability to acquire mathematical concepts and express understanding (Schultz, Colarusso, & Strawderman, 1989).

CURRICULUM FOR SCIENCE

The science curriculum for ages five to eight continues to build on the experiences children had in the preschool years. Unlike mathematics, which has sequential characteristics, science is holistic in nature. The child is continually encountering information about the world and adding to his or her schema, or store of knowledge. Children's natural interest and curiosity makes them avid explorers of scientific phenomena during these years.

How Young Children Learn about Science

The science curriculum can be predominantly child centered and child initiated because knowledge is acquired best through firsthand investigation and experimentation. A requirement for preoperational and concrete operational thinking, an understanding of science should be approached from hands-on study at all ages. The nature of the child's thinking in each of these stages has implications for how the science program is planned.

Preoperational children of ages five and six learn about science within their cognitive limitations. Because they cannot mentally reason about concepts, they must carry out actions to understand their importance. But even with concrete actions, their perceptions limit their understanding. For example, even though a child can pour a container of liquid into vessels of two different shapes, he or she is influenced by the appearance of a change in quantity and does not understand that the quantity remains the same. Children are also affected by their level of egocentricity. They focus on their own view of events and can address only one aspect of a situation at a time.

Five- and six-year-olds cannot anticipate results or consequences of future actions. This limits their ability to predict what they have not yet experienced. The question, "What do you think might happen if . . .?" is very difficult for them to grasp. Likewise, this limitation makes it difficult for children to link cause and effect or see a pattern in a series of events. The science curriculum for preoperational children should be composed of firsthand experience and exploration of objects. Harlen (1985, p. 129) recommends that activities for preoperational children include the following:

1. Looking, handling, using other senses on material collected and displayed in the classroom
2. Collecting things and sorting
3. Trying things out
4. Making things, particularly models, that in some way 'work'
5. Taking things apart and reconstructing them
6. Talking about what has been observed and sometimes recording the narrative in pictures and models and in words
7. Discussing ideas and trying to think of explanations for things that have been noticed

As children make the transition from preoperational to concrete operational thinking, they can use thought instead of, or in addition to, action to approach their understanding of science. They can grasp the entirety of a process, as well as the individual parts or steps. They are able to understand how more than one variable or characteristic of a phenomenon can affect an outcome, and they begin to understand another person's viewpoint or physical perspective of an event or object. Because the transition to concrete operational thinking is gradual, the ability to use rational thinking is first possible with familiar concepts and information. The more complex a problem or situation, the less likely it is that the child will be able to use rational thinking to reach a solution. Physical manipulation of the information will be needed.

Children in the primary grades also bring developing literacy and social skills to the science curriculum. They can use numbers and written words to express their reflections on science investigations. They can extend their period of work and collaborate with their peers in taking turns, making predictions, and discussing their findings (Charlesworth & Lind, 1990).

As a result of acquiring these new competencies, the possibilities for working with science concepts can be expanded. Children can now gain information from books, films, and other, more abstract, resources. They can also learn that they can make a change during an investigation and understand how their action affected a result. Harlen (1985, p. 132) suggests that children in the primary grades can benefit from the following elements:

1. A wider range of objects and events to observe and relate to their existing experience
2. Tasks that require close observation of detail and sequence of events
3. Investigations of the effect on some object or system of changing a variable systematically, keeping other things the same
4. Tasks that require a search for patterns or relations in observations
5. Problems that demand fair comparisons between objects or materials
6. Encouragement to try to explain how things work
7. Having expectations of finding answers to their own questions by systematic and controlled investigation, rather than just "doing something and seeing what happens"

Trends and Issues in Science

Concern about the low quality of science curriculum in U.S. schools has been expressed for many years. The criticism about poor science instruction includes comments about elementary school science programs. Numerous reports on science education have described the curriculum used in the 1980s to be obsolete. Allan Bromley, science adviser to President Bush, declared, "In a great many cases, precollege education in the past decade has been literally perpetuating a fraud on the younger generation" (Bromley, 1989, p. 203).

Bromley's observation was supported by the 1986 study of school science conducted by the National Assessment of Education Progress (NAEP) (Mullis & Jenkins, 1988). Not only did U.S. students perform more poorly than students from other countries, but girls lagged behind boys, and black and Hispanic students' performance was lower than that of their white peers.

The poor quality of science instruction at the elementary level had been reported earlier. Dueschl (1983) reported that science instruction at the elementary level was infrequent and ineffective. Causes of poor science instruction had been attributed by elementary teachers to inadequate background in science, inadequate time and space, and inadequate science equipment (Hove, 1970); researchers in the late 1980s felt little had changed since these conditions were reported (Tilgner, 1990).

In 1987, the National Science Teachers Association (NSTA) developed criteria for excellence that addressed the requirements for a quality science program for students, curriculum, instruction, and teachers in kindergarten through third grade. Cliatt and Shaw (1992, p. 14) summarized the characteristics of an exemplary science program as follows:

Students

Acquire effective health habits

Recognize people's relationship to the environment

Bring varied resources to problem solving

Curriculum

Provides planned programs for all students, emphasizing hands-on learning

Presents knowledge and experiences that students can apply to their lives now and in the future

Instruction

Offers many problem-solving activities applicable to the daily life of students

Provides enough materials for all students to conduct experiments

Integrates science into other content areas on a regular basis

Teachers

Learn new methods and ideas for implementing them

Provide varied experiences with the content, processes, and other dimensions of science

Provide experiences from many sources, including the life, physical, and environmental sciences; technology; and current community and societal problems

The National Science Foundation funded an effort to reform science education in U.S. elementary and secondary schools. *Project 2061* suggests implementing four common themes—materials, energy, information, and systems—that are introduced in kindergarten and studied throughout the school years (Tilgner, 1990). This project and other efforts to improve science curriculum seek to meet the criteria of an exemplary science program proposed by the National Science Teachers Association. In the following sections we describe a science curriculum for kindergarten and primary grades that reflects a developmental approach, and we review the criteria for excellence just described.

Planning the Science Program

Goals for the Science Program. The main goal for the science program for children ages five to eight is to help children understand the world around them. To accomplish this major goal, three subgoals should be met: children should understand the ideas or concepts of science; they should acquire science process skills; and they should establish certain attitudes about science. Before a child can gain an understanding of science concepts, however, the following three objectives of the science program must be met (Harlen & Jelly, 1989, p. 7). Children should learn

1. What the characteristics of things (living and nonliving) are and how these characteristics can be used to classify and label things;
2. How things work or interact with other things; and
3. What is needed to change something from one position, state, or form to another

The way in which children learn about their world involves the use of the science process, including observing, classifying and comparing, measuring, communicating, experimenting, and relating, inferring, or applying. In chapter 7 we described the science process in terms of preschool experiences. In this chapter we will discuss the process in terms of curriculum for five- to eight-year-old children.

Incorporating the Science Process.   The science program for young children is designed around the science process. Whether students are engaging in a single experience or conducting a series of experiences for a broader topic, some or all of the process skills may be applied. Figure 10.6 explains the process skills as they apply to kindergarten and primary-grade children.

One example of a science activity is a nature walk to observe plants. Two science processes that children will use are observing and communicating. On the walk, the students will use observation skills to explore the variety of plants in the immediate environment. Upon returning to the classroom, they can communicate their thoughts on their observations by discussing, drawing pictures, or writing about their findings.

A longer project to study seeds can incorporate more process skills. Students can classify types of seeds and plants and observe progress of growth. They can predict which seeds will have the largest plants; measure plant growth and control variables

1. *Observing.* Using the senses to gather information.

2. *Comparing.* Looking at similarities and differences in real objects. In the primary grades, students begin to compare and contrast ideas and concepts.

3. *Classifying.* Grouping and sorting according to categories, such as size, shape, color, use, and so on.

4. *Measuring.* Quantitative descriptions made by an observer either directly through observation or indirectly with an instrument.

5. *Communication.* Communicating ideas, directions, and descriptions orally or in written form such as pictures, maps, graphs, or journals so others can understand what you mean.

6. *Inferring.* Based on observations but suggests more meaning about a situation than can be directly observed. When children infer, they recognize patterns and expect these patterns to recur under similar circumstances.

7. *Predicting.* Making reasonable guesses or estimations based on observations or data.

8. *Hypothesizing.* Formal conditional statements about a phenomenon being investigated. The typical form of a hypothesis: if . . . then . . . . For a primary child an example would be: If water is put in the freezer overnight, then it freezes.

9. *Defining and controlling variables.* Determining which variables in an investigation should be studied or controlled to conduct a controlled experiment. For example, when we find out if a plant grows in the dark, we must also grow a plant in the light.

Figure 10.6   Science Process Skills

R. Charlesworth & K. K. Lind, *Math and Science for Young Children.* (Delmar, 1990), p. 48. Used by permission of the publisher.

by varying the amount of moisture and light that plants will receive; and observe the effect on the plants. Teacher and students should consciously plan to use science process skills and actively think about the components of the process as they are incorporated into science curriculum experiences.

The Role of the Environment

A quality science program requires a large amount of storage space. The classroom science center will need to have adequate space for small groups and individuals to be able to conduct investigations and other science activities. The center will need to have a number of locations where materials can be stored. Table tops, bulletin boards, and storage cabinet surfaces will be needed for exhibits, projects that are in progress, and permanent components of the science program, such as pets, terraria, aquaria, and insect cages. Not to be forgotten are the essential elements needed for science activities: natural light, a source of water, electricity, and reference materials.

Rotating science materials will be a frequent task for the teacher and students. As materials are brought to the classroom, they are made available for examination and exploration. When work is completed for a thematic unit, materials and equipment that are no longer needed are returned to storage to be replaced by items needed for new topics of study.

With the various types of activities that may be occurring at the same time, careful planning is necessary for traffic flow and management of different types of activities. Display areas should be separated from working areas. Storage facilities should be located in an area that is accessible for the appropriate activities.

The science center requires a management plan. Hands-on activities will require that students know how to use science equipment and materials safely. Procedures for conducting investigations and appropriate behaviors to use when working in the center should be clearly understood and observed by the students. Planned activities should be reviewed to determine whether they can be conducted independently or whether adult guidance or supervision is required (Cliatt & Shaw, 1992).

The teacher will need additional storage beyond what is available in the center. If the teacher is fortunate enough to have a storage closet, materials and equipment should be organized and stored in clearly labeled containers. A school resource area may be available at many sites, but teachers frequently find themselves transporting needed items back and forth from home when space for storage is not available at the school.

Teachers will also need to plan ahead to acquire materials needed for classroom science activities. Much of the permanent equipment will be supplied by the school as part of classroom resources. Materials can also be salvaged from home and recycled for the classroom. Parents are frequently helpful in locating free and low-cost materials. If newsletters are sent home well ahead of the implementation of science activities, parents can save and send needed items to the teacher.

Not to be overlooked is the outdoor environment as a natural resource for science experiences. Many investigations can easily be transported outdoors, where there is room to move about. Of course, some activities should be conducted outdoors only. Many times, commercial resources present science activities in an artificial format; such activities could be better learned by going outside and experiencing things firsthand. For example, a lesson on different types of clouds accompanied by pictures is a poor substitute for observing clouds over a period of days or weeks until all types of clouds have been observed.

The Role of the Teacher

The teacher is actively involved as a guide, respondent, and facilitator in implementing the science curriculum. When children are engaged in observation, investigation, and experimentation, the teacher observes and questions as the children conduct the activity. As observer, the teacher determines when children need additional resources or would benefit from responding to careful questioning.

The teacher also needs to anticipate the kind of time and grouping that is required for science activities. At times, children should pursue their own interests individually; at other times, a cooperative group effort will enhance learning opportunities. Prior to whole-class or teacher-directed activities, the teacher will want to plan demonstrations or otherwise prepare students for a science activity. The teacher needs to be aware of

Role	Purposes
Providing the materials, time, and physical arrangement for children to study and interact with things from their environment	For children to have the evidence of their own senses, to raise questions, to find answers to them by doing things, to have concrete experience as a basis for their thinking, and to be able to check ideas they develop against the behavior of real things
Designing tasks that encourage discussion among small groups of children	For children to combine their ideas, to listen to others, to argue about differences, and to refine their own ideas through explaining them to others
Discussing with children as individuals and in small groups	For children to explain how they arrive at their ideas; for teachers to listen, to find out the evidence children have gathered and how they have interpreted it, to encourage children to check findings, and to review their activities and results critically
Organizing whole-class discussions	For children to have the opportunity to describe their findings and ideas to others, to hear about others' ideas, to comment on alternative views and to defend their own; for teachers to offer ideas and direct children to sources that will extend the children's ideas
Teaching the techniques of using equipment and conventions of using graphs, tables, charts, and symbols	For children to have available the means to increase the accuracy of their observations and to choose appropriate forms for communication as the need arises
Providing books, displays, visits, visitors, and access to other sources of information	For children to be able to compare their ideas with those of others, to have access to information that may help them to develop and extend their ideas, to raise questions that may lead to further inquiry

Figure 10.7   The Teacher's Role in Science Experiences
W. Harlen, *Teaching and Learning Primary Science.* (Teachers College, 1985), p. 159. Used by permission of the publisher.

which process skills will facilitate students acquiring knowledge from activities and must guide them accordingly on how to use the skills in the procedures they will follow. If rules or policies need to be established, the teacher needs to make sure that the children understand how to proceed before the activity begins. The teacher's role has been charted in terms of components and processes of skill development. Figure 10.7 outlines the role of the teacher in different kinds of student activities.

Organizing the Science Program

Components of the Science Program.   The world of science offers unlimited possibilities for organizing the science program. In the large field of biological and physical sciences, the teacher has many interesting topics from which to select. Seefeldt and Barbour (1990) suggest that science topics should be selected from the ideas students are most interested in and closest to. They also caution that there needs to be a balance between biological and physical sciences, because children tend to be more interested in biological topics.

Public school teachers are likely to have a basal science program adopted by the school district. If the teacher is free to develop the curriculum, the basal program may be used as a resource. The components of the science program for kindergarten developed by D. C. Heath (Barufaldi, Ladd, & Moses, 1984) included topics in both biological and physical sciences. The components of *Heath Science* (Level K) are as follows:

UNIT I: LEARNING ABOUT OURSELVES
Chapter A: You and Me

Chapter B: The Five Senses

Chapter C: Using the Senses to Learn About Cooking

UNIT II: THE WORLD AROUND US
Chapter A: Plants

Chapter B: Animals

Chapter C: Habitat

Chapter D: The Physical World

UNIT III: OBJECTS AND MATERIALS
Chapter A: Sorting and Classifying with Attribute Blocks

Chapter B: Sequencing with Pattern Blocks

Chapter C: Sense of Touch

Chapter D: Quantifying with Cubes

Chapter E: Exploring with Magnets

Chapter F: Investigating the Properties of Sand and Water

Chapter G: Comparing Weight

The teacher may look to other resources for components of the science program. The *Windows on Science Program* (Westley, 1988) is a hands-on, ungraded science program developed for children from prekindergarten through second grade. The program consists of six resource books that include topics in both biological and physical sciences: *Seeds and Weeds; Insects and Other Crawlers; Rocks, Sand, and Soil; Water and Ice; Constructions;* and *Light, Color, and Shadows.* Each book has twenty-eight investigations, called Windows. This program can be used either as the framework for a science program or as a resource.

Teachers may wish to select and develop their own topics. In *Helping Children Explore Science* (Cliatt & Shaw, 1992), a sourcebook for children ages four to eight, the authors suggest nine major topics: (1) the human body; (2) animals; (3) plants; (4) nature; (5) the earth and its weather; (6) space; (7) water, air, and light; (8) heat, sound, and machines; and (9) magnets and electricity. Each category has subtopics and suggested activities for investigation.

It should be obvious that the possibilities for selecting topics and organ...
science program are open ended. There are topics that children will want to ...
that may not have been addressed in any of the resources discussed here. The
important consideration is that the science program be structured in such a way that
the children are empowered through hands-on, child-directed experiences to be the
active learners along with the teacher. Equally important is the nature of local or
regional science opportunities that occur as a result of climate and geography.
Children will be more interested in science experiences that directly relate to where
they live. Lindberg summarized the ultimate goal as "students experiencing the
process of science while they sought to answer questions *they* wanted to know the
answers to, discovering in the process that science was something you *do*"
(Lindberg, 1990, p. 80).

Designing Curriculum for the Science Program

The science curriculum just described is organized as a content area; that is, the
activities are focused on the teaching of science concepts. Various types of activities
from other content areas may be included in the range of experiences, but the predominant focus is on learning science.

A significant alternative method is to design the curriculum within thematic topics,
where all content areas are equally important to the exploration and knowledge is

ı the thematic experiences. Science concepts are learned within the
xt of the unit theme. Growth in all content areas through integrated, the-
riences is the major goal of the curriculum. Through this process, the child
understand the connections in learning and the holistic nature of learning
₂ world.

curriculum activities presented next reflect these two approaches. The first
includes individual activities that can be used with any age group from five to
We will explain a variety of interesting activities from science topics. The sec-
section of science curriculum will be representative of science integrated with
other content areas. We will describe examples of science units that are based on a
theme or special topic in science.

Experiences That Promote Science

Dried Apples

Science topic: Plants

Science processes used: Observation, predicting, communicating, inferring

Description: Have students peel apples with a potato peeler, remove the core,
and slice the apples. String the slices in bright sunlight and observe them over a
period of time as they dry. When the children sample dry apple slices, have them
slice a fresh apple and compare them for color, texture, and taste.

Materials needed: Apples; potato peelers; knives; string (Barufaldi, Ladd, &
Moses, 1984)

Comparing Seeds

Science topic: Plants

Science processes used: Predicting, classifying, inferring

Description: Collect a variety of fruits, such as apples, pears, peaches, cherries,
melons, and strawberries. Cut open the fruit and have the children locate and
describe the seeds. Have them compare the number and type of seeds and where
they are located on or in the fruit.

Materials needed: Fruits of several types; knives; paper plates or paper towels

Seed Collections

Science topic: Plants

Science processes used: Collecting data, classifying, communicating

Description: Take a nature walk in the fall to collect seeds. Give each child a
shopping bag and have the children collect as many different seeds as they can find.

Have the children work in small groups to compare the types of seeds they found for similarities and differences. Combine all of the seeds in each group and ask the children to group the seeds from each type of plant together. Let each pick a seed to describe. As an extension of the activity, children could count and graph the number of seeds they found for six or seven types of seeds.

Materials needed: Shopping bags; large paper; marking pens for graphing

Bug Models

Science topic: Animals (insects)

Science processes used: Observing, identifying, communicating

Description: Use collected insects to encourage children to make model representations. Let the children examine the insects in an insect cage or small jar. Provide magnifying glasses for examination of the insect's body parts. Encourage the children to make a model of the insect using play dough and scrap materials. Upon completion, the children can explain their model or write about the insect and their model.

Materials needed: Play dough; scrap materials; insects; paper and pencils (Westley, 1988)

Bark Rubbings

Science topic: Plants

Science processes used: Observing, communicating

Description: Following a discussion about trees, tree parts, and the characteristics of bark, take children out to observe the bark of different trees. Give each child a large piece of paper and a large beginner's crayon. Have the child choose the tree for a rubbing. Attach the paper to the tree and show the child how to use the side of the crayon to make the rubbing. Children can compare the completed drawings and discuss the comparisons of the trees.

Materials needed: Large sheets of paper; wax crayons (Richards, 1989)

Watching Shadows

Science topic: Light and shadows

Science processes used: Observing, experimenting, inferring

Description: Children are interested in shadows. They can trace the movement of the sun and earth and describe the way shadows are affected. Take them out several times during a sunny day and let them compare the size and directions of the shadows. Let them experiment with different objects and the shadows they can make.

Materials needed: None

Making Shadows

Science topic: Light and shadows

Science processes used: Observing, experimenting, inferring

Description: Children can experiment with shadows indoors. Project a strong light on a white wall or newsprint. Encourage the children to experiment with the shadows they can make with their bodies. Encourage them to make puppets out of paper taped to a Popsicle stick or attached to their fingers. Show the children how to vary the types of shadows they can make by varying the distance between the light and the wall.

Materials needed: Light; white surface on a wall; paper; scissors; tape; Popsicle sticks

Introduction to Magnets

Science topic: Magnets

Science processes used: Observing, experimenting, inferring

Description: Give each child a magnet. Place a collection of small objects, both metal and nonmetal, on the table. Let the children experiment with the objects that are attracted to the magnet. Have the children sort the objects into two piles: those that are attracted by the magnet and those that are not attracted by the magnet. Encourage the children to hypothesize why objects are attracted to a magnet.

Materials needed: Magnets; small classroom objects

Integrated Experiences That Promote Science

The science activities described in the previous section can be meaningful in themselves or used as part of a series of activities to explore a broader concept. Science is meaningful in a more comprehensive manner when experiences are correlated with other content areas. Moreover, science can be a starting point for cross-disciplinary curriculum. Science is excellent as the core of integrated curriculum because children love science as a content area, it lends itself to involvement and hands-on activities, and all subject areas are enhanced by the thinking skills used with the science processes. Figure 10.8 illustrates how Mechling and Kepler (1991) charted science process skills used across the curriculum.

A unit on studying the September harvest moon demonstrates how a science topic can be the focus of a unit that integrates science across the curriculum. Students observe the cycle of one new moon to another during the period of one month. They observe and sketch the moon each night to record its phases. In a second activity, the students compare the sizes of the rising full moon with its appear-

PROCESS SKILLS *ACROSS* THE CURRICULUM
Read left to right and see how process skills are used across the curriculum.

Science	Reading	Math	Social Science
Classifying	Comparing and contrasting characteristics	Sorting, sequencing	Comparing ideas
Collecting data	Taking notes	Collecting data	Collecting data
Interpreting data	Organizing facts, recognizing cause and effect	Analyzing	Interpreting data
Communicating results	Logically arranging information	Graphing, constructing tables	Making maps
Predicting	Predicting	Predicting	Predicting

Figure 10.8   Integrating Science Process Skills
K. R. Mechling & L. E. Kepler, "Start with Science." *Instructor* (March 1991), p. 37.

ance higher in the sky by tracing the moon on a paper held up to a window. To extend the understanding of the significance of the moon, for social studies students can study historical lore connecting the phases of the moon to weather changes; for art they can conduct a nighttime art project by the light of the moon; and for math they can compare how the moon's different gravitational force would affect the weight of objects. These are but some of the many activities that can be designed to make a study of the moon more interesting and informative (Kepler, 1991).

INTEGRATING CURRICULUM IN LANGUAGE ARTS, MATHEMATICS, AND SCIENCE

An integrated unit designed for first grade originated with children's literature. *If You Give a Mouse a Cookie*, by Laura Joffe Numeroff, was used as the focus for a unit on mice. As part of the science content, students observed and measured a mouse. They wrote their own mouse stories for a book in language arts and discussed the kinds of food that mice like to eat. Many of the activities designed for the unit integrated several areas of the curriculum. The Summary of Activities section of their unit, presented next, gives a description of the activities. (See Appendix C for the complete unit and lesson plans.)

Summary of Activities

1. Mouse observation. Both language arts and science are integrated in this activity of observing a real mouse. Children will be using the language arts skills of listening and answering questions, along with following directions. Science will be experienced through observing the different characteristics of the mouse and classifying differences and similarities between a real mouse and a fictional one.

2. Mice puppets. Integration of language arts, social studies, and art can be experienced through this activity of creating mice puppets. The children will be using their language arts skills of listening and following directions. Social studies will be represented through cooperation and sharing by the children. The art activity will include drawing and coloring the mice and gluing them on paper bags. Theater arts can be incorporated through play acting *If You Give a Mouse a Cookie.*

3. Mouse shapes and sizes. This activity integrates art, math, science, and language arts. The art activity involves drawing different sizes and shapes of mice. Students use math when they measure the different mice and compare them with real mice. Science is incorporated through measuring and predicting.

4. Mouse story. This activity involves dictating a mouse story to the teacher and drawing pictures to illustrate the story. It integrates language arts and fine arts.

5. Mouse party. This activity integrates health and physical education, social studies, music, and mathematics. Nutrition is studied through the different foods brought to the mouse party. Movement and music are experienced as children sing and dance to mouse songs. Art is involved in making the costumes and decorations for the party. Social studies is incorporated through a discussion of proper party manners, and math is integrated when measuring different ingredients for the mouse food.

Summary

In this chapter we described the curriculum in language arts, mathematics, and science suitable for children from age five to eight. At these ages, children are in a transitional period; the curriculum also undergoes a transition. Children are making the transition from the preoperational period to the concrete operational period in the later early childhood years. They are also making a transition from preschool into elementary school. The curriculum is transitional in language arts, as literacy becomes well established in most children by the time they are eight years old and in the third grade. Mathematics and science curricula also are designed to complement the emerging literacy and cognitive abilities of the children.

Although acquisition of literacy is a major accomplishment during this period, children also continue to add to and refine their ability to speak. Oral language development is important in continuing the language foundation needed to acquire and use concepts and apply them to written language. Therefore, the curriculum in kindergarten and primary grades includes emphasis on oral language development.

Children who have special language needs particularly need attention to language development. Whether they are speakers of a dialect or speakers of another language, they need abundant opportunities to add Standard English to their speaking vocabulary. These children need to interact with peers who are skilled speakers of English. Through social and instructional contexts they benefit from opportunities to listen and speak throughout the day. Group discussions, projects, teacher-led lessons, and working periods in learning centers all afford children from various language backgrounds opportunities to speak about things based on common interests.

The process of emerging literacy continues within each child. Some will progress more rapidly than others, depending on the type of home environment and preschool experiences they have available to them. The emergent literacy or whole-language activities used in the preschool continue in kindergarten. As children approach the stage where the ability to interpret written language from books becomes a reality, teachers must make decisions about the role of phonics and beginning reading skills in their reading program. The philosophy of the nature of beginning reading and the conflict between skills approaches to reading versus the whole-language approach causes further conflict in many school districts.

Although there is no definitive resolution regarding the opposing philosophies, teachers need to understand the causes of the disagreement so that they can make informed decisions about how they think a quality reading program should be designed. To that end, we described several possibilities for primary-grade language arts programs, which ranged from totally whole-language instruction to a blend of whole-language and reading skills instruction.

To further assist teachers in developing an appropriate language arts program, we described stages of literacy acquisition, beginning with the foundations stage, when children experiment with emergent writing and reading and acquire many of the characteristics of literacy on an individual basis. In the second stage, they master the forms of printed language. They learn to use phonic elements, grammar, and punctuation in their writing and reading efforts. Through extensive practice in reading and writing, they are able to put together the elements of printed language until they are able to read on their own.

During stage three, children become independent readers. They refine their knowledge about printed language and can use their emerging skills in more complex and lengthy reading and writing experiences. They engage in extended practice and become interested in both narrative and expository reading and writing.

The mathematics curriculum also enables students to progress to more complex levels using higher levels of cognition as concrete operational thinking is acquired. The sequence of concrete to abstract and simple to complex is particularly significant as children encounter new mathematical concepts. Because mathematics is sequential in nature, the teacher needs to understand how concepts build on previous mathematical experiences. Extensive use is made of concrete materials when learning new skills, and many opportunities are made available for children to apply their mathematical skills and problem-solving abilities in real-life applications. Like the language arts curriculum, the trend in mathematics is to its application in context and not as a set of isolated skills. In addition, the importance of immersing young children in the use of technological tools and applications is part of the curriculum from the preschool years through higher education.

Science curriculum, conversely, is more holistic. Children need ongoing encounters with the same science concepts in many contexts to fully understand the implications and applications of the science process. Whether children are in the preschool years, kindergarten, or the primary grades, they are using the science processes of observing, classifying and comparing, measuring, communicating, experimenting, and relating, inferring, or applying as part of their basis of understanding scientific phenomena.

There are extensive possibilities in physical and biological science that teachers and children can pursue. Although children tend to favor biological themes, they need a balance of both in the curriculum. Young children benefit from integrated experiences with science when all components of the curriculum can contribute to the child's understanding and use of the science process. As national efforts are made to improve the quality of the science curriculum, beginning with very young children, teachers are placing more emphasis on planning and implementing improved curriculum in their classrooms. This includes the design of units of study based on science topics that facilitate comprehensive experiences in a variety of activities over a period of time, including real experiences with living things and materials and phenomena of the world around.

Summary Statements

1. Curriculum designed for children between the ages of five and eight can be called transitional because children are making the transition to literacy and from the preoperational period to the concrete operational period.
2. The language arts curriculum is a continuum from the preschool years into the primary years.
3. Oral language development continues during these years as students extend and refine language abilities.
4. Children with language differences especially need many experiences to use oral language as they learn Standard English.
5. Many ongoing classroom activities promote the use of oral language, such as group discussions, cooperative group activities, and class projects.
6. Educators differ in their opinions as to how young children should be taught to read. This is an extension of the debate regarding emergent literacy versus reading readiness skills in preschool classrooms.
7. In the primary grades, the differences in approaches to reading instruction comprise the whole-language versus phonics debate.
8. One trend in language arts instruction is to use the best of both practices based on the learning needs of individual children.
9. A quality language arts program contains a balance between child-initiated and teacher-directed experiences and emergent experiences supported with systematic instruction.
10. Students gradually develop competence in reading and writing during kindergarten and the primary years with individual variations.
11. The classroom environment that is conducive to helping children progress in language skills has a well-appointed language arts center that supports many student-initiated reading and writing experiences.
12. The teacher's role for students making the transition to literacy is to guide, facilitate, and assess and evaluate progress.
13. Much of systematic instruction in the language arts occurs informally within whole-language and integrated theme activities, supplemented by direct teaching when needed.
14. The child can be thought of as proceeding through three stages toward literacy: stage one,

setting foundations for literacy; stage two, learning about print and understanding printed language; and stage three, becoming independent readers.
15. There are several models of classroom organization for language arts in kindergarten and primary grades, including nonability grouping, literature-based instruction, and content-area grouping.
16. There are students who do not acquire literacy within a normal time span and need intervention before serious reading problems develop.
17. Mathematics curriculum also considers the child's transition from preoperational to concrete operational thinking and includes abundant opportunities with concrete materials.
18. One current trend in mathematics curriculum and instruction is a movement away from teaching skills and drills to an approach that prepares students to solve unconventional problems.
19. One important goal for the mathematics program is to ensure that practices are developmentally appropriate.
20. Curriculum and instruction in mathematics is based on hands-on activities that achieve a balance between teacher-directed, systematic instruction and informal, real-life activities.
21. Current technology is a part of mathematics curriculum; young children learn how and why to use computers and calculators with mathematics.
22. Mathematics instruction for children who experience developmental delays or have handicaps in cognitive abilities must be adapted to developmental levels rather than chronological ages.
23. Some children have difficulty performing successfully in mathematics instruction because of delayed motor skills or receptive and expressive difficulties.
24. Science is best studied from a hands-on approach through firsthand investigation and experimentation.
25. As learners make the transition from preoperational to concrete operational thinking, they can move from totally active experiences to activities where they can use thought processes to understand concepts.
26. As cognitive abilities mature, new competencies permit students to acquire science information from a variety of sources, such as videos, films, and books.

27. There is national concern about the poor quality of science programs and the low priority given to science instruction in elementary schools.
28. As a result of the effort to reform science education, new approaches to science are being developed and implemented.
29. Quality science programs for young children incorporate the science process in curriculum and instruction.
30. The classroom and teacher roles reflect the child-centered approach to science that focuses on the student's involvement in planning and learning.

Study Questions

1. In what way are children age five to eight considered transitional learners?
2. Why is it important to continue oral language development after students have begun the transition to literacy?
3. How do teachers attend to the needs of diverse speakers whose strongest language is not Standard English?
4. How can oral language be strengthened and extended within classroom experiences and instruction?
5. Why do kindergarten and primary-grade teachers face a dilemma when organizing the language arts program?
6. What issues must these teachers resolve when deciding how to best teach children who are making the transition to literacy?
7. What are some possibilities for resolving the whole-language versus phonics debate in reading instruction?
8. How would you organize the language arts program in kindergarten and the primary grades using the models described in the chapter?
9. How does the beginning reader move through stages of reading ability between kindergarten and third grade? What implications do these stages have for instruction?
10. How does the teacher achieve a balance between systematic instruction and child-initiated experiences in the language arts program?
11. Why is early intervention important for children who experience difficulty learning to read?
12. Why can the mathematics program be described as a continuum between preschool and primary years?
13. Why are mathematics specialists recommending a different approach to mathematics instruction for future students?
14. What kinds of changes are recommended?
15. Why does the mathematics program need to be developmentally appropriate?
16. Why are integrated or real-life experiences particularly significant in mathematics?
17. How should students learn about computer and calculator technology in mathematics activities?
18. Why should teachers be cautious about selecting and using computer software?
19. In what way is the mathematics curriculum hierarchical and sequential?
20. What difficulties do students with learning disabilities encounter when trying to understand and perform in mathematics? How can the teacher help them?
21. Why do preoperational and concrete operational thinking students need firsthand, real-life experiences in science?
22. What additional cognitive strategies can concrete operational students use in learning science concepts?
23. What are some investigation activities that primary-grade children can use to experience science concepts?
24. Why do science experts have concerns about elementary science programs?
25. How are new science programs different from more traditional programs?
26. How is the science process an integral part of science curriculum?
27. How are science topics selected in kindergarten and primary-grade classrooms?
28. Why is the use of thematic units a good approach to the development of meaningful science experiences?

References

Abramson, S., Seda, I., & Johnson, C. (1990). Literacy development in a multilingual kindergarten classroom. *Childhood Education, 67,* 68–72.

Adams, M. J. (1990). *Beginning to read: Thinking and learning about print.* Cambridge, MA: MIT Press.

Adams, M. J., Allington, R. L., Chaney, J. H., Goodman, Y. M., Kapinus, B. A., McGee, L. M., Richgels, D. J., Schwartz, S. J., Shannon, P., Smitten, B., & Williams, J. P. (1991). Beginning to read: A critique by literacy professionals and a response by Marilyn Jager Adams. *The Reading Teacher, 44,* 370–395.

Barufaldi, J. P., Ladd, G. T., & Moses, A. J. (1984). *Heath science* [Level K]. Lexington, MA: D. C. Heath.

Bredekamp, S. (Ed.). (1987). *Developmentally appropriate practice in early childhood programs serving children from birth through age 8.* Washington, DC: National Association for the Education of Young Children.

Bromley, D. A. (1989). A conversation with D. Allen Bromley by B. J. Culliton. *Science, 246,* 203.

Bullough, R. V., & Beatty, L. F. (1991). *Classroom applications of microcomputers* (2nd ed.). New York: Merrill/Macmillan.

Carter, L. G. (1984). The sustaining effects of compensatory and elementary education. *Educational Researcher,* 4–13.

Chall, J. (1967). *Learning to read: The great debate.* New York: McGraw–Hill.

Chall, J. (1983). *Learning to read: The great debate* (Updated ed.). New York: McGraw–Hill.

Charlesworth, R. C., & Lind, K. K. (1990). *Math and science for young children.* Albany, NY: Delmar.

Clay, M. M. (1979). *The early detection of reading difficulties* (3rd ed.). Portsmouth, NH: Heinemann.

Clements, D. H. (1985). *Computers in early and primary education.* Englewood Cliffs, NJ: Prentice–Hall.

Clements, D. H. (1987). Computers and young children: A review of research. *Young Children, 40,* 4–44.

Cliatt, M. J. P., & Shaw, J. M. (1992). *Helping children explore science.* New York: Merrill.

Commission on Reading, National Academy of Education. (1985). *Becoming a nation of readers.* Washington, DC: National Institute of Education.

Cunningham, P. M., Hall, D. P., & DeFee, M. (1991). Non–ability grouped, multilevel instruction: A year in a first–grade classroom. *The Reading Teacher, 44,* 566–571.

Danielson, K. E. (1990). Creating interest in words with literature. *Childhood Education, 66,* 220–225.

Dueschl, R. A. (1983). The elementary level science methods course: Breeding ground of an apprehension toward science? A case study. *Journal of Research in Science Teaching, 20,* 322–326.

Dutton, W. H., & Dutton, A. (1991). *Mathematics children use and understand.* Mountain View, CA: Mayfield.

Enright, D. S., & McCloskey, M. L. (1985). Yes Talking! Organizing the classroom to promote second language acquisition. *TESOL Quarterly, 15,* 431–453.

Fields, M. V., Spangler, K. L., & Lee, D. M. (1991). *Let's begin reading right* (2nd ed.). Columbus, OH: Merrill.

Flesch, R. (1955). *Why Johnny can't read.* New York: Harper & Row.

Fountas, I. C., & Hannigan, I. L. (1989). Making sense of whole language: The pursuit of informed teaching. *Childhood Education, 65,* 133–137.

Freppon, P. A., & Dahl, K. L. (1991). Learning about phonics in a whole language classroom. *Language Arts, 68,* 190–196.

Gaskins, R. W., Gaskins, J. C., & Gaskins, I. W. (1991). A decoding program for poor readers—and the rest of the class, too. *Language Arts, 68,* 213–225.

Glazer, J. I. (1986). *Literature for young children* (2nd ed.). Columbus, OH: Merrill.

Glazer, J. I., & Lamme, L. L. (1990). Poem picture books and their uses in the classroom. *The Reading Teacher, 44,* 102–108.

Gluck, D. H. (1991). Helping students understand place value. *Arithmetic Teacher, 38,* 10–13.

Graves, D. H. (1983). *Writing: Teachers and children at work.* Portsmouth, NH: Heinemann.

Harlen, W. (1985). *Teaching and learning primary science.* New York: Teacher's College Press.

Harlen, W., & Jelly, S. (1989). *Developing science in the primary classroom*. Portsmouth, NH: Heinemann.

Haugland, S. W., & Shade, D. D. (1988). Developmentally appropriate software for young children. *Young Children*, *43*, 37–43.

Hill, L. B., & Hale, M. G. (1991). Reading recovery: Questions classroom teachers ask. *The Reading Teacher*, *44*, 480–483.

Holdaway, D. (1979). *Foundations of literacy*. Sydney: Ashton Scholastic.

Hoskisson, K. (1975). The many facets of assisted reading. *Elementary English*, *52*, 312–315.

Hove, E. (1970). Science scarecrows. *School Science and Mathematics*, *70*, 322–326.

Hudelson, S. (1984). Kan yu ret and rayt in Ingles: Children become literate in English as a second language. *TESOL Quarterly*, *18*, 221–238.

Jewell, M. G., & Zintz, M. V. (1986). *Learning to read naturally*. Dubuque, IA: Kendall/Hunt.

Kamii, C. (1982). *Number in the preschool and kindergarten*. Washington, DC: National Association for the Education of Young Children.

Kepler, L. (1991, September). Shine on harvest moon. *Instructor*, 54–55.

Lindberg, D. L. (1990). What goes 'round comes 'round. Doing science. *Childhood Education*, *67*, 79–81.

McCracken, M., & McCracken, R. A. (1979). *Reading and writing language: A practical guide for primary teachers*. Winnipeg: Peguis.

Mechling, K. R., & Kepler, L. E. (1991, March). Start with science. *Instructor*, 35–37.

Mullis, I. V. S., & Jenkins, L. B. (1988). *The science report card: Elements of risk and recovery: Trends and achievement based on the 1986 national assessment*. Princeton, NJ: Educational Testing Service.

National Council of Supervisors of Mathematics. (1988). Essential mathematics for the 21st century (Position paper).

National Science Foundation. (1983). *Educating America for the 21st century: A report to the American people and the National Science Board*. Washington, DC: Author.

Newman, J. M., & Church, S. M. (1990). Commentary: Myths of whole language. *The Reading Teacher*, *44*, 20–27.

Papert, S. (1980). *Mindstorms: Children, computers, and powerful ideas*. New York: Basic Books.

Pardo, L. S., & Raphael, T. E. (1991). Classroom organization for instruction in content areas. *The Reading Teacher*, *44*, 556–565.

Quintero, E., & Velarde, M. C. (1990). Intergenerational literacy: A developmental, bilingual approach. *Young Children*, *45*, 10–15.

Reutzel, D. R., & Cooter, R. B. (1991). Organizing for effective instruction: The reading workshop. *The Reading Teacher*, *44*, 548–555.

Richards, R. (1989). *An early start to nature*. New York: Simon & Schuster.

Sanacore, J. (1991). Expository and narrative text: Balancing young children's reading experiences. *Childhood Education*, *67*, 211–214.

Schultz, K. A., Colarusso, R. P., & Strawderman, V. W. (1989). *Mathematics for every young child*. Columbus, OH: Merrill.

Seefeldt, C., & Barbour, N. (1990). *Early childhood education: An introduction* (2nd ed.). Columbus, OH: Merrill.

Steen, L. A. (1990, April). Making math matter. *Instructor*, 21–23.

Tilgner, P. J. (1990). Avoiding science in the elementary school. *Science Education*, *74*, 421–431.

Urzua, C. (1987). "You stopped too soon": Second language children composing and revising. *TESOL Quarterly*, *21*, 279–303.

Webb, A., Bowers, R., Hietpas, L., Lang, T., & McKinley, L. (1991). Four teachers pilot a whole language program. *Childhood Education*, *67*, 155–160.

Westley, J. (1988). *Insects and other crawlers*. Sunnyvale, CA: Creative Publications.

Willis, S. (1992, January). Mathematics education standards 'Revolution' takes hold. *ASCD Curriculum Update*, 1–3.

CHAPTER ELEVEN

The Transitional Curriculum: Ages Five to Eight

Social Studies and Physical Education

CURRICULUM FOR SOCIAL STUDIES

In the preschool years, social development is the basis for devising the social science curriculum. In the years between age five and age eight, the curriculum for social development or social science is commonly labeled as *social studies;* however, the major components or topics are similar to the categories used with young children. Social development is still an important consideration in the kindergarten and primary grades. In addition to expanding socialization skills, students in the latter early childhood years are developing attitudes and values about themselves and other people. The curriculum for social studies includes activities for both advancing socialization skills and broadening students' understanding about the world and its people.

Social Development for Ages Five to Eight

In chapter 8 we described the preschool child as gradually becoming less egocentric and developing the ability to understand that others may think and feel differently than they do. As the young child enters school, this ability continues to mature and enables the child's social cognition to include social role taking, or the ability to put oneself in another's place and anticipate what another person may feel or think. Development of social cognition allows children to better understand others and themselves, leading to interests in initiating friendships (Shantz, 1975). Children also understand that people interpret situations differently, though they may not understand the source or cause of those differences (Selman, 1976).

As young children enter school, they are moving into what Erikson called the stage of industry versus inferiority. Until they reach puberty, these young children will be developing a sense of adequacy as they become adept at reading, writing, and mathematics. If they are successful academically, they come to see themselves as competent learners. Likewise, if they are successful in using their social skills, they perceive themselves as liked by their peers. Children who do not overcome barriers to successful adaptation to school or fail to learn satisfactorily can develop a sense of inferiority or a lack of self-esteem.

Unfortunately, not all children achieve social and academic success. Many factors can affect the child's positive socialization in the first years of school. Differences in child-rearing practices and value systems can make it difficult for some children to fit into the school structure, which traditionally has reflected a middle-class perspective. Diversity among family structures, economic conditions among families, and ethnic and cultural variations in the child's background can make it difficult for the child to feel comfortable in the school environment (Hale-Benson, 1986; Lane, 1986). Children who have been neglected and abused and children with handicaps have special challenges in their efforts to feel successful and accepted (Meddin & Rosen, 1986; White & Phair, 1986). Although these factors affect socialization in preschool years, they can be even more significant during early elementary school years. When they enter the primary grades, children are more aware of the need to conform to the social standards of their class and school and expectations for behavior. They are also more perceptive as to whether they are accepted by their peers as part of a classroom social group.

The school is a major force for socialization, and the teacher plays an important role in guiding all children toward becoming successful members of the classroom community (McNeil, 1969). There are practices the teacher can use to maximize positive socialization in students in kindergarten and primary classrooms. Cooperative and sharing behaviors can be acquired through teacher modeling and guidance. The teacher can use coaching, direct teaching, and reinforcing to nurture appropriate social behaviors. Frequent group experiences, including activities among cooperative learning groups, can help children understand that they can work together and support one another (Deutsch, 1963; Kamii, 1986; Roopnarine & Honig, 1986; Veach, 1986).

The ages between five and eight are also important for moral development (Kamii, 1986). Whereas children have previously made objective judgments in moral reasoning, they now become more subjective—that is, they consider the other person's intentions when making moral judgments about them. Learning to understand the intention of others is a difficult process, which continues through adulthood (Kohlberg, 1973).

There seems to be a relationship between the development of moral reasoning and social behavior. In a study of first-grade students, those with indications of higher moral reasoning were also more successful socially (Enright & Sutterfield, 1980). Children who had good social skills were better able to judge the intentions of other children and were able to take their needs into account (Dodge, Murphy, & Buchsbaum, 1984). Children who were more advanced in moral reasoning had more successful social interactions and were sought out or approached more frequently by other children.

Paralleling moral development is the formation of attitudes and values. Values and attitudes are learned; moreover, they are acquired through the attitudes and values that are experienced by children through interactions with the people they come in contact with in their family and community (Seefeldt, 1989). The child's formation of values and attitudes begins in very early childhood years and is influenced by family, school peers, adults at the school, and other groups outside the school. Young children learn the values and habits of their family and immediate community through daily life. They likewise learn the values of the school culture through daily experiences in the school community. Therefore, it is important that parents and teachers take seriously their role in establishing values and attitudes. This is especially true in teaching the values and attitudes of living in a democratic society. In our society, we wish to promote the idea that all are equal and have equal rights to dignity and respect.

Not everyone in our society receives equal treatment, and children can become prejudiced at a very young age (Allport, 1952). Children can be influenced by stereotypes, prejudices, and discriminatory practices as early as age two (Derman-Sparks, 1992). Prejudice is a serious problem in this country, especially against minorities. Teachers can work toward establishing an environment that ensures equal treatment for all students. They will want to understand that diversity among children includes differences in gender, abilities, linguistic capabilities, class, and culture (Byrnes & Kiger, 1992). A first step in this process is for teachers to develop their own awareness of differences in the backgrounds of their children and how it affects them as they live and learn together. West (1992) explains that cultural differences can include perceptions about sex roles, orderliness, noise level, and the importance of the group rather than competition between individuals. Toward eliminating prejudice, as their understanding of differences develops, teachers can better model and teach equality and fairness toward all students and expect the same attitudes from the children (Greenberg, 1992; Seefeldt, 1989).

Activities for Nurturing Continued Social Development

Social development in kindergarten and primary classrooms is nurtured through the daily process of living, playing, learning, and working together. Social and moral development as well as the formation of values and attitudes are formed within the environment and practices for social living and learning that are established by the teacher. The major goals for social development are for children to extend their own socialization skills and to develop an appreciation for themselves and others through membership in their school community group. The teacher helps students reach these goals through modeling appropriate attitudes and behaviors and establishing classroom practices and activities that enable students to practice social role taking and cooperation in a democratic environment.

The teacher's initial task is to establish a classroom climate that nurtures cooperation and mutual respect. A conscious effort is made to establish a noncompetitive atmosphere where all children participate in shared learning. The teacher's orientation and leadership shifts the emphasis from teacher-directed instruction to mediated leadership that fosters peer interaction (Atkinson & Green, 1990).

The desired classroom climate established by the teacher promotes self-esteem and respect for self and others. Students learn how to be good citizens in the process of acquiring democratic values and behaviors. Through participating in group life, communicating with others, and solving problems cooperatively, students experience social and academic success (Holmes, 1991). A sense of belonging and self-worth develops from learning together through participatory roles facilitated by the teacher (Johnson & Johnson, 1987).

The teacher uses several strategies to actualize the noncompetitive, shared learning environment. These strategies involve discussions, cooperative learning groups, and democratic decision making.

Class Discussions.   Class discussions are a vehicle whereby teachers can help students learn rights and responsibilities and develop respect for themselves and others. Through the medium of discussion, children can express their developing awareness of the many differences and similarities among people in the United States, as well as those represented by children in their classroom. They can share their family lifestyles and traditions with one another and broaden their understanding and appreciation of individual and group differences (Holmes, 1991).

Cooperative Learning Groups.   Cooperative learning groups facilitate shared learning and group interactions. Instead of working alone, students work in small groups that are heterogeneous in development, ability, background, and gender. To function successfully in the group, students must learn and use interpersonal skills. The teacher plans activities that will build group cohesiveness and positive interactions. Through successful participation in group efforts, low-achieving students can feel they are making positive contributions to the group, while more able students can try out leadership roles (Lyman & Foyle, 1990). Students learn from each other as they observe, imitate, and discuss ideas with their peers (Atkinson & Green, 1990).

Democratic Decision Making.   Democratic values are learned through democratic decision making in group living and learning. Throughout the school year, students and teachers work together in setting learning goals and classroom rules and solving social problems that arise in the classroom. Choices are made about what and how they will learn, particularly when planning projects or thematic units. When a unit of study is developed, the process of brainstorming together and planning and implementing activities to accomplish unit learning objectives actualize democratic practices in learning. Individual and group work that is planned includes assigning varied responsibilities, monitoring progress of unit activities, and reporting the final results (Holmes, 1991).

Social problem solving can be addressed in democratic decision-making activities. The teacher can lead group discussions intended to elicit suggestions for resolving the issue at hand. Class meeting techniques can be used (Glasser, 1969) to ensure that each child has the opportunity to speak, that children are guided in seeing and understanding the viewpoints of others, and that a solution to the problem is reached through consideration of the consequences of making suggestions and reaching conclusions.

Citizenship learning and socialization skills are part of the total school curriculum, but they are also part of the social studies curriculum. In the next section we will consider how to organize or structure social studies in kindergarten through third grade, as well what major role integrated learning has in the social science curriculum.

Social Studies Curriculum in Kindergarten and the Primary Grades

The preschool social science curriculum is divided into the categories of history, geography, economics, sociology, and anthropology; these subjects also form the framework for social studies in elementary and secondary school. In earlier chapters we explained that studies in these areas are adapted to the experiences and abilities of children in the preoperational stage of development. In this chapter, social studies will be discussed using the same categories, but learning experiences for kindergarten and primary-grade children will reflect their growing ability to understand concepts from a broader and more complex perspective. Moreover, social studies curriculum design will be approached from an integrated organization, reflecting the most meaningful way that young children can learn about themselves and others in their world.

The social studies curriculum emerges from the children in the individual classroom. The ethnic and cultural backgrounds of the students and the makeup of their larger community and region form the foundation for the topics and content to be studied. For example, children who live in Arizona will attend classes that have a different mix of cultures than would be found in Alaska or Wisconsin. Differences within cultures and ethnic groups can also be affected by where children live. The Hispanic culture in southern Florida may be affected by influences from Cuba and South America, whereas the Hispanic culture in California and Texas may have stronger influences and traditions from Mexico. When developing goals for social studies, the unique characteristics of each region's student population will affect the learning experiences that will be planned.

Goals for Social Studies

History.   Children in kindergarten and the primary grades are beginning to develop concepts related to history. Two of the concepts, change and time, help children understand the notion of the past. Children first understand the passage of time through understanding the role of routines during the day. They can move from experiences measuring time to understanding that history is the study of things that happened in time that has passed. A sense of change that occurs over time also leads to an understanding of the meaning of history. Children can move from understanding changes in themselves to recognizing changes in their home and neighborhood. Through intergenerational contacts, they learn about continuity in life and that people of different ages represent the passage of time (Seefeldt, 1989). Holidays mark the passage of time during a calendar year, as well as celebrations people observe today that were also observed in the past.

Geography. Learning geography helps children understand that the earth is the home of humans. Geography helps them to be able to locate where places and things can be found on earth. As children move toward concrete operational thinking, they begin to discriminate between living and nonliving things. They begin to understand that nonliving things cannot move themselves but can be moved by an outside force (Piaget, 1965).

Some concepts that can be understood between age five and eight include the following: the land and water surfaces on earth; earth as a member of the solar system; the way seasonal and climatic changes occur on earth; and spatial directions. With an understanding of location and spatial directions, children can be introduced to the use of simple maps. They can learn how to represent places and locations by using such things as blocks and boxes. For example, kindergartners enjoy laying out an outline of a house using unit blocks. Drawing streets for small vehicles are also possibilities for beginning mapping experiences.

Geography concepts can be applied first within the local community and then within the immediate neighborhood surrounding the school. Nearby land and water surfaces, characteristics of local climate, and mapping of community places in relationship to the location of the school can lead to mapping more varied area characteristics at farther distances from the school and community.

Economics. Preschool children can understand what is involved in the buying and selling of goods and services. They have all gone shopping at some point in their lives and have experienced the exchanges of money, bank checks, and charge cards for groceries or clothes. Kindergarten and primary-grade children can understand the relationship between labor and production of goods and the economic characteristics of neighborhoods. They can understand, for example, the need to work to earn money, the concept of supply and demand, the implications of overproduction and scarcity, and the idea of savings (Seefeldt, 1989). Learning activities that will foster an understanding of these concepts include field trips to grocery stores, freight yards, banks, drug stores, construction sites, and shopping malls.

Children can explore what it means to be a consumer. They can learn how consumers become informed about goods that are available for purchase through advertising and the difference between producing goods and providing services.

Sociology and Anthropology. Young children need to learn about people and how they organize themselves into groups and communities. Preschool children can understand the family as the basic social unit, and primary-grade children can learn about communities beyond the local level. Children can also relate to how people live in other countries. They can become aware that we need to understand the similarities and differences in how people live in the nearby community as well as other parts of the world. Children in transition from preoperational thinking to concrete operational thinking can begin to use reasoning to understand the causes of war and the implications of racial and ethnic differences. Children need to discuss international topics so they can have a perception of people beyond U.S. stereotypes. Discussing global topics will facilitate acquisition of international concepts. These studies must begin with young children if they are to build positive attitudes toward the diversity of people in the United States and other countries and avoid prejudices that can influence their points of view (Moyer, 1970).

Current Issues.   Information in social studies is constantly changing. We live in a rapidly changing world; and because of the availability of visual information about current events on television, children can develop an awareness of changing situations and conditions in countries that are nearby as well as distant. For example, primary-grade children may be made aware of information about new countries that are being carved out of the former Soviet Union or are seeking to regain the historic status they had in decades prior to the world wars. Current issues, such as ecology and environmental protection, being addressed by various media resources and local community groups and organizations are also part of young children's awareness.

Primary-grade children are able to study topics about their own community that can relate to topics in other parts of the world. They can develop an awareness of why economic issues can affect how countries react to the way they use their environment. By being shown concrete examples of conflicting needs of different populations in their own community, children can be guided in beginning to understand conflicts in other nations. For example, awareness of a local controversy over the location of a garbage dump site or an issue about the amount of garbage that accumulates in the community can establish a foundation for understanding that there are various types of pollution in the world that are addressed differently in individual countries because of differing circumstances.

Young children can understand principles of patriotism. They can appreciate why flags are used as symbols for a state or country, why we recite the "Pledge of Allegiance," and why countries have a national anthem. Especially in the 1990s, children can become aware that countries experience change and that change in government can result in changes in how people live and work.

Designing Curriculum for Social Studies

In chapter 10 we described curriculum for the language arts as a holistic process whereby children acquire the ability to read and write in an interrelated fashion, not as separate processes or areas of learning. Literacy in language arts was defined as the ability to use written language. Literacy is also connected to other areas of learning because progress in one area affects other areas. The interrelatedness of learning extends to the development of integrated curriculum in social studies.

The California plan for revising the social science curriculum, titled *History–Social Science Framework for California Public Schools, Kindergarten through Grade Twelve,* (California State Board of Education, 1988) can serve as a model for integrated curriculum design. The curriculum for kindergarten through twelfth grade

(K–12) is based on the concept of literacy. The term *literacy* has been best understood as the integrated process that explains the emerging ability for children to be able to use written language. In the California plan, the focus on literacy has been applied to social studies; that is, the aim is for students to become literate in social science. Components of the social science curriculum are organized into historical literacy, ethical literacy, cultural literacy, geographic literacy, economic literacy, and sociopolitical literacy under the goal of knowledge and cultural understanding. Other related goals in the curriculum include understanding democracy and civic values and attaining skills such as basic study skills, critical thinking skills, and social participation skills. The three major goals and their related strands provide a framework for the integrated curriculum (Alexander & Crabtree, 1988). Figure 11.1 illustrates the integrated curriculum framework.

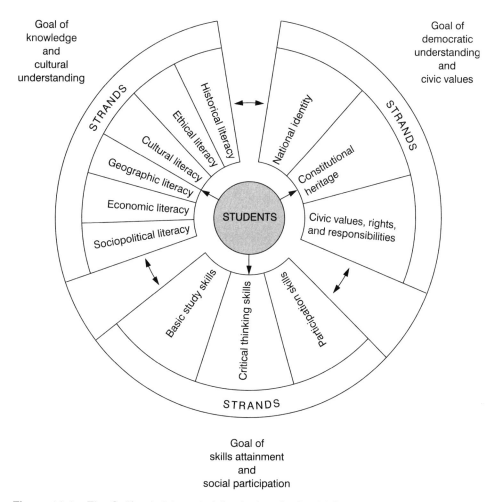

Figure 11.1   The California Integrated Curriculum for Social Science Literacy

F. Alexander & C. Crabtree, *California's New History: Social Science Curriculum Promises Richness and Depth. Educational Leadership, 46,* p. 11.

The California curriculum uses history as the integrative core and focuses on the multicultural nature of American society throughout its history. "Throughout all these studies, the framework's integrative approach establishes human events in their geographic setting, analyzes the interplay of historical times and geographic place, and integrates the social sciences in order to bring the explanatory perspectives of economics, sociology, and political science to each year's study" (Alexander & Crabtree, 1988, p. 11).

The literacy curriculum in the California plan is introduced in kindergarten and repeated each in year in more depth. The intent is to enrich and extend the curriculum to enable the children to use geographic location and historical time beyond that currently offered by most social science curricula. The course titles for kindergarten through third grade demonstrate this approach:

Kindergarten: Learning and Working Now and Long Ago

Grade 1: A Child's Place in Time and Space

Grade 2: People Who Make a Difference

Grade 3: Continuity and Change

The curriculum for kindergarten and the primary grades uses fairy tales, biographies, legends, and historical stories from children's literature to help young children understand history and historical people. With this approach, students learn about the past through story narrative.

How, then, do teachers of young children from five to eight years old plan and implement curriculum for social studies? The California model is one of a comprehensive social studies curriculum that is interrelated rather than composed of independent components. To be consistent with the focus of this text, the social studies curriculum to be described will build on developmental continuity between the preschool and primary years. The social science topics about understanding oneself, other people, and society that were listed in the preschool social science curriculum will be further developed to include topics that explore the elements of social science in more depth.

The topics will be developed with the students' cognitive abilities in mind. We will consider the child's development toward using written language and making cognitive advances into concrete operational thinking, as well as the principles of learning that have been basic to all curriculum development throughout the text. Reconstruction of knowledge through active participation in hands-on learning and student involvement in planning are basic to the way the curriculum is organized. The topics discussed below focus on having global awareness, integrating social science with whole language, and celebrating holidays. Then, a thematic, integrated unit designed according to the model used in chapter 9 will be introduced to exemplify social studies as integrated curriculum.

Topics in Global Awareness. One of the goals of the social science curriculum is for young children to understand people from other cultures and countries. Three topics for global awareness are designed for different levels of development as children

make the transition from preschool into the primary grades. The topics—Silkworms and the Orient, Toys, and the Global Community—involve activities that complement changing development and experiences in learning about other cultures.

Silkworms and the Orient

This study of silkworms integrates science and social studies and is suitable for kindergarten children (Cole, 1988). It originates with how silkworm thread was discovered in China and developed to make silk fabric. Children are introduced to the topic through a story about silkworms. The unit focuses on growing silkworms in the classroom and observing their life cycle from eggs to adult moths. The students can make some of the cocoons into silk thread and see the eggs laid by the moths after they emerge from the cocoon. Cole gives information on how to obtain silkworm eggs and how to care for and feed the worms until they spin their cocoon. Science concepts learned from following the life cycle of the moth are important in building foundations for understanding other types of life cycles, the process of metamorphosis, and the care of silkworms at different stages of the life cycle.

Cole suggests other activities that help children develop an appreciation for people from an Oriental culture. Field trips to such places as an Oriental garden or market would familiarize children with Oriental customs and foods. Community members from the Far East can be invited to visit the classroom to share information about their native country. Children can also be invited to bring household items from their home that are from China, Japan, or other Far Eastern countries. Cooking experiences should include preparation of Oriental dishes. Books about boys and girls from Oriental cultures should be read to the class and placed in the library center.

Toys

A study of toys and play can help children understand that toys are universals that are present in all cultures around the world. Students can understand similarities and differences among people through a unit study of toys and the roles they play in children's lives (Swiniarski, 1991). A unit on toys could be organized around different types of toys. Animal toys, fashion toys, war toys, toys as national symbols, and toys as representative of folklore or fairy tales are just a few of the types of toys that can be studied.

Toys such as Babar and Pinocchio offer insights into children's literature from other countries. Toys from popular cultures—such as Mickey Mouse and Barbie from the United States and Sooty from Great Britain—can be recognized by children in many countries.

Some toys are more classic and reflect the historical heritage of a country. Nested dolls from the former Soviet Union, Chinese kites, and dragon puppets are traditional toys from various parts of the world. Cultures can be compared through toys that are representative of a country's traditions or customs. Bride and groom dolls, toy vehicles, miniature dwellings, and toy environments such as farms or medieval castles can be used to compare current and historical life-styles.

With toys of various types as the core of a unit, experiences can be developed to integrate learning across the curriculum. Children can make toys from various media, explore children's literature related to toys, and make puppets representing other cultures.

The study of toys from an international perspective can be developed into extended projects and used as sources for writing stories and reports and discussing social issues. Swiniarski reported on a first-grade project that involved making a catalog of international toys that the class had collected and an exhibit of the collected toys. The toys reflected the ethnic and racial backgrounds of the children in the class.

A Global Community Study

A unit for third-grade students (Peters, 1991) had as its purpose to introduce students to different cultures and physical environments from a global perspective. A strategy called Student Awareness of Global Environments (SAGE) was used to gather and report information about other cultures and environments. Working in small, cooperative groups, students worked to research and interpret data on culture traits such as diet, clothing, shelter, education, and family structures of different cultures. The types of physical characteristics of a country—such as vegetation, wildlife, weather, temperature, rainfall, and natural resources—were matched with the environmental characteristics of the country. Data on natural and cultural characteristics were used to understand the people who occupy the area. The effects of the country's physical characteristics on the cultural traits were explored for relationships between the two; the reverse issue could also be applied, regarding how the inhabitants of an area affect the natural environment of the country.

Topics Integrating Whole Language and Literature.   Language and literature can be the vehicles for designing social studies topics. In the two examples that follow, principles from whole language are used to investigate topics that could lead children to become involved in social action. Children's literature is used as a source of understanding and appreciating cultural differences.

Whole Language Lessons for Promoting Social Action

The authors (Freeman & Freeman, 1991) of this curriculum topic support the thesis that students should be involved in their own learning and that authentic learning materials are the best source of information for social studies curriculum. Their suggestions for improving curriculum follow the changes initiated by California's *History–Social Science Framework* (California State Board of Education, 1988) discussed earlier. They present a model of social studies that addresses the inclusion of whole-language principles in social studies instruction.

Freeman and Freeman draw a parallel between instruction in language and instruction in social studies in the shift from education that transmits knowledge to education as construction of knowledge. They further propose that cooperative groups investigating long-term projects place students as active players in their own learning. Moreover, they believe that students can put knowledge into action by initiating social change. Freeman and Freeman believe this approach is particularly suitable for students who have limited English proficiency and who benefit from engaging in learning that is related to their own lives. For these students, active involvement in cooperative projects creates more opportunities to develop second-language proficiency.

The model the authors propose centers on a study of the community. As they study the community, students can focus on how the environment affects community life. To better understand the characteristics of the community, students can examine and compare two communities and determine the advantages and disadvantages of living in each community. Language and vocabulary development are used in reporting the analysis. Reading can be used to further understand how various environments affect how people live.

As students conduct an in-depth study of the quality of life in their community, they can identify ways in which their community can be improved; further, they can design an action plan where they can contribute to the desired improvement.

Whole-language activities related to the topic include class discussions, group research and writing, and definitions of what students can do to improve the quality of life. Talking, reading, and writing will be used to accomplish all the goals of their investigation. The approach to learning uses the students' background knowledge and facilitates the development of proficiency in oral and written language.

Students in a large urban city in Texas studied two areas within the city to compare what was available for elementary students to do after school. The students discovered that one area they studied had many resources, whereas the other did not. The students devised a plan for after-school activities for children in the targeted area and approached two churches with their concern. One church not only became interested but coordinated efforts with the neighborhood elementary school to conduct after-school activities both at the church and at the school. The students studied their community from the perspective of the availability of the quality of life for children in different areas of the city. When they understood that there was a lack of resources for children in one of the areas, they designed a plan that engaged them in the process of social action to improve the situation.

Children's Literature and Social Studies

Children's literature can foster social science concepts, especially in developing an understanding and appreciation of multiple cultures. Barnes (1991) proposed that, in addition to understanding cultural differences, children can understand how cultures are the same—that is, the universals that all cultures share. Some of the cultural universals that can be explored include language, government, economic systems, religion, family, and education.

Barnes suggests that children's literature is more meaningful than are texts that supposedly help people learn about their own culture. Children's books can be helpful in learning about the form that cultural universals take, no matter which culture the child is in. Barnes suggests books that will familiarize children with cultural understanding; his suggestions include topics that are related to family relationships, daily living, race, and cultural rituals such as weddings, funerals, graduations, and christenings. Each of these acculturation topics can be developed into a thematic unit using topical literature and related, integrated experiences.

Multicultural literature written for children can be used to meet the goal of helping children grow in their understanding of themselves and others (Norton, 1990). Using Native American literature as an example, Norton suggests a comprehensive sequence of study that includes traditional literature; autobiographies; biographies; historical fiction and nonfiction; and contemporary fiction, biography, and poetry, in five phases of study. The sequence would be followed to study one cultural group at a time. Although the process is most appropriate for upper elementary and secondary students, second- and third-grade students could engage in the process with literature written for primary-grade children.

Holiday Celebrations

When teachers of young children consider social studies, one of the topics they usually think of is the celebration of holidays. Although there is an abundance of ideas on how to study and experience holiday celebrations, many of the existing activities have become stereotyped or sterile. Curriculum themes for holidays can be fresh and innovative if teachers and children plan thematic units based on children's interests and backgrounds.

One way to get a new perspective is to have a brainstorming session at the beginning of the year to include parents, children, and teachers. The planning group can focus on theme ideas that are appealing to them and can bring new approaches to understanding holidays (Nunnelley, 1990). The unit developed for the theme can follow the same steps as in chapter 9, with parents taking an active part in all steps, including planning and implementation. It is recommended that each theme involve one main event, such as a field trip, party, production of a play, or celebration of a special event.

Older children can take a broader, global approach to holiday observances. For example, a group of teachers and students planned a two-month study of holiday celebrations around the world in November and December. Between November 1 and December 31, they observed fifteen celebrations, from Mexico, England, the United States, Germany, Africa, Japan, Vietnam, Israel, Sweden, and Poland. The unit, called "Holiday Express," involved research, writing, learning geographic locations, and learning about cultural differences in important holidays and observances. In addition to making and posting a master plan for all the countries they would "visit," the students participated in the National Geographic Kids Network and exchanged information about traditional holiday celebrations by computer with students from other countries (Beach, Hinojosa, & Tedford, 1991).

Designing Integrated, Thematic Units in Social Studies

Earlier we discussed how literature can serve as the source of information to learn about other cultures. In one example, in a unit planned for primary-grade children and initiated with children's literature, activities were planned that would involve learning about life on a different continent and dealing with frustration. Laurel, a second-grade teacher, designed a thematic unit that integrated social studies and language arts with her class. She used *Alexander and the Terrible, Horrible, No Good, Very Bad Day* by Judith Viorst as the focus of her unit. (The entire unit, including the unit plan and the lesson plans, is described in Appendix D.) Students in her class were able to learn about Australia and how people speak and live differently in that country. Among the unit activities Laurel and her students planned were those that involved learning how to waltz, to sing the song "Waltzing Matilda," and to participate in singing the song and waltzing as a music activity. Students learned new vocabulary words that are unique to Australia and participated in related activities that incorporate other content areas into the unit experiences. Laurel listed the following activities for five lessons in the unit:

1. The teacher will read to the class the literature selection *Alexander and the Terrible, Horrible, No Good, Very Bad Day,* followed by a discussion of the story. The children will write and illustrate a sequel to the story, describing what might have happened the next day.

2. The class will locate the continent of Australia on a map and draw a map of the continent. This will be followed by an identification game in which children select a picture, identify it, and become familiar with the person, place, or thing that is characteristic of Australia.
3. A dentist (maybe a student's parent) will visit the class to discuss the importance of caring for one's teeth (in the story, Alexander has to go to the dentist). The class will participate by using a model of teeth and demonstrating proper dental hygiene techniques.
4. The children will construct a graph charting the least favorite vegetable of the class.
5. The children will become familiar with an Australian song through singing and dancing.

Both social development and social studies objectives were fulfilled through this unit. Children learned how to cope with feelings at the same time that they were learning about people in Australia. They learned that Australian children speak and live differently than children in the United States. At the same time, they were made aware of the similarities between children in both countries when they try to deal with difficult days in their lives.

CURRICULUM FOR PHYSICAL EDUCATION

Although much attention is paid to the need for play in the preschool years, the same cannot be said for the elementary school years; moreover, the emphasis on play periods for five-year-olds may be very different among programs at different settings. Child-care centers and private schools are more likely to devote time for unstructured play than are public schools. Five- to eight-year-olds continue in their need for activities that promote motor development; however, schools and homes do not always provide the kinds of physical activities that are desirable.

Physical Development of Children Ages Five to Eight

We have described motor development in the preschool years more specifically as perceptual–motor development, and we divided the skills into fine motor and gross motor skills. Play for preschool children was discussed in terms of physical play and its relationship to social and cognitive development. The indoor and outdoor preschool play environments provide for fine and gross motor skills in a context of play experiences that encompass sociodramatic play, cognitive play, and creative expression within play activities that involve physical activities.

Gross motor and fine motor skills, body awareness, spatial awareness, balancing, and integrated movement as described for preschool children continue to develop in the early elementary years (Frost, 1992). The rapid rate of growth during the preschool years slows down with major development now occurring in the trunk and limbs (Schickedanz, Hansen, & Forsyth, 1990). Childhood obesity can occur, a condition that is prevalent and increasing among children of these ages (Epstein, Wing, & Valoski, 1985).

Motor development during these years is a process of improving fine and gross motor skills. Children acquire improved skills rapidly and become competent at physical games. The child in the primary grades enjoys demonstrating the skills that are being acquired. Hughes (1991) gives the example of the young boy who begged his parents for a skateboard and then derived much satisfaction from daily performances of the latest accomplishments that had been mastered. Children become interested in gymnastics, dance lessons, and organized sports. Improvement in fine motor skills makes hobbies possible, such as assembling models, sewing, making crafts, and participating in other activities that require dexterity. Many children become adept at writing and are able to use smaller writing. However, not all children develop this fine motor maturity and are penalized if school expectations for handwriting are too difficult for their level of fine motor development.

Motor development is interrelated with social and cognitive development. As children move from preoperational to concrete operational thinking, their emerging cognitive and social-emotional needs affect their play interests. In the primary grades, children become more aware of peer approval. It is very important to them to be accepted by the group. Cognitive abilities make it possible for children to engage in games with rules, increasing the opportunities to engage in group activities and enjoy organized sports, which require group efforts and competition.

Games with rules can involve gross or fine motor skills. The typical games familiar in American culture—such as baseball, soccer, hide-and-seek, and hopscotch—exercise gross motor skills. Marbles, checkers, and jacks require fine motor skills, whereas Monopoly and other board games advance intellectual skills. Children between the ages of five and eight enjoy all of these opportunities for participating in physical activity and games that require physical and mental competence.

There are issues and lack of agreement concerning what kinds of physical activities should be promoted and how much importance should be given to physical development in kindergarten and primary grades. The issues that are most common relate to the following questions: What emphasis should be placed on physical education in the primary grades? Should physical education curriculum involve structured or unstructured play periods? And what is the appropriate role for organized sports in the early elementary grades?

Planning for Physical Development

The preschool teacher has the primary responsibility for all areas of the curriculum in most program settings. This organization changes radically in elementary schools as specialist teachers assume some of the instruction of young students. As early as kindergarten, children may be served by a music teacher, physical education teacher, computer center technologist, and art teacher. If the school is limited in special teachers, the physical education teacher is the specialist most likely to be hired. The common perception, then, is that physical education is a separate subject of the curriculum. The physical education teacher plans the physical education program as a structured curriculum with goals and objectives for motor development and physical fitness. The classroom teacher no longer has the responsibility for physical development beyond fine motor skills related to classroom experiences. It is possible that no one has the responsibility for the child's total physical development and for providing a balance between exercise and fitness and play opportunities that foster the interrelated benefits of social, cognitive, expressive, and physical play.

Furthermore, there is great concern that physical development is neglected in elementary schools. Concurrent with the back-to-basics movement in the latter 1980s, less time was devoted to physical education and more time was scheduled for academic instruction. There is evidence that physical fitness has declined in the last decades. Kenneth Cooper, a prominent fitness expert, reported that children in 1986 were heavier, fatter, and in poorer aerobic condition than were children in 1976 (Dart, 1990). Although some of the problem is attributed to increased television watching and poor diet, decreased emphasis in the public schools on physical education is also a major factor (Coop & Rotella, 1991).

The issue of participation in organized sports in early elementary years is another concern in planning for physical development in elementary schools. There was a time in past decades when unstructured play periods were part of the school day. Children had time to be outdoors and to select their own play activity. Although they were likely to organize group games during these periods, the activities were supervised by, but not directed by, adults. In schools today, most outdoor periods are limited to adult-directed physical education periods. Adults select and direct the activities, and children are required to participate. In addition, many primary-grade children participate in organized sports after school. Time for unstructured play after school and on weekends has diminished for many children. As a result, some of the advantages of unstructured, child-initiated play are lost. Games that are initiated and conducted by children promote social and psychological development in addition to physical development. Children create the games and rules and learn leadership skills, diplomacy, and compromise within the social group engaged in the games. These possibilities are lost in adult-directed sports. Not only is the child relegated to an adult-controlled world, but the spontaneous qualities of child-initiated play and games are lost to school-age children.

There are negative physical consequences of overemphasis on organized sports. Children who participate excessively in organized sports can experience burnout (Rotella, Hanson, & Coop, 1991). In addition, they are subject to sports injuries (Taft, 1991). Young children who participate in organized sports may experience injuries from overuse, such as tendinitis and stress fractures. Taft states that children seldom experience this kind of injury in free-play sports because children will stop playing when they are tired or feel pain. In organized sports, however, adults tend to encourage children to train, exercise, and compete at a level that is not appropriate to their level of development. Moreover, when parents encourage children to participate in more than one organized sport, the possibilities for injury or overuse of muscles and tendons may be compounded.

Designing Curriculum for Physical Development and Education

The Role of the Teacher.   Although the classroom teacher may not have a responsibility for developing a curriculum for physical development, the teacher should be responsible for ensuring that kindergarten and primary-grade children have a balance between unstructured and structured play during the school day. If present policies preclude outdoor play periods for young kindergarten and elementary children, the teacher should seek to inform administrators about the need for unstructured play. Developmentally, these children need the social, cognitive, and physical benefits of outdoor play on a well-designed, safe playground just as much as do younger preschool children. Although primary-grade students are interested in organized games, they still engage in sociodramatic play during these years. After they are eight or nine years old, this interest diminishes; nevertheless, kindergarten, first-grade, and second-grade children still benefit from sociodramatic play in overall development.

The classroom teacher can plan and develop physical activities that are suitable for children who are making the transition to the primary-grade years. With the child's advancing abilities in physical skills and changing interests in games with rules, the teacher organizes the classroom and outdoor environment to accommodate a range in children's physical and cognitive development and interests. Many of the activities used with preschool children are appropriate for five- to eight-year-olds. As school-age children begin to need more challenges in materials and equipment, new possibilities are added to the opportunities available for play.

The emerging ability to concentrate on games with rules creates a demand for board and card games. The teacher begins with easy games with simple rules that are easily understood and followed. Carpentry tools requiring more physical coordination can be added to the simple tools made available to preschool children. Small motor abilities can be fostered through handicraft materials for leather work, embroidery, beadwork, and painting and glazing child-made clay pieces. These activities also promote creativity and pride in accomplishment. More complex manipulative materials that focus on higher cognitive skills are enjoyed, as well as more challenging art activities and drawing materials.

Large motor skills also develop through an evolving interest in games with rules. Although the children may be most interested in baseball, there are other games that encourage beginning group play and motor skill development. Croquet, tetherball, volleyball, and basketball are commonly available. Badminton is another possible game for beginners (Eliason & Jenkins, 1990). The classroom teacher can see that these large motor games are accessible for outdoor play periods.

The Role of the Physical Education Teacher.   There are guidelines for organized curriculum for exercise and fitness for young elementary school children. Responding to information that young American children are declining in fitness, the President's Council on Physical Fitness and Sports conducted a nationwide study confirming that American youth are not in good physical condition. The report proposed that schools need to again emphasize physical education. Primary-age children need daily physical education periods that provide exercise and physical fitness. A typical physical education period would include both fitness and exercise. Figure 11.2 lists suggestions for activities that would be presented in a typical physical education class (Greene & Adeyanju, 1991).

It is recommended that physical fitness and exercise activities used with elementary school children be those that students are most likely to continue as adults. Walking, aerobic dance, calisthenics, swimming, bicycling, and jogging are among the possibilities that children will enjoy and continue later in life.

Figure 11.2 Typical Physical
Education Class Activities
L. Greene & M. Adeyanju, *Exercise
and Fitness Guidelines for
Elementary and Middle School
Children. The Elementary School
Journal, 91*, p. 441.

Activity	Time (minutes)
Presentation of fitness or health concept:	
Teacher discussion and explanation	1–2
Student participation and related activity	1–2
Brief discussion	1–2
Warm-up or muscular fitness exercise	2–3
Aerobic exercise	6–10
Skill development	9–17
Cool down	2

The physical education program should also inform students about fitness and health. Children need to know why they need to engage in physical activities and exercise and how they can lead a healthy life-style. The lesson format in Figure 11.2 begins with an opportunity that allows the teacher to introduce and explain health and fitness concepts. The goal of promoting a healthy life-style should be encouraged through observance of the following guidelines (Greene & Adeyanju, 1991, p. 442):

1. Stress the importance of aerobic conditioning and total body fitness, and promote an understanding of the physiological concepts of fitness.
2. Teach children to become responsible for their own fitness. Demonstrate to them the importance of sufficient physical activity to stimulate normal growth and development.
3. Provide experiences that will enable children to understand the necessity of maintaining good health-related fitness.
4. Incorporate motivational schemes to promote positive attitudes toward physical fitness.
5. Discuss with students the immediate and long-term effects of health-related fitness.
6. Provide information on running economy and pacing oneself when exercising.
7. Allow children to test their knowledge about health-related fitness and total fitness.

Although the guidelines just mentioned were designed for physical education teachers, they can apply to classroom teachers as well. All teachers can promote healthy life-styles and stress the need for physical fitness. Physical education and regular classroom teachers can work together in planning and providing activities for fine and gross motor skills and health and physical fitness.

The Integrated Curriculum for Physical Development

Can integrated curriculum that centers on physical development and education be designed in kindergarten and the primary grades? Many resources on curriculum design do not include motor development as one of the content areas to be addressed in curriculum development. Physical movement is sometimes identified merely as movement and grouped with music. The categorization of physical education as a component of education separate from classroom instruction also reduces the interest in using physical development and education as a focus for integrated curriculum design. There are good examples of how integrated curriculum can be designed and implemented, however. *Integrated Learning Activities for Young Children* (Trostle & Yawkey, 1990) contains many examples of activities that feature or incorporate physical education or movement education. Two examples from this resource are provided in Figure 11.3 and Figure 11.4. The first, titled "Phys. Ed." (Figure 11.3), has children use an art activity to create movement pictures. In a writing activity, the children

---

PHYSICAL EDUCATION (Movement Education)

Overview: The children learn how nice it is to feel good physically. They depict movement activities in a creatively pictoral way and then learn the steps involved in their favorite sport. Later, they write exercise routine booklets so all the children can play.

Objective: Expanding physical education knowledge and creativity.

Supplies: Construction paper; glue or paste; small tan or brown circles; mats; crayons or felt-tip markers

Words You'll Like: *sports, sportswear, circle, movement, physical exercise, routine, booklet, authors*

Getting Started
Distribute ten tan or brown one-inch circles to each youngster. Also provide colored construction paper, crayons, and glue. The children randomly paste the circles on the colored paper. They draw faces, hats, sportswear, and scenery around and on the circles to depict their favorite or imaginary movement or sport. Help them write titles for their movement pictures at the bottom of the page. Titles for the movement pictures from one group of creative first-graders included Playing Football, Strike One, Super Skaters, Physical Ed., Bowling Boys, and Swim and Sun.

Target
Ask the youngsters to display their pictures from Getting Started. They imitate the sport or movement they have drawn. Then vote on one activity that they would most like to learn. Compile with the youngsters a set of written directions for mastering the skills involved in the sport. Provide the necessary equipment or supplies, if possible. Youngsters may wish to learn somersaulting, bowling, kite flying, bicycle riding, skipping, rope jumping, ball throwing, or basket weaving. Invite them to pretend that they are a famous person while they perform each of the skills.

Figure 11.3 Integrated Curriculum for Physical Education (pp. 439–440)
S. L. Trostle & T. D. Yawkey, *Integrated Learning Activities for Young Children.* (Allyn & Bacon, 1990), pp. 97–98. Reprinted by permission of the publisher.

Moving Ahead

The children become authors. They work in teams of three or four and compile an exercise routine booklet. In the booklet, they write the exercises they feel are most interesting for their classmates. The list might include *As If* exercises or skills, such as *Make believe that you are a famous gymnast:*

1. Do a forward roll.
2. Do a backward roll.
3. Hop ten times on your left foot.
4. Do a headstand.
5. Count to twenty while standing on one foot.

Let's Talk

1. Ask each child to relate an experience to his or her Getting Started movement picture. Write one sentence on a language experience chart for each of the storytellers.
2. Discuss feelings (a) when we cannot perform a certain exercise or sport, (b) when we are learning the sport, and (c) after we have succeeded in mastering skills.
3. Invite the youngsters to locate pictures of famous athletes. Discuss the achievements and contributions of each famous athlete.

Figure 11.3 Integrated Curriculum for Physical Education *(continued)*

describe exercise routines that are compiled into a booklet. The class selects a sport and exercise routine they wish to learn. Other related activities include language experience stories and discussions about the process of learning a sport.

The second activity, "In the Air" (Figure 11.4) is related to basketball. Students engage in an activity to keep balloons in the air and pretend to be Harlem Globetrotters. Games are played that involve passing the balloon in creative ways. In addition, air-filled balloons are compared with helium-filled balloons. Written messages are put into balloons for another child in the class to read.

There are many other topics that come to mind that can correlate physical education with other components of the curriculum. The history of baseball can be studied to explore changes in rules, equipment, and uniforms. Students might learn about early baseball fields and how foods served at baseball games became popular. Students might visit a local school team or professional team workout to learn the role of physical fitness in preparing for participation in a sport. Books describing what has been learned can be written for the class library, and a mural depicting a baseball game might be created.

Another unit might be based on jump ropes and jump rope chants. Children might look to other children and older members of the community for different chants that are used for jumping rope. They could also research print resources with the librarian's assistance. Different types of jump ropes could be studied, as well as jumping with a single rope or a pair of ropes. Contests might be conducted for the

IN THE AIR (Physical Education)

Overview: The youngsters pass air-filled ballons and basketballs as team members and team leaders. Pretending to be famous pilots and the Globetrotters enhances the activities.

Objective: Cooperating with teammates to manipulate balloons and basketballs.

Supplies: Air-filled balloons; floor mats; two basketballs

Words You'll Like: *balloon, flight, airplane, pilot, Harlem Globetrotters, airport, helium, parallel*

Getting Started

Ask the youngsters to pretend that an air-filled balloon is an airplane that contains many frightened passengers, and they are the pilots. It is up to them to keep the plane in flight at all times. The youngsters stand in a circle as they bounce and toss the balloon from one pilot to another.

Target

Divide the youngsters into two equal groups. The children pretend to be the Harlem Globetrotters. Each group chooses a leader. Place a basketball in front of the straight line of children. The leader sends one basketball down the line in three unique ways, such as bouncing twice between children, bouncing under the leg, or bouncing behind the back. Each of the three times the leader sends the ball to the others in his or her group, the ball travels a new way. The last child in line to receive the ball runs the ball to the front of the line. A new leader takes

Figure 11.4   Integrated Curriculum for Physical Education (pp. 441–442)

S. L. Trostle & T. D. Yawkey, *Integrated Learning Activities for Young Children.* (Allyn & Bacon, 1990), pp. 101–102. Reprinted by permission of the publisher.

highest number of completed jumps, most improved jumper, and so on. Students might write letters to another class inviting them to come and learn new chants.

Brainstorming with parents and other teachers could result in a number of interesting topics that integrate physical education with other content areas. Once an interesting topic has been planned and implemented, others will follow. The physical education teacher is a valuable resource for planning integrated units. The librarian can also be helpful in researching information and locating books on famous athletes, stories about sports that include children, and other books that relate to a physical education topic.

The units that appear in the appendixes all contain examples of physical development activities that support the theme of the unit. Activities that require the children to use fine or gross motor skills have been described for each unit in the curriculum web and summary of activities. In addition, attention has been given to the inclusion of activities for health, safety, and nutrition. Through incorporation of physical education in integrated curriculum, children can be reminded of the importance of physical exercise and fitness.

the front of the line after the previous leader has had three turns to send the ball. The other line of children passes a second ball in a similar fashion. Which team was faster?

Moving Ahead

The youngsters, divided into two teams, form two parallel lines. The first child in line, the leader, passes a balloon (an airplane) to the next child in the line in a unique way. The airplane must not touch the ground and no hands are allowed. Play the game like the Target ball game; now each team member serves as a leader (or pilot) once. The others pass the balloon in the same fashion as the team leader. The first team to complete passing the balloon, with every child being a leader one time, is named "Champion Pilots." Ideas for no-hands balloon passing include passing under the chin, under the arm, between the feet, from head to head, or between the knees.

Let's Talk

1. Observe and compare a helium-filled balloon with a regular, air-filled balloon. Discuss the properties of a variety of gases.
2. Obtain several helium balloons. Help the youngsters to think of messages that they would like to send to others. The messages are written on small slips of paper, along with the names of the children in the classroom. The messages are inserted into the balloons. Release the balloons into the classroom. Each child finds a new balloon and reads the message inside.

Figure 11.4 Integrated Curriculum for Physical Education *(continued)*

Summary

Children who are making the transition from preschool into kindergarten and the primary grades are in the later years of early childhood education. The curriculum that is planned for them reflects the continuing importance of development, both to ensure that experiences are developmentally appropriate and to accommodate curriculum activities to changing development.

Children from ages five to eight are continuing to acquire social skills. They are more aware of peer perception and acceptance. They are developing moral reasoning in the process of developing attitudes and values. In addition to acquiring their own values, they are becoming aware of the values and attitudes of others. Teachers have the responsibility to guide children in avoiding prejudice and stereotypic attitudes toward students from different ethnic and economic groups. This goal of equality and fairness for all students is nurtured through a positive classroom climate that nurtures cooperation, mutual respect, self-esteem, and good citizenship practices.

The social studies curriculum also addresses the goal of helping students to understand themselves and others. The social studies components of history, geography, economics, sociology, and anthropology are taught within an integrated organization of content. A model integrated curriculum developed by the state of California is used as an example of how the social studies curriculum can be organized into a meaningful context. Though the California plan uses history as the integrative core for the social studies curriculum, examples of topics ranging from Oriental silkworms to untraditional ways to celebrate holidays were also described as approaches to integrating the curriculum.

The curriculum for physical development and physical education changes as children move from preschool to elementary school programs. One difference is that the need for play and physical activity may not receive the priority that it should have. Another difference is that the physical education teacher usually has the responsibility for developing the curriculum for physical development.

There are issues regarding physical education and development in the primary grades. One concern is the poor fitness level of American children and the recommendation that public schools devote more time and effort to helping children develop fitness programs and healthy life-styles. Another concern is whether physical activities should be limited to formal physical education periods. Because children in kindergarten and the primary grades benefit

from unstructured outdoor play periods, there is a need for teachers and other school personnel to advocate for young children to have the opportunity for daily outdoor play beyond formal physical education periods. Parents and teachers also need to be aware of potential problems in overstressing organized sports for primary-grade children and seek to ensure opportunities for unstructured play outside of school.

Curriculum for physical development and physical education should respond to the changing physical and cognitive abilities of the students. Opportunities for games with rules for fine motor and gross motor skills should be provided. Though much of the time devoted to providing opportunities to engage in games with rules falls within the physical education curriculum, the classroom teacher can also help ensure a balanced curriculum in physical development and make equipment and materials available for group games.

The integrated curriculum is appropriate for physical education topics. Although teachers may be less familiar with using the process with physical education, there are many topics that can be designed into thematic units with supportive experiences drawn from other content areas.

Summary Statements

1. Children from five to eight years old are still acquiring socialization skills; however, they are now more aware whether they are accepted by their peers.

2. Children need to experience both social and academic success during the latter early childhood period.

3. Moral development allows children to become aware of the role of intent when making moral judgments.

4. Attitudes and values are being acquired as a part of moral development.

5. Teachers need to guide children toward accepting and appreciating people of all cultures as part of moral development to avoid developing attitudes of prejudice.

6. The classroom climate established by the teacher can nurture democratic values and attitudes.

7. Classroom strategies such as class discussions, cooperative learning groups, and democratic decision making can nurture democratic values and attitudes.

8. The social studies curriculum in kindergarten and primary grades reflects the child's emerging cognitive skills, which are moving toward concrete operational thinking.

9. The most effective context for social studies is an integrated organization that incorporates the components of the social studies curriculum as well as other content areas.

10. Students need to study current issues such as environmental protection and the changing world order because social studies as a field is constantly changing.

11. The literacy curriculum for social studies developed by the state of California serves as a model for integrated curriculum.

12. Teachers can develop many topics for children to study that are concerned with understanding ourselves and others.

13. The curriculum for physical education also is developed for emerging physical and cognitive skills; however, a physical education teacher now has the major responsibility for providing the formal curriculum.

14. Gross and fine motor skills develop rapidly during the ages from five to eight.

15. Primary-grade children are becoming interested in games with rules. Some games—such as card and board games—involve fine motor skills, whereas others—such as tetherball and baseball—involve gross motor skills.

16. Because American children are generally unfit, more emphasis needs to be given to physical fitness and exercise in elementary schools.

17. The physical education program should achieve a balance between fitness and exercise during each class period.

18. Adults should be cautious about young children's participation in organized sports because of the danger of injuries.

19. Young children need to have opportunities for free play and free play sports to balance organized activities and sports.

20. Children in the later early childhood years still need opportunities for social, cognitive, and sociodramatic play.

21. The physical fitness and exercise activities used with children in the primary grades should be those that students are most likely to continue as adults.

22. The physical education curriculum can be integrated with other content-area subjects.

23. Cooperative planning between the classroom teacher and the physical education teacher may be required to develop thematic units centered on physical education and development.

Study Questions

1. How does the social studies curriculum for the primary grades differ from the preschool curriculum? How is it similar?

2. Why is Erikson's industry versus inferiority stage significant for young children in the primary grades?

3. How does peer approval affect social behaviors of young children entering elementary school?

4. What role should the teacher have in the young child's moral development?

5. How can an attitude of prejudice be prevented in young children?

6. Why are class discussions effective for developing democratic values and practices?

7. How does decision making facilitate understanding of the democratic process?

8. How do young children from ages five to eight learn about history?

9. Can primary-grade children construct maps? What kinds?

10. Why do young children need to be conscientious consumers?

11. Why do young children need to understand changes in countries at the present time?

12. What are some current social studies issues that young children could address (beyond the examples given in the text)?

13. What is meant by a literacy curriculum in social studies?

14. Why does the social studies curriculum need to include topics from a global perspective?

15. Why is children's literature especially helpful in planning integrated social studies curriculum?

16. Why do public schools devote less time for outdoor play than other school settings that serve children five to eight years old?

17. What does motor development imply for curriculum development in the early elementary grades?

18. How do games with rules relate to cognitive and physical development in kindergarten and primary-grade children?

19. Why should the physical education program focus on physical fitness and exercise?

20. Why are public schools accused of neglecting physical development in elementary schools?

21. What kinds of games do young children in kindergarten and the primary grades enjoy? How should the teacher introduce games with rules?

22. Why do kindergarten and primary-grade children need free play in addition to a period for physical education?
23. How would you describe a quality program for physical fitness and exercise for children in the primary grades?
24. What is the classroom teacher's role in nurturing physical development?
25. Why should the physical education program stress long-term health and fitness?

References

Alexander, F., & Crabtree, C. (1988). California's new history: Social science curriculum promises richness and depth. *Educational Leadership, 46*, 10–13.

Allport, G. (1952). *The nature of prejudice.* New York: Doubleday Anchor Books.

Atkinson, A. H., & Green, V. P. (1990). Cooperative learning: The teacher's role. *Childhood Education, 66*, 8–11.

Barnes, B. R. (1991). Using children's literature in the early anthropology curriculum. *Social Education, 55*, 17–18.

Beach, L., Hinojosa, B. L., & Tedford, A. C. (1991, November/December). Holiday express: A cross–curricular, multicultural geography unit on holidays around the world. *Instructor,* 25–29.

Byrnes, D. A., & Kiger, G. (1992). *Common bonds: Anti–bias teaching in a diverse society.* Wheaton, MD: Association For Childhood Education International.

California State Board of Education. (1988). *History–social science framework for California public schools, kindergarten through grade twelve.* Sacramento: Author.

Cole, E. (1988, Spring). Silkworms and the Orient. *Texas Child Care Quarterly,* 28–33.

Coop, R. H., & Rotella, R. J. (1991). Sport and physical skill development in elementary schools: An overview. *The Elementary School Journal, 91*, 409–412.

Dart, B. (1990, January 19). Exercise urged for youngsters. *News and Observer,* p. 1D.

Derman-Sparks, L. (1992). "It isn't fair!" Antibias curriculum for young children. In B. Neugebauer (Ed.), *Alike and different: Exploring our humanity with young children* (pp. 2–10). Washington, DC: National Association for the Education of Young Children.

Deutsch, M. (1963). Minority group and class status as related to social and personality factors in scholastic achievement. In M. Grossack (Ed.), *Mental health and segregation.* New York: Springer.

Dodge, K., Murphy, R. R., & Buchsbaum, K. (1984). The assessment of intention-cue detection skills in children: Implications for developmental psychopathology. *Child Development, 55*, 163–173.

Eliason, C. F., & Jenkins, L. (1990). *A practical guide to early childhood curriculum* (4th ed.). Columbus, OH: Merrill.

Enright, R. D., & Sutterfield, S. J. (1980). An ecological validation of social cognitive development. *Child Development, 51*, 156–161.

Epstein, L. H., Wing, R. R., & Valoski, A. (1985). Childhood obesity. *Pediatric Clinics of North America, 32*, 363–379.

Freeman, D. E., & Freeman, Y. S. (1991). "Doing" social studies: Whole language lessons to promote social action. *Social Education, 55*, 29–32, 66.

Frost, J. L. (1992). *Play and playscapes.* Albany, NY: Delmar.

Glasser, W. (1969). *Schools without failure.* New York: Harper & Row.

Greenberg, P. (1992). How to institute some simple democratic practices pertaining to respect, rights, responsibilities, and roots in any classroom (without losing your leadership position). *Young Children, 47*, 10–17.

Greene, L., & Adeyanju, M. (1991). Exercise and fitness guidelines for elementary and middle school children. *The Elementary School Journal, 91*, 437–444.

Hale-Benson, J. (1986). Research in review: Black children: Their roots, culture, and learning styles. In J. B. McCracken (Ed.), *Reducing stress in young children's lives* (pp. 122–129). Washington, DC: National Association for the Education of Young Children.

Holmes, E. E. (1991). Democracy in elementary school classes. *Social Education, 55*, 176–178.

Hughes, F. P. (1991). *Children, play, and development*. Boston: Allyn & Bacon.

Johnson, D. W., & Johnson, R. (1987). *Learning together and alone: Cooperative, competitive, and individualistic learning* (2nd ed.). Englewood Cliffs, NJ: Prentice–Hall.

Kamii, C. (1986). Viewpoint: Obedience is not enough. In J. B. McCracken (Ed.), *Reducing stress in young children's lives* (pp. 93–95). Washington, DC: National Association for the Education of Young Children.

Kohlberg, L. (1973). Moral development and the new social studies. *Social Education, 37*, 369–375.

Lane, M. (1986). Reaffirmations: Speaking out for children. A child's right to the valuing of diversity. In J. B. McCracken (Ed.), *Reducing stress in children's lives* (p. 130). Washington, DC: National Association for the Education of Young Children.

Lyman, L., & Foyle, H. C. (1990). *Cooperative grouping interactive learning: Students, teachers, administrators*. Washington, DC: National Education Association.

McNeil, E. (1969). *Human socialization*. Belmont, CA: Brooks/Cole.

Meddin, B. J., & Rosen, A. L. (1986). Child abuse and neglect: Prevention and reporting. In J. B. McCracken (Ed.), *Reducing stress in young children's lives* (pp. 78–82). Washington, DC: National Association for the Education of Young Children.

Moyer, J. (1970). *Bases for world understanding and cooperation*. Washington, DC: Association for Supervision and Curriculum Development.

Norton, D. E. (1990). Teaching multicultural literature in the reading curriculum. *The Reading Teacher, 44*, 28–40.

Nunnelley, J. C. (1990). Beyond turkeys, santas, snowmen and hearts: How to plan innovative curriculum themes. *Young Children, 45*, 24–29.

Peters, R. (1991, February). Introducing students to the global community. *Teaching K–8*, 61–62.

Piaget, J. (1965). *The moral judgment of the child*. (M. Gabain, Trans.). New York: Free Press. (Original work published 1932).

Roopnarine, J. L., & Honig, A. (1986). Research in review: The unpopular child. In J. B. McCracken (Ed.), *Reducing stress in young children's lives* (pp. 110–115). Washington, DC: National Association for the Education of Young Children.

Rotella, R. J., Hanson, T., & Coop, R. H. (1991). Burnout in youth sports. *The Elementary School Journal, 91*, 421–428.

Schickedanz, J. A., Hansen, K., & Forsyth, P. D. (1990). *Understanding children*. Mountain View, CA: Mayfield.

Seefeldt, C. (1989). *Social studies for the preschool-primary child*. Columbus, OH: Merrill.

Selman, R. (1976). Social-cognitive understanding: A guide to educational and clinical practice. In T. Lickona (Ed.), *Moral development and behavior: Theory, research, and social issues* (pp. 219–240). New York: Holt, Rinehart & Winston.

Shantz, C. U. (1975). The development of social cognition. In E. M. Hetherington (Ed.), *Reviews of child development research* (Vol. 5, pp. 257–323). Chicago: University of Chicago Press.

Soderman, A. K. (1986). Dealing with difficult young children: Strategies for teachers and parents. In J. B. McCracken (Ed.), *Reducing stress in young children's lives* (pp. 116–121). Washington, DC: National Association for the Education of Young Children.

Swiniarski, L. (1991). Toys: Universals for teaching global education. *Childhood Education, 67*, 161–163.

Taft, N. (1991). Sports injuries in children. *The Elementary School Journal, 91*, 429–436.

Trostle, S. L., & Yawkey, T. D. (1990). *Integrated learning activities for young children*. Boston: Allyn & Bacon.

Veach, D. M. (1986). Choice with responsibility. In J. B. McCracken (Ed.), *Reducing stress in young children's lives* (pp. 96–98). Washington, DC: National Association for the Education of Young Children.

West, B. (1992). Children are caught—between home and school, culture and school. In B. Neugebauer (Ed.), *Alike and different: Exploring our humanity with young children* (pp. 127–139). Washington, DC: National Association for the Education of Young Children.

White, B. P., & Phair, M. A. (1986). "It'll be a challenge!" Managing emotional stress in teaching disabled children. In J. B. McCracken (Ed.), *Reducing stress in young children's lives* (pp. 136–140). Washington, DC: National Association for the Education of Young Children.

CHAPTER TWELVE

Teaching in the Real World

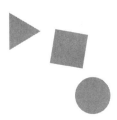

In this book we have tried to help teachers and future teachers of young children in the early childhood years become informed about quality educational programs. We have discussed some of the issues, problems, and possibilities involved with the practices used with curriculum and instruction in early childhood programs today. One purpose of this book has been to describe how teachers can develop curriculum and learning experiences that are appropriate for the young children they teach.

Following are some basic principles that have formed the foundation for characterizing quality early childhood programs:

1. Children in early childhood programs come from diverse backgrounds and have different abilities and interests. The quality early childhood program responds to and supports these differences.
2. Various theories of learning and development affect the nature of programs for young children. Teachers in quality early childhood programs understand these influences and the way in which they affect their program.
3. Current trends in early childhood education can have both positive and negative affects on efforts to implement quality programs. Program planners and teachers need to be able to put these influences into proper perspective if they are to develop and maintain a quality program.
4. The development of young children serves as a major criterion in how quality programs are designed and implemented.
5. The developmental continuum across age and grade levels should serve as a significant guide in designing quality early childhood programs that are developmentally appropriate.
6. During the preschool and primary-grade years, children move from what Piaget termed the preoperational period to the concrete operational period. The quality early childhood program responds to individual variations in developmental progress by providing educational experiences that support development rather than expect all children to achieve predetermined levels of maturity at the same rate.
7. An integrated curriculum supports a child-centered approach to curriculum design that facilitates learning as a holistic experience. The quality early childhood program utilizes child planning and parent planning in curriculum design so that learning experiences support individual and group interests and backgrounds.
8. Thematic integrated curriculum provides a focus for curriculum design that encourages children to understand the relationships and connections in knowledge. The quality early childhood program uses grouping and instructional strategies that will support children's reconstruction of knowledge as they encounter and interact with new information in learning experiences.

9. The teacher in a quality early childhood program understands how to organize the indoor and outdoor learning environments to support learning experiences that are appropriate for developmental and cultural differences in young children.
10. The early childhood teacher understands that young children live in a changing world and that early childhood programs will need to be prepared for children with diverse circumstances and needs. The effective early childhood teacher in a quality early childhood program expects to continue his or her own development as a teacher to meet the challenges presented by changing circumstances.

Because there are various types of early childhood settings and because early childhood programs vary within a community, between communities, and among different areas of the nation, early childhood teachers work under diverse kinds of circumstances. How teachers in early childhood programs design and implement curriculum and instruction in their own program setting depends on their unique backgrounds and experiences and the way in which their individual teaching styles fit into the particular environment where they work with young children. The early childhood teacher seeking employment will want to be aware of the different possibilities that are available in the community. In addition, the teacher entering the profession will want to be aware of the philosophy and approach being used in the early childhood setting where employment is sought to determine what type of a program is in place or being developed. Many teachers feel that they have no choice, that they must take whatever teaching opportunity is available. If this is the case, and the program is not appropriate, the teacher might work toward improving the situation or seek a better position in another setting. On the other hand, the teacher might have the opportunity to join a group of teachers who are in the process of restructuring their program and curriculum to be developmentally appropriate. Moreover, there are early childhood settings in many states that have been offering developmentally appropriate quality programs for many years. The teachers hired to join this type of setting have the advantage of being able to learn from fellow teachers.

In the following sections, nine early childhood educators are introduced. Their stories can serve to illustrate the opportunities and realities that exist in current programs for young children. The reader is invited to evaluate the potential for developing, improving, or advocating a developmentally appropriate early childhood program in each setting.

Beth

Beth has been teaching first grade in a suburban school district for six years. She is working on a master's degree in early childhood education. She considers herself well informed about issues and practices in the field. Although her school district has a reputation for being progressive and is highly respected in the immediate area, Beth is frustrated. She has a new principal who is very concerned with her success as an administrator. The principal is worried about achievement test scores in her school and how they will reflect upon her effectiveness as an administrator. She expects teachers in her school to focus on a skills approach to teaching and learning that will result in good test scores. Beth is particularly frustrated with the new principal because the school district encourages her to attend staff development sessions on whole language and strategies for implementing integrated curriculum with a child-centered approach. Beth knows that the school district supports developmentally appropriate curriculum, but it is discouraged in her particular school. She resists using precious time and energy to be an assertive advocate for an appropriate program for her first-grade children. Beth is uncertain how to proceed with curriculum planning because she is not clear about the future direction of her particular school and how much of her recent training she should try to implement with her students. The school has two vacancies for teachers in first-grade classrooms. Beth will be involved in interviewing candidates. She is uncertain about what information she should share about the school with prospective teachers during their visits.

Renee

Renee teaches kindergarten in the same school district as Beth. She originally taught in a child development laboratory school in a university in the Midwest. She has relocated to the Southwest because there are more teaching opportunities in this area, where the population is steadily increasing each year. When Renee first arrived, she, too, was discouraged because the school where she was teaching was very academically oriented and she found the program to be rigid and demanding compared with the developmental program she taught previously. When the school district opened a new school at the beginning of the current year, Renee was chosen to be one of the kindergarten teachers. The principal had a background in early childhood education; moreover, the school had applied for and received a grant to develop innovative programs. Renee is very pleased to be able to try new approaches in her classroom. She is confident that she and her fellow teachers are creating an exciting program for young children. However, she sometimes has moments of doubt because standardized achievement tests are administered in her school. She and her colleagues are afraid that if test scores drop they will be required to return to a more academic approach. Usually, though, she enjoys the opportunity to be the kind of teacher she has envisioned being. Another kindergarten teacher will be hired for a new classroom next year. Renee hopes that the new teacher will be knowledgeable about a developmentally based program and will bring new ideas and strategies to share with her and the other early childhood teachers.

Yolanda

Yolanda has taught for twenty years. She has worked with young Hispanic children in a small rural school district for most of those years. Yolanda is Hispanic herself and feels that she can help these young children in her preschool classroom for four-year-olds. Although the school district has limited funds, and the children come from families who are poorly paid farm workers, Yolanda's school has been recognized as an exemplary school by the state. For several years the school has served as a family resource center in the community. Families are an important part of the program and parents volunteer regularly to assist in classrooms. Yolanda and her fellow teachers design the curriculum to reflect the children's backgrounds and learning levels and the population of the community. They look to parents and community businesses to help them provide learning experiences that will broaden the world where these young children live. Walking field trips to nearby locations are a frequent activity. Yolanda uses thematic curriculum for social studies but also believes that structured teaching, using direct strategies, is important. She uses commercial curriculum materials and learning centers to extend learning experiences for her children. Yolanda hopes that new teachers hired for her school will understand the cultural backgrounds of the children in her community and be prepared to continue the type of program that nurtures this particular population of children.

Susan

Susan is a teacher in a private early childhood center that combines a preschool program with child care. The center calls itself a child enrichment center. It is located in a community of professional parents. The center is new and well equipped. There is a beautiful playscape, and each classroom has computers and an abundance of software. Susan has a degree in music but no teaching certificate. Her training for her position has been primarily through local workshops given by a junior college. Susan is very interested in using the fine arts in her classroom. She supplements supplies that the center provides with materials that she buys herself. Susan also buys resource and idea books through catalogs at the center. She is beginning to understand a little about designing curriculum around a theme. She is currently trying out some ideas she found in one of her books. She is thinking about the possibility of contacting a nearby university to work toward becoming certified, but she likes the freedom she has to pursue her own ideas as a teacher at the center. The pay is poor compared with the salaries of public school teachers; however, Susan enjoys her small class of children, which would be much larger in a public school setting in her community. She also has an interest in opening her own center and further developing the expressive arts for young children. One frustration that Susan encounters is the frequent change in teachers at the center. The turnover is so high that teachers do not have time to adjust to the children and the program before they have moved on to find a position that offers higher pay.

Rollo and Nancy

Rollo operates his own early childhood center. He lives in a small city on the East Coast. Rollo and his wife, Nancy, have two children in elementary school. They are very interested in new trends in life-styles and in teaching children to be socially responsible. Rollo opened the New Age School for children from age two to five. He perceives his program to be suitable for parents who want a school that reflects the values of their upper-middle-class culture. Children attend the preschool program for a half day. Child-care services are not a part of the program. Rollo's background is in psychology, and Nancy has a master's degree in English. Both of them have taken courses in early childhood education through an extension program offered by a local college. They opened the school originally for their own children. The program features expressive experiences and trips to museums and other cultural centers, activities which Rollo and Nancy believe are missing in other preschool settings. The curriculum reflects an awareness of ecology, animal rights, natural foods, and the fine arts. They prefer to hire teachers with a liberal arts background who agree with their philosophy of education. This is possible because policies requiring teacher certification do not apply to private and parochial schools in their state. They train their staff themselves and hold several orientation sessions each year for prospective parents. The school has a waiting list; therefore, Rollo and Nancy are considering opening a second center or expanding the current program.

Gladys

Gladys is an African-American teacher at a public school in Oregon that serves children from many cultural backgrounds. The school includes a program for non-English-speaking four-year-olds, as well as kindergarten through third grade. The school is located within a housing development for families with low income. Because all types of families seek work in the area, the children represent twelve different cultural backgrounds. Language acquisition is the most important component of the curriculum. Curriculum development is usually centered on different cultures represented by the children in the school. Gladys teaches second grade. Most of her children have acquired some facility in English, but there are a few every year who are still very limited in the use of expressive English or unfamiliar with Standard English. Gladys and her fellow teachers do a great deal of team planning. They also exchange children throughout the day to better place the children in activities that are appropriate for their level of language and cognitive development. Curriculum planning is done by teams of teachers representing at least two grade levels; but, frequently, multiage grouping across three grade levels is more useful for the children. Several new teachers will be hired for the coming school year. Gladys and her colleagues hope the new teachers will quickly adjust to the style of teaching they have developed in the school. They have also heard rumors that their principal will be transferred to a larger school. They are uneasy about having a new principal next year who might not understand and support their program.

Loretta

Loretta is the principal in an inner-city elementary school. Her school includes kindergarten through fifth grade. In addition, an early childhood wing for children with disabilities has programs for three- to five-year-olds; these children, who have various special needs, also participate in regular classroom activities. Until recently, the school district required an academic approach to curriculum and instruction. Loretta belongs to a national early childhood organization, as does the early childhood supervisor for the district. As a result of the efforts of Loretta and the supervisor to inform district administrators about the inappropriate practices that are currently in use in early childhood classrooms, the district has decided to develop a model early childhood program in Loretta's school that will use multiage grouping to try to eliminate the high numbers of children failing the primary grades. Although all of Loretta's teachers in kindergarten through third grade have expressed an interest in the training being offered to prepare for implementing the new program, Loretta has some concerns. She believes that some of her teachers are reluctant to leave self-contained classrooms and a more traditional curriculum. She is considering suggesting that some teachers might like to transfer to another school in the district and then replacing them with either new or experienced teachers who have a more flexible approach to teaching. She is also concerned that she will not have time to participate in the training and curriculum development process. Her school experiences crises frequently, and Loretta has a Reading Recovery program starting up this semester as well. She is looking for volunteers to serve as reading tutors and makes frequent visits to local organizations that might be interested in helping. Loretta sometimes feels that she is trying to implement more than she and the teachers can manage. On the other hand, she feels she owes it to the students and parents to provide the best early childhood education possible. She and the teachers are hoping that the district will be able to provide financial support for the materials needed to implement the new model that will be developed.

Loisa

Loisa has been teaching for five years. She is married and has three children; two are in high school and one is in middle school. Loisa completed her training to become an elementary teacher twenty years ago but did not begin teaching until her children were well along in school. Loisa teaches first grade. The state education agency recently rewrote learning objectives for kindergarten and the primary grades that focus on development rather than skills. Loisa is uneasy about using the new objectives. She believes she is a competent teacher, a firm believer in giving children a good start in the first grade. Loisa feels very comfortable with the commercial textbooks and materials purchased by her school and uses them to make sure that her children acquire the skills they need to achieve in school. However, the school district is pushing a developmental approach using the developmental objectives that will require her to design her own curriculum. She has studied the new objectives and finds them to be very general and vague. Loisa has agreed to attend meetings where the new developmental objectives will be explained and where there will be discussions about how the objectives can be used to design curriculum experiences for children with different rates of development. Loisa has her doubts about the changes that are being discussed and is concerned that too much work will be required to prepare for teaching. She wants to keep an open mind but is confused by the many terms—such as *alternative assessments, emergent literacy,* and *outcome-based learning*—that are being discussed by her fellow teachers. She feels that it has taken her this long to master how to teach first grade and does not want to have to start over with some new fad that probably will change yet again.

Teachers who are moving into professional teaching positions may find themselves teaching with early childhood educators similar to those described above. They may find that teaching in the real world is either very similar to or different from approaches to teaching suggested in this text. Whatever the educational environment in which teachers of young children find themselves, there will be opportunities to work toward developing a quality program in their classroom. They may find themselves in the position of becoming advocates for the type of program they believe is best for young children. As professionals in the field of early childhood education, they will want to maintain currency with new developments. To achieve this status, they will want to consider joining two organizations that address issues and disseminate information about early childhood education in the United States. Both the Association for Childhood Education International and the National Association for the Education of Young Children welcome new members and publish excellent journals and educational materials.

Today's new teachers will become tomorrow's educational leaders. There is much work to be done to improve early childhood education in this country. Early childhood educators in the twenty-first century will be continually adjusting their programs as society, children, and educational resources continue to evolve and change. The early childhood educator can make a difference in the lives and learning of very young children. The challenge is awesome, as is the opportunity.

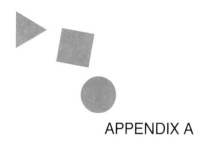

APPENDIX A

Preschool Unit: "Seeds"

UNIT PLAN OUTLINE

Unit Topic: Seeds

Overview or Rationale for the Unit: To motivate, stimulate, and interest the children in learning and developing concepts associated with seeds, specifically the following:

1. All growing things develop from some sort of seed.
2. Seeds are different from one another in color, shape, size, and texture.
3. Seeds need several things in order to grow.
4. We eat some seeds.

Developmental Stage: Cognitive Development

Grade Level: Kindergarten

Brainstorming Web: See Figure A.1.

List of Activities to Be Used for Five Lesson Plans

1. Stories about seeds (teacher directed)
2. Seed walk excursion (teacher–child initiated)
3. Examining and dissecting seeds (teacher–child initiated)
4. Seed collage (child initiated)
5. Counting seeds (child initiated)
6. Dictated story (teacher–child initiated)
7. Picture-card sequence of seed growth (child initiated)

8. Songs about seeds (teacher–child initiated)
9. Pretending to be seeds: music/movement (teacher–child initiated)
10. Compare and contrast different seeds (child initiated)
11. Seed shaker instruments (child initiated)
12. Classify different seeds (child initiated)

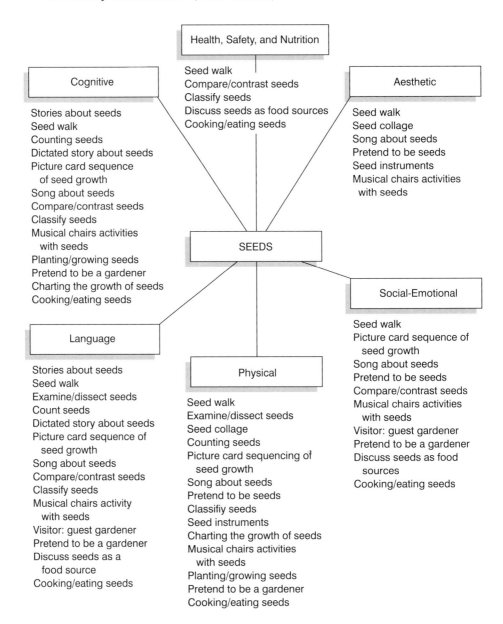

Health, Safety, and Nutrition
Seed walk
Compare/contrast seeds
Classify seeds
Discuss seeds as food sources
Cooking/eating seeds

Cognitive
Stories about seeds
Seed walk
Counting seeds
Dictated story about seeds
Picture card sequence
   of seed growth
Song about seeds
Compare/contrast seeds
Classify seeds
Musical chairs activities
   with seeds
Planting/growing seeds
Pretend to be a gardener
Charting the growth of seeds
Cooking/eating seeds

Aesthetic
Seed walk
Seed collage
Song about seeds
Pretend to be seeds
Seed instruments
Musical chairs activities
   with seeds

SEEDS

Language
Stories about seeds
Seed walk
Examine/dissect seeds
Count seeds
Dictated story about seeds
Picture card sequence of
   seed growth
Song about seeds
Compare/contrast seeds
Classify seeds
Musical chairs activity
   with seeds
Visitor: guest gardener
Pretend to be a gardener
Discuss seeds as a
   food source
Cooking/eating seeds

Physical
Seed walk
Examine/dissect seeds
Seed collage
Counting seeds
Picture card sequencing of
   seed growth
Song about seeds
Pretend to be seeds
Classifiy seeds
Seed instruments
Charting the growth of seeds
Musical chairs activities
   with seeds
Planting/growing seeds
Pretend to be a gardener
Cooking/eating seeds

Social-Emotional
Seed walk
Picture card sequence of
   seed growth
Song about seeds
Pretend to be seeds
Compare/contrast seeds
Musical chairs activities
   with seeds
Visitor: guest gardener
Pretend to be a gardener
Discuss seeds as food
   sources
Cooking/eating seeds

Figure A.1   Brainstorming Web

13. Musical chairs activity with seed packages (teacher–child initiated)
14. Visitor: guest gardener (teacher/guest directed)
15. Planting and growing seeds (teacher–child initiated)
16. Pretending to be a gardener in dramatic play (child initiated)
17. Charting the growth of seeds (teacher directed)
18. Discuss seeds as food sources (teacher–child initiated)
19. Cooking/eating seeds (teacher–child initiated)

Unit Objectives

1. As a result of reading and listening to stories about seeds and going on a seed walk, students will be able to dictate their thoughts about seeds in story form.
2. As a result of taking a nature walk to find seeds, students will understand that seeds come from many plants, trees, and other vegetation and that they vary tremendously in size, color, shape, and texture.
3. By examining and dissecting seeds, the students will develop a general understanding of the complexity of seeds.
4. Students will be able to make unique seed collages with a variety of seeds after comparing and contrasting their different types.
5. After discussing and reading about the growth process of seeds, children will be able to place sequence cards of seed growth in order.
6. As a result of learning a song about the growth of seeds, students will be able to pretend to be seeds; musical background will accompany.
7. Following an activity in examining and dissecting seeds, students will understand that seeds can be organized or classified according to their color, shape, size, and texture.
8. As a result of collecting seeds on the nature walk, students will be able to make rhythm instruments using a variety of seeds.
9. By classifying seeds, students will be able to participate in a musical chairs activity with seed packages.
10. As a result of visiting with a gardener, the students will be able to plant their own seeds.
11. The students will be able to chart the growth of their own seeds as a result of planting seeds.
12. By observing the actions of the guest gardener, students will be able to pretend to be a gardener in dramatic play.
13. Through listening to stories about seeds that are eaten, children will be able to participate in a discussion about seeds as a food source.
14. As a result of participating in a cooking activity with seeds, the children will learn of the nutritional value of seeds.

Assumptions about Previous Knowledge

1. Knowledge of story structure
2. Knowledge of the terms *before* and *after*

Summary of Activities

1. The teacher begins each lesson with a series of books that introduce the topic, which involves seeds in a unique way. Through these readings and the discussions that follow, language arts is integrated into every lesson in the unit.
2. The students will take an excursion around the school grounds and collect as many different kinds of seeds as they can find. The activity involves cognitive development using concepts in science. It also integrates language, aesthetic, and social development through discussions among the students. Physical skills are used in the process of walking and collecting leaves.
3. The teacher and the students will discuss the characteristics of a variety of seeds. They will look at size, shape, color, texture, and the parent plant. They will then dissect several seeds, taking note of the differences among them. This activity involves oral language, social skills through cooperative activities, and fine motor skills for dissecting the seeds.
4. Students will be instructed to construct a seed collage using seeds, glue, and construction paper. The activity provides for aesthetic development as the children construct their unique collage. Fine motor skills are integrated in that the children must be able to manipulate the materials and use the glue.
5. The students are given a muffin tin labeled with the numbers 1 through 10. They are then instructed to place the correct amount of seeds in the appropriate cup. The children will use cognitive skills when counting and fine motor skills for handling the seeds.
6. As a class, the students will dictate a story to the teacher, who will, in turn, write the children's thoughts in story form.
7. When provided with a series of pictures showing the growth of a seed at various stages, the students will place them in appropriate order. In doing so, children will be using cognitive thinking skills as well as language and social skills to reach a consensus within their cooperative learning group.
8. The teacher will introduce a song about seeds. Language skills will be integrated into this expressive arts activity.
9. The children will be asked to pretend to be a sprouting seed; background music will be provided. They will be using motor skills and developing an appreciation for music and its different tempos.
10. The teacher will read to the children about the differences between seeds. The children will then be given a variety of seeds to compare and contrast in a group discussion. Speaking and cognitive skills will be used.
11. The seeds collected on the nature excursion will be used to make rhythm instruments. Children will play their instruments to pieces of recorded music. They will be developing aesthetic appreciation for a variety of forms of music and using motor skills to construct and use the instruments.
12. Students will use the muffin tins and seeds that were used in a counting activity for a classification experience. They will classify seeds according to color, shape, size, and texture. Both cognitive and fine motor skills will be used.
13. Children will be given a selection of seeds to use in an adapted version of musical chairs. The teacher will stop the music at various intervals and ask

those who have a seed with a specific characteristic to sit down. Students will use cognitive skills to identify their seeds. Social skills will be integrated through participation in the group activity.

14. The guest gardener will read books to the children on planting and growing seeds. The group will then discuss the process of planting seeds. Students will demonstrate listening skills, show respect for others who are speaking, and actively participate in the discussion.

15. Children will work under the direction and supervision of the teacher and guest gardener in planting their own seeds. Students will be required to listen carefully and follow directions in order to successfully complete the task. They will be using fine motor skills to plant their seeds and oral language to explain the steps they took in the planting process.

16. The children will be provided with various gardening supplies for use in the dramatic play center. They will be using motor skills and symbolic play to engage in sociodramatic experiences.

17. After their seeds begin to grow, students will discuss the changes and will record the growth of their seeds on a chart. Language and cognitive skills will be used in conjunction with working with peers.

18. After listening to stories about seeds that we eat, children will be allowed to share individual experiences they have had with eating various seeds. Socialization skills will be used in the group discussion.

19. During the cooking activity, the teacher will ask the children to gather the necessary ingredients for making peanut butter. They will be measuring and adding ingredients under the teacher's direction. They will use cognitive, socialization, and physical skills.

LESSON PLAN 1

Lesson Title: An Introduction to Seeds

Lesson Objectives

1. As a result of reading and listening to stories about seeds and going on a seed walk, students will be able to dictate their thoughts about seeds in story form.
2. As a result of taking a nature walk to find seeds, students will understand that seeds come from many plants, trees, and other vegetation and that they vary tremendously in size, color, shape, and texture.
3. By examining and dissecting seeds, the students will develop a general understanding of the complexity of seeds.
4. Students will be able to make unique seed collages with a variety of seeds.

Developmental and/or Content Areas that Have Been Integrated: Cognitive, physical, social-emotional, language, and aesthetic experiences have been integrated into the lesson.

Lesson Procedures

1. In a whole-group setting, read *Seeds and More Seeds,* by Millicent E. Selsam. Discuss the book and plan the nature excursion to be taken. Describe things the students can look for and write them on a chart.
2. Take a nature walk around the school grounds looking for seeds. Let the children collect into a shopping bag any seeds they find. Encourage conversation among the children.
3. In small groups, have the children talk about what they saw on the walk or collected in their bags. Then guide the children in cutting an apple and examining the seeds and the star shape made by the seeds. Show other types of seeds and discuss edible versus inedible seeds. Guide the children in discussing differences in size, shape, and color of the seeds. Children can have their apple for a snack.
4. In the art center, provide the children with an array of seeds and let them make their seed collage.
5. Place in the mathematics center a muffin tin that is labeled with the numbers 1 to 10. Show the children how to place the correct number of seeds in each cup.

Materials Needed

Shopping bag

Book

   Seeds and More Seeds, by Millicent E. Selsam

Apples

Bird seed

Glue

Muffin tin (labeled 1 through 10)

Large paper

Writing utensil

Evaluation

Teacher

   Were the activities developmentally appropriate?

   Did the children acquire an understanding of seeds?

Activity

   Were the children interested?

   Did the children participate?

Students

   What comments and actions did the student use that suggest a broader understanding of the nature and function of seeds?

LESSON PLAN 2

Lesson Title: Seed Growth

Lesson Objectives

1. After discussing and reading about the growth process of seeds, children will be able to place sequence cards of seed growth in order.
2. As a result of learning a song about the growth of seeds, students will be able to pretend to be seeds.

Developmental and/or Content Areas That Have Been Integrated: Cognitive, physical, aesthetic, social-emotional, and language activities have been integrated.

Lesson Procedures

1. The teacher reads from the following books:
    The Tiny Seed, by Eric Carle

    How a Seed Grows, by Joseph Low

    The Wonders of Seeds, by Alfred Stefferund

    A discussion of seeds follows.
2. Children will work in small groups to determine the growth sequence of plants. The teacher provides a series of sequence cards showing the development of a plant from a seed. Children work cooperatively to put the cards in their correct sequence.
3. The teacher guides the students in learning "The Garden Song" to a record. The song describes the seed as a tiny, still object; then it slowly begins to grow with the help of sun and water.
4. After learning the garden song, children are asked to pretend that they are the little seed that gradually grows. As the song is played, the children assume a position as a tiny seed. As they sing along, they act out the growing process. The teacher participates with the children as they move and pantomime the actions suggested by the song.

Materials Needed

Books
   The Tiny Seed, by Eric Carle
   How a Seed Grows, by Joseph Low
   The Wonders of Seeds, by Alfred Stefferund
Sequence cards
Record
   "The Garden Song"

Evaluation

Teacher

Did the students understand stages of a seed's growth into a plant from the stories and discussion?

Activity

Did the children enjoy the activities?

Did the activity spark the children's desire to grow their own seeds?

Students

Did the students work cooperatively in the center activity?

Were the students interested in the activity?

LESSON PLAN 3

Lesson Title: Seeds Are Different

Lesson Objectives

1. Following an activity in examining and dissecting seeds, students will understand that seeds can be organized or classified according to their color, shape, size, and texture.
2. As a result of collecting seeds on the nature walk, students will be able to make rhythm instruments using a variety of seeds.
3. By classifying seeds, the students will be able to participate in a musical chairs activity with seed packages.

Developmental and/or Content Areas That Have Been Integrated: Cognitive and physical development have been integrated.

Lesson Procedures

1. In a whole-group setting, read *Bean and Plant,* by Christine Back. Discuss the differences and similarities among seeds.
2. Have the children classify seeds in a muffin tin by some category, including size, shape, color or texture.
3. Play musical chairs in a large-group activity. Place seed packages on chairs. When the music stops, the teacher will call out a characteristic of seeds to identify. If the chair has seeds with that characteristic, the child may sit down. For example, the teacher may say, "Everyone who has black seeds may sit down."
4. Place a variety of books about seeds and plants in the class library.
5. Have the children make their own rhythm instruments using seeds in the art center. Paper rolls from toilet tissue may be used to construct a seed shaker. Instruments are played to several musical pieces.

Materials Needed

Book
Bean and Plant, by Christine Back
Muffin tins
Collection of seeds
Glue music

Evaluation

Teacher
Were the activities developmentally appropriate?
Did the children understand that seeds can have differences and similarities?
Activity
Were the children interested?
Did they participate?
Students
Did the children participate?
Did they demonstrate an understanding of how to classify seeds?

LESSON PLAN 4

Lesson Title: Planting and Growing Seeds

Lesson Objectives

1. As a result of visiting with a gardener, the students will be able to plant their own seeds.
2. The students will be able to chart the growth of their own seeds.
3. By observing the actions of the guest gardener, the students will be able to pretend to be a gardener in a dramatic play.

Developmental and/or Content Areas That Have Been Integrated: Cognitive, physical, aesthetic, social-emotional, and language activities have been integrated.

Lesson Procedures

1. The teacher introduces the class visitor, a gardener in the community. The gardener first asks the children what they already know about seeds and then reads to the class from the following books: *Planting Seeds,* by Millicent

Selsam, and *Hidden Magic of Seeds,* by Dorothy Shuttesworth. The guest gardener and students discuss what is involved in planting seeds. The children are asked what they believe to be the magic of seeds.

2. In small-group activities, students are asked to sort and match a mixture of seeds by color and shape. They are asked to select some seeds for planting.

3. Children are assisted in planting their seeds in small containers. Throughout the process, questioning and discussing are constant. Following the activity, students are asked to explain the process to another child.

4. The teacher introduces a chart on which students measure and record the growth of their plant. Growth on charts of the same seed types will be compared, as well as growth on charts of different seed types.

5. Tools and equipment for gardening are placed in the dramatic play center for role-playing activities.

Materials Needed

Books

Planting Seeds, by Millicent Selsam

Hidden Magic of Seeds, by Dorothy Shuttesworth

Assortment of seeds

Soil, water, containers

Growth charts

For dramatic play:

Gloves

Hat or bonnet

Small hand shovel

Buckets

Water sprinkler

Evaluation

Teacher

Did the children understand the gardener's questions?

Did they understand how to plant and care for their seeds?

Activity

Did the children enjoy interacting with the gardener?

Did they enjoy planting their seeds?

Students

Could the students sort and match their seed assortment?

Did they work cooperatively with the other students?

Were they able to describe the planting process?

LESSON PLAN 5

Lesson Title: We Eat Some Seeds

Lesson Objectives

1. Through listening to stories about seeds that are eaten, children will be able to participate in a discussion about seeds as food sources.
2. As a result of participating in a cooking activity with seeds, the children will learn of the nutritional value of seeds.

Developmental and/or Content Areas That Have Been Integrated: Cognitive, physical, social-emotional, language, and nutrition activities have been integrated.

Lesson Procedures

1. The teacher reads the book, *Seeds We Eat,* and a section from *Science Fun with Peanuts and Popcorn.* The teacher and the children share their experiences in eating seeds.
2. The teacher introduces the activity of making peanut butter to small groups. She asks the students to recall the ingredients that are needed. Students are then assigned to different tasks for making peanut butter. Some will shell peanuts and remove skins, others will gather the supplies needed, and so on.
3. The teacher asks the children to review the process of making peanut butter. For each cup of peanuts, students will measure one teaspoonful of vegetable oil and add it before placing the ingredients in a food processor.
4. After the peanut butter is made, students make their own sandwiches to enjoy.

Materials Needed

Books
> *Seeds We Eat,* by Shelley Harper
> *Science Fun with Peanuts and Popcorn,* by Rose Wyler

Peanuts
Vegetable oil
Measuring spoons
Food processor
Butter knives
Bread

Evaluation

Teacher

Were the children provided with plenty of examples of seeds that are eaten?

Did the children have sufficient opportunity to participate?

Activity

Did the children enjoy the activities?

Were they able to follow the directions for making peanut butter and work cooperatively?

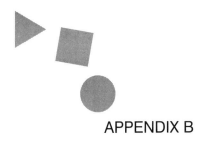

APPENDIX B

Preschool Unit: "Farm Animals"

UNIT PLAN OUTLINE

Unit Topic: Farm Animals

Overview or Rationale for the Unit: Because children generally like animals and have an innate curiosity about them, implementing a farm animal unit is a way to channel their interest and facilitate a rich learning experience. The suggested trip to a farm will especially help to build a larger background knowledge base for future learning.

Developmental Stage: Preoperational

Grade Level: Kindergarten

Brainstorming Web: See Figure B.1.

List of Activities to Be Used for Five Lesson Plans

1. Visit a farm.
2. Make a big book, using pictures from the field trip.
3. Observe eggs in an incubator set up in the science center.
4. Sing "Old McDonald."
5. Chart students' favorite animals from the song.
6. Work with number line made of duck feet shapes on the floor.
7. Write "I Went Walking" story.
8. Make a mural.
   use fingerpaint with grain

   use animal sponge painting

9. Square dance
10. Reenact The Barn Dance in dramatic play center.
11. Match pictures to animal sounds tape.
12. Make pancakes.

Unit Objectives

1. As a result of visiting a farm, children will be able to contribute something of their experience to a big book story.
2. As a result of watching eggs in an incubator, children will gain an understanding of how chicks are developed in eggs.
3. As a result of choosing their favorite animal from the song "Old McDonald," children will be able to determine the class's overall favorite.

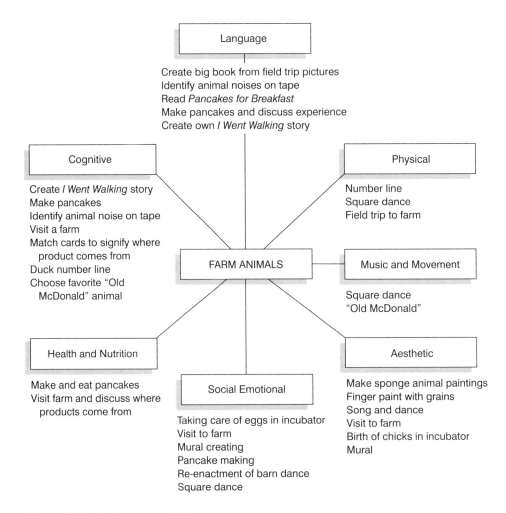

Language

Create big book from field trip pictures
Identify animal noises on tape
Read *Pancakes for Breakfast*
Make pancakes and discuss experience
Create own *I Went Walking* story

Cognitive

Create *I Went Walking* story
Make pancakes
Identify animal noise on tape
Visit a farm
Match cards to signify where product comes from
Duck number line
Choose favorite "Old McDonald" animal

Physical

Number line
Square dance
Field trip to farm

FARM ANIMALS

Music and Movement

Square dance
"Old McDonald"

Health and Nutrition

Make and eat pancakes
Visit farm and discuss where products come from

Social Emotional

Taking care of eggs in incubator
Visit to farm
Mural creating
Pancake making
Re-enactment of barn dance
Square dance

Aesthetic

Make sponge animal paintings
Finger paint with grains
Song and dance
Visit to farm
Birth of chicks in incubator
Mural

Figure B.1 Brainstorming Web

4. As a result of working with manipulatives and a number line, children will be able to match the numeral to the set to which it corresponds for sets of objects from one to ten.
5. As a result of listening to the story *I Went Walking,* children will be able to make predictions and finish repetitive sentences.
6. As a result of participating in the reading of *I Went Walking* in class, children will be able to "write" (using emergent literacy) their own story about the animal that was looking at them at the farm.
7. As a result of working with paint, paper, yarn, hay, sponges, etc., children will be able to contribute to the creation of a class mural.
8. As a result of listening to the story *The Barn Dance* and being given square dancing directions, children will participate in a simple dance.
9. As a result of listening to *The Barn Dance* and using associated props, children will re-create the story during center time.
10. As a result of listening to a tape of animal sounds, children will be able to identify the animal and match the corresponding picture to the sound.
11. After hearing *Pancakes for Breakfast,* children will be able to recall where the ingredients for pancakes come from.
12. As a result of making pancakes, children will understand how to use a measuring cup and measurement terms.

Assumptions about Previous Knowledge

We assume that the child has an adequate vocabulary and language skills to participate in the activities and that the child has had some previous experience with art activities.

Summary of Activities

1. **Visit a Farm.** Students will visit a farm and be shown pigs, cows, horses, ducks, and sheep. They will pet the animals, feed the chickens, and see a cow being milked. This activity involves cognitive development as the children observe the animals. It integrates language development in the discussions that take place during the field trip, and social development is facilitated in the children's interactions. Motor skills are being used as the children walk on the farm and feed the animals.
2. **Make a Big Book.** During the field trip, the teacher will take pictures to be displayed in the classroom. The children will sequence the pictures according to the day's activities and then dictate a story reenacting their trip. The teacher will record their responses and give them each one page of the story to illustrate. The pages will be put together to form a class big book that will be put in the reading center. This activity uses cognitive and language skills when the children recall their farm experiences in sequence. Fine motor skills are being developed as the children create their illustrations, which also promotes aesthetic development.
3. **Observe Eggs in an Incubator.** The teacher will set up the eggs in an incubator to be kept in the science center. She will discuss the concept of

"touching only with the eyes." She will place a calendar in the center, and the children will mark off each date and count how many days the eggs had been there before they hatched. This activity encourages cognitive and language development as the children observe and discuss what is happening each day. It also facilitates social development as the children exercise control and care for the eggs. Observing new life is an aesthetic experience that can be woven into discussion.

4. **Sing "Old McDonald" and Chart the Favorite Animal.** The class will sing "Old McDonald" together. Then they will place their name card under their favorite animal drawn on a large chart. The class will determine which animal has the largest number of names under it and thus identify it as the favorite animal. Second and third choices will also be determined. This activity promotes language development, because the children are expressing which is their favorite animal. Cognitive skills are being used to determine the favorite animals. The music enhances aesthetic development.

5. **Duck Feet Number Line.** A large number line will be placed on the floor with the numbers 1 to 10 written on duck feet. The child will stand on the first footprint and the teacher will give the child a set of plastic ducks, ranging in quantity from one to ten. The child will be asked to waddle to the number that corresponds to the number of ducks he or she is given. This activity can also be done with two children instead of a teacher. This activity uses physical skills as the child waddles to the correct number. It uses cognitive skills as the child matches the numeral to the corresponding set. If this activity is done with two children, they will develop socially as a result of their interactions.

6. **Write an "I Went Walking" Story.** The teacher will read *I Went Walking* to the class and then ask the children to choose an animal that was looking at them when they went to the farm and "write" a story about it. This activity facilitates the children's cognitive and language development when they create their own story and recall the story they heard. Sharing their stories with one another integrates their social and emotional development, while the actual creation of their story uses motor skills.

7. **Make a Mural.** During large-group time, the teacher will provide a large farm scene backdrop made on butcher paper and give instructions for the children to add their favorite farm animal or the one they wrote about in the walking story. The mural will be completed in small groups with the help of a parent. This activity facilitates children's cognitive and language development when they create their own animal for the mural and when they work together cooperatively. Fine motor skills are being used, and the art activity stimulates their aesthetic development.

8. **Square Dance.** The teacher will read *The Barn Dance,* by Bill Martin, Jr., and John Archimbault. Then the children will listen to a square dance tape and specific commands, such as the Virginia Reel, and the teacher will explain and demonstrate the caller's directions. Students will learn and participate in the square dance. Dancing facilitates the social development of the children, as well as their physical development. Aesthetic development is enhanced as children respond to music with body movement.

9. **Reenact the Barn Dance in the Dramatic Play Center.** The dramatic play center should be arranged as a simulation of the barn in *The Barn Dance* book. A table with a red-and-white checkered tablecloth, a small bale of hay, and a prop box complete with cowboy boots, hats, kerchiefs, and child-size musical instruments (such as fiddles or guitars) will encourage the children to reenact the book in their dramatic play. This activity facilitates the children's social development through play and enhances their language development as they role play.

10. **Match Pictures to Animal Sounds.** In the listening center, children will listen to a tape of farm animal sounds and pick the corresponding animal from animal pictures. The answer will be given after each sound so that the child can self-correct his or her choice. This listening activity promotes cognitive, listening, and language development skills.

11. **Pancake Party.** The teacher will read *Pancakes for Breakfast,* by Tomi dePaola. After the reading, the teacher will write the correct measurements of the ingredients on a large chart. The children will divide into small groups and follow the directions on the chart with the help of volunteer fifth graders. Cognitive and language development is encouraged as children "read" the recipe chart and measure the ingredients. Vocabulary is developed as groups discuss the ingredients and cooking and measuring terms. Nutrition and health concepts are also incorporated into the activity. Social development is involved as children interact with other students.

LESSON PLAN 1

Lesson Title: Field Trip to Farm

Lesson Objectives

1. As a result of visiting a farm, children will be able to contribute something of their experience to a big book story.
2. As a result of watching eggs in an incubator, children will gain an understanding of how chicks are developed in eggs.

Developmental and/or Content Areas that Have Been Integrated: This lesson involves cognitive development in observing scientific concepts. Language development is facilitated through the children's interactions. Physical skills will be used as children walk on the farm, and an appreciation for the beauty found in their environment will be facilitated through observation and conversation during the field trip.

Lesson Procedures
Introduction.   Students will visit a farm and pet and feed the animals. They will be encouraged to notice sounds and movements of the animals. The teacher will take

pictures of the day's activities. When the class returns, the teacher will mount the pictures on tagboard and display them at large-group time.

Development.   Students will be encouraged to describe what is happening in the photos and to arrange them in sequential order as a reenactment of the day's events. Together they will then dictate a story retelling their experience on the farm.

The teacher will give each student one page of the story and allow them to illustrate it. Then the teacher will build a big book and make it available in the reading center for the children.

The teacher will set up eggs in an incubator in the science center. The teacher will discuss with the children what the incubator is and the importance of "touching only with their eyes." The teacher will place a calendar in the center and each day the children can mark off the date and count how many days the eggs had been there before they hatched.

Summary Review.   At large-group time, children will read together the big book and further discuss their field trip. Children will be encouraged to explain their illustrations and share observations of the eggs in the incubator.

Materials Needed

Tagboard

Marking pens

Photographs

Crayons

Incubator

Calendar

Paper

Evaluation

Teacher

Did the children understand the activities from the explanations given?

Were materials used appropriate and adequate?

Activity

Did the children enjoy the activity?

Were the children able to carry out the activity?

Were the children able to carry out the activity with little assistance?

Students

Did all students participate?Were the children able to use descriptive language to discuss the field trip and contribute to the big book story?

LESSON PLAN 2

Lesson Title: Graphing Children's Favorite Farm Animals

Lesson Objectives

1. As a result of choosing their favorite animal from the song "Old McDonald," children will be able to determine the class's overall favorite.
2. As a result of working with manipulatives and a number line, children will be able to match the numeral to the set to which it corresponds for sets of objects from one to ten.

Developmental and/or Content Areas That Have Been Integrated: This lesson promotes cognitive development through counting, sequencing, and corresponding number to numeral. Physical development is integrated as children waddle, imitating a duck's movement. Aesthetic appreciation is incorporated through the song.

Lesson Procedures
Introduction.   Children will sing "Old McDonald" as a class. Then they will be asked which was their favorite farm animal and be instructed to place their name strip under a picture of that animal on a wall chart.

Development.   The children will then count together to see which was the class favorite, the second favorite, and so on. Then they will sing the song again with the favorite animal first, the second favorite next, and so on. In the math center, a large number line will be placed on the floor with the numerals 1 to 10 written on duck prints. Working in pairs, one child will give the other child a number of ducks, and the second child will waddle to the corresponding numeral.

Materials Needed

Classroom chart of farm animals
Name strips
Plastic ducks
Duck footprints

Evaluation

Teacher
    Did the children understand how to do the activities?
    Were the materials appropriate and adequate?
Activity
    Did the children enjoy the activities?
    Were the children able to carry out the activities successfully?

Students

Did all the students participate? Was descriptive language used to compare choices for the animal chart?

Were children able to match the set of ducks to the appropriate numeral?

LESSON PLAN 3

Lesson Title: I Went Walking

Lesson Objectives

1. As a result of listening to the story *I Went Walking,* the children will be able to make predictions and finish repetitive sentences.
2. As a result of participating in the reading of *I Went Walking,* the children will be able to "write" (using emergent literacy) their own story about the animal that was looking at them at the farm.
3. As a result of working with paint, paper, yarn, dried hay, sponges, grains, colors, etc., the children will be able to contribute to the creation of a class farm mural.

Developmental and/or Content Areas That Have Been Integrated: This activity facilitates the children's cognitive and language development when they create their own story of an animal they could see looking at them. Sharing their stories with one another and working cooperatively to create a class mural develops their social skills. Fine motor skills are being used in both activities, and the art activity stimulates their aesthetic development.

Lesson Procedures

Introduction.   Students will listen as the teacher reads the story *I Went Walking,* by Sue Williams. The teacher will encourage students to predict what will happen and will use the repetitive structure of the story to facilitate the children "reading" along.

Development

1. The book *I Went Walking* will be put in the writing center and children will be supplied with paper, pencils, and colors to "write" their own "I Went Walking" story. The teacher can encourage the students to write about an animal they saw at the farm.
2. In large-group time, children can share their stories with one another. The teacher can ask questions that will encourage them to elaborate on their stories, thereby extending their language skills.
3. While still in large-group time, the teacher will provide a large farm scene backdrop made on butcher paper to which the children will add their favorite

farm animal. The teacher will give directions for the use of animal-shaped sponges, paint, construction paper, paste, and scissors. Yarn, cotton, and straw will be provided for them to add creative details of their choosing. The teacher will point out that the green fingerpaint has grains in it, representing what the animals eat. Children can use the paint to create the grass for their animal creation.

4. The children will be divided into small groups and will take turns working on the mural. A volunteer parent will provide assistance and stimulate the children to talk about what they are doing.

Summary.   During large-group time, after the mural is finished, the process of creating the mural will be discussed by the class. Then the teacher can reenact the story *I Went Walking.* The teacher can point to a particular animal on the mural and ask, "I went walking, and what did I see?" The child who created the animal the teacher is pointing to can complete the question with, "I saw a _____ looking at me."

Materials Needed

Book
    I Went Walking, by Sue Williams
Construction paper
Finger paint
Grains (oats or wheat)
Butcher paper
Yarn, straw, paste, cotton
Scissors
Animal-shaped sponges

Evaluation

Teacher
    Did the children understand how to participate in the activities?
    Were there enough materials?
    Were they appropriate?
Activity
    Did the children enjoy writing their story and making the mural?
    Could they use the materials with little difficulty?
Students
    Did all the students participate?
    Did their stories give indications of development and progress?
    Did they use expanded language in their conversations?

LESSON PLAN 4

Lesson Title: The Barn Dance

Lesson Objectives

1. As result of listening to *The Barn Dance* and being given square dancing directions, children will participate in a simple dance.
2. As a result of listening to *The Barn Dance* and using associated props, children will re-create the story during center time.
3. As a result of listening to a tape of animal sounds, children will be able to guess the animal and match the corresponding picture to the sound.

Developmental and/or Content Areas That Have Been Integrated: This lesson facilitates the social development of the children as they play act the story in their center. The dance also facilitates social development and physical development. Aesthetic development is enhanced as children respond to music with body movement. Listening to animal sounds on a tape helps the children develop listening and cognitive skills.

Lesson Procedures

Introduction. The teacher will read *The Barn Dance,* by Bill Martin, Jr., and John Archimbault. As the story is read, the teacher will point out the rhythm and rhyme of the language in the story and the beauty of the illustrations.

Development.

1. During large-group time, the children will listen to a square dance tape with simple commands, such as the Virginia Reel. The teacher will explain and demonstrate the caller's directions and help the children participate in a square dance.
2. In the listening center, children will listen to a tape of farm animal sounds and pick the corresponding animal from animal pictures. The answer will be given after each sound so that children can self-correct their answers.
3. The dramatic play/housekeeping center will be arranged as a simulation of the barn in *The Barn Dance*. A table with a red-and-white checkered tablecloth, a small bale of hay, and a prop box complete with cowboy boots, hats, kerchiefs, and child-sized musical instruments (such as guitars or fiddles) will encourage the children to reenact the story in their dramatic play.

Summary. During large-group time, after the children have had a chance to work in the centers, the teacher will guide them to summarize the caller's commands from the square dance tape. A list of commands can be made on the chalkboard and the children can come up two at a time to demonstrate each command.

Materials Needed

Book

The Barn Dance, by Bill Martin, Jr., and John Archimbault

Tape of animal sounds

Square dance tape

Props for housekeeping center

Evaluation

Teacher

Did the children understand how to do the square dance steps?

Were the dance instructions simple enough and demonstrated clearly enough for the children to successfully participate in the dance activity?

Activity

Did the children voluntarily participate in the barn dance dramatic play opportunity?

Were the children able to follow the caller's instructions for the square dance on the tape?

Students

Were all of the children able to participate in following the directions on the square dance tape?

Did all of the students voluntarily participate in the dance activity?

Did the students match the correct pictures to the animal sounds?

LESSON PLAN 5

Lesson Title: Pancake Party

Lesson Objectives

1. After listening to *Pancakes for Breakfast,* the children will be able to identify where the ingredients for pancakes come from.
2. As a result of making pancakes, the children will understand how to use a measuring cup and measurement terms.

Developmental and/or Content Areas That Have Been Integrated: Cognitive and language development is encouraged as children "read" the recipe on the large chart and measure the ingredients. Vocabulary is developed as groups discuss where the ingredients came from and as they use cooking and measuring terms. Nutrition and health concepts are also discussed during this activity, as well as when the children eat their pancakes. Social development is also involved as children interact during the activity.

Lesson Procedures

Introduction.   During large-group time, the teacher will read *Pancakes for Breakfast,* by Tomi dePaola. After the reading, the teacher will help students recall information about the story by asking questions such as the following:

> What did the lady use to make her pancakes?
>
> Where did she get the eggs, milk, butter, and syrup?
>
> What happened to her pancakes?
>
> Did she still get to have pancakes for breakfast?

Development

1. While still in large group-time, the children will discuss how pancakes are made at their respective houses. The teacher will record the children's responses on a large recipe chart. The teacher will adapt their contributions to include correct measurements and ingredients for pancakes.
2. After the chart is completed, the class will divide into small groups. With the help of fifth-grade students, each group will follow the directions to mix and make pancakes. After they have finished cooking, the children will eat the pancakes.

Summary and Review.   During large-group time, the teacher will encourage the students to talk about their cooking experience. The teacher will ask them to describe the sequence of the mixing and cooking and evaluate how well they did in making the pancakes.

Materials Needed

Cooking utensils
    Griddles
    Spoons
    Bowls
    Measuring cups
Ingredients for pancakes
    Milk
    Butter
    Pancake mix
    Eggs

Book

Pancakes for Breakfast, by Tomi dePaola

Evaluation

Teacher

Were there adequate materials for the cooking activity?

Were the questions appropriate for the study to encourage recall and discussion?

Were the fifth-grade students able to lead their group?

Activity

Did the children enjoy making and eating the pancakes?

Were the children able to work successfully with older students?

Were adequate measures taken for the safety of the children while they were cooking?

Were all of the students included in the mixing and cooking?

Students

Were the students able to retell the story and learn about the origin of the ingredients for pancakes?

Did all children participate?

Did the students measure ingredients properly?

Did they understand measurement procedures?

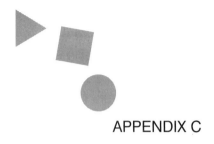

APPENDIX C

Kindergarten–Primary Unit:
If You Give a Mouse a Cookie

UNIT PLAN OUTLINE

Unit Topic: Mice

Overview or Rationale for the Unit: The unit is based on the story *If You Give a Mouse a Cookie*. Students will be able to learn about the differences and similarities between a real and a fictional mouse.

Developmental Stage: Preoperational and Concrete Operational

Grade Level: First Grade

Brainstorming Web: See Figure C.1.

List of Activities to Be Used for Five Lesson Plans

1. Observe real mouse.
2. Sing songs about mice.
3. Discuss different foods mice eat. Have children make and eat food.
4. Talk about manners and how we should ask for things we want.
5. Create mice puppets to be used in dramatization of book.
6. Have children dictate stories to teacher about mice.
7. Count how many different things the mouse asked for.
8. Move to music and role play mouse movements.

9. Draw what you would want if you were a mouse; explain why you would want these things.
10. Measure a real mouse.

Curriculum Web: See Figure C.2

Unit Objectives

1. As a result of observing a mouse, students will understand different characteristics of mice.
2. As a result of observing a mouse and listening to the story *If You Give a Mouse a Cookie,* students will understand and be able to discuss the differences and similarities between a real mouse and a storybook mouse.
3. As a result of observing a mouse, listening to the story *If You Give a Mouse a Cookie,* and participating in an art activity, students will be able to create mice puppets and cut out a picture representing the thing they would desire if they were a mouse.

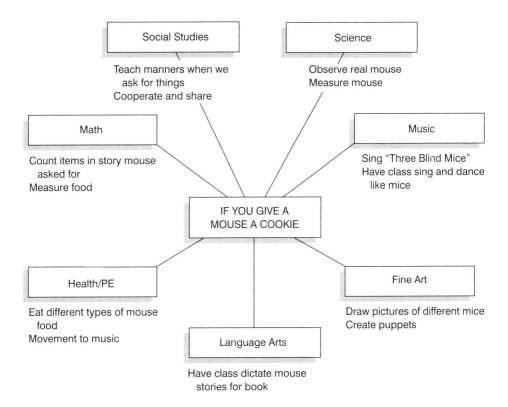

Figure C.1   Brainstorming Web

4. As a result of drawing and measuring mice of different sizes, students will understand how mice can be measured.
5. As a result of studying individual mice drawings, students will be able to discuss a mouse's shape.
6. As a result of measuring a real mouse, students will be able to determine the length of the mouse's tail and the size of the body.

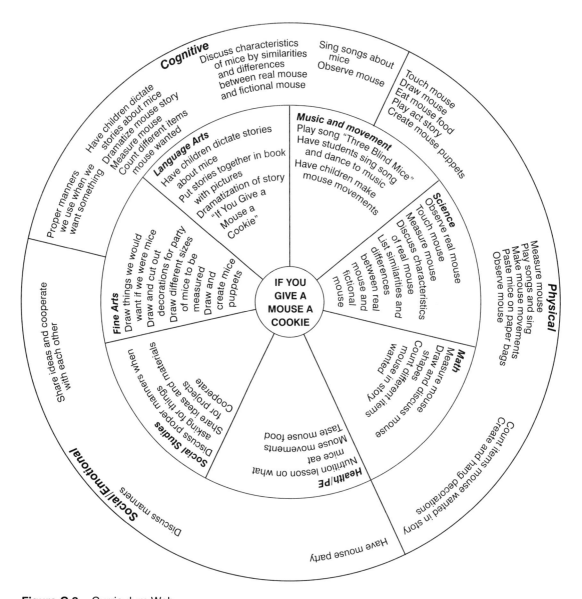

Figure C.2   Curriculum Web

7. As a result of their experiences with mice, students will be able to dictate or write and illustrate their own story about mice.

8. As a result of observing a mouse and listening to the story *If You Give a Mouse a Cookie,* students will be able to distinguish between what a real mouse and a storybook mouse would eat.

9. As a result of participating in a music activity with the song "Three Blind Mice," students will be able to sing and role play mouse movements to the music.

Assumptions about Previous Knowledge.   Students will know what mice are. Students will have had previous experiences with mice or heard stories about mice.

Summary of Activities

1. **Mouse Observation.** Both language arts and science are integrated in this activity of observing a real mouse. Children will be using language arts skills of listening and answering questions, along with following directions. Science can be seen through the actual manipulation of the real mouse, observance of the different characteristics of the mouse, and classification of the differences and similarities between a real and fictional mouse.

2. **Mice Puppets.** The integration of language arts, social studies, and art can be seen in this activity of creating mice puppets. The children will be using their language arts skills of listening and following directions. Social studies will be observed through cooperation and sharing skills. The art activity in this lesson will include drawing the mice, gluing them on the paper bags, and coloring the mice. The theater arts can be incorporated through role playing the story *If You Give a Mouse a Cookie.*

3. **Mouse Shapes and Sizes.** This activity integrates art, mathematics, science, and language arts. The art activity is the drawing of different sizes and shapes of mice. The math activity involves measuring the drawn mice and comparing the measurement with that of a real mouse. Language arts is again experienced through listening and speaking skills. Science is incorporated through measuring and predicting.

4. **Mouse Story.** This activity of dictating or writing individual mouse stories and drawing pictures to illustrate the story integrates language arts and fine arts. Students use their creative abilities for creating and illustrating the story.

5. **Mouse Party.** The integration of health, social studies, music, fine arts, and math can be observed through this activity. The study of nutrition occurs as a result of the different foods used at the mouse party. Physical education can be seen in the movement that the children use as they dance and act like mice. Music is incorporated in the music and movement as they sing along to the song. Art is involved in the making of the decorations and costumes for the party. Social studies occurs in socialization skills during the party and the discussion of proper manners. Math is integrated through measurement of different ingredients for the mouse food.

LESSON PLAN 1

Lesson Title: Mouse Observation

Lesson Objectives

1. As a result of observing a mouse, students will understand different characteristics of mice.
2. As a result of observing a mouse and listening to the story *If You Give a Mouse a Cookie*, students will understand and be able to discuss the differences and similarities between a real mouse and a storybook mouse.

Developmental and/or Content Areas that Have Been Integrated: The content areas of science and language arts will be integrated. The activity will involve science through observation and deductions made through the observation. The activity will be physical in that children will be allowed to touch and hold the mouse. Language arts is integrated through the discussion about the similarities and differences between the real and fictional mouse.

Lesson Procedures

1. **Planning Time.** Students and teacher will discuss what they know about mice. They will then discuss observing a real mouse before it is brought to class. The teacher will discuss rules about how to handle the mouse and things to avoid when holding the mouse.
2. **Observation Time**. The teacher will bring a real mouse to class in a glass aquarium. Students will be allowed to come to the science center in groups of five. Students will be allowed to hold and pet the mouse during the observation. The teacher will point out different characteristics of the mouse and encourage the children to discuss their own observation.
3. **Recall Time**. The teacher will conduct the class in a discussion of the different characteristics of mice. The characteristics will be listed on the board. The children will be encouraged to suggest differences and similarities between the real and the fictional mouse. The differences and similarities will be listed on the board.

Materials Needed

Mouse
Mouse house (aquarium)
Book
   If You Give a Mouse a Cookie

Evaluation

Teacher

Were the activities conducted in a meaningful way with the students?

Was the teacher able to maintain the students' interest in the activities?

Activity

Did the children enjoy participating in the activities?

Were the children interested in observing and holding the mouse?

Did the children understand how to compare the real and fictional mouse?

Students

Did each student handle the mouse carefully?

Did each student contribute to the discussions?

LESSON PLAN 2

Lesson Title: Mice Puppets

Lesson Objectives: As a result of observing a mouse, listening to the story *If You Give a Mouse a Cookie,* and participating in an art activity, students will be able to create mice puppets and cut out a picture representing the thing they would desire if they were a mouse.

Developmental and/or Content Areas That Have Been Integrated: This lesson integrates art with social studies and language arts. It requires that students use their creative abilities to draw and create mice puppets. It will also require the students to work together and be involved in socialization activities. Children will use language arts as they talk to each other and the teacher, and they will use listening skills to follow directions.

Lesson Procedures

1. **Planning Time.** Students will talk about the story and start to think about what they would want if they were a mouse. The teacher will give the class directions about how they will go about creating their puppets and drawing a mouse with one item they would want if they were a mouse.
2. **Activity Time**. The students will each get a brown paper bag, which they will be able to transform into mice puppets. Every student will receive drawing paper and crayons to draw their mouse and the one thing they would ask for if they were a mouse. The students then will cut out their mice and glue them on the brown paper bag. They will also cut out the item that they would ask for if they were a mouse. The class would role play the story *If You Give a*

Mouse a Cookie with their puppets but instead of saying the items the mouse in the story asked for they would use the items that they drew in class.

3. **Discussion Time**. Students will talk about why they chose the items they selected for the activity. The teacher will ask the students to contribute responses to the other students' ideas.

Materials Needed

Brown paper bags

Scissors

Glue

Drawing paper

Crayons

Evaluation

Teacher

Was enough time provided for completing the puppets?

Was the class managed so that all students participated in the role play? Were all students included in the discussion?

Activity

Were the students able to manage the materials to construct the puppets?

Did the students seem interested in the role play activity?

Students

Did all students participate in the activities?

Did the students work in a cooperative manner?

LESSON PLAN 3

Lesson Title: Mouse Shapes and Sizes

Lesson Objectives

1. As a result of drawing and measuring mice of different sizes, students will understand how mice can be measured.
2. As a result of studying individual mice drawings, students will be able to discuss a mouse's shape.
3. As a result of measuring a real mouse, students will be able to determine the length of the mouse's tail and the size of the body.

Developmental and/or Content Areas That Have Been Integrated: This lesson includes the integration of art, mathematics, science, and language arts. Children use social and emotional skills in cooperating and sharing materials and information. Science and math are used in measuring different parts of the mouse's body. Art is used in drawing mice.

Lesson Procedures

1. **Planning Time.** The teacher will plan the activity of measuring the mouse with the class by first talking about and predicting how big the children think mice are. The responses can be written on a large chart or chalk board. The teacher will provide appropriate instructions for drawing mice.
2. **Activity Time**. Students will draw mice of different shapes and sizes. They will cut out their mice and tape them on the board. Students will use a ruler or measuring tape to measure the mice. The teacher will assist in the measuring process. The real mouse will be measured and the measurements put on the board next to the students' earlier predictions. The class will discuss the predictions compared with the measuring results.
3. **Discussion Time**. The class will discuss the different measurements of their mice and compare measurements of the real mouse with drawn mice.

Materials Needed

Scissors

Drawing paper

Crayons

Measuring tape or ruler

Real mouse

Evaluation

Teacher

Did the students understand the purpose for drawing mice?

Did they understand the value in measuring the real mouse?

Was the measuring activity conducted so that all students could feel involved?

Activity

How did comparing the measurements of the drawn mice with that of the real mouse benefit the students?

Were they interested in discussing the different mice drawings?

Students

Were all students engaged in attending to the measuring activities?

Did all students exhibit an interest in using the ruler or tape measure?

Did students understand how to use a measuring tool?

LESSON PLAN 4

Lesson Title: Mouse Story

Lesson Objectives: As a result of their experiences with mice, students will be able to dictate or write and illustrate their own story about mice.

Developmental and/or Content Areas That Have Been Integrated: This lesson integrates art and language arts. Fine motor skills are used for writing and illustrating the story. Art is integrated in the illustration, and language arts is involved in dictating or writing the story.

Lesson Procedures

1. **Planning Time**. The teacher and students will discuss some ideas for writing or dictating a story about mice. Some of the ideas can be listed on the board. Students are encouraged to be creative in extending their own ideas for a story.
2. **Activity Time**. The students individually work on writing or dictating their story. Each child then illustrates their story. Completed stories are bound into a class book.
3. **Discussion Time**. Students can read or tell their story and discuss their picture. Children are encouraged to respond to other students' stories. Suggestions might be made to revise or extend stories.

Materials Needed

Drawing paper

Crayons

Notebook or materials to construct a book for the stories

Evaluation

Teacher

Was the teacher able to manage dictation from individual students?

Were students encouraged to work at their own ability level in writing or dictating their stories?

Activity

Did all of the students seem interested in creating a story and illustration?

Were the students able to give supportive and constructive comments to
other students' stories?

Students

Did all of the students complete their story?

Did each student use the time well?

LESSON PLAN 5

Lesson Title: Mouse Party

Lesson Objectives

1. As a result of observing a mouse and listening to the story *If You Give a
   Mouse a Cookie,* students will be able to distinguish between what a real
   mouse and a storybook mouse would eat.
2. As a result of participating in a music activity with the song "Three Blind
   Mice," students will be able to sing and role play mouse movements to the
   music.

Developmental and/or Content Areas That Have Been Integrated: This lesson
integrates health, social studies, mathematics, music, and movement. Social studies
involves the use of proper manners at a meal. Music and movement involve the song
and dance movements. Math is incorporated through measuring ingredients for food,
and health involves eating different types of food.

Lesson Procedures

1. **Planning Time**. Students and teacher will discuss and plan the mouse party.
   The students will each participate in creating the decorations for the party, as
   well as their costumes. The teacher will help set the guidelines for behavior
   during the party.
2. **Activity Time**. Students will cut out mice ears and tails, which they will wear
   to the party. They will create decorations for the party, which will be hung
   around the room. In small groups, food trays will be prepared for the party.
   Two trays of food will be made. One tray will have the items the mouse in *If
   You Give a Mouse a Cookie* wanted. The other tray will have what real mice
   will eat.
   Following the eating activity, the teacher will play the song "Three Blind
   Mice." The students will sing along and dance and role play mice movements
   to the music.
3. **Recall and Review Time**. The class will review what they have learned
   about what mice eat. They will compare the types of food the real mouse eats
   with the types of food the fictional mouse eats.

Materials Needed

Mouse
Food (cheese, grains, cookies, milk, etc.)
Record of "Three Blind Mice"
Colored paper for tails and ears
Materials for room decorations

Evaluation

Teacher
Were the students prepared appropriately for the activities?
Was the teacher able to manage the activities smoothly?
Were all students able to participate in food preparation?
Was enough time allotted for the activities related to the party?
Activity
Was there enough food for all to sample?
Did the students enjoy role playing mice?
Students
Were all students actively involved in the activities?
Did each student contribute to the review at the end of the activities?

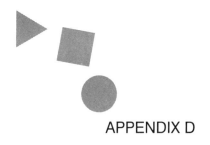

Primary Unit: *Alexander and the Terrible, Horrible, No Good, Very Bad Day*

UNIT PLAN OUTLINE

Unit Topic: *Alexander and the Terrible, Horrible, No Good, Very Bad Day,* by Judith Viorst

Overview or Rationale for the Unit   *Alexander and the Terrible, Horrible, No Good, Very Bad Day* is a familiar story to most children who have experienced days when nothing seems to go quite right. By introducing Alexander to the children, they will relate to him and realize that life does, indeed, have its ups and downs but that in some situations they can control the outcome and in other situations the result is simply unavoidable—even if you live in Australia! The goals of this unit are to incorporate meaningful activities to develop the children's knowledge and skills in all of the cognitive, social-emotional, and physical development areas; to develop self-esteem, a sense of competence, and positive feelings toward learning; and to view each child at different levels of ability as well as integrate all of the content areas of language arts, social studies, science, mathematics, and fine arts that are woven throughout the story.

Developmental Stage: Transitional period moving from preoperational to concrete operational (five- to eight-year-olds)

Grade Level: Second Grade

Brainstorming Web: See Figure D.1.

Figure D.1   Brainstorming Web

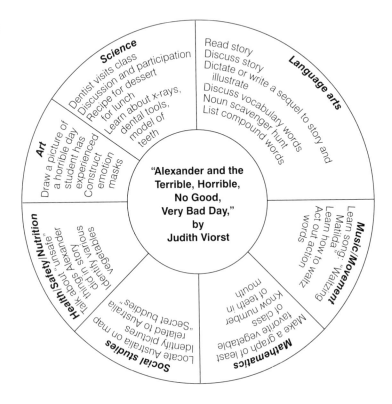

List of Activities to Be Used for Five Lesson Plans

1. The teacher will read to the class the literature selection, *Alexander and the Terrible, Horrible, No Good, Very Bad Day,* followed by a discussion of the story. The children will write and illustrate a sequel to the story of what might have happened the next day.
2. The class will locate the continent of Australia on a map, and the children will draw a map of the continent. This will be followed by an identification game in which children select a picture, identify it, and become familiar with the person, place, or thing that is characteristic of Australia.
3. A dentist will visit the class to discuss the importance of care for the teeth. The class will participate using a model of teeth and demonstrating proper dental hygiene techniques.
4. The children will construct a graph charting the least favorite vegetable of the class.
5. The children will become familiar with an Australian song through singing and dancing.

Curriculum Web: See Figure D. 2.

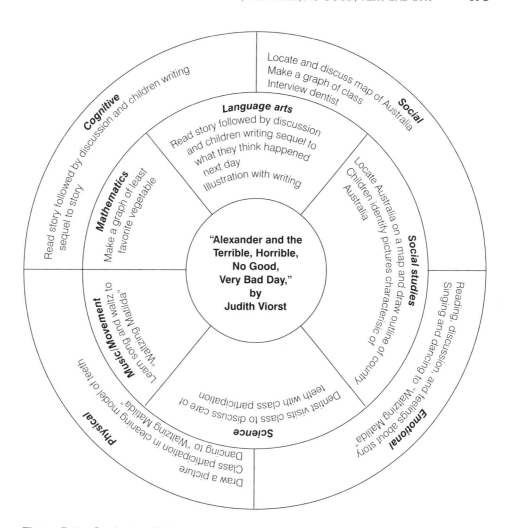

Figure D.2   Curriculum Web

Unit Objectives

1. Students will understand that it is not unusual to have a bad day.
2. Students will be able to distinguish between safe and unsafe practices.
3. Students will understand the importance of proper dental hygiene and the way to avoid cavities.
4. Students will be able to locate Australia on a map; know that it is not only a separate country, but also one of the seven continents; and be familiar with certain characteristics of the country.
5. Students will be able to construct a graph charting the least favorite vegetable of the class.

6. Students will be able to understand the process of creative thinking when writing a sequel to the story.
7. Students will be exposed to Australian idioms in the lyrics of the song "Waltzing Matilda."
8. Students will have an opportunity to dance a waltz to "Waltzing Matilda."

Assumptions about Previous Knowledge

1. Students should be familiar with daily practices that promote oral hygiene.
2. Students should have basic familiarity with safe and unsafe practices.
3. Students should be familiar with construction of graphs.
4. Students should know basic geography skills concerning direction and location.
5. Students should have a basic interest in the topic of literature selection and knowledge of listening, discussing, reading and writing skills.
6. Students will have had some exposure to music and movement to music.

Summary of Activities
Physical Activities

1. **Music/Movement**. Students will become familiar with the Australian song "Waltzing Matilda" and acquainted with the steps to the waltz. This activity would initially be teacher directed, with the words to the song being taught by the teacher or played on a record or tape. Special terms would be defined for the students. Basic steps to the waltz would be demonstrated for the students. The students would then divide into pairs singing and dancing to the song. (teacher directed)
2. **Science**. The dentist will discuss the importance of caring for the teeth with class participation using a model of teeth and demonstrating proper dental hygiene techniques. This activity would initially be teacher directed, with discussion, but would be followed by a hands-on activity of brushing and flossing the large model of teeth. Each child will receive his or her own personal toothbrush and floss from the dentist.
3. **Language Arts**. The students will use creative thinking abilities to write a sequel to the story of what might have happened to Alexander the next day. This activity would be an informal handwriting exercise providing flexibility in fine motor skills in a less structured environment. (child initiated)

Cognitive Activities
1. **Language Arts**. The teacher will read the literature selection, followed by a class discussion of the story. The children will write a sequel to the story of what might have happened the next day and include an illustration. This activity would be done in a reading circle with all of the children. It would begin as a teacher-directed activity with reading of the story, followed by discussion in comprehension, safety practices, vocabulary words, nouns, and

compound words. As a child-initiated activity, children would use their own creative thinking abilities by writing a sequel to the story of what they think might have happened to Alexander on the next day. This exercise would accommodate children as emerging writers at various stages of development and with varying ability to actively reconstruct knowledge.

2. **Mathematics**. Students will construct a graph charting the least favorite vegetable of the class. Discussion would begin with a teacher-directed question, such as when the class remembered the vegetable that Alexander hated in the story. After their responses to the question, the discussion would lead to other vegetables that the children consider their least favorite. The students would be divided into small groups to decide what is the least favorite vegetable of the whole group. The results from the groups would be given to the teacher, who would then graph a large chart of the least favorite vegetables in the class.

Social-Emotional Activities

1. **Social Studies**. Students will locate Australia on a map or globe and will draw a map of the continent. This will be followed by an identification game. A large Manila envelope with various pictures of persons, places, and things are passed around to each child. Each child is to select a picture from the envelope and identify it, and the class then discusses its relevance to Australia.

2. **Language Arts**. The class will discuss the story. This activity touches on many aspects of social studies learning by exploring Alexander's day, his experiences with friends and his teacher, his relationship with his family and the dentist, etc. By discussing Alexander's social experiences, the students are able to understand the importance of positive peer relationships, class rules, and self-control.

LESSON PLAN 1

Lesson Title: Have You Ever Had a Bad Day?

Lesson Objectives

1. The students will understand that it is not unusual to have a bad day.
2. The students will be able to distinguish between safe and unsafe practices.
3. The students will be able to understand the process of creative thinking when writing a sequel to the story.

Developmental and/or Content Areas that Have Been Integrated: Language arts, social studies, and art activities have been integrated into the lesson.

Lesson Procedures: Students will be read the literature selection, *Alexander's Terrible, Horrible, No Good, Very Bad Day*, by Judith Viorst. This will be followed by discussion of the story with such topics as what unsafe actions Alexander performed that could have been prevented; what his relationships were with family, friends, and teachers; why his trip to the dentist's office was unpleasant, etc. The students would then have an opportunity to write a sequel to the story and imagine what they think might have happened to Alexander the next day. The students will create an illustration to go with their sequel.

Materials Needed

Book

> *Alexander and the Terrible, Horrible, No Good, Very Bad Day,* by Judith Viorst

Chalkboard and chalk or easel with large writing tablet with marker

Paper and pencil

Evaluation

Teacher

> Was the discussion led in such a manner that most of the students felt they were actively involved?

Activity

> Did the students enjoy the story?

> Were the children interested in writing and illustrating the sequel to the story?

Students

> Did each student attempt to do his or her best in writing and illustrating the sequel to the story?

> Did each student focus on the discussion that followed the reading of the story?

LESSON PLAN 2

Lesson Title: Where IS Australia, Anyway?

Lesson Objectives: Students will be able to locate the country of Australia on a map; know that it is not only a separate country but also one of the seven continents; and be familiar with certain characteristics of the country.

Developmental and/or Content Areas That Have Been Integrated: Language arts, social studies, and art activities have been integrated into the lesson.

Lesson Procedures: The lesson will begin with a discussion of Alexander's references to going to Australia whenever he is unhappy with a situation. The students will then find Australia on a map and be able to draw an outline of the country. The class will play a game in which a large Manila envelope containing various magazine pictures of persons, places, and things that are characteristic of Australia will be passed to each student. The student will identify the picture and understand its association with Australia.

Materials Needed

Large world map showing the country of Australia

Paper and crayons or markers

Large Manila envelope

Magazine pictures of persons, places, or things characteristic of Australia

Evaluation

Teacher

Was the discussion conducted in a relevant manner?

Were the students encouraged to participate in the discussion?

Activity

Were the students interested in the discussion and the game?

Were the pictures used for the game relevant to Australia?

Students

Was each student able to locate and draw an outline of Australia?

Did each student actively participate in the game?

LESSON PLAN 3

Lesson Title: Cavities Make for a Very Bad Day!

Lesson Objectives: Students will understand the importance of proper dental hygiene and the way to avoid cavities.

Developmental and/or Content Areas That Have Been Integrated: Science, social studies, language arts, and mathematics activities have been integrated into the lesson.

Lesson Procedures: A dentist will visit the class to discuss the importance of proper dental hygiene. The dentist will show various charts, X rays taken of patients' teeth, and examples of tools used in the office. A hands-on model of teeth will be displayed for the children to look at and will be used by the dentist to show the proper procedure for cleaning the teeth with a toothbrush and floss. The students will learn the total number of teeth in the human mouth. The children will also be able to participate in cleaning a model of the teeth. At the close of the visit, the dentist will give each of the students his or her own toothbrush and floss to take home.

Materials Needed

Dental charts

X rays

Dental tools

Model of teeth

Toothbrushes

Floss

Chalkboard and chalk

Evaluation

Teacher

Was the dentist able to communicate effectively with the students?

Activity

Were all students able to participate in the lesson procedures?

Students

Did the students understand the importance of regular brushing and flossing?

Could the students demonstrate the proper way to brush their teeth?

LESSON PLAN 4

Lesson Title: Terrible, Horrible, No Good, Very Bad Veggies!

Lesson Objectives: Students will be able to construct a graph charting the least favorite vegetable of the class.

Developmental and/or Content Areas That Have Been Integrated: Mathematics, language arts, science, and social studies activities have been integrated into the lesson.

Lesson procedures: Students will be asked if they remember what vegetable (lima beans) Alexander hated in the story. The students will then be told they are going to construct a graph to show which vegetable is the least favorite of the class. Various common vegetables will be shown to the students through pictures or actual vegetables bought at the store. The students will initially be divided into small groups to decide which is their least favorite vegetable among their own group. Then the results will be given to the teacher to be graphed on a class chart to determine the least favorite vegetable of the whole class.

Materials Needed

Pictures of vegetables or actual vegetables bought at store.

Mimeographed copies of graphing chart for individual students

Large graphing chart in front of room for showing totals of least favorite vegetables

Evaluation

Teacher

Was the teacher able to clearly explain the procedures for making the chart?

Activity

Were all of the students able to participate in the graphing activity?

Students

Were the students able to complete the graphing chart within their small group?

LESSON PLAN 5

Lesson Title: "Waltzing Matilda"

Lesson Objectives

1. Students will be exposed to Australian idioms in the lyrics of the song "Waltzing Matilda."
2. Students will have an opportunity to dance a waltz to "Waltzing Matilda."

Developmental and/or Content Areas That Have Been Integrated: Music and movement, language arts, and social studies activities have been integrated into the lesson.

Lesson Procedures: Students will become familiar with the words and tune to the Australian song "Waltzing Matilda." There will be a discussion of unfamiliar terms such as *swagman* ("hobo"), *billabong* ("spring"), *billy* ("small pot of water"), *jumbucks* ("sheep"), and *tuckerbag* ("travel sack") included in the song and an explanation of their meaning. After becoming familiar with the song, the students will be divided in pairs to learn how to do a waltz. The students will then try waltzing to the song.

Materials Needed

Words to "Waltzing Matilda"

Tape or record of "Waltzing Matilda"

Evaluation

Teacher

Was the teacher able to clearly explain the unfamiliar terms during the discussion?

Was the teacher able to teach the students how to do a waltz?

Activity

Was the waltz within the students' ability level?

Students

Did each student participate in singing the song and waltzing?

Index

ISBN 0- 02- 429471- 3